D0474714

THE GOOD HOTEL GUIDE 2020
GREAT BRITAIN & IRELAND

Editors

Ian Belcher

Nicola Davies

Joanna Symons

THE GOOD HOTEL GUIDE LTD

The Good Hotel Guide Ltd

This edition first published in 2019 by
The Good Hotel Guide Ltd

Chief executive: Richard Fraiman

Contributing editors:
Rose Shepherd
Emma Grundy Haigh
Maggie O'Sullivan
Bonnie Friend

Production: Hugh Allan
Managing editor: Alison Wormleighton
Designer: Stuart Sutch
Text editor: Daphne Trotter
Computer consultant: Vince Nacey
Website design: Matt Preston, Cotswolds Online Services
Researcher: Cristina Recio-Corral

A CIP catalogue record for this book may be found in the British Library.

ISBN 978-0-9932484-4-3

Cover photograph: The Star at Harome

Printed and bound in Malta by Gutenberg Press Ltd

*'A good hotel is where
the guest comes first'*

Hilary Rubinstein, founding editor
(1926–2012)

The Pig at Bridge Place, Bridge

CONTENTS

www.goodhotelguide.com

Our website has many handy features to help you get the most out of your Guide.

- **Explore offers and discounts**
- **View special collections**
- **Read the latest news**
- **Search for a hotel near you**
- **Search for a hotel near a particular destination**
- **Submit a review**
- **Join the Good Hotel Guide Readers' Club**
- **Order a copy of the printed Guide**

DESKTOP

TABLET   SMARTPHONE

Make it even easier to get on the Good Hotel Guide website while you're on the go: add an icon to the home screen of your iPhone or iPad for one-touch smartphone access. Go to **www.goodhotelguide.com** on your mobile browser. Tap on the rectangle with an arrow pointing upwards, at the bottom of the screen. Then tap on the + sign ('Add to Home Screen') that pops up.

INTRODUCTION

How times change. Developments in hospitality over the four decades the Guide has been published have been huge. The first edition featured 320 hotels offering half board from as little as £11 per person a day. Showers were dodgy, lighting dismal, in-room TV rare, Wi-Fi non-existent and food variable. Prices, in line with standards and expectations, have risen sharply since then.

The values that underline the Guide have not changed. As its founder, Hilary Rubinstein, wrote in the first edition: 'We loathe the safe, boring hotel that insulates its guests from their environment. We treasure the personal and idiosyncratic.' The Guide remains committed to selecting the very best hotels, inns and B&Bs in Great Britain and Ireland without fear, favour or free hospitality. Not a penny is paid for an entry in the print edition. Selections are made solely on merit, based on reports from readers, backed where necessary by our inspectors, whose anonymous visits help settle arguments.

This year's Guide, with 830 hotels, inns and B&Bs in the UK and Ireland, has been edited by two distinguished journalists: Ian Belcher, winner of several national travel writing awards, and Joanna Symons, former commissioning editor for the Daily Telegraph's travel section. They have brought their considerable professional skills to the task of separating the great from the good, and the unusual from the ordinary. They point out that the test of a good hotel, whether a luxury manor house or a small B&B, remains the same – great hospitality, attention to detail, and friendly, attentive service.

The Guide's range of entries is deliberately eclectic. Pride of place is given to our ten winners of a César, our top annual award. This year the winners include an informal dining pub in a fishing village, a Peak District longhouse and a lively Irish B&B. Some of our favourite entries include great value places with double rooms from as little as £75 a night for B&B.

To help you find your perfect hotel, there are Editor's Choice selections in 16 categories, ranging from romantic, value, gardens and weddings, to gastropubs, seaside, walking and dog-friendly. These special hotels are chosen by the Guide's editorial team after analysis of readers' and inspectors' reports.

The Guide could not exist without its thousands of loyal readers, whose reports are its lifeblood. One comment from a long-time reader was: 'I can't think of a book which over the years has given me more pleasure.' We hope this edition will carry on the good work, so please keep writing to us.

Adam Raphael
July 2019

HOW TO USE THE GOOD HOTEL GUIDE

MAIN ENTRY

The 433 main entries, which are given a full page each, are those we believe to be the best of their type in Great Britain and Ireland.

Colour bands identify each country; London has its own section.

An index at the back lists hotels by county; another lists them by hotel name.

Hotels appear alphabetically under the name of the town or village. If the Shortlist (see opposite) also has one or more entries for the same town or village, a cross-reference to the Shortlist appears at the bottom of the panel.

The maps at the back of the book are divided into grids for easy reference. A small house indicates a main entry, a triangle a Shortlist one.

This hotel is making its first appearance, is returning after an absence, or has been upgraded from the Shortlist.

This hotel has agreed to give Guide readers a 25% discount off its normal bed-and-breakfast rate for one night only, subject to availability. Terms and conditions apply.

We name readers who have endorsed a hotel; we do not name inspectors, readers who ask to remain anonymous, or those who have written a critical report.

We try to indicate whether a hotel can accommodate wheelchair-users. It's always worth calling the hotel to check the details of wheelchair access.

We give the range of room or B&B prices for 2020, or the 2019 prices when we went to press. The price for dinner is for a set meal, or the average cost of three courses from an à la carte menu.

The panel provides useful information, such as contact details, number of bedrooms and facilities.

Sample entry (Blackaddie House, Sanquhar)

404　SCOTLAND　　www.goodhotelguide.com

SANQUHAR Dumfries and Galloway　　MAP 5:E2

BLACKADDIE HOUSE　NEW

Sweet flows Rabbie Burns's beloved River Nith, past the garden of an old manse that the poet knew well. Owned by Jane and Ian McAndrew, it is swept up from the Shortlist on a wave of reader approval. Traditional bedrooms are supplied with home-made shortbread and tablet. The River Suite's French doors open on to a patio above the water. Grouse has a super-king-size four-poster, spa bath and monsoon shower. 'We were more than happy with our accommodation, but the real star was the food.' Ian McAndrew trained under Anton Mosimann at the Dorchester, and in 1980 became the youngest British chef to hold a Michelin star. His five-course menu (with either/or choices) and tasting menu highlight fine Scottish produce. Typical dishes: halibut, black rice, brown shrimps, sea purslane, spinach; seared roe deer loin, acidulated chocolate, braised red cabbage, burnt onion, braised walnuts, millefeuille potatoes, lightly pickled raspberries. Guests, too, can be lightly pickled from a tempting wine list. 'Dinner was simply wonderful.' 'Ian and Jane could not have been more welcoming.' A breakfast of smoked haddock and poached egg 'was simply divine.' (Mr and Mrs Murray, Michael Asquith, PK)

25% DISCOUNT VOUCHERS

Blackaddie Road
Sanquhar DG4 6JJ

T: 01659 50270
E: ian@blackaddiehotel.co.uk
W: blackaddiehotel.co.uk

BEDROOMS 7, plus two 2-bed self-catering cottages, 1 suitable for disabled (from Autumn 2019).
OPEN all year.
FACILITIES bar, restaurant, breakfast/function room, library, conservatory, free Wi-Fi, in-room TV (Freeview), wedding/function facilities, 2-acre grounds, cookery school, fishing, parking, public rooms wheelchair accessible.
BACKGROUND MUSIC in public areas.
LOCATION outskirts of village.
CHILDREN all ages welcomed.
DOGS allowed in most bedrooms (£10 per night), public rooms, not in restaurant.
CREDIT CARDS Amex, MC, Visa.
PRICES per room B&B single £105–£230, double £125–£250. Set menu £65, tasting menu £80.

HOW TO USE THE GOOD HOTEL GUIDE

SHORTLIST ENTRY

The shortlist complements our main section by including interesting
new entrants and a selection of places in areas where we have limited choice.
It also includes some hotels that have previously been in the Guide but have
not had sufficient feedback this year.

Shortlist hotels
are included in
both indexes at
the back of the
book, with (S)
indicating that
it is a Shortlist
entry.

This hotel is
making its first
appearance in
the Shortlist or is
returning after
an absence.

We give the range of
room or B&B prices
for 2020, or the 2019
prices when we went
to press.

Many readers
tell us they find
background music
irritating. We
tell you if music
is played and
where you might
encounter it.

We list the principal
credit cards accepted
by the hotel (with
MC standing for
Mastercard).

This hotel has agreed to give Guide readers a
25% discount off its normal bed-and-breakfast
rate for one night only, subject to availability.
Terms and conditions apply.

---

638 ENGLAND SHORTLIST   www.goodhotelguide.com

YORK Yorkshire
BAR CONVENT
Serenity is assured at this B&B in England's
oldest active convent, next to the city's medieval
walls. The Grade I listed building still houses a
community of sisters, who share their peaceful
garden, domed chapel and antique religious
texts with guests. Simple, immaculate bedrooms
(some designed by Olga Polizzi) have a
'wickedly comfortable' bed and a well-equipped
refreshment tray. Open during the day, the café,
in a Victorian atrium, serves an award-winning,
slap-up breakfast, beers and wine, meals, coffee
and cake. There's a communal kitchen for DIY
dinners; the pick of York's eateries are on the
doorstep. Guests enjoy a discounted entrance
to the exhibition in the on-site Living Heritage
Centre, and the convent, founded in 1686.

MAP 4:D4
17 Blossom Street
York YO24 1AQ
T: 01904 643238
W: bar-convent.org.uk

BEDROOMS 20. 4 with shared
bathrooms.
OPEN all year except some days over
Christmas.
FACILITIES lift (to 1st and 2nd floors),
sitting room, kitchen, licensed café,
meeting rooms, free Wi-Fi, in-room
TV (Freeview), 34-acre garden,
Victorian atrium, 18th-century chapel,
museum, shop.
BACKGROUND MUSIC none.
LOCATION 5 mins' walk from the
railway station.
CHILDREN all ages welcomed (well-
equipped guest kitchen, with a
washing machine (small additional
charge)).
DOGS assistance dogs only.
CREDIT CARDS MC, Visa.
PRICES per room B&B £40–£140.

YORK Yorkshire
THE BLOOMSBURY   NEW
A scenic riverside walk away from the city centre,
Steve and Tricia Townsley's three-storey Victorian
town house B&B offers an exceptional Yorkshire
welcome. The 'charming' hosts greet guests with a
hot drink and 'something sweet' on arrival. Most
of the traditionally furnished bedrooms are up the
original staircase. 'Extremely comfortable' and
well equipped, they are supplied with tea- and
coffee-making facilities, a safe, iron and alarm
clock. In the sedate dining room overlooking
a flowery courtyard garden, the 'very tasty'
breakfast offers locally sourced fare: sausages and
thick-cut bacon from the butcher 200 yards away;
roasted ground coffee from an independent coffee
merchant nearby; 'fabulous porridge with a tot of
whisky!' Off-street parking is a bonus.

25% DISCOUNT VOUCHERS

MAP 4:D4
127 Clifton
York YO30 6BL
T: 01904 634031
W: thebloomsburyguesthouse.com

BEDROOMS 4. 1 on ground floor.
OPEN all year except 23 Dec–end Jan.
FACILITIES sitting/dining room, free
Wi-Fi, in-room TV (Freeview),
terrace, 'secret' courtyard garden,
parking.
BACKGROUND MUSIC 'relaxing hits'
from the 1990s to the present day in
dining room at breakfast.
LOCATION within a mile of the City
centre, 10–15 min. walk from York
Minster.
CHILDREN not under 17.
DOGS not allowed (resident dog).
CREDIT CARDS MC, Visa.
PRICES per person B&B single £60–£70,
double £40–£60. 2-night min. stay.

CÉSARS 2020

We give our César awards to the ten best hotels of the year. Named after César Ritz, the most celebrated of hoteliers, these are the Oscars of hotel-keeping.

NEWCOMER OF THE YEAR
North House, Cowes
Just minutes from the yacht-filled Solent lies Luke Staples and Lewis Green's chic, immaculately run boutique hotel, with top-notch, locally sourced food, a pretty garden for alfresco dining, hands-on owners and charming young staff.

SEASIDE HOTEL OF THE YEAR
The Old Coastguard, Mousehole
Readers feel thoroughly spoilt at the Inkin brothers' informal dining pub in a pretty fishing village. Most bedrooms have a sea view. In sunny weather, you can eat local seafood on the terrace in the palm-filled garden. Simple things done with style.

COUNTRY HOUSE HOTEL OF THE YEAR
Old Downton Lodge, Ludlow
Deep in the countryside, Willem and Pippa Vlok have created superb accommodation in historic farm buildings around parterre gardens. From dinner in a room resembling a medieval great hall, to a perfect breakfast, everything delighted our inspectors.

B&B OF THE YEAR
Underleigh House, Hope
Perfect hosts Vivienne and Philip Taylor set high standards at their Peak District longhouse home. Three of four well-equipped guest bedrooms are suites. A log burner warms the cosy lounge. Breakfast brings an array of fresh and very local produce.

ROMANTIC HOTEL OF THE YEAR
Southernhay House, Exeter
Silk, Spice… the bedrooms at Deborah Clark and Tony Orchard's boutique hotel recall the original owner. A Georgian Orientalist and diplomat, he'd have enjoyed drinks on the pretty veranda, alfresco meals, a free-standing bath in a glamorous bedroom.

🏆 INN OF THE YEAR
The Pipe and Glass Inn, South Dalton

With a cosy, beamed bar and Michelin-starred cooking in the child-friendly, veggie-friendly restaurant, James and Kate Mackenzie's former coaching inn is a winner. Smart bedrooms have a terrific bathroom, and everything in the garden is edible.

🏆 SCOTTISH LUXURY HOTEL OF THE YEAR
The Airds Hotel, Port Appin

From cream teas by the fire to drinks on the loch shore, Shaun and Jenny McKivragan's former ferry inn is a place for indulgence. Bedrooms have designer fabrics, Bulgari toiletries; dinner brings superb West Coast produce. Breakfast is exceptional.

🏆 WELSH HOTEL OF THE YEAR
The Angel Hotel, Abergavenny

William Griffiths's Georgian former coaching inn is the very model of a town hotel; family run, with friendly staff, a relaxed locals' bar, eclectic menus, modern artworks. Afternoon tea is a particular treat, with cakes from the hotel's own bakery.

🏆 IRISH B&B OF THE YEAR
The Quay House, Clifden

Generosity of spirit abounds at Julia and Paddy Foyle's fun B&B, filled with entertaining auction finds. Bedrooms have immense character, a terrace or balcony, perhaps a harbour view. Breakfast in the conservatory is all you could ask – and more.

🏆 RESTAURANT-WITH-ROOMS OF THE YEAR
Read's, Faversham

Our inspectors loved everything at David and Rona Pitchford's Georgian manor house, but it's Mr Pitchford's cooking that really sets it apart. A typical dish: roast Kentish lamb, smoked potato purée, haggis and lovage tart, roasted onion, lamb sauce.

REPORT OF THE YEAR COMPETITION

Readers' contributions are the lifeblood of the Good Hotel Guide. Everyone who writes to us is a potential winner of the Report of the Year competition. Each year we single out the writers of the most helpful reports. These correspondents win a copy of the Guide and an invitation to our annual launch party in October.

This year's winners are:
Steven Hur of Winchester
Liz Saunders of Gerrards Cross
Mary Wilmer of Cambridge
Steve Jack of York
Sue and John Jenkinson of Exbourne
David Ganz of Cambridge
Frances Thomas of Aylesbury
Suzanne Lyons of Barnstaple
Andrew Wardrop of London
David Birnie of Edinburgh

JOIN THE GOOD HOTEL GUIDE READERS' CLUB

Send us a review of your favourite hotel.
As a member of the club, you will be entitled to:
- A pre-publication discount offer
- Personal advice on hotels
- Advice if you are in dispute with a hotel
- Monthly emailed Guide newsletter

The writers of the ten best reviews will each win a free copy of the Guide and an invitation to our launch party. And the winner of our monthly web competition will win a free night, dinner and breakfast for two at one of the Guide's top hotels.

Send your review via
our website: www.goodhotelguide.com
or email: editor@goodhotelguide.com
or fax: 020 7602 4182
or write to:
Good Hotel Guide
50 Addison Avenue
London W11 4QP
England

EDITOR'S CHOICE

From glamorous spa hotels to great value B&Bs and
dog-friendly pubs with treats behind the bar, here are
some of the places that have caught our eye this year.
Turn to the full entry for the bigger picture.

The Ship Inn, Elie

THE LORD POULETT ARMS
HINTON ST GEORGE
West Country fixtures The Beckford Arms and The Talbot have a new sister here, a historic thatched village pub with stylish bedrooms, high-class cooking, lovely courtyard gardens, and – such novelty! – a Basque pelota wall and a pétanque piste. (Page 199)

THE SHIP INN
ELIE
Rachel and Graham Bucknall continue to innovate at this seaside pub with its own beach cricket team, promoted to a full entry after our inspectors pronounced it a corker. A new sea-view private dining room doubles as a pavilion. (Page 370)

THE DEVONSHIRE ARMS
BOLTON ABBEY
Works of art from the collection at Chatsworth hang on the walls of the Duke and Duchess of Devonshire's Dales country house hotel, which joins sister property The Cavendish in the Guide, with special praise from our inspector for the chef and sommelier. (Page 105)

THE PIG AT BRIDGE PLACE
BRIDGE
A Jacobean manor house has become the latest in the Pig family. Every part of this Piggy was quite all right with our inspectors, from the shabby chic aesthetic to the kitchen-garden menus. We're fans of the Pig brand. Honk if you support us. (Page 117)

THE GREAT HOUSE
LAVENHAM
Plus ça change. . . New proprietor Dominique Tropeano has retained the cherished French ambience created by former owners the Crépys. Behind its Georgian facade this ancient, timber-framed building lives on as a fine restaurant-with-rooms. (Page 215)

THE ST TUDY INN
ST TUDY
Wine producer Mark Hellyar and chef/director Emily Scott have created a smart but approachable pub-with-rooms in a picture-postcard village. Bedrooms are painted in those dreamy soft greys that Farrow & Ball calls white. Ms Scott cooks with flair and imagination. (Page 293)

THE OLD MANOR HOUSE
HALFORD
Serendipity led trusted readers to Jane and William Pusey's 16th-century manor house B&B. They found a winning combination of attention to detail, a perfect balance of historic character and modern convenience, and a friendly ambience. (Page 188)

23 MAYFIELD
EDINBURGH
A rave report from an inspector for Ross Burnie's family-run B&B gains it full Guide status. From rosemary water and home-made fudge in the bedroom to a candlelit breakfast, everything at this Victorian merchant's house is splendid. (Page 369)

THE COACH HOUSE
BRECON
With Georgian elegance, modern comforts, plus pikelets and rarebits for breakfast, Kayt and Hugh Cooper's Georgian coach house turned contemporary town house B&B ticks all the boxes for trusted readers. A Brecon beacon of warm hospitality. (Page 427)

THE DUNCOMBE ARMS
ELLASTONE
A heartening tale of a village inn saved from ruin by locals. . . Johnny and Laura Greenall have done a bang-up job, transforming a Victorian boozer into a stylish pub with annexe rooms and first-rate cooking, earning the nod from our inspectors. (Page 172)

AUGILL CASTLE
KIRKBY STEPHEN
This Victorian fantasy castle in the Eden valley, with views of fells and dales, enchants all who stay. Most bedrooms have a four-poster, some a real fire. The Gatehouse suite occupies one of two towers, with private garden. (Page 210)

LEWTRENCHARD MANOR
LEWDOWN
'The herbaceous borders full of flowers, a granite fountain always playing. . . imagine it on a sunlit evening.' Victorian genius Sabine Baring-Gould extols his own creation, this glorious Jacobean-style manor replete with ornate plasterwork and antiques. (Page 218)

LA SABLONNERIE
LITTLE SARK
Arrive by horse-drawn carriage at this 16th-century stone farmhouse on a car-free island ablaze with gorse in summer. Sleep in a rustic cottage bedroom. Take a dip in the pools of Venus and Adonis. Dine in a rose-filled garden. (Page 459)

HAZLITT'S
LONDON
You can repose on a bed adorned with gilded cherubs and steep in a vintage roll-top bath at this sumptuous boutique hotel in raffish Soho, adorned with silks and velvets, portraits and porcelains, the last home of 18th-century essayist William Hazlitt. (Page 57)

LANGAR HALL
LANGAR
With poetry on the walls and a canopy four-poster, Bohemia room is the honeymooners' choice at this Georgian mansion in the Vale of Belvoir. Others prefer Cartland room, beloved of the doyenne of romantic fiction, the late Dame Barbara. (Page 212)

CASTLE LESLIE
GLASLOUGH
Rooms come with tales of wartime espionage, whirlwind romance and royal visits, at Samantha Leslie's ancestral lakeside pile. Book flamboyant Aggie's room with four-poster, a roll-top bath in a curtained alcove. Have a lie-in: breakfast ends at 11 am. (Page 477)

THE PIG AT BRIDGE PLACE
BRIDGE
The latest in the Pig family occupies a fabulous Jacobean manor and former music venue that hosted the likes of Led Zeppelin. Climb a stairway to the heaven of a four-poster room, or sleep in a hop pickers' hut, on stilts, by the river. (Page 117)

COES FAEN
BARMOUTH
Rooms come with luxury extras at this astonishing B&B overlooking the Mawddach estuary. Perhaps a Welsh slate steam room; an outdoor cedar hot tub; a rock terrace with views of Snowdonia. And Tuscan style dinners? La dolce vita! (Page 423)

GLENAPP CASTLE
BALLANTRAE
A fountain sparkles on the forecourt of this turreted, Scottish baronial-style castle, reached by a wooded drive. Bedrooms have sea or garden views, The Penthouse offers a sauna and roof terrace. Dine as the sun sets over Ailsa Craig and the Mull of Kintyre. (Page 358)

NO.15 GREAT PULTENEY
BATH
The Hideout Suite at this glamorous boutique hotel has everything for a sybaritic weekend, with statement art and lighting, a sitting room with a real-flame gas fire, a Sonos music system, hot tub and steam-room shower. (Page 86)

Castle Leslie, Glaslough

THE SCARLET
MAWGAN PORTH
A contemplative, adults-only space, this Ayurvedic-inspired spa has an inside-outside feel, with cliff-top hot tubs, an indoor pool with sea views, a reed-filtered outdoor pool. Herbs and heat, salt and seaweed are all deployed for your well-being. (Page 236)

WHATLEY MANOR
EASTON GREY
The 'superb' Aquarius Spa at this luxury hotel is housed in a mellow Cotswold stone building, with underwater recliners in the indoor/outdoor pool. It is strong on facials and massage – Thai, Swedish, hot stone, 'Melting Away'. . . A place to be pampered. (Page 168)

SEAHAM HALL
SEAHAM
A tunnel leads from the hotel to the Serenity Spa, creating a heightened sense of escape. Extensive facilities include a hammam, an Indian steam room, outdoor hot tubs, an ice fountain and a Zen garden with infinity hydrotherapy pool. (Page 296)

ST BRIDES SPA HOTEL
SAUNDERSFOOT
Gaze out from the marine hydrotherapy pool at this cliff-top hotel, and experience the illusion of being in the sea. Treatment rooms for couples have full-height sliding windows. Specialities include vinotherapy (exfoliation, not a nice glass of Pinot!). (Page 452)

LONGUEVILLE MANOR
ST SAVIOUR
Within a walled Victorian kitchen garden, the new Cottage Garden spa offers therapies based on fruit and herbs, massage with natural oils from Jersey brand Manomara, facials and more. The focus is on beauty and rejuvenation. (Page 463)

GILPIN HOTEL
AND LAKE HOUSE
WINDERMERE
Perched in the tree canopy, the Swedish-style Jetty Spa offers treatments for Lake House guests. Or stay in a Spa Lodge with steam room, outdoor sauna and hydrotherapy tub, and book in-room treatments. Gilpin guests have use of nearby Choices Health Club. (Page 345)

CHEWTON GLEN
NEW MILTON
From the ozone-treated pool and outdoor hot tubs, to crystal steam rooms and aromatherapy saunas, this spa sets the standard. There are top-to-toe beauty treatments, yoga and Tai Chi, all in a lovely New Forest setting. (Page 245)

DART MARINA
DARTMOUTH
Children are welcome in the afternoons to enjoy the pool, spa bath, steam room and fitness suite at this hotel on the River Dart. The signature massage and facial treatments, body wraps and manicures, will appeal more to harassed parents. (Page 157)

MALLORY COURT
LEAMINGTON SPA
In the grounds of an Arts and Crafts country house, the Elan Spa has a fitness room with static bikes, treadmills and exercise pool – or facials and massage for those who simply want to unwind. Perhaps a hot stone massage, or a chakra well-being ritual. (Page 216)

BINGHAM RIVERHOUSE
RICHMOND-UPON-THAMES
Guests at this riverside hotel wishing for an 'eco-wellbeing escape' can stroll around to sister operation Bhuti for a ho-leaf and rosemary muscle melt massage or honey radiance facial. There are fitness classes, yoga, a vegan café. (Page 282)

Chewton Glen, New Milton

Talland Bay Hotel, Talland-by-Looe

ROMNEY BAY HOUSE
NEW ROMNEY

In the elemental landscape of Romney Marsh, between English Channel and golf course, this remote 1920s house, built for Hedda Hopper by Clough Williams-Ellis, is an oasis of warmth and civilisation. Bring boots and binoculars, not bucket and spade. (Page 246)

TRESANTON
ST MAWES

Olga Polizzi's labour of love has been contrived from a former yacht club and fishermen's cottages to create a harmonious whole. Works of Cornish art hang in sea-facing bedrooms. Dine alfresco, enjoy the beach club, sail on a vintage yacht. (Page 292)

RATHMULLAN HOUSE
RATHMULLAN

Overlooking the long sea arm of Lough Swilly, this Georgian house in wooded grounds on the Wild Atlantic Way, is family-run and family-friendly. There are play facilities, an indoor pool, a choice of dining options, a beach at the end of the garden. (Page 491)

THE GALLIVANT
CAMBER

Miles of unspoilt beach lie beyond the only sand dunes in East Sussex, across the road from this fun hotel modelled on a California beach motel. There is a laid-back vibe, seaside-chic style, freshly caught fish on the menu, golf nearby. (Page 133)

THE ROYAL HOTEL
VENTNOR

Set on the cliff top, in sub-tropical gardens with pool and geranium terrace, this 19th-century former coaching inn found great favour this year. The style is country house, smart but relaxed, with fine cooking of local ingredients. (Page 335)

TALLAND BAY HOTEL
TALLAND-BY-LOOE

There is such a spirit of caprice about this cliff-top hotel, with its playful décor, its sub-tropical gardens filled with whimsical sculptures. A place for leisure and pleasure, with sea views from many bedrooms, alfresco dining on the terrace. (Page 317)

THE PIERHOUSE
PORT APPIN

At the northernmost point of the Seafood Trail, with spectacular views across Loch Linnhe to Lismore, this friendly hotel incorporates the quaint Victorian piermaster's house. A shellfish platter served on the bar terrace is heaven. (Page 398)

SOAR MILL COVE HOTEL
SALCOMBE

Binoculars are supplied for dolphin-spotting at this much-loved, family-friendly hotel. Bedrooms have glass doors leading to patio or balcony, views of cove and coastal gardens, or National Trust countryside. Wild-flower walks and beach days beckon. (Page 294)

PORTH TOCYN HOTEL
ABERSOCH

The first generation of children to stay at this family-run hotel will be grandparents or great-grandparents now, but the timeless beauty of the view across Cardigan Bay, the fun of a safe sandy beach, great food and warm hospitality are as they ever were. (Page 421)

THE BLAKENEY HOTEL
BLAKENEY

Kids enjoy crabbing and mud, glorious mud, on the quay at this well-run hotel. Older guests prefer local crab in a sandwich with chilled Picpoul de Pinet. All love north Norfolk's unspoilt beaches, the indoor pool, seal trips to Blakeney Point. (Page 101)

GORDON'S
INVERKEILOR
Fine dining and friendly informality are as perfectly balanced here as Garry Watson's modern cooking and use of Scottish produce, in such dishes as North Sea turbot, chargrilled sweetcorn, crispy chicken wings, mushroom purée, burnt cabbage. (Page 379)

THE COTTAGE IN THE WOOD
BRAITHWAITE
You are invited to 'taste Cumbria' in an eyrie dining room among the treetops. Ben Wilkinson uses local and foraged ingredients in such dishes as Herdwick hogget loin, roast sweetbread, asparagus, anchovy, almond. Views and setting equal the food. (Page 114)

GRASSINGTON HOUSE
GRASSINGTON
John Rudden shows great attention to detail at this Georgian house on the village square. Even the butter is home made. Dishes range from simple fish and chips to, perhaps, Yorkshire lamb loin, breast, braised shoulder, potato, peas, wild garlic. (Page 186)

THE LITTLE GLOSTER
GURNARD
Fun dining meets fine dining beside the Solent. Ben Cooke's menus include sharing plates, chargrilled steaks, local seafood. Flair and ingenuity show in such dishes as day-boat hake, smoked haddock and saffron velouté, crispy pancetta, bronze sea fennel. (Page 187)

THE MASH INN
RADNAGE
Nick Mash reconnects with the land at this red brick village pub. Jon Parry forages, ferments and cures. Ingredients, home grown or sourced from the Mash family farm, appear in such dishes as smoked Romanesco soup; pork belly, burnt apple sauce. (Page 275)

RESTAURANT JAMES SOMMERIN
PENARTH
Acclaim, as ever, for this family-run seafront venture. Diners can watch as Michelin-starred Mr Sommerin and his brigade prepare such dishes as wild sea bass, samphire, ginger, artichoke; Welsh lamb, coconut, butternut squash, cumin, mint. (Page 449)

LAKE ISLE
UPPINGHAM
There is no lake and no isle here at the Burtons' market-town restaurant, just a passion for food, wine and WB Yeats. Stuart Mead uses local produce in such dishes as grilled sea bream, summer vegetables, white clams, Ibérico ham, miso broth. (Page 333)

THE SEAFOOD RESTAURANT
PADSTOW
Forty years on (and more), the Steins' flagship is in full sail. Stéphane Delourme uses Rick Stein's recipes to create seafood classics, from fish and chips and Padstow lobster to Singapore chilli crab. (Page 262)

CROSSWAYS HOTEL
WILMINGTON
David Stott and Clive James run a very happy ship at their house beneath the South Downs. David's monthly-changing menus include the day's fish catch, maybe roast rack of local lamb, port, redcurrant and rosemary jelly. Breakfast is no less of a joy. (Page 342)

BLACKADDIE HOUSE
SANQUHAR
Readers rave about this riverside manse, with special praise for Ian McAndrew's inventive menus. Maybe butter-poached ling; ragout of beef, baby leeks from the garden; pressed pheasant and foie gras terrine, pease pudding, apple purée. (Page 404)

Lake Isle, Uppingham

Widbrook Grange, Bradford-on-Avon

TALLAND BAY HOTEL
TALLAND-BY-LOOE
You don't have to be a sausage dog to qualify for a breakfast banger and chicken dinner at this cliff-top hotel. You're welcome (accompanied) on the beach, in the brasserie or on the terrace; you can borrow a blanket, shower under a tap; £12.50 a day. (Page 317)

THE CASTLE HOTEL
BISHOP'S CASTLE
Great walkies start at the front door of this 18th-century hotel. Feeding trays, food and bowls are provided at no charge, plus refrigerator space. You can eat with your canine companion in the back bar. Leads, towels, torches available on request. (Page 100)

WIDBROOK GRANGE
BRADFORD-ON-AVON
Dog-friendly rooms have garden access at this farmhouse turned hotel (dog bed provided). Fido can join you as you chow down in the conservatory. Doggy afternoooon tea brings wet food, organic biscuits and puppichino. They'll even throw in a tennis ball. (Page 112)

THE FALCONDALE
LAMPETER
Pooches and their people can dine together from separate menus at this Italianate villa. A blanket, water bowl and treats are provided on arrival, and Freya the husky can advise on great doggy days out. £10 per dog a night. (Page 439)

FOREST SIDE
GRASMERE
There are six dog-friendly rooms at this fabulous hotel in 43 acres of wooded grounds. A bed, bowls, water, food and treats are supplied to pups prepared to mind their Ps and Qs. Maximum two at £25 per dog per night (assistance dogs stay free). (Page 183)

PRINCE HALL
TWO BRIDGES
You can dine with your dog in the bistro at this 18th-century manor on Dartmoor (up to two stay free; £15 for each extra dog). Bowls, fridge and treats are provided, with outside tap, bucket, sponge and towels for mucky pups; grooming by arrangement. (Page 330)

MOOR OF RANNOCH
RESTAURANT & ROOMS
RANNOCH STATION
A wee sausage at breakfast and a cosy fireside cushion await canine guests at this remote hotel in a vast moorland landscape. A hose pipe and towels are provided for muddy paws, and no area is off limits, but dogs must be on a lead around wildlife. (Page 401)

THE LUTTRELL ARMS HOTEL
DUNSTER
Canine guests are welcomed with their own bed and 'plenty of fuss' at this historic hotel. Most bedrooms and the bar are dog friendly. The beach is nearby. Ask advice on the best walks. A 'small additional fee' applies. (Page 161)

THE DOG AT WINGHAM
WINGHAM
It would be a funny kind of Dog that sniffed at canine guests, and your four-legged friend is positively welcomed in all areas of this pub/restaurant-with-rooms, where biscuits and water bowls await in the bar; £25 per stay. (Page 346)

THE CAT INN
WEST HOATHLY
Harvey the spaniel welcomes canine company at this cosy, beamed village pub. Winnie the Pooh's Ashdown Forest offers great walking, and when it's time for a little something there are dog-friendly tables in the bar. (Page 339)

LORDS OF THE MANOR
UPPER SLAUGHTER
In a gentle Cotswold landscape, this cherished 17th-century manor house and former rectory is furnished with antiques, the walls hung with portraits of past rectors. You can take tea by the fire or in lovely gardens, dine formally or informally. (Page 332)

LIME WOOD
LYNDHURST
Starry and glamorous yet relaxed, this rebuilt and extended Georgian lodge offers all you could look for in a country house hotel and spa. A perfect blend of traditional hospitality and 21st-century luxury, in a bucolic New Forest setting. (Page 229)

HAMBLETON HALL
HAMBLETON
The superlative staff, outstanding cuisine and sumptuously appointed bedrooms have won unstinting praise this year for the Harts' former hunting lodge turned hotel. Beautifully landscaped gardens are bordered by shimmering Rutland Water. (Page 190)

DOUNESIDE HOUSE
TARLAND
The Edwardian interiors of this Scots Revival former holiday home of the MacRobert family have been lovingly preserved in a recent makeover. Furnished with antiques, it stands in beautifully landscaped gardens. At dinner Scottish ingredients shine. (Page 412)

HOTEL ENDSLEIGH
MILTON ABBOT
A very special place, Olga Polizzi's ducal fishing lodge stands in an Arcadian landscape with the Tamar running through. The relaxed chic style mixes contemporary touches with period furnishings, in perfect harmony with the historic building. (Page 240)

THE MUSTARD SEED
AT ECHO LODGE
BALLINGARRY
Flower-filled public rooms, elegant dining and the welcoming host win praise for this hotel, a fine 19th-century parochial house and former nunnery, in terraced gardens. Traditionally styled bedrooms have truly charming individual touches. (Page 467)

LITTLE BARWICK HOUSE
BARWICK
Afternoon tea by the fire or in the beautiful garden are among the joys at this family-run Georgian country house. They call it a restaurant-with-rooms, and dinner is a feast, but it's not the entire raison d'être. Stay, be spoilt, unwind. (Page 81)

HARTWELL HOUSE
AYLESBURY
Once home to French royalty in exile, this National Trust-owned mansion brims with antiques, paintings, tapestries. Despite the grandeur, it's unstuffy. Play croquet. Dress down for the café/bar, dress up for fine dining. (Page 76)

THE PRIORY
WAREHAM
Flower-filled gardens border the River Frome from this 16th-century former priory. You can take lunch alfresco, afternoon tea by the fire in a cosy lounge, dine very well in the Garden restaurant. Some bedrooms are in the Boathouse on the riverbank. (Page 337)

BODYSGALLEN HALL AND SPA
LLANDUDNO
Coats of arms adorn this 17th century mansion in magnificently restored gardens and parkland, run as a hotel and spa by the National Trust, with views of Snowdonia. Tea in a panelled lounge, fine dining and an aura of professionalism are hallmarks. (Page 441)

GOLDSTONE HALL
MARKET DRAYTON

Come to this Georgian manor house in summer to see the roses. Come at any time to enjoy produce from one of the UK's largest hotel vegetable gardens, with herb walkway (more than 200 varieties), heritage vegetables and double-tiered herbaceous border. (Page 232)

LINDETH FELL
BOWNESS-ON-WINDERMERE

Gardens laid out by unsung Edwardian genius Thomas Mawson surround this B&B overlooking Lake Windermere. Here are Mawson's trademark terraces, lawns, dry-stone walls, glorious plantings, a private tarn in grounds that melt into the landscape. (Page 111)

GRAVETYE MANOR
EAST GRINSTEAD

'In setting a garden, we are painting,' wrote William Robinson, who owned this Elizabethan manor from 1884. Disdaining Victorian formality, Robinson favoured a natural style. Discover a wild garden, flower garden, orchard, lake and meadow in 1,000 wooded acres. (Page 163)

GREYWALLS
GULLANE

An Arts and Crafts 'golf box' designed by Edwin Lutyens stands in gardens attributed to Gertrude Jekyll, with arched gateways in high walls framing views, a sunken croquet lawn, a lavender border, a ha-ha beside Muirfield golf course. (Page 378)

THE PIG NEAR BATH
PENSFORD

A kitchen garden lies at the heart of every Pig, and this Georgian manor with deer park has the largest, with smokehouse, glasshouse, wild-flower orchard, fruit cages and hives. Enjoy home-grown produce in the Conservatory, spa treatments in a 'potting shed'. (Page 267)

VIEWMOUNT HOUSE
LONGFORD

Four landscaped acres surround this 17th-century mansion. Guests will discover a Japanese garden with pagoda and wisteria pergola, a blue garden, a white garden with lily pond, an orchard – and a herb garden to supply the kitchen. (Page 486)

FISCHER'S AT BASLOW HALL
BASLOW

Five acres of gardens surround this Jacobean-style mansion, with clipped box and yews, cottage garden borders, an arboretum, a kitchen garden. Guests, free to wander, find hidden paths, a pond, a 'secret' bridge, specimen trees. (Page 83)

BOATH HOUSE
AULDEARN

You can eat alfresco at the café in the walled garden of this Georgian mansion in parkland. Hens, hives, orchard, potager, glass houses and herb parterres supply the kitchen. Herbaceous borders supply flowers, the lake is stocked with trout. (Page 357)

THE SALUTATION
SANDWICH

'Lutyens's most intricate Wrenaissance house and garden ensemble', this red brick mansion overlooks 3.7 acres of walled gardens for all seasons, a plant-lover's paradise painstakingly restored and home to a summer opera festival. (Page 295)

THE GROVE
NARBERTH

Walking trails thread through 28-acre grounds at this 17th-century-cum-Victorian mansion. Explore four acres of kitchen and walled gardens, terraces, a pond, a stream, an apple orchard and fruit garden, beehives, ancient oaks, mighty beeches. (Page 446)

Fischer's at Baslow Hall, Baslow

The Horn of Plenty, Tavistock

KYLESKU HOTEL
KYLESKU
Loch Glendhu laps the shore below Tanja Lister and Sonia Virechauveix's former coaching inn, which stands against a backdrop of mountains in a Highland wilderness. From decked terrace or light-filled bar, watch seals, otters, golden eagles. (Page 386)

HAZEL BANK
BORROWDALE
Perched above Rosthwaite, the MacRaes' Victorian villa gazes out across the beautiful Borrowdale valley to Great Gable and the 'Jaws of Borrowdale', Kings How and Castle Crag. Rear-facing rooms look on to woodland where you might see Squirrel Nutkin. (Page 106)

HELL BAY HOTEL
BRYHER
On a tiny, rugged island, Robert Dorrien-Smith's stylish hotel enjoys a glorious situation, in grounds bordered by a beach washed by the Atlantic. Bedrooms have a terrace or balcony. Drinks on the Sunset Deck are a little taste of heaven. (Page 128)

STOBERRY HOUSE
WELLS
Frances and Tim Meeres Young's exceptional B&B stands in landscaped parkland, overlooking the gem of a city and its cathedral, with views over the Vale of Avalon to Glastonbury Tor, steeped in the legend of King Arthur, topped by roofless St Michael's Tower. (Page 338)

CURRAREVAGH HOUSE
OUGHTERARD
At the gateway to the Connemara mountains, Henry and Lucy Hodgson's Victorian country house lies in wooded grounds bordering island-studded Lough Corrib. Every bedroom – some with dual aspect – has a view of the lough or Benlevy (Mount Gable). (Page 490)

THE ZETTER
LONDON
At street level, Clerkenwell may be characterful but it's not very scenic. Book a rooftop deluxe studio at this Victorian warehouse turned boutique hotel, however, and from your terrace you can enjoy panoramic views of the glorious gallimaufry of a city. (Page 65)

THE WHITE HORSE
BRANCASTER STAITHE
In the big-sky Norfolk landscape, the Nye family's inn has views across tidal salt marshes and sandy beach to Scolt Head Island. Eat on the terrace or in the dining room with its wall of windows. The top bedroom has a telescope. Birdwatchers' bliss. (Page 115)

HARBOURMASTER HOTEL
ABERAERON
It is not just the views of the harbour that beguile at Glyn and Menna Heulyn's waterfront hotel, with bobbing boats and sails red in the sunset. The Georgian quayside itself, with its brightly coloured houses against a backdrop of hills, is a charm. (Page 418)

THE SEASIDE BOARDING HOUSE
BURTON BRADSTOCK
There are fabulous views over Lyme Bay from Mary-Lou Sturridge and Tony Mackintosh's hotel above Chesil Beach. All bedrooms look out to sea or along the cliffs. The dining room opens out on to the terrace for an airy, outside-in feel. (Page 131)

THE HORN OF PLENTY
TAVISTOCK
Most bedrooms have balcony or private terrace views over the lush, verdant Tamar valley, at Julie Leivers and Damien Pease's former mine captain's house in beautifully tended grounds with manicured lawns, rhododendrons, mature trees. (Page 319)

OLD WHYLY
EAST HOATHLY
Dinner under a vine-covered pergola
with fellow guests on a summer's night
epitomises a stay at Sarah Burgoyne's
Georgian manor house in glorious gardens.
Her spaniel, Puzzle, is a chatty host. Eggs
are from the hens, honey from hives in the
orchard. (Page 164)

THE OLD RECTORY
BOSCASTLE
There are romantic associations with
Thomas Hardy at the Searles' Victorian
rectory B&B. The bed might be an antique
carved one. Breakfast brings eggs from the
hens, home-grown tomatoes, honey from
the bees that pollinate the fruit trees in
lovingly tended gardens. (Page 108)

TIMBERSTONE
CLEE STANTON
Tracey Baylis and Alex Read are the
warmest of hosts at this conversion of two
old cottages. Modern-rustic bedrooms have
countryside views. One has an in-room
bath and balcony. Supper is convivial,
breakfast a feast. (Page 147)

SHALLOWDALE HOUSE
AMPLEFORTH
There are dreamy views to the Howardian
hills from Anton van der Horst and
Phillip Gill's 1960s house in leafy, hillside
gardens. From fresh-baked scones to
freshly squeezed orange juice at breakfast,
everything is just about perfect. (Page 72)

94DR
EDINBURGH
A very special place, avers a fellow Guide
hotelier, of Paul Lightfoot and John
MacEwan's Victorian town house near
Holyrood Park. Special and beautiful, with
period features, personable hosts, super
bathrooms and a spectacular breakfast.
(Page 367)

THE OLD RECTORY
PWLLHELI
The welcome from Lindsay Ashcroft, and
husband Gary's breakfasts win praise for
this B&B in a Georgian rectory surrounded
by mature grounds on the Llyn peninsula.
Book a session with a visiting artist and
paint your own souvenir. (Page 450)

SEA MIST HOUSE
CLIFDEN
Hens cluck away in the flower-filled
garden of Sheila Griffin's Georgian house
B&B. There are wood-burning stoves,
artworks everywhere, new-laid eggs at
breakfast, of course, with soda bread,
pancakes, honey from happy bees.
(Page 474)

THE OLD MANOR HOUSE
HALFORD
You can ask for a picnic then fish in the
River Stour, which borders the landscaped
gardens of the Puseys' 16th-century manor
house filled with antiques and curios. A
full English breakfast of local produce sets
you up for the day. (Page 188)

NUMBER THIRTY EIGHT
CLIFTON
BRISTOL
Hit the heights at Adam Dorrien-Smith's
Georgian merchant's house overlooking
Clifton Down. Stylish, uncluttered
interiors, stunning views, swish
bathrooms, lovely service, cream teas and
a top-notch breakfast more than repay the
uphill climb. (Page 123)

SWAN HOUSE
HASTINGS
Brendan McDonagh is a legendarily kind
and friendly host at this Tudor house
tucked away behind the High Street.
A log fire burns in the beamed sitting
room. Bedrooms are simple but beautiful.
A great breakfast is cooked to order.
(Page 195)

Number Thirty Eight Clifton, Bristol

The Roseleigh, Buxton

THE OLD RECTORY
BOSCASTLE
It's the little things that mean so much at Sally and Chris Searle's B&B – free laundry, a morning paper, fresh flowers and produce from the beautiful organic garden, eggs from the hens, a lift into Boscastle for dinner. Doubles from £75, single £60. (Page 108)

NEWBEGIN HOUSE
BEVERLEY
Georgian elegance, a walled garden, rooms filled with antiques, generous extras (fresh milk, biscuits, chocolate), and an award-winning breakfast are all yours at Nuala and Walter Sweeney's lovely home for a modest £90–£100 (single £60). (Page 95)

THE ROCK INN
NEWTON ABBOT
With double rooms from as little as £110, a small charge for an extra bed for a child, a three-course dinner for £24.95, and Dartmoor on the doorstep, the Graves family's friendly inn offers bargain breaks at any time of year. (Page 250)

NO. 33
HUNSTANTON
B&B starts at £95 a room (add £10 for an infant's bed, deduct £10 if staying solo) at Jeanne Whittome's stylish seaside B&B. A cream tea is served on arrival, and guests are presented with a discount voucher to spend at the owner's deli. (Page 203)

BROWNBER HALL
NEWBIGGIN-ON-LUNE
When Amanda and Peter Jaques-Walker left London in 2016 to take over this Dales country house, they clearly left behind London notions of pricing. With singles from £70, doubles from £100, they run this smart B&B in a spirit of real generosity. (Page 247)

TRELASKE HOTEL & RESTAURANT
LOOE
Hazel Billington and Ross Lewin, hands-on hosts at this small hotel, have priced their rooms to be affordable; eschewing the word 'luxury', they offer a delightful home-from-home. Doubles start at £110 – and, at £30–£35, dinner is value indeed. (Page 224)

THE OLD VICARAGE
DOLFOR
Double rooms at Helen and Tim Withers's eco-friendly Victorian vicarage in the Cambrian mountains start at £95 (£70 for a single guest). A family can stay for £150, and an imaginative mezze platter is just £12. The warm hospitality is free. (Page 431)

JURA HOTEL
CRAIGHOUSE
You could pitch your tent in the field in front of the McCallum family's hotel overlooking the Sound of Jura and pay as little as £5, but for £100 more you can have a snug double room, a comfy bed and your own bathroom. A bar meal won't break the bank. (Page 365)

THISTLEYHAUGH FARM
LONGHORSLEY
If you could put a price on the warmth of welcome from Enid Nelless at this family-run Georgian farmhouse B&B, it would certainly be far higher than the £110 they charge for a double room (single £70). Great breakfasts, home-made shortbread and hugs. (Page 223)

THE ROSELEIGH
BUXTON
In a lovely situation overlooking the Pavilion Gardens lake, Gerard and Maggi Heelan's Victorian B&B is a veritable snip. Traditionally furnished rooms cost £35–£56 per person. The opera house is nearby. Readers sing the praises. (Page 132)

The Rose & Crown, Romaldkirk

THE FELIN FACH GRIFFIN
FELIN FACH

Twenty years after Edmund Inkin bought the first of the three dining pubs he owns with brother Charles, the formula is still a winner. Shabby chic decor, delicious food, an inclusive ambience, sustainability, support for the community, perfectly judged simplicity. (Page 435)

THE RED LION FREEHOUSE
EAST CHISENBURY

From a burger in the beer garden or bar, to Michelin-starred cooking, Guy and Brittany Manning will provide at their thatched village pub. Boutique guest-house rooms have decking almost on the banks of the Avon. Better than ever, say our readers. (Page 162)

THE ROSE & CROWN
SNETTISHAM

Top marks to Jeannette and Anthony Goodrich for the enthusiasm they bring to their pretty 14th-century pub, which serves pub classics and more ambitious fare. Traditional charm is matched by friendly staff, a happy vibe and decor with touches of humour. (Page 304)

THE WELLINGTON ARMS
BAUGHURST

Fluffy tea cosies, fine china, new-laid eggs, home-grown produce and resident Jacob's sheep add to the off-beat appeal of Simon Page and Jason King's pub. Bedrooms are beautifully appointed, and Mr King's cooking has an unfussy elegance. (Page 89)

THE CRICKET INN
BEESANDS

You can eat a soup of locally caught crab in the nautical-themed restaurant at Rachel and Nigel Heath's Victorian pub overlooking Start Bay, as waves crash on the shingle beach. New England-style bedrooms are fresh and appealing. (Page 93)

THE INN AT WHITEWELL
WHITEWELL

A distinctly Merrie England ethos pleases readers at Charles Bowman's eccentric inn on the River Hodder. Blazing log fires, locally shot game, cask-conditioned ales, four-poster rooms, antiques, oil paintings, and a subversive sense of humour add to a potent mix. (Page 341)

THE ROSE & CROWN
ROMALDKIRK

A chorus of acclaim this year for Cheryl and Thomas Robinson's 18th-century coaching inn turned village pub par excellence. The quality of local ingredients shines in David Hunter's seriously great grub. Rooms are splendidly non-chintzy. (Page 283)

THE GREYHOUND INN
LETCOMBE REGIS

First out of the traps this year among Oxfordshire pubs, Martyn Reed and Catriona Galbraith's red brick village local wins high approval for maintaining traditional values while innovating with jazz, pizza, garden parties. Phil Currie cooks with flair. (Page 217)

THE SUN INN
DEDHAM

The Sun has been on the rise since Piers Baker took on what was then a grotty local boozer in 2003. A 15th-century coaching inn, it perfectly fulfils the roles of friendly local, smart hotel and modern restaurant with Italian-inspired cooking. (Page 159)

THE BLACK SWAN
RAVENSTONEDALE

Cosy and quirky, Louise Dinnes's Victorian pub ticks so many boxes. Friendly staff, public rooms filled with clocks and curios, individually styled bedrooms, first-rate modern cooking, a garden with rushing brook, and the Eden valley on the doorstep. (Page 277)

WOOLLEY GRANGE
BRADFORD-ON-AVON
One of the first country house hotels to welcome families, this mellow Wiltshire manor continues to delight all ages. Extensive grounds contain a grass maze and play garden with tractor; indoors, there's a crèche, games room, pool and spa. (Page 113)

ROUNDWOOD HOUSE
MOUNTRATH
Set in 18 acres near the unspoilt Slieve Bloom mountains, this is a wonderfully relaxed and relaxing family home. Cots, kid's supper and child beds are offered, with babysitting on request – though it's worth staying in for Paddy Flynn's superb dinners. (Page 488)

TREFEDDIAN HOTEL
ABERDOVEY
Generations of families have enjoyed the view across Cardigan Bay from this popular hotel that's just a five-minute dash from the beach. But first you have to tear yourself away from the games room, indoor pool, putting green and tennis court. (Page 419)

CHEWTON GLEN
NEW MILTON
Be warned: you'll raise children's expectations sky high by taking them to this super-luxury hotel. Will anything ever match sleeping in a Treehouse suite with hot tub, 35 feet above ground? Or fun and games in the new fairytale children's club? (Page 245)

THE WHITE HOUSE
HERM
There's something of Kirrin Island about car-free Sark, where children can be let off the leash. The Famous Five would have had an awfully jolly holiday at this traditional country house in gardens with tennis, croquet and solar-heated pool. (Page 458)

MOONFLEET MANOR
FLEET
'I'm bored' is just not an option at this friendly hotel on the Dorset coast. A huge indoor games room, swimming pools for all ages, a skittle alley and fossil hunts are on tap; an Ofsted crèche, high tea and baby listening give parents a break. (Page 180)

THE COLONSAY
COLONSAY
Children love the adventure of a ferry ride to an island. Here there are bikes to hire, dolphins and seals to spot and white-sand beaches – as well as the purest of air. Not to mention board games, a kid's menu and a laid-back vibe. (Page 363)

CALCOT
TETBURY
This converted Cotswold farmhouse has just the right level of sophistication to make it feel special, offset by an unstuffy atmosphere, a superb spa, crèches and children's clubs for under- and over-eights and bikes for cycling round the grounds. (Page 321)

THE NARE
VERYAN-IN-ROSELAND
A great place for three-generation family holidays; adults are cosseted by immaculate service and comfort, while children are kept busy with lovely Carne beach, swimming pools, tennis and family painting sessions with a resident artist. (Page 336)

THE BLAKENEY HOTEL
BLAKENEY
Even north Norfolk's glorious beaches have their drizzly days, and families will find happy refuge here in the games room (pool, table tennis, darts) and indoor pool. Children's lunch and tea is served, as well as half portions from the adult menu. (Page 101)

The Blakeney Hotel, Blakeney

The Traddock, Austwick

EES WYKE COUNTRY HOUSE
NEAR SAWREY

Wherever you walk around here, you find yourself in the footsteps of Beatrix Potter, who spent family holidays at this country house, now run as a hotel by Richard Lee. Her farmhouse, Hill Top, is nearby. A newly opened path runs by Esthwaite Water to Hawkshead. (Page 243)

LLANTHONY PRIORY HOTEL
LLANTHONY

A circular walk, taking in two miles of Offa's Dyke, will present you with an eagle's eye view of Victoria and Geoff Neal's historic hotel and abbey ruins. A hearty meal, not frugal monkish fare, will be served up on your return. (Page 444)

THE TRADDOCK
AUSTWICK

Guide books, maps and a packed lunch can be supplied at the Reynoldses' Dales hotel. Whether you're up for the Yorkshire Three Peaks Challenge or a stroll in the Forest of Bowland, you can reward yourself on your return with afternoon tea in the lounge. (Page 75)

PENDRAGON COUNTRY HOUSE
CAMELFORD

Whether you choose to follow the Coastal Path or stride out on Bodmin Moor from Sharon and Nigel Reed's small hotel, they will provide a pick-up-and-drop-off service. Set off with a superb breakfast under your belt. (Page 136)

KNOCKENDARROCH HOTEL
PITLOCHRY

More than 40 miles of signed routes around Pitlochry lead through woodland, along the loch side, by river and burn, to the Linn of Tummel waterfall, to Scotland's smallest distillery. Struan and Louise Lothian, hosts at this hotel, are happy to advise. (Page 394)

BIGGIN HALL
BIGGIN-BY-HARTINGTON

Help yourself to a complimentary packed lunch before setting off from James Moffett's manor house hotel to explore the Peak District, discover Dovedale, perhaps to follow the old railway track bed of the Tissington and High Peaks Trails. (Page 98)

SHEEDY'S
LISDOONVARNA

The Wild Atlantic Way, the Cliffs of Moher and the eerie karst moonscape of the Burren are on the doorstep of this 18th-century mansion. Hosts Martina and John Sheedy are happy to share their local knowledge and provide maps. (Page 485)

DOLFFANOG FAWR
TYWYN

Guests wishing to tackle the Cadair range can request a lift from Alex Yorke and Lorraine Hinkins's Snowdonia guest house and walk back. There are forest, river and mountain walks, a hot tub for a soak on your return. (Page 454)

TUDOR FARMHOUSE
CLEARWELL

Guests can roam 14 acres of ancient grassland without even leaving the property at Hari and Colin Fell's boutique hotel, but the Forest of Dean beckons, with its four-mile sculpture trail. Ask for information and guides. (Page 146)

THE GURNARD'S HEAD
ZENNOR

The Inkin brothers' dining pub is a popular watering hole for hikers on the Coastal Path. Set out from here to explore cliffs and coves, see seals basking on the Carracks, discover the farm source of Moormaid of Zennor ice cream. (Page 351)

AUSTWICK HALL
AUSTWICK
The interiors are a riot of antiques, paintings and ethnic art at Eric Culley and Michael Pearson's historic house, rebuilt in the 1700s and once home to a kinsman of the Inglebys of Ripley Castle. A sculpture trail threads through woodland gardens. (Page 74)

THE GUNTON ARMS
THORPE MARKET
A deer park surrounds this pub, filled by its art dealer owner, Ivor Braka, with works by the likes of Damien Hirst, Julian Opie, Gilbert and George. There are pieces by Tracey Emin, but bedrooms do not reflect her housekeeping standards. (Page 324)

HOWTOWN HOTEL
ULLSWATER
Your bedroom door will have a brass knocker but no key at the Baldrys' gloriously old-fashioned hotel, where a gong still summons guests to dine. Electric blankets, Imperial Leather soap, sherry trifle. . . Who needs a time machine? (Page 331)

ARTIST RESIDENCE OXFORDSHIRE
SOUTH LEIGH
Charlotte and Justin Salisbury collaborated with artists the Connor Brothers to transform this thatched pub, dreaming up a fictional previous owner, Mr Hanbury. Surprising artworks and upcycled furniture adorn bar and rustic-luxury bedrooms. (Page 308)

POOL HOUSE
POOLEWE
All rooms are themed and filled with antiques at the personable Harrison family's former fishing lodge. Hand-painted crusaders adorn reception. One bedroom has a canopied 1912 claw-foot bath. Another evokes the Italian Renaissance. (Page 396)

WIDBROOK GRANGE
BRADFORD-ON-AVON
From the vintage milk float on the terrace to such adornments and amenities as a dressmaker's form, a top-hat lampshade, an antique typewriter, Nick Dent's farmhouse hotel is paraphernalia heaven. There is even an upcycled cycle, a bike-cum-basin stand. (Page 112)

THE PIG ON THE BEACH
STUDLAND
You can sleep in a thatched folly with four-poster in the prolific kitchen garden at this most higgledy-piggledy Piggy, all gargoyles, pointy gables, chimneys and towers. Hogwarts meets Hansel and Gretel. (Page 313)

LOW MILL GUEST HOUSE
BAINBRIDGE
The Workshop bedroom at Jane and Neil McNair's smart 18th-century watermill and former doll's house museum contains the winding gear of the sack hoist and a large pulley wheel. The spur wheel and grinding stones are in the lounge. (Page 79)

GLAZEBROOK HOUSE
SOUTH BRENT
If there was such a thing as a drawing of a muchness it would hang at Fran and Pieter Hamman's frabjous Alice in Wonderland-themed hotel. Cheshire Cat room, with illuminated coffee table and shareable shower, will make you grin from ear to ear. (Page 306)

CLEY WINDMILL
CLEY-NEXT-THE-SEA
If you choose the Wheel Room at the Goldees' iconic tower mill, you'll have to sign a waiver form and climb a ladder. Your reward – panoramic views on all sides. The circular Stone Room has a door on to an oak balcony that wraps around the tower. (Page 148)

Artist Residence Oxfordshire, South Leigh

Lympstone Manor, Exmouth

ASKHAM HALL
PENRITH

The chapel, a French drawing room, medieval hall, gardens and nearby church are at your disposal if you wed at this battlemented ancient pile. Relax in the spa beforehand, party in the Bank Barn, sleep in a four-poster room. (Page 264)

BODYSGALLEN HALL AND SPA
LLANDUDNO

A photographer's dream, this Elizabethan manor house stands in gardens and parkland, with mountain views. A spa, oak-panelled drawing room, romantic four-poster suite, stone cottages with roses round the door. . . What more could you ask? (Page 441)

JUDGES
YARM

Up to 75 people can attend your garden wedding ceremony in the Gazebo at this smart hotel (smaller gatherings in the lounge, garden room and conservatory restaurant). You want a Daimler? A magician? A string quartet? They have the contacts. (Page 349)

LYMPSTONE MANOR
EXMOUTH

It will be a while before guests can raise a flute of Lympstone Manor bubbly from the vineyard, but Michael Caines's Georgian manor in parkland on the Exe estuary affords a glorious setting and a gourmet experience. (Page 177)

MORSTON HALL
HOLT

A more intimate venue, this long-time Guide favourite is renowned for Galton Blackiston's Michelin-starred cooking. Ceremonies are held in the conservatory or gardens. Opt for exclusive use and guests will be welcomed with a cream tea. (Page 200)

THE PAINSWICK
PAINSWICK

Have a civil ceremony in the lounge or on the terrace of this beautiful Palladian mansion with wisteria-draped loggia, or make your vows at St Mary's church. Spa treatments and the four-poster George's Suite are a bride's dream. (Page 263)

THE COLONSAY
COLONSAY

Whether you elect to hold your wedding in the lovely gardens or indoors (and this is the rainy Hebrides), the remote and beautiful situation of this hotel makes for an unforgettable day. There are self-catering cottages if there's no room at the inn for all guests. (Page 363)

HILTON PARK
CLONES

Formal gardens and pleasure grounds surround this Italianate ancestral home. A roofed colonnade has been restored to create a wedding space. Or request a humanist ceremony in the rose garden by the lake. A house-party atmosphere prevails. (Page 475)

THE SALUTATION
SANDWICH

The owners of this beautiful, Queen Anne-style Lutyens house with Arts and Crafts gardens choose to host a small number of weddings each year, and to make them very special. There are no packages; everything is bespoke. (Page 295)

MONTAGU ARMS
BEAULIEU

From an intimate ceremony in the Paris Room to a large gathering in the Terrace restaurant, with Gertrude Jekyll-inspired gardens outside and four-poster suites above, this New Forest hotel can lay on the full Monty. (Page 92)

Each of these hotels has a tennis court (T) and/or a swimming pool (S)

The Grand Hotel, Eastbourne

ENGLAND

Hartwell House & Spa,
Aylesbury (T,S)

Park House,
Bepton (T,S)

Burgh Island Hotel,
Bigbury-on-Sea (T,S)

The Blakeney Hotel,
Blakeney (S)

The Devonshire Arms,
Bolton Abbey (S)

Widbrook Grange,
Bradford-on-Avon (S)

Woolley Grange,
Bradford-on-Avon (S)

The Lygon Arms,
Broadway (S)

Hell Bay Hotel,
Bryher (S)

Brockencote Hall,
Chaddesley Corbett (T)

Tor Cottage,
Chillaton (S)

Corse Lawn House,
Corse Lawn (T,S)

North House,
Cowes (S)

The Rectory Hotel,
Crudwell (S)

Dart Marina,
Dartmouth (S)

Old Whyly,
East Hoathly (T,S)

Gara Rock,
East Portlemouth (S)

The Grand Hotel,
Eastbourne (S)

Whatley Manor,
Easton Grey (S)

Starborough Manor,
Edenbridge (T,S)

Summer Lodge,
Evershot (T,S)

Moonfleet Manor,
Fleet (S)

Fowey Hall,
Fowey (S)

The Old Manor House,
Halford (T)

Hambleton Hall,
Hambleton (T,S)

The Pheasant,
Harome (S)

Augill Castle,
Kirkby Stephen (T)

Mallory Court,
Leamington Spa (S)

Lime Wood,
Lyndhurst (S)

Bedruthan Hotel and Spa,
Mawgan Porth (T,S)

The Scarlet,
Mawgan Porth (S)

Budock Vean,
Mawnan Smith (T,S)

Mullion Cove Hotel,
Mullion Cove (S)

Chewton Glen,
New Milton (T,S)

Askham Hall,
Penrith (S)

Star Castle,
St Mary's (T,S)

Soar Mill Cove Hotel,
Salcombe (T,S)

Seaham Hall,
Seaham (S)

Plumber Manor,
Sturminster Newton (T)

Cliveden House,
Taplow (T,S)

Calcot,
Tetbury (T,S)

The Royal Hotel,
Ventnor (S)

The Nare,
Veryan-in-Roseland (T,S)

Gilpin Hotel and Lake House,
Windermere (S)

Middlethorpe Hall & Spa,
York (S)

SCOTLAND

Glenapp Castle,
Ballantrae (T)

Shieldaig Lodge,
Gairloch (T)

Douneside House,
Tarland (T,S)

WALES

Trefeddian Hotel,
Aberdovey (T,S)

Porth Tocyn,
Abersoch (T,S)

Gliffaes,
Crickhowell (T)

Bodysgallen Hall & Spa,
Llandudno (T,S)

The Lake,
Llangammarch Wells (T,S)

CHANNEL ISLANDS

The White House,
Herm (T,S)

The Atlantic Hotel,
St Brelade (T,S)

Greenhills,
St Peter (S)

Longueville Manor,
St Saviour (T,S)

IRELAND

Ballyvolane House,
Castlelyons (T)

Killiane Castle,
Drinagh (T)

Castle Leslie,
Glaslough (T)

Marlfield House,
Gorey (T)

Rosleague Manor,
Letterfrack (T)

Currarevagh House,
Oughterard (T)

Rathmullan House,
Rathmullan (T,S)

Coopershill,
Riverstown (T)

Ballymaloe House,
Shanagarry (T,S)

Each of these hotels
has at least one
bedroom equipped
for a visitor in a
wheelchair. You
should telephone to
discuss individual
requirements.

Coes Faen, Barmouth

LONDON
The Goring
The Zetter
The Zetter Townhouse Clerkenwell
The Zetter Townhouse Marylebone

ENGLAND
The Wentworth,
Aldeburgh
Rothay Manor,
Ambleside
Hartwell House & Spa,
Aylesbury
Red Lion Inn,
Babcary
Barnsley House,
Barnsley
The Cavendish,
Baslow
No. 15 Great Pulteney,
Bath
Park House,
Bepton
The Blakeney Hotel,
Blakeney
The Lord Crewe Arms,
Blanchland
The Crown Hotel,
Blandford Forum
The Devonshire Arms,
Bolton Abbey
Leathes Head Hotel,
Borrowdale

The Millstream,
Bosham
Lindeth Fell,
Bowness-on-Windermere
Widbrook Grange,
Bradford-on-Avon
Woolley Grange,
Bradford-on-Avon
The White Horse,
Brancaster Staithe
The Mason's Arms,
Branscombe
The Pig at Bridge Place,
Bridge
The Lygon Arms,
Broadway
The Pig in the Forest,
Brockenhurst
The University Arms,
Cambridge
Pendragon Country House,
Camelford
Blackmore Farm,
Cannington
Brockencote Hall,
Chaddesley Corbett
Crouchers,
Chichester
Captain's Club Hotel,
Christchurch
Kings Head Hotel,
Cirencester
Beech House & Olive Branch,
Clipsham

Hipping Hall,
Cowan Bridge

Clow Beck House,
Croft-on-Tees

Dart Marina,
Dartmouth

The Red Lion Freehouse,
East Chisenbury

The Grand Hotel,
Eastbourne

Whatley Manor,
Easton Grey

The Duncombe Arms,
Ellastone

Summer Lodge,
Evershot

Lympstone Manor,
Exmouth

The Carpenters Arms,
Felixkirk

Fowey Hall,
Fowey

The Pig at Combe,
Gittisham

Forest Side,
Grasmere

The Pheasant,
Harome

Castle House,
Hereford

Augill Castle,
Kirkby Stephen

Northcote,
Langho

Mallory Court,
Leamington Spa

Lewtrenchard Manor,
Lewdown

Lime Wood,
Lyndhurst

The Sands Hotel,
Margate

Bedruthan Hotel and Spa,
Mawgan Porth

The Scarlet,
Mawgan Porth

Budock Vean,
Mawnan Smith

Hotel Endsleigh,
Milton Abbot

Chewton Glen,
New Milton

Jesmond Dene House,
Newcastle upon Tyne

The Packhorse Inn,
Newmarket

The Assembly House,
Norwich

Hart's Hotel,
Nottingham

Old Bank,
Oxford

Old Parsonage,
Oxford

Tebay Services Hotel,
Penrith

The Yorke Arms,
Ramsgill-in-Nidderdale

The Black Swan,
Ravenstonedale

The Coach House
at Middleton Lodge,
Richmond

Boskerris Hotel,
St Ives

Idle Rocks,
St Mawes

Seaham Hall,
Seaham

St Cuthbert's House,
Seahouses

La Fleur de Lys,
Shaftesbury

Brocco on the Park,
Sheffield

The Rose & Crown,
Snettisham

Glazebrook House,
South Brent

The Pipe and Glass Inn,
South Dalton

The Crown,
Stoke by Nayland

Plumber Manor,
Sturminster Newton

The Royal Oak,
Swallowcliffe

Cliveden House,
Taplow

The Horn of Plenty,
Tavistock

The Hare and Hounds,
Tetbury

The Royal Oak,
Tetbury

The Gunton Arms,
Thorpe Market

Titchwell Manor,
Titchwell

Tuddenham Mill,
Tuddenham
The Royal Hotel,
Ventnor
The Nare,
Veryan-in-Roseland
Gilpin Hotel and Lake House,
Windermere
Middlethorpe Hall & Spa,
York

SCOTLAND
Loch Melfort Hotel,
Arduaine
Boath House,
Auldearn
Glenapp Castle,
Ballantrae
Coul House,
Contin
**The Three Chimneys
and The House Over-By,**
Dunvegan
Prestonfield,
Edinburgh
Ballathie House,
Kinclaven
Kylesku Hotel,
Kylesku
Langass Lodge,
Locheport
The Peat Inn,
Peat Inn
The Green Park,
Pitlochry
Viewfield House,
Portree
Blackaddie House,
Sanquhar
Kinloch Lodge,
Sleat
The Inn at Loch Tummel,
Strathtummel
Douneside House,
Tarland
Tiroran House,
Tiroran

WALES
Harbourmaster Hotel,
Aberaeron

Trefeddian Hotel,
Aberdovey
Coes Faen,
Barmouth
Gliffaes,
Crickhowell
Penbontbren,
Glynarthen
Tyddyn Llan,
Llandrillo
Bodysgallen Hall & Spa,
Llandudno
The Lake,
Llangammarch Wells
The Grove,
Narberth
Restaurant James Sommerin,
Penarth
Twr y Felin Hotel,
St David's
St Brides Spa Hotel,
Saundersfoot

CHANNEL ISLANDS
Greenhills,
St Peter

IRELAND
The Mustard Seed at Echo Lodge,
Ballingarry
Stella Maris,
Ballycastle
Gregans Castle Hotel,
Ballyvaughan
The Quay House,
Clifden
Castle Leslie,
Glaslough
Rayanne House,
Holywood
Brook Lane Hotel,
Kenmare
No.1 Pery Square,
Limerick
Viewmount House,
Longford

LONDON

Big Ben, London

LONDON

ARTIST RESIDENCE LONDON

♺ Previous César Winner

Forget starving in a garret. Artists need their creature comforts like the rest of us, and find them at Charlotte and Justin Salisbury's hip hotels (see also Brighton, South Leigh). Here, a 19th-century pub has been reinvented, with 'quirky rooms full of character, retro touches, upcycled industrial metal and wood used for floors, ceilings and other furnishings'. Even the smallest rooms have an espresso machine, a fridge, limited-edition prints, a rainfall shower. Larger ones have a super-king-size bed, vintage furniture. The Art Deco-style Club Suite has leather club armchairs, a velvet sofa, roll-top bath and walk-in shower. À la carte breakfast, in the all-day Cambridge Street Kitchen with its neon art and long copper counter, might be a cold-pressed juice, granola, smashed avocado on sourdough, eggs any way, pancakes with bacon, a full English. Staff are 'cheerful and helpful'. Cocktails are shaken in the cellar bar, while dinner brings such fare as sirloin steak, beer onions, malted shiitakes, smoked anchovy butter. It has all come a long way since Justin first conceived the wheeze of inviting artists to stay at his parents' Brighton B&B in exchange for decorating the rooms.

52 Cambridge Street
Pimlico
London SW1V 4QQ

T: 020 3019 8610
E: london@artistresidence.co.uk
W: artistresidence.co.uk

BEDROOMS: 10. 2 suites.
OPEN: all year.
FACILITIES: cocktail bar, restaurant, club room lounge, games/private dining room, small 'hidden' garden, free Wi-Fi, in-room TV (Freeview), unsuitable for disabled.
BACKGROUND MUSIC: in public areas.
LOCATION: Pimlico, underground Pimlico.
CHILDREN: all ages welcomed, cot available for larger rooms, no extra beds for children sharing.
DOGS: only allowed in the restaurant.
CREDIT CARDS: Amex, MC, Visa.
PRICES: room £285–£475. Cooked breakfast from £7, full English £12, à la carte £40. 1-night bookings sometimes refused weekends.

SEE ALSO SHORTLIST

LONDON

MAP 2:D4

THE CAPITAL

'On arrival we discovered that our package
included afternoon tea, which we enjoyed before
a concert at Cadogan Hall.' A cream tea with
smoked salmon and cream cheese on beetroot
bread, 'amazing little cakes', elderflower jelly.
What could be nicer? Our readers had a 'splendid'
stay at this 'intimate luxury hotel'. Built in 1970
for David Levin as a red brick 'grand hotel in
miniature', it and little sister The Levin (see
entry) are now owned by Warwick Hotels. 'Old-
fashioned London hospitality' extends to children,
with kids' bathrobes and slippers, maybe a little
gift. Bedrooms are smart and contemporary,
with marble bathroom, espresso machine,
minibar, every possible service from shoeshine to
babysitting and turn-down. You can relax in the
comfortable restaurant and watch frantic shoppers
hurry by with Harrods carrier bags. New chef
Adam Simmonds's tasting menus include such
dishes as hake, roasted cauliflower, jalapeño
sauce, coriander and lime dressing; London cure
salmon, cucumber chutney, horseradish yoghurt.
'We enjoyed dinner, entertained by a delightful
waitress from Northern Ireland.' Breakfast brings
'an extensive buffet, wonderful eggs Benedict'.
(Jill and Mike Bennett)

22–24 Basil Street
Knightsbridge
London SW3 1AT

T: 020 7589 5171
E: reservations@capitalhotel.co.uk
W: capitalhotel.co.uk

BEDROOMS: 49. 9 suites.
OPEN: all year, restaurant closed Sun.
FACILITIES: sitting room, bar,
restaurant, free Wi-Fi, in-room TV
(Sky), car park, access to nearby health
club/spa, lift, restaurant wheelchair
accessible, no adapted toilet.
BACKGROUND MUSIC: in public areas.
LOCATION: central, underground
Knightsbridge, private car park.
CHILDREN: all ages welcomed.
DOGS: only assistance dogs.
CREDIT CARDS: Amex, MC, Visa.
PRICES: per room B&B £285–£575.
Seasonal menu £45–£55, tasting menu
£75 (plus 12½% discretionary service
charge). Car park £40 a day.

SEE ALSO SHORTLIST

LONDON

DURRANTS

'I have stayed at this lovely hotel for many years, and it still pleases in every respect,' writes a reader in 2019, of this cherished London institution, contrived from four knocked-through Georgian town houses. Founded in 1790, 'solid, respectable and unchanging', it is approaching its centenary in the ownership of the Miller family. 'I love the entrance, the restaurant and the enlarged area for seating, by using the former breakfast room. For somewhere so spotlessly clean and well polished, it is hard to beat at the price.. Another reader, on a fifth visit, reports a 'shabby bathroom' and 'slow breakfast service', but for a long-time devotee, any shortcomings are outweighed by the slightly offbeat charm. Bedrooms have classical and antique furniture and a bathroom with L'Occitane toiletries. A coal fire burns in the clubby George bar, while in the panelled restaurant, at Sunday lunchtime, the carver trundles his trolley of excellent roasts. The food is traditionally British (shepherd's pie, liver and bacon), with occasional flourishes of pancetta or Parmesan shavings. Breakfast is served until 11.30. 'Smoked haddock and poached egg were delicious.' (Ralph Wilson, RC, KS)

26–32 George Street
Marylebone
London W1H 5BJ

T: 020 7935 8131
E: enquiries@durrantshotel.co.uk
W: www.durrantshotel.co.uk

BEDROOMS: 92. 7 on ground floor, not adapted for wheelchair.
OPEN: all year, restaurant closed 25 Dec evening.
FACILITIES: lifts, bar, restaurant, lounge, function rooms, free Wi-Fi, in-room TV (Freeview), use of nearby fitness club, public areas wheelchair accessible, no adapted toilet.
BACKGROUND MUSIC: none.
LOCATION: off Oxford Street, underground Bond Street, Baker Street.
CHILDREN: all ages welcomed.
DOGS: allowed in George bar only.
CREDIT CARDS: Amex, MC, Visa.
PRICES: per room B&B single from £190, double £190–£592. Set menu £20–£33, à la carte £55.

SEE ALSO SHORTLIST

LONDON

MAP 2:D4

THE GORING

'We enjoyed our very expensive one-night stay,' writes a reader who pushed the boat out at Jeremy Goring's grand Edwardian hotel, the last of its kind in London to be run by the founding family. Astonishingly, in the heart of Belgravia, it has a one-acre garden. From the cheapest street-facing rooms, to deluxe doubles with marble bathroom, and luxury garden-view rooms with silk-lined walls, all benefit from 24-hour room service and shoeshine. A room above the entrance was 'very nice, especially two quite lovely armchairs'. Minor 'blemish': a 'hazardous deep-angled step' in the bathroom. On the ground floor, where footmen in scarlet tailcoats buzz about, the bar can be abuzz too: 'We were twice placed on the fringes.' However, 'public areas are in perfect condition', staff are 'plentiful and courteous', and the dining room, designed by David Linley, is 'a joy to behold'. Here is seriously upmarket cooking. Thumbs up for Yorkshire grouse; glazed lobster omelette, perhaps with duck-fat chips, lobster Caesar salad. Breakfast is 'relaxed', with 'plenty of choices'. A separate seafood restaurant, run by Michelin-starred Nathan Outlaw, opens this year. (Anthony Bradbury, H and AM)

15 Beeston Place
Grosvenor Gardens
London SW1W 0JW

T: 020 7396 9000
E: reception@thegoring.com
W: thegoring.com

BEDROOMS: 69. 2 suitable for disabled.
OPEN: all year.
FACILITIES: lifts, lounge, bar, restaurant, private dining rooms, free Wi-Fi, in-room TV (Sky), civil wedding licence, business centre, fitness room, veranda, 1-acre garden (croquet), public rooms wheelchair accessible, adapted toilet.
BACKGROUND MUSIC: none.
LOCATION: Belgravia, mews parking, underground Victoria.
CHILDREN: all ages welcomed.
DOGS: only assistance dogs allowed.
CREDIT CARDS: Amex, MC, Visa.
PRICES: B&B single from £455, double from £485, D,B&B double from £525. À la carte (3 courses) from £64, pre-theatre dinner (2 courses) £37.

SEE ALSO SHORTLIST

LONDON

THE GRAZING GOAT

In 'a great location' in vibrant 'Portman Village', tucked away behind Oxford Street, this 'all-day café/bar/restaurant-with-rooms' has a relaxed vibe. There are pavement tables in front, clatter and chatter in a buzzy bar with stripped wooden floor. Some bedrooms are 'quite a climb'. Our inspector's bags were carried up to a top-floor room with rooftop views, 'beautifully furnished in simple modern style', and quiet, even with the sash window open. There were teapigs tea and cafetière coffee, decaf on request. An 'exceptional' bathroom had a limestone floor, a freestanding bath, walk-in shower and Aesop toiletries. All rooms are air conditioned, with a king-size bed, room service. In the first-floor restaurant, menus use carefully sourced ingredients for such dishes as venison shoulder and loin, beetroot, cavolo nero, red wine jus; beluga lentil salad, broccoli, truffle dressing; pan-fried hake, celeriac, hispi cabbage, lobster sauce. Breakfast is à la carte, with juices, free-range eggs, smoked ham hock, pancakes, chorizo, red onion and spinach omelette, a full English with Cumberland sausage. One 'for the young or the young at heart'. See also sister operation, The Orange.

6 New Quebec Street
Marble Arch
London W1H 7RQ

T: 020 7724 7243
E: reservations@thegrazinggoat.co.uk
W: thegrazinggoat.co.uk

BEDROOMS: 8.
OPEN: all year.
FACILITIES: bar, dining room, patio, free Wi-Fi, in-room TV.
BACKGROUND MUSIC: all day in bar.
LOCATION: central, underground Marble Arch.
CHILDREN: all ages welcomed.
DOGS: allowed in public rooms, not in bedrooms.
CREDIT CARDS: Amex, MC, Visa.
PRICES: room £210–£250. À la carte £35, set menus £27–£46, breakfast mains from £7.50, full English £12.50.

SEE ALSO SHORTLIST

LONDON

HAZLITT'S

Named after former resident and essayist William Hazlitt, this 'stunningly individual' hotel, owned by Peter McKay and Douglas Blain, is a sensuous escape from Soho directly outside. The 'exquisitely restored' Georgian town house adheres to Mr McKay's belief that atmosphere is the most important thing. Guests step into 'an island of civility' where rich velvets, silks and tapestries are joined by gilt-framed portraits, antiques and porcelain. The plush drawing room, occupied by resident cat Sir Godfrey, is stocked with books including first editions of Harry Potter, signed by regular guest JK Rowling – a literary link to when Jonathan Swift and William Wordsworth were visitors. The bedrooms, named after Hazlitt's cohort, mix sumptuous details with quirky features: a bed from the House of Commons, a bath filled from the beak of a life-size eagle tap. 'Our shower was as big as some chain hotel bathrooms.' At the front, triple glazing; at the back, 'we slept with windows ajar and heard no noise'. Breakfast, including a Cumbrian bacon baguette, is served in the room. Light bites are available at any time, but Soho's eateries are mere yards away. (The Rookery is a sister – see main entry.)

6 Frith Street
Soho
London W1D 3JA

T: 020 7434 1771
E: reservations@hazlitts.co.uk
w: hazlittshotel.com

BEDROOMS: 30. 2 on ground floor.
OPEN: all year.
FACILITIES: lift, library, private lounge/meeting room, free Wi-Fi, in-room TV (Sky), public rooms wheelchair accessible, adapted toilet.
BACKGROUND MUSIC: none.
LOCATION: centre of Soho, underground Tottenham Court Road, Leicester Square.
CHILDREN: all ages welcomed.
DOGS: not allowed.
CREDIT CARDS: Amex, MC, Visa.
PRICES: per room B&B single from £169, double £232–£483. À la carte £25.

SEE ALSO SHORTLIST

LONDON

THE LEVIN

The show-stopper at this small hotel is Sharon Marston's April Light, a 60-foot cascade of polished steel, polymer and glass-fibre optics, which hangs in the central stairwell, scattering colours and light. The Levin, like its neighbour, The Capital (see entry), was the creation of David Levin, designed in glamorous 1930s style, and now part of the Warwick group. Smart, contemporary bedrooms have Porta Romana lighting, fabrics by Designers Guild and William Yeoward. All are air conditioned, with hand-stitched Savoir bed, minibar, espresso machine, a marble bathroom with under-floor heating. 'We enjoyed our stay, with a lovely room and bathroom,' wrote trusted Guide readers, who dined well at The Capital. Cross-fertilisation between the sibling operations allows guests to stay at The Levin and take afternoon tea or dinner next door, charging it to their room. Similarly, if you crave a freshly cooked breakfast, The Capital will provide it. But the Levin's 'well-organised buffet breakfast, in a corner of the lounge, offers fresh fruit and juice, cereals and yogurt, hot dishes, breads for toasting, pastries, cheese and cold meats... What more does one need?' (Jill and Mike Bennett)

28 Basil Street
Knightsbridge
London SW3 1AS

T: 020 7589 6286
E: reservations@thelevinhotel.co.uk
W: thelevinhotel.co.uk

BEDROOMS: 12.
OPEN: all year.
FACILITIES: lobby, library, bar/brasserie, free Wi-Fi, in-room TV (Sky), babysitting, valet parking, access to nearby health club/spa, unsuitable for disabled.
BACKGROUND MUSIC: in restaurant and lobby.
LOCATION: central, underground Knightsbridge.
CHILDREN: all ages welcomed.
DOGS: only guide dogs allowed.
CREDIT CARDS: Amex, MC, Visa.
PRICES: per room B&B (continental, included when booked directly with hotel) from £210.

SEE ALSO SHORTLIST

LONDON

MAP 2:D4

NUMBER SIXTEEN

⚘ Previous César Winner

'No bland corporate anonymity here.' Beyond the
portico of a white stucco Victorian mansion lies a
truly boutique hotel, part of Kit and Tim Kemp's
Firmdale group. Interiors have been designed in
Kit Kemp's bright, modern style, with bold use
of colour that never jars. Two drawing rooms
with floor-to-ceiling windows are filled with
paintings, sculpture and objets d'art chosen by the
Kemps. An orangery overlooks a walled garden
with fishpond and gazebo, a leafy sanctuary in the
heart of London – and if that's not enough green
for you, Kensington Gardens and Hyde Park are a
stroll away. You can eat indoors or out, light bites,
club sandwiches, salads, steaks, fishcakes – or take
'afternoon tea' at any time for a very reasonable
(for London) £22. The ambience is deliberately
'home-from-home', with 'helpful staff', child-size
bathrobes and a book of London activities for
young guests. Bedrooms range from single to the
Sumner Room with king-size bed and sofa bed.
Two can interconnect for a family. All have a
'wonderfully comfortable' bed, an oak and granite
bathroom, Kit Kemp's RIKRAK bath products.
Twenty-four-hour room service and breakfast in
bed, if desired, add to a sense of being cosseted.

16 Sumner Place
South Kensington
London SW7 3EG

T: 020 7589 5232
E: sixteen@firmdale.com
W: firmdale.com

BEDROOMS: 41. 1 on ground floor.
OPEN: all year.
FACILITIES: drawing room, library,
conservatory, free Wi-Fi, in-room TV
(Sky), civil wedding licence, garden.
BACKGROUND MUSIC: in library.
LOCATION: Kensington, underground
South Kensington.
CHILDREN: all ages welcomed.
DOGS: small dogs sometimes allowed
(phone to discuss).
CREDIT CARDS: Amex, MC, Visa.
PRICES: room single from £228, double
£282–£360. Continental breakfast £18,
cooked items £5.50 each, 2-course
à la carte from £32.

SEE ALSO SHORTLIST

LONDON

THE ORANGE

Across from the pocket park of Orange
Square, with its statue of a young Mozart, this
'upmarket pub/café/restaurant' is a sister to The
Grazing Goat (see entry). Both are creations
of the Bernardi brothers' Cubitt House group,
characterised by casual sophistication. 'A
conversion of a beautifully proportioned Georgian
building.' The Orange is set over three floors
with a private dining room in the old brewery
beneath. 'Beautifully crafted bedrooms' at the top
have exposed roof timbers, bare floorboards, air
conditioning, a king-size bed, modern artwork,
what they term 'countryside chic'. In the street-
level bar they serve coffees, cocktails, craft beers,
more than 30 wines by the glass. The first-floor
dining room menu offers such 'well-presented'
dishes as fried hake, cauliflower, forced rhubarb,
smoked almonds; truffle potatoes, wild garlic,
goat's curd, artichokes, cured egg yolk, as well as
wood-fired pizzas. 'We were pleased we chose to
eat in.' Breakfast can include chilli cornbread with
smashed avocado; smoked salmon and poached
egg, hollandaise on muffin. Sloane Square, the
King's Road and the Royal Hospital, Chelsea (for
the flower show), are nearby.

37 Pimlico Road
Pimlico
London SW1W 8NE

T: 020 7881 9844
E: reservations@theorange.co.uk
W: theorange.co.uk

BEDROOMS: 4.
OPEN: all year.
FACILITIES: restaurant, 2 bars, private
dining room, free Wi-Fi, in-room
TV, ground-floor pub/dining area
wheelchair accessible, adapted toilet.
BACKGROUND MUSIC: in public areas.
LOCATION: Pimlico, underground
Sloane Square.
CHILDREN: all ages welcomed.
DOGS: allowed in bedrooms by prior
agreement, public rooms, except first-
floor dining room.
CREDIT CARDS: Amex, MC, Visa.
PRICES: per room £205–£240. À la carte
£36, set menus £27–£39, breakfast
cooked dishes from £7.50, full English
£12.50.

SEE ALSO SHORTLIST

LONDON

PORTOBELLO HOTEL

It's not alone in claiming to be 'London's first boutique hotel', but the 'charming, quirky' Portobello is assuredly one of its most extraordinary. Since taking over the property – comprising two adjoining neoclassical mansions – in 2014, Peter and Jessica Frankopan have been gently upgrading, while preserving original features. Bedrooms range from 'tiny, beautifully coloured' box-room singles to signature rooms, via comfy, cosy, jolly good, roomy and splendid. All have own-brand luxury bath products, robes, slippers, minibar. One has a Victorian canopy shower bath, another a circular bed, yet another a four-poster from Hampton Court Palace, French doors, an iron-lace balcony overlooking the garden. The drawing room has an honesty bar and a short menu, so you can pair a bottle of bubbly (a nod to the hotel's flamboyant history of models, musicians and movie stars) with a BLT sandwich or boeuf bourguignon. A help-yourself breakfast of porridge, cereal, cold meats and cheeses is laid out on a Welsh dresser; cooked dishes to order cost extra; all served on vintage china finds from nearby Portobello Road market. The Canal House, Amsterdam, is a sister (see Guide website).

22 Stanley Gardens
Notting Hill
London W11 2NG

T: 020 7727 2777
E: stay@portobellohotel.com
W: portobellohotel.com

BEDROOMS: 21.
OPEN: all year.
FACILITIES: lift, drawing room/ breakfast room with honesty bar, free Wi-Fi, in-room TV, unsuitable for disabled.
BACKGROUND MUSIC: 'chill-out' in drawing room.
LOCATION: Notting Hill, underground Notting Hill Gate.
CHILDREN: all ages welcomed.
DOGS: allowed in one room, not in breakfast room.
CREDIT CARDS: Amex, MC, Visa.
PRICES: per room B&B single £185–£195, double £225–£435. Cooked breakfast £6–£10. One-night bookings sometimes refused Sat and public holidays.

SEE ALSO SHORTLIST

LONDON

MAP 2:D4

THE ROOKERY

There may now be USB charge sockets in all
bedrooms, but this hotel retains such an air of a
bygone age that you half expect Dr Johnson to
swing by from his house a stroll away. Owned
by Peter McKay and Douglas Blain, founding
members of the Spitalfields Trust, this huddle
of knocked-through 18th-century houses is
replete with antique furniture, crackling fires,
'gilt-framed portraits', rich silks and velvets. 'A
soothing space' infused with a club-like calm,
it is a world away from surrounding, trendy
Clerkenwell and Smithfield (the meat market,
a triumph of Victorian architecture, is close by).
Walls are painted in heritage shades. Bedrooms
have a 17th-century carved oak bed or four-poster,
a minibar, new-fangled air conditioning. Junior
suites, with a panelled sitting room, have a vintage
roll-top bath, walk-in shower, a throne loo. From
the Rook's Nest suite, with Victorian bathing
machine, a staircase leads to a sitting room under
a 40-foot spire. There are cordials from the
Conservatory's honesty bar, victuals and breakfast
from a room-service menu including freshly
baked pastries, smoothies, a smoked salmon bagel
or bacon sandwich. (See also sister hotel, Hazlitt's.)

12 Peter's Lane
Cowcross Street
London EC1M 6DS

T: 020 7336 0931
E: reservations@rookery.co.uk
W: rookeryhotel.com

BEDROOMS: 33. 1 on ground floor.
OPEN: all year.
FACILITIES: conservatory lounge,
meeting rooms, free Wi-Fi, in-room
TV (Sky), small patio garden,
unsuitable for disabled.
BACKGROUND MUSIC: none.
LOCATION: Clerkenwell, underground
Farringdon, Barbican.
CHILDREN: all ages welcomed.
DOGS: not allowed.
CREDIT CARDS: Amex, MC, Visa.
PRICES: per room £250–£350. Breakfast
from around £11, à la carte (from
limited room-service menu) £28.

SEE ALSO SHORTLIST

LONDON

SAN DOMENICO HOUSE

Osbert Lancaster dubbed the style 'Pont Street Dutch', but behind the gabled red brick facade of twin Victorian mansions, you are in Italy. This is the old Sloane Hotel, reinvented by the Pugliese Melpignano family (see Guide website for sister hotel Masseria San Domenico, Savelletri di Fasano). It has been lavishly styled and furnished, with antiques, mirrors, oil portraits in gilt frames, urns, lamps, statuary, chinoiserie, ormolu and putti. Bedrooms have air conditioning, a minibar, a marble bathroom, Molton Brown toiletries, swags and drapes. Suites, perhaps with four-poster, have a sitting area with sofa, comfy chairs and antique table. The cheapest rooms are surprisingly affordable for this area, three minutes from Sloane Square, the Royal Court Theatre and the King's Road. Manager Giambattista La Torre presides over 'charming, helpful' Italian staff. There is no gym, but you can give the lift a miss and ascend the stairs to the spectacular roof terrace for a breakfast of freshly squeezed orange juice, pastries, cooked items to order; maybe later a salad or pasta from the room-service menu. When it rains, there is a breakfast room, a restful drawing room. Reports, please.

29–31 Draycott Place
Chelsea
London SW3 2SH

T: 020 7581 5757
E: info@sandomenicohouse.com
W: sandomenicohouse.com

BEDROOMS: 19.
OPEN: all year.
FACILITIES: lift, lounge, breakfast room, roof terrace, free Wi-Fi, in-room TV (Freeview), unsuitable for disabled.
BACKGROUND MUSIC: in lounge and breakfast room.
LOCATION: Chelsea, underground Sloane Square.
CHILDREN: all ages welcomed.
DOGS: not allowed.
CREDIT CARDS: Amex, MC, Visa.
PRICES: room £220–£700. Continental breakfast £18, cooked £24.

SEE ALSO SHORTLIST

LONDON

THE VICTORIA

A busy, multi-tasking pub, 'school-run coffees in the morning, great food and pub atmosphere at night'. In a leafy suburb close to Richmond Park and a short train ride from central London, Paul Merrett's Victorian gastropub with rooms indeed keeps busy through the day, from the cappuccino crowd to dinner. Bedrooms, in converted stables, are of a kind, each with a coffee machine, a queen-size bed, a shower room. The bar has bare floorboards, fringed lamps, plum-coloured chesterfields and fun wallpaper (Lisa Bliss's 'Stag Head'). Interesting bar food includes samosas, crisp squid with wasabi and lime mayo, pulled pork bap). In the conservatory restaurant or the walled garden, Mr Merrett serves modern British food with an Asian twist, rigorously sourced with an eye to animal welfare and sustainability (Dingley Dell pork, rare breed artisan sausages, MSC-approved day-boat fish). There is a children's menu; good veggie options. Typical dishes: porcini risotto, rocket, truffle oil; chargrilled Barnsley chop, imam bayildi, coriander yogurt. A 'great' breakfast brings American pancakes, bacon in a brioche bap, smashed avocado on wholemeal. A good stop-over for Heathrow travellers.

10 West Temple Sheen
Mortlake
London SW14 7RT

T: 020 8876 4238
E: reservations@victoriasheen.co.uk
W: victoriasheen.co.uk

BEDROOMS: 7. 3 on ground floor.
OPEN: all year.
FACILITIES: bar, restaurant, free Wi-Fi, in-room TV, garden, play area, unsuitable for disabled.
BACKGROUND MUSIC: in pub and dining room, occasional live music events.
LOCATION: Mortlake, 10 mins' walk from trains to Waterloo/Clapham Jct, car park.
CHILDREN: all ages welcomed.
DOGS: allowed in pub and garden.
CREDIT CARDS: MC, Visa.
PRICES: per room B&B £135–£145 (continental breakfast), £140–£150 (cooked). À la carte £33 (plus discretionary 12½% service charge).

SEE ALSO SHORTLIST

LONDON

MAP 2:D4

THE ZETTER

A design-led boutique hotel with impressive green credentials (it pumps water from its own 1,500-foot borehole), this former Victorian warehouse embodies the renaissance of East London. Part of the Zetter group (see next two entries), it's ideally located in buzzing Clerkenwell, close to the City and British Museum yet just ten minutes from the West End by taxi (or astride one of the hotel's complimentary Brompton bikes). Rooms vary in size, from small to extremely spacious; rooftop studios have a private balcony or terrace, one with a roll-top bath for alfresco bathing. All enjoy Zetter's signature cutting-edge design, an honesty tray of food and drink and a selection of Penguin paperbacks, as well as a monsoon shower and REN toiletries. On the ground floor, locals tap away at their laptops (the hotel partners with a shared workspace company) while diners tuck into all-day modern British dishes prepared by Ben Boeynaems: garden pea chilled soup with mint, this morning's ricotta; or loin of fallow deer, heritage beetroots, caramelised endive, glazed faggot, sautéed chanterelles. Breakfast is a feast of hot and cold options, with a classic brunch the order of the day at weekends.

St John's Square
86-88 Clerkenwell Road
London EC1M 5RJ

T: 020 7324 4444
E: info@thezetter.com
W: thezetter.com

BEDROOMS: 59. 2 suitable for disabled.
OPEN: all year.
FACILITIES: 2 lifts, atrium, bar/restaurant, terrace (alfresco dining), free Wi-Fi, in-room TV (Freeview, some with Smart TV), in-room spa treatments, reduced rates at local gym, bicycles to borrow, NCP 5 mins' walk, public areas wheelchair accessible, adapted toilet.
BACKGROUND MUSIC: in bar/restaurant.
LOCATION: Clerkenwell, NCP garage 5 mins' walk, underground Farringdon.
CHILDREN: all ages welcomed.
DOGS: only guide dogs allowed.
CREDIT CARDS: Amex, MC, Visa.
PRICES: per room £297–£534. Breakfast buffet £15.50, full English £16, à la carte £40.

SEE ALSO SHORTLIST

LONDON

THE ZETTER TOWNHOUSE CLERKENWELL

♛Previous César Winner

Wit and whim go hand in hand at Mark Sainsbury and Michael Benyan's 'brilliantly quirky' Georgian town house in a cobbled corner of Clerkenwell. Standing opposite the original Zetter (see previous entry), it was devised as the eclectic home of eccentric Great-Aunt Wilhelmina, and it brims with oddities collected on her travels. The lounge, with velvet sofas and winged armchairs, displays a stag's head, oil paintings and taxidermied birds, all under the watchful eye of a parasol-wielding stuffed cat. Pleasing touches fill the equally eccentric bedrooms, some with a four-poster, one with a gaudy fairground reclamation headboard: lots of books, hot-water bottles in hand-knitted covers; a drench shower, REN toiletries in the bathroom. Wilhelmina and her companion, Uncle Seymour, lay out a feast for afternoon tea: truffled sausage roll and devilled eggs alongside puffy scones, ruffles of vanilla choux, and finger sandwiches. In the apothecary-style bar, a resident mixologist shakes heady pre-dinner gin cocktails, before guests venture into a neighbourhood with many dining options. Breakfast is served in the lounge.

25% DISCOUNT VOUCHERS

49–50 St John's Square
Clerkenwell
London EC1V 4JJ

T: 020 7324 4567
E: reservations@thezetter.com
W: www.thezettertownhouse.com/
   clerkenwell

BEDROOMS: 13. 1 suitable for disabled.
OPEN: all year.
FACILITIES: cocktail lounge, private dining room, games room, free Wi-Fi, in-room TV (Freeview), civil wedding licence, cocktail lounges wheelchair accessible.
BACKGROUND MUSIC: all day in cocktail lounge.
LOCATION: Clerkenwell, underground Farringdon.
CHILDREN: all ages welcomed.
DOGS: assistance dogs only.
CREDIT CARDS: Amex, MC, Visa.
PRICES: per room B&B £222–£582 (includes £16 continental breakfast, which can be traded for equivalent cooked option, including a full English). À la carte £30.

SEE ALSO SHORTLIST

LONDON

MAP 2:D4

THE ZETTER TOWNHOUSE MARYLEBONE

Choose Lear's Loft bedroom at this Georgian town house and you can dance to the light of the moon on a roof terrace with alfresco copper bath, then phone down for mince and slices of quince and a runcible spoon. The one-time home of Edward Lear, that Victorian purveyor of literary nonsense, is run as a wonderfully outré hotel by Mark Sainsbury and Michael Benyan, who have 'styled it as the London home of wicked Uncle Seymour', filling it with 'artefacts from his grand European tour'. It is as 'dotty as the Clerkenwell version' and original Zetter (preceding entries). The atmosphere is clubby, with a cocktail bar (Seymour's Parlour) 'more like a drawing room than a bar'. Bedrooms are a riot. One has a four-poster with a Union Jack canopy, another an in-room bath set in a gold-tiled alcove. Each has a raindance shower (walk-in or over-bath), minibar, ground coffee, organic tea, novels, REN toiletries, robes and slippers. 'Every detail is carefully thought out.' The atmosphere is 'warm and inclusive'. There's afternoon tea with cream scones. Light bites cater to Seymour's English tastes, with a Scotch egg, potted salmon, truffled sausage roll with brown sauce.

28–30 Seymour Street
Marylebone
London W1H 7JB

T: 020 7324 4544
E: reservations@thezetter.com
W: www.thezettertownhouse.com/
    marylebone

BEDROOMS: 24. 2 suitable for disabled.
OPEN: all year.
FACILITIES: lift, cocktail lounge/
restaurant, free Wi-Fi, in-room TV
(terrestrial).
BACKGROUND MUSIC: all day in cocktail
lounge.
LOCATION: central, underground
Marble Arch.
CHILDREN: all ages welcomed.
DOGS: only guide dogs allowed.
CREDIT CARDS: Amex, MC, Visa.
PRICES: per room B&B £222–£882
(includes £16 continental buffet, which
can be traded for equivalent cooked
option, including a full English). À la
carte £35.

SEE ALSO SHORTLIST

Golden Cap, Jurassic Coast, Dorset

ENGLAND

ALDEBURGH Suffolk

MAP 2:C6

THE WENTWORTH

In 'a great location, just across from the beach',
Michael Pritt's Victorian hotel has been family
owned and run since 1920. 'It always delights
us,' say readers who visit every year. 'We never
get bored.' Mr Pritt 'has just the right recipe –
informality and courtesy'. The bedrooms are
individually designed, 'good and well appointed',
many with a sea view. Seven are in Darfield
House, set back, with a secluded garden and
outdoor seating. 'The place is a tradition,' our
reader continues. 'A lot of older people come
here, but so what? I'm old myself.' A younger
visitor had a quibble: 'There's no night porter
and they lock the communal areas at midnight
to set the alarm, so we had to rush to finish our
board game (because we're cool).' Still, 'staff were
accommodating and service was generally good'.
In the sea-facing dining room, Tim Keeble's short
menus include local seasonal ingredients, maybe
lemon sole with cream and Parmesan; pan-fried
duck breast with black cherry sauce; Thai green
vegetable curry. 'The food is not outstanding, but
it's good, the breakfasts especially so.' Work up an
appetite: 'A 7 am walk with the dogs, along the
path by the sea, is heaven.' (Simon Rodway)

25% DISCOUNT VOUCHERS

Wentworth Road
Aldeburgh IP15 5BD

T: 01728 452312
E: stay@wentworth-aldeburgh.co.uk
w: wentworth-aldeburgh.com

BEDROOMS: 35. 7 in Darfield House
opposite, 5 on ground floor, 1 suitable
for disabled.
OPEN: all year except maybe 2 weeks
in Jan.
FACILITIES: 2 lounges, bar, restaurant,
private dining room, conference room,
free Wi-Fi, in-room TV (Freeview),
2 terrace gardens, courtyard garden,
public rooms wheelchair accessible,
adapted toilet.
BACKGROUND MUSIC: none.
LOCATION: seafront, 5 mins' walk from
centre.
CHILDREN: all ages welcomed.
DOGS: allowed in bedrooms (£2 per
dog per night) and public rooms, not
in restaurant.
CREDIT CARDS: Amex, MC, Visa.
PRICES: per room B&B £113–£330,
D,B&B £135–£370. Set dinner
£24–£30. 1-night bookings refused Sat.

AMBLESIDE Cumbria

MAP 4: inset C2

ROTHAY MANOR

The flower-bedecked balconies at this manor
house hotel offer spectacular views to Wansfell
Pike. Dating from 1823, it stands in wooded
grounds on the edge of Ambleside. 'Young and
ambitious' owners, Jamie and Jenna Shail, have
been updating the interiors since taking over in
2016 – eight guest rooms were renovated this
year. Trusted readers who knew the place of old
were 'very impressed' to find it 'maintained to a
high standard'. All bedrooms have a mini-fridge,
Noble Isle toiletries, fluffy robes. One of two
dog-friendly ground-floor rooms has an accessible
bathroom, the other a small courtyard garden.
Balcony rooms have a luxurious bathroom, a
coffee machine. The look is contemporary, with
Farrow & Ball finishes, designer wallpaper. The
latest innovation: a hot-tub suite. At dinner,
chef Daniel McGeorge's cooking is 'a class act'.
Seasonal, locally sourced dishes include Lavinton
lamb loin, sweetbreads, rib, roots, sea buckthorn,
cime di rapa. From a no-less-ambitious vegetarian
menu: goat's cheese and honey pastilla, cucumber,
spring onion, olive. Your dog can join you in the
lounge, where simpler fare includes fish of the
day, and a Cumbrian staple, sticky toffee pudding.

25% DISCOUNT VOUCHERS

Rothay Bridge
Ambleside LA22 0EH

T: 015394 33605
E: hotel@rothaymanor.co.uk
W: rothaymanor.co.uk

BEDROOMS: 19. 2 in bungalow in the
grounds, 1 suitable for disabled.
OPEN: all year except 3 weeks Jan.
FACILITIES: lounge, drawing room, bar,
2 dining rooms, free Wi-Fi, in-room
TV (Sky), civil wedding licence,
1-acre garden (croquet), public rooms
wheelchair accessible.
BACKGROUND MUSIC: all day in bar and
restaurant.
LOCATION: ¼ mile SW of Ambleside.
CHILDREN: all ages welcomed.
DOGS: allowed in 4 bedrooms, public
rooms, not restaurant, £20 per dog
per stay.
CREDIT CARDS: Amex, MC, Visa.
PRICES: per room B&B small single
£110, double £165–£250, D,B&B
£215–£365. Dinner £49–£55, tasting
menu £65. Normally min. 2-night
bookings Sat.

SEE ALSO SHORTLIST

AMPLEFORTH Yorkshire   MAP 4:D4

SHALLOWDALE HOUSE

Phillip Gill and Anton van der Horst's 'warm welcoming' B&B is adored by a cohort of regular returnees. 'It felt like coming home,' writes a reader after this year's visit. 'It is a perfect venue for a real treat.' The afternoon teas with home-made scones were greatly enjoyed, as were Phillip's 'outstanding seasonal' dinners. 'They were obviously prepared by a confident, imaginative cook.' An endive gratin was followed by a slow-cooked duck leg, and a delicious apricot and almond tart. 'We left room for the cheeseboard, knowledgeably presented by Anton.' Public rooms in the architect-designed 1960s house are filled with antiques, 'enticing bookcases and amazing art'. They look out across 'beautiful gardens', planted by Anton, to the Howardian hills. 'Our spacious bedroom was well equipped, with Penhaligon toiletries, binoculars on the windowsill – even a bowl of chocolates to dip into while watching the rabbits on the lawn.' After an 'excellent breakfast' ('What makes the Shallowdale House scrambled eggs so good?'), there are 'some great (hilly) walks straight from the house'. Helmsley and the delightful Scampston Garden are a short drive away. (Mary Hewson, and others)

West End
Ampleforth YO62 4DY

T: 01439 788325
E: stay@shallowdalehouse.co.uk
w: shallowdalehouse.co.uk

BEDROOMS: 3.
OPEN: all year except Christmas/New Year, 'occasionally at other times'.
FACILITIES: drawing room, dining room, sitting room/library, in-room TV (Freeview), 2½-acre gardens, unsuitable for disabled.
BACKGROUND MUSIC: none.
LOCATION: edge of village.
CHILDREN: not under 12.
DOGS: not allowed.
CREDIT CARDS: MC, Visa.
PRICES: per room B&B single £115–£140, double £135–£170. Set dinner £48 (min. 48 hours' notice). 1-night bookings occasionally refused weekends.

ARUNDEL Sussex

MAP 2:E3

THE TOWN HOUSE

Visitors to Lee and Katie Williams's town-centre restaurant-with-rooms this year raved about 'everything: the food, the accommodation, the location – all was perfect'. Across from the walls of the castle dating back to the 11th century, the Regency town house opens straight on to the street. Hungry guests should take a moment before perusing the 'well-thought-out' menus to admire the 'ornate walnut, carved and gilded, 16th-century Florentine ceiling, worthy of a visit in its own right'. Lee serves 'well-proportioned, cooked-to-perfection' dishes. For instance, roast Barbary duck breast, rösti potato, braised red cabbage, rhubarb jus; pan-fried Skrei cod, buttered savoy, mashed potato, braised red wine bacon and lentil sauce. Steep stairs from a side entrance lead to 'clean, comfortable' bedrooms. Top-floor rooms offer splendid views across the town and over the castle grounds. A 'well-appointed, well-lit room' had good storage, a clean contemporary bathroom, real coat-hangers, tea/coffee-making facilities, biscuits in a jar. Come morning, 'the freshly cooked breakfast was excellent'. The owner and staff were 'welcoming, the food was top notch, price extremely reasonable'.

65 High Street
Arundel BN18 9AJ

T: 01903 883847
E: enquiries@thetownhouse.co.uk
W: www.thetownhouse.co.uk

BEDROOMS: 5.
OPEN: all year except 25/26 Dec, 1 Jan, two weeks in mid-Nov, restaurant closed Sun–Tues.
FACILITIES: restaurant, free Wi-Fi, in-room TV (Freeview), unsuitable for disabled.
BACKGROUND MUSIC: in restaurant.
LOCATION: top end of High Street.
CHILDREN: all ages welcomed.
DOGS: only guide dogs allowed.
CREDIT CARDS: MC, Visa.
PRICES: per room B&B £75–£150 (2-room family suite £190), D,B&B (mid-week) £150–£190. Set lunch £19–£23, à la carte £33–£40. 1-night bookings refused weekends in high season.

AUSTWICK Yorkshire

MAP 4:D3

AUSTWICK HALL

The Guide's recommendation inspired one gratified reader to book a stay at Eric Culley and Michael Pearson's characterful B&B in a Yorkshire Dales village: 'I'm pleased to be able to agree with the enthusiastic comments.' Beyond the Tuscan porch, interiors are lavishly furnished and embellished with ornaments, antiques, ethnic items, 'decent, well-framed art'. An imperial staircase leads from the Great Hall to spacious bedrooms. In Four-Poster Room, a gilded Buddha contemplates his navel. Blue Room has a beautiful rococo bed. 'My room was generously furnished. The polished floorboards were pleasantly creaky. Sleeping with the window open I could hear no sounds other than morning birdsong.' Bathrooms have 'a large roll-top bath'; three, a separate shower. The 'very good' breakfasts were a 'civilised, unhurried affair, taken in a sumptuously furnished dining room', although freshly squeezed orange juice and slightly larger cooked portions would have been appreciated. Afterwards, you might sit in the lounge or the 'very interesting' Italianate gardens, follow a sculpture trail, or steep in the wood-fired hot tub. For dinner, try the nearby Traddock (next entry). (Trevor Lockwood, and others)

Townhead Lane
Austwick LA2 8BS

T: 01524 251794
E: info@austwickhall.co.uk
W: austwickhall.co.uk

BEDROOMS: 4.
OPEN: all year except 24–26 Dec.
FACILITIES: hall, drawing room, dining room, free Wi-Fi, in-room TV (Freeview), 14-acre gardens, hot tub, unsuitable for disabled.
BACKGROUND MUSIC: none.
LOCATION: edge of village.
CHILDREN: 16 and upwards welcomed.
DOGS: not allowed.
CREDIT CARDS: MC, Visa.
PRICES: per room B&B single £110–£140, double £125–£155. 1-night bookings refused bank holiday weekends.

AUSTWICK Yorkshire

MAP 4:D3

THE TRADDOCK

Previous César Winner

'We have stayed many times, and it remains a
favourite,' writes a trusted reader after this year's
visit to the Reynolds family's popular, dog-friendly
Dales hotel. Built around the 1740s, the house
was extended in Victorian times and continues
to evolve. Two bedrooms have just been added
to a mix that ranges from decent-sized doubles
with bath and/or shower to generous suites. All
have period furniture, Molton Brown toiletries,
home-baked biscuits. The largest, Kickers
Ghyll, 'was huge, with a massive bathroom with
a freestanding bath and an excellent separate
shower'. Our reader's wife loved the traditional
styling; he found it old-fashioned, but, 'that said,
it was quiet and comfortable'. Downstairs there
are acres of space for relaxing by open fires or on
a sunny terrace. 'The staff are brilliant, friendly
and efficient.' New chef Shaun Burke cooks such
imaginative seasonal dishes as Yorkshire pig,
sour cabbage, date and apple; smoked quinoa,
nut crumb, mushroom textures, garden herbs.
Breakfast includes smoothies, local sausages,
Manx kippers, eggs Benedict. Walkers can order
a packed lunch. 'We will certainly return.' (Peter
Anderson, FK)

25% DISCOUNT VOUCHERS

Austwick LA2 8BY

T: 01524 251224
E: info@thetraddock.co.uk
W: thetraddock.co.uk

BEDROOMS: 14. 1 on ground floor.
OPEN: all year.
FACILITIES: 3 lounges, bar, 2 dining
rooms, function facilities, free Wi-Fi,
in-room TV (Freeview), 1½-acre
grounds (sun deck), ground-floor
restaurant wheelchair accessible.
BACKGROUND MUSIC: in public areas
except 1 lounge.
LOCATION: 4 miles NW of Settle.
CHILDREN: all ages welcomed.
DOGS: allowed in bedrooms and on
lead in public rooms, not in dining
rooms, but owners may eat in bar area
with their dogs (£5 per dog per night).
CREDIT CARDS: MC, Visa.
PRICES: per room B&B double
£95–£230. À la carte £40. 1-night
bookings refused Sat.

AYLESBURY Buckinghamshire

HARTWELL HOUSE

'The three generations were happy with the day. We relaxed over croquet, some played tennis, and we had the library for ourselves.' Praise this year for this Jacobean-cum-Georgian mansion in an Arcadian landscape, from readers who celebrated a significant anniversary there. Owned by the National Trust, it houses beautiful antiques and paintings. 'The rooms are grand but also relaxing.' Hartwell was once home to the exiled Louis XVIII with Queen Marie-Joséphine. She, liking a drink, would surely have admired today's wine list with good choice by the glass. A staircase adorned with statues leads to spacious bedrooms and opulent suites. 'We loved the historic items in our large first-floor room, at the front, in this case a tapestry.' Brunches, lunches and afternoon tea are served in the café bar. Dinner in the restaurant is formal but unstuffy; dress smartly. Daniel Richardson's creative modern fare includes pan-fried hake fillet, saffron and potato gnocchi, leek flavours, white wine fish and tomato sauce. 'Dinner was excellent, especially the succulent guineafowl.' Service is 'unobtrusive and exceptional'. 'We were all delighted with our stay.' (Alice and John Sennett, MC)

Oxford Road
Stone
Aylesbury HP17 8NR

T: 01296 747444
E: info@hartwell-house.com
W: www.hartwell-house.com

BEDROOMS: 48. 16 in stable block, some on ground floor, 1 (main house) suitable for disabled.
OPEN: all year, closed for lunch Mon/Tues.
FACILITIES: great hall, morning room, drawing room, library, 2 dining rooms, function facilities, free Wi-Fi, in-room TV (Sky, Freeview), civil wedding licence, spa (swimming pool), 94 acres of gardens and parkland, tennis, public rooms wheelchair accessible.
BACKGROUND MUSIC: none.
LOCATION: 2 miles W of Aylesbury.
CHILDREN: not under 6.
DOGS: allowed in some annexe bedrooms with access to grounds.
CREDIT CARDS: Amex, MC, Visa.
PRICES: per room B&B single £210, double £340–£780. À la carte £53.

BABBACOMBE Devon

MAP 1:D5

CARY ARMS & SPA

'The lodging-houses at Bablicome are magnificent to be seen, And the accommodation there would suit either king or queen.' The poet William Topaz McGonagall extols the beauties of Babbacombe, where Lana de Savary's hotel sits just above the beach, at the foot of a wooded corniche road. It was newly built when Edward VII came by rowing boat for a Devonshire cream tea. He would not know it today, with its spa, coastal-chic bedrooms, glamorous suites, beach huts with mezzanine bedroom, glass doors, sun deck with Adirondack loungers. All rooms are supplied with a decanter of sloe gin, White Company toiletries, robes. All but one have a terrace or balcony. Our inspector's room was 'spacious and attractive', with a 'magnificent view of Torbay'. He rated the 'genuine welcome', the dog-friendliness, the 'relaxed, intimate atmosphere' of the lounge and 'strong sense of fisherman's pub' in the bar. Steve Poyner has been promoted to head chef. Expect 'gastro food cooked simply', River Exe mussels, Brixham fish and chips, West Country beef fillet, veggie options. New, too, this year are watery activities: kayaking, paddle-boarding, mackerel fishing, sailing on a classic wooden yacht. Reports, please.

Beach Road
Babbacombe TQ1 3LX

T: 01803 327110
E: enquiries@caryarms.co.uk
W: caryarms.co.uk

BEDROOMS: 18. 6 in beach huts, 2 beach suites. Plus 5 self-catering cottages.
OPEN: all year.
FACILITIES: saloon, bar, restaurant, free Wi-Fi, in-room TV (Freeview), civil wedding licence, spa (treatment rooms, hydrotherapy pool, mini-gym, steam room, sun deck), garden, sun terraces, unsuitable for disabled.
BACKGROUND MUSIC: all day in inn, saloon and bar.
LOCATION: by beach, 2¼ miles N of Torquay harbour.
CHILDREN: all ages welcomed.
DOGS: allowed in some rooms, part of restaurant.
CREDIT CARDS: Amex, MC, Visa.
PRICES: per room B&B double £265–£450. À la carte £40. 1-night bookings often refused weekends.

BABCARY Somerset

THE RED LION

'We are very likely to return,' enthuses one reader about this quintessential Somerset pub, which makes a good pit stop for journeys to and from the West Country. Flagstone floors, exposed beams and open fires all feature; as does 'a small selection of real ales', a wine list selected from Berry Bros. & Rudd, and a covered smoking area for those who enjoy a quiet 'pipe and a pint' before dinner. The half-dozen bedrooms are in The Barn, a few yards from the main building, and are 'spacious and tastefully furnished', with well-chosen artwork, faux-fur throws and large, 'comfortable' bed. Some bathrooms feature a bath and shower, others a shower only. Dinner, in the cosy bar or in the slightly more formal restaurant, comes courtesy of new chef Richard Ford, and might include a 'delicious' chicken liver parfait 'with just the right amount of melba toast', followed by 'tasty pork belly' and perhaps a 'greatly successful' rice pudding with apricots. Service, though 'friendly', can be 'a little haphazard'. Breakfast, taken in The Den, includes a selection of hot dishes cooked to order. 'Very much enjoyed.' (John Charnley, and others)

Babcary TA11 7ED

T: 01458 223230
E: info@redlionbabcary.co.uk
W: redlionbabcary.co.uk

BEDROOMS: 6. All in converted barn, 1, on ground floor, suitable for disabled.
OPEN: all year.
FACILITIES: bar, snug, restaurant, private dining room, seasonal pizza bar, meeting/function facilities, free Wi-Fi in rooms and reception, in-room TV (BT), garden (play area), bar is wheelchair accessible.
BACKGROUND MUSIC: in bar area.
LOCATION: 5 miles E of Somerton.
CHILDREN: all ages welcomed.
DOGS: allowed in bar only.
CREDIT CARDS: Amex, MC, Visa.
PRICES: per room B&B single £95–£115, double £115–£125. À la carte £29.

BAINBRIDGE Yorkshire

MAP 4:C3

LOW MILL GUEST HOUSE

In the heart of Wensleydale, Jane and Neil McNair welcome guests to their 18th-century watermill on the River Bain. 'Beautifully restored, full of character and quirkiness', it has everything you'd look for in a high-end hotel, with working mill apparatus to boot. The 'amazing', huge, dual-aspect, beamed Workshop room has a freestanding copper bath and walk-in deluge shower room, a log-burner, an emperor-size bed, a patchwork sofa – and the mill machinery. The Kiln room has a king-size sleigh bed, a separate lounge area, a river view. 'The fudge is a real treat – Temple Spa products, too.' The hosts 'clearly and rightly' show great pride in what they have achieved, and a sense of fun is everywhere apparent. The lounge, warmed by a range fire, houses the grinding stones and spur wheel. Two or three nights a week, a dinner of home-cooked local produce is served in 'generous portions'. Maybe chicken and mushroom pie with hash browns; mushroom ragout, soft polenta. Breakfast brings the full Yorkshire and its veggie counterpart, smoked salmon, blueberry pancakes, home-made bread and jams. 'Jane and Neil's attention to detail makes this guest house so special.' (C and PB, and others)

25% DISCOUNT VOUCHERS

Bainbridge
Leyburn DL8 3EF

T: 01969 650553
E: lowmillguesthouse@gmail.com
W: lowmillguesthouse.co.uk

BEDROOMS: 3.
OPEN: all year except Christmas–27 Dec, dinners served three nights a week (check in advance).
FACILITIES: lounge, dining room, free Wi-Fi, in-room TV (Freeview), ¼-acre riverside garden with seating, secure bicycle storage, unsuitable for disabled.
BACKGROUND MUSIC: none.
LOCATION: 5 miles E of Hawes.
CHILDREN: not under 15.
DOGS: allowed in bedrooms, not in dining room, on lead in other public areas.
CREDIT CARDS: MC, Visa.
PRICES: per room B&B single £90–£160, double £110–£180. Dinner £22–£28. 1-night bookings refused some Sats, bank holidays.

SEE ALSO SHORTLIST

BARNSLEY Gloucestershire

BARNSLEY HOUSE

There is 'a romantic air' to this Cotswold stone
mansion, built in the 1690s and extended in the
1820s. Today a hotel and spa, it is part of the
Calcot Collection (see entry for Calcot, Tetbury).
Within, wood fires burn in 'little fireplaces in
small, cosy lounges', furnished in a blend of
period and contemporary styles. Bedrooms are
in the main house and annexes. A duplex Stables
Suite has a sitting area and bathroom at ground
level, a bedroom 'up a steep flight of stairs'. Not
ideal! A request to be moved was 'impeccably'
handled, and a house room proved 'lovely, with
a nice bathroom', a bath and walk-in shower.
All rooms are supplied with biscuits, magazines,
Arran Aromatics toiletries. The Rosemary Verey
Suite, with private courtyard, conservatory and
grotto, recalls the renowned garden designer
who created the gardens here in the 1950s, with
laburnum walk, parterres, a pond garden. The
kitchen garden supplies the Potager restaurant, a
'charming, long room with tall windows', where
menus include such dishes as haunch of venison,
mashed potato, roasted pumpkin, cavolo nero,
pine nuts. You can eat more simply and cheaply in
The Village Pub, run by the same team.

Barnsley
Cirencester GL7 5EE

T: 01285 740000
E: info@barnsleyhouse.com
W: barnsleyhouse.com

BEDROOMS: 18. 7 in stableyard, 4 in
courtyard, 1 in cottage, 1 suitable for
disabled.
OPEN: all year.
FACILITIES: 2 lounges, bar, restaurant,
cinema, meeting room, free Wi-Fi,
in-room TV (Sky, Freeview), civil
wedding licence, 11-acre garden (spa,
hydrotherapy pool), restaurant and
lounge wheelchair accessible.
BACKGROUND MUSIC: in lounge and
restaurant.
LOCATION: 5 miles NE of Cirencester.
CHILDREN: not under 14.
DOGS: allowed in stableyard rooms, not
grounds or public areas.
CREDIT CARDS: Amex, MC, Visa.
PRICES: per room B&B single
£262–£632, double £280–£650, family
£320. À la carte £45 (pub £32). 1-night
bookings sometimes refused.

SEE ALSO SHORTLIST

BARWICK Somerset

MAP 1:C6

LITTLE BARWICK HOUSE

'Hospitality was as good as ever, with a welcome log fire on a chilly day.' Guests are warmly received at Emma and Tim Ford's Georgian country house, set in mature gardens. It is the kind of place that draws people back ('our fourth time here'; 'our first visit and not our last'). Afternoon tea (part of the half-board package) brings 'generous slices of cake, shortbread to die for'. You do well to hold back, though. Dinner, cooked by Tom Ford and son Olly and served in a 'large, airy dining room', is, say trusted readers, 'amazing', 'immaculately prepared, and presented with finesse'. The Fords met at Sharrow Bay, Ullswater, in its day the very prototype of a fine country house hotel, where Tim worked under the legendary Francis Coulson. His menus showcase West Country produce in such dishes as rump of lamb, baby spinach, dauphinoise potato; fillet of Red Ruby beef, shallot purée, in a red wine sauce. Bedrooms and bathrooms 'match the quality of the food', with a 'comfy bed, a generous hospitality tray, high-quality toiletries' – and one change this year – 'only five scatter cushions in our room'. Breakfast is 'up to the usual high standard'. (MC, F and IW, and others)

25% DISCOUNT VOUCHERS

Rexes Hollow Lane
Barwick
Yeovil BA22 9TD

T: 01935 423902
E: info@littlebarwick.co.uk
W: littlebarwick.co.uk

BEDROOMS: 7. 1 for week-long let.
OPEN: all year except Christmas Day, New Year, 3 weeks in Jan, every Sun, Mon, lunchtime Tues.
FACILITIES: 2 lounges, restaurant, conservatory, free Wi-Fi, in-room TV (Freeview), 3½-acre garden (terrace, paddock), restaurant wheelchair accessible.
BACKGROUND MUSIC: none.
LOCATION: ¾ mile outside Yeovil.
CHILDREN: not under 5.
DOGS: allowed in bedrooms, sitting rooms, only assistance dogs in restaurant.
CREDIT CARDS: MC, Visa.
PRICES: per room B&B single occupancy £90–£160, double £126–£195. Set 3-course dinner £50–£55. 1-night bookings sometimes refused weekends.

BASLOW Derbyshire

MAP 3:A6

THE CAVENDISH

'Comfortable, pretty and very English', the
Duke and Duchess of Devonshire's smart hotel
on the Chatsworth Estate delighted readers this
year. They received 'a warm welcome' from a
member of staff, who carried their bags up, and
'reappeared within minutes with a small jug of
cold milk for our minibar'. Their bedroom had
'a lovely brass bed, a wonderful view beyond
the old apple tree laden with fruit, to the fields'.
Even 'standard' rooms are tip-top, with comfy
armchairs, Temple Spa toiletries, Chatsworth
biscuits, prints and paintings. Superior rooms
have a sofa, perhaps a four-poster. Coach house
rooms have antiques from the stately home.
Bathrooms are 'modern and efficient'. In the
Gallery restaurant, chef Adam Harper uses local
and estate produce in such complex dishes as
saddle of hogget, kidney and smoked pancetta
suet pie, red cabbage, yeast, roast root vegetables,
fondant potato. You can eat more simply and very
well in the Garden Room – maybe fish pie, a rib-
eye steak. At breakfast there is freshly squeezed
orange juice, organic porridge, yogurts from the
farm shop, eggs Benedict, poached kippers, the
full Chatsworth. 'We loved it.' (Catrin Treadwell)

25% DISCOUNT VOUCHERS

Church Lane
Baslow DE45 1SP

T: 01246 582311
E: reception@cavendishbaslow.co.uk
W: cavendishbaslow.co.uk

BEDROOMS: 28. 2 on ground floor, 4 in
converted coach house, 2 suitable for
disabled.
OPEN: all year.
FACILITIES: lounge/bar, 2 restaurants,
2 private dining rooms, function
facilities, free Wi-Fi, in-room TV
(Freeview), civil wedding licence,
½-acre grounds, public rooms
wheelchair accessible.
BACKGROUND MUSIC: background in
Garden Room.
LOCATION: on edge of village.
CHILDREN: all ages welcomed.
DOGS: only guide dogs allowed.
CREDIT CARDS: Amex, MC, Visa.
PRICES: per room B&B single £120–
£430, double £140–£450. Tasting menu
£85. Set menus £43–£63, Garden
Room à la carte £30. 1-night bookings
sometimes refused weekends,
Christmas.

BASLOW Derbyshire   MAP 3:A6

FISCHER'S AT BASLOW HALL

On the edge of the village, with the Peak District on the doorstep, this Jacobean-style Edwardian manor house stands in a beautifully tended garden with sculpted box and yews, potager and arboretum. 'We had a delightful stay,' say readers this year, which also saw owners Max and Susan Fischer open a striking teal blue wine events room. Main house bedrooms are country house style, looking across the garden to the Derbyshire dales. All have an espresso machine, handmade biscuits and organic toiletries. Annexe rooms are contemporary, with bold decor, their own walled garden. 'Our tranquil, spacious garden room, opening on to a leafy courtyard, was simply but tastefully decorated, with a modern bathroom.' At dinner, in the Michelin-starred restaurant or at the kitchen tasting bench, James Payne is now head chef, while Max Fischer remains executive, cooking 'with flair and just enough modernity': perhaps best end of Derbyshire lamb, sticky rib, crispy sweetbread, pesto; from the vegetarian menu, asparagus and artichoke tartlet, truffle dressing, crispy egg. Breakfast brings freshly squeezed juice, honey from the hives. 'We very much enjoyed our stay.' (SB, RC, and others)

Calver Road
Baslow DE45 1RR

T: 01246 583259
E: reservations@fischers-baslowhall.co.uk
W: fischers-baslowhall.co.uk

BEDROOMS: 11. 5 in Garden House, 4 on ground floor.
OPEN: all year except 25/26 Dec, restaurant closed Mon.
FACILITIES: lounge/bar, main dining room, drawing room, wine room, function facilities, free Wi-Fi, in-room TV (Freeview), civil wedding licence, 5-acre grounds, restaurant and lounge wheelchair accessible.
BACKGROUND MUSIC: in bar/lounge.
LOCATION: edge of village, 5 miles NE of Bakewell.
CHILDREN: all ages welcomed, no under-8s in restaurant.
DOGS: not allowed.
CREDIT CARDS: Amex, MC, Visa.
PRICES: per room B&B single £185–£225, double £260–£325, D,B&B £367–£432. Set menu £65–£79, tasting menu £88.

BASSENTHWAITE LAKE Cumbria

THE PHEASANT

Close to the northernmost of the Lakes, under
Wythop Woods in the shadow of Skiddaw, this
300-year-old coaching inn, managed by Matthew
Wylie, is 'a very special place', say fans. The
rerouting of the A66 along the old lakeside rail
trackbed has left the inn sitting pretty 'behind
a ridge of land separating it effectively from
road noise'. You'll find fresh flowers on arrival,
in a traditionally styled bedroom furnished
with antiques – either in the main house or a
garden lodge. 'Our bedroom was spacious, with
a super-king-size bed, separate sitting area, lots
of storage, really good bathroom.' You can eat
in the 'popular and fun' bistro (burger, fish and
chips. meze platter), take a light lunch in the
'remarkable' panelled bar with blazing fire,
where John Peel used to drink in his 'coat so gay'
(hounds are welcome). In the 'classy restaurant',
the short menu might include canon of lamb,
haggis, pomme purée, celeriac, red wine jus.
'Food and service in both bistro and restaurant
were excellent.' A 'lounge with a log fire, lots of
comfortable chairs', copies of Country Life make
this 'ideal for a winter stay'. Packed lunches can
be ordered for a day out osprey-spotting.

Bassenthwaite Lake
Cockermouth CA13 9YE

T: 017687 76234
E: reception@the-pheasant.co.uk
W: the-pheasant.co.uk

BEDROOMS: 15. 2 on ground floor in
lodge.
OPEN: all year except 25 Dec,
restaurant open Sun lunch, Thurs–Sat
eve.
FACILITIES: 2 lounges, bar, bistro,
restaurant, private dining room,
Wi-Fi, in-room TV (Freeview),
40-acre grounds, lake 200 yds,
wheelchair accessible, adapted toilet,
access to nearby spa, pool.
BACKGROUND MUSIC: in bistro.
LOCATION: 5 miles E of Cockermouth,
¼ mile off A66 to Keswick.
CHILDREN: not under 8, except in
bistro.
DOGS: allowed in 4 bedrooms (£10
charge), public rooms.
CREDIT CARDS: MC, Visa.
PRICES: per room B&B £110–£210.
Set menu (restaurant) £45, à la
carte (bistro) £30. 1-night bookings
occasionally refused Sat.

BATH Somerset

MAP 2:D1

APSLEY HOUSE

A 'delightful young couple', Miroslav Mikula and Katarzyna Kowalczyk are the 'friendly, helpful' managers at Nicholas and Claire Potts's Georgian house. Built, it is said, by the Duke of Wellington for his mistress, it is less grand than His Grace's London mansion of the same name, but it has 'comfortable, well-proportioned rooms, tastefully decorated in a unique style'. Even the snuggest, Vitoria, has a king-size bed, slipper bath and walk-in shower. Mornington, once a kitchen (it still has a bread oven), has a silk-dressed four-poster ('excellent lighting'), and French doors that open on to a pretty garden. Or choose ground-floor Copenhagen, named in honour of that great warhorse, which, with Mornington, can form a family suite. A 'spacious, comfortable' drawing room with chandelier and open fire has a leather chesterfield sofa, grand piano and bar. At breakfast guests decide between 'good cereals, fruit, smoked salmon, poached eggs, bagels'. Here, on a hilltop, you are a half-hour walk from the centre (frequent buses to the door), and there is 'much appreciated parking in a city where space is at a premium'. And the views over Bath are equally, if not more, spectacular at night.

141 Newbridge Hill
Bath BA1 3PT

T: 01225 336966
E: claireypotts@btinternet.com
W: apsley-house.co.uk

BEDROOMS: 12. 1 on ground floor, plus 1 self-catering 2-bedroom apartment in coach house.
OPEN: all year except 24–26 Dec.
FACILITIES: bar/drawing room, dining room, free Wi-Fi, in-room TV (Freeview), ¼-acre garden, parking, unsuitable for disabled.
BACKGROUND MUSIC: Classic FM in drawing and dining rooms.
LOCATION: 1¼ miles W of city centre.
CHILDREN: all ages welcomed.
DOGS: only guide dogs allowed.
CREDIT CARDS: MC, Visa.
PRICES: per room B&B single £99–£250, double £99–£280. 1-night bookings refused Sat in peak season.

SEE ALSO SHORTLIST

BATH Somerset

NO.15 GREAT PULTENEY

It promises 'luxury for the curious', and Christa and Ian Taylor's boutique hotel on a grand neoclassical street does not disappoint. The Grade I listed building has been given a 'stylish', 'quirky' make-over, with copious chandeliers and statement lighting, displays of brass instruments, dinky handbags, plates, kaleidoscopes . . . 'Fabulously helpful' staff are clearly happy in their work. Some compact bedrooms on the top 'Artists' Floor' have a bespoke mural. Themed deluxe doubles have exotic bird wallpaper on the ceilings, parrot lamps. Coach house rooms, behind a mock-Gothic facade, sport muted shades, bright splashes of colour and larky artwork, a rain shower, perhaps a bath, mood lighting. Toiletries are by Aromatherapy Associates. In The Dispensary, with its antique apothecary cabinets, breakfast choices include organic porridge, eggy bread with forest fruits and vanilla mascarpone, eggs Florentine. At dinner, chef Marcus Bradley's dishes range from simple beer-battered cod goujons and burgers, to exotic panko king prawn and squid, miso mayo, gochujang chilli sauce, burnt lime. 'A must-stay hotel', a reader writes, a far cry from its dour days as a temperance hotel for Second World War veterans.

25% DISCOUNT VOUCHERS

15 Great Pulteney Street
Bath BA2 4BR

T: 01225 807015
E: enquiries@no15greatpulteney.co.uk
W: no15greatpulteney.co.uk

BEDROOMS: 40. 8 in coach house, 1 suitable for disabled.
OPEN: all year, all-day menu in bar, restaurant open daily for breakfast, dinner Tues–Sat, brunch on Sun.
FACILITIES: lift, lounge, bar, restaurant, private dining room, free Wi-Fi, in-room TV (Sky), spa (treatments, hot tub, sauna), small garden terrace, parking permits, public rooms wheelchair accessible.
BACKGROUND MUSIC: all day in lounge, bar and restaurant.
LOCATION: central.
CHILDREN: all ages welcomed.
DOGS: allowed in bedrooms, bar, not in restaurant.
CREDIT CARDS: Amex, MC, Visa.
PRICES: per room B&B £115–£296. À la carte £35. 1-night bookings sometimes refused weekends.

SEE ALSO SHORTLIST

BATH Somerset

THE QUEENSBERRY

'The situation is perfect, central, by the Assembly Rooms and Circus,' readers write of Laurence and Helen Beere's self-consciously quirky hotel. Boldly patterned wallpapers and muted contemporary hues blend with Georgian proportions throughout the four honey-toned town houses. Junior suites, with elegant period windows and fireplace, are forged from the old drawing rooms; one suite has a leather chaise longue in the bathroom; smaller doubles have an en suite shower room. While the contemporary styling is harmonious, one reader did baulk at a see-through plastic chair. However, 'the bathroom was excellent'. In the snug Old Q bar, where you can order cocktails and light meals, a spoof of the Queensberry Rules prohibits finger-clicking, audible obscenities and shouting into mobile phones. Things get more serious in the basement Olive Tree restaurant, where Michelin-starred chef Chris Cleghorn's tasting menus cater to carnivores, vegetarians and vegans. Typical dishes include fallow deer, golden raisin, sprout, bitter chocolate; barbecue cauliflower, sea beet, hen of the woods, hazelnuts. By all means order à la carte. 'Service is attentive.' The valet parking is a bonus.

25% DISCOUNT VOUCHERS

4–7 Russel Street
Bath BA1 2QF

T: 01225 447928
E: reservations@thequeensberry.co.uk
W: thequeensberry.co.uk

BEDROOMS: 29. Some on ground floor.
OPEN: all year, restaurant closed Mon, midday Tues–Thurs.
FACILITIES: lift, residents' drawing room, bar, 2 sitting rooms, restaurant, meeting room, free Wi-Fi, in-room TV (Freeview), 4 linked courtyard gardens, unsuitable for disabled.
BACKGROUND MUSIC: in restaurant and bar.
LOCATION: near Assembly Rooms.
CHILDREN: all ages welcomed.
DOGS: assistance dogs only.
CREDIT CARDS: Amex, MC, Visa.
PRICES: per room B&B £125–£475. Tasting menus £68–£85, à la carte £55. 1-night bookings sometimes refused weekends.

SEE ALSO SHORTLIST

BATH Somerset

THE ROYAL CRESCENT
HOTEL & SPA

Here is an exemplary hotel, according to
a discerning Guide reader. 'Elegant and
comfortable', it has 'an air of confidence' that sets
guests at ease. It occupies two mansions at the
centre of the glorious sweep of a Grade I listed
Georgian crescent. Once home to intellectual and
social reformer Elizabeth Montagu, who hosted
the likes of Joshua Reynolds and Fanny Burney,
it was later transformed into a top-notch hotel,
bought by the Topland group in 2012. To the fore,
a lawn overlooks Royal Victoria Park; behind is a
secluded garden and a spa. Luxurious bedrooms,
in the main building and annexes, are supplied
with Floris toiletries. A family suite occupies a
pavilion across the garden. The staff are 'friendly
and helpful', 'only too happy to provide a service'.
You can dine in the restaurant, the bar or alfresco.
In the restaurant, David Campbell's 'outstanding'
menus include such modern dishes as Everleigh
Farm venison, smoked potato, haggis croquette,
spiced pear, chard. He creates separate menus
for vegetarians and children. Breakfast, picnic
hampers and a champagne tea invite you to
indulge. 'Not cheap, but worth every penny.' (RC)

16 Royal Crescent
Bath BA1 2LS

T: 01225 823333
E: info@royalcrescent.co.uk
W: royalcrescent.co.uk

BEDROOMS: 45. 10 in Dower House,
14 in annexes, 8 on ground floor.
OPEN: all year.
FACILITIES: lift, bar, drawing room,
library, restaurant, function facilities,
free Wi-Fi, in-room TV (Sky,
Freeview), civil wedding licence,
1-acre garden, spa (12-metre pool),
public rooms wheelchair accessible.
BACKGROUND MUSIC: in library and
restaurant.
LOCATION: ½ mile from High Street.
CHILDREN: all ages welcomed, not
under 13 in spa.
DOGS: allowed in some bedrooms,
public rooms, not in restaurant or bar.
CREDIT CARDS: Amex, MC, Visa.
PRICES: per room B&B £330–£960.
À la carte £72, tasting menu £82. Min.
2-night stay on Saturdays.

SEE ALSO SHORTLIST

BAUGHURST Hampshire

MAP 2:D2

THE WELLINGTON ARMS

'The best B&B we've ever stayed in', the 'Welly' is a small but beautifully formed foodie pub on the Hampshire–Berkshire border. Owned and run by Simon Page and chef Jason King, this 'dog-friendly' place with an 'immaculate garden' mixes designer decor (Farrow & Ball paint, Osborne & Little fabrics) with a Good Life-style ethos: the kitchen garden produces the herbs and vegetables; fruit comes from the owners' trees; ice cream, bread and chutney are all home-made; there's even a flock of Jacob sheep in a field behind the pub. 'Delicious' and 'unfussy' dishes, served in the tiny, informal dining room, might include roast rack of home-reared Jacob lamb with bashed carrot, parsnip and butternut squash, mint sauce; perhaps a scoop of marmalade ice cream to finish. Bedrooms are all 'beautifully appointed'; two have a slate floor, oak beams and exposed brickwork; one has a cast iron stove and bespoke turned oak bed. Luxury touches include Malin+Goetz toiletries. Breakfast features the freshest eggs cooked in a multitude of ways, as well as warm croissants or sourdough toast with home-made jam and honey. An 'amazing' pub with a 'comfy, country atmosphere', say Guide readers.
(R and RH)

Baughurst Road
Baughurst RG26 5LP

T: 0118 982 0110
E: hello@thewellingtonarms.com
W: thewellingtonarms.com

BEDROOMS: 4. 3 in converted outbuildings.
OPEN: all year, restaurant closed Sun night.
FACILITIES: bar, restaurant, free Wi-Fi, in-room TV (Freeview), 2-acre garden, parking.
BACKGROUND MUSIC: in bar and restaurant.
LOCATION: equidistant between Reading, Basingstoke and Newbury.
CHILDREN: all ages welcomed.
DOGS: allowed in 1 bedroom (£10 per night), public areas.
CREDIT CARDS: MC, Visa.
PRICES: per room B&B £125–£220. À la carte £35.

BEAMINSTER Dorset

MAP 1:C6

THE OLLEROD

Since Chris Staines and Silvana Bandini bought
The Ollerod 18 months ago, its transformation
into a 'restaurant-led' establishment has continued
apace. Refurbishment of the main areas is now
complete, and a new treatment room has been
added for facials and massage. But Rome wasn't
built in a day – or in 18 months – and the much-
needed bedroom revamp is still ongoing. In the
meantime, all have been kitted out with Frette
linen, a Nespresso machine and organic toiletries
and, inspectors note, they are 'well insulated'
from traffic noise on the road outside. Chris, a
former Michelin-starred chef, cooks seasonal
dishes from local ingredients (his 15-leaf salad
comes entirely from the hotel kitchen garden).
Dinner, in the informal conservatory restaurant,
can be from the à la carte menu – perhaps roast
loin of Jurassic Coast lamb, confit aubergine,
wild garlic, sweetbread and monk's beard – or
from a selection of small plates including Middle
Eastern spiced lamb shoulder, hummus, yogurt
and pomegranate. Breakfast is a highlight: a
'small buffet' of pastries, local yogurt, home-made
granola, an 'excellent kipper'. Inspectors' verdict:
'The food was a plus point, and everyone was
very friendly.'

3 Prout Bridge
Beaminster DT8 3AY

T: 01308 862200
E: reception@theollerod.co.uk
W: theollerod.co.uk

BEDROOMS: 13. 4 in coach house, 4 on
ground floor.
OPEN: all year.
FACILITIES: lounge, bar, sun room,
conservatory, restaurant, free Wi-Fi,
in-room TV (Freeview), civil wedding
licence, ⅓-acre walled garden, covered
terrace.
BACKGROUND MUSIC: in public rooms.
LOCATION: 100 yards from centre.
CHILDREN: all ages welcomed.
DOGS: allowed in 2 bedrooms, bar and
terrace, not in restaurant (£15 per dog
per night).
CREDIT CARDS: Amex, MC, Visa.
PRICES: per room B&B £125–£285.
À la carte £40.

BEAULIEU Hampshire

MAP 2:E2

THE MASTER BUILDER'S

Nautical styling is spliced with New Forest hospitality at this 'friendly' riverside hotel, once the home of Henry Adams, master shipbuilder to Nelson. In a 'lovely setting' in the village of Buckler's Hard, the 'unpretentious' hotel with 'delightful staff' is filled with maritime memorabilia. Rooms, in the main house and newer wing, mine the same nautical seam without being 'over-insistent'. The latter are 'modern, comfortable and tastefully furnished', with blue-and-white striped cushions and throws; the former have a more period feel, with antique furniture and vintage prints. Two dining options: the Yachtsman's bar, overlooking the ancient shipyard, serves fish and chips, salads and pizzas; the Riverview restaurant, under head chef Alicia Storey, specialises in innovative, seasonal dishes such as grilled mackerel, kohlrabi, globe artichokes and salsify, or pan-fried stone bass, toasted crevette, tenderstem, fennel and saffron beurre d'or. Breakfast, perhaps porridge followed by The Master Builder's Full English, 'is a fine start to any day', and can be offset by a variety of local activities, from canoeing and paddle-boarding on the Beaulieu river to cycling and walking. (LH)

Buckler's Hard
Beaulieu SO42 7XB

T: 01590 616253
E: enquiries@themasterbuilders.co.uk
W: hillbrookehotels.co.uk/the-master-
builders

BEDROOMS: 26. 18 in newer Henry Adams wing.
OPEN: all year.
FACILITIES: lounge, bar, restaurant, terrace with river views, free Wi-Fi, in-room TV (Freeview), civil wedding licence, ½-acre garden, bar and restaurant wheelchair accessible, no adapted toilet.
BACKGROUND MUSIC: in bar and restaurant.
LOCATION: 6 miles NE of Lymington.
CHILDREN: all ages welcomed.
DOGS: allowed in some bedrooms, lounge, the Yachtman's bar, not in restaurant.
CREDIT CARDS: Amex, MC, Visa.
PRICES: per room B&B £135–£200, D,B&B £190–£255. À la carte £45.

BEAULIEU Hampshire

MONTAGU ARMS

'Our sixth visit, and a wonderful end to our holiday,' write readers who stopped over at this wisteria-smothered hotel in an unspoilt New Forest village. Built in 1888, in Arts and Crafts style, it hosted Sir Arthur Conan Doyle while he wrote The White Company. Now, whether or not in homage, its 'comfortable, well-equipped' bedrooms sport White Company toiletries. Most have a handmade, king-size bed, some a highly ornate four-poster, one has beautiful stained glass. Hayloft suites have a freestanding bath and private terrace. The big news this year was the arrival of chef Matthew Whitfield, from New York's triple-Michelin-starred Eleven Madison Park. He works with locally sourced and home-grown organic produce, apples from the orchard, eggs from the hens, to create dishes served in the Terrace restaurant, overlooking the 'most attractive' garden. Typical of his repertoire are glazed Pennington lamb belly, salt-baked celeriac, rosemary and hazelnut; turbot, curried mussels, Cornish saffron, broccoli and almond. Provenance is no less important at Monty's Inn, where you might enjoy a ploughman's with real ale from Ringwood Brewery. 'As ever the ambience was great.' (RC, MK-O)

Palace Lane
Beaulieu SO42 7ZL

T: 01590 612324
E: reservations@montaguarmshotel.
co.uk
W: montaguarmshotel.co.uk

BEDROOMS: 24. 2 new Hayloft suites.
OPEN: all year, Terrace restaurant closed Mon, Tues lunch.
FACILITIES: lounge, conservatory, library/bar/brasserie, restaurant, free Wi-Fi, in-room TV (Freeview), civil wedding licence, 3-acre garden, access to spa at Careys Manor (6 miles away), public rooms wheelchair accessible.
BACKGROUND MUSIC: Classic FM all day in reception.
LOCATION: village centre.
CHILDREN: all ages welcomed.
DOGS: assistance dogs allowed.
CREDIT CARDS: Amex, MC, Visa.
PRICES: per room B&B £219–£399. Tasting menu £90, à la carte £60 (Terrace restaurant), £28 (Monty's Inn). 1-night bookings sometimes refused Fri/Sat, peak season.

BEESANDS Devon

MAP 1:E4

THE CRICKET INN

Rachel and Nigel Heath's Victorian fishermen's inn has a wonderful position overlooking Start Bay. It is a 'really attractive, relaxing place, in a village that retains a quiet atmosphere', thanks, perhaps, to the approach via 'narrow, winding lanes'. Guests of all ages enjoy crab soup, flame-grilled steaks, the catch of the day, maybe fish and chips alfresco, cooked by son Scott Heath and Stuart Downie. 'Food was very good, especially the fresh fish.' The bar has a nautical feel, with crab pots and model boats, while the light and airy bedrooms have a New England ethos. With sea in front and hills behind, the opportunities for cricket are limited, yet each room is named after a cricket ground, with Oval offering 'panoramic sea views' from its large bay window. Family rooms sleep three or four. Trueman and Botham suites have a king-size four-poster. One reader praised the housekeeping and the 'well-planned bedroom and bathroom'. Music plays in the bar where, it is said, pre-Rolling Stones, Keith Richards and Mick Jagger performed their first public gig. After a breakfast of Devon produce, stir your stumps and walk the South West Coast Path. (LW)

Beesands
Kingsbridge TQ7 2EN

т: 01548 580215
E: sally@thecricketinn.com
w: thecricketinn.com

BEDROOMS: 7. 4 in extension.
OPEN: closed Christmas Day.
FACILITIES: bar, restaurant (alfresco dining), private dining facilities, free (intermittent) Wi-Fi, in-room TV (Freeview), parking, restaurant and bar wheelchair accessible, adapted toilet.
BACKGROUND MUSIC: all day.
LOCATION: in village, on South West Coast Path.
CHILDREN: all ages welcomed, children's menu, family rooms.
DOGS: allowed (in bar only).
CREDIT CARDS: MC, Visa.
PRICES: per room B&B £110–£150, D,B&B £150–£190 (up to £50 per couple for dinner). À la carte £30. Min. 2-night stay preferred at weekends.

BEPTON Sussex

MAP 2:E3

PARK HOUSE, HOTEL & SPA

'All aspects of the hotel hit the standard: staff
service, decor, food quality, ambience.' New
endorsements for this Edwardian country house
hotel under the South Downs. Founded by Ioné
and Michael O'Brien when rationing was still
in force, it is today, under grandson Seamus, all
about living it large, with a spa, a six-hole, 18-tee
golf course, pools indoors and out. 'Grounds and
amenities were impressive, especially the two
grass tennis courts.' The 'immaculate' main house
bedrooms are pretty and traditional, some with a
separate seating area, balcony or terrace. Nine are
in separate cottages. 'We stayed in Polo Cottage
[Cowdray Park is nearby], close to the main hotel
and manageable for my disabled bro.' There is
a happy ethos: 'From the moment we arrived,
we were greeted with enormous smiles from the
friendly staff.' In dining room or conservatory,
overlooking the croquet lawn, Callum Keir's
three-course menus include such dishes as baked
cod, Puy lentils, curried cauliflower; corn-fed
chicken, lime and chilli honey-roasted parsnips.
An 'utterly delicious' breakfast brings free-
range eggs, kippers, oak-smoked haddock. (Max
Lickfold, Ben Rymer)

Bepton Road
Bepton
Midhurst GU29 0JB

T: 01730 819000
E: reservations@parkhousehotel.com
W: parkhousehotel.com

BEDROOMS: 21. 5 on ground floor, 1
suitable for disabled, 9 in cottages in
grounds.
OPEN: all year, except 23–27 Dec.
FACILITIES: drawing room, bar, dining
room, conservatory, function rooms,
free Wi-Fi, in-room TV (Sky), civil
wedding licence, 10-acre grounds,
spa, heated indoor and outdoor
swimming pools, public rooms and
spa wheelchair accessible.
BACKGROUND MUSIC: in restaurants.
LOCATION: village centre.
CHILDREN: all ages welcomed.
DOGS: allowed in some bedrooms with
garden access, not public rooms.
CREDIT CARDS: Amex, MC, Visa.
PRICES: per room B&B £150–£320,
D,B&B £230–£340. Set dinner £45.
Min. 2-night stay Fri/Sat.

BEVERLEY Yorkshire

MAP 4:D5

NEWBEGIN HOUSE

A stay at the Georgian family home of Nuala and Walter Sweeney, he a former MP, is 'memorable for all the right reasons'. With many beautiful original features, the house is filled with antiques and paintings, clocks, books, mirrors. The 36-foot-long Drawing Room, the largest of three guest bedrooms, has a fireplace at each end, and three sash windows. It sleeps up to five, and has something of the feeling of a playroom, complete with rocking horse, comfy armchair, photos and ornaments. It overlooks a quiet one-way street, with shutters to screen out the light and 'intermittent' traffic noise. Iveson gazes on to the 'wonderful' walled garden, which, with the orchard, has been newly landscaped. Its bathroom has a claw-footed bath. Readers who stayed in all three rooms liked best the peace of Appleton, which has the strongest lights for reading, and a good shower. Pleasing extra touches include fresh milk in a mini-fridge, biscuits, chocolate, fine china. Nuala cooks an award-winning breakfast using local produce and offering 'a wide choice'. There is secure parking, so leave the car and take a stroll to the town centre to visit the Saturday market, Gothic minster and Georgian Quarter.

10 Newbegin
Beverley HU17 8EG

T: 01482 888880
E: wsweeney@wsweeney.karoo.co.uk
W: newbeginhousebbbeverley.co.uk

BEDROOMS: 3.
OPEN: all year except when owners take a holiday.
FACILITIES: sitting room, dining room, small conference facilities, free Wi-Fi, in-room TV (Freeview), ¾-acre walled garden, unsuitable for disabled.
BACKGROUND MUSIC: none.
LOCATION: central.
CHILDREN: all ages welcomed.
DOGS: not allowed.
CREDIT CARDS: none accepted.
PRICES: B&B per room single £60, double £90–£100. 1-night bookings refused during the Early Music Festival and the Folk Festival.

BIGBURY-ON-SEA Devon

MAP 1:D4

BURGH ISLAND HOTEL

♥ Previous César Winner

Tucked into a hillside on a tidal island, this sleek, white, concrete hotel has a seagoing aspect. Built in 1929 for a wealthy industrialist, it hosted the likes of Nancy Cunard, Noël Coward and Josephine Baker. The place is shipshape under new owner Giles Fuchs, with refurbished public areas retaining the glamorous Art Deco style. The Burgh Island experience begins with a ride across the sands on the 'sea tractor'. Morning teas and coffees are brought to rooms and suites, supplied with chocolates, water, fluffy robes. From first class to steerage, each has a full or partial sea view, some a lounge with Deco armchairs, a balcony or terrace. You can hire Agatha Christie's beach retreat, the Artist's Studio, or a dog-friendly apartment above the 14th-century Pilchard Inn, which now has a downstairs café serving food all day. There are cocktails and a lounge menu in the Palm Court bar with its glazed 'peacock' dome. Dinner in the Ballroom (now open to non-residents) is a black-tie affair. Chef Tim Hall is still on board, cooking 30-mile menus of such dishes as pan-fried cod, clam chowder, smoked cod beignet. A dip in the natural seawater Mermaid Pool is a must.

Burgh Island
Bigbury-on-Sea TQ7 4BG

T: 01548 810514
E: reception@burghisland.com
W: burghisland.com

BEDROOMS: 25. 1 suite in Beach House in grounds, apartment above Pilchard Inn.
OPEN: all year, except Jan.
FACILITIES: lift, bar, 2 restaurants, ballroom, sun lounge, billiard room, private dining room, spa, free Wi-Fi, civil wedding licence, 17-acre grounds, sea bathing pool, tennis court.
BACKGROUND MUSIC: background in public rooms, live music on Mon, Wed, Sat nights in summer.
LOCATION: off Bigbury beach; private garages on mainland.
CHILDREN: not under 5, no under-13s at dinner.
DOGS: allowed in Agatha's Beach House and the Artist's Studio.
CREDIT CARDS: MC, Visa.
PRICES: per room B&B £195–£580, D,B&B £295–£680. À la carte £75. 1-night bookings refused Sat, some bank holidays.

BIGBURY-ON-SEA Devon   MAP 1:D4

THE HENLEY

'An idyllic place… absolute heaven.' So say regular visitors to this dog-friendly B&B with 'fabulous views' over Bigbury Bay. New arrivals receive 'a really warm welcome' from the 'charming and friendly' hosts, Martyn Scarterfield and Petra Lampe. There is a Three Bears choice of bedrooms – small, medium and a large, each just right in its way. A dual-aspect room has 'stunning panoramic coastal views'. All are homely in the best sense, supplied with biscuits and sherry. In an Edwardian house built as a holiday home, rattan chairs and potted palms abound, especially in the light-filled breakfast room overlooking the Avon estuary. You can sit out on the decking – or by a wood-burning stove in a lounge. Dogs are welcomed by the owner's Labrador, Caspar. At night, with three days' notice, residents can dine in. Martyn's limited but 'tasty, generously portioned' three-course menus might include melon with Parma ham and figs, a steak or fresh fish, pear and frangipane pudding. Breakfast choices include an 'excellently cooked' full Devon, eggs Benedict, kippers, smoked salmon. Steps lead to the beach; the South West Coast Path runs right by. 'No doubt we will be back once again!' (SR, SH)

Folly Hill
Bigbury-on-Sea TQ7 4AR

T: 01548 810240
E: thehenleyhotel@btconnect.com
W: thehenleyhotel.co.uk

BEDROOMS: 4.
OPEN: Mar–end Oct, restaurant closed Sun eve.
FACILITIES: 2 lounges, dining room, reception, free Wi-Fi, in-room TV (Freeview), small terraced garden (steps to beach, golf, sailing, fishing), South West Coast Path nearby, unsuitable for disabled.
BACKGROUND MUSIC: jazz/classical in the evenings in lounge, dining room.
LOCATION: 5 miles S of Modbury.
CHILDREN: not under 12.
DOGS: allowed in bedrooms (not on bed), lounges, not in dining room (£7 per dog per night).
CREDIT CARDS: MC, Visa.
PRICES: per room B&B single £103, double £140–£170, D,B&B (2-night min.) single £134, double £195–£225. Set dinner £36. 1-night bookings sometimes refused weekends.

BIGGIN-BY-HARTINGTON Derbyshire   MAP 3:B6

BIGGIN HALL

'The garden views were entertaining at
mealtimes. There seemed to be more hens on
the lawn this time.' A trusted reader on a third
visit captures the spirit of James Moffett's manor
house hotel in a 'delightful Peak District location'.
'Not posh, but straightforward', it 'continues to
improve'. New arrivals are offered complimentary
beer or Prosecco. The handling of a late-booking
change was 'most gracious'. Bedrooms, in main
house and annexes, are traditionally styled, some
have antiques, maybe a half-tester or four-poster.
A small twin-bedded suite had a sitting room
and fridge. All rooms have fresh milk. One
sitting room has 'a wood stove in a fireplace said
to be several hundred years old'. The other is
'essentially an interesting library with charming
furniture'. In the beamed, candlelit restaurant,
Mark Wilton's 'really good' dishes include slow-
braised lamb rump, bubble and squeak, honey-
roasted baby carrots, red wine sauce. Vegans
have their own menu. 'Breakfast is help yourself,
plenteous, varied and freshly cooked.' A self-
service free packed lunch with decent 'freshly
made sandwiches' is provided for walkers. 'All
in all, amazing value. We will stay again.' (John
Barnes, DL)

25% DISCOUNT VOUCHERS

Biggin-by-Hartington
Buxton SK17 0DH

T: 01298 84451
E: enquiries@bigginhall.co.uk
W: bigginhall.co.uk

BEDROOMS: 21. 13 in annexes, some on
ground floor.
OPEN: all year, restaurant closed Mon
lunch.
FACILITIES: sitting room, library, dining
room, meeting room, Wi-Fi (in sitting
rooms, some bedrooms), in-room TV
(Freeview), civil wedding licence,
8-acre grounds, restaurant, toilet
wheelchair accessible.
BACKGROUND MUSIC: in restaurant.
LOCATION: 8 miles N of Ashbourne.
CHILDREN: not under 12.
DOGS: allowed in annexe bedrooms,
not main house.
CREDIT CARDS: MC, Visa.
PRICES: per room B&B single from
£89, double £120–£320. À la carte £32,
Indulgence menu Fri and Sat (for
whole table) £70 per person, including
wine. 1-night bookings sometimes
refused weekends.

BILDESTON Suffolk

MAP 2:C5

THE BILDESTON CROWN

A 'cosy, friendly restaurant-with-rooms', this timber-frame, 15th-century former merchant's house has been an inn for some 400 years. It is owned by Suffolk farmer and businessman James Buckle, who supplies produce to the kitchen, while Hayley and Chris Lee, manager and head chef, run the business. The style is 'traditional English but playful', says a Guide insider, the bedrooms are 'full of character and charm'. They are individually styled, each different. One triple-aspect room has an antique four-poster with damask bed coverings. A real princess might prefer a French-inspired king-size bed finished in silver, a huge walk-in shower and a double-ended bateau bath. 'Artwork adorns the walls' in public rooms with 'crackling log fires' and 'very soft pop music'. 'Food is at the heart of the place.' In the candlelit restaurant, Chris Lee's short menus showcase Suffolk ingredients, perhaps loin of local rabbit, duck liver, beetroot, fennel and endive. Veggie options include truffle tortellini, salsify, Roscoff onions. Service was 'charming'. Breakfast is 'good and plentiful', with 'delicious orange juice, butter on a stone slab, a tasty vegetarian special made just for me'. (RF)

25% DISCOUNT VOUCHERS

104 High Street
Bildeston IP7 7EB

T: 01449 740510
E: reception@thebildestoncrown.
co.uk
W: thebildestoncrown.com

BEDROOMS: 12.
OPEN: all year, no accommodation 24–26 Dec, New Year's Day.
FACILITIES: 2 bars, restaurant, 2 private dining areas, lift, free Wi-Fi, in-room TV (Freeview), courtyard, 3 small patios, parking, mobile phone reception variable, restaurant and bar wheelchair accessible, adapted toilet.
BACKGROUND MUSIC: in public areas.
LOCATION: village centre 10 mins' drive from Lavenham.
CHILDREN: all ages welcomed.
DOGS: allowed in some rooms and in bar, not in restaurant.
CREDIT CARDS: Amex, MC, Visa.
PRICES: per room B&B single £70–£180, double £95–£180. À la carte £40.

BISHOP'S CASTLE Shropshire

THE CASTLE HOTEL

Built in 1719 for the Duke of Chandos, on the bailey of a Norman hilltop castle, Henry Hunter's 'really lovely hotel in a truly quirky village' is sister to the highly regarded Pen-y-Dyffryn, Oswestry (see entry). 'This was our third visit to what has become our favourite hotel,' writes one of many approving readers this year. Smart, contemporary, 'immaculate' bedrooms, some for a family, some with in-room bath, overlook the town to Shropshire's vaunted blue hills, or to the south-facing gardens with tables for alfresco eating and drinking. 'Staff are friendly and helpful.' Steve Bruce's 'superb' locally sourced dishes range from gastropub classics (beer-battered hake and chips, Welsh lamb burger) to more inventive fare, especially for veggies (black garlic risotto, butternut squash ragout, field mushroom, crispy leeks). A rare complaint came from regular guests who, on successive nights, found service slow, dinner disappointing. Nothing but praise, however, for the 'excellent breakfast menu' with pancakes, free-range eggs Benedict, the full Shropshire. Dogs can stay at no charge and are not merely welcome but 'positively encouraged'. (Mr and Mrs J Glynn, Sue Cook, and many others)

25% DISCOUNT VOUCHERS

Market Square
Bishop's Castle SY9 5BN

T: 01588 638403
E: stay@thecastlehotelbishopscastle.co.uk
W: thecastlehotelbishopscastle.co.uk

BEDROOMS: 12.
OPEN: all year except first week Jan.
FACILITIES: 3 bar areas, dining room, free Wi-Fi, in-room TV (Freeview), in-room spa treatments, patio, terrace, garden, parking, bars and restaurant wheelchair accessible.
BACKGROUND MUSIC: in bar areas.
LOCATION: in small market town centre.
CHILDREN: all ages welcomed.
DOGS: allowed in bedrooms, bar, at owner's side at meal times in dog-friendly areas, not in restaurant, welcome pack, no charge.
CREDIT CARDS: MC, Visa.
PRICES: per room B&B single £100–£115, double £110–£195, D,B&B single £128–£143, double £168–£253. À la carte £30. 1-night bookings sometimes refused Sat.

BLAKENEY Norfolk

MAP 2:A5

THE BLAKENEY HOTEL

♛ Previous César Winner

Widescreen vistas of salt marshes and big skies surround this family-friendly, quayside hotel. Helmed by Emma Stannard, with 'universally friendly and efficient staff', the north Norfolk grand dame is approaching its centenary. The inside, however, hits a contemporary note, with soothing greens, creams and greys, nature prints, comfy seating and log fires, plus those 'wonderful estuary views'. Holidays can be busy with families but the upstairs lounge is a tranquil retreat. Bedrooms are 'comfortable' and 'tasteful'. 'Mine was no less attractive for being just slightly down at heel,' says a regular reader this year. 'It had all one could want.' More expensive rooms have more still, proper coffee, perhaps a four-poster, a balcony, a garden patio. Interconnecting rooms suit guests with children. Adam Thompson's locally sourced dishes, served 'attentively and pleasantly' in the stylish restaurant, include the likes of grilled plaice, mash, roast fennel, courgettes, chive butter sauce. Breakfast 'has something for everyone'. Indoors, a games room, a heated pool; outdoors, a windswept coast, seal-watching, crabbing, dune-backed beaches. (Susan Willmington, AW, PR, and others).

The Quay
Blakeney
Holt NR25 7NE

T: 01263 740797
E: reception@blakeneyhotel.co.uk
W: blakeney-hotel.co.uk

BEDROOMS: 64. 16 in Granary annexe opposite, some on ground floor, 1 suitable for disabled.
OPEN: all year.
FACILITIES: lift, lounges, bar, restaurant, Wi-Fi, in-room TV (Freeview), function facilities, heated indoor swimming pool, steam room, mini-gym, games room, terrace, ¼-acre walled garden, public rooms wheelchair accessible, adapted toilet.
BACKGROUND MUSIC: none.
LOCATION: on the quay.
CHILDREN: all ages welcomed.
DOGS: allowed in some bedrooms, not in public rooms.
CREDIT CARDS: Amex, MC, Visa.
PRICES: per person B&B £122–£194, D,B&B (2-night min.) £134–£206. À la carte £35. 1-night bookings sometimes refused weekends, bank holidays.

BLANCHLAND Northumberland   MAP 4:B3

THE LORD CREWE ARMS

♛ Previous César Winner

You can drink champagne in the vaulted bar, as
W H Auden did, dine among the ancient stone
walls like Philip Larkin, or sleep in a room once
used by Benjamin Britten, at this hotel in the
monastic buildings of a dissolved abbey. The
heart of a north Pennines village, it is owned by
the Calcot Collection (see Calcot, Tetbury), and
retains the 'feeling of a heritage', with beamed
ceilings, 'a maze of corridors', and an inglenook
big enough to hide a Jacobite general in the 1715
Rising. Bedrooms, in the main house, miners'
cottages and at The Angel opposite, range from
'cosy' to 'champion', their colours inspired by the
Northumbrian landscape. Suites have their own
front door, a log-burner. 'My room was warm,
the bed comfortable, bathroom splendid (but the
lighting dim for reading),' writes a reader who
was frustrated by a mix-up over his booking.
Where was Tommy Mark, the 'genial Geordie'
manager, always so solicitous? Simon Hicks's
'honest British dishes', perhaps chicken from
Thistleyhaugh Farm, Longhorsley (see entry),
with haggis and sausage patty, leeks, mustard
cream sauce, hit the spot. Breakfast brings freshly
squeezed juice, 'decent cooked dishes'.

The Square
Blanchland DH8 9SP

T: 01434 675469
E: enquiries@
   lordcrewearmsblanchland.co.uk
W: lordcrewearmsblanchland.co.uk

BEDROOMS: 21. 7 in adjacent miners'
cottages, 10 in The Angel across the
road, some on ground floor, 1 suitable
for disabled.
OPEN: all year.
FACILITIES: 2 lounges, restaurant,
Gatehouse events space, free Wi-Fi,
in-room TV (Freeview), civil wedding
licence, beer garden, public rooms not
suitable for wheelchair.
BACKGROUND MUSIC: in dining room
and bar.
LOCATION: in Blanchland village on the
B6306, 9 miles S of Hexham.
CHILDREN: all ages welcomed.
DOGS: 'well-behaved dogs' allowed in
bedrooms, public rooms, not in dining
room.
CREDIT CARDS: Amex, MC, Visa.
PRICES: per room B&B £139–£264.
À la carte £32.

BLANDFORD FORUM Dorset

MAP 2:E1

THE CROWN HOTEL

'Well-regarded' brewers Hall and Woodhouse
have owned this Georgian town-centre inn since
1931. For one reader it is but 'a useful stopping
place', for another 'there's no better place for
a choice of Badger Ales'. A ghostly cloaked
highwayman and a lady in a crinoline are said
to like it so much that they've never left. Guests
graze (veggie platter, ploughman's, fish and chips)
in the panelled Pantry draped with vintage items
of kitchen equipment, or choose from a longer
menu in the dining room among gilt-framed
paintings (steak and Tanglefoot pie, chargrills,
stuffed aubergine). On sunny days people eat
and drink alfresco on a veritable 'piazza' among
clipped hedges and lollipop topiary. 'Handsome
accommodation' includes bedrooms that take
inspiration from Jane Austen, with 'interesting
portraits and engravings, antique or faux-antique
lamps, a vintage designer kettle'. A luxury room
has a modern four-poster, copper bath, Cole &
Son's pretty 'Winter Birds' wallpaper. The clubby
common room has 'leather armchairs, a roaring
fire'. The service may be 'polite and adequate', or
'friendly and helpful'. Thumbs up for the cooked
breakfast – thumbs down for the buffet. 'All in all,
an odd mix but a tempting one.'

West Street
Blandford Forum DT11 7AJ

T: 01258 456626
E: crownhotel.reception@
    hall-woodhouse.co.uk
W: crownhotelblandford.co.uk

BEDROOMS: 27. 1 suitable for disabled.
OPEN: all year.
FACILITIES: lift, bar, common room,
restaurant, function suite, free Wi-Fi,
in-room Smart TV (Freeview), civil
wedding licence, garden terrace,
public areas wheelchair accessible,
adapted toilet.
BACKGROUND MUSIC: in public rooms.
LOCATION: edge of town centre, 1 min.
from High Street.
CHILDREN: all ages welcomed.
DOGS: allowed in some bedrooms by
arrangement for an additional charge,
in bar, not in restaurant.
CREDIT CARDS: Amex, MC, Visa.
PRICES: per room B&B £90–£170.
À la carte £40.

BLEDINGTON Gloucestershire   MAP 3:D6

THE KING'S HEAD INN

On a wide village green guarded by ochre-
hued houses, Archie and Nicola Orr-Ewing's
'photogenic' 16th-century pub extends a 'relaxed
yet professional' welcome. A reader, arriving
on a cold night this year, was 'greeted warmly
and shown to a courtyard room' with an offer
of help with luggage. The 'wonderfully quiet'
room, a 'harmonious mix of eclectic furniture,
patterned wallpaper, and rugs', came with tea-/
coffee-making facilities, bottles of mineral water,
a 'lovely if slightly cramped bathroom'. Other cosy
rooms sit above the pub, some with a Provençal
feel, some overlooking the Green; all with
newly revamped bathroom. In the low-roofed,
'atmospheric' bar, with a fire, stone flags, 'high-
backed settles, and much mellow timber', locals
and visitors mingle over pints of Hook Norton.
While Calvin Mallows's locally sourced seasonal
dishes have won many plaudits, our reader found
dinner a 'slightly mixed affair', with a thumbs-up
for the Cornish bream, and a chilli cheeseburger
(beef from the family farm), but with a butternut
squash salad 'that really could have tried harder'.
After a 'more than solid sleep', breakfast, in
the light-filled dining room, was 'terrific'. (IB,
and others)

The Green
Bledington OX7 6XQ

T: 01608 658365
E: info@kingsheadinn.net
W: thekingsheadinn.net

BEDROOMS: 12. 6 in courtyard annexe,
some on ground floor.
OPEN: all year except 25/26 Dec.
FACILITIES: bar, restaurant, snug,
courtyard, free Wi-Fi, in-room TV
(Freeview), children's play area.
BACKGROUND MUSIC: most of the day,
in bar.
LOCATION: on village green.
CHILDREN: all ages welcomed.
DOGS: allowed in bar and certain
bedrooms by arrangement, not in
restaurant.
CREDIT CARDS: MC, Visa.
PRICES: per room B&B single £80–£105,
double £110–£140, D,B&B double
£170–£200. À la carte £35. 1-night
bookings refused Sat.

BOLTON ABBEY Yorkshire

MAP 4:D3

THE DEVONSHIRE ARMS [NEW]

You can arrive by helicopter at the Duke and Duchess of Devonshire's hotel 'in extensive lawned grounds with a view towards the River Wharfe'. Our inspectors, more circumspect, came by car, to be 'greeted by both the receptionist and a porter as we offloaded suitcases'. These were 'whisked' to a bedroom with 'quality period furnishing', a minute bathroom but a garden view. The nicest rooms are in the 17th-century wing, some with a four-poster, overlooking the Italian box garden. All have coffee machine, mini-fridge, fresh milk, a hamper of Yorkshire treats. In the restaurant, Paul Leonard's menus are a paean to local and home-grown produce. 'Cooking is of a high order. As amuse-bouche, we had rabbit goujons, salmon rolls and Wensleydale tarts, followed by langoustine, salted beetroot salad, smoked duck, wild mushroom raviolo, cured mackerel with warm apple dressing, a fine cheese selection.' The wine list 'has the weight of an ecclesiastical bible'; the sommelier 'knows his stuff'. You can eat à la carte in the jazzy brasserie from a wide-ranging menu. After breakfast, take advantage of the spa, or the complimentary access to ruined Bolton Abbey. (See also main entry for The Cavendish, Baslow.)

Bolton Abbey Estate
Bolton Abbey
Skipton BD23 6AJ

T: 01756 718100
E: reception@thedevonshirearms.co.uk
W: thedevonshirearms.co.uk

BEDROOMS: 40. Some on ground floor, 1 suitable for disabled.
OPEN: all year, restaurant closed Mon eve, brasserie open all week.
FACILITIES: 4 lounges, brasserie, restaurant, private dining rooms, Wi-Fi, in-room TV, civil wedding licence, spa (indoor pool, spa bath), gardens, helicopter pads, public areas wheelchair accessible, adapted toilet.
BACKGROUND MUSIC: in public areas.
LOCATION: 6 miles E of Skipton.
CHILDREN: all ages welcomed.
DOGS: allowed in most bedrooms, public areas, not spa or dining areas.
CREDIT CARDS: Amex, MC, Visa.
PRICES: per room B&B single £149–£359, double £169–£379, DB&B £309–£519. À la carte £35 (brasserie), tasting menu (restaurant) £85.

BORROWDALE Cumbria

MAP 4: inset C2

HAZEL BANK

♀ Previous César Winner

'Great hotel, great food,' enthuse American readers in 2019, rating Gary and Donna MacRae's 'Lakeland gem' as the 'best hotel of our five-week European trip – and we stayed in some superb places'. Sitting above Rosthwaite, with views across the Borrowdale valley to Scafell Pike and Great Gable, the Victorian house was visited regularly by Hugh Walpole, providing inspiration for the family home in his novel Rogue Herries. Expect less drama today. The 'wonderful hosts' extended a 'warm and very personal greeting' before ushering readers to an 'immaculately appointed' room, with 'good views of surrounding hills, a carafe of sherry, home-made chocolates and shortbread'. Restraint is called for, however. The 'engaging, discreet and efficient' MacRaes preside over the 'charming dining room', while Donna and new chef Darren Cornish, a MasterChef finalist, use seasonal, locally sourced ingredients in such dishes as Herdwick lamb saddle, crisped breast, king carrot, lamb jus. An 'excellent' breakfast fuels fell walks from the front door. 'The hosts' undoubted aim is to ensure every guest comes away with a powerful glow of satisfaction.' (David Dalton-Leggett, and others)

25% DISCOUNT VOUCHERS

Borrowdale
Keswick CA12 5XB

T: 017687 77248
E: info@hazelbankhotel.co.uk
W: hazelbankhotel.co.uk

BEDROOMS: 7. 1 on ground floor with walk-in shower.
OPEN: 25 Jan–1 Dec.
FACILITIES: lounge, dining room, drying room, free Wi-Fi, in-room TV (Freeview), 4-acre grounds (croquet, woodland walks).
BACKGROUND MUSIC: Classic FM at breakfast.
LOCATION: 6 miles S of Keswick on B5289 to Borrowdale.
CHILDREN: not under 16.
DOGS: not allowed.
CREDIT CARDS: MC, Visa.
PRICES: per person B&B single occupancy £135–£150, double £75–£90, D,B&B single £169–£194, double £109–£134. Set dinner £39. Min. 2-night bookings except by special arrangement.

SEE ALSO SHORTLIST

BORROWDALE Cumbria

MAP 4: inset C2

LEATHES HEAD HOTEL

'In a beautiful setting, with valley and fell views all around', this country house, built for the daughter of a Liverpool ship owner, retains the leisured ambience of its Edwardian past. Bedrooms are traditionally styled, although with modern comforts. The dual-aspect original master bedroom looks across the valley towards Derwentwater and Catbells. Its bathroom has a bath and separate monsoon shower. All rooms have room service, smart Gilchrist and Soames toiletries. Throughout, the hotel is spruce, 'smart, clean and in good repair'. Manager Leigh O'Donoghue presides over 'accommodating' staff. You can take afternoon tea under a parasol on the terrace – a sighting of red squirrels, the icing on the cake. A reader admired chef Noel Breaks's cooking. 'The food is a major delight – we ended up eating in every night.' He uses locally grown, reared and foraged produce to create such dishes as rack of Yew Tree Farm hogget, turnips, fondant potato, roasted shallot; confit cabbage, Jersey Royals, broccoli and blue cheese purée, mustard-seed vinaigrette. A 'very good breakfast' includes home-made bread and free-range eggs. Pretty Grange village is a stroll away.

Borrowdale
Keswick CA12 5UY

T: 017687 77247
E: reservations@leatheshead.co.uk
W: leatheshead.co.uk

BEDROOMS: 11. Some on ground floor, 1 suitable for disabled.
OPEN: all year except Christmas and Jan (but open New Year).
FACILITIES: lounge, bar, Conservatory restaurant, free Wi-Fi, in-room TV (Freeview), civil wedding licence, drying room, terrace, 3-acre grounds, public rooms wheelchair accessible.
BACKGROUND MUSIC: in public rooms.
LOCATION: 4½ miles S of Keswick.
CHILDREN: not under 15.
DOGS: allowed in some bedrooms and public areas.
CREDIT CARDS: Amex, MC, Visa.
PRICES: per room B&B £100–£190, D,B&B £160–£285. Set dinner £45.

SEE ALSO SHORTLIST

BOSCASTLE Cornwall   MAP 1:C3

THE OLD RECTORY

'A super place. The real deal.' Praise from Guide insiders for Chris and Sally Searle's B&B, in the rectory where Thomas Hardy courted Emma Gifford. Sally's grandmother's childhood and marital home, it is infused with 'comfort and charm'. The garden supplies cut flowers, produce for the table. Rectory bedrooms have period furnishings. Emma's Room has a power shower, original thunderbox toilet, garden views ('even in February, lots of early camellias out, and displayed in a mantelpiece jug'). Mr Hardy's Room has an antique carved bed, the 'cosy' Rector's Room a whirlpool bath and Victorian fireplace. The Old Stable, a dog-friendly annexe room, has a separate entrance, wood-burning stove, king-size bed and sofa bed. A generosity of spirit seals the deal: 'Daily paper outside your door by 7.30; no charge for laundry if staying three nights or more; free transport to Boscastle eateries, nicest residents' sitting room, great choice of breakfast ingredients.' These include eggs from the resident hens, 'nicely done bacon and fried egg, good smoked salmon, good kipper'. 'Their gorgeous golden retriever comes to check out guests if she can get away with it!' Well located for the Coast Path. (AKH)

St Juliot
Boscastle PL35 0BT

T: 01840 250225
E: sally@stjuliot.com
W: stjuliot.com

BEDROOMS: 4. 1 in stables (connected to house via conservatory).
OPEN: normally Feb–end Oct, 'but please check', limited evening meals by arrangement.
FACILITIES: sitting room, breakfast room, conservatory, free Wi-Fi, in-room TV (Freeview), 3-acre garden (croquet lawn, 'lookout', walled kitchen garden), unsuitable for disabled.
BACKGROUND MUSIC: none.
LOCATION: 2 miles NE of Boscastle.
CHILDREN: not under 12.
DOGS: up to 2 allowed, only in stable room (£10 per dog/stay).
CREDIT CARDS: MC, Visa.
PRICES: per room B&B single £60–£108, double £75–£120. 1-night bookings only accepted if a late vacancy or quiet period.

BOSHAM Sussex

MAP 2:E3

THE MILLSTREAM

We have readers who have been returning for more than 20 years to the Wild family's traditional hotel 'in a picturesque village' once known for oyster fishing. It began life as three 17th-century workmen's cottages bordered by a stream, subsuming more over time, to become the seamless operation of today. The pretty, light-washed bedrooms are 'comfortable and well furnished'; all have a coffee machine, biscuits, paraben-free toiletries, fresh milk in an 'all-important silent fridge'. The best have a seating area, bathroom with freestanding bath and separate shower, French doors to a south-facing private garden. However, one guest disliked his room in the modern extension. Monochrome photographs of local beauty spots are displayed throughout the hotel. In the elegant restaurant, chef Neil Hiskey's contemporary British dishes include guineafowl breast, boudin blanc, hispi cabbage, tarragon croquettes. You can eat more simple fare in the brasserie, maybe tempura cod, Thai green curry, honey-roast ham. Morning brings a decent buffet, 'a good choice of hot breakfasts, cooked to order'. 'A craft centre, coffee shop, pub, church and quay are a short walk away.' (Ian Marshall, JB)

25% DISCOUNT VOUCHERS

Bosham Lane
Bosham
Chichester PO18 8HL

T: 01243 573234
E: reception@millstream-hotel.co.uk
W: millstreamhotel.com

BEDROOMS: 35. 2 in cottage, 7 on ground floor, 2 suitable for disabled.
OPEN: all year.
FACILITIES: lounge, bar, restaurant (pianist Sat eve), brasserie, conference room, free Wi-Fi, in-room TV (Freeview), civil wedding licence, front lawn (alfresco dining), residents' garden (stream, gazebo), public areas wheelchair accessible.
BACKGROUND MUSIC: all day in bar, lounge and restaurants.
LOCATION: 4 miles W of Chichester.
CHILDREN: all ages welcomed.
DOGS: not allowed.
CREDIT CARDS: MC, Visa.
PRICES: per room B&B £135–£245, D,B&B £180–£310. À la carte £43 (restaurant), £25 (brasserie). 1-night bookings sometimes refused Sat.

BOURTON-ON-THE-HILL Gloucestershire   MAP 3:D6

THE HORSE AND GROOM

♥ Previous César Winner

A new manager and a new chef last year for
this popular Cotswold inn in which guests feel
they can 'genuinely relax'. The inn is on a busy
road but soundproofing is 'good', and trusted
reviewers 'weren't at all disturbed by the traffic'.
After a 'warm welcome', they were shown to a
'lovely, spacious' room with 'good lighting and
two comfortable chairs'. King- or super-king-size
beds are 'comfortable', 'spotless' bathrooms have a
bath and a shower; one room has doors on to the
garden. 'Good food' is the main draw, and Katie
Jackson's à la carte menu changes daily. Eat in the
rustic-style bar or the restaurant. Perhaps Naked
beef burger, bacon, Double Gloucester, chips,
Tandoori aïoli; beer-battered haddock, chips,
minted crushed peas, tartare sauce. 'Good, fresh
orange juice' and 'very good local produce' at
breakfast, 'especially bacon and sausages' and 'the
eggs Florentine'. 'Slow service' and housekeeping
that could be 'more professional' are minor niggles
this year. But it's in a 'good location with great
walks along the South Cotswold Way, around
Batsford Arboretum, Bourton House garden and
Sezincote'. 'We will stay again.' (Sue and John
Jenkinson, Suzanne Lyons, and others)

Bourton-on-the-Hill
Moreton-in-Marsh GL56 9AQ

T: 01386 700413
E: enquiries@horseandgroom.info
W: horseandgroom.info

BEDROOMS: 5.
OPEN: all year round.
FACILITIES: bar, restaurant, garden, free
Wi-Fi, in-room TV (Freeview), 1-acre
garden, public rooms wheelchair
accessible (toilets not adapted,
upstairs).
BACKGROUND MUSIC: in bar and
restaurant.
LOCATION: village centre.
CHILDREN: all ages welcomed.
DOGS: allowed in most bedrooms
and bar.
CREDIT CARDS: MC, Visa.
PRICES: per room B&B £110–£210.
À la carte £30. 1-night bookings
refused weekends.

BOWNESS-ON-WINDERMERE Cumbria   MAP 4: inset C2

LINDETH FELL

'The Kennedys certainly know how to welcome their guests and to make every minute special,' report visitors staying for lunch this year. This 'delightful', wisteria-draped Edwardian country house B&B, surrounded by Lakeland fells and encircled by spectacular garden and grounds (with croquet, bowls and putting on tap), has a period feel. Arriving guests may be treated to cream tea in the peach-coloured lounge filled with squashy sofas, family snaps and books. Alternatively, take tea on the terrace overlooking the garden. There's a light period touch in the bedrooms, too (some snug, some with lake views), plus an espresso machine, decanter of sherry, good toiletries, fluffy robes, slippers. Light bites and wine are served all day in the tartan-carpeted dining room with glorious fell views, as well as cheese, meat or fish platters from 12 pm to 8 pm or Sunday lunch (both by prior arrangement). The 'splendid' breakfast includes home-made yogurt and marmalade, French pastries; for the full works choose between a Cumberland grill, finnan haddock, or veggie with free-range eggs. Feast at your leisure, and then wander through the garden with its own tarn, or take a cruise on Lake Windermere.

25% DISCOUNT VOUCHERS

Lyth Valley Road
Bowness-on-Windermere LA23 3JP

T: 015394 43286
E: kennedy@lindethfell.co.uk
W: lindethfell.co.uk

BEDROOMS: 14. 1, on ground floor, suitable for disabled.
OPEN: all year except 24–26 Dec, 2 Jan–8 Feb, open New Year.
FACILITIES: 2 lounges, bar, entrance hall with seating, dining room, Wi-Fi, in-room TV (Freeview), 7-acre grounds (terrace, gardens, lawn games), complimentary access to local gym, spa, pool 5 mins' drive away.
BACKGROUND MUSIC: classical in dining room, bar.
LOCATION: 1 mile S of Bowness.
CHILDREN: all ages welcomed.
DOGS: only assistance dogs allowed.
CREDIT CARDS: MC, Visa.
PRICES: per room B&B single from £105, double from £210. Pre-ordered Sunday lunch £24.50, evening platters £14.50. 1-night bookings sometimes refused.

SEE ALSO SHORTLIST

BRADFORD-ON-AVON Wiltshire   MAP 2:D1

WIDBROOK GRANGE

'The place abounds with creative uses of old,
mainly farm, paraphernalia.' Guide inspectors
enjoyed Nick Dent's diverting Georgian
farmhouse turned dog-friendly hotel with most
rooms in converted outbuildings. After an
'enthusiastic' welcome from the manager, they
were shown to a 'spacious' stables room with 'nice
old agricultural bits and pieces ranged outside'. It
had an emperor-size bed, leather wing armchairs
and 'an old suitcase that worked well as the
receptacle for hospitality drinks'; a bath with a
good shower over, Bramley toiletries. Main-house
rooms are smarter, perhaps with in-room bath.
Intriguing upcycling is a constant feature: mirrors
in old windows, lights in milk pails, shelves from
wooden crates. In a 'light, modern' dining room
with a display of garden tools, guests sit down
at 'tables of mixed shapes and sizes', to Sándor
Szücs's 'unusual combinations and flavours'. For
instance, marinated duck breast, calabrese rice,
roasted golden beetroot, carrot mash, green tea-
cured parsnips, apple gin glaze. There are vegan,
gluten-free and children's menus. Breakfast
brings kippers, egg and soldiers. Sister pub
The Boathouse, opposite, overlooks the canal.
(N and CH)

Trowbridge Road
Widbrook
Bradford-on-Avon BA15 1UH

T: 01225 864750
E: stay@widbrookgrange.co.uk
w: widbrookgrange.co.uk

BEDROOMS: 19. 15 in outbuildings, 1
suitable for disabled.
OPEN: all year.
FACILITIES: gin bar, snug, restaurant,
conservatory, Wi-Fi, in-room TV
(Freeview), civil wedding licence,
function facilities, 11-acre grounds,
11-metre indoor heated swimming
pool, gym, giant chess, parking, public
rooms wheelchair accessible.
BACKGROUND MUSIC: soft all day in
public rooms.
LOCATION: 2 miles S of Bradford-on-
Avon.
CHILDREN: all ages welcomed.
DOGS: allowed in courtyard bedrooms
(£15 per dog per night), public rooms,
not restaurant.
CREDIT CARDS: Amex, MC, Visa.
PRICES: per room B&B double
£110–£220, family room £170–£235.
À la carte £35, tasting menu £59.

SEE ALSO SHORTLIST

BRADFORD-ON-AVON Wiltshire   MAP 2:D1

WOOLLEY GRANGE

The first of Nigel Chapman's Luxury Family Hotels (see also Fowey Hall, Fowey, and Moonfleet Manor, Fleet) occupies a 'pretty, rambling' Jacobean manor house in 'lovely grounds' with 'views across the Wiltshire countryside'. The formula is a winner, providing a spa and fine dining for adults, indoor and outdoor swimming pools, and all-day fun for children. There are 'lots of small, cosy sitting rooms with wood fires and squashy sofas', a kids' club, baby-listening and baby-minding, nature trails, a grass maze and fairy garden, eggs to collect, fruit to pick, a playroom with air hockey, table football. Four-legged guests get a welcome pack and outdoor shower. Accommodation includes family rooms, suites (sleeping up to seven) and interconnecting rooms, some in annexes, some contemporary in style, some traditional. The walled garden, supplying fresh produce, is home to the White Witch of Woolley and her tiny cottage. The kitchen is home to wizard Jethro Lawrence, who creates such dishes as lamb rump, samphire, baby gem, mashed potato, grelots; 'plenty of fish and vegetarian options'. There is an all-day lounge menu, children's high tea. Breakfast is served with a daily newsletter.

Woolley Green
Bradford-on-Avon BA15 1TX

T: 01225 864705
E: info@woolleygrangehotel.co.uk
W: woolleygrangehotel.co.uk

BEDROOMS: 25. 11 in annexes, 2 on ground floor, 1 suitable for disabled.
OPEN: all year.
FACILITIES: 2 lounges, 2 restaurants, cinema, 2 private dining rooms, free Wi-Fi, in-room TV (Freeview), crèche, spa, heated indoor and outdoor swimming pools, civil wedding licence, 14-acre grounds, wheelchair accessible.
BACKGROUND MUSIC: in restaurants.
LOCATION: 1 mile NE of Bradford-on-Avon, 8½ miles SE of Bath.
CHILDREN: all ages welcomed.
DOGS: allowed in bedrooms, public rooms, not restaurants.
CREDIT CARDS: Amex, MC, Visa.
PRICES: per room B&B double £179–£319, family £219–£469. À la carte £40. 1-night bookings sometimes refused weekends.

SEE ALSO SHORTLIST

BRAITHWAITE Cumbria

THE COTTAGE IN THE WOOD

'Everything about this small, personal hotel was faultless, from the accommodation, food and helpful staff to the overall atmosphere.' Readers loved this year's stay at Kath and Liam Berney's restaurant-with-rooms on Whinlatter Pass. Surrounded by England's only true mountain forest, the former coaching inn has views towards Skiddaw and the Northern Fells, close-ups of red squirrels and deer. Light contemporary-style bedrooms range from very snug to the garden room with separate entrance, seating area and wet room. Oak and Ash rooms have a whirlpool bath and a shower. 'Our room, overlooking the terrace and mountains, was in perfect order, always clean and fresh when we returned in the evening.' In the dining room with panoramic views and wraparound terrace, chef Ben Wilkinson's 'awesome dinners' include ingredients raised, grown or foraged in Cumbria. For instance, Herdwick hogget loin, spiced carrot, Puy lentils, fried sweetbread, Roscoff onion; hen of the woods, Old Winchester gnocchi, roast butternut squash, tenderstem broccoli, charred hispi. 'Liam acted as sommelier at night and chef in the morning (great breakfast, by the way).' 'Thoroughly recommended.' (NL, and others)

Magic Hill
Whinlatter Forest
Braithwaite CA12 5TW

T: 017687 78409
E: relax@thecottageinthewood.co.uk
W: thecottageinthewood.co.uk

BEDROOMS: 9. 1 in the garden with separate entrance.
OPEN: all year except 25/26 Dec, 2nd and 3rd week Jan, closed Sun, Mon.
FACILITIES: lounge, restaurant, free Wi-Fi, in-room TV (Freeview), drying room, secure bicycle storage, terraced garden, 2 acres of woodland, restaurant and public areas wheelchair accessible, adapted toilet.
BACKGROUND MUSIC: none.
LOCATION: 5 miles NW of Keswick.
CHILDREN: not under 10.
DOGS: not allowed.
CREDIT CARDS: MC, Visa.
PRICES: per room D,B&B double £210–£300. Set dinner £50, tasting menu £70. 1-night bookings refused weekends.

BRANCASTER STAITHE Norfolk

MAP 2:A5

THE WHITE HORSE

♥Previous César Winner

'A lovely hotel with efficient, friendly staff,' declares a trusted Guide reader this year after a third visit to the Nye family's inn, which gazes across tidal salt marshes to Scolt Head Island and the open sea. The contemporary en suite bedrooms nod to the surroundings with breezy tones of turquoise, green, lavender and sand. Eight rooms, each with a terrace, occupy a garden extension, blending into the landscape with grass and sedum roofs. 'Our comfortable room, overlooking the marshes, was well appointed with a good bathroom and plenty of storage.' Light sleepers might request a room away from the restaurant. In the bar and light-washed conservatory dining room with its alfresco deck, Fran Hartshorne's locally sourced menus 'are heavily accented towards fish' but also serve Norfolk lamb, beef and vegetarian options including chargrilled leeks, gnocchi, goat's curd, hazelnut dressing. 'I had a memorable baked ray wing with grapes and almond – a dish I'm determined to cook myself.' Guests can pick up kippers or salmon from the smokehouse in the garden. 'Breakfast was OK with good croissants. We will return.' (Peter Anderson)

Main Road
Brancaster Staithe PE31 8BY

T: 01485 210262
E: reception@whitehorsebrancaster.
   co.uk
W: whitehorsebrancaster.co.uk

BEDROOMS: 15. 8 on ground floor in annexe, 1 suitable for disabled.
OPEN: all year.
FACILITIES: public bar, open-plan lounge areas, conservatory restaurant, dining room, free Wi-Fi, in-room TV (Freeview), ½-acre garden (terrace, covered sunken garden), in-room therapies, public rooms wheelchair accessible, adapted toilet.
BACKGROUND MUSIC: 'subtle' in restaurant.
LOCATION: centre of village.
CHILDREN: all ages welcomed.
DOGS: allowed in garden rooms (£10 per night), bar.
CREDIT CARDS: Amex, MC, Visa.
PRICES: per room B&B £120–£200, D,B&B (Sun–Thurs in low season only, except bank holidays and school holidays) £170–£250. À la carte £30.

BRANSCOMBE Devon   MAP 1:C5

THE MASON'S ARMS

Cosy hotel or traditional pub? This 14th-century
thatched inn offers the best of both, and will
certainly 'tempt us from London again', says a
recent visitor. The setting, in a 'most attractive'
village (said to be the longest in England), a
ten-minute stroll from a lovely shingle cove,
and near the Coastal Path, is idyllic. Rooms in
the main building and in separate cottages are
'comfortable' and decorated in contemporary
style; the ground-floor cottage rooms open on to
the gardens. Hand-pumped ale in the convivial
bar and 'excellent' (if 'a little slow') food in the bar
or beamed restaurant, where the emphasis is on
fresh local produce (key suppliers are shown on
a produce map). The Branscombe lobster proved
'a particular treat' for one reader. Other delights
include the Mason's seafood platter, featuring
their own hot-smoked salmon, mackerel fillet
soused in cider, Devon crab meat. Plenty of decent
pub grub, too, including pizzas, burgers, pies and
steak. Breakfast is 'exceptional', with a selection
of fruit including 'fresh watermelon, pineapple'.
Tables, both inside and out, are 'constantly filled',
testament to the 'very friendly and helpful' staff.
(Martin Daly, SJ)

Branscombe EX12 3DJ

T: 01297 680300
E: masonsarms@staustellbrewery.
   co.uk
W: www.masonsarms.co.uk

BEDROOMS: 27. 14 in cottages, 1 suitable
for disabled.
OPEN: all year.
FACILITIES: bar, restaurant, free Wi-Fi
(in main bar), in-room TV, garden
with outdoor seating, public rooms
accessible to some wheelchairs (minor
steps), adapted toilet (reached via
outside route).
BACKGROUND MUSIC: none.
LOCATION: village centre.
CHILDREN: all ages welcomed.
DOGS: allowed in a few bedrooms
(£10 per dog per night), in bar and on
terraces.
CREDIT CARDS: Amex, MC, Visa.
PRICES: per room B&B £95–£155.
À la carte £28.

BRIDGE Kent

MAP 2:D5

THE PIG AT BRIDGE PLACE `NEW`

A new entry to the Guide this year, the latest addition to the Pig litter (see index) is set in a Jacobean manor house just outside Canterbury. 'Any fan of the other Pigs would love this one too,' says our inspector. From the 'helpful' receptionist who 'insisted on carrying our bags up four floors' to the 'charming' waiters, staff have 'the same boundless enthusiasm' found at the other Pig hotels. The house oozes period features – panelled rooms, secret stairs, quiet nooks for 'curling up with a book' – as well as a 'cosy' bar and lounge. Bedrooms in the main building have signature Pig comforts: 'crisp linen', Roberts radio, snack drawer 'full of temptations', and Bramley toiletries. All are up several flights; adjacent coach house rooms are 'spacious, with their own entrance off the garden'. Hop Pickers' Huts are smart-rustic rooms on stilts by the river. Food comes from the kitchen gardens or within a 25-mile radius. Dinner is 'expertly cooked and served' in the shabby-chic Coach House restaurant. Breakfast is a hot dish from a limited menu; cereal, fruit, cheese, breads and pastries, or a full cooked breakfast. The courtyard looked 'a lovely place to sit on a sunny day'.

Bourne Park Road
Bridge
Canterbury CT4 5LF

T: 01227 830208
E: reservations@thepighotel.com
W: thepighotel.com/at-bridge-place

BEDROOMS: 30. 7 in main house, 13 in coach house, 4 on ground floor, 2 suitable for disabled, 2 family-friendly lodges, 1 converted barn, and 7 Hop Pickers' Huts.
OPEN: all year.
FACILITIES: restaurant, bar/lounge, snugs, study, two treatment rooms, gardens, terrace, wheelchair access to restaurant, adapted toilet.
BACKGROUND MUSIC: in public areas.
LOCATION: on edge of village, 3 miles S of Canterbury.
CHILDREN: all ages welcomed.
DOGS: allowed in grounds only (not the kitchen garden).
CREDIT CARDS: Amex, MC, Visa.
PRICES: Per room £110–£235. Breakfast buffet £12, cooked breakfast £16, à la carte £42. 2-night bookings only at weekends.

BRIGHTON Sussex

ARTIST RESIDENCE BRIGHTON

Pure Evil has been unleashed this past year at
Charlotte and Justin Salisbury's funky hotel.
The graffiti artist was one of two brought in to
work on bedroom murals at the original Artist
Residence. 'At the top of a delightful Regency
square looking down to the derelict West Pier', it
is praised by trusted readers for its 'enthusiastic
young staff' and a bedroom 'with character'.
A 'tiny lift' bore them up to the fourth floor,
to a 'comfy sea-view room with repurposed
furnishings, a mock-antler chandelier, a large,
comfortable bed'. Even rooms classed as 'tiny'
have original artist decor, a minibar, espresso
machine, Bramley toiletries. A new loft room
has an in-room roll-top bath, a walk-in rainfall
shower, limited-edition prints. Balcony rooms
come in various sizes and guises. In The Set
restaurant, Dan Kenny uses local and foraged
ingredients in such dishes as glazed monkfish,
octopus, seaweed, butterbeans, olives. One small
request: 'A little more cleaning of the industrial
chic decor, please.' At breakfast, 'super squeezed
juice and a bacon roll with fried egg and tangy
Cheddar set us up for a morning in the Lanes,
ten minutes' walk away.' (Desmond and Jenny
Balmer, K and VS)

34 Regency Square
Brighton BN1 2FJ

T: 01273 324302
E: brighton@artistresidence.co.uk
W: artistresidence.co.uk/our-hotels/
   brighton

BEDROOMS: 24.
OPEN: all year, restaurant closed 25/26
Dec.
FACILITIES: lift, lounge, cocktail bar,
private bar (events), restaurant,
ping-pong/meeting room, free Wi-Fi,
in-room TV (Freeview), unsuitable
for disabled.
BACKGROUND MUSIC: in public areas.
LOCATION: town centre.
CHILDREN: all ages welcomed (under-
16s not unsupervised in bedrooms).
DOGS: allowed in some bedrooms (£15
per dog per night).
CREDIT CARDS: Amex, MC, Visa.
PRICES: room £85–£325. Cooked
breakfast from £6, full English/veggie
£10, à la carte £32. 1-night bookings
refused weekends.

SEE ALSO SHORTLIST

BRIGHTON Sussex

MAP 2:E4

DRAKES

'One of the nicest locations we've stayed at.'
Trusted readers enjoyed a night's stay at Andy
and Gayle Shearer's boutique hotel on the
seafront, with 'panoramic views' of sea and the
Palace Pier. A signature room was 'sun-drenched
and stylishly designed, with emperor-size bed,
a freestanding bath in the bay window'; in the
wet room a good power shower. Bedrooms,
some city-facing, range from snug to 'beautifully
spacious'. All have cafetière coffee, fresh milk on
request, waffle robes, complimentary slippers,
White Company toiletries. The ground-floor,
sea-facing cocktail bar 'felt oddly poky' for a space
with such potential, but the restaurant, on the
lower ground floor, proved 'a very pleasant place'
with 'comfortable furnishings, smart, minimalist
design, ambience and acoustics just right'. Chef
Andy Vitez impressed with 'a delicious amuse-
bouche of duck rillettes with Bloody Mary gel',
then 'delicate, tasty scallop ceviche, with a yuzu
sorbet, chilli gel, coriander leaves'. Braised rabbit
was 'delicate in taste but slightly under-seasoned'.
Breakfast, charged extra, has such unusual
offerings as huevos rancheros and (how very
Brighton!) quinoa salad. (Anna and Bill Brewer,
and others)

25% DISCOUNT VOUCHERS

43–44 Marine Parade
Brighton BN2 1PE

T: 01273 696934
E: info@drakesofbrighton.com
W: drakesofbrighton.com

BEDROOMS: 20.
OPEN: all year.
FACILITIES: lounge/bar, restaurant,
meeting/private dining room, free Wi-
Fi, in-room TV (Sky), civil wedding
licence, off-road parking, unsuitable
for disabled.
BACKGROUND MUSIC: in bar and
restaurant.
LOCATION: ½ mile from centre, on
seafront.
CHILDREN: all ages welcomed.
DOGS: only assistance dogs allowed.
CREDIT CARDS: Amex, MC, Visa.
PRICES: room only £120–£360, DB&B
£190–£430. Breakfast £7.50–£15,
5-course tasting menu £65, table
d'hôte menu £37–£48. Min. 2-night
stay Fri and Sat, but check availability.

SEE ALSO SHORTLIST

BRILL Buckinghamshire

THE POINTER

The Pointers were a prominent local family, but
as a motif for an inn with an outdoorsy, farm-
to-fork ethos, a gun dog does very nicely.
'In an elevated position above beautiful
Buckinghamshire', the '18th-century red brick
pub' is a big amenity for this 'exceptionally
friendly village', the inspiration for Bree in
Tolkien's The Lord of the Rings. One of its USPs
is a butcher's shop, selling meats from traditional
breeds, raised to high standards on local farms and
by owner Harry Aubrey-Fletcher's family on their
Chilton estate. With produce from a vegetable
garden in Ludgershall, these are mainstays of
new chef Gavin Sinden's farm and fine-dining
menus, which offer such earthy dishes as pan-
fried ox tongue, mashed Maris Pipers, cavolo
nero, glazed carrots – and such fishy ones as
grilled plaice, sea vegetables, beurre noisette.
Also new this year are four inn bedrooms. An
inspector's room last year, in a cottage annexe,
was 'Farrow & Ball grey with rustic touches'. All
rooms have a Hypnos bed, coffee machine, roll-
top bath and waterfall shower, White Company
toiletries. After breakfast you can borrow Hunter
wellies for a short stroll to one of Britain's oldest
windmills. (NH)

27 Church St
Brill HP18 9RT

T: 01844 238339
E: reservations@thepointerbrill.co.uk
W: thepointerbrill.co.uk

BEDROOMS: 8. 4 in cottage a few yards
from main building, 2 on ground
floor.
OPEN: all year.
FACILITIES: restaurant, bar, garden,
free Wi-Fi in main building, in-room
TV, bar wheelchair accessible, adapted
toilet.
BACKGROUND MUSIC: Spotify playlists.
LOCATION: centre of village.
CHILDREN: all ages welcomed, blow-up
beds provided.
DOGS: allowed in bedrooms (£20 per
dog per night), in bar, garden, but not
in restaurant.
CREDIT CARDS: MC, Visa.
PRICES: per room B&B double
£120–£160. À la carte £43, farm
menu (Tues–Fri lunch, Tues–Thurs
dinner) £22.

BRISTOL

MAP 1:B6

BACKWELL HOUSE

Something old, something new. Many of the furnishings at this Georgian 'country house' hotel and wedding venue have been upcycled from materials reclaimed on site. Close to Bristol Airport and the city centre, the mansion that spawned its own cricket team and saw WG Grace play on the lawn is run by Guy Williams with owners the Hobbs family. Guide insiders this year 'never saw a manager', but service was 'always helpful'. After a 'good welcome' they were shown 'up a fine staircase… to our room'. It had limited storage, but 'the best reading lights we've found in a hotel'. One room has a roll-top bath on a dais by the window, another 'a sink made from an antique suitcase', 'a strong shower'. All rooms have views over walled garden, grounds and 'rolling fields'; also ground coffee, fresh milk. Downstairs, the ambience is 'convivial, with leather armchairs, wood-burning stoves'. Josh Hutson cooks such dishes as lamb rump, sweetbread, broad beans, pearl onion, artichokes; 'fluffy' chocolate mousse. Breakfast was 'adequate' though with 'a large TV showing news above our heads'. 'The staff seemed to care about the hotel as they might a well-loved family home.' (C and AR, NG)

Farleigh Road
Bristol BS48 3QA

T: 01275 794502
E: enquiries@backwellhouse.co.uk
W: backwellhouse.co.uk

BEDROOMS: 9.
OPEN: all year except Christmas (phone for details).
FACILITIES: bar, lounge, breakfast room, restaurant, conservatory, meeting room/snug, free Wi-Fi, in-room TV (Freeview), civil wedding licence, cinema room, ornamental walled garden, parking, public rooms wheelchair accessible, adapted toilet.
BACKGROUND MUSIC: in public areas.
LOCATION: in the country, 8 miles from Bristol.
CHILDREN: not under 12.
DOGS: not allowed.
CREDIT CARDS: Amex, MC, Visa.
PRICES: per room B&B £95–£245. Fixed-price dinner £29–£35.

BRISTOL

BROOKS GUESTHOUSE

In 'a great location' close to St Nicholas market, in the old city centre, this 'very good value, really friendly' B&B was the third of Carla and Andrew Brooks's growing stable of properties. Befitting its home in a refurbished 1950s office block, the lounge's retro leather sofas and cowhide rug on a pale wooden floor emit an air of mid-century cool. Upstairs, the bright if 'compact' rooms have pretty Cole & Son wallpapers, real coat-hangers, a hospitality tray with tea, coffee, biscuits; a bathroom with power shower. Guests opting for a less conventional stay head to the rooftop where, amid tubs of shrubs, four 'sleek, shiny' Airstream-type caravans offer a higher form of glamping. A larger one, sleeping four, was 'very nicely and comfortably done up' with a 'strong shower' and fun strips of coloured lights. 'The interior was very clever and cool,' reports a younger reader. 'A good place for a family. The roof's amazing Astroturf felt like a garden.' Weekends up there may have a louder party atmosphere. An 'excellent' breakfast in the open-plan kitchen brings organic yogurt and home-made fruit compote, a full English, eggs any way.

Exchange Avenue
St Nicholas Market
Bristol BS1 1UB

T: 0117 930 0066
E: info@brooksguesthousebristol.com
W: brooksguesthousebristol.com

BEDROOMS: 27. 4 in Airstream-style caravans on roof.
OPEN: all year except 24–26 Dec.
FACILITIES: lift, lounge/breakfast room, honesty bar, free Wi-Fi, in-room TV (Freeview), courtyard and rooftop garden, unsuitable for disabled.
BACKGROUND MUSIC: in lounge and breakfast area.
LOCATION: central, next to St Nicholas Market.
CHILDREN: all ages welcomed.
DOGS: only assistance dogs.
CREDIT CARDS: Amex, MC, Visa.
PRICES: per room B&B single £89–£149, double £99–£169. Min. 2-night stay Sat.

BRISTOL

MAP 1:B6

NUMBER THIRTY EIGHT CLIFTON

♀ Previous César Winner

'The friendly staff, super-comfortable bedrooms and great views make this a very special place.' Inspectors in 2019 loved their stay at Adam Dorrien-Smith's bay-fronted Georgian merchant's house turned B&B above the city, overlooking Clifton Down. Interiors are 'soothingly tasteful and uncluttered', with eclectic artwork on panelled walls painted in muted shades, chairs upholstered in velvet and tweed. Cocktails and cream teas are served in a sitting room with a log-burner, or on a terrace with rooftop vistas. 'We were welcomed warmly, given a parking permit and upgraded to a suite. "It seems a shame not to show off a lovely room like this," said the manager.' And lovely it was, 'as big as a starter flat, with a sitting area, a very comfortable super-king-size bed, good lighting, a Roberts radio, minibar, fresh milk, bottled water'. The stylish bathroom had a powerful shower. Some rooms have a tin or copper roll-top bath, dual-aspect windows. The house is unstaffed from 8pm. Breakfast choices include a full English, smashed avocado on sourdough, smoked salmon, eggs Benedict. Many restaurants are very close by.

38 Upper Belgrave Road
Clifton
Bristol BS8 2XN

T: 0117 946 6905
E: info@number38clifton.com
W: number38clifton.com

BEDROOMS: 12.
OPEN: all year.
FACILITIES: lounge, breakfast room, meeting space, free Wi-Fi, in-room TV (Freeview), terrace, limited number of parking permits on request, unsuitable for disabled.
BACKGROUND MUSIC: in public areas 8 am–8 pm.
LOCATION: 2½ miles from city centre.
CHILDREN: not under 12.
DOGS: not allowed.
CREDIT CARDS: Amex, MC, Visa.
PRICES: per room B&B single £115–£240, double £130–£255, cooked breakfast £5 surcharge.

BROADWAY Worcestershire

THE BROADWAY HOTEL

On fine days, guests eat and drink alfresco in
front of this 15th-century inn, watched over by
two towering clipped yews. Behind the 'antique
facade', 'designer look' meets 'olde-worlde
charm'. The double-height Jockey bar has 'a large
fireplace, rugs on a wood floor', comfy seating,
a wall of Lisa Bliss teal stags' head wallpaper.
Part of Cotswold Inns and Hotels, the Broadway,
'while friendly and personal, clearly has
professionally trained management'. Equestrian-
themed bedrooms are each named after a famous
horse – a nod to Cheltenham races. A room
approached via 'creaky stairs' and a minstrels'
gallery above the bar had 'dashing feature fabrics',
chocolate and cream decor, lattice casements, a
'rather poky' bathroom, all 'smart, well thought
out' rather than luxurious. One reader, visiting
for a funeral reception this year, found his 'spirits
lifted' by the hotel's 'terrific savoury pastries'.
For more substantial fare, don the nosebag for
Eric Worger's imaginative dishes in Tattersall's
Brasserie. Maybe sea bass, miso-glazed carrots,
king oyster mushroom, langoustine tortellini and
bisque. Next morning, breakfast on eggs Royale
with smoked salmon before romping home. (IB)

25% DISCOUNT VOUCHERS

The Green
Broadway WR12 7AA

T: 01386 852401
E: info@broadwayhotel.info
W: cotswold-inns-hotels.co.uk/the-
broadway-hotel

BEDROOMS: 19. 1 on ground floor,
2 self-catering cottages nearby.
OPEN: all year.
FACILITIES: sitting room, bar, brasserie,
free Wi-Fi, in-room TV (Freeview),
courtyard, garden (residents-only
terrace), car park, unsuitable for
disabled.
BACKGROUND MUSIC: ambient in public
areas.
LOCATION: village centre, 'best to
request a parking space before you
arrive, especially in summer'.
CHILDREN: all ages welcomed
(children's menu).
DOGS: well-behaved dogs allowed in
some bedrooms and in public areas,
not in restaurant.
CREDIT CARDS: Amex, MC, Visa.
PRICES: per room B&B £180–£280,
D,B&B £240–£340. À la carte £39.

SEE ALSO SHORTLIST

BROADWAY Worcestershire

THE LYGON ARMS

'Bravo! I spent three marvellous days at The Lygon Arms in the Cotswolds.' A reader in 2019 raves about her stay at this Elizabethan coaching inn with roots in the 1300s. In the guestbook, the names of Elizabeth Taylor and Richard Burton (though not of earlier guests Charles I and Oliver Cromwell) recall a glamorous heyday, but the hotel had lost some of its lustre before a rescue by Iconic Luxury Hotels (see also Chewton Glen, New Milton; and Cliveden, Taplow). Now it is 'lovely, relaxed, gorgeous', its 'quirky features enhanced with beautiful fabrics and colours'. From cosy bedrooms to historic suites, all have an espresso machine, maybe furniture by Gordon Russell (see next entry). Dog-friendly courtyard suites open on to a landscaped terraced garden. You can dine in the wine bar (panini, pasta, pizzette), in cosy lounges or 'the stunning Great Hall, with its barrel ceiling, huge fireplace' and minstrels' gallery. Ales Maurer's modern British menus include such dishes as herb crust lamb canon, wild garlic leaves, radish, spinach; for vegans, heritage cauliflower, spring greens, walnut pesto. 'The food was amazing, the whole hotel so lovely, the staff perfect, a real heaven.' (S and TB, and others)

High Street
Broadway WR12 7DU

T: 01386 852255
E: reservations@lygonarmshotel.co.uk
W: lygonarmshotel.co.uk

BEDROOMS: 86. 26 on ground floor, some in cottages, some courtyard suites, 2 suitable for disabled.
OPEN: all year.
FACILITIES: 7 lounge areas, wine bar/restaurant, bar/grill, in-room TV (Freeview), free Wi-Fi, civil wedding licence, 3-acre garden, indoor pool, spa, public areas (not spa) wheelchair accessible, adapted toilet.
BACKGROUND MUSIC: in lounges.
LOCATION: village centre.
CHILDREN: all ages welcomed.
DOGS: min. 1-year-old allowed in some bedrooms, all lounges (£25 per dog per night).
CREDIT CARDS: Amex, MC, Visa.
PRICES: per room B&B £205–£465. À la carte £40. 1-night bookings sometimes refused Sat, always at Christmas/New Year.

SEE ALSO SHORTLIST

BROADWAY Worcestershire

MAP 3:D6

RUSSELL'S

In a picturesque village of honey-stone houses, antique shops and galleries, Andrew and Gaynor Riley's restaurant-with-rooms occupies a 17th-century building overlooking the green. It was once the workshop of Sir Gordon Russell, pioneer of utility furniture, but there is nothing utilitarian about the Rileys' operation. Bedrooms share a tastefully neutral palette, but each is special in its own way, says a reader who stayed for seven nights. Some have 'wonderful' beams, exposed stone walls. The swishest has a separate seating area, a marble bathroom with spa bath and walk-in shower. Room 4 has 'some awkward projections and sloping ceilings' – all part of its charm – and 'windows looking up the grassy climb to Broadway Tower', a Georgian folly, brainchild of Capability Brown. Chef Jorge Santos's daily-changing, locally sourced menus include such dishes as pan-fried wild halibut, seafood bouillabaisse, Parmesan gnocchi; cumin-roasted rack and belly of Lighthorne lamb, sweet potato and spinach curry, pickled cauliflower, tomato jus; always a vegetarian option. The imaginative prix fixe menu is a steal, with one of the dozen house wines. Service is 'excellent'.

20 High Street
Broadway WR12 7DT

T: 01386 853555
E: info@russellsofbroadway.co.uk
W: russellsofbroadway.co.uk

BEDROOMS: 7. 3 in adjoining building, 2 on ground floor.
OPEN: all year, restaurant closed Sun night and bank holiday Mon.
FACILITIES: residents' lounge, bar, restaurant, private dining room, free Wi-Fi, in-room TV (Freeview), patio (heating, meal service), restaurant and bar wheelchair accessible.
BACKGROUND MUSIC: in restaurant.
LOCATION: village centre.
CHILDREN: all ages welcomed, under-2s stay free.
DOGS: allowed in certain bedrooms, public rooms.
CREDIT CARDS: MC, Visa.
PRICES: per room B&B £140–£300. Set dinner (Mon–Fri) £23–£27, à la carte £50. 1-night bookings refused weekends.

SEE ALSO SHORTLIST

BROCKENHURST Hampshire

MAP 2:E2

THE PIG IN THE FOREST

Innovative hotelier Robin Hutson turned to pig husbandry in 2011, alchemising this New Forest hunting lodge into the mother of his still-growing family of Pig hotels (see index). 'It has lots to recommend it', not least 'the huge grounds, beautiful, huge vegetable garden, fields with chickens, pigs, sheep and horses'. Interiors are styled by Judy Hutson, who has given the public rooms her trademark shabby-chic look, perhaps a stuffed fish, vintage decanters, pot-herbs, mismatched chairs. Bedrooms, all soothing neutrals, earth tones and botanical prints, are found in the main house and stables, ranging from 'snug' ('the big bed took up the space') with monsoon shower, to the Pig House, with kitchenette, log-burner, showers, bath, via 'comfy-luxe' (with shower and freestanding bath), lodges and a cabin. The kitchen garden, the engine of the operation, supplies ingredients for such dishes as Beaulieu Estate pheasant, Puy lentils, purple sprouting broccoli; South Coast pollack, parsnip purée, chorizo salsa. 'The very pretty, large conservatory dining room was packed and noisy, but service was excellent from delightful young staff.' The breakfast buffet is 'a feast'. (A and BB, C and AR)

Beaulieu Road
Brockenhurst SO42 7QL

T: 01590 622354
E: info@thepighotel.com
W: thepighotel.com

BEDROOMS: 31. 10 in stable block (100 yds), some on ground floor, 2 lodges and a cabin in the garden, 1 courtyard room suitable for disabled.
OPEN: all year.
FACILITIES: lounge, library, bar, restaurant, free Wi-Fi, in-room TV (Freeview), civil wedding licence, treatment rooms, kitchen garden, 6-acre grounds, public rooms wheelchair accessible, adapted toilet.
BACKGROUND MUSIC: in public areas.
LOCATION: 1 mile E of Brockenhurst village.
CHILDREN: all ages welcomed.
DOGS: guide dogs only.
CREDIT CARDS: Amex, MC, Visa.
PRICES: room £160–£420. Breakfast £12–£16, à la carte £35. 1-night bookings refused weekends, Christmas, New Year.

SEE ALSO SHORTLIST

BRYHER Isles of Scilly

HELL BAY HOTEL

♧ Previous César Winner

'Hell by name, quite the opposite by nature,'
declares a reader after visiting Robert Dorrien-
Smith's 'gloriously located' hotel on the smallest
of the inhabited islands of Scilly. 'Our stay was
heavenly.' Set behind secluded beaches guarded
by a cluster of islets, the 'thoughtfully converted'
cottage and clapboard chalets have interiors
with an airy blend of creams, blues and greens.
Alongside Lloyd Loom furniture, there are
Malabar fabrics, cushions made on Tresco, cheery
ocean paintings. 'Our suite had a balcony with
lovely views, comfortable armchairs, a kitchenette
with milk and bottled water replaced daily.'
Another fully detached suite mimics a traditional
gig (boat) shed. Public rooms complement the
scenery with a 'fabulous' collection of Cornish art,
including pieces by Dame Barbara Hepworth. It's
not the only good taste found in the hotel. Richard
Kearsley's daily-changing, islands-sourced menus
are 'a consistent highlight'. For instance, slow-
braised Tresco beef, soft truffle polenta, crispy
onion, red wine jus. Staff are 'charming, friendly,
efficient'. A deck allows guests to toast sunset over
Gweal hill. Small wonder then that 'we didn't
want to leave'. (IB)

Bryher
Isles of Scilly TR23 0PR

T: 01720 422947
E: contactus@hellbay.co.uk
W: hellbay.co.uk

BEDROOMS: 25 suites. In 5 buildings,
some on ground floor.
OPEN: mid-Mar–mid-Oct.
FACILITIES: lounge, games room, bar,
2 dining rooms, free Wi-Fi, in-room
TV (Freeview), gym, grounds
(heated swimming pool, playground,
par-3 golf), public rooms wheelchair
accessible, adapted toilet (island
reached by ferry).
BACKGROUND MUSIC: none.
LOCATION: W side of island, boat from
St Mary's (reached by boat/plane from
mainland).
CHILDREN: all ages welcomed.
DOGS: allowed (charge), not in
restaurant.
CREDIT CARDS: MC, Visa.
PRICES: per person B&B single
£119–£394, double £95–£315, D,B&B
double £140–£360. Set dinner £48.
Min. 2-night weekend bookings.

BUDE Cornwall

MAP 1:C3

THE BEACH

Overlooking Summerleaze surfers' beach, with its
1930s tidal pool and brightly coloured beach huts,
the Victorian Summerleaze Court Hotel has been
reinvented in hip New England style. 'Innovative'
owners Susie and Will Daniel have created 'a
mecca for the young of Bude', who drink cocktails
in the bar or on the sea-facing terrace. The staff
are 'friendly and helpful', says a reader after a
fourth visit. Some sea-view bedrooms have a
Juliet balcony or private terrace. All have limed
oak furniture, Lloyd Loom chairs, muted decor.
Two 2-bedroom suites have a lounge, freestanding
bath and walk-in shower. A new chef this year,
Jamie Coleman, has impressive credentials,
having worked under Gordon Ramsay and
Michael Caines. His locally sourced menus
include such dishes as Cornish scallops, fried fish
of the day with crab cake, Jerusalem artichoke,
savoy cabbage; venison loin, smoked potato,
parsnip, kale, juniper jus. 'The accommodation
was good,' writes another reader, though she
was disappointed to be seated at the back of the
restaurant, when her booking for a window
table was somehow overlooked. Breakfast, on
the terrace in summer, is 'comprehensive'.
(FM, and others)

25% DISCOUNT VOUCHERS

Summerleaze Crescent
Bude EX23 8HJ

T: 01288 389800
E: enquiries@thebeachatbude.co.uk
W: thebeachatbude.co.uk

BEDROOMS: 18. 1 on ground floor,
1 family suite.
OPEN: all year except Christmas.
FACILITIES: lift, bar, lounge area,
restaurant, free Wi-Fi, in-room TV
(Freeview), terrace, ground floor
wheelchair accessible, adapted toilet.
BACKGROUND MUSIC: all day in public
areas.
LOCATION: above Summerleaze beach.
CHILDREN: all ages welcomed,
children's menu.
DOGS: allowed in 1 dog-friendly suite
only, not in public areas except the
terrace.
CREDIT CARDS: Amex, MC, Visa.
PRICES: per room B&B £125–£255,
D,B&B £184–£314. À la carte £30.50.

BURFORD Oxfordshire

THE LAMB INN

On a quiet side street in this photogenic town on the River Windrush, the Lamb has been receiving guests since the 1750s. Not the butcher, the baker, the candlestick-maker, but weaver, cooper and chandler once occupied the 16th-century cottages from which it is forged. Beams, flagstone floors and open fires in 'three linked lounges' contribute to 'a wonderful atmosphere'. Bedrooms, some with mullioned windows, have a smart country style, perhaps an antique half-tester bed, white-painted beams, a bathroom with log-filled fireplace. All have fine fabrics, an espresso machine, home-made flapjacks, Molton Brown toiletries. Guests can dine in the 'busy' and sometimes 'noisy' bar, the lounge or alfresco, on superior pub classics (crayfish and haddock fishcakes, venison burger, good vegan options). In the newly refurbished restaurant, a recent visitor found the dinner menu 'a little dull'. Maybe pavé of seatrout, crab fishcake, almonds, saffron sauce. Breakfast brings 'big jugs of freshly squeezed juices, organic Cotswold preserves', freshly baked pastries, smoked Bibury trout with scrambled eggs, Wiltshire cured ham, eggs Florentine.

25% DISCOUNT VOUCHERS

Sheep Street
Burford OX18 4LR

T: 01993 823155
E: info@lambinn-burford.co.uk
W: cotswold-inns-hotels.co.uk/the-lamb-inn

BEDROOMS: 17. 1 with private garden, 1 on ground floor.
OPEN: all year.
FACILITIES: 3 lounges, bar, restaurant, free Wi-Fi, in-room TV (Freeview), courtyard, ½-acre walled garden.
BACKGROUND MUSIC: subtle in all public areas.
LOCATION: 500 yds from High Street.
CHILDREN: all ages welcomed.
DOGS: allowed by prior arrangement in some bedrooms, bar, lounges, garden, not in restaurant (£20 per night for 1, £10 for each additional dog).
CREDIT CARDS: Amex, MC, Visa.
PRICES: per room B&B single £130–£210, double £160–£310, D,B&B (double) £220–£370. À la carte £40.

SEE ALSO SHORTLIST

BURTON BRADSTOCK Dorset

MAP 1:D6

THE SEASIDE BOARDING HOUSE

In 'a wonderful cliff-top location', this 'large white edifice above Chesil Beach' is run as a restaurant-with-rooms by Mary-Lou Sturridge and Tony Mackintosh, late of London's Groucho Club. The vibe is carefree, the style drawing inspiration from Edwardian seaside hotels, with a dash of Edward Hopper's Cape Cod. Furniture from the 1920s and 1980s, ornamental flotsam and jetsam, nautical paintings, Peter Blake prints and bare floorboards set the tone in bar and restaurant, with a row of French doors opening on to the terrace. Bedrooms, all with some view of the sea, ranked 'double', 'larger' and 'largest', are 'nicely kitted out', 'elegant and unfussy', with Roberts radio, books, shower or claw-footed bath. Breakfast brings freshly squeezed OJ, kipper, eggs Benedict. You can eat in or alfresco, for dinner maybe half-lobster, chips and salad; rump of lamb, haricot bean and tomato stew. Of course, sunshine is not guaranteed. A reader who came by in a 'ferocious gale', if not blown away by 'a certain seaside charm', was happy with 'good' fishcakes for lunch. 'We are tempted to visit properly,' he wrote, adding that he felt it 'could be boisterous'. (John Barnes, MA)

Cliff Road
Burton Bradstock DT6 4RB

T: 01308 897205
E: info@theseasideboardinghouse.
com
W: theseasideboardinghouse.com

BEDROOMS: 9.
OPEN: all year.
FACILITIES: cocktail bar, restaurant, library, function facilities, in-room TV on request, free Wi-Fi, civil wedding licence, terrace, lawn, restaurant and bar wheelchair accessible.
BACKGROUND MUSIC: classical music in bar.
LOCATION: ½ mile from village centre, 3½ miles SE of Bridport.
CHILDREN: all ages welcomed.
DOGS: allowed in some bedrooms, bar, library and on terrace, not in restaurant.
CREDIT CARDS: Amex, MC, Visa.
PRICES: per room B&B £205–£265.
À la carte £35. 1-night bookings refused Sat.

BUXTON Derbyshire   MAP 4:E3

THE ROSELEIGH

Overlooking gardens designed by Joseph Paxton, close to Buxton's opera house, this is an 'excellent B&B' in an 'attractive, convenient location', write trusted readers after a return visit this year. The Grade II listed property, built in 1871, is owned by 'pleasant, attentive' Gerard and Maggi Heelan. 'When our room's shaver point failed, it was fixed as soon as we mentioned it.' Front bedrooms overlook the forest-garlanded lake; all are sympathetic to the house's Victorian roots with leather wingback chairs and dark wood; some have an antique-style brass bed. 'Nice details include flannels in the bathroom, although the elaborate swan towel arrangement on our bed had disappeared, perhaps it was "so last year".' The warmly traditional sitting room is well stocked with guides, maps and books, backed up by the owners' detailed knowledge about the Peak District (both were tour guides, Gerard also drove a London Routemaster bus). A wide-ranging breakfast includes 'delicious home-made banana loaf', although the 'quiet canned classical muzak' was less admired. During the Buxton Festival, when Roseleigh is busy, its reception posts a daily events schedule. (Stephen and Pauline Glover)

19 Broad Walk
Buxton SK17 6JR

T: 01298 24904
E: enquiries@roseleighhotel.co.uk
W: roseleighhotel.co.uk

BEDROOMS: 14. 1 on ground floor.
OPEN: all year except 1 Dec–23 Jan.
FACILITIES: lounge (computer for guests' use), breakfast room, free Wi-Fi, in-room TV (Freeview), parking, unsuitable for disabled.
BACKGROUND MUSIC: classical/baroque in breakfast room.
LOCATION: central.
CHILDREN: not under 6.
DOGS: not allowed.
CREDIT CARDS: MC, Visa.
PRICES: per person B&B single from £45, double £35-£56. 1-night bookings usually refused weekends, bank holidays (call to check).

CAMBER Sussex

MAP 2:E5

THE GALLIVANT

'Great to cross over the road to an incredible beach where you can stroll for miles,' writes a reader who spent 'a great weekend' at Harry Cragoe's restaurant-with-rooms. Lying between Rye Golf Club and Camber village, with high dunes to the fore, it draws inspiration from a Californian beach motel, with casual seaside-chic style. Some bedrooms have a decked patio; 12 open on to the coastal garden. Snug cabin-style rooms, lined with reclaimed pine and oak, have a slate-clad wet room, espresso machine and fresh milk. The newest garden rooms have white beamed ceilings, oak floors, rugs made from recycled ocean plastic. There is a sitting room with open fire, a snug, library and bar. In the light-filled dining room, menus are sourced from local producers, fishermen and foragers, for such dishes as Romney salt marsh lamb; Dungeness skate wing, three-cornered leek risotto, cauliflower. 'The staff were nice; good restaurant, and very good fish.' An 'excellent breakfast' brings local apple and freshly squeezed orange juice, 'fab home-made granola', home-cured bacon, own-recipe sausages, free-range eggs – maybe a Bloody Mary from the recovery station. (Danielle Hommel)

New Lydd Road
Camber TN31 7RB

T: 01797 225057
E: reservations@thegallivant.co.uk
W: thegallivant.co.uk

BEDROOMS: 20. All on ground floor, 12 with direct access to garden.
OPEN: all year.
FACILITIES: bar, sitting room, reading room, restaurant, private dining room, free Wi-Fi, in-room TV (Freeview), civil wedding licence, function facilities, spa treatment room, terrace, car park, 1-acre garden, restaurant and bar wheelchair accessible.
BACKGROUND MUSIC: in bar and restaurant.
LOCATION: 3¾ miles SE of Rye.
CHILDREN: babies up to 18 months and children 12 and older welcome.
DOGS: allowed in some bedrooms, bar, terrace.
CREDIT CARDS: MC, Visa.
PRICES: per room B&B £135–£325, D,B&B £205–£395. À la carte £38.

CAMBRIDGE Cambridgeshire

DUKE HOUSE

Liz and Rob Cameron's 'beautifully presented' B&B is 'well located', in 'walking distance of the whole city'. The ducal theme runs throughout, recalling that HRH Prince Richard lived here while studying architecture at Magdalene in the 1960s, when he made many of the alterations guests see today. As second son, he can have had no notion that he would soon be Duke of Gloucester, or that he would be commemorated in the immaculate white-and-cream Gloucester room, with its Victorian fireplace, bath and separate walk-in shower. Kent, in the house next door, is 'perfect, with great facilities', decorated in Jane Churchill Cassina Aqua linen; a bathroom with shower and underfloor heating. Cambridge, with sitting area and private balcony, sleeps three. At breakfast there are organic yogurts, butter, bread and granola, compotes made with fruit from local growers, free-range eggs, salmon from River Farm Smokery, apple juice from Cambridgeshire orchards, 'everything you could wish for'. All guests have use of the chic Duchess sitting room and balcony. Help with parking can be arranged. The green oasis of Christ's Pieces is just a step away; Michelin-starred Midsummer House restaurant is very close. (MB)

1 Victoria Street
Cambridge CB1 1JP

T: 01223 314773
E: info@dukehousecambridge.co.uk
W: dukehousecambridge.co.uk

BEDROOMS: 5. 1 in adjacent cottage, plus self-catering apartment.
OPEN: all year except over Christmas period.
FACILITIES: sitting room, breakfast room with courtyard, balcony, free Wi-Fi, in-room TV (Freeview), limited parking (by arrangement), unsuitable for disabled.
BACKGROUND MUSIC: during breakfast.
LOCATION: city centre.
CHILDREN: babies and over-10s welcomed.
DOGS: not allowed.
CREDIT CARDS: MC, Visa.
PRICES: per room B&B single £125–£165, double £140–£195. 1-night bookings refused weekends.

SEE ALSO SHORTLIST

CAMBRIDGE Cambridgeshire

MAP 2:B4

UNIVERSITY ARMS [NEW]

A 19th-century coaching inn beside grassy
Parker's Piece has been redesigned by John
Simpson architects (who have worked on projects
at Kensington Palace and The Queen's Gallery),
with Edwardian-style interiors by Martin
Brudnizki. Rooms range from 'cosy' to suites,
the latter with shelves of books related to one or
other Cambridge luminary. Walls are painted in
restful Cambridge blues. A reader thought the
library would have been 'a good setting', were it
not for the 'noisy tourists'. A reservation made 'via
the Marriott central system' resulted in a mix-up,
compensated with an upgrade upon check-in.
There is no background music, but recordings,
in the loos, of Alan Bennett reading The Wind
in the Willows. In your room you'll find Hilaire
Belloc's Cautionary Tales. Take a lesson from the
vulture, don't eat between meals, but save yourself
for lunch or dinner at Parker's Tavern, an all-day
bistro where Tristan Welch cooks such British
classics as sole with coastal herbs and brown
shrimps; a daily 'Hobson's choice' pie; braised
Lake District pig, salt-baked apple. 'The food
was reasonable, the wine excellent.' Breakfast is
a buffet. 'The best thing about the hotel was the
quality and helpfulness of the staff.'

Regent Street
Cambridge CB2 1AD

T: 01223 606066
E: enquiries@universityarms.com
W: universityarms.com

BEDROOMS: 192, 10 suitable for
disabled.
OPEN: all year.
FACILITIES: library, bar/bistro,
ballroom, meeting rooms, fitness
centre, in-room TV, free Wi-Fi,
bicycles, limited guest parking.
BACKGROUND MUSIC: none.
LOCATION: city centre.
CHILDREN: all ages welcomed,
children's menu, interconnecting
rooms.
DOGS: only assistance dogs allowed.
CREDIT CARDS: Amex, MC, Visa.
PRICES: per person B&B £144–£640.
À la carte £35.

SEE ALSO SHORTLIST

CAMELFORD Cornwall   MAP 1:C3

PENDRAGON COUNTRY HOUSE

We can't say whether King Arthur stabled
Llamrei in the equestrian centre next door, but the
once and future king lives on in this small hotel
near Tintagel, named after Uther Pendragon.
'Owners Sharon and Nigel Reed have "excellent
hospitality skills",' report our inspectors in 2019.
The former Victorian rectory is 'furnished with
good taste'. Lounges have roaring fires, leather
sofas, paintings, antiques, a well-stocked honesty
bar. A suit of armour guards the hall. Bedivere
room, with four-poster, was 'VERY comfortable',
with sherry, 'high-quality teas, a proper teapot,
milk from a little fridge on the landing, super
home-made biscuits', local toiletries. The 'huge
bathroom' had a cast iron roll-top bath. Other
'cosy' rooms have a shower. In the conservatory
dining room (no round table), guests can enjoy a
home-cooked dinner. 'Ham hock terrine, chutney,
lovely salad garnishes; sea bass with five different
home-grown vegetables; a fabulous chocolate
confection' were 'superb'. A 'scrumptious'
breakfast has home-baked bread, a continental
buffet, Pendragon rarebit, Cornish kipper, free-
range eggs. 'No lunch needed here!' (Saskia Nolet,
John and Jerelyn Walters, and others)

25% DISCOUNT VOUCHERS

Old Vicarage Hill
Davidstow
Camelford PL32 9XR

T: 01840 261131
E: enquiries@
   pendragoncountryhouse.com
W: pendragoncountryhouse.com

BEDROOMS: 7. 1 on ground floor
suitable for disabled.
OPEN: all year except Christmas,
restaurant closed Sun eve.
FACILITIES: sitting room, lounge with
honesty bar, dining room, games room
(pool table), free Wi-Fi, in-room TV
(Freeview), 1¾-acre grounds.
BACKGROUND MUSIC: none.
LOCATION: 3½ miles NE of Camelford.
CHILDREN: all ages welcomed.
DOGS: allowed in ground-floor
bedroom (£5 charge), lounge but not
restaurant, except guide dogs.
CREDIT CARDS: Amex, MC, Visa.
PRICES: per room B&B single £75,
double £110–£150, D,B&B single
£90–£100, double £145–£200. Set
menu £28–£35.

CANNINGTON Somerset

MAP 1:B5

BLACKMORE FARM

On the family dairy farm on the edge of the Quantock hills, Ann and Ian Dyer run this 15th-century manor house with chapel as a 'warm, welcoming' B&B. There are three 'amazing large rooms' in the main house – one with four-poster under the cruck-framed roof. Further rooms (four new this year) are in a converted barn, with fridge, toaster, microwave. The Cider Press, for four, has a kitchen with a working Aga, a patio and small garden, while two can cosy up in the shepherd's hut. Breakfast is taken at a carved-oak refectory table, by a 'fantastic log fire', in the Great Hall, its walls hung with trophy heads, pikes and halberds, a suit of armour in attendance. Free-range eggs are from Blackmore's hens, award-winning sausages and traditionally cured bacon from Pyne's of Somerset. These can be bought at the farm shop (scheduled to relocate to an old mill), where the café serves cream teas, home-made puddings and ice cream, quiches, panini, preserves. You can assemble a picnic and walk the nearby Coleridge Way, or visit the poet's cottage in Nether Stowey. For dinner stroll to the nearby Malt Shovel pub or, suggests Mr Dyer, take a short drive to The Hood Arms, Kilve.

Blackmore Lane
Cannington TA5 2NE

T: 01278 653442
E: info@blackmorefarm.co.uk
W: blackmorefarm.co.uk

BEDROOMS: 14. 6 on ground floor in annexes, 1 in shepherd's hut in grounds, 1 suitable for disabled.
OPEN: all year.
FACILITIES: lounge/TV room, Great Hall/breakfast room, free Wi-Fi, in-room TV (Freeview), 1-acre garden (stream, coarse fishing), children's play area, farm shop/café, lounge and dining room wheelchair accessible.
BACKGROUND MUSIC: none.
LOCATION: 3 miles W of Bridgwater.
CHILDREN: all ages welcomed.
DOGS: allowed in some bedrooms by prior arrangement, not in public rooms.
CREDIT CARDS: MC, Visa.
PRICES: per room B&B single £75–£90, double £120–£140. 1-night bookings refused bank holiday weekends.

CARTMEL Cumbria

AYNSOME MANOR

'In a lovely location in quiet countryside',
Christopher and Andrea Varley's 400-year-old
manor house stands in wooded grounds with
views across the Vale of Cartmel. Its ethos is
traditional 'and not the worse for that', says one
regular visitor. 'The welcome and friendliness
of the staff and owners are outstanding,' say
others. An inviting lounge has a blazing log
fire. Bedrooms have pine furniture, perhaps
floral wallpaper, beams or a fine outlook; some
have been updated since last year; a noisy boiler
replaced. 'Room 12 was a good size with modern
bathroom.' Especially appreciated was a book on
'the magic and mystery of the Lake District'. In
the panelled Georgian dining room, chef Gordon
Topp's 'daily-changing and varied' five-course
menus include such locally sourced dishes as roast
sirloin of Cumbrian beef on creamed potato,
red onion marmalade, Burgundy wine jus. 'We
liked the option to have as few as two courses or
as many as five, and a well-chosen wine list that
allows guests to order house wine not only by
the glass or bottle but also in litre and half-litre
carafes.' Breakfast is 'excellent'. 'You soon realise
why guests return year after year.' (B and JH)

Aynsome Lane
Cartmel
Grange-over-Sands LA11 6HH

T: 015395 36653
E: aynsomemanor@btconnect.com
W: aynsomemanorhotel.co.uk

BEDROOMS: 12. 2 in cottage (with
lounge) across courtyard.
OPEN: all year except 23–27 Dec,
2–29 Jan, lunch served Sun only, Sun
dinner for residents only.
FACILITIES: 2 lounges, bar, dining
room, free Wi-Fi, in-room TV
(Freeview), ½-acre garden, unsuitable
for disabled.
BACKGROUND MUSIC: none.
LOCATION: ¾ mile N of village.
CHILDREN: all ages welcomed.
DOGS: allowed, not in public rooms or
unattended in bedrooms (£7 nightly
charge).
CREDIT CARDS: Amex, MC, Visa.
PRICES: per room B&B £95–£160,
D,B&B £150–£199. Set dinner £24–
£39. 1-night bookings occasionally
refused weekends.

CHADDESLEY CORBETT Worcestershire   MAP 3:C5

BROCKENCOTE HALL

Imagine that a 'stylishly renovated' château has been lifted from the Loire valley and set down in 'magnificent' parkland with lake, fountain and 17th-century dovecote, all in deepest Worcestershire. Part of the Eden Collection (see also Mallory Court, Leamington Spa), the hotel has a 'splendid hallway with deep, cosy seats by a fireplace', beyond which bedrooms range from 'classic' to 'feature suite'. A 'very spacious' first-floor room was 'tastefully but soberly decorated, with well-chosen pictures each side of a marble fireplace'. Extra touches included 'fresh fruit, jars of nuts, pickles, mini-bottle of milk in a fridge'. A bathroom had luxury toiletries, a bath and separate shower. At dinner, Tim Jenkins's menus (one for veggies) include 'interesting surprises… pre-starters in amazing upside-down glasses with a hollow; roasted granola on starters'. Typical dishes: pan-fried hake, roasted cauliflower, braised chicory, golden raisins and white balsamic; salt-baked Jerusalem artichokes, sprout leaves, baked yeast with chestnut dressing. Breakfast, overseen by a 'pleasant and jovial maître', brought 'smoked haddock, perfect poached eggs'. 'A beautiful place.' (F and IW, SJ)

Chaddesley Corbett DY10 4PY

T: 01562 777876
E: info@brockencotehall.com
W: brockencotehall.com

BEDROOMS: 21. Some on ground floor, 1 suitable for disabled.
OPEN: all year.
FACILITIES: lift, hall, lounge, conservatory, bar, library, restaurant, function facilities, free Wi-Fi, in-room TV (Freeview), civil wedding licence, 72-acre grounds (gardens, lake, fishing, croquet, tennis), public rooms wheelchair accessible, adapted toilet.
BACKGROUND MUSIC: all day in public areas.
LOCATION: 3 miles SE of Kidderminster.
CHILDREN: all ages welcomed.
DOGS: not allowed.
CREDIT CARDS: Amex, MC, Visa.
PRICES: per room B&B single from £130, double £140–£270. Market menu £38–£49, seasonal menu £45–£60, tasting menu (whole table) £75.

CHESTER Cheshire

MAP 3:A4

EDGAR HOUSE

A glass of fizz and handmade brownies or truffles
set the tone on arrival at Tim Mills and Michael
Stephen's boutique hotel atop the Roman city
walls. Its garden terrace overlooks the River Dee.
A Georgian villa built for a snuff manufacturer,
it has been done over by the owners with wit and
flair, the style 'refreshingly different'. Playful
touches include an honesty bar in a black-painted
telephone kiosk, artwork by notorious forger
John Myatt. The lounge has 'soft fabric sofas',
dramatic decor. A junior suite has 'a huge copper
bath' against exposed brick, burgundy walls and
blinds, clever lighting, 'top-quality bedding', a
wet room with raindance shower, a lounge with a
chesterfield, Zoffany London 1832 map wallpaper.
A garden terrace room has a modern four-poster,
Cole & Son Woods and Pears wallpaper. In
Twenty2 restaurant, Andy Scott's tasting menus
(veggies have one, too) change every six weeks and
include such dishes as 'Around the World chicken
(a journey of flavours inspired by Morocco, the
Caribbean and Thailand)'; 'wild mushroom and
lentil strudel', smoked cauliflower cheese. 'We
left with a warm feeling generated by the general
atmosphere and charming staff.'

22 City Walls
Chester CH1 1SB

T: 01244 347007
E: hello@edgarhouse.co.uk
W: edgarhouse.co.uk

BEDROOMS: 7.
OPEN: all year, restaurant Wed–Sat.
FACILITIES: garden lounge, mini-
cinema, restaurant, free Wi-Fi,
in-room TV (Smart TV), sun terrace,
riverside garden (alfresco meals),
free allocated parking, restaurant
wheelchair accessible, adapted toilet.
BACKGROUND MUSIC: Classic FM
in lounge, music in restaurant,
'appropriate to relaxing setting'.
LOCATION: central, on the river.
CHILDREN: not under 14.
DOGS: not allowed in hotel, but
welcome in garden and when dining
outside.
CREDIT CARDS: MC, Visa.
PRICES: per room B&B single
£135–£255, double £149–£269, D,B&B
double £280–£359. Tasting menu £59.
Min. 2-night stay when incl. Sat.

SEE ALSO SHORTLIST

CHETTLE Dorset

MAP 2:E1

CASTLEMAN

If you're in search of 'a comfortable and homely experience', look no further than Barbara Garnsworthy's former dower house in an 'unspoilt' estate village within the former royal hunting ground of Cranborne Chase. Trendy it is not, but it 'captures an age of country house hospitality' and 'pampers its clients'. The building incorporates a 17th-century farmhouse, extended in the 1800s, with two-storey, Tudor-style canted bays. Drawing rooms have Regency plasterwork and a Jacobean fireplace from a cannibalised house in London. An impressive 18th-century staircase leads up to large bedrooms in a variety of styles, furnished with antiques, perhaps a four-poster. All bathrooms have a power shower; three have a roll-top bath. A family room has bunks for the children. Richard Morris and Barbara Garnsworthy cook a daily-changing menu using local, home-grown and foraged produce, fruits from orchard and hedgerow, wild garlic, game from surrounding estates. Maybe peppered fillet steak; wild halibut fillet, samphire, tarragon, chilli and lemon butter; venison and mushroom pie. At breakfast there is freshly squeezed orange juice, Loch Fyne kippers, eggs any which way, home-baked bread. (B and JH)

25% DISCOUNT VOUCHERS

Chettle
Blandford Forum DT11 8DB

T: 01258 830096
E: enquiry@castlemanhotel.co.uk
W: castlemanhotel.co.uk

BEDROOMS: 8. 1 family room.
OPEN: 5 Mar–end Jan, except 25/26, 31 Dec, restaurant closed midday except Sun.
FACILITIES: 2 drawing rooms, bar, restaurant, free Wi-Fi, in-room TV (Freeview), 2-acre grounds (stables for visiting horses), riding, fishing, shooting, cycling nearby, public rooms wheelchair accessible.
BACKGROUND MUSIC: none.
LOCATION: village, 1 mile off A354 Salisbury–Blandford.
CHILDREN: all ages welcomed.
DOGS: only guide dogs.
CREDIT CARDS: MC, Visa.
PRICES: per room B&B single £85, double £110–£125, D,B&B double (midweek only) £140–£160. À la carte £36, midweek supper from £16.

CHICHESTER Sussex

CROUCHERS

Between cathedral city and marina, set a little back from the main road, Lloyd van Rooyen and Gavin Wilson's smart, contemporary hotel centres on a farmhouse in a pastoral setting. Rooms range from 'cosy' to 'luxe'. Most are in a converted barn, coach house and stables. 'Everything is praiseworthy,' vouched trusted readers, whose luxe room was at the rear. It had French doors on to 'an individual nook with wrought iron table and chairs overlooking a field', 'quality modern furniture in dark, rough-hewn wood', a four-poster, a 'state-of-the-art bathroom' with a good shower over the bath. Snugger, road-facing rooms are not such a good choice. In the 'elegant' Potager restaurant, new chef David Smith uses local and home-grown produce in such dishes as slow-cooked fillet and cutlet of South Downs lamb, gratin potatoes, roasted Crouchers vegetables. If you prefer simple pub grub, there is the bar, while for those who like their cucina more rustica, the Cider House rules: also new since last year, and two minutes' walk away, it serves a wide choice of pizzas and pastas in an informal setting. In sum, an innovative operation, 'well above our expectations'. (F and IW)

Birdham Road
Chichester PO20 7EH

T: 01243 784995
E: enquiries@crouchershotel.co.uk
W: crouchersorchards.co.uk

BEDROOMS: 26. 23 in converted coach house, barn and stables, 10 with patio, 2 suitable for disabled.
OPEN: all year.
FACILITIES: lounge, bar, restaurant, free Wi-Fi, in-room TV (Freeview), civil wedding licence/function facilities, courtyard, 2-acre garden, restaurant and bar wheelchair accessible with adapted toilet.
BACKGROUND MUSIC: in public areas.
LOCATION: 3 miles S of town centre.
CHILDREN: all ages welcomed.
DOGS: allowed in some bedrooms, bar, not in restaurant.
CREDIT CARDS: Amex, MC, Visa.
PRICES: per room B&B single £149.50–£239.50, double £160–£250, D,B&B single £173–£263, double £207–£297. Set menus £19–£24.50, à la carte £40.

SEE ALSO SHORTLIST

CHILLATON Devon

MAP 1:D3

TOR COTTAGE

Maureen Rowlatt is the 'charming' hostess at this B&B in a private valley, surrounded by gardens that extend into woodland and fields – an ideal spot for exploring Dartmoor and the Tamar valley. A welcoming trug is filled with fudge, fresh fruit, flowers and sparkling wine, while the in-room fridge provides a degree of self-sufficiency. Guests may swim in the heated pool, or sit and watch for herons and deer. Four bedrooms are in the garden – one with log-burner, conservatory and terrace; another with a log fire and a garden by a stream. Individually styled, they include a room aiming for a 1920s mood with an Art Deco-style cabinet and fireplace tiles, feather decorations and a porthole; another has a New England feel (much light timber, maple furnishings). No cooked dinner, but the hosts can supply a platter of sandwiches, salad, pasties, lemon posset, cheeses. For dining, there are many nearby Guide hotels – perhaps The Horn of Plenty, Tavistock (see entry), 15 minutes away by car. Breakfast, in the conservatory or outdoors, offers abundant fruit, home-made muesli and Greek yogurt, kedgeree, full English or a vegetarian version with sauté potatoes or hash browns. Reports, please.

Chillaton
Lifton PL16 0JE

T: 01822 860248
E: info@torcottage.co.uk
W: torcottage.co.uk

BEDROOMS: 5. 4 in garden.
OPEN: Feb–mid-Dec.
FACILITIES: sitting room, large conservatory, free Wi-Fi in reception and public areas, in-room TV (Freeview), 28-acre grounds (2-acre garden, heated outdoor swimming pool, 12 by 6 metres, May–Sept until 11.30 am and evenings by arrangement) with pool house, river (fishing ½ mile).
BACKGROUND MUSIC: none.
LOCATION: ½ mile S of Chillaton, 6½ miles N of Tavistock.
CHILDREN: not under 15.
DOGS: only guide dogs allowed.
CREDIT CARDS: MC, Visa.
PRICES: per room B&B single £98, double £130–£150. Platters £32 for 2. Normally min. 2 nights, 'but check availability'.

CHRISTCHURCH Dorset

MAP 2:E2

CAPTAIN'S CLUB HOTEL

'A great stay, great staff, accommodation, food, and all in a lovely river setting.' A resounding endorsement from a reader this year for Robert Wilson and Tim Lloyd's hotel on the banks of the Stour. A warm welcome included birthday wishes to his wife, and an upgrade to a 'fabulous suite with two luxury bathrooms, huge lounge, fully fitted kitchen (fresh milk and bottled water in the fridge), floor-to-ceiling windows overlooking river, terrace and jetty'. Fabulous indeed, but even 'just' a room comes with a Nespresso machine, room service, Aromatherapy Associates toiletries. With the look of a cruise ship, the hotel has a free-and-easy vibe. Boating folk moor and come aboard for all-day dining in the bar, lounge or alfresco. In the restaurant 'with a glass-covered waterfall', a 'perfect fillet steak' came with 'triple-cooked chips and trimming'. Andrew Gault's menus include plenty of fresh fish, perhaps baked halibut, leek stir fry, prawn wonton, crispy leeks, ginger and lemongrass sauce, and good veggie options. Nor does breakfast disappoint, with everything from the full English to hummus on granary toast, and an anti-oxidant smoothie. 'A worthy entry.' (Ian Malone)

Wick Ferry
Christchurch BH23 1HU

T: 01202 475111
E: tim@captainsclubhotel.com
W: captainsclubhotel.com

BEDROOMS: 29. 2 suitable for disabled.
OPEN: all year.
FACILITIES: lifts, open-plan bar/lounge/restaurant, function facilities, free Wi-Fi, in-room TV (Sky, Freeview), civil wedding licence, riverside terrace, spa (hydrotherapy pool, treatments, sauna), moorings for guests, public rooms wheelchair accessible.
BACKGROUND MUSIC: in public areas, live music some evenings.
LOCATION: on the river.
CHILDREN: all ages welcomed.
DOGS: allowed in suites, on terrace, areas of bar/lounge (£20 per dog per night).
CREDIT CARDS: MC, Visa.
PRICES: per room B&B doubles £159–£299, suites (3–6 guests) £219–£699. À la carte £40. 1-night bookings normally refused Sat.

CIRENCESTER Gloucestershire

MAP 3:E5

KINGS HEAD HOTEL

A man walks into a bar – not the cue for a joke, but a Guide inspector, incognito, to check out this historic coaching inn which has a comedy club in the cellar. The main building dates from 1860, but 'the hotel consists of a number of ancient buildings' dating back to the 1600s and beyond. In 2014 it reopened after a top-to-toe make-over, but original features survive. 'An inner courtyard forms a large bar and dining area with sofas, a wood-burning stove, a Copernicus globe light fitting.' Bedrooms, from classic to 'feature', have air conditioning, an espresso machine, comfy seating, restful decor, perhaps 'a large zinc bath alongside the four-poster bed', a wet room with monsoon shower, 'a fridge with fresh milk'.

In the restaurant, its walls crammed with 'a serendipitous collection of prints, photos and artwork', 'friendly, pleasingly efficient' waiting staff deliver 'well-judged portions' of such dishes as smoked pork belly, braised cheek, confit onion mash, cavolo nero, swede purée, pork jus; market fish; wild garlic gnocchi. Breakfast brings freshly squeezed orange juice, local bacon, Gloucester Old Spot sausages. Full marks for 'an obvious desire to get things right'.

24 Market Place
Cirencester GL7 2NR

T: 01285 700900
E: info@kingshead-hotel.co.uk
W: kingshead-hotel.co.uk

BEDROOMS: 46. 1 suitable for disabled, 6 apartments.
OPEN: all year.
FACILITIES: lifts, lounge/bar, restaurant, study, meeting/private dining rooms, free Wi-Fi, in-room TV (Freeview), civil wedding licence, spa, roof terrace, public rooms wheelchair accessible, adapted toilet.
BACKGROUND MUSIC: in public areas.
LOCATION: town centre, limited secure parking (£15 a day).
CHILDREN: all ages welcomed.
DOGS: allowed by arrangement in most bedrooms (£20 per dog per night), lounge, not in restaurant or spa.
CREDIT CARDS: MC, Visa.
PRICES: per room B&B single £117–£209, double £119–£239. À la carte £37. 1-night bookings sometimes refused.

CLEARWELL Gloucestershire

MAP 3:D4

TUDOR FARMHOUSE

♀ Previous César Winner

'A wonderful find. We had a lovely few days.'
Praise from readers in 2019 for Hari and Colin
Fell's Elizabethan farmhouse-cum-boutique
hotel in a Forest of Dean village. Bedrooms,
some in converted outbuildings, have neutral
decor, beams, many original features. They range
from Hatchling to Hen to Cockerel to suites,
all supplied with a Nespresso machine, fridge,
Bramley toiletries. 'Steep stairs' (not for the
chicken-hearted) led to a barn bedroom with an
'arched window looking over the fields where
sheep and horses graze', a small bathroom with a
whirlpool bath. Another reader, on a third visit,
loved the Byre, 'a characterful ground-floor junior
suite, beautifully fitted out and immaculately
clean', with roll-top bath and monsoon shower.
Chef Rob Cox's modern British dishes use home-
grown and local produce. Perhaps 'delicious
white onion soup with duck egg yolk, beautifully
presented plaice, mussels and sea vegetables,
delicious pork belly and dark chocolate tart'.
Staff are 'delightful and helpful'. At breakfast the
'excellent buffet, poached and creamy scrambled
eggs', local apple juices are 'worth getting up for'.
(Sara Price, Andrew and Moira Kleissner)

25% DISCOUNT VOUCHERS

High Street
Clearwell GL16 8JS

T: 01594 833046
E: info@tudorfarmhousehotel.co.uk
w: tudorfarmhousehotel.co.uk

BEDROOMS: 20. 8 on ground floor, 4 in
farmhouse, 9 in barn, 7 in cider house.
OPEN: all year.
FACILITIES: lounge, bar, 2 dining
rooms, free Wi-Fi, in-room TV
(Freeview), 14-acre grounds (garden,
ancient grassland), restaurant and
lounge wheelchair accessible, adapted
toilet.
BACKGROUND MUSIC: in restaurant and
lounge at lunch and dinner.
LOCATION: 7 miles SE of Monmouth.
CHILDREN: all ages welcomed.
DOGS: allowed in 3 bedrooms, grounds,
not in public rooms.
CREDIT CARDS: Amex, MC, Visa.
PRICES: per room B&B £129–£299,
D,B&B £209–£389. Tasting menu £60,
à la carte £42. Min. 2-night stay at
weekends, some bank hols.

CLEE STANTON Shropshire

MAP 3:C5

TIMBERSTONE

'We are greeted as if we are the most important people in the world,' says a regular guest at this Shropshire B&B, lovingly created by Tracey Baylis and Alex Read from two 300-year-old cottages. Others are equally warmly received, perhaps with a pot of tea and a plate of biscuits in the lovely, light sitting/dining room, before being shown to one of five comfortable bedrooms, each with king-size bed, fine linen and tea- and coffee-making facilities. One room has a double-ended slipper bath opposite the bed, and French doors opening on to a balcony; another has oak beams and tranquil garden views. Guests staying for a simple supper are asked by Tracey, who has worked with Michelin-starred chef Shaun Hill, what they would like – 'I get the impression that she would provide any outlandish choice,' says one reader. Meals are 'served at a communal table' with Alex 'ever watchful that glasses are not empty'. Breakfast is a feast of local, organic and Fairtrade produce, served with home-made jams and bread. A great base for exploring the foodie town of Ludlow, five miles away. (David Bartley, and others)

25% DISCOUNT VOUCHERS

Lackstone Lane
Clee Stanton SY8 3EL

T: 01584 823519
E: timberstone1@hotmail.com
W: timberstoneludlow.co.uk

BEDROOMS: 4. Plus garden cabin retreat for 2.
OPEN: all year.
FACILITIES: lounge/dining room, conservatory, free Wi-Fi, in-room TV (Freeview), ½-acre garden.
BACKGROUND MUSIC: none.
LOCATION: 5 miles NE of Ludlow.
CHILDREN: all ages welcomed.
DOGS: allowed by arrangement (£10 per night), not in dining room.
CREDIT CARDS: MC, Visa.
PRICES: per room B&B single £90, double £100–£120. Set menus £25–£30. Min. 2-night booking in cabin retreat.

CLEY-NEXT-THE-SEA Norfolk   MAP 2:A5

CLEY WINDMILL   NEW

All hotels demand upkeep, though it is rare for owners to have to replace a fan wheel or fit new sails. But, then, there is nothing ordinary about Julian and Carolyn Goldee's B&B. A 'beautifully converted', five-storey tower mill overlooking the River Glaven and reed beds, it achieves main entry status this year, with Rachael and Jeremy Parke now manager and chef. Our inspectors were 'greeted cheerfully by the receptionist, who came out when she saw us arrive'. Bedrooms, some in outbuildings, are intensely characterful, from the ground-level Boat House, with four-poster and courtyard access, to the circular Stone Room with wrap-around balcony, and the Wheel Room, reached by a ladder. 'Our first-floor room was large, with a sofa, super-king-size bed, antiques, individual touches, a fridge with fresh milk, a roll-top bath (no shower).' A three-course dinner brought 'delicious scallops and pancetta in a light sauce, a sublime dish of pork three ways, Bakewell tart with berry sauce'. Everything is cooked from scratch; let them know ahead of time if you wish to dine. Breakfast, too, proved 'lovely', with 'local kippers and kedgeree'. A walk to Cley beach was 'exhilarating'. (SF)

The Quay
Cley-next-the-Sea NR25 7RP

T: 01263 740209
E: info@cleywindmill.co.uk
W: cleywindmill.co.uk

BEDROOMS: 9. 1 in Boat House, 1 in Long House, 2 self-catering apartments, some ground-floor rooms suitable for more able wheelchair-users, but bathrooms not adapted.
OPEN: all year, self-catering only over Christmas/New Year.
FACILITIES: bar/lounge, dining room, Wi-Fi, in-room TV (Freeview), civil wedding licence, ¼-acre garden.
BACKGROUND MUSIC: in dining room at dinner.
LOCATION: in northerly village next to River Glaven, under a mile from the sea.
CHILDREN: all ages welcomed, sofa or air bed £30.
DOGS: allowed in 1 room.
CREDIT CARDS: MC, Visa.
PRICES: per room B&B £159–£245 based on 2 sharing. Set menu £32.50. Min. 2-night stay weekends.

CLIPSHAM Rutland

MAP 2:A3

BEECH HOUSE & OLIVE BRANCH

♀ Previous César Winner

'My favourite place to stop when travelling north. It's the tops.' Readers enthuse over this 'excellent' enterprise, centred on a village pub/restaurant created in the 1890s from three farm labourers' cottages. It was brought back from the dead in 1999 by a trio including owners Ben Jones and Sean Hope. From the A1 it is two miles down a tree-lined lane to the Olive Branch, with a pub shop selling wines and hand-made chocolates. You can eat 'lunch for less' in the bar or go the whole hog in the dining room. Sean Hope uses locally sourced, home-grown or foraged ingredients, herbs and salads from their polytunnel, in such 'fantastic' dishes as roast lamb rump, petit ratatouille, potato terrine, rocket pesto. In Beech House opposite, bedrooms have a luxury bed with handmade, pocket-sprung mattress, a double-ended bath, a power shower. First-floor Double Cream has a roll-top bath in the window overlooking fields, a French linen press. Chocolate is a family suite with wet room and wheelchair access. Breakfast brings squeeze-it-yourself orange juice, 'superb' kedgeree, 'plump' kippers, local sausages and bacon. Staff are jolly and smiling; 'I never witnessed one grump.' (R and MM-D)

Main Street
Clipsham LE15 7SH

T: 01780 410355
E: beechhouse@theolivebranchpub.com
W: theolivebranchpub.com

BEDROOMS: 6. 2 on ground floor, family room (also suitable for wheelchair) in annexe.
OPEN: all year, pub closed evening 25 Dec, 1 Jan.
FACILITIES: pub, dining room, breakfast room, free Wi-Fi, in-room TV (Freeview, Netflix), small terrace, garden, public rooms wheelchair accessible, adapted toilet.
BACKGROUND MUSIC: classical/jazz in pub.
LOCATION: in village 7 miles NW of Stamford.
CHILDREN: all ages welcomed.
DOGS: allowed in ground-floor bedrooms and bar.
CREDIT CARDS: MC, Visa.
PRICES: per room B&B £115–£205, D,B&B £175–£260. Set 5-course dinner £40, à la carte £39.

CORSE LAWN Gloucestershire

CORSE LAWN HOUSE

'Little has changed' at this 'beautifully maintained and furnished' pink brick Queen Anne mansion. Guests on a return visit after many years likened it to a wonderful 'time warp'. Bought by the Hines family in 1978, the handsome house now rambles comfortably through sympathetic additions, with Baba, the senior in the mother-son team, keeping 'an eagle eye on everything' including the 'brilliant, friendly and attentive staff'. Inside is pure country house with a plush palette, equestrian prints and several watercolours by Baba's great-grandmother. There are settles and old photographs in the snug bar, a fire and relaxed seating in the drawing room. Light, airy, individually decorated bedrooms with large period windows have a 'comfortable king-size bed, a large bathroom with fluffy robes, good towels and Duck Island toiletries'. 'We appreciated the delicious shortbread in the rooms along with leaf tea, coffee and fresh milk in the fridge.' Local boy and new chef Chris Monk, who trained in the kitchens here, might serve miso-sesame skrei cod; maple-glazed celeriac. Breakfast ('near-perfect') has home-made muesli, sausages cooked to a family secret. (BG, and others)

25% DISCOUNT VOUCHERS

Corse Lawn GL19 4LZ

T: 01452 780771
E: enquiries@corselawn.com
W: corselawn.com

BEDROOMS: 18. 5 on ground floor.
OPEN: all year except 24–26 Dec.
FACILITIES: 2 drawing rooms, snug bar, restaurant, bistro, private dining/meeting rooms, free Wi-Fi, in-room TV (Sky, BT, Freeview), civil wedding licence, 12-acre grounds (croquet, tennis, indoor heated swimming pool), unsuitable for disabled.
BACKGROUND MUSIC: none.
LOCATION: 5 miles SW of Tewkesbury on B4211.
CHILDREN: all ages welcomed.
DOGS: allowed in bedrooms, on lead in public rooms, not in eating areas.
CREDIT CARDS: Amex, MC, Visa.
PRICES: per room B&B single £75–£85, double £110–£160. Set dinner (restaurant) £34, (bistro) £24, à la carte £35.

COWAN BRIDGE Lancashire

MAP 4: inset D2

HIPPING HALL

In the Lune valley, between the Lake District and Yorkshire Dales, this 'comfortable hotel with modern, well-appointed bedrooms' was Andrew Wildsmith's first foray into the hospitality field (see also Shortlist entry for The Ryebeck, Bowness-on-Windermere, and main entry for Forest Side, Grasmere). Set in 12-acre grounds with a beck running through, it is 'a wonderful place'. The heart of the operation is the 15th-century dining room with open fire, where chef Oli Martin displays 'considerable flair' in his use of seasonal, locally sourced ingredients. Dinner is a 12-course tasting menu, one for omnivores and one for vegetarians, both short on hyperbole, long on flavours. For instance: local Goosnargh chicken, seaweed, shiitake; chalk-stream trout, buttermilk, roe; celery fettucine, fig leaf, smoked almond. Service is 'first class' from 'really friendly staff'. The bedrooms in the main house, cottage and converted stables were styled by Mr Wildsmith with designer James Mackie. The five rooms in the stables have a luxury bathroom and private terrace. Attention to detail shows in bespoke tweeds, paint finishes, and Sedbergh bath products. 'We recommend it highly.' (DG)

Cowan Bridge
Kirkby Lonsdale LA6 2JJ

T: 01524 271187
E: info@hippinghall.com
w: hippinghall.com

BEDROOMS: 15. 3 in cottage, 5 in stables, 1 room suitable for disabled.
OPEN: all year, restaurant closed Mon, Tues.
FACILITIES: lounge, orangery, bar, restaurant, 'chef's kitchen', civil wedding licence, free Wi-Fi, in-room TV (Freeview), civil wedding licence, 12-acre grounds, orangery, restaurant and lounge wheelchair accessible.
BACKGROUND MUSIC: in lounge, restaurant.
LOCATION: 2 miles SE of Kirkby Lonsdale, on A65.
CHILDREN: all ages welcomed, not under 12 in restaurant.
DOGS: allowed in stable bedrooms (max. 2), orangery.
CREDIT CARDS: Amex, MC, Visa.
PRICES: per room B&B £179–£299, D,B&B £299–£419. Dinner tasting menu £70.

COWES Isle of Wight

♛ NORTH HOUSE

NEW

César award: newcomer of the year

'In the heart of West Cowes, five minutes from
the ferry', up 'a steep side road', this Grade II
listed town house has been given a stylish make-
over by Lewis Green and Luke Staples of interiors
store Staples and Green, nearby. Our inspectors
this year found Mr Green and his wife, Charlotte,
'hands-on owners, chatting to guests, checking
that all ran smoothly'. Their bedroom was
'smartly decorated in muted colours, with seagrass
flooring, big, comfortable bed, soft but effective
lighting'. Among 'nice touches' were 'fresh milk,
home-made biscuits, REN toiletries'. Some rooms
have both a freestanding bath and a monsoon
shower; three have a sea view; others overlook a
courtyard garden, with tables for alfresco dining
(garden chairs could do with some TLC) and a
small pool. The restaurant has a 'subtle seaside
feel, with tongue-and-groove walls, nautical-
themed photos and prints', doors on to the
garden. 'Dinner is excellent, using local produce,
lobster, crab, charcoal-cooked steaks.' 'Very good'
breakfasts bring pastries, fruit, smoked salmon,
with cooked dishes at weekends. 'A model of how
a good small hotel should be run.' (JS)

Sun Hill
Cowes PO31 7HY

T: 01983 209453
E: reception@northhousecowes.co.uk
W: northhousecowes.co.uk

BEDROOMS: 14.
OPEN: all year, restaurant closed Mon,
Tues (except bank hols).
FACILITIES: bar, library, restaurant,
private dining room, free Wi-Fi,
in-room TV (Freeview), civil wedding
licence, garden, outdoor heated
swimming pool.
BACKGROUND MUSIC: in bar and
restaurant.
LOCATION: in centre of Old Town.
CHILDREN: all ages welcome.
DOGS: allowed in some bedrooms,
bar, library, in restaurant by special
request.
CREDIT CARDS: Amex, MC, Visa.
PRICES: per room B&B £145–£245.
À la carte £36.

CROFT-ON-TEES Yorkshire

MAP 4:C4

CLOW BECK HOUSE

'A hearty welcome' awaits guests at Heather and David Armstrong's farmhouse which has been in the host's family since 1904. There are six guest bedrooms in annexe buildings, 'set around a beautifully landscaped, immaculately kept garden'. Wherever you look, something diverts the eye. There is a fishpond, a bird house, ceramic pigs, a miniature cricket team on a lawn; plenty to entertain the children, plus seats and benches everywhere, from which guests enjoy 'views across fields towards the village and the River Tees'. In one bedroom a young Audrey Hepburn gazes from the wall. Another has 'an old, black, cast iron fire surround fixed on the wall as decoration'. Most now have a king- or super-king-size bed. In a bathroom, 'teddy bears' bath-time' tiles raised a smile. Extras include fresh milk, chocolates, home-made biscuits, good toiletries, an umbrella, you name it. Breakfast and an evening meal are served in an orangery-like room with 'polished slate and timber floor, unusual artwork', a large stone fireplace lending 'a manor-house feel'. David cooks, with local produce, 'farmhouse-style' dishes in large portions. Everything about the place is generous. More reports, please.

Monk End Farm
Croft-on-Tees DL2 2SP

T: 01325 721075
E: reservations@clowbeckhouse.co.uk
W: clowbeckhouse.co.uk

BEDROOMS: 6 in garden buildings, some on ground floor, 1 suitable for disabled.
OPEN: all year except Christmas and New Year.
FACILITIES: lounge, restaurant, free Wi-Fi, in-room TV (Freeview), small conference facilities, 2-acre grounds on 100-acre farm.
BACKGROUND MUSIC: classical, 'easy listening' in restaurant.
LOCATION: 3 miles SE of Darlington.
CHILDREN: all ages welcomed.
DOGS: not allowed.
CREDIT CARDS: Amex, MC, Visa.
PRICES: per room B&B single £90, double £140. À la carte £37.

CROSTHWAITE Cumbria

THE PUNCH BOWL INN

In 'one of the prettiest villages in south Lakeland', Richard Rose's former 18th-century coaching inn is firmly on Cumbria's culinary map. In late 2018 the talented Arthur Bridgeman Quin headed to France for a sabbatical – the prize for winning the annual William Heptinstall Award for young chefs. The Punch Bowl kitchen continued to uphold his 'keep it simple' values and respect for local produce. As we go to press, Simon Hill is slated to arrive from Andrew Pern's Michelin-starred kitchen at The Star Inn, Harome (see entry): expect a twist on modern classics, and great things. Meanwhile, plans are afoot for a new venture with Arthur (be excited). This is a lovely old pub with 'lots of atmosphere', especially in the front room with log-burner. Bedrooms, each named after a past vicar of neighbouring St Mary's parish church, some with views of the Lyth valley, are high spec, with heated limestone bathroom floor, free-standing bath (two baths in top-storey Noble, under the eaves) and power shower. Two rooms have a four-poster built from reclaimed elm. Danson has gnarly oak beams, a small fireplace. After breakfast, hikers pick up their Wainwright and walk. (S and KT, DP)

Crosthwaite
Kendal LA8 8HR

T: 015395 68237
E: info@the-punchbowl.co.uk
W: the-punchbowl.co.uk

BEDROOMS: 9.
OPEN: all year.
FACILITIES: bar, bar dining area, restaurant, free Wi-Fi, in-room TV (Freeview), civil wedding licence, 2 terraces, bar and restaurant wheelchair accessible, adapted toilet.
BACKGROUND MUSIC: in public areas.
LOCATION: 5 miles W of Kendal, via A5074.
CHILDREN: all ages welcomed.
DOGS: allowed in bar only.
CREDIT CARDS: Amex, MC, Visa.
PRICES: per room B&B £110–£345. À la carte £35. 1-night bookings usually refused 25 Dec, 31 Dec.

CRUDWELL Wiltshire   MAP 3:E5

THE RECTORY HOTEL

When music industry executive Alex Payne set out in 2016 to transform this Georgian country house, he brought in Dan Brod and Charlie Luxton of the Beckford Arms, Tisbury (see entry). They are responsible for the stylish interiors of this limestone mansion, built for the rector of All Saints and his 14 children. 'One of the biggest improvements' has been the addition of a cocktail bar, opening on to a garden with a swimming pool and a 13th-century dovecote. Even a 'small' bedroom proved spacious, with 'comfortable king-size bed'. Fresh milk was available, while a cafetière was provided. 'Nice touches' were the home-made shortbread, 'lovely' local toiletries. Some larger rooms have an in-room roll-top bath. In the restaurant, head chef Darren Stephens's 'excellent, creative' cooking includes such dishes as loin of fallow deer, celeriac purée, cavalo nero and cassis onion – always a vegetarian option. Similarly appealing fare is available in sister pub The Potting Shed across the road. Breakfast choices include eggs Benedict, toasted sourdough bread with avocado, smoked salmon, French toast with maple syrup and bacon. 'We had a very enjoyable stay and would return.' (T and AR)

Crudwell
Malmesbury SN16 9EP

T: 01666 577194
E: info@therectoryhotel.com
W: therectoryhotel.com

BEDROOMS: 18. 3 in cottage in garden.
OPEN: all year.
FACILITIES: living room, drawing room, dining room, card room, bar, in-room TV (Freeview, film library), free Wi-Fi, meeting facilities, civil wedding licence, 3-acre garden, heated outdoor swimming pool (10 by 15 metres, May–Oct), restaurant and bar wheelchair accessible.
BACKGROUND MUSIC: sometimes, in public areas.
LOCATION: 4 miles N of Malmesbury.
CHILDREN: all ages welcomed.
DOGS: allowed in 3 bedrooms and public rooms, not in dining room.
CREDIT CARDS: Amex, MC, Visa.
PRICES: per room B&B £150–£295. À la carte £35. Min. 2-night bookings at weekends, usually.

DARTMOUTH Devon

MAP 1:D4

BAYARDS COVE INN

'Nothing is too much trouble' at this timber-framed pub-with-rooms, a few steps from Bayards Cove, where the Pilgrim Fathers departed for America. The town's second-oldest building, Charles Deuchar's historic inn, with 14th-century bones, takes 'a very personal approach to service' that 'really made our stay'. Upstairs, a 'larger than anticipated' room 'has all the hallmarks of the building's age', with uneven walls and floors, 'but is cosy, with custom-made tweed curtains, headboard and cushions', an 'extremely comfy' bed, a sofa, 'biscuits, loose leaf tea and coffee'; a shower room, White Company toiletries. Most rooms have original features, from beams to windows with muntins, some sport nautical-themed artwork, a model boat. Menus, in the bar and restaurant, have pleasingly 'local credentials', notably the seafood. Daytime fare includes haddock and bacon chowder, fresh crab sandwiches. Come evening, Devon-style moules frites in Heron Valley cider, cream and chorizo; fish of the day, salsa verde, olives, baby plum tomatoes and new potatoes. The inn is 'so well placed for exploring Dartmouth', but also ideal for 'a night away to feel indulgent without breaking the bank'. (BF)

27 Lower Street
Dartmouth TQ6 9AN

T: 01803 839278
E: info@bayardscoveinn.co.uk
W: bayardscoveinn.co.uk

BEDROOMS: 7. 2 family suites.
OPEN: all year.
FACILITIES: bar, restaurant, free Wi-Fi, in-room TV (Freeview), bicycle storage, private parking nearby (reservation required, £15 per day), public areas wheelchair accessible, adapted toilet.
BACKGROUND MUSIC: in public areas.
LOCATION: in centre, close to waterfront.
CHILDREN: all ages welcomed.
DOGS: allowed throughout (£12 per dog per night).
CREDIT CARDS: Amex, MC, Visa.
PRICES: per person B&B single £95–£200, double £95–£220. À la carte £35. Min. 2-night stay at weekends.

SEE ALSO SHORTLIST

DARTMOUTH Devon

MAP 1:D4

DART MARINA

'Yet again, everything was of the highest standard.' Regular visitors once more praise Richard Seton's spa hotel overlooking the River Dart (come by boat, by all means). Credit, also, to his manager: 'Paul Downing is brilliant at his job!' All the smart, modern bedrooms have a river view. Even a smaller one, with sliding doors and balustrade, 'was comfortable, well appointed, with a king-size bed'. Air conditioning, fresh milk and a good bathroom were appreciated. Trade up for a balcony, a junior suite with dual-aspect lounge, a garden suite with wet room and drench shower. The latest wheeze is Cloud Nine summer pop-up bar, serving pints of prawns, pulled pork sliders. Dine inside or out. A lounge menu offers lighter fare, while in the dining room, Peter Alcroft exploits freshly landed fish and seasonal local produce to create such 'inventive, delicious' dishes as pan-fried sea bass, confit fennel, olives, saffron potato, orange and wild fennel butter sauce. One reader rated the food 'good, but not excellent'. Breakfast brings a 'wonderful buffet, superb cooked dishes'. The staff are 'attentive and friendly'; this is 'obviously a happy ship'. (Eric and Mary Woods, John Charnley)

Sandquay Road
Dartmouth TQ6 9PH

T: 01803 832580
E: reception@dartmarina.com
W: dartmarina.com

BEDROOMS: 49. 4 on ground floor, 1 suitable for disabled, plus 4 apartments.
OPEN: all year.
FACILITIES: lounge/bar, restaurant, free Wi-Fi, in-room TV (Freeview), river-front lawn, spa (heated indoor swimming pool, 8 by 4 metres, gym), lounge and restaurant wheelchair accessible.
BACKGROUND MUSIC: in restaurant and lounge/bar during the day.
LOCATION: on waterfront.
CHILDREN: all ages welcomed.
DOGS: allowed in some bedrooms and lounge, not in restaurant.
CREDIT CARDS: MC, Visa.
PRICES: per room B&B single £153–£213, double £180–£480, D,B&B double £250–£550. À la carte £37. 1-night bookings usually refused weekends at peak times.

SEE ALSO SHORTLIST

DEDHAM Essex   MAP 2:C5

DEDHAM HALL & FOUNTAIN HOUSE RESTAURANT

Wisteria festoons Wendy and Jim Sarton's peaceful manor house, in a picture-postcard village at the heart of Constable country. Surrounded by brimming gardens with duck pond, it has 'nothing chichi' about it, just a 'warm and comforting' ambience, cosy parlours with beamed ceilings, cottage-style bedrooms exposing their oak ribs. The pricing is reasonable and no-nonsense: all rooms cost the same. Most are in converted buildings around the barn-cum-studio where residential art courses are held. We hear tales of the hosts' kindness – a welcome with tea and home-made brownies by the fire; the day they got up at 5.30 am to cook breakfast for guests who had to make an early start. At night Wendy cooks a three-course dinner of local ingredients with choices at each course, always a vegetarian option. Maybe duck breast with green peppercorn gravy; mushroom and cream cheese pancakes. Art is in the air here: Constable attended school in Dedham; Munnings is remembered at the museum in his former home. After a freshly cooked breakfast you can cross the bridge over the River Stour into Suffolk and take a stroll to Flatford Mill.

25% DISCOUNT VOUCHERS

Brook Street
Dedham
Colchester CO7 6AD

T: 01206 323027
E: sarton@dedhamhall.co.uk
W: dedhamhall.co.uk

BEDROOMS: 20. 16 in annexe around art studio, some on ground floor suitable for disabled.
OPEN: all year except Christmas–New Year.
FACILITIES: 2 lounges, bar, dining room, restaurant, studio, free Wi-Fi, in-room TV, 6-acre grounds (pond, gardens), lounge and dining room wheelchair accessible.
BACKGROUND MUSIC: none.
LOCATION: end of village High Street (set back from road).
CHILDREN: all ages welcomed.
DOGS: allowed in some bedrooms, not in public rooms.
CREDIT CARDS: MC, Visa.
PRICES: per room B&B single £75, double £120, D,B&B single £105, double £180. À la carte/fixed-price dinner, for guests only (or by prior arrangement), £35.

DEDHAM Essex

MAP 2:C5

THE SUN INN

An eye-catching hand-painted pub sign marks your arrival at Piers Baker's ancient butter-yellow inn on the Essex–Suffolk border, just down the road from rowing boats bobbing on the River Stour. The hub of the village, the 'genial' bar oozes 'easy community feel'; it's just the spot to people-watch across the 'gorgeous elm bar top', with a refreshing drink. In the next room the 'cosy' lounge is stuffed with a mishmash of sofas and armchairs, vintage books, board games. In the made-to-last 15th-century building (an Elizabethan staircase, timber framing), the decor is bang up to date. 'Pleasingly decorated' bedrooms (sizes vary, two accessed via the terrace) overlook the garden, the street or St Mary's church with its soft peal. 'Our well-lit, comfortably sized room had crisp linens, puffy pillows, a woollen throw; a vintage-style chest; a large skylight with window shades. We faced the beer garden, but no noise bothered us.' Modern English pub food is given an Italian twist by chef Jack Levine. Try the spaghetti alle vongole; Dingley Dell pork cotoletta. Breakfast ('exceptional') has made-to-order omelettes, ideal fuel for exploring the gentle pleasures of Constable country.

High Street
Dedham
Colchester CO7 6DF

T: 01206 323351
E: office@thesuninndedham.com
W: thesuninndedham.com

BEDROOMS: 7. 2 across the terrace, approached by Elizabethan staircase.
OPEN: all year except 25/26 Dec.
FACILITIES: lounge, bar, dining room, free Wi-Fi, in-room TV (Freeview), 1-acre walled garden (covered terrace, children's play area, garden bar), unsuitable for disabled.
BACKGROUND MUSIC: all day in public areas.
LOCATION: village centre.
CHILDREN: all ages welcomed.
DOGS: in bar and Oak Room, in guest bedrooms by arrangement and subject to terms and conditions (not in dining room).
CREDIT CARDS: Amex, MC, Visa.
PRICES: per room B&B single £90–£135, double £150, D,B&B double £200. À la carte £28.50.

DODDISCOMBSLEIGH Devon

THE NOBODY INN

♲ Previous César Winner

Buried deep in the countryside, Sue Burdge's inn is so much the model of an olde worlde Devon pub that it 'could have been created by a set designer'. To get there, you plunge down a rabbit warren of narrow, winding lanes. The bar is 'beguiling', with beams, brasses and blazing log-burner, the counter 'stacked with bottles and barrels of every kind of drink imaginable'. This is 'somewhere memorable', though not without its irritations, some a result of the age of the building (a shower was 'a bit tight' for a reader standing five foot six inches). Bedrooms range from very small (four-foot bed, separate bathroom) to tolerably spacious, with 'a big, comfortable bed' and en suite shower. One bed has 'a beautiful, hand-carved headboard'. A decanter of sherry is a nice touch. The staff, when not fraught, are 'welcoming, well practised and very able'. The food sometimes misses the mark, but the NoBody Pie has proved a palpable hit. More ambitious dishes might include ten-day corned beef, hashed with onions, potato, peppers, kale, veal jus, fried duck egg. Come in winter and hope to be snowed in for weeks, so you can sample the 260-odd whiskies. (J and MB, and others)

Doddiscombsleigh
Exeter EX6 7PS

T: 01647 252394
E: info@nobodyinn.co.uk
W: nobodyinn.co.uk

BEDROOMS: 5.
OPEN: all year except 24/25, 31 Dec, 1 Jan, restaurant closed Sun, Mon, but bar menu available.
FACILITIES: 2 bars, restaurant, free Wi-Fi (improving but may be patchy), in-room TV (Freeview), garden, patio, parking, dining room wheelchair accessible, no adapted toilet.
BACKGROUND MUSIC: none.
LOCATION: in village, 8 miles SW of Exeter.
CHILDREN: not under 5.
DOGS: allowed, on lead, in bar only.
CREDIT CARDS: MC, Visa.
PRICES: per room B&B single £59–£90, double £79–£110, D,B&B single £79–£105, double £110–£140. À la carte £32.

DUNSTER Somerset

MAP 1:B5

THE LUTTRELL ARMS HOTEL

You can eat by a blazing fire, or alfresco in a leafy garden overlooked by hilltop Dunster Castle, at Nigel and Anne Way's historic hotel. Dating in part from the 1400s, and at the heart of a medieval village on the edge of Exmoor, it has 'the ambience of a proper old coaching inn done right'. Interiors have oak beams, leaded casements, yawning fireplaces. Some bedrooms have a four-poster, one a 17th-century carved overmantel. Each room is different, some have a private terrace and garden access, ideal for dogs and accompanying owners. 'A lovely four-poster room' overlooking the Yarn Market was 'spacious, warm, with a nice seating area', a little chatter from below until closing time. Food is served all day in a bar adorned with horse brasses and weaponry, 'popular with shooting parties and dog owners', maybe chicken Kiev, oak-smoked salmon linguine. In Psalter's restaurant, named after the Luttrell Psalter, a treasure of the British Library, locally sourced menus include such dishes as poached turbot, charred baby gem, brown shrimps, pickled samphire, buttermilk dressing. Breakfast brings grilled kippers, eggs Benedict, local sausages, Dunster honey.

32–36 High Street
Exmoor National Park
Dunster TA24 6SG

T: 01643 821555
E: enquiry@luttrellarms.co.uk
W: luttrellarms.co.uk

BEDROOMS: 29. Some on ground floor, 1 with 'easy access'.
OPEN: all year.
FACILITIES: lounge, 2 bars, snug, restaurant, function rooms, free Wi-Fi, in-room TV (Freeview), civil wedding licence, courtyard, garden (alfresco dining), bar and restaurant wheelchair accessible.
BACKGROUND MUSIC: in restaurant.
LOCATION: village centre, 3½ miles SE of Minehead.
CHILDREN: all ages welcomed; some rooms not suitable for under-14s, call to check availability.
DOGS: allowed in most bedrooms, bar, not in restaurant.
CREDIT CARDS: Amex, MC, Visa.
PRICES: per room B&B single £82.50–£162.50, double £125–£175. À la carte £35. Min. 2-nights weekends.

EAST CHISENBURY Wiltshire

THE RED LION FREEHOUSE

⚘ Previous César Winner

On the banks of the River Avon, in a 'charming' village, stands 'a pub-with-rooms that has real character and is clearly popular with the locals'. Trusted Guide readers on a return visit this year reported that Michelin-starred chef/proprietors Guy and Brittany Manning continue to run it with style. 'We were delighted to discover that the menu is even better than we recalled.' In the bar and dining room, 'friendly, knowledgeable staff' serve 'exceptional' and 'delicious' modern British dishes. Perhaps roast halibut with Cornish mussels; herb-roast guineafowl, potato millefeuille and Wye valley asparagus. Bedrooms, in the Troutbeck Guesthouse across the road, enjoy a private wooden deck with river views; each has rich soothing hues, contemporary bathroom, king-size bed. 'Delightfully appointed' Manser is dog-friendly; Benjamin has a roll-top, claw-foot bath. 'We awoke to the sight of the River Avon, a grebe on the water, and beyond, rolling fields with sheep. Bliss.' Breakfast, including a full English, home-made muffins and jams, is 'splendid'. 'It goes from strength to strength. We would go out of our way to stay here again.' (Terence Bendixson, Chris and Erika Savory)

East Chisenbury
Pewsey SN9 6AQ

T: 01980 671124
E: troutbeck@redlionfreehouse.com
W: redlionfreehouse.com

BEDROOMS: 5. On ground floor, in adjacent building; 1 (with wet room) suitable for disabled.
OPEN: all year except Christmas Day, kitchen closed Sun evening, all day Mon/Tues.
FACILITIES: bar/restaurant, private dining room, free Wi-Fi, in-room TV (Freeview), 1-acre garden.
BACKGROUND MUSIC: in pub/restaurant.
LOCATION: in village, 6 miles S of Pewsey.
CHILDREN: all ages welcomed.
DOGS: allowed.
CREDIT CARDS: Amex, MC, Visa.
PRICES: per room B&B £155–£275, D,B&B £195–£275. À la carte £45.

EAST GRINSTEAD Sussex

MAP 2:D4

GRAVETYE MANOR

♆ Previous César Winner

'Whenever a special date crops up, we make a beeline for Gravetye and have never been disappointed.' Guide stalwarts vouch for Jeremy and Elizabeth Hosking's luxury country house hotel, an Elizabethan manor house (Relais & Châteaux), surrounded by woodland, with gardens laid out by William Robinson, exponent of the 'wild' garden style. Andrew Thomason is the consummate manager, his staff are 'charm personified'. Bedrooms, some with a four-poster, some more contemporary, have many thoughtful touches – 'home-made biscuits, bottled water, a jar of sweets, books, postcards, orchids, Noble Isle toiletries.' Another trusted reader, who last year asked for kiwi fruit, this year found some 'prepared and waiting in the fridge'. Downstairs, 'a splendid log fire' was burning in a panelled lounge. A new, glass-walled dining room brings the gardens inside. 'Magician' George Blogg holds a Michelin star for such creative offerings as 'out-of-this-world mini-beetroot meringues, partridge several ways, perfectly cooked veal sweetbreads, strawberry and beetroot soufflé with liquorice ice cream'. Breakfast is 'everything it should be'. (Francine and Ian Walsh, Bill Bennett)

25% DISCOUNT VOUCHERS

Vowels Lane
West Hoathly
East Grinstead RH19 4LJ

T: 01342 810567
E: celine@gravetyemanor.co.uk
W: gravetyemanor.co.uk

BEDROOMS: 17.
OPEN: all year.
FACILITIES: 2 lounges, bar, restaurant, 2 private dining rooms, free Wi-Fi, in-room TV (Sky), civil wedding licence, 1,000-acre grounds (woodland, ornamental and kitchen gardens, meadow, orchard, lake, croquet lawn, glasshouses), restaurant wheelchair accessible.
BACKGROUND MUSIC: in bar.
LOCATION: 4 miles SW of East Grinstead.
CHILDREN: not under 7.
DOGS: not allowed.
CREDIT CARDS: Amex, MC, Visa.
PRICES: per room B&B £278–£850. Set dinner £35–£50, tasting menu £95, seasonal menu £80. 1-night bookings sometimes refused weekends.

EAST HOATHLY Sussex   MAP 2:E4

OLD WHYLY

'You are essentially staying in someone's beautiful
farmhouse, with an exquisite garden and delicious
breakfast.' A reader reaffirms her support this
year for Sarah Burgoyne's 'wonderful' B&B. A
Georgian red brick manor house, it adjoins a
private estate near Lewes. Interiors are filled with
period furnishings, paintings, family possessions.
Spacious, tranquil country house bedrooms have
Irish linen, Egyptian cotton sheets, wool blankets.
In summer you can take tea beneath a vine-
covered pergola, swim in the outdoor pool, work
up an appetite on the tennis court. At night the
hostess, who took a cookery course in Paris, serves
a three-course dinner, by candlelight or alfresco.
Guests gather for drinks before sitting down
to, for example, fresh figs, buffalo mozzarella,
wild rocket; pork fillet, apples, prunes, mashed
potato; wild blackberry jelly with double cream.
Breakfast brings orchard fruits, honey from the
hives, eggs from free-roaming hens and ducks.
With Glyndbourne just four miles away, it's a
perfect spot for opera buffs: 'Her tiffin box picnics
continue to be the best.' Don't turn up too late. 'It's
worth arriving in time for tea and home-baked
cake.' (Catrin Treadwell)

London Road
East Hoathly BN8 6EL

T: 01825 840216
E: stay@oldwhyly.co.uk
W: oldwhyly.co.uk

BEDROOMS: 4.
OPEN: all year.
FACILITIES: drawing room, dining
room, free Wi-Fi, in-room TV
(Freeview), 4-acre garden, heated
outdoor swimming pool (14 by
7 metres), tennis, unsuitable for
disabled.
BACKGROUND MUSIC: none.
LOCATION: 1 mile N of village.
CHILDREN: all ages welcomed.
DOGS: allowed in drawing room, not
in dining room or unattended in
bedrooms.
CREDIT CARDS: none.
PRICES: per room B&B £98–£150,
D,B&B £136–£188. Set dinner £38,
hamper £40 per person. 1-night
bookings may be refused weekends in
summer season.

EAST PORTLEMOUTH Devon   MAP 1:E4

GARA ROCK   `NEW`

High on the south Devon coast, Gara Rock re-enters the Guide following a stylish revamp, and a relaunch as a 'well-being retreat'. Once a row of remote coastguard cottages, more recently a smaller hotel, this gleaming construction of glass, steel and white paint is commended by inspectors for its position overlooking the sea, 'lovely' beach below, and direct access to the South West Coast Path – walkers and their dogs can enjoy refreshments on the large terrace with panoramic views. Recent additions include a contemporary lounge area with soothing vintage tones, simple driftwood walls and sisal rugs, and a ten-seat cinema room, with five screenings each day. There are new loft bedrooms, 'well-appointed' junior suites, plus cottages and apartments. The refurbished restaurant has floor-to-ceiling windows offering 'stunning views', and 'a good choice of food and wine'. Though not fully finished at the time of going to press, and beset by teething problems, Gara Rock 'has huge potential', say admirers of the glamorous indoor and outdoor pools and spa, and the 'friendly staff'. (A and CR, Chris and Erika Savory)

East Portlemouth
Salcombe TQ8 8FA

T: 01548 845946
E: info@gararock.com
W: gararock.com

BEDROOMS: 30, Accessed externally, 1 suite separate from hotel.
OPEN: all year.
FACILITIES: restaurant, private dining area, lounge bar, spa, cinema room, terrace, indoor and outdoor pool, free Wi-Fi, in-room TV, civil wedding licence, public rooms wheelchair accessible, adapted toilet on floor below, reached via lift.
BACKGROUND MUSIC: in public areas.
LOCATION: on cliff-top, 1 mile SE of East Portlemouth.
CHILDREN: all ages welcomed.
DOGS: allowed in some rooms, grounds, lounge bar and restaurant.
CREDIT CARDS: Amex, MC, Visa.
PRICES: per room B&B £135–£548.
À la carte £36.

EASTBOURNE Sussex   MAP 2:E4

BELLE TOUT LIGHTHOUSE

To the lighthouse! And if you have a mind to visit
this unique B&B, make it soon. In 1999 it had to
be moved from the crumbling chalk cliff edge; in
around a decade it will be in peril again. Built in
1831 of Aberdeen granite, and decommissioned
in 1902, it is owned by David and Barbara Shaw,
managed by Ian Noall. It stands as a beacon of
hospitality in a remote landscape of sheep-grazed
downs, with views to the Seven Sisters and Beachy
Head. One bedroom, the Keeper's Loft, in the
actual tower, has a ladder to a double bed. In the
adjoining house, the Captain's Cabin has a feature
brick wall, fireplace, sea views. All rooms have
immaculate white decor, decent en suite facilities,
a basic hospitality tray. A cosy upstairs sitting
room with 'leather sofas, a working fire, fresh
flowers, copies of Sussex Life', lets guests meet for
drinks, before driving to East Dean's Tiger Inn
or enjoying supper from the village deli. Later,
they can ascend to the lantern to gaze at the dark
sky. A 'wonderful' breakfast, cooked to order in a
small kitchen alongside the breakfast room, brings
'good coffee', a daily special, perhaps poached
eggs and prosciutto. 'We loved this place.' More
reports, please.

Beachy Head Road
Eastbourne BN20 0AE

T: 01323 423185
E: info@belletout.co.uk
W: www.belletout.co.uk

BEDROOMS: 6. 5 in house, 1 in
lighthouse tower (bunk bed).
OPEN: all year except Christmas/New
Year.
FACILITIES: 2 lounges, breakfast room,
free Wi-Fi (in some rooms and some
public areas), in-room TV (Freeview),
terrace, garden, unsuitable for
disabled.
BACKGROUND MUSIC: none.
LOCATION: 3 miles W of Eastbourne,
2 miles S of East Dean village (pub,
deli).
CHILDREN: not under 15.
DOGS: not allowed.
CREDIT CARDS: MC, Visa.
PRICES: per room B&B £160–£240. Min.
2 nights, though 1-night bookings
may be accepted (check for availability
in the week before proposed stay).

EASTBOURNE Sussex

MAP 2:E4

THE GRAND HOTEL

One of the largest hotels in the Guide but 'with such kind staff and a beautiful situation'. A great, white Victorian edifice, the Grand is part of the small Elite Hotels group, but there is nothing elitist here. Readers are charmed by the family-friendliness. It might be 'all very glamorous', they'll turn down your bed, shine your shoes, but the clientele is 'mixed and of varying degrees of smartness (nice to see children)'. Traditionally styled bedrooms have towelling robes, an espresso machine, 24-hour room service. A reader's third-floor suite had 'a fruit bowl, nougat, shortbread, a small decanter of sherry'; a breakfast table at its sitting-room window exploited 'super sea views'. Slight niggles: 'captive coat-hangers, so-so lighting'. 'A beautiful outdoor pool, spa, gym and small playroom' are at guests' disposal. In the Garden restaurant, Keith Mitchell's modern classics include crumbed plaice fillet, pea purée, tomato salsa, gherkin mayonnaise and fries. In the Mirabelle restaurant Stephanie Malvoisin's fine dining menu has a European accent, maybe chicken breast, celeriac purée, French lentils, parsnip. Breakfast is 'excellent'. (MG)

King Edwards Parade
Eastbourne BN21 4EQ

T: 01323 412345
E: enquiries@grandeastbourne.com
W: grandeastbourne.com

BEDROOMS: 152. 1 suitable for disabled.
OPEN: all year, Mirabelle closed first 2 weeks Jan.
FACILITIES: 5 lounges, bar, 2 restaurants, function facilities, lifts, free Wi-Fi, in-room TV (BT, Freeview), civil wedding licence, terrace, spa/health club (indoor and outdoor pools), 2-acre garden, public areas wheelchair accessible.
BACKGROUND MUSIC: in lounges, live music at weekends.
LOCATION: seafront, outside centre.
CHILDREN: all ages welcomed.
DOGS: allowed in bedrooms, not in public rooms, £20 a night.
CREDIT CARDS: Amex, MC, Visa.
PRICES: per room B&B £150–£730, D,B&B £239–£804. Set dinner £46 (Mirabelle), £42 (Garden).

EASTON GREY Wiltshire   MAP 3:E5

WHATLEY MANOR   `NEW`

'As soon as you pull up, a besuited employee emerges, bags are lifted, car keys handed over for valet parking.' Inspectors were impressed by a stay at this luxury hotel and 'superb' spa (Relais & Châteaux). One of the more 'modestly priced' rooms ('there are huge suites') was 'lovely, with blue and cream, broad-striped silk wallpaper, two pink armchairs placed for watching TV, a wood-clad bathroom with a shower over a curved bath, candles, robes, slippers, L'Occitane toiletries'. The spa has an indoor/outdoor pool and an 'assortment of beautifully designed, differently heated rooms – sauna, steam room, caldarium'. A stroll revealed gardens divided into 'rooms', 'many lawned, with a water feature'. There are 'impressive' public spaces, a 'welcoming' bar. In the dining room, Michelin-starred chef Niall Keating cooks tasting menus for omnivores, pescatarians and vegetarians. There is simpler fare in the brasserie ('excellent chargrilled prawns, perfectly cooked lamb loin, lemon posset and raspberry sorbet'); small plates in the Green Room. A 'beautifully presented' breakfast brings 'excellent crisp croissants, perfectly poached eggs with smoked salmon'. One's cup runneth over.

Easton Grey SN16 0RB

T: 01666 822888
E: reservations@whatleymanor.com
W: whatleymanor.com

BEDROOMS: 23, Some on ground floor, 1 suitable for disabled.
OPEN: all year, restaurant closed Mon, Tues (brasserie open all week).
FACILITIES: 3 lounges, 2 bars, brasserie, restaurant, cinema, gym, spa, free Wi-Fi, in-room TV (Sky, Freeview), civil wedding licence, conference facilities, 12-acre garden, public areas wheelchair accessible, adapted toilet.
BACKGROUND MUSIC: in public areas.
LOCATION: 6½ miles from Tetbury.
CHILDREN: over-11s welcomed.
DOGS: allowed in some rooms (treats and toys, £30 per night), public areas, not in restaurant.
CREDIT CARDS: Amex, MC, Visa.
PRICES: per room B&B £249–£549. Tasting menus (dining room) £120, à la carte (brasserie) £40, small plates (Green Room) £4–£8.

ECKINGTON Worcestershire

MAP 3:D5

ECKINGTON MANOR

Pickles entrepreneur Judy Gardner preserved the historic character of a timber-frame farmhouse and outbuildings when she restored and converted them to create a stylish restaurant-with-rooms. 'Classic' ground-floor bedrooms have a Fired Earth shower room, White Company toiletries. 'Beautifully decorated', pricier rooms have hand-painted silk wallpaper, antiques, exposed beams, perhaps a log-burner or an in-room bath. One niggle that a reader, staying in a Cider Mill room, reported was poor internet connection and an 'alarming' number of spiders. A state-of-the-art cookery school is housed in a former Dutch barn. In May 2019 a new head chef, Mehdi Amiri (early years at Le Manoir aux Quat'Saisons, most recently Executive Chef at Swinton Park), was appointed and will no doubt make good use of ingredients gleaned from Eckington's farm, orchard, vegetable and herb gardens. New dishes on the menu include Eckington spring lamb, ras-el-hanout, lamb fat carrot, pickled garden vegetables, wild garlic pesto. Foraging classes and wine courses are held. Gardens with sculptures add to the charms. Also enjoyed – the bar, the 'first class' service and the 'charming sitting room'. (SR, and others)

Hammock Road
Eckington WR10 3BJ

T: 01386 751600
E: info@eckingtonmanor.co.uk
W: eckingtonmanor.co.uk

BEDROOMS: 17. All in courtyard annexes, some on ground floor.
OPEN: all year except 25/26 Dec, restaurant closed Sun evening, Mon, Tues.
FACILITIES: lift, 2 sitting rooms (one with bar area), restaurant, function rooms, free Wi-Fi, in-room TV (Freeview), civil wedding licence, cookery school, 260-acre grounds (lawns, herb garden, orchard, farm), public areas wheelchair accessible, adapted toilet.
BACKGROUND MUSIC: in garden bar and restaurant.
LOCATION: 4 miles SW of Pershore.
CHILDREN: not under 8.
DOGS: allowed in 1 bedroom, not in public rooms.
CREDIT CARDS: MC, Visa.
PRICES: per room B&B £179–£279. Set dinner £48.

EDENBRIDGE Kent   MAP 2:D4

STARBOROUGH MANOR

Approached by a long, tree-lined drive, Daisy
and Clive Hayley's B&B is the 'perfect weekend
getaway', an ideal base for exploring Kent's stately
homes and castles. It even has a 'castle' on site
– an 18th-century neo-Gothic garden house on
an island in the middle of a lake. Surrounded by
parkland, the red brick Georgian manor house
'has been adapted over the years, being largely
Victorian in its current form', say readers, full
of praise for the 'extremely friendly hosts', the
'lovely views over the peaceful setting'. Bedrooms
have a mix of period and contemporary furniture,
restful, pale decor, soft blues and hues. This is
a popular wedding venue, and newlyweds can
book the 'gorgeous, high-ceilinged' honeymoon
suite. A family might take the Blue Suite with two
bedrooms. All rooms have 'soft robes and towels',
Penhaligon toiletries. Dinner is not provided, but
for a £25 charge, guests have use of the dining
room and 'lovely, large kitchen', where, in the
morning, a freshly cooked breakfast is served,
with a 'delicious array' of home-made muesli
and granola, Greek yogurt, cinnamon plums,
blueberry pancakes. One for 'people who like to
chat and get to know their hosts'.

Moor Lane
Marsh Green
Edenbridge TN8 5QY

T: 01732 862152
E: daisy@starboroughmanor.co.uk
W: starboroughmanor.co.uk

BEDROOMS: 4 (incl. 1 suite with
2 bedrooms, 4 sharing).
OPEN: all year.
FACILITIES: 2 sitting rooms, dining
room, kitchen/breakfast room,
laundry for guests' use, function
facilities, free Wi-Fi, in-room TV
(Freeview), 4-acre gardens in 13-acre
grounds (parkland, tennis, heated
outdoor swimming pool in season),
unsuitable for disabled.
BACKGROUND MUSIC: none.
LOCATION: 1½ miles W of Edenbridge.
CHILDREN: all ages welcomed.
DOGS: not allowed.
CREDIT CARDS: Amex, MC, Visa.
PRICES: per person B&B £70–£72.50,
single occupancy £90–£110. 1-night
bookings usually refused weekends
in summer.

SEE ALSO SHORTLIST

EGTON BRIDGE Yorkshire

MAP 4:C5

BROOM HOUSE AT EGTON BRIDGE

'We had a delightful stay.' Guests were impressed by Georgina and Michael Curnow's well-located B&B within the North York Moors national park. It has views over the Esk valley. The handsome sitting room, with its warm, earthy tones, stone fireplace, antique scales and typewriter, has squashy sofas under huge windows overlooking the garden. Further serenity is offered in the nine bedrooms, each with a 'comfortable' bed, a hospitality tray with tea and coffee facilities, a bathroom with Scottish Fine Soaps toiletries. Some mix traditional and contemporary decor, including a dual-aspect double with fireplace and sofa, while beamed attic rooms (one compact), reached by steep stairs, offer far-reaching valley views and country style. Readers stayed in the two-bed May Barn with exposed brickwork, Farrow & Ball tones, a claw-footed bath (with views), a private entrance, patio and sitting room. Everything was 'well thought through' by the 'excellent hosts'; it offered 'a lot of space for the price'. Scrambled eggs, 'particularly good', starred in Michael's locally sourced, if slightly short, breakfast menu. Bram Stoker's stomping ground in Whitby is a ten-minute jaunt away.

Broom House Lane
Egton Bridge YO21 1XD

T: 07423 636783
E: mail@broom-house.co.uk
W: broom-house.co.uk

BEDROOMS: 9. 2 (1 on ground floor) in converted barn suite.
OPEN: Mar–Nov.
FACILITIES: lounge, breakfast room, free Wi-Fi, in-room TV (Freeview), 1-acre garden.
BACKGROUND MUSIC: in breakfast room.
LOCATION: ½ mile W of village.
CHILDREN: all ages welcomed (by arrangement).
DOGS: not allowed.
CREDIT CARDS: MC, Visa.
PRICES: per room B&B £89–£200. Min. 2-night bookings preferred at weekends.

ELLASTONE Staffordshire   MAP 3:B6

THE DUNCOMBE ARMS   [NEW]

There is a 'physical warmth immediately
discernible' upon entering this 1850s village
pub close to the Peak District national park. It
is hard to believe that the place was boarded up
and decaying before a local couple, Johnny and
Laura Greenall, breathed new life into it. Guide
inspectors were greeted on arrival by a 'polite
and friendly' young woman, and shown to one
of ten bedrooms in Walnut House annexe. It
was 'tastefully furnished, with leaf-patterned
wallpaper', hung with some of the modern
artwork that abounds throughout and is for sale.
'A French window opened on to a paved terrace
with a view over gently undulating fields and
wood.' There was a coffee machine, milk in a
fridge in the lobby. Six rooms have a bath and
shower, four a shower only. In the dining room,
busy on a Wednesday night, cooking is 'of a high
order. We enjoyed heritage Isle of Wight tomatoes
and white crab meat', with avocado mousse
(smallish portions), roast cod in a fish bisque and
'a perfectly timed Hereford rib-eye steak with
Béarnaise sauce'. The service was 'bumpy' but
at breakfast (with scrambled egg on sourdough,
tempting pastries) 'a very personable manageress
provided prompt attention'.

Ellastone
Ashbourne DE6 2GZ

T: 01335 324275
E: hello@duncombearms.co.uk
W: duncombearms.co.uk

BEDROOMS: 10. In Walnut House
annexe, 2 family rooms, 1 suitable for
disabled.
OPEN: all year.
FACILITIES: bar, dining room, private
dining room, free Wi-Fi, no mobile
signal, garden (alfresco dining, fire
pit), car park, electric charging points,
bar and dining room wheelchair
accessible, adapted toilet.
BACKGROUND MUSIC: quiet in bar and
restaurant.
LOCATION: on B5032, 5 miles SW of
Ashbourne.
CHILDREN: all ages welcomed.
DOGS: allowed in some bedrooms
(£20 charge), bar (dog-friendly tables
for dining).
CREDIT CARDS: MC, Visa.
PRICES: per room B&B £160–£190.
À la carte £40, market menu (Mon–
Thurs) £18.50–£22.50.

ERMINGTON Devon

MAP 1:D4

PLANTATION HOUSE

There are no 'airs and graces' at this Georgian rectory-cum-hotel in the gentle South Hams countryside between Dartmoor and the South Devon coast. Bedrooms are contemporary in style with wicker chairs, a 'comfortable king-size bed'; some have abstract artwork, some bold colours. All are supplied with fresh-cut flowers, fruit, biscuits, mineral water, White Company bath products. New arrivals are welcomed with home-made cake and tea or coffee. Chef/patron Richard Hendey is a 'welcoming', genial and considerate host. He and John Raines cook 'uncommonly good' dishes with 'subtle combinations of flavours'. Their menus are an essay in localism and seasonality, with fish from nearby sea and river, home-grown and gathered ingredients. For instance, crisp-skinned, slow-cooked Devon duckling, caramelised St Clement jus, wild garlic dauphinoise, stir-fried broccoli, roast baby onion. There is a vegetarian option, and everything that can be is made in-house. At breakfast a 'wide-ranging choice' includes freshly squeezed orange juice, home-baked bread and croissants, 'the best ever' home-smoked haddock, and four-minute ten-second boiled eggs with asparagus and toast soldiers. 'A real treat.' (JB)

Totnes Road
Ermington
Plymouth PL21 9NS

T: 01548 831100
E: info@plantationhousehotel.co.uk
W: plantationhousehotel.co.uk

BEDROOMS: 8.
OPEN: all year, restaurant (dinner only) closed some Sun evenings.
FACILITIES: lounge/bar, 2 dining rooms, free Wi-Fi, in-room TV (Freeview), in-room massage, terrace, 1-acre garden, restaurant wheelchair accessible.
BACKGROUND MUSIC: in public rooms 'whenever required or when deemed suitable'.
LOCATION: 10 miles E of Plymouth.
CHILDREN: all ages welcomed.
DOGS: allowed in 1 bedroom, not in public rooms.
CREDIT CARDS: Amex, MC, Visa.
PRICES: per room B&B single £95–£195, double £110–£195. Set dinner £40 (items can be charged separately). 1-night bookings sometimes refused bank holiday weekends.

EVERSHOT Dorset

THE ACORN INN

Guide regulars were drawn to this former 16th-century coaching inn 'partly for its excellent location; partly because of the Thomas Hardy connection'. Perhaps its mention in Tess of the d'Urbervilles also attracted Scarlett Johansson and Darcey Bussell. Whatever the reason, the historic pub-with-rooms, managed by Richard and Natalie Legg for Red Carnation group (see Summer Lodge, Evershot, next entry), clearly has its devotees. Chef Robert Ndungu's seasonal fare, served in a dining room with a carved acorn fireplace, is described as 'straightforward' by one reader who enjoyed 'an enormous helping of whitebait', a 'good Thai green curry'. A lounge has leather chairs, shelves of books, period prints; the atmospheric bar a roaring fire, exposed stones, old photographs. Upstairs, bedrooms can be snug. 'Our room was fine with a super-king-size bed and sofa; a slightly cramped bathroom, but tons of hot water.' Other rooms might have an antique four-poster, a warm colour scheme; a spacious loft suite, in uplifting yellows and blues, has a double and single room, lounge, both bath and shower. Staff are 'helpful, friendly'; breakfast is 'excellent'. (JB, and others)

28 Fore Street
Evershot DT2 0JW

T: 01935 83228
E: stay@acorn-inn.co.uk
W: acorn-inn.co.uk

BEDROOMS: 10.
OPEN: all year.
FACILITIES: 2 bars, restaurant, lounge, free Wi-Fi, in-room TV (Sky, Freeview), skittle alley, beer garden, access to spa, gym at sister hotel opposite (£15 per day), bar and restaurant wheelchair accessible, toilet not adapted.
BACKGROUND MUSIC: in bar and restaurant.
LOCATION: in village, 10 miles S of Yeovil.
CHILDREN: all ages welcomed.
DOGS: allowed (£12 charge per dog per night, water bowls, towels, treats).
CREDIT CARDS: Amex, MC, Visa.
PRICES: per room B&B £105–£230. À la carte £35. Min. 2-night stay at weekends during peak season.

EVERSHOT Dorset

MAP 1:C6

SUMMER LODGE

'We will stay there again soon – if I can afford it,' wrote a reader after a first visit to this country house hotel (Relais & Châteaux) last year. Things must be going well – he's been back, to find everything 'pretty faultless'. A former dower house built in 1798, at the heart of Thomas Hardy's Wessex, it received an extension in 1893 to designs drawn up by Hardy himself. Today it is managed by Alexandra and Jack Mackenzie for Bea Tollman's Red Carnation group (see previous entry, The Acorn Inn). 'Jack Mackenzie showed us around, took us to our bedroom, helped carry our luggage.' That 'beautifully furnished' room had 'nice little touches' like 'fresh flowers, fruit, shortbread biscuits'. The styling is glamorous, with lavish drapes, room service, robes, slippers, REN toiletries. 'Staff are so professional, well trained and friendly.' Chef Steven Titman cooks 'a memorable meal' with local and home-grown produce. Maybe Cornish brill, sweetcorn purée, baby fennel, lobster mousseline, lobster cognac cream. There is a children's menu, and under-12s dine in the conservatory. A 'delightful' breakfast brings a great cold selection, rolls and croissants from the village bakery. (Ian Dewey)

9 Fore Street
Evershot DT2 0JR

T: 01935 482000
E: summerlodge@rchmail.com
W: summerlodgehotel.co.uk

BEDROOMS: 24, 6 in coach house, 3 in courtyard house, 5 in cottages, 1 on ground floor suitable for disabled.
OPEN: all year.
FACILITIES: lounge, drawing room, restaurant, conservatory, meeting room, free Wi-Fi, in-room TV (Sky), indoor pool, spa, civil wedding licence, 4-acre grounds, public rooms wheelchair accessible.
BACKGROUND MUSIC: in bar/whisky lounge.
LOCATION: 10 miles S of Yeovil.
CHILDREN: all ages welcomed.
DOGS: allowed in some bedrooms, lounge.
CREDIT CARDS: Amex, MC, Visa.
PRICES: per room B&B double £215–£615. Set-price dinner £56–£71, tasting menu £85, à la carte £38 (conservatory). 1-night bookings sometimes refused.

EXETER Devon

♛SOUTHERNHAY HOUSE   **NEW**

César award: romantic hotel of the year

'One of the loveliest hotel experiences I've had in a long time,' writes a Guide inspector in 2019, of a stay at this 'romantic' Georgian town house, 'on a pretty square' a stroll from the cathedral. Run as a hotel by Deborah Clark and Tony Orchard, it is promoted to a full entry. Arriving late for a dinner reservation, our reporter was met by 'the warmest, most helpful of individuals… they couldn't have been nicer'. Even 'intimate' bedrooms are not poky, while luxury ones have a super-king-size bed, big bathroom overlooking the garden, with bath and walk-in shower. All have a minibar, REN toiletries and comfy seating. 'Our room was exquisite, superbly designed, from the bag of local fudge to the info folder. There were no rough edges.' In the 'peaceful dining room', dinner was 'beautifully served' by 'charming' waiting staff. Short, intelligent menus include such dishes as heritage tomato salad, whipped feta, polenta croutons, basil vinaigrette. Breakfast, 'again beautifully presented', brings 'an individual bottle of orange juice, mini-pastry, mini-granola and yogurt' before a choice of hot dishes. 'Honestly, I couldn't fault it.'

36 Southernhay East
Exeter EX1 1NX

T: 01392 439000
E: home@southernhayhouse.com
W: southernhayhouse.com

BEDROOMS: 11.
OPEN: all year.
FACILITIES: bar menu, private dining, free Wi-Fi, in-room TV (Freeview), small lawn, veranda, terrace, civil wedding licence, public rooms wheelchair accessible.
BACKGROUND MUSIC: in public areas.
LOCATION: central Exeter.
CHILDREN: all ages welcomed.
DOGS: bar, terrace only.
CREDIT CARDS: MC, Visa.
PRICES: per room B&B £110–£283. À la carte £35.

SEE ALSO SHORTLIST

EXMOUTH Devon

MAP 1:D5

LYMPSTONE MANOR

'The food is, of course, the highlight, closely followed by the extremely comfortable room, lovely surroundings and professional, friendly service.' An 'excellent' birthday stay at Michael Caines's beautifully restored Georgian manor house, in grounds bordering the Exe estuary, was a treat for a regular reader this year. 'The welcome is smilingly professional,' relates another, who was given 'an informed tour of the house' on the way to a bedroom with estuary view. 'Hand-painted wallpaper of local birdlife impresses, ditto the artwork liberally scattered.' Each room has work by local watercolourist Rachel Toll, complimentary G & T, a capsule coffee machine. Some have a balcony, side-by-side copper baths, a terrace with soak tub and fire pit. There are three dining rooms and, at dinner, three menus – à la carte, 'Signature' (with veggie alternatives), and 'Taste of the Estuary'. Local produce shines in such dishes as Lyme Bay lemon sole, broccoli, button onions, white wine foam; Darts Farm beef fillets, horseradish and shallot confit, celeriac purée, mushrooms, red wine sauce. Mr Caines is 'very much a presence and clearly takes enormous pride in his venture'. (RB, and others)

Courtlands Lane
Exmouth EX8 3NZ

T: 01395 202040
E: reservations@lympstonemanor.
   co.uk
W: lympstonemanor.co.uk

BEDROOMS: 21. 5 on ground floor, 1 suitable for disabled.
OPEN: all year.
FACILITIES: 3 dining rooms, reception lounge, lounge, bar, 28-acre grounds (vineyard), free Wi-Fi, in-room TV (Freeview), civil wedding licence, public areas wheelchair accessible, adapted toilet.
BACKGROUND MUSIC: all day in public rooms.
LOCATION: in centre, close to waterfront.
CHILDREN: all ages welcomed (no under-5s in restaurant).
DOGS: in 2 bedrooms.
CREDIT CARDS: Amex, MC, Visa.
PRICES: per room B&B £340–£1,139, D,B&B £610–£1,409. 8-course tasting menu £155, seafood menu £145, à la carte £135 (discretionary service charge of 12½% is added to food).

FAVERSHAM Kent

♦ READ'S

César award: restaurant-with-rooms of the year

'From the moment the front door opened,
we were made to feel most welcome.' Guide
inspectors were deeply impressed this year
when visiting David and Rona Pitchford's
restaurant-with-rooms in a Georgian manor
house on the outskirts of this market town.
'The staff were professional and delightful,
friendly but not intrusive.' Traditional-style
bedrooms are furnished with antiques. 'Laurel
had a comfortable, handsome four-poster, a
well-proportioned, rather elegant bathroom.
The physical space and uncluttered style
transmit wonderful feelings of contentment.
However, it's when you visit the restaurant that
you comprehend just how special this place is.'
Classically trained Mr Pitchford exploits produce
from the walled kitchen garden, local meat and
game in his set-price menus. His 'superb' dishes
included 'mouth-wateringly thin slices of Serrano
ham, caramelised figs; salted beetroot with
Stilton-infused sauce; skate wing with capers and
lime'. Breakfast, in a 'bright, airy room', brought
'home-made jams and lemon curd', all prepared
with 'the same care, love, dedication. We look
forward to going back.' (LK, and others)

Macknade Manor
Canterbury Road
Faversham ME13 8XE

T: 01795 535344
E: rona@reads.com
W: reads.com

BEDROOMS: 6.
OPEN: all year except 4 days at
Christmas, first 2 weeks Jan, 2 weeks
Sept, restaurant closed Sun/Mon.
FACILITIES: sitting room/bar, 3 dining
rooms, free Wi-Fi, in-room TV
(Freeview), civil wedding licence,
4-acre garden (terrace, outdoor
dining), restaurant wheelchair
accessible.
BACKGROUND MUSIC: none.
LOCATION: ½ mile SE of Faversham.
CHILDREN: all ages welcomed.
DOGS: allowed in bedrooms only.
CREDIT CARDS: MC, Visa.
PRICES: per room B&B single
£140–£195, double £180–£210, D,B&B
single £185–£250, double £290–£320.
Set dinner £60, tasting menu £65.

FELIXKIRK Yorkshire

MAP 4:C4

THE CARPENTERS ARMS

You can order a York Brewery ale or a Pornstar Martini in the bar of this village inn, itself a winning cocktail of the traditional and the modish. A trusted reader sums it up as 'a fashionable place' for the well-to-do, 'to which locals come to eat'. The pub bedrooms are 'very comfortable', with a king-size double bed. More 'wow', indeed bow-wow, are dog-friendly Garden Rooms, set around a landscaped garden, each with private terrace and views over the Vale of Mowbray. They have a super-king-size bed, plush seating, perhaps a working fireplace. Some rooms interconnect; all have a minibar, fluffy towels, robes, H2K toiletries. Tracy Cooper's menus range from pub classics and sharing boards to such 'first-rate' dishes as rack of Yorkshire lamb, confit rosemary shallot, dauphinoise potato, spring cabbage, red wine reduction. Owners Provenance Inns place heavy emphasis on sourcing locally. Fruit and vegetables and cut flowers are from a garden above the village. The 'very tempting' breakfast includes freshly squeezed orange, rare breed pork sausages, home-made black pudding. 'A nice building in a great location with friendly and helpful staff… would stay again.' (RG, and others)

25% DISCOUNT VOUCHERS

Felixkirk
Thirsk YO7 2DP

T: 01845 537369
E: enquiries@
   thecarpentersarmsfelixkirk.com
W: thecarpentersarmsfelixkirk.com

BEDROOMS: 10. 8 in single-storey garden annexe, 1 suitable for disabled.
OPEN: all year.
FACILITIES: bar/sitting area, restaurant, private dining room, free Wi-Fi, in-room TV (Freeview), terrace (alfresco meals), garden, public rooms on ground floor wheelchair accessible, toilet adapted.
BACKGROUND MUSIC: 'generally at mealtimes' in bar and garden room.
LOCATION: in village 3 miles NE of Thirsk.
CHILDREN: all ages welcomed.
DOGS: welcomed in garden bedrooms, bar and some dining areas.
CREDIT CARDS: Amex, MC, Visa.
PRICES: per room B&B £120–£200, D,B&B £175–£255. À la carte £30.

FLEET Dorset

MOONFLEET MANOR

There is much to fire the young imagination
at this 17th-century manor house above Chesil
beach, the setting for John Meade Falkner's 1898
tale of smuggling, Moonfleet. Owned by Luxury
Family Hotels, with 'two swimming pools, a
huge games room', football pitch, fossil hunts and
more, it has 'everything children could want'.
The service and welcome are 'brilliant', though a
reader found occasional communication problems
with the 'keen-to-please' staff. 'Bedrooms were
very good, beds comfortable, every extra you
could need.' An Ofsted crèche frees parents for
pampering in the spa – or a glass of fizz on the
terrace. At night, 'You could have the children
eat between 5 and 6.30; the hotel then provides
a listening service, while adults go down and
have a nice meal'. A nice meal, indeed. Michael
Culley sources local ingredients for such dishes
as pan-fried Lyme Bay scallops; Jurassic Coast
lamb rump, dauphinoise potato, golden beetroot,
kalettes, red wine jus. A hot buffet breakfast,
'but they would also cook you individual dishes
from a menu. A good choice.' Picnic hampers
are available for the beach. This family hotel 'did
exactly what it said on the tin'. (CH, and others)

Fleet Road
Fleet DT3 4ED

т: 01305 786948
E: info@moonfleetmanorhotel.co.uk
w: moonfleetmanorhotel.co.uk

BEDROOMS: 36. 3 in coach house, 3 in
villa, 3 ground floor.
OPEN: all year.
FACILITIES: 2 lounges, snug, restaurant,
playroom, crèche, cinema, Wi-Fi,
in-room TV (Freeview), civil wedding
licence, indoor swimming pools,
terrace, 5-acre garden (play areas),
public areas wheelchair accessible.
BACKGROUND MUSIC: in restaurant.
LOCATION: 7 miles W of Weymouth.
CHILDREN: all ages welcomed, last
entrance for children in dining room
7.30 pm.
DOGS: allowed in bedrooms, on lead
in public rooms, not in restaurant or
play areas.
CREDIT CARDS: Amex, MC, Visa.
PRICES: per room B&B £109–£549,
D,B&B £179–£619. À la carte £40.
1-night bookings sometimes refused.

FOWEY Cornwall

MAP 1:D3

FOWEY HALL

♔ Previous César Winner

'An eligible, self-contained gentleman's residence, very unique… with every modern convenience.' So Kenneth Graham describes Toad Hall, which he modelled on this Victorian mansion, a baroque extravaganza with sumptuous interiors, overlooking the Fowey estuary. Now part of the Luxury Family Hotels group, it 'ticks all the luxury boxes', while being as child- and dog-friendly as you please. Family and interconnecting rooms sleep up to six. Mansion bedrooms are traditionally styled, those in the courtyard annexe more contemporary. 'A large mansion room had all the comforts, a super big bathroom, all lovely and warm.' There are shrimp nets, buckets and spades at the door, a zip wire and trampoline in the garden; a crèche, baby-listening, an indoor pool, a games room, cream teas, high teas; for adults the spa and a choice of family meals or fine dining. New chef Wesley Pratt uses produce from trusted local suppliers in such dishes as Cornish bouillabaisse with chive crème fraîche; crispy duck leg salad; vegetable and braised lentil curry – for children toad-in-the-hole and Mr Toad's shakes. At breakfast there is a 'groaning' buffet, 'fabulous' cooked dishes. 'We loved it so.'

Hanson Drive
Fowey PL23 1ET

T: 01726 833866
E: info@foweyhallhotel.co.uk
W: foweyhallhotel.co.uk

BEDROOMS: 36. 8 in coach house, some on ground floor, 2 suitable for disabled.
OPEN: all year.
FACILITIES: 2 lounges, library, 2 restaurants, free Wi-Fi, in-room TV (Freeview), crèche, games rooms, civil wedding licence, spa, 12-metre indoor pool, 5-acre grounds, public rooms wheelchair accessible, adapted toilet.
BACKGROUND MUSIC: in restaurants.
LOCATION: ½ mile from town centre.
CHILDREN: all ages welcomed.
DOGS: allowed in main house bedrooms (£15), in public areas on lead, not in restaurant.
CREDIT CARDS: Amex, MC, Visa.
PRICES: per room B&B £139–£249. Set dinner £30–£38, à la carte £43. 1-night bookings refused weekends.

SEE ALSO SHORTLIST

GITTISHAM Devon

MAP 1:C5

THE PIG AT COMBE

'A superb hotel,' reports a trusted reader in 2019, of Robin Hutson's Elizabethan manor at the end of a mile-long drive. 'Stunning grounds, a beautiful main house, helpful young staff. A lovely experience all round.' Rooms range from 'cheap and cheerful' with monsoon shower, and 'comfy-luxe' with shower and in-room bath, to the Laundry with a circular copper bath, the Horsebox, Hayloft, and cottages. 'We had a perfect little cottage with two generously sized bedrooms and bathrooms, living room, tiny kitchen with all we could need.' Public rooms have the signature artful scruffiness of the Pig group (see index), with comfy sofas in the 'magnificent' Great Hall-turned-bar. Guests eat in the panelled dining room; more simply in (or outside) The Folly, with wood-fired oven. The kitchen garden and Devon larder supply much fresh produce. 'Our starters were delicious (with a vegetable I didn't know existed), mains less good, but redeemed by perfect desserts (best sorbets ever).' After breakfast, a recommended walk affords sightings of 'pigs, ducks, hens, white doves, pheasants, little lambs roaming. We very much hope we can go back (our wallets permitting).' (Sybille Raphael, and others)

Gittisham
Honiton EX14 3AD

T: 01404 540400
E: reservations@thepighotel.com
W: thepighotel.com

BEDROOMS: 30. 10 in stable yard, 5 in cottages (2 for family), 3 rooms suitable for disabled.
OPEN: all year.
FACILITIES: bar, 2 lounges, restaurant, Folly (communal dining), private dining rooms, free Wi-Fi, in-room TV (Freeview), civil wedding licence, spa treatment rooms, 3,500-acre grounds, public rooms wheelchair accessible, adapted toilet.
BACKGROUND MUSIC: in public areas.
LOCATION: on outskirts of village.
CHILDREN: all ages welcomed.
DOGS: not allowed.
CREDIT CARDS: Amex, MC, Visa.
PRICES: room £150–£450. À la carte £35, continental breakfast £12, cooked £16. 1-night bookings sometimes refused.

GRASMERE Cumbria

MAP 4: inset C2

FOREST SIDE

⚜ Previous César Winner

'Simply awesome,' writes a reader this year,
about this 'fabulous' hotel on wooded slopes
overlooking Grasmere. A Victorian slate and
stone mansion and sometime walkers' hostel, it
has been all but rebuilt in modern-rustic style
by Andrew Wildsmith (see also Hipping Hall,
Cowan Bridge). Instead of partition walls and
mangy flooring, it now offers bespoke beds,
Herdwick wool carpets, Zoffany fabrics, Cole &
Son wallpaper. All bedrooms, though varying
in size, have the same little luxuries: fine china,
a 'fantastic' bathroom, Bramley toiletries.
Outside, monster rhododendrons have gone, the
kitchen garden is reborn, an old fernery is to be
restored. Michelin-starred chef Kevin Tickle
draws inspiration from the landscape in devising
tasting menus for omnivores and vegetarians,
which might run from golden beetroot, cuckoo
flower, smoked ewe's curd, puffy barley, to Yorkie
rhubarb in several guises, thick custard, brown
butter. 'Efficient, friendly staff. Amazing meal.'
Breakfast, including foraged mushrooms, duck
eggs, local bacon, was 'delightful while watching
red squirrels'. (Lynn Annette Middleton, and
others)

Keswick Road
Grasmere LA22 9RN

T: 015394 35250
E: info@theforestside.com
W: theforestside.com

BEDROOMS: 20. 1 suitable for disabled.
OPEN: all year, restaurant closed Mon/
Tues, and Wed lunch.
FACILITIES: lounges, bar, restaurant,
function/private dining rooms, civil
wedding licence, free Wi-Fi, in-room
TV (Freeview), terrace, 43-acre
grounds with kitchen garden, public
rooms wheelchair accessible, adapted
toilet.
BACKGROUND MUSIC: in public areas.
LOCATION: outskirts of village.
CHILDREN: all ages welcomed.
DOGS: allowed in some bedrooms
(max. 2 per room, £25 per dog
includes welcome pack).
CREDIT CARDS: Amex, MC, Visa.
PRICES: per room B&B £229–£419,
D,B&B £329–£559. Tasting menus £80
(six courses), £105 (ten courses).

GRASMERE Cumbria

MAP 4: inset C2

THE GRASMERE HOTEL   NEW

'Kevin and Nicki Winsland, with their daughters
Charlotte and Bex, have created a hotel of great
charm and warmth.' Readers enthuse over a stay
at this small Victorian country house with gardens
running down to the River Rothay, in a village
for ever associated with Wordsworth. 'From the
moment we were greeted by Charlotte, we felt
we were welcomed into their home as guests.'
The bedrooms, each named after a Lake poet,
are smart-contemporary, with bath or shower.
'Ruskin overlooks the car park at the front
with glorious views to Helm Crag and the hills
beyond.' It has 'a well-equipped bathroom', plenty
of hot water for a soak after a hike. Log fires
burn in a 'comfortable lounge' where drinks and
canapés are served before a four-course dinner
cooked by Kevin, with local, seasonal ingredients.
'We particularly enjoyed oak-smoked wild
Lakeland venison, celeriac, apple slaw, dressed
with chocolate vinaigrette. Roast breast of corn-
fed guineafowl, black garlic, salsify, kale and wild
mushrooms were cooked to perfection.' Breakfast
'is the same high standard'. Now, 'One question:
why is the hotel on the Shortlist?' Answer: it no
longer is. (Bob and Jean Henry)

Broadgate
Grasmere LA22 9TA

T: 015394 35277
E: info@grasmerehotel.co.uk
W: grasmerehotel.co.uk

BEDROOMS: 11. Some on ground floor.
OPEN: all year except 31 Dec–26 Jan.
FACILITIES: two lounges, restaurant,
free Wi-Fi, in-room TV (Freeview),
½-acre garden, unsuitable for disabled.
BACKGROUND MUSIC: in lounge and
restaurant during mealtimes.
LOCATION: in village.
CHILDREN: over-10s welcomed.
DOGS: allowed, by arrangement, in
some ground-floor bedrooms, not in
public rooms.
CREDIT CARDS: MC, Visa.
PRICES: per room B&B single £69–£74,
double £126–£158. Set dinner £35
(£29 for residents). 2-night min. stay
normally required (check for 1-night
availability), Sat and bank holiday
Sun night reservations must include
dinner.

GRASMERE Cumbria

MAP 4: inset C2

OAK BANK

An anniversary in 2020, and a valediction: a century after this Victorian private house first opened to paying guests, and 13 years after they took over, Glynis and Simon Wood are preparing to retire. They will be missed by those readers who have 'stayed many times and always enjoyed the visit'. The spruce and contemporary interiors include bedrooms ranging from the smallest 'standard' with shower room, to a spacious 'superior'; all have still and sparkling water, Bath House toiletries. Second-floor superior-view rooms have a double-ended bath with rain shower over; king-size beds perfectly positioned to enjoy spectacular mountain views through big windows. A fire burns in the newly refurbished lounge with huge, modern armchairs, neutral decor, while in the dining room and conservatory, Matt Clarke's 'delicious and imaginative gourmet' dishes include Goosnargh duck breast, spring roll, king carrot, tenderstem broccoli, soy and sesame jus. Breakfast brings fresh-baked bread and croissants, a daily smoothie, a kipper. As we go to press, the hotel is up for sale. We hope that whoever follows will continue to offer the fine hospitality of these 'very friendly hosts'. (WS, and others)

25% DISCOUNT VOUCHERS

Broadgate
Grasmere LA22 9TA

T: 015394 35217
E: info@lakedistricthotel.co.uk
W: lakedistricthotel.co.uk

BEDROOMS: 13. 1 on ground floor.
OPEN: all year except 15–26 Dec, 5–23 Jan, 2–13 Aug.
FACILITIES: lounge, bar, restaurant, conservatory dining room, free Wi-Fi, in-room TV (Freeview), ½-acre garden, unsuitable for disabled.
BACKGROUND MUSIC: classical at breakfast, 'easy listening' at dinner.
LOCATION: just outside village centre.
CHILDREN: all ages welcomed (not under 10 in restaurant or public rooms after 6 pm).
DOGS: allowed in 3 bedrooms, front lounge.
CREDIT CARDS: MC, Visa.
PRICES: per room B&B single £82–£156, double £82–£190. À la carte £38, tasting menu £65. 1-night bookings usually refused weekends.

GRASSINGTON Yorkshire   MAP 4:D3

GRASSINGTON HOUSE   NEW

'Grassington House provided all I could want for
a most enjoyable break in this busy but beautiful
village.' A full entry this year for Sue and John
Rudden's restaurant-with-rooms overlooking the
cobbled square. Behind the slightly austere facade
of a Georgian limestone house lie lavish interiors.
Bedrooms range from the modest – 'a small but
comfortable second-floor double', say, with 'a very
powerful shower' – to No. 6, the full Hollywood,
with chandelier, ornate silvered furniture,
freestanding claw-footed bath and separate
shower room. All have home-made biscuits, robes,
organic toiletries. John Rudden is 'a very inventive
chef'. Witness fillet mignon with rag pudding,
cabbage faggot, carrot purée, red wine jus. 'Rag
pudding is his own creation: a parcel of shredded
beef wrapped in suet, it looks and tastes delicious.'
A shame, however, about the restaurant's piped
pop. Attention to detail is evident at breakfast,
when 'even the butter was home-made, and
freshly squeezed juices came in generous glasses.
The bacon and sausages came from John's pigs,
the salmon was smoked on the premises. It's
rare for breakfast to be so good that the memory
lingers all day.' (Trevor Lockwood)

5 The Square
Grassington
Skipton BD23 5AQ

T: 01756 752406
E: bookings@grassingtonhouse.co.uk
W: grassingtonhouse.co.uk

BEDROOMS: 9.
OPEN: all year except Christmas Day.
FACILITIES: lounge, bar, restaurant, free
Wi-Fi, in-room TV, civil wedding
licence, function facilities, terrace,
cookery classes, parking, public rooms
wheelchair accessible.
BACKGROUND MUSIC: in public areas.
LOCATION: in village square, 16 mins'
drive from Skipton.
CHILDREN: all ages welcomed.
DOGS: allowed in bar and terrace only.
CREDIT CARDS: MC, Visa.
PRICES: per room B&B single £117,
double £135–£175. Tasting menu £50
for 2, market menu (lunch Mon–Sat,
early dinner Tues–Thurs) £18–£20,
à la carte £30.

GURNARD Isle of Wight

MAP 2:E2

THE LITTLE GLOSTER

A Scandinavian breeze flows through this pretty corner of the Isle of Wight. Visitors in 2019 share Guide inspectors' enthusiasm for the 'lovely, fresh food', 'amenable service', and sweeping Solent views from inside and out at this buzzing restaurant-with-rooms set right on the water. Ben Cooke's 'short, tasty menu' is served in the open-plan, wood-floored dining room, all whitewashed walls and lots of light: perhaps seared white fish, sprouting broccoli, fennel; Uffa ricotta and Parmesan ravioli, sage butter, toasted hazelnuts. The Scandi feel extends from the restaurant into the three smart bedrooms in an adjoining building. Each has 'fabulous' sea views, and the two at the front look out from a private garden terrace or a large decked balcony. Rooms have 'generous' refreshments (espresso machine, teapigs tea, fresh milk, jelly babies), and binoculars to track yachting activity or seabirds. Wake up to the sound of the sea, and a 'well-cooked' breakfast, ordered the night before, perhaps avocado and poached egg on sourdough dusted with chilli and mint, fresh pastries, a full English. Afterwards, enjoy 'great walks' to Cowes along the blustery promenade.

31 Marsh Road
Gurnard PO31 8JQ

T: 01983 298776
E: info@thelittlegloster.com
w: thelittleglosterrooms.com

BEDROOMS: 3. All in adjoining building.
OPEN: all year except 4–20 Nov, 23–26 Dec, 30 Dec–13 Feb, restaurant closed Sun evening, Mon–Wed Oct–Apr, Sun evening and Mon/Tues June–Sept.
FACILITIES: bar, restaurant, free Wi-Fi, in-room TV (Freeview), seaside garden, public rooms wheelchair accessible.
BACKGROUND MUSIC: in dining room.
LOCATION: on the coast, a 5-min. drive west of West Cowes.
CHILDREN: all ages welcomed.
DOGS: allowed in restaurant (not bedrooms).
CREDIT CARDS: MC, Visa.
PRICES: per room B&B £130–£240. À la carte £35. 1-night bookings sometimes refused.

HALFORD Warwickshire   MAP 3:D6

THE OLD MANOR HOUSE   `NEW`

Surrounded by 'lovely grounds' rolling down to
the River Stour, this 'beautiful, well-preserved'
16th-century manor house enters the Guide this
year on the urging of trusted readers. High marks
for the 'timeless, relaxing atmosphere' and 'warm
professional welcome'. The 'project' of hands-on
Jane Pusey; she is helped by husband, William,
and Gertie and Summer, 'a pair of flat-coated
retrievers of impeccable manners'. Books, curios
and antiques fill the large, elegant drawing room.
'It feels like staying at a friend's home.' Bedrooms
are full of character: mullioned windows, wonky
exposed beams, a chest-of-drawers-sized alcove.
'Our room was huge, with a very comfortable
king-size bed draped in crisp bedlinen,
independently controlled heating, good lighting;
fluffy towels, a bathroom with bath and powerful
separate shower.' Good secondary glazing ensured
a perfectly quiet night. One quibble: 'Not enough
seating, given the size of the room.' 'Breakfast
had no real choice but an excellent full English
of local produce, plus muesli, superb home-made
preserves (and a small jar of Marmite, much to my
pleasure).' No fresh orange juice, but 'very good
coffee'. (Sue and John Jenkinson)

Halford
Shipston-on-Stour CV36 5BT

T: 01789 740264
E: oldmanorhalford@btinternet.com
W: oldmanor-halford.co.uk

BEDROOMS: 3.
OPEN: 28 Feb–14 Dec.
FACILITIES: hall, dining room, drawing
room, free Wi-Fi, in-room TV
(Freeview), 3½-acre grounds.
BACKGROUND MUSIC: none.
LOCATION: northern edge of village.
CHILDREN: over-5s welcomed.
DOGS: allowed (confirm when
booking), not in dining room.
CREDIT CARDS: MC, Visa.
PRICES: per room B&B single £65–£85,
double £110–£120. Phone to check for
1-night bookings.

HALNAKER Sussex

MAP 2:E3

THE OLD STORE

There are treats in store for guests behind the chequerboard facade of this B&B, in a pretty South Downs village close to Chichester. Patrick and Heather Birchenough, the 'accommodating, very thoughtful' hosts, welcome new arrivals with tea and 'delicious' cakes ('the whole downstairs smelled pleasantly of baking'). The sitting room is snug: a sofa and armchair, a 'massive model train in a display case'. One bedroom is on the ground floor; the others are reached by 'quite narrow' stairs. Some have beams; one looks across farmland to Chichester. The look is perhaps a little dated – here a wicker sofa, there a padded headboard. However, a 'gorgeous' bed, a 'wonderful walk-in shower', toiletries from 'a local soap maker', fresh milk and a 'nicely equipped hospitality tray' are 'the things that really matter' (shame about the instant coffee). Breakfast is served in 'a sun-filled room' with old milk bottles on a beam recalling the building's past as a village grocer's. shop. The buffet offers fresh fruit salad, 'really tasty fresh-pressed apple juice', home-made bread and preserves, smoked salmon, pancakes with bacon and maple syrup. The muesli is 'possibly the nicest in England'.

Stane Street
Halnaker
Chichester PO18 0QL

T: 01243 531977
E: theoldstore4@aol.com
W: theoldstoreguesthouse.co.uk

BEDROOMS: 7. 1 on ground floor with step between bathroom and bedroom.
OPEN: Mar–Dec.
FACILITIES: lounge, breakfast room, free Wi-Fi, in-room TV (Freeview), ¼-acre garden with seating.
BACKGROUND MUSIC: none.
LOCATION: 4 miles NE of Chichester.
CHILDREN: all ages welcomed.
DOGS: not allowed.
CREDIT CARDS: MC, Visa.
PRICES: per person B&B single £63–£120, double £85–£125, family from £115 (higher for Goodwood 'Festival of Speed' and 'Revival' meetings). 1-night bookings refused weekends, sometimes other nights in high season.

HAMBLETON Rutland

MAP 2:B3

HAMBLETON HALL

♥Previous César Winner

'I find it difficult to make any original comments,' writes a Guide regular after this year's visit to Tim and Stefa Hart's much-loved hotel (Relais & Châteaux) with grounds reaching down to Rutland Water. 'All the superlatives have been used by other guests. We have never before stayed in such a comfortable hotel with such helpful staff and imaginative food.' Another trusted reader adds, 'The standard of service is beyond anything we could ever imagine. The team all go the extra mile.' Built as a fox-hunting lodge for a wealthy brewer in 1881, and later as a society hotspot, it has elegant, individually designed bedrooms with sumptuous fabrics and richly patterned wallpaper. Most overlook the lake; all have garden views, fresh flowers, and biscuits from the hotel's famous bakery. In the restaurant (after 37 years, this holds the UK's longest-retained Michelin star), chef Aaron Patterson's sophisticated, locally sourced, seasonal menus include Launde Farm lamb, Mediterranean vegetables, ewe's curd. 'Long may Hambleton last,' one guest writes. 'We suspect it will.' Hart's Hotel, Nottingham (see entry) is a sister hotel. (David Bartley, Caroline Faircliff, and others)

Hambleton
Oakham LE15 8TH

T: 01572 756991
E: hotel@hambletonhall.com
W: hambletonhall.com

BEDROOMS: 17. 2-bedroom suite in cottage.
OPEN: all year.
FACILITIES: lift, hall, drawing room/bar, restaurant, 2 private dining rooms, free Wi-Fi, in-room TV (Sky), civil wedding licence, 17-acre grounds (tennis, swimming pool (heated May–Sept), croquet, vegetable garden), public rooms wheelchair accessible.
BACKGROUND MUSIC: none.
LOCATION: 3 miles SE of Oakham.
CHILDREN: all ages welcomed.
DOGS: allowed in bedrooms (not unattended), hall, not in public rooms.
CREDIT CARDS: Amex, MC, Visa.
PRICES: per room B&B single £210–£225, double £295–£750. Set dinner £78, tasting menu £95. 1-night bookings normally refused weekends (call to check).

HAROME Yorkshire

MAP 4:D4

THE PHEASANT

'So glad it's in your guide – keep it in.' A strong
endorsement this year for Jacquie Pern and
Peter Neville's hotel overlooking a duck pond.
It occupies a former smithy, village shop and
barns, brought together as one harmonious
whole. The bedroom styling is contemporary
and confident, busy with patterns. All have a
fridge with fresh milk, complimentary sloe gin,
Cowshed toiletries. The three lounges are 'so
comfy and well maintained'; one, by the bar, 'cosy
with a designer wood-burner'. There Swim in
the indoor pool, or relax on seats under the apple
tree. There is a bar and lounge menu, while, in the
restaurant, Peter Neville's menus, for omnivores,
vegetarians and 'chicks', showcase home-grown
and Yorkshire produce, in such dishes as North
York Moors pheasant pie, savoy cabbage, roasted
quince, barley, smoked butter potatoes. 'The
staff are young, enthusiastic, hard working.' Pop
radio music one night jarred, but breakfast in the
conservatory was 'bathed in Classic FM'. And
what a breakfast! 'Possibly the best ever', with
'extensive buffet', freshly squeezed orange juice.
'A first-class stay, a lovely place indeed.' (Peter and
Anne Davies, RG)

Mill Street
Harome YO62 5JG

T: 01439 771241
E: reservations@thepheasanthotel.
    com
W: thepheasanthotel.com

BEDROOMS: 16. 3 on ground floor,
4 in courtyard, 1 in cottage, 1 room
in hotel suitable for disabled.
OPEN: all year.
FACILITIES: bar, lounge, conservatory,
restaurant, free Wi-Fi, in-room TV
(Freeview), civil wedding licence,
heated indoor swimming pool, terrace,
public areas wheelchair accessible.
BACKGROUND MUSIC: in public areas.
LOCATION: village centre.
CHILDREN: all ages welcomed.
DOGS: allowed in 2 bedrooms, on
terrace and in garden, not in public
rooms.
CREDIT CARDS: MC, Visa.
PRICES: per room B&B single
£105–£240, double £190–£280, D,B&B
single £145–£280, double £270–£360.
Tasting menu £75, à la carte £46.

HAROME Yorkshire

MAP 4:D4

THE STAR INN

♛ Previous César Winner

In 'a lovely village' on the edge of the North Yorkshire moors, Andrew Pern's 'stylish old inn' is a mix-and-thatch of ancient cruck-framed pub, dining extension, and lodgings in a converted building opposite. The 'characterful' accommodation presents difficult choices. Will it be a spa bath or a snooker table? Perhaps that ground-floor room with upright piano? The low-beamed bar is similarly eccentric, with oak furniture by Robert (Mouseman) Thompson, and a coffee loft above. The great draw, however, is Mr Pern's Michelin-starred cooking of local, home-grown, shot or foraged ingredients, in such dishes as Star hive honey-glazed gammon, spiced pineapple, smoked bacon ice cream, sage-cured egg yolk, chestnut mushroom shavings, sauce 'Perpignan'. Service was 'first class'. Pull up a button-back chair in the colourful restaurant, or eat alfresco – 'in summer the garden is a wonderful place to lunch'. An 'amazing' breakfast, served in The Wheelhouse, under a high, beamed ceiling, 'at a vast circular table, like something out of Camelot', included 'great-tasting cooked options', smoked salmon, rollmops, juices. 'We can't wait to go back.' (RC, SH)

High Street
Harome
Helmsley YO62 5JE

T: 01439 770397
E: admin@thestarinnatharome.co.uk
w: thestaratharome.co.uk

BEDROOMS: 9. All in Cross House Lodge, opposite, 4 on ground floor.
OPEN: all year, restaurant closed midday Mon, last orders Sun 6 pm.
FACILITIES: lounge, restaurant, The Wheelhouse private dining room, free Wi-Fi in reception, in-room TV (Freeview), civil wedding licence, terrace, 2-acre garden, restaurant wheelchair accessible.
BACKGROUND MUSIC: in lounge and dining room.
LOCATION: village centre.
CHILDREN: all ages welcomed.
DOGS: allowed in 3 bedrooms by arrangement, not in restaurant or pub.
CREDIT CARDS: MC, Visa.
PRICES: per room B&B £150–£270. Market menu £20–£25, à la carte £60, tasting menu £85.

HARWICH Essex

MAP 2:C5

THE PIER AT HARWICH

You can sit on the terrace at the Milsom family's hotel overlooking harbour and estuary, and watch supper being landed. There is such a sea-going feel about Harwich, this year celebrating the 400th anniversary of the Pilgrim Fathers' Mayflower voyage, captained by local man Christopher Jones. Bedrooms, in the main Victorian building and the former Angel pub, range from smallish to the Mayflower Suite with seating area and telescope. They have a king-size bed, 'quality tea and coffee', fresh milk in a minibar, posh toiletries, but may feel slightly 'corporate'. Soundproofing could be better. The young staff are 'willing, open in manner'. A Gin Library and small plates are found in the NAVYÄRD bar, while in the first-floor brasserie with 'industrial lamps, leather banquettes, an attractive exposed-brick wall', the menu includes Colchester oysters, Harwich crab; feather blade of beef, Parmesan polenta, hispi cabbage, red wine jus, salsa verde. Breakfast, served by a 'lovely, bustly woman, quick with jokes', brought 'expertly fried egg, avocado at peak ripeness' for a Guide insider – for others, maybe, smoked haddock rarebit, or omelette with San Daniele ham, smoked Cheddar, rocket.

25% DISCOUNT VOUCHERS

The Quay
Harwich CO12 3HH

T: 01255 241212
E: pier@milsomhotels.com
W: milsomhotels.com

BEDROOMS: 14. 7 in annexe, 1 on ground floor suitable for disabled.
OPEN: all year.
FACILITIES: bar, lounge (in annexe), restaurant, private dining room, small lift, free Wi-Fi, in-room TV (Sky, BT, Freeview), civil wedding licence, balcony, small front terrace; restaurant, bar wheelchair accessible.
BACKGROUND MUSIC: in the bar.
LOCATION: on quay, in old town.
CHILDREN: all ages welcomed.
DOGS: allowed in bedrooms, bar, lounge.
CREDIT CARDS: Amex, MC, Visa.
PRICES: per room B&B £135–£300. À la carte £35.

HASTINGS Sussex

MAP 2:E5

THE OLD RECTORY

Trusted friends of the Guide rated this boutique B&B, on the fringe of the Old Town, 'the nicest' they had stayed in. The Georgian rectory, standing behind an apron of front garden, has been transformed by its designer/owner, Lionel Copley, who also co-owns Swan House (see next entry). Bare wooden floors and muted paint finishes mix with bespoke hand-painted wallpapers, artfully distressed and antique furniture with modern, sometimes quirky pieces. A chair 'made entirely of deer skin (ears still in place)' worried one reader, but who would not love Ebenezer bedroom with its wall of Wedgwood calendar plates, or All Saints Suite, with vintage French bed, bathroom and wet room? All rooms come with fresh milk and home-baked biscuits. Tracey-Anne Cook and Helen Styles are the 'dynamic, warm, friendly' managers, while in the hand-painted breakfast room, with doors open on to the beautiful walled rear garden on fine days, a locally sourced menu includes organic apple juice, smoked haddock, a kipper with parsley butter, tomatoes with basil, home-made sausages and preserves, French toast with vanilla strawberries: fuel for a day in Hastings Country Park or a stroll along the beach.

25% DISCOUNT VOUCHERS

Harold Road
Hastings TN35 5ND

T: 01424 422410
E: info@theoldrectoryhastings.co.uk
W: theoldrectoryhastings.co.uk

BEDROOMS: 8. One 2-bed suite.
OPEN: all year except 1 week Christmas, 1 week Jan, open for New Year.
FACILITIES: 2 lounges (honesty bar), breakfast room, treatment rooms, sauna, free Wi-Fi, in-room TV (Freeview), civil wedding licence, 1-acre walled garden, unsuitable for disabled.
BACKGROUND MUSIC: in breakfast room and main lounge.
LOCATION: edge of Old Town (limited parking spaces, complimentary permits).
CHILDREN: not under 10.
DOGS: not allowed.
CREDIT CARDS: Amex, MC, Visa.
PRICES: per room B&B single £90–£115, double £110–£175. 1-night bookings refused weekends.

HASTINGS Sussex   MAP 2:E5

SWAN HOUSE

'Possibly the friendliest place I have ever stayed in,' writes a reader in 2019, of Brendan McDonagh's 'exquisitely beautiful' Tudor black-and-white B&B in a quiet Old Town cul-de-sac. 'Every one of the bedrooms is perfection,' says another, who stayed every week for a year. 'From the moment you arrive there is a warm welcome and you are offered refreshments.' The front door leads straight into the lounge/breakfast room, 'with roaring log fire in winter', blond sofas, bare floorboards. Designer flourishes are the work of Brendan's partner, Lionel Copley (see previous entry, The Old Rectory). A ground-floor bedroom has double wooden doors on to a pretty patio garden. Upstairs rooms, furnished 'in a way that suits the property's old style', have beams, wonky floors, 'super-comfy bed with the highest quality sheets'. Brendan cooks breakfast to order with 'home-made preserves and freshly squeezed juices. All the food is delicious but I can highly recommend the eggy bread with bacon!' There are many nearby options for eating out and, of course, 'Brendan is always helpful with dinner recommendations and sorting taxis'. 'Highly and warmly recommended.' (Duncan Sprott, and others)

25% DISCOUNT VOUCHERS

1 Hill Street
Hastings TN34 3HU

T: 01424 430014
E: info@swanhousehastings.co.uk
w: swanhousehastings.co.uk

BEDROOMS: 5. 1 on ground floor, 2 adjoining.
OPEN: all year except 24–26 Dec.
FACILITIES: lounge/breakfast room, free Wi-Fi, in-room TV, patio garden, secure allocated parking 10 mins' walk away (permits supplied), unsuitable for disabled.
BACKGROUND MUSIC: none.
LOCATION: in Old Town, near seafront.
CHILDREN: 5 and upwards in Renaissance Suite, by prior arrangement.
DOGS: not allowed.
CREDIT CARDS: Amex, MC, Visa.
PRICES: per room B&B single £99–£110, double £120–£150. 1-night bookings usually refused weekends but check, £10 supplement for Sat night only, if available.

HATHERSAGE Derbyshire

THE GEORGE HOTEL

The legend of Robin Hood runs through the
village where Little John is said to be buried, and
another merry man, veteran hotelier Eric Marsh,
owns this ancient coaching inn. 'Still a favourite'
of trusted readers, it is a place with heart and
character. Log fires burn in public rooms and
'the pluses far outweigh the minuses', a regular
visitor tells us. Although one guest had qualms
about the service, others found it 'very friendly'
with 'attention to detail'. Front rooms overlook a
main road, those at the back have 'not such a good
view, but are very quiet'. You can eat casually
from the lounge menu (grills, sandwiches, pasta),
with choices for children, or more formally in
the dining room, for such dishes as chargrilled
Castlegate rib-eye steak, portobello mushroom,
tomatoes, hand-cut chips, chimichurri; seafood
mixed grill; spiced pumpkin katsu, sticky rice,
coconut curry. It was 'fine but not outstanding',
though one reader was impressed with 'the way
they dealt with my gluten-free diet'. Everyone
agrees that 'breakfast was good'. 'The highlight
of the day, including pancakes with blueberry
compote.' (Steve Hur, Peter Anderson, and others)

Main Road
Hathersage S32 1BB

T: 01433 650436
E: info@george-hotel.net
W: george-hotel.net

BEDROOMS: 24.
OPEN: all year.
FACILITIES: lounge/bar, restaurant,
2 function rooms, free Wi-Fi, in-room
TV, civil wedding licence, courtyard,
restaurant wheelchair accessible, no
adapted toilet.
BACKGROUND MUSIC: light jazz in
restaurant.
LOCATION: in village centre, parking.
CHILDREN: all ages welcomed.
DOGS: not allowed.
CREDIT CARDS: Amex, MC, Visa.
PRICES: per room B&B single £85–£143,
double £95–£184. Set menu £33.50–
£39.95, early bird menu £16.85–£20
(weekdays, 6.30–7.30), à la carte £35.
1-night bookings sometimes refused.

HEREFORD Herefordshire   MAP 3:D4

CASTLE HOUSE

'It is difficult to find any fault,' write trusted
readers this year, after staying at the Watkins
family's 'individual, independent, truly welcoming
hotel'. Occupying a Regency villa near the
cathedral, it has a wide choice of bedrooms,
some in the main hotel, some in a Georgian
town house. All have artwork, antiques, milk in
a mini-fridge, fruit, flowers, sherry, L'Occitane
toiletries. Some have garden access, an underfloor-
heated bathroom. 'Room 25 was smallest in
the town house but wonderfully and elegantly
fitted.' Staff were 'welcoming, helpful, smiley'.
In the restaurant, Gabor Katona's 'excellent'
dishes use 'local ingredients, many grown in
the kitchen garden of the owner's farm' to give
classic British fare a contemporary twist. For
instance, braised venison haunch, blackberries,
roast squash, hazelnut and parsley dumplings.
You can eat more informally in the brasserie, bar
and alfresco. 'Superb breakfasts included the best
scrambled egg I've ever had in a hotel.' Beside the
terraced garden, in the old moat – all that remains
of Hereford Castle – 'the sight of swimming
otters was a highlight of our visit'. (Sue and John
Jenkinson, Stephen and Pauline Glover)

25% DISCOUNT VOUCHERS

Castle Street
Hereford HR1 2NW

T: 01432 356321
E: reception@castlehse.co.uk
W: castlehse.co.uk

BEDROOMS: 24. 8 in town house (a short
walk away), some on ground floor,
1 suitable for disabled.
OPEN: all year.
FACILITIES: lift (in main house only),
lounge, bar/bistro, restaurant, free
Wi-Fi, in-room TV (Freeview), civil
wedding licence, terraced garden,
ground floor wheelchair accessible.
BACKGROUND MUSIC: occasionally in
restaurant, bistro and reception.
LOCATION: central.
CHILDREN: all ages welcomed.
DOGS: not allowed except in garden,
on a lead.
CREDIT CARDS: Amex, MC, Visa.
PRICES: per room B&B single
£140–£210, double £155–£250, D,B&B
double £200–£305. Tasting menu £50,
à la carte (restaurant) £40, (bistro) £30.

HETTON Yorkshire
MAP 4:D3

THE ANGEL INN

'A peaceful, scenic place to unwind', amid 'beautiful surroundings' in a Dales village, the Angel continues its ascent from drovers' inn to foodie heaven. Touted as the original gastropub, it is now owned by Michael and Johanna Wignall with James and Josephine Wellock. Mr Wignall brings the cachet of two Michelin stars, and his dishes are certainly more gastro than pub. Thick chips are on offer, but instead of battered fish expect, maybe, skrei cod, haricot blanc, sea vegetables, gnocchi cassoulet. There's a six-course tasting menu, and other menus for vegetarians and children. Bedrooms and suites are in a converted barn and cottage. Our inspector had a 'light and attractive' cottage room, with 'ivory walls' and fine china on the tea tray, 'a small terrace for alfresco refreshment'. There was a 'well-stocked honesty bar', a bathroom with bath and shower, Rituals toiletries. At dinner, 'first-class trout salad and perfectly cooked, well-presented turbot' were enjoyed. The welcome was 'warm and friendly'. Breakfast brought such unusual offerings as beetroot black pudding with the full veggie. Despite a few teething problems, we come down firmly on the side of The Angel.

25% DISCOUNT VOUCHERS

Hetton
Skipton BD23 6LT

T: 01756 730263
E: reservations@angelhetton.co.uk
W: angelhetton.co.uk

BEDROOMS: 9. 5 in barn conversion, 4 in cottage, 1 on ground floor suitable for disabled.
OPEN: all year except 2–31 Jan, rooms and restaurant closed Tues, Wed.
FACILITIES: bar, restaurant, private dining room, civil wedding licence, terrace, in-room TV (Freeview), free Wi-Fi, some public areas wheelchair accessible.
BACKGROUND MUSIC: none.
LOCATION: village centre.
CHILDREN: all ages welcome, children's menu.
DOGS: allowed in 2 bedrooms and bar.
CREDIT CARDS: Amex, MC, Visa.
PRICES: per room B&B £130–£185, D,B&B £230–£285. Tasting menu £65, à la carte £45 (vegetarian £34).

HINTON ST GEORGE Somerset

MAP 1:C6

THE LORD POULETT ARMS   NEW

'A wonderful, historic pub at the heart of a magnificent village in deepest countryside.' The thatched Lord Poulett Arms is now under new ownership – a sister to The Beckford Arms, Tisbury, and The Talbot Inn, Mells (see entries). Our inspectors stepped inside to find it 'heaving'. Public rooms are 'splendidly atmospheric, with a spectacular central fireplace', furniture of 'character and age'. All bedrooms have a king- or super-king-size bed, comfy seating, Bramley toiletries. Two are small, with separate bathroom. A 'spectacular' room, reached by an external staircase, 'could have hosted a party. The style was rustic chic, but the modern shower room had everything you might wish for', not to speak of a retro in-room bath on 'lion paws'. Beyond the window the clematis was in full cry. Dinner was served by 'enchanting waitresses'. Philip Verden cooks a seasonally changing menu of local ingredients. 'Twice-baked goat's cheese soufflé was exquisite, the Mendip lamb tender and cooked as requested; tonka bean crème brûlée with pistachio ice cream delicious.' Breakfast brings a 'well-stocked buffet', smoked salmon, the full Somerset. 'If you like staying in a pub, this is as good as it gets.'

High Street
Hinton St George TA17 8SE

T: 01460 73149
E: info@lordpoulettarms.com
W: lordpoulettarms.com

BEDROOMS: 6. 4 with en suite, 2 with private bathroom, 1 for family.
OPEN: all year except 25 Dec.
FACILITIES: bar, restaurant, private dining room, in-room TV (Freeview), free Wi-Fi, 1-acre grounds, unsuitable for disabled.
BACKGROUND MUSIC: throughout pub.
LOCATION: in village, 4 miles NW of Crewkerne.
CHILDREN: all ages welcomed.
DOGS: in 1 bedroom and all public areas.
CREDIT CARDS: MC, Visa.
PRICES: B&B per room single £75–£95, double £85–£120, D,B&B £145–£170. À la carte £35.

HOLT Norfolk

MAP 2:A5

MORSTON HALL

'The drama of dinner is played out in fine style' at Tracy and Galton Blackiston's 'gorgeous' restaurant-with-rooms in a coastal village. The house, dating in parts from 1640, shows its venerable age in the beams in bedrooms, each named after a local stately home. Characterful Mannington is under the eaves. Blickling (Anne Boleyn's birthplace) has a 'great' bathroom with roll-top bath and walk-in shower. Rooms in the garden pavilion have a seating area with a coal-effect fire, a private terrace – Lavender's seating area is scented by the real thing. The staff are 'warm, friendly and enthusiastic', wrote a reader who rates the place 'top of my list' among Michelin-starred restaurants. Cooked in tandem with Greg Anderson, Mr Blackiston's daily-changing, seven-course menus – including such dishes as wild Stiffkey sea bass, whey butter sauce, or Richard Vaughan's Middle White suckling pig – are theatrically presented in conservatory dining rooms: 'The young waiters (all wearing gloves) have to explain each serving.' Breakfast brings freshly squeezed orange juice, locally pressed apple juice, locally smoked haddock, home-smoked salmon. Seal-spotting boat trips depart from close by. (JB)

Morston
Holt NR25 7AA

T: 01263 741041
E: reception@morstonhall.com
W: morstonhall.com

BEDROOMS: 13. 6 on ground floor, 100 yds from house, in garden pavilion, 1, in main house, suitable for disabled.
OPEN: all year except 24–26 Dec, 1–31 Jan.
FACILITIES: reading lounge, sun lounge, conservatory, restaurant, free Wi-Fi, in-room TV (Freeview), civil wedding licence, 3-acre garden (pond, croquet), restaurant wheelchair accessible, adapted toilet.
BACKGROUND MUSIC: none.
LOCATION: 2 miles W of Blakeney.
CHILDREN: all ages welcomed, children's suppers.
DOGS: allowed in bedrooms, some public rooms, not in restaurant.
CREDIT CARDS: Amex, MC, Visa.
PRICES: per person D,B&B single occupancy £250–£310, double £180–£210. Set dinner £90.

SEE ALSO SHORTLIST

HOPE Derbyshire

MAP 3:A6

♀UNDERLEIGH HOUSE

César award: B&B of the year

'Near the end of a quiet cul-de-sac lane', within the Peak District national park, Vivienne and Philip Taylor welcome guests to their 19th-century farmhouse B&B, 'overlooking the beauty of Hope valley'. There are four guest bedrooms – three of them a suite, including one with French doors opening on to the garden. An inspector this year received 'a warm and friendly welcome from the extremely hospitable' hostess, and was shown to Derwent suite. It had 'a cosy and comfortable, newly carpeted bedroom, a well-appointed modern bathroom with state-of-the-art walk-in shower, a sitting room at a lower level, with a small fridge and local beer'. A 'wonderful' breakfast is served communally on pretty china, in a beamed former shippon, or cattle shed. It includes 'a huge array of marinated dried fruits, home-made muesli, freshly squeezed orange juice, local black pudding and eggs'. There is a lounge with log-burner, a terrace with tables and chairs, hanging baskets and bird feeders. Great walking starts from the door. In all, 'a homely environment run by experienced and committed owners who set and maintain the highest standards'.

Lose Hill Lane
off Edale Road
Hope S33 6AF

T: 01433 621372
E: underleigh.house@btconnect.com
W: underleighhouse.co.uk

BEDROOMS: 4. 3 suites with a private lounge.
OPEN: all year except mid-Dec to mid-Feb.
FACILITIES: lounge, breakfast room, free Wi-Fi, in-room TV (Freeview), ¼-acre garden, unsuitable for disabled.
BACKGROUND MUSIC: none.
LOCATION: 1 mile N of Hope.
CHILDREN: not under 12.
DOGS: allowed in 1 suite by prior arrangement, not in public rooms.
CREDIT CARDS: MC, Visa (payment by debit card preferred).
PRICES: per room B&B single £80–£110, double £100–£130. 1-night bookings normally refused Fri/Sat, bank holidays.

HOUGH-ON-THE-HILL Lincolnshire   MAP 2:A3

THE BROWNLOW ARMS

On cold days a roaring log fire toasts the beamed bar at this 'winning combination of gastropub, local inn and restaurant-with-rooms' in a 'pretty old village'. But it is the warmth and enthusiasm of hostess Lorraine Willoughby that still more impresses readers, who praise her 'boundless energy', her 'life-and-soul personality'. 'Ripples of laughter run through the dining rooms,' one related. Lorraine and husband Paul have been here, on and off, for decades (they sold the inn in 2008 and so missed it that they bought it back five years on). Cosy, traditional bedrooms have some hefty antique mahogany pieces. 'Our light pastel room was enchanting, spotless, well lit.' There is no residents' lounge, but guests sink into a winged armchair in the 'atmospheric' bar. At dinner in the 'stunning, grey-panelled' dining room, Ruaraidh Bealby's award-winning menus include such dishes as cod fillet, broccoli velouté, pickled wild mushrooms, herb potato croquette, toasted hazelnuts. There is 'a small but interesting wine list, with tempting bin ends'. Breakfast is 'appetising, promptly served, piping hot'. 'Very good value. Absolutely deserves its place in the GHG.' (RG)

High Road
Hough-on-the-Hill
Grantham NG32 2AZ

T: 01400 250234
E: armsinn@yahoo.co.uk
W: thebrownlowarms.com

BEDROOMS: 5. 1 on ground floor in barn conversion.
OPEN: all year except 25/26 Dec, 31 Dec/1 Jan, restaurant closed Sun evening, Mon, Tues midday.
FACILITIES: bar, 3 dining rooms, free Wi-Fi, in-room TV (Freeview), unsuitable for disabled.
BACKGROUND MUSIC: in public areas.
LOCATION: rural, 2 miles E of town centre.
CHILDREN: no under-8s in restaurant in the evening.
DOGS: only guide dogs allowed.
CREDIT CARDS: MC, Visa.
PRICES: per room B&B single £80, double £130, À la carte £40.

HUNSTANTON Norfolk

MAP 2:A5

NO. 33

New arrivals at this boutique B&B, in a 'quiet, attractive street' close to the seafront, are welcomed with 'delicious' afternoon tea and cakes. The creation of experienced hotelier Jeanne Whittome, it has been 'designed and furnished to a high standard', with 'bold, contemporary and unique' decor. Stylish bedrooms are painted in soft greys, with maybe one wall of statement wallpaper, and have a king-size bed, a bath and walk-in drench shower. Extras include cafetière coffee and biscuits. One ground-floor room has an in-room bath beneath a 'delightful' tiled fire surround, Zoffany's 'Gondolier' wallpaper; another has access to a courtyard. A four-poster room has a balcony with a glimpse of the sea. 'Immaculate housekeeping made our visit a pleasure.' If you want more space, there are suites down the road at Thornham, above Ms Whittome's deli, supplier of all manner of good things for a cooked or continental breakfast – home-made granola, free-range eggs, croissants and bagels. You can order a hamper to take with you when exploring the north Norfolk coast. The concierge service will help with restaurant bookings, bicycle hire, sailing, walking, bird tours and more.

33 Northgate
Hunstanton PE36 6AP

T: 01485 524352
E: reception@33hunstanton.co.uk
W: 33hunstanton.co.uk

BEDROOMS: 5. 1 on ground floor.
OPEN: all year.
FACILITIES: small sitting room, breakfast room, free Wi-Fi, in-room TV (Freeview), small garden.
BACKGROUND MUSIC: none.
LOCATION: town centre.
CHILDREN: well-behaved children welcomed, Z-bed for childen under 14 (max. 1 per room).
DOGS: allowed in bedrooms, not in dining room, max. 1 per room (£5 per night).
CREDIT CARDS: MC, Visa.
PRICES: per room B&B double (Hunstanton) £95–£150, suites (Thornham) £140–£205, single occupany discount £10 a night, third person £30, infant £10.

HUNTINGDON Cambridgeshire   MAP 2:B4

THE OLD BRIDGE

When the proprietors are a Master of Wine and an interior designer, you can count on a smart bedroom and a decent vino. So it is at Julia and John Hoskins's ivy-clad hotel, centred on a Georgian house, with the Great Ouse flowing just behind. 'Excellent,' reports a trusted reader after a visit this year. 'It was a pleasure to stay.' From single to four-poster bedrooms, all are a warm elegant blend of the traditional and contemporary. One room has a Rajput-style mirror, another a tiger print carpet and cushions (a mini-Fenland safari), another offers a contemporary country mood. Some enjoy river views, a spacious bathroom with bath and walk-in shower; all get Noble Isle toiletries. A 'decent-sized room' had 'plenty of storage, a nice modern bathroom, though the shower was a bit compact'. Triple glazing cuts out the noise from the busy roads outside. Guests can take tea by the fire, have a snack in the patio garden. Jack Woolner's modern British cooking, served by 'efficient, cheerful staff', was much admired. Gravadlax, with 'just right' horseradish sauce, then crown of pheasant with boulangère potatoes and red cabbage were 'fab'. 'We will return.' (Peter Anderson, and others)

1 High Street
Huntingdon PE29 3TQ

T: 01480 424300
E: oldbridge@huntsbridge.co.uk
W: huntsbridge.com

BEDROOMS: 24. 2 on ground floor.
OPEN: all year.
FACILITIES: lounge, bar, restaurant, private dining room, wine shop, business centre, free Wi-Fi, in-room TV (Freeview), civil wedding licence, 1-acre grounds (riverside patio for private events), parking, unsuitable for disabled.
BACKGROUND MUSIC: none.
LOCATION: 500 yds from town centre, station 10 mins' walk.
CHILDREN: all ages welcomed.
DOGS: allowed in 2 bedrooms, lounge and bar, not in restaurant.
CREDIT CARDS: MC, Visa.
PRICES: per room B&B single from £99, double £148–£230. À la carte £38.

ILMINGTON Warwickshire

MAP 3:D6

THE HOWARD ARMS

Shakespeare was at work up the road in Stratford when this inn was built, overlooking the green in a 'lovely' Cotswolds village. In 2015 two families took it over to rescue it from decline, and love's labours have not been lost. It is 'the perfect village pub', with 'log fires, nooks and crannies. . . a great atmosphere'. Bedrooms have a mix of antique and new furnishings, some are in a modern annexe. Main pub rooms are more quaint, and sloping ceilings in three of them restrict the space. No such problem in the charming Old Beam Room (shower only); all other rooms have a bath and shower. Extras include a coffee percolator, gingerbread, Temple Spa toiletries. In the mezzanine dining area, with a 'beautiful arched window' on to the green, Gareth Rufus cooks pub classics and more inventive dishes (pan-fried chicken breast, chorizo, sautéed potatoes, purple sprouting, tomato coulis; pan-fried stone bass, warm niçoise salad, poached egg, lemon dressing). At breakfast there is freshly squeezed orange juice, 'an especially good cooked selection'. 'We'll return when we're back seeing anything at the RSC.' Try to catch the local Morris dancers, with Britain's oldest hobby horse. (S and JJ)

Lower Green
Ilmington
Stratford-upon-Avon CV36 4LT

T: 01608 682226
E: info@howardarms.com
W: howardarms.com

BEDROOMS: 8. 4 in extension, 1 on ground floor.
OPEN: all year.
FACILITIES: snug, bar, restaurant, free Wi-Fi, in-room TV (Freeview), terrace, garden (alfresco dining), bar wheelchair accessible, toilet not adapted.
BACKGROUND MUSIC: all day in public areas.
LOCATION: 8 miles S of Stratford-upon-Avon, 6 miles NE of Chipping Campden.
CHILDREN: all ages welcomed, travel cots and Z-beds.
DOGS: allowed in bar and on patio only.
CREDIT CARDS: Amex, MC, Visa.
PRICES: per room B&B single £112–£130, double £120–£160. À la carte £32. 1-night bookings sometimes refused.

ILSINGTON Devon

ILSINGTON COUNTRY HOUSE

'This place has a lot going for it.' A trusted reader commends this country house hotel and spa, 'beautifully located' on the edge of Dartmoor national park. Owned and run by the Hassell family since 1998, with 'friendly, helpful and efficient' staff, it is 'very quiet', with comfy, relaxing lounges. Rooms, which are being upgraded, have a neutral palette and splashes of bright colour. Dog-friendly rooms include those on the ground floor with garden access. Two second-floor rooms offer long views across the countryside; a smart bathroom with a roll-top bath and separate shower. There are family suites, and singles with a fine outlook. Dining is similarly flexible. The Blue Tiger bistro's all-day menu includes a sharing platter of cold meats or fish, all smoked or cured in-house. In the dining room, Mike O'Donnell, also in his 22nd year here, exploits local produce – moorland meats, fish from Brixham – in such dishes as pan-fried lamb fillet, black pudding, niçoise vegetables, rosemary jus; seared red mullet, saffron-scented mash, red wine reduction, chive, vanilla and avruga caviar oil. 'We couldn't fault anything, food-wise.' Breakfast eggs are laid by the house hens. (PA)

Ilsington TQ13 9RR

T: 01364 661452
E: hotel@ilsington.co.uk
W: ilsington.co.uk

BEDROOMS: 25. 6 on ground floor.
OPEN: all year except Jan.
FACILITIES: lift, 2 lounges, bar, restaurant, bistro, conservatory, function facilities, spa, free Wi-Fi, in-room TV (Freeview), 10-acre grounds, spa/public rooms wheelchair accessible.
BACKGROUND MUSIC: in bar, restaurant at dinner.
LOCATION: just W of village, 7 miles NW of Newton Abbot.
CHILDREN: all ages welcomed.
DOGS: allowed in some bedooms, 1 lounge area, bar, conservatory, garden (on lead).
CREDIT CARDS: MC, Visa.
PRICES: per room B&B single £100–£200, double £135–£290. Set dinner £41, tasting menu (Fri, Sat) £58. 1-night bookings refused peak times.

KELMSCOTT Oxfordshire

MAP 3:E6

THE PLOUGH

In 'a gorgeous village hidden away on the banks of the Thames', this 17th-century inn is owned by Sebastian and Lana Snow, who also have the Five Alls, a stroll along the Thames Path at Lechlade (see Shortlist). It would rate inclusion here 'for the setting alone', say Guide insiders. It is popular with locals, 'the sort of place where you'd better join in if you want to enjoy it', and not mind if you hear the murmur of voices from the garden if your room overlooks it. The bedroom style is casual chic, the walls painted in muted shades with coir flooring. All have a king-size bed, a walk-in shower (or, perhaps, a double-ended bath). You can eat in the dog-friendly bar, with 'flagstone floor, stone walls, mismatched tables and chairs', or in the restaurant, choosing from either of the menus. The first has superior pub classics (burger, cottage pie, fish and chips); the second, changing daily, is a showcase for local produce (maybe duck breast, mash, broccoli, red wine jus; a pie in 'perfect shortcrust'). Breakfast brings 'nice croissants', local bacon, Kelmscott sausage. William Morris's 'loveliest haunt of ancient peace', Kelmscott Manor, opens Wednesday and Saturday in summer.

Kelmscott
Lechlade GL7 3HG

T: 01367 253543
E: info@theploughinnkelmscott.com
W: theploughinnkelmscott.com

BEDROOMS: 8.
OPEN: all year except 25 Dec, no food Sun eve, Mon.
FACILITIES: bar, restaurant, private dining room in Hideaway bar, free Wi-Fi, in-room TV (Freeview), garden (alfresco drinks and meals).
BACKGROUND MUSIC: all day in restaurant, Hideaway bar.
LOCATION: 3 miles E of Lechlade.
CHILDREN: all ages welcomed.
DOGS: allowed in all public rooms, not in bedrooms.
CREDIT CARDS: MC, Visa.
PRICES: per room B&B single £90–£140, double £110–£140. À la carte £33 (restaurant), £26 (bar).

KING'S LYNN Norfolk   MAP 2:A4

BANK HOUSE

We hear glowing accounts of this Georgian bank-turned-boutique hotel. It stands by the historic Custom House and River Ouse in 'this fascinating town with, they claim, more Grade I listed buildings than York'. Owned by Jeannette and Anthony Goodrich, it is managed by Michael Baldwin. He brings the same energy to the enterprise as the Goodriches do to sister hotel The Rose & Crown, Snettisham (see entry). Smart bedrooms, most with river view, have Regency cartoons, antiques and modern art. Extras include ground coffee, Molton Brown toiletries, the owners' guide to King's Lynn. 'We enjoyed our stay in the King's Room, on the building's quieter side, overlooking the square,' writes a trusted reader in 2019. 'Spacious bathroom, excellent lighting, two armchairs by a desk in a bay window.' Dine casually in the Counting House, or more formally in the River Room, Old Kitchen or Billiards Room, on 'enormous portions' of Stuart Deuchars's locally sourced dishes (sharing plates, burgers, mussels and fries; slow-cooked lamb shoulder, celeriac fondant, warm apple and red cabbage chutney). Service is 'excellent', breakfast 'exceptional, particularly the eggs Benedict'. 'We hope to return.' (Michael Gwinnell, Ian Walsh)

King's Staithe Square
King's Lynn PE30 1RD

T: 01553 660492
E: info@thebankhouse.co.uk
W: thebankhouse.co.uk

BEDROOMS: 12.
OPEN: all year except 25 Dec.
FACILITIES: bar, 3 dining rooms, meeting/function rooms, vaulted cellars for private functions, free Wi-Fi, in-room TV (Freeview), riverside terrace, courtyard, all public rooms wheelchair accessible, adapted toilet.
BACKGROUND MUSIC: 'mellow jazz and offbeat pop' in public areas ('turned off on demand').
LOCATION: central.
CHILDREN: all ages welcomed.
DOGS: allowed in Counting House, bar, terrace, 2 bedrooms.
CREDIT CARDS: Amex, MC, Visa.
PRICES: per room B&B single £85–£120, double £115–£220, D,B&B single £105–£140, double £170–£275. Pre-theatre dinner £15–£20, à la carte £32.

SEE ALSO SHORTLIST

KIRKBY LONSDALE Cumbria

MAP 4: inset C2

THE SUN INN

`NEW`

'Once we had found our way there via the one-way streets of Kirkby Lonsdale, we were shown up to a lovely corner room overlooking an alleyway and the church.' Praise this year from readers, for Iain and Jenny Black's 400-year-old inn in a market town between the Lake District and Yorkshire Dales. Bedrooms have handmade furniture, Swaledale wool carpets, Bath House toiletries, original features (one door is 5 foot high). Most have a bath and rainhead shower. 'The bed was comfortable, with not too many cushions to remove, and the bathroom was bright and reasonably spacious.' There are light bites and Cumbrian ales in the dog-friendly, atmospheric bar with log-burner. In the restaurant, 'the staff were all helpful and friendly'. New chef Joe Robinson's 'imaginative and good' dishes might include a 'really tasty starter of ewe's curd ravioli with lemon'; chalk-stream trout, broccoli, roast stem, mussels, confit potato. In the morning there is a 'generous breakfast buffet with fresh pastries, fruit and compote. No freshly squeezed orange juice, but a berry smoothie, local eggs and bacon.' The hotel has no garden but a walk through the churchyard leads to river and woodlands. (Sara Price)

25% DISCOUNT VOUCHERS

6 Market Street
Kirkby Lonsdale LA6 2AU

T: 01524 271965
E: email@sun-inn.info
W: sun-inn.info

BEDROOMS: 11.
OPEN: all year.
FACILITIES: bar, restaurant, free Wi-Fi, in-room TV (Freeview), parking (permits supplied), bar and restaurant wheelchair accessible adapted toilet.
BACKGROUND MUSIC: in bar.
LOCATION: town centre.
CHILDREN: all ages welcomed.
DOGS: allowed in bedrooms, public rooms (separate dog-friendly area in restaurant).
CREDIT CARDS: MC, Visa.
PRICES: per room B&B single £90–£130, double £105–£192, D,B&B £165–£256. À la carte £34. 1-night bookings sometimes refused Sat.

KIRKBY STEPHEN Cumbria

AUGILL CASTLE

♞ Previous César Winner

'A very special place.' 'Utterly charming.' 'It's
not the Ritz, but you will feel like a lord.' Lavish
and frequent praise in 2019 for Wendy and
Simon Bennett's Victorian fantasy castle in the
Eden valley. 'Simon, Wendy and the team have
provided a place with a magical feel that draws
you in and asks you to stay for longer.' Bedrooms
are filled with antiques, and abound in character.
Castle rooms, most with four-poster, have views to
the Yorkshire Dales and Lakeland Fells, perhaps
a brightly burning fire. The Gatehouse occupies
an entire tower. Annexe rooms have their own
garden. A reader, hosting guests for a birthday
house party, relates: 'Every one of them came back
from their first visit to their room with the same
excited look of appreciation.' The 'superb' dinner
is a social affair, taken communally. New 'Umbria
meets Cumbria' menus include such dishes as
wild mushroom lasagne; Tuscan slow-roasted
lamb shank with tomato and olives. Sunday
night is pizza night. The atmosphere is pure fun,
with roaring fires, squashy sofas, honesty bar
and 'legendary' home-made cake. Children can
feed the hens and collect the eggs for breakfast.
(Maurice Hall, Liz Saunders, and many others)

25% DISCOUNT VOUCHERS

South Stainmore
Brough
Kirkby Stephen CA17 4DE

T: 01768 341937
E: enquiries@stayinacastle.com
W: stayinacastle.com

BEDROOMS: 17. 2 on ground floor,
9 in stables, orangery, coach house,
1 suitable for disabled.
OPEN: all year, dinner nightly (excl.
Tues, Wed), children's suppers daily.
FACILITIES: hall, drawing room, library,
sitting room, conservatory bar, dining
room, cinema, free Wi-Fi, in-room
TV (Freeview), civil wedding licence,
20-acre grounds (landscaped garden,
tennis), public rooms wheelchair
accessible, adapted toilet.
BACKGROUND MUSIC: none.
LOCATION: 3 miles NE of Kirkby
Stephen.
CHILDREN: all ages welcomed.
DOGS: allowed in 2 bedrooms.
CREDIT CARDS: Amex, MC, Visa.
PRICES: per room B&B £180–£280. Set
dinner £25–£30. 1-night bookings
often refused school holidays, Sat (but
call to check).

LACOCK Wiltshire

SIGN OF THE ANGEL

'Enter by a narrow flagstone passageway and low, latched doorways' to discover the very model of 'an olde worlde hostelry'. Tom and Jack Nicholas and Jon Furby have taken care of creature comforts at their 15th-century coaching inn, all of a piece with this 'exquisitely preserved' National Trust village, while losing nothing of the atmosphere. Narrow stairs lead to 'delightful, authentic but comfortable' bedrooms, with leaded windows, low beams, a double or king-size bed, antique and shabby-chic furniture. A Roberts radio replaces TV; the welcome tray has chocolate treats. Afternoon tea is served in a panelled sitting room. In one of three 'charming' dining areas, 'some with a huge fireplace', our inspectors were brought 'nice bread' and canapés while perusing Mr Furby's locally sourced menus. 'Really delicious dishes, with imaginative combinations.' For instance, steamed Devon mussels, chowder sauce, leek, caviar; roasted spring lamb, dumplings, spinach and rosemary crumb, smoked garlic sauce. A 'fine breakfast' brings 'lovely jams', poached haddock, 'excellent scrambled egg', 'good coffee'. There are tables and chairs in the orchard garden.

6 Church Street
Lacock SN15 2LB

T: 01249 730230
E: info@signoftheangel.co.uk
W: signoftheangel.co.uk

BEDROOMS: 5.
OPEN: all year except New Year's Eve (phone to check festive dates).
FACILITIES: bar, 3 dining rooms, residents' sitting room, private dining room, free Wi-Fi, no mobile phone signal, cottage garden (alfresco drinking and eating), restaurant and garden wheelchair accessible.
BACKGROUND MUSIC: in restaurant, radio option in sitting room.
LOCATION: in village, 4 miles S of Chippenham.
CHILDREN: all ages welcomed.
DOGS: allowed in bedrooms (£15 charge for cleaning), public rooms.
CREDIT CARDS: Amex, MC, Visa.
PRICES: per room B&B single £80–£110, double £110–£150. À la carte £36.

LANGAR Nottinghamshire

LANGAR HALL

'We arrived on a golden Indian summer late afternoon to a warm welcome, culminating in tea on the lawn, looking beyond the ha-ha to a field.' A much-loved hotel, this apricot-washed Georgian mansion in the Vale of Belvoir lies at the end of a lime avenue, beside the church of St Andrew. 'A charming place, relaxed and caring', it is run by Lila Arora, granddaughter of the late chatelaine, Imogen Skirving. Bedrooms (three in a separate wing) are characterful, with views over parkland ornamented with sculptures. From pretty Marks, named after Imogen's brother, and decorated with Louise Body's 'Pavilion Birds' wallpaper, to four-poster Bohemia with poetry on the walls, via The Nursery and Barbara Cartland room (beloved of the romantic novelist), each is a picture, and each picture tells a story. 'The warmth of the welcome carried on to our excellent dinner in a beautiful, classical dining room.' Gary Booth's menus include such dishes as assiette of Langar lamb, beetroot, home-made ricotta, pistachio pesto. There are niggles (a limp kipper, a mix-up over a booking), but 'the delightful ambience and excellent dinner cancelled out the shortcomings'. (Jock and Jane Macdonald, and others)

Church Lane
Langar NG13 9HG

T: 01949 860559
E: info@langarhall.co.uk
W: langarhall.com

BEDROOMS: 13. 1 on ground floor, 3 in annexe, 1 in garden chalet, 1 pod.
OPEN: all year.
FACILITIES: Study/sitting room, bar, garden room, main dining room, Indian room, free Wi-Fi, in-room TV (Freeview), civil wedding licence, 30-acre grounds (gardens, children's play area), restaurant wheelchair accessible.
BACKGROUND MUSIC: at lunch and dinner.
LOCATION: 12 miles SE of Nottingham.
CHILDREN: all ages welcomed.
DOGS: in bedrooms, sitting room and bar, not in restaurant.
CREDIT CARDS: Amex, MC, Visa.
PRICES: per room B&B single £110–£180, double £125–£225, Agnews/Pod £110–£125. Set dinner (Fri, Sat) £54.50, other nights £39–£44.50.

LANGHO Lancashire

MAP 4:D3

NORTHCOTE

In an 'outstanding location' in the Ribble valley, Northcote is known principally for its restaurant, but it is also a luxury hotel (Relais & Châteaux). A manor house built for a Victorian textile baron has burgeoned, as the operation has grown in scale and ambition. It began some 40 years ago as a restaurant-with-rooms, achieved Michelin stardom under Nigel Haworth, and retains it under Lisa Goodwin-Allen. Despite a change of ownership, the key players remain, including MD Craig Bancroft. 'Comfortable, well-equipped' bedrooms in main house and garden lodge are crisply contemporary with dramatic flashes of colour. Most have a bath and separate walk-in shower. Superior lodge rooms have a balcony or terrace overlooking garden and valley. All have a minibar, Temple Spa toiletries, evening turn-down. Vegetables, fruit and flowers are home grown; the bees supply honey, the bar's cocktails supply a buzz. Ms Goodwin-Allen's menus for omnivores and veggies feature such dishes as wild turbot, bourguignon, parsley; Yorkshire duck, smoked bacon, turnip, parsley; slow-cooked Copper Maran egg, 'baked potato' flakes. The breakfast choice is 'comprehensive'. Reports on the new regime, please.

25% DISCOUNT VOUCHERS

Northcote Road
Langho
Blackburn BB6 8BE

T: 01254 240555
E: reception@northcote.com
W: northcote.com

BEDROOMS: 26. 8 in garden lodge, 8 on ground floor, 2 suitable for disabled.
OPEN: all year.
FACILITIES: lift, 2 lounges, bar, restaurant, private dining/meeting room, chef's table, cookery courses, free Wi-Fi, in-room TV (Sky), civil wedding licence, 3-acre garden, public areas wheelchair accessible.
BACKGROUND MUSIC: evening in bar.
LOCATION: 5½ miles N of Blackburn, on A59.
CHILDREN: all ages welcomed.
DOGS: not allowed.
CREDIT CARDS: Amex, MC, Visa.
PRICES: per room B&B single £175–£585, double £218–£650, D,B&B double £260–£780. À la carte £75, set menu £70, vegetarian £63, tasting menu £90, vegetarian £72 (guests must dine Sat and Sun).

LASTINGHAM Yorkshire

MAP 4:C4

LASTINGHAM GRANGE

'Loved it all.' 'A slice of heaven.' Readers have an abiding fondness for this small hotel, a wisteria-swathed 17th-century stone farmhouse, owned by the Wood family since the 1950s. Despite its High Street address, it sits pretty in ten acres of lovely gardens, fringing the North York Moors. Within it is, indeed, 'rather dated'. However, a reader this year was 'made very welcome and comfortable, and the rooms have all the modern toys like an espresso machine'. Brothers Bertie and Tom Wood and their mother, Jane, are kind hosts. 'We enjoyed a friendly welcome from Bertie and Tom, then morning coffee and a light lunch with a newspaper, before setting off over the moors.' Sandra Thurlow's nightly-changing, locally sourced menus cater to hungry walkers with such dishes as poached Whitby halibut with Pernod hollandaise; nut and lentil loaf; braised venison in Madeira sauce. At breakfast there are locally smoked kippers, York ham, the full Monty. 'The bill was less than we expected. When we pointed out some small omissions they said "Oh, never mind, as long as you're happy." Can you beat that for personal care and service?' 'We shall certainly return!' (Richard Bright, and others)

25% DISCOUNT VOUCHERS

High Street
Lastingham YO62 6TH

T: 01751 417345
E: jane.wood@lastinghamgrange.com
W: lastinghamgrange.com

BEDROOMS: 11. Plus self-catering cottage in village.
OPEN: all year except 17 Nov–6 Mar.
FACILITIES: hall, lounge, dining room, laundry facilities, free Wi-Fi, in-room TV (Freeview), 10-acre grounds (terrace, garden, orchard, croquet, boules), restaurant wheelchair accessible.
BACKGROUND MUSIC: none.
LOCATION: 5 miles NE of Kirkbymoorside.
CHILDREN: all ages welcomed.
DOGS: allowed in bedrooms with prior consent, lounge, garden but not in dining room.
CREDIT CARDS: Amex, MC, Visa.
PRICES: per room B&B single £140–£144, double £165–£220, D,B&B double £225–£290. À la carte £42.

LAVENHAM Suffolk

MAP 2:C5

THE GREAT HOUSE   `NEW`

Behind its Georgian front, the timber-framed Great House is as old as its neighbours in this former medieval wool town. Run as a restaurant-with-rooms since 2018 for Dominique Tropeano, owner of Colchester Zoo, it happily retains the French ambience created by former owners the Crépys. Our inspectors in 2019 received 'an impeccable welcome from a young member of staff'. Their room, Bastille, was 'lovely, with separate sitting area, minibar, tiny TV'. Welcoming touches include a decanter of sherry. Bastille has an oak bed; Élysée, overlooking the market square, two king-size beds, velvet chaises longues. Bohème, under the eaves, is indeed petite, with cubbyhole bathroom. 'Mind-your-head beams are everywhere.' For the convivial, there is a small bar and some outside seating. In the dining room, at feeding time on a Friday night, 'every table was taken'. Guillaume Dericq combines local ingredients with Gallic flair to create dishes like roasted saddle of Suffolk venison, parsnip and parsley root mash, juniper sauce. 'Turbot, oddly, was lukewarm, though the plate was hot, and it tasted nice.' Service was slow, the staff were 'a bit harassed'. Breakfast brings 'very good croissants'.

Market Place
Lavenham CO10 9QZ

T: 01787 247431
E: info@greathouse.co.uk
W: greathouse.co.uk

BEDROOMS: 5.
OPEN: open 1 Feb–31 Dec, restaurant closed Sun eve, Mon.
FACILITIES: restaurant (2 rooms), free Wi-Fi, in-room TV (BT, Freeview), patio dining area, unsuitable for disabled.
BACKGROUND MUSIC: in restaurant.
LOCATION: town centre (free public car park).
CHILDREN: all ages welcomed.
DOGS: only assistance dogs allowed.
CREDIT CARDS: Amex, MC, Visa.
PRICES: per room with continental breakfast, B&B £164–£184. Set dinner £37.50, tasting menu £58, à la carte £46 (Sat only). 1-night bookings sometimes refused Sat.

SEE ALSO SHORTLIST

LEAMINGTON SPA Warwickshire   MAP 2:B2

MALLORY COURT   NEW

An Arts and Crafts house in 'beautiful'
landscaped gardens, run as a country house hotel,
is promoted from the Shortlist this year at the
urging of a trusted reader. Recent extensions,
housing a gym, spa and guest accommodation,
are 'designed to resonate sympathetically with
the older building'. A 'smallish' annexe room
had 'a comfortable bed, a coffee pod machine, a
bath with overhead shower'. Some rooms have a
more contemporary edge, others open on to the
herb garden; all have bathrobes, slippers, ESPA
toiletries. In the original house's 'most attractive
wood-panelled dining room, with mullioned
windows and thick glazing bars', Paul Evans's
ambitious dishes use seasonal and home-grown
produce, perhaps South Coast hogget loin and
belly, salt-baked kohlrabi, fermented black garlic,
ewe's curd, lamb jus. In the 'light, stylish' annexe
brasserie, 'twice-baked cheese soufflé and a duck
confit with plenty of meat (slightly salty jus)' were
enjoyed. A 'first-rate breakfast' (rather wasted on
laptop-browsing conference delegates) included
'delicious scrambled egg, tender, thick bacon,
tasty black pudding. Service was very courteous,
supervised by an alert manager.' (Robert Gower)

Harbury Lane
Bishop's Tachbrook
Leamington Spa CV33 9QB

T: 01926 330214
E: reception@mallory.co.uk
W: mallory.co.uk

BEDROOMS: 43, 11 in Knight's Suite,
12 in Orchard House, 2 suitable for
disabled.
OPEN: all year.
FACILITIES: 2 lounges, brasserie (Thurs
jazz pm), restaurant, lift, Wi-Fi,
in-room TV (Freeview), civil wedding
licence, function facilities, fitness suite,
spa (indoor pool), 10-acre garden,
terrace, public rooms wheelchair
accessible.
BACKGROUND MUSIC: in public rooms.
LOCATION: Bishop's Tachbrook, 3 miles
from Leamington Spa.
CHILDREN: all ages welcomed.
DOGS: in some bedrooms, gardens, not
in public rooms, charges apply.
CREDIT CARDS: Amex, MC, Visa.
PRICES: per room B&B single from
£124, double £129–£401. À la carte
£65, table d'hôte menu £37, tasting
menu £65.

LETCOMBE REGIS Oxfordshire

MAP 2:C2

THE GREYHOUND INN

In the Vale of the White Horse guests enjoy 'delicious' food, 'exceptional' accommodation, and a 'fine welcome' at this 18th-century country pub with 'a lovely beer garden'. Owners Martyn Reed and Catriona Galbraith have 'given the red brick building a new lease of life', transforming it into both an idyllic retreat and the focal point of 'a village full of birdsong', with events including jazz and pizza nights, garden parties, a monthly quiz. Downstairs, dining areas branch from the earthy-hued main bar (craft ales, well-chosen wine), with leather club chairs around brick fireplaces. Here, visitors and regulars enjoy chef Phil Currie's 'imaginative' menus, served by 'friendly staff': such dishes as cider-braised lamb, beetroot dauphinoise, salsa verde, kale; leek and roasted cauliflower lasagne, truffled ricotta. Upstairs, the 'comfortable' bedrooms have a contemporary country style with mellow beams and splashes of colour from cushions, throws and artwork. All have fresh milk, home-made biscuits, a Roberts radio; and a 'smart, well-lit bathroom' with Bramley toiletries, a bath, a monsoon shower, or both. Breakfast brings 'a small buffet, good cooked dishes'. (AT, and others)

25% DISCOUNT VOUCHERS

Main Street
Letcombe Regis
Wantage OX12 9JL

T: 01235 771969
E: info@thegreyhoundletcombe.co.uk
W: thegreyhoundletcombe.co.uk

BEDROOMS: 8.
OPEN: all year except 24/25 Dec, 5–16 Jan, Mon lunchtime.
FACILITIES: bar with snug, 3 dining rooms (1 available for private dining/meetings), function room, free Wi-Fi, in-room TV (Freeview), garden, bar/restaurant, garden wheelchair accessible, adapted toilet.
BACKGROUND MUSIC: occasionally in public rooms.
LOCATION: in village, 2 miles SW of Wantage.
CHILDREN: all ages welcomed.
DOGS: allowed in 3 bedrooms, bar, garden, not dining rooms.
CREDIT CARDS: MC, Visa.
PRICES: per room B&B single £80–£130, double £95–£155, D,B&B £155–£205. À la carte £35, 2-course Midweek Fix dinner (Wed) £14.

LEWDOWN Devon

LEWTRENCHARD MANOR

A 'wonderful hotel' with that 'special feel' of family ownership, Sue and James Murray's manor house delights with its 'history, beauty and style'. Standing in gardens laid out by Walter Sarel, the apparently Jacobean house is largely a rebuild by the Revd Sabine Baring-Gould, hyperactive Victorian author, antiquarian and folk-song collector. It has Renaissance woodwork, a Jacobean ceiling, rococo fireplace, friezes, panels and pilasters. Rooms are filled with antiques and oil paintings, 'roaring fires creating a great atmosphere'. The welcome is 'genuinely friendly'. A first-floor room was a 'truly large suite' with 'soft, easy chairs, a king-size bed', period furniture. 'We could not have asked for anything nicer.' Classic rooms, two with four-poster, overlook gardens and parkland. Tom Browning, promoted to head chef this year, uses produce from the kitchen garden in such 'impeccable' dishes as curry-roasted cod loin, cauliflower, caper and raisin dressing, served in the panelled dining room hung with gilt-framed portraits. 'Food and service were a delight.' Breakfast brings freshly squeezed juice, local bacon, scrambled eggs. 'Full marks in our book!' (ID)

Lewdown
Okehampton EX20 4PN

T: 01566 783222
E: info@lewtrenchard.co.uk
W: lewtrenchard.co.uk

BEDROOMS: 14. 1 in folly, 4 with separate entrance, 1 suitable for disabled.
OPEN: all year.
FACILITIES: front-hall lounge, bar, library, restaurant, function facilities, free Wi-Fi, in-room TV (Freeview), civil wedding licence, 12-acre gardens, public rooms wheelchair accessible.
BACKGROUND MUSIC: none.
LOCATION: rural, 10 miles N of Tavistock.
CHILDREN: all ages welcomed.
DOGS: allowed in bedrooms (not unattended), in public rooms, not in restaurant.
CREDIT CARDS: Amex, MC, Visa.
PRICES: per room B&B single £145–£235, double £180–£280, D,B&B double £270–£370. Set dinner £50, tasting menu £74–£89. 1-night bookings sometimes refused Sat.

LIFTON Devon

MAP 1:C3

THE ARUNDELL ARMS

People get hooked on Adam Fox-Edwards's country sports hotel close to Dartmoor, with its tackle shop in an original cock-fighting pit, ghillies for hire, and 20 miles of fishing on the Tamar and tributaries. In the family for nearly 60 years, it has 'tastefully decorated, country house-style bedrooms', some in a former Victorian tailor's shop opposite. 'Our superior room was fine,' relates a trusted reader. 'Lots of wardrobe space. Small study with a tea tray. Excellent king-size bed', though the bathroom 'needed some TLC'. There is a 'comfortable lounge', a bar with a good menu of 'well-presented' dishes (eg, venison burger; mixed grill of sea fish). Simple fare is served in the old police station and court-turned-pub, with barred windows (just the place for a lock-in!). But the main event is Steve Pidgeon's five-course tasting menu in the restaurant. 'The food was extremely good. Delicious cauliflower soup, trio of fish, sorbet, pan-fried guineafowl' with 'well-judged' wine pairing. Unusually, staff seemed affected by a 'general malaise', which took the shine off. Breakfast brought 'the best scrambled egg and bacon eaten for some time'. (Ian Dewey, A K-H, and others)

Fore Street
Lifton PL16 0AA

T: 01566 784666
E: reservations@arundellarms.com
W: arundellarms.com

BEDROOMS: 27. 4 on ground floor, 4 in adjacent Church Cottage.
OPEN: all year.
FACILITIES: lounge, bar, pub, restaurant, private dining and meeting rooms, free Wi-Fi (some bedrooms, public rooms), in-room TV (Freeview), civil wedding licence, 1-acre garden, lake, 20 miles of private fishing, unsuitable for disabled.
BACKGROUND MUSIC: none.
LOCATION: 3 miles E of Launceston.
CHILDREN: all ages welcomed.
DOGS: allowed except in restaurant and on river bank.
CREDIT CARDS: Amex, MC, Visa.
PRICES: per room B&B single from £120, double £160–£195, D,B&B single from £150, double £260–£295. Tasting menu £49.50, à la carte (bar) £32.

LIVERPOOL Merseyside

MAP 4:E2

2 BLACKBURNE TERRACE

Practically within earshot of the Liverpool
Philharmonic, in the city's cultural quarter, this
pitch-perfect B&B has been attracting ecstatic
reviews since it opened in 2014. Guide readers
were given 'a warm welcome' by owners Sarah
and Glenn Whitter, she a former primary school
teacher, he an interior designer, musician and
composer, and what a composition is this! A fine
late Georgian terrace house behind a screen of
trees, it has been made over from top to toe in
'inspirational' style. From the 'shattered' mirror in
the hall – as if the Lady of Shalott had paused to
check her hair – to a double-height top suite with
views over rooftops to the Anglican cathedral,
everything is on song. Here are oversized lamps,
an orange velvet-upholstered ottoman, works
by Turkish artist Ayse Kucuk, a bathroom with
freestanding bath against a raw stone wall. Each
of the 'exquisite' rooms has top-quality Egyptian
bedlinen, a Sonos music system, luxury bath foam,
hand-made chocolates, a tot of artisan gin. Guests
relax with a book in the drawing room or pretty
garden, while in the dining room 'a fabulous
breakfast' brings 'an enormous buffet', rare breed
meats, smoked salmon, veggie options.

Liverpool L8 7PJ

T: 0151 708 5474
E: info@2bbt.co.uk
W: 2blackburneterrace.com

BEDROOMS: 4.
OPEN: all year except 24 Dec–1 Jan.
FACILITIES: drawing room, dining
room, free Wi-Fi, in-room smart TV
(Freeview), walled garden, unsuitable
for disabled.
BACKGROUND MUSIC: classical at
breakfast.
LOCATION: city centre.
CHILDREN: not under 10.
DOGS: not allowed.
CREDIT CARDS: MC, Visa.
PRICES: per room B&B £160–£290.

SEE ALSO SHORTLIST

LODSWORTH Sussex   MAP 2:E3

THE HALFWAY BRIDGE

'Well placed for visiting the historic market towns' of Midhurst and Petworth, Sam and Janet Bakose's 18th-century inn proved more than halfway decent on a Guide inspection. Bedrooms are across and down a country lane, in converted stables, 'set in a patch of garden with picnic tables and games'. A deluxe room was 'not quite boutique', with 'uncontroversial flower prints, thick beige curtains, dark wood furniture, good storage and lighting', milk and mineral water in a mini-fridge, underfloor heating, local toiletries in the bathroom. After dark, follow the motion sensors to eat in one of the 'snug dining spaces'. Chef Clyde Hollett presides here and at sister hotel The Crab & Lobster, Sidlesham (see entry), surf to Lodsworth's turf. The food is 'a happy discovery' with praise for the 'delectable modern platings and perfectly cooked dishes', perhaps hake, citrus-crushed potatoes, red pepper purée, samphire, cashew nut pesto; leek, spinach and Sussex Cheddar croquettes, baby leeks, tomato, sage sauce. Breakfast brings 'gorgeously tart' berry compote, first-rate scrambled eggs, 'a generous serving of smoked salmon'. All this, and 'since dinner was so good, we stayed for lunch'.

Lodsworth
Petworth GU28 9BP

T: 01798 861281
E: enquiries@halfwaybridge.co.uk
W: halfwaybridge.co.uk

BEDROOMS: 7. In converted barns, 165 yds from main building.
OPEN: all year.
FACILITIES: bar, restaurant, free Wi-Fi, in-room TV (Freeview), bar terrace, small beer garden, unsuitable for disabled.
BACKGROUND MUSIC: 'quiet' in bar and restaurant.
LOCATION: 3 miles W of Petworth, on A272.
CHILDREN: all ages welcomed.
DOGS: allowed in bar area only.
CREDIT CARDS: Amex, MC, Visa.
PRICES: per room B&B single £95–£115, double £150–£230. Set lunch menu £26, à la carte £32. 1-night bookings refused Fri and Sat.

LONG SUTTON Somerset

MAP 1:C6

THE DEVONSHIRE ARMS

Philip and Sheila Mepham's gabled dining-pub-with-rooms 'by the village green' is a consistent hit with returning Guide readers who find it 'as good as ever'. Nine bedrooms, two in a separate cottage, are decorated in country-chic style. Some rooms have a bath, some a shower, and some a combination of the two, though one visitor this year reports a 'lack of attention to detail' in the bathrooms. Bedrooms are 'well furnished and comfortable'. 'There is no passing traffic, so peace prevails.' No guest lounge, but a pretty garden for alfresco eating. The 'real attraction' at this former hunting lodge is the 'excellent' food served in the restaurant, which shares the surprisingly contemporary open-plan space with the bar. Start perhaps with home-cured salmon, confit beetroot, wasabi crumb and dill crème fraîche, and follow with pan-roasted cod, pearl barley, chorizo, greens and tarragon sauce vierge; a lemon and blueberry torte. Breakfast is 'rather perfunctory', the buffet lacking 'fruit, cold meats and cheeses'; but the 'very good sausages' and croissants more than pass muster. A rural gem in a 'great location' with staff who are 'efficient and friendly'. (Robert Cooper, PA)

Long Sutton TA10 9LP

T: 01458 241271
E: info@thedevonshirearms.com
W: thedevonshirearms.com

BEDROOMS: 9. 2, on ground floor, in annexe behind main building.
OPEN: all year except 24–26 Dec.
FACILITIES: open-plan bar and restaurant, private dining room, free Wi-Fi, in-room TV (Freeview), courtyard, garden (croquet lawn, vegetable garden), public areas wheelchair accessible, no adapted toilet.
BACKGROUND MUSIC: in bar.
LOCATION: by the village green.
CHILDREN: all ages welcomed.
DOGS: allowed in bar only.
CREDIT CARDS: MC, Visa.
PRICES: per room B&B £90–£160, D,B&B £130–£220. À la carte £30. 1-night bookings sometimes refused weekends.

LONGHORSLEY Northumberland

THISTLEYHAUGH FARM

⚜ Previous César Winner

'A twisty road' leads to this 'beautiful' Georgian farmhouse B&B in 'a wonderful location' on an organic livestock farm on the River Coquet. The Nelless family have farmed here for four generations, raising sheep, cattle and poultry to high welfare standards. This is a real home-from-home, its rooms 'full of nooks and crannies, and lots of beautiful furniture and ornaments'. A 'large, well-equipped' bedroom had fresh milk in a fridge, home-made shortbread, 'exquisite bedlinen with drawn threadwork', a bathroom with 'a splendid roll-top bath and a powerful shower over it'. Another room sports a king-size American four-poster. But it is Mrs Nelless who 'makes it so special', with her friendly, open manner and a hug for one departing guest. A 'lovely' breakfast, served beneath an antique grandfather clock, sets guests up for a walk on Longhorsley Moor, or a drive to the coast. Other choices include a full English with Stornoway black pudding, local bacon and sausages; smoked salmon and scrambled egg. Dinner is no longer offered, but there is pub grub to be had at the Shoulder of Mutton in Longhorsley, and Morpeth is a seven-mile drive. (PB)

25% DISCOUNT VOUCHERS

Longhorsley
Morpeth NE65 8RG

T: 01665 570629
E: thistleyhaugh@hotmail.com
w: thistleyhaugh.co.uk

BEDROOMS: 4.
OPEN: Feb–Christmas (closed at Christmas).
FACILITIES: 2 lounges, garden room, dining room, free Wi-Fi, in-room TV (Freeview), ¼-acre garden (summer house), fishing, shooting, golf, riding nearby.
BACKGROUND MUSIC: none.
LOCATION: 10 miles N of Morpeth, W of A697.
CHILDREN: all ages welcomed.
DOGS: not allowed (kennels nearby).
CREDIT CARDS: MC, Visa.
PRICES: per room B&B single £80, double £110.

LOOE Cornwall

MAP 1:D3

TRELASKE HOTEL & RESTAURANT

'We have stayed at this hotel for many years; it is still brilliant.' High praise in 2019 for Hazel Billington and Ross Lewin's 'small, beautiful' hotel, between the historic fishing ports of Looe and Polperro. Hazel is a 'fantastic hostess, friendly and helpful'. Alongside three 'comfortable, spacious' main house rooms, there are four larger, 'lovely, clean' garden rooms with a private balcony or a patio, offering 'fantastic' views of rolling Cornish countryside or of the hotel's four acres of tranquil gardens. All have harmonious neutral and earthy hues. Ross, an 'excellent chef', produces 'first-class' dishes exploiting 'the finest' Cornish ingredients. A daily-changing dinner menu, largely dictated by the sea's fresh bounty, is 'superb, especially the fish', perhaps Looe day-boat lemon sole, crushed new potatoes, chives, garam oil. It comes with a 'good wine list' and 'lovely puddings'. The 'excellent breakfast' garners approbation in equal measure, 'especially the local sausages and bacon'. Readers invariably mention how 'very welcome' they always feel here. Many share the view that they would 'never stay anywhere else in Cornwall'. (Ann Simons, YW, and others)

25% DISCOUNT VOUCHERS

Polperro Road
Looe PL13 2JS

T: 01503 262159
E: info@trelaske.co.uk
W: trelaske.co.uk

BEDROOMS: 7. 4 garden rooms, on ground floor, in adjacent building.
OPEN: Mar–Nov.
FACILITIES: 2 lounges, dining room, free Wi-Fi (in main house), in-room TV (Freeview), function facilities, terrace (summer barbecues), 4-acre grounds, bar and restaurant wheelchair accessible.
BACKGROUND MUSIC: in lounge bar and restaurant.
LOCATION: 2 miles W of Looe, 3 miles NE of Polperro.
CHILDREN: all ages welcomed.
DOGS: allowed in 2 bedrooms (£7.50 per night), gardens, not in public rooms.
CREDIT CARDS: MC, Visa.
PRICES: per room B&B £110–£135, D,B&B £175–£190. Set dinner £30–£35. 1-night bookings sometimes refused.

SEE ALSO SHORTLIST

LORTON Cumbria

MAP 4: inset C2

NEW HOUSE FARM

A cream tea on arrival and a hot tub in the grounds are among the pleasures that make Hazel Thompson's B&B, in fans' eyes, 'the best in the Lakes'. It is much in demand for private functions, especially as a wedding venue, when the surrounding fells are a spectacular backdrop for photography. The rustic bedrooms, in the farmhouse and converted outbuildings, are redecorated every year. The Stables and Old Dairy each have a carved antique oak four-poster, the latter a Victorian-style bathroom with freestanding slipper bath, the former a bath with air jets. Swinside has a brass bed, a double power shower, a view of Swinside itself, source of the house spring water. None has a television, but there are 15 acres of fields, woods and streams to explore, fells to climb – and packed lunches to order. A 'roaring log fire' burns in the tea room with tables in the old cow byres, where such local favourites as Cumbrian sausages and ham, sticky toffee pudding, Lakeland ice creams, Solway shrimps, and scones with Cumberland butter are served. Check they're open before dropping in, especially in summer when it's snowing confetti. Cockermouth (and dinner) is just six miles away.

Lorton
Cockermouth CA13 9UU

T: 07841 159818
E: hazel@newhouse-farm.co.uk
W: newhouse-farm.com

BEDROOMS: 5. 1 in stable, 1 in Old Dairy.
OPEN: all year, tea room closed end Oct–mid-Mar, every Sat.
FACILITIES: entrance hall, 2 lounges, dining room, free Wi-Fi, civil wedding licence, 17-acre grounds (garden, hot tub, streams, woods, field, lake and river, safe bathing 2 miles), unsuitable for disabled.
BACKGROUND MUSIC: none.
LOCATION: on B5289, 2 miles S of Lorton.
CHILDREN: not under 6.
DOGS: 'clean and dry' dogs with own bed allowed in bedrooms (£10 per night), not in public rooms.
CREDIT CARDS: MC, Visa.
PRICES: per room B&B £140–£180. 1-night bookings usually refused weekends in peak season.

LOWER BOCKHAMPTON Dorset   MAP 1:D6

YALBURY COTTAGE

♻ Previous César Winner

'An example of how really good management can
make a stay memorable,' writes a Guide regular
this year, after visiting Ariane and Jamie Jones's
small thatched hotel in the heart of Thomas
Hardy country. 'Ariane and her staff took what
appeared to be a genuine interest in us and
they (lads under training) took the trouble to
remember our names: a very personal experience.'
'Comfortable' bedrooms, in a modern extension,
display 'a simple country style with floral prints'.
All have tea and coffee facilities, fresh milk; a
bathroom with bath and shower over. There may
be a tiny price to pay for a room's 'lovely outlook'
over sheep-filled fields: 'All very bucolic, until we
were woken at 5.30 am by bleating right outside
the window.' Still, as a reader suggests, this is
'really a restaurant-with-rooms', with 'emphasis
on the excellent cooking'. In the beamed dining
room, Jamie Jones's locally sourced seasonal
French dishes include roast lamb rump, yeast
purée, sticky red onion, ricotta beignets, roast
garlic and rosemary sauce. 'Cheese soufflé,
scallops and lamb were all faultless.' Breakfast
brings Bridport kippers, eggy bread with maple
syrup. (Robert Cooper, PA, LH and JF)

25% DISCOUNT VOUCHERS

Lower Bockhampton
Dorchester DT2 8PZ

T: 01305 262382
E: enquiries@yalburycottage.com
W: yalburycottage.com

BEDROOMS: 8. 6 on ground floor.
OPEN: all year except 23 Dec–17 Jan.
FACILITIES: lounge, restaurant, free Wi-
Fi, in-room TV (Freeview), garden
with outdoor seating.
BACKGROUND MUSIC: 'easy listening' in
lounge in evening.
LOCATION: 2 miles E of Dorchester.
CHILDREN: all ages welcomed, no
under-12s in restaurant after 8 pm.
DOGS: allowed in bedrooms, lounge,
not in restaurant.
CREDIT CARDS: MC, Visa.
PRICES: per room B&B single £75–£85,
double £99–£125, D,B&B single
£95–£115, double £165–£185. À la
carte £34.50–£39.50.

LUDLOW Shropshire

MAP 3:C4

♀OLD DOWNTON LODGE

César award: country house hotel of the year

A drive through 'miles of very narrow roads' led
trusted readers to this restaurant-with-rooms,
deep in the Shropshire countryside. A 'brilliant'
conversion of barns and farm buildings, it is
laid out around parterre gardens. Willem and
Pippa Vlok are the 'hands-on' owners. Each
of the rustic bedrooms is unique: a superior
ground-floor room, typically, was 'sumptuous',
with stone-flagged floor, 'medieval in feel but
with all the comforts of a deluxe modern hotel,
including a state-of-the-art bathroom. Everything
is immaculate.' Old stables now make for an
inviting guest lounge, while 'the dining room,
with its Tudor decor, is spectacular'. Here, chef
Karl Martin's menus shout of quality ingredients,
from rose veal, miso, celeriac, cabbage, truffle,
through mackerel, scallop, beetroot, horseradish,
to rhubarb, sorrel, milk. 'They have numerous
awards for their wine list.' The service is 'prompt
and effective' from 'superbly trained' staff. A
'totally delightful breakfast served by charming
local ladies' brought 'the lightest, fluffiest'
scrambled eggs with excellent smoked salmon.
(Ian and Francine Walsh, Patience Churcher)

Downton on the Rock
Ludlow SY8 2HU

T: 01568 771826
E: bookings@olddowntonlodge.com
W: olddowntonlodge.com

BEDROOMS: 10. In buildings round
courtyard.
OPEN: all year, except Christmas,
restaurant closed Sun, Mon.
FACILITIES: sitting room, dining room,
'museum' (function room), free Wi-Fi,
in-room TV (Freeview), civil wedding
licence, 1-acre courtyard, 2 Tesla car
chargers, unsuitable for disabled.
BACKGROUND MUSIC: soft classical in
sitting and dining rooms.
LOCATION: 6 miles W of Ludlow.
CHILDREN: over-12s only.
DOGS: allowed in some bedrooms
by prior arrangement, not in public
rooms.
CREDIT CARDS: Amex, MC, Visa.
PRICES: per room B&B £155–£245,
D,B&B £215–£305. Market menu (2–3
courses) £40–£50, tasting menus (6
courses) £65, (9 courses) £80.

SEE ALSO SHORTLIST

LYMINGTON Hampshire   MAP 2:E2

BRITANNIA HOUSE

Built in 1865 as the Britannia Commercial Hotel, this 'homely' B&B sits in a quiet location close to the quay with its web of cobbled streets. 'It's a good base for exploring this lively small coastal town', once famed for its salt industry. Indeed, a little decorative seasoning has been sprinkled on the interiors by 'amiable' Tobias Feilke, an owner liked for his 'personal' approach. The stylish lounge has a rich gold and blue palette, plush fabrics, squashy sofas and book-lined shelves by a marble fireplace. Elsewhere, classical wallpaper is decorated with hats – naval caps or an explorer's leather trilby – next to a suit of armour and display of pipes. The 'delightful' bedrooms maintain an eclectic style. One has a Greek column, classical statue and artwork, a window overlooking the courtyard garden; another sports a decorative canopy over a king-size bed, black-and-gold imperial furnishings, Chinese calligraphy. A two-storey apartment has a light-washed sitting room with leather chesterfield sofas, balcony overlooking the quay to the Isle of Wight. Breakfast, taken in a country-style kitchen with much mellow pine, has a continental buffet, an 'exceptional' full English.

25% DISCOUNT VOUCHERS

Station Street
Lymington SO41 3BA

T: 01590 672091
E: enquiries@britannia-house.com
w: britannia-house.com

BEDROOMS: 5. 2 on ground floor, one 2-storey apartment.
OPEN: all year.
FACILITIES: lounge, kitchen/breakfast room, free Wi-Fi, in-room TV (Freeview), courtyard garden, parking, unsuitable for disabled.
BACKGROUND MUSIC: none.
LOCATION: 2 mins' walk from High Street/quayside, close to station.
CHILDREN: not under 8.
DOGS: not allowed.
CREDIT CARDS: MC, Visa.
PRICES: per room B&B single £95–£139, double £109–£139. 1-night bookings refused weekends.

LYNDHURST Hampshire

MAP 2:E2

LIME WOOD

At the end of a long drive past rustic cabins, a helipad and a forest-fringed meadow, this 21st-century rebuild of a Georgian lodge is a 'highly professional, near faultless' modern country house hotel. 'We were greeted warmly as we climbed out of our car at the entrance,' reports a Guide insider, before being shown around, with bags taken to the room. A range of 'light, tastefully neutral' or earth-toned accommodation includes cosy rooms, overlooking garden and forest with a king-size bed, robes, minibar and Bamford toiletries. Two-storey lodges include one with a four-poster, open fire and stand-alone bath in a bay window surrounded by trees; wooden cottages with kitchenette suit a family. Public rooms, including a marble-topped bar lined with leather chairs, have a bright, uplifting mood, eclectic artwork and 'many quiet spots for afternoon tea'. The spa is 'slick and beautiful'. In the 'elegant, relaxed, slightly dimly it' restaurant, Luke Holder and Angela Hartnett's seasonal Italian fare includes Parmesan gnocchi, morels, wild garlic; lamb chops, garlic, sweetbread Bolognese. 'Perhaps wait until you have eaten to study the dining room's Tracey Emin nudes.'

Beaulieu Road
Lyndhurst SO43 7FZ

T: 02380 287177
E: info@limewood.co.uk
W: limewoodhotel.co.uk

BEDROOMS: 32. 5 on ground floor, 2 suitable for disabled, 16 in pavilions and cottages in the grounds.
OPEN: all year.
FACILITIES: lifts, 2 bars, 3 lounges, 2 restaurants, private dining rooms, free Wi-Fi, in-room TV (Freeview), civil wedding licence, spa (indoor pool), 14-acre gardens, cookery school, public rooms wheelchair accessible.
BACKGROUND MUSIC: all day in public areas.
LOCATION: in New Forest, 12 miles SW of Southampton.
CHILDREN: all ages welcomed.
DOGS: allowed in outside bedrooms, not in main house.
CREDIT CARDS: MC, Visa.
PRICES: room £345–£1,250. Breakfast £22, à la carte £65. 1-night bookings refused most weekends.

SEE ALSO SHORTLIST

MARAZION Cornwall

MAP 1:E1

MOUNT HAVEN HOTEL & RESTAURANT

NEW

The Mount is St Michael's, a tidal island best viewed from your bedroom balcony or the terrace of this hotel, set at a high point above the town, overlooking the bay. An old Guide favourite, it was sold in 2016 to James and Mary (Lord and Lady) St Levan, who also own the Godolphin Arms (Shortlist). It gains a full entry this year at the urging of a trusted reader who knew it well in the past and has found standards more than maintained after a 'smart' refurbishment. 'Comfy' rooms at the rear have space for a child's bed. Dog-friendly rooms have garden access, outside seating. Our reader's room had an updated bathroom with 'powerful shower'. All bedrooms have organic toiletries, tea and coffee. In the morning chef Ross Sloan might be seen on the beach, foraging. The emphasis is on local produce. Small plates are served in the bar (Porthilly oysters, damson and Helford Blue tart), while in the restaurant, the menu might include John Dory, oyster and potato fritter, mussels cooked with seaweed. Breakfasts were good, too. 'My partner really enjoyed the poached eggs and ham on English muffin, with hollandaise.' Above all, 'great service'. (Steve Hur, and others)

Turnpike Road
Marazion TR17 0DQ

T: 01736 719937
E: reception@mounthaven.co.uk
W: mounthaven.co.uk

BEDROOMS: 20, some on ground floor.
OPEN: annual closure possible Jan–Mar (check website).
FACILITIES: bar, restaurant, free Wi-Fi, in-room TV (Freeview), sun terrace, ½-acre grounds.
BACKGROUND MUSIC: in bar and restaurant.
LOCATION: 4 miles E of Penzance.
CHILDREN: all ages welcomed (please notify if you are travelling with children or need a room for more than two guests).
DOGS: allowed in Garden Haven rooms (£15 per night per dog, bowl, bed, treats provided), in bar, not in restaurant.
CREDIT CARDS: MC, Visa.
PRICES: per room B&B £100–£300. À la carte set-price dinner £27.50–£33.50 (2/3 courses).

SEE ALSO SHORTLIST

MARGATE Kent

MAP 2:D5

SANDS HOTEL

JMW Turner would take the steam packet down the Thames to Margate. Today Londoners can hop aboard the fast train at St Pancras mid-morning, and enjoy lunch with a sea view at Nick Conington's 'friendly' hotel. The 'smart renovation' of the Victorian building is part of Margate's renaissance, driven by the opening of Turner Contemporary gallery. There are sea-facing bedrooms with a balcony; others look towards the Old Town with its vintage shops and cafés. Two undercroft rooms have mood lighting, and daylight through a light well ('on the whole the approach works nicely'). Most rooms have a bath and walk-in shower. All have climate control, a mini-fridge, Noble Isle toiletries. 'A nice touch was home-made chocolate chip cookies, replenished every day.' In the 'lovely first-floor dining room' with floor-to-ceiling windows, or on the terrace, Ross Barden's menus are strong on locally farmed or fished produce – maybe Romney Marsh lamb rump, galette potato, shallot, black garlic vinaigrette; almond-crusted cod, kale, Jerusalem artichoke, brown shrimp butter. At breakfast there is porridge with banana, honey and chia seeds; smashed avocado on sourdough; kippers, eggs Benedict, the full English.

Marine Drive
Margate CT9 1DH

T: 01843 228228
E: info@sandshotelmargate.co.uk
W: sandshotelmargate.co.uk

BEDROOMS: 20. 1 with wheelchair access and wet room.
OPEN: all year.
FACILITIES: lift, bar, restaurant, free Wi-Fi, in-room TV (Freeview), civil wedding licence, roof terrace, ice-cream parlour, public areas wheelchair accessible.
BACKGROUND MUSIC: varied, in public areas.
LOCATION: town centre.
CHILDREN: all ages welcomed.
DOGS: not allowed.
CREDIT CARDS: Amex, MC, Visa.
PRICES: per room B&B £140–£200, D,B&B £200–£260. À la carte £40.

SEE ALSO SHORTLIST

MARKET DRAYTON Shropshire

GOLDSTONE HALL

'Hands-on owners, attention to detail and a warm and friendly ambience.' All-round plaudits this year for John and Sue Cushing's Georgian manor house hotel. Further praise too for the 'stunning gardens'. Opened to the public each summer under the National Garden Scheme, they 'reflect the care and attention' offered to guests. At their heart is one of the country's largest kitchen gardens – a source of fruit, vegetables and herbs for new head chef Liam Philbin's 'beautifully presented' modern British dishes, perhaps halibut, white beans, monk's beard, baby turnips, yeasted cauliflower purée; home-grown poached rhubarb. Downstairs, a 'bright, inviting' drawing room and oak-panelled lounge. Upstairs, 'very comfortable' bedrooms, perhaps with a brass bed, antique four-poster or locally crafted super-king-size wooden bed. Some enjoy garden views, others have rugs on oak floors. All have a fridge with milk, home-made cookies, a bathroom with bath and separate shower. A 'delicious breakfast', served in the orangery overlooking the walled garden, includes freshly squeezed juice, 'super-tasty Staffordshire oatcake', a 'perfect poached egg'. 'We'll be back!' (Kath and Liam Berney, R and JF)

25% DISCOUNT VOUCHERS

Goldstone Road
Market Drayton TF9 2NA

T: 01630 661202
E: enquiries@goldstonehall.com
w: goldstonehall.co.uk

BEDROOMS: 12. 2 on ground floor.
OPEN: all year.
FACILITIES: bar, lounge, drawing room, dining room, orangery, free Wi-Fi, in-room TV (Sky, Freeview), function facilities, civil wedding licence, 5 acres of grounds (walled garden, kitchen garden, Great Lawn), public rooms, garden wheelchair accessible.
BACKGROUND MUSIC: in bar and dining room.
LOCATION: 5 miles S of Market Drayton.
CHILDREN: all ages welcomed.
DOGS: not allowed.
CREDIT CARDS: Amex, MC, Visa.
PRICES: per room B&B single £95–£115, double £150–£180, D,B&B single £138–£158, double £246–£276. Set dinner £49.

MARTINHOE Devon   MAP 1:B4

HEDDON'S GATE HOTEL

Guests feel 'thoroughly spoilt' at this welcoming
hotel, tucked away in wooded seclusion at the
end of a quarter-mile private drive. Owners
Mark and Pat Cowell go out of their way to
assure visitors' comfort, providing complimentary
afternoon tea and cake in the large lounge or
on the terrace. Front-facing bedrooms have
panoramic valley views. Those at the rear look
on to woodland. Some are bright and modern,
some more traditional. Dual-aspect Beech
has the best outlook. Oak, the original master
bedroom, has an 1840s half-tester bed; Laurel,
antique stained-glass windows. 'Chestnut had
a Victorian bed of a strange shape but perfectly
comfortable, two ornate chairs plus a table and
chair. The large bathroom had a bath and separate
shower.' Breakfast brings 'a vast range of packet
cereals', fresh fruit, berry compote ('our favourite,
wonderful with yogurt'), smoked salmon,
pancakes with lemon, or a full English – fuel
for walkers planning to follow the South West
Coast Path, which runs below. Take it at a table
in the lounge if you want your dog with you. The
Cowells no longer offer an evening meal, but the
National Trust-run Hunter's Inn is just half a mile
away. More reports, please.

25% DISCOUNT VOUCHERS

Martinhoe
Barnstaple EX31 4PZ

T: 01598 763481
E: stay@heddonsgatehotel.co.uk
W: heddonsgatehotel.co.uk

BEDROOMS: 11.
OPEN: 15 Mar–11 Nov, group bookings
over Christmas and New Year.
FACILITIES: lounge, bar, boxed-games
room, TV room, breakfast/dining
room, free Wi-Fi, in-room TV
(Freeview), no mobile phone signal
(guests may use landline free of
charge), sun terrace, 2½-acre grounds,
unsuitable for disabled.
BACKGROUND MUSIC: none.
LOCATION: 6 miles W of Lynton.
CHILDREN: all ages welcomed.
DOGS: allowed in bedrooms (not
unattended), and in public rooms,
except dining room.
CREDIT CARDS: Amex, MC, Visa.
PRICES: per room B&B single £50-£120,
double £100-£155, 1-night bookings
refused bank holiday weekends.

MARTINHOE Devon

MAP 1:B4

THE OLD RECTORY HOTEL

Previous César Winner

The 'attentive hosts', 'friendly' ambience and
the 'very beautiful' situation are the standouts
at this Georgian rectory in 'what must be one of
the most tranquil places in the whole country'. 'It
takes some finding,' readers say, 'but it's worth the
search.' In 2008, Huw Rees and Sam Prosser took
over what was then a rather staid country house
hotel in a hamlet on the Exmoor coast. They
threw out the chintz, and gave the place a 'clean,
smart' make-over. 'The bedrooms are delightful,
as are sitting areas, which are beautifully
furnished, especially the orangery.' 'Our
comfortable room overlooked the garden with its
waterfall and little stream, a delight to the eye and
ear.' Afternoon tea is 'a sociable event'; 'Hugh's
cakes are worth returning early for'. In the same
way, 'pre-dinner drinks in the conservatory are a
great way of meeting other guests'. Thomas Frost,
who has worked for Michelin-starred super-chef
Michael Caines, creates such 'interesting dishes'
as wild garlic soup; Lundy turbot with Noilly
Prat sauce. Breakfast choices include local apple
juice, fruit smoothie; smoked salmon. 'Huw and
Sam have created a great hotel… We have already
booked to return.'

Berry's Ground Lane
Martinhoe EX31 4QT

T: 01598 763368
E: reception@oldrectoryhotel.co.uk
W: oldrectoryhotel.co.uk

BEDROOMS: 11, 2 on ground floor, 3 in
coach house.
OPEN: Mar–early Nov.
FACILITIES: 2 lounges, orangery,
dining room, free Wi-Fi, in-room TV
(Freeview), 3-acre grounds, public
rooms including restaurant wheelchair
accessible, toilet not adapted.
BACKGROUND MUSIC: 'very quiet' in
dining room only.
LOCATION: 4 miles W of Lynton.
CHILDREN: not under 14.
DOGS: not allowed.
CREDIT CARDS: Amex, MC, Visa.
PRICES: per room B&B double £190–
£245, D,B&B £230–£290, for single
deduct £15 (B&B) or £45 (D,B&B).
À la carte £35, 1-night bookings
occasionally refused weekends.

MAWGAN PORTH Cornwall

MAP 1:D2

BEDRUTHAN HOTEL AND SPA

♻ **Previous César Winner**

It is not that they've put away childish things at
this contemporary hotel set into the hillside above
Mawgan Porth beach. It remains very family-
friendly, but there's plenty for adults, too, from a
spa with a sensory garden, to cocktails on the bar
terrace, a tranquillity space, sunset suppers in the
Herring restaurant. 'My single room was crisp
and comfortable,' writes a trusted reader. 'Despite
being very small, it avoided being institutional.'
Her son, his wife and children 'seemed happy
enough' with a family room in 'an outlying
concrete stretch of the complex'. All rooms have
light Scandi styling, fresh milk, local toiletries.
Some have a sea view through floor-to-ceiling
windows; a private patio. On an Easter weekend
the place was 'packed to the gills, and for most of
the time guests and their children were managed
brilliantly'. School holidays are busy, and
'meaningful changes' are afoot for other times.
At night, Gareth Saddler's locally sourced dishes
include gurnard, salsify, spring onions, warm
potted crab. There's a children's menu in the Wild
Café, while kids' clubs and activities, evening
entertainment and babysitting give parents a
break. (Susan Willmington)

Trenance
Mawgan Porth TR8 4BU

T: 01637 860860
E: stay@bedruthan.com
W: bedruthan.com

BEDROOMS: 101. 1 suitable for disabled,
apartment suites in separate block.
OPEN: all year except 2 weeks Jan.
FACILITIES: lift, bar, restaurant, café,
lounge, free Wi-Fi, in-room TV
(Freeview), spa (indoor pool), civil
wedding licence, 5-acre grounds (3
heated pools, tennis), several areas
wheelchair accessible.
BACKGROUND MUSIC: in restaurant, café
and bar.
LOCATION: 4 miles NE of Newquay.
CHILDREN: all ages welcomed.
DOGS: allowed in some bedrooms,
some public areas (£12 per dog).
CREDIT CARDS: MC, Visa.
PRICES: per room B&B single from £80,
double £165–£335, D,B&B £217–£387.
Set dinner £38 (Herring), à la carte £26
(Wild Café).

MAWGAN PORTH Cornwall   MAP 1:D2

THE SCARLET

Shhh! It's adults only at this 'truly special' cliff-top hotel, which, say readers this year, 'achieves a wonderful balance of chic luxury, tranquillity and culinary delight'. No finger-paints or pirate ship – for those, check out sister hotel Bedruthan (previous entry). Here you can soak in an outdoor hot tub, unwind in the spa, chill out in meadow gardens, sit by a lounge fire. Bedrooms range from 'Just Right' to 'Indulgent'. 'Unique' rooms have an oval bath at the foot of the bed, a monsoon shower, a rooftop sitting room overlooking the Atlantic. All rooms have a private garden, terrace or balcony, sea views. 'We loved the fact that tea and coffee would be delivered to our room at any time by a cheerful member of the team.' 'The real stand-out, though, has to be the food… beautifully cooked, and simple, elegant presentation' in the Atlantic-view restaurant. From Mike Francis's imaginative seasonal menus: pan-fried pollack, baby globe artichokes, roast garlic potato gnocchi, gremolata. Vegans are well served. 'Breakfast is perfectly proportioned, imaginative.' 'Will we return? Absolutely. I cannot fault this hotel.' (Beth Carruthers, Ros Quinlivan, and many others)

Tredragon Road
Mawgan Porth TR8 4DQ

T: 01637 861800
E: stay@scarlethotel.co.uk
W: scarlethotel.co.uk

BEDROOMS: 37. 2 suitable for disabled.
OPEN: all year except 2–31 Jan, house parties Christmas (4 days) and New Year (3 days).
FACILITIES: lift, 2 lounges, bar, library, restaurant, free Wi-Fi, in-room TV (Freeview), civil wedding licence, spa, terrace, meadow garden, public areas wheelchair accessible, adapted toilet.
BACKGROUND MUSIC: all day in bar and restaurant.
LOCATION: 4 miles NE of Newquay.
CHILDREN: not allowed.
DOGS: allowed in five selected bedrooms, some public areas.
CREDIT CARDS: MC, Visa.
PRICES: per room B&B single £200–£460, double £220–£480. Set dinner £46. 1-night bookings refused Fri/Sat.

MAWNAN SMITH Cornwall

MAP 1:E2

BUDOCK VEAN

NEW

In 'glorious' grounds', Martin Barlow's hotel, golf resort and spa on the Helford river returns to a full entry this year thanks to a trusted reader and frequent guest who loves 'the personalised hospitality and the attention of good staff'. The refurbished 18th-century manor house contains bedrooms 'to suit all purses', and is praised for 'comfort and cleanliness', good lighting and an 'excellent bathroom'. Traditional superior rooms face the garden and golf course. Signature rooms have a more contemporary luxury feel, a new bathroom. All are supplied with robes, slippers, Elemis toiletries. A Cornish cream tea awaits the return of hungry walkers and kayakers. A cosy lounge has a log fire in a curved stone fireplace; the spa lounge opens on to a terrace. In the restaurant (formal dress required), chef Darren Kelly's locally sourced 'consistently well-presented and superbly flavoured' dishes include the likes of grilled hake, sauté potatoes, red chard, crab and samphire butter; from a vegetarian menu, vegan chickpea patties with tomato and red pepper sauce. There are children's sailing lessons, on- and offshore fishing. 'A deserved entry for so many reasons.' (Mary Coles, Suzanne Lyons)

25% DISCOUNT VOUCHERS

nr Helford Passage
Mawnan Smith
Falmouth TR11 5LG

T: 01326 252100
E: relax@budockvean.co.uk
W: budockvean.co.uk

BEDROOMS: 56. Plus 4 self-catering cottages, 1 suitable for disabled; wheelchair access from rear of hotel.
OPEN: all year except 2–24 Jan.
FACILITIES: lift, 2 lounges, cocktail bar, conservatory, bar, restaurant, free Wi-Fi, in-room TV (Freeview), civil wedding licence, 65-acre grounds, spa, sauna, indoor swimming pool, bar and public lounges wheelchair accessible.
BACKGROUND MUSIC: 'gentle' live piano or guitar music in evening in restaurant.
LOCATION: 6 miles SW of Falmouth.
CHILDREN: all ages welcomed.
DOGS: allowed in most bedrooms, terrace, not in public rooms.
CREDIT CARDS: MC, Visa.
PRICES: per person B&B £73–£146, D,B&B £100–£172. Set dinner £46.

MELLS Somerset

THE TALBOT INN

♧Previous César Winner

'Very much the country pub, with a warm buzz
to it', this old coaching inn, built around a cobbled
courtyard, stands at the heart of a historic stone
village. It is a 'gem', say readers, with 'friendly,
attentive staff', a popular locals' bar. Bedrooms
range from small to 'very large', but all have a
king- or emperor-size bed, Welsh blankets, a
comfy armchair or sofa, seagrass flooring, works
by local artists, Bramley toiletries. A garden-
facing room has a four-poster, roll-top bath and
shower room. A double with separate access and
vaulted ceiling can connect with a twin room and
share a bathroom. Richie Peacocke has moved
to sister hotel The Beckford Arms, Tisbury
(see entry) and it is now chef Dave Waine who
devises menus of West Country and home-grown
produce, pub classics, day-boat fish, a daily pie,
served in the bar, snug, courtyard, map room or
alfresco. Perhaps fennel-cured Brixham hake,
mussels, new potatoes, samphire, aïoli, sourdough
crumbs. On Saturday night there are charcoal
grills in the lovely beamed coach house, which
opens also for Sunday lunch roasts. The rolling
Mendip hills are on the doorstep for walking,
cycling and top-of-the-world views.

Selwood Street
Mells
Frome BA11 3PN

T: 01373 812254
E: info@talbotinn.com
W: talbotinn.com

BEDROOMS: 8. 1 on ground floor.
OPEN: all year except 25 Dec.
FACILITIES: sitting room, bar,
restaurant, coach house grill room,
free Wi-Fi, in-room Smart TV
(including Freeview), cobbled
courtyard, small garden.
BACKGROUND MUSIC: in public areas.
LOCATION: in village.
CHILDREN: all ages welcomed.
DOGS: allowed in 1 bedroom (£10 one-
off charge), and in all public areas.
CREDIT CARDS: MC, Visa.
PRICES: per room B&B £100–£160
(family suite £200). À la carte £30.
1-night bookings refused weekends.

MEVAGISSEY Cornwall

MAP 1:D2

TREVALSA COURT

'Sitting on the cliff-tops on the outskirts of Mevagissey', John and Susan Gladwin's small hotel is 'relaxed and informal with a nicely varied age range of guests', writes a trusted reader this year. A 1930s house with panelled dining room, big Gothic fireplaces, stone-mullioned windows, it stands in a sub-tropical garden, 'a wonderful place to unwind, take a clotted cream tea, or begin the stroll down to the private beach'. Most of the light bedrooms have splashes of seaside colour and a sea view 'as far as the South Devon headlands and distant Dartmoor'. Some have a shower-only wet room, some a bath with shower over. All provide bathrobes, White Company toiletries. 'I always choose a small but comfortable ground-floor one with its own access to the garden, and a small but spotless bathroom.' Chef Adam Cawood chooses ingredients from the sea and local farms for such dishes as seared mackerel fillets, granola, pickled cucumber, peanut emulsion; ten-hour slow-cooked braised beef brisket, Helford Blue soufflé, braised red cabbage; wild garlic tart. 'Service can be a bit slow, but that's because food is individually prepared and always worth waiting for.' (Mike Craddock)

School Hill
Mevagissey PL26 6TH

T: 01726 842468
E: stay@trevalsa-hotel.co.uk
W: trevalsa-hotel.co.uk

BEDROOMS: 15. Family suite on ground floor with own entrance.
OPEN: 12 Feb–20 Nov (phone to check if open at Christmas, New Year).
FACILITIES: lounge, bar, restaurant, free Wi-Fi, in-room TV (Freeview), 2-acre garden, summer house, public rooms wheelchair accessible.
BACKGROUND MUSIC: all day in bar.
LOCATION: on cliff-top, at edge of village.
CHILDREN: all ages welcomed.
DOGS: allowed in bedrooms (not unattended), not in restaurant, in other public rooms with consent of other guests.
CREDIT CARDS: Amex, MC, Visa.
PRICES: per room B&B single £70–£120, double/family £110–£295. À la carte £35. 1-night bookings refused high season.

SEE ALSO SHORTLIST

MILTON ABBOT Devon

HOTEL ENDSLEIGH

♦ Previous César Winner

Et in Arcadia we go – to Olga Polizzi's Regency
cottage-orné, in gardens and pleasure grounds
with woodland walks and waterfalls, arboretum,
fount and follies. The house was built as a fishing
lodge for the Duchess of Bedford by Jeffry
Wyatville, with landscaping by Humphry Repton,
who confessed he 'never so well pleased himself'.
Readers have been every bit as pleased by the
'wonderful grounds' with 'the wide meander of
the Tamar' running through, the 'library full of
real books', the 'charm' of the decor, the 'historical
authenticity'. Bedrooms have gorgeous original
features, hand-painted wallpaper, a roll-top bath,
perhaps, too, a walk-in shower, Mitchell and
Peach toiletries, teas and coffees delivered on
request. Even a small room overlooking the car
park did not disappoint. A new chef this year,
Tom Ewings, sources produce from local growers,
suppliers, fishermen and foragers, to create such
dishes as brill, shellfish and saffron chowder,
grilled baby leek; venison ragout, baby turnips,
pickled red cabbage, shallot purée, braised onion,
cavolo nero. A ghillie is available for fishing days.
See also the entry for Tresanton, St Mawes, Mrs
Polizzi's seaside hotel.

Milton Abbot
Tavistock PL19 0PQ

T: 01822 870000
E: info@hotelendsleigh.com
W: hotelendsleigh.com

BEDROOMS: 18. 1 on ground floor, 3 in
stables, 1 in lodge (1 mile from main
house), 1 suite suitable for disabled.
OPEN: all year.
FACILITIES: drawing room, library, card
room, bar, 2 dining rooms, free Wi-Fi,
in-room TV (Freeview), civil wedding
licence, 108-acre estate (fishing,
ghillie), public rooms wheelchair
accessible, adapted toilet.
BACKGROUND MUSIC: none.
LOCATION: 7 miles NW of Tavistock.
CHILDREN: all ages welcomed.
DOGS: allowed in bedrooms, lounges,
not in restaurant, or library at tea
time.
CREDIT CARDS: Amex, MC, Visa.
PRICES: per room B&B £202–£460,
D,B&B £242–£565. Set dinner
£28–£52.50. 1-night bookings refused
Fri, Sat.

MOUSEHOLE Cornwall

⚘THE OLD COASTGUARD

César award: seaside hotel of the year

'They really want to give you a treat and spoil you.' 'A lovely, relaxing couple of days.' Much praise this year for Charles and Edmund Inkin's 'buzzy' dining pub, sister to The Gurnard's Head, Zennor, and The Felin Fach Griffin, Felin Fach, Wales (see entries). 'Classy' bedrooms overlook the pretty village and harbour, towards St Clement's Island. 'Mine had a lounge and delightful balcony.' 'No. 8 was a tight fit; no wardrobe, but a good-sized bed, bathroom, two comfy chairs. All rooms have a Roberts radio, woollen blankets, Bramley toiletries. The trademark Inkin style embraces a blazing fire, bare floorboards, unmatched furniture. 'The lovely restaurant looks out to sea. Service was friendly and attentive', if 'a little chaotic' at busy times. Matthew Smith uses locally sourced ingredients in such dishes as fish stew, mussels, new potatoes, fennel, sea vegetables, aïoli. 'Breakfast could hardly be bettered, from slices of melon to delicious vine tomatoes with the bacon and sausage.' A fire in June forced the closure of the hotel, but it is due to reopen in autumn 2019. (Mike Craddock, Sue and John Jenkinson, and others)

25% DISCOUNT VOUCHERS

The Parade
Mousehole
Penzance TR19 6PR

T: 01736 731222
E: bookings@oldcoastguardhotel.co.uk
W: oldcoastguardhotel.co.uk

BEDROOMS: 14.
OPEN: all year except 24/25 Dec.
FACILITIES: bar, sun lounge, restaurant, free Wi-Fi, sea-facing garden with path to beach, restaurant and bar wheelchair accessible.
BACKGROUND MUSIC: Radio 4 at breakfast, selected music at other mealtimes.
LOCATION: 2-min. walk from village, 3 miles S of Newlyn.
CHILDREN: all ages welcomed.
DOGS: allowed in bedrooms (treats, towels, dog bowls), not in dining room.
CREDIT CARDS: MC, Visa.
PRICES: per room B&B single from £110, double £150–£250. Set dinner £19.50–£27, à la carte £29. 1-night bookings only rarely refused.

MULLION COVE Cornwall

MULLION COVE HOTEL

'Perched high on the Lizard cliffs with views out to sea and the sound of waves at night, the setting could not be more romantic.' A reader was impressed this year by the location of this Edwardian cathedral of a hotel, built by the Great Western Railway, now owned by the Grose family. Most bedrooms offer a 'spectacular' outlook; all have splashes of colour, and tea-/coffee-making facilities. Premier sea-view rooms include home-made biscuits, a Nespresso machine, robes, slippers. A Guide regular found his room 'generously sized, luxuriously appointed, if a little old-fashioned in decor'. Seasonal Cornish produce takes centre stage, both in the bar, where bistro fare includes mackerel fillets and crab salad, and in the Atlantic View restaurant, where returnees rave over Paul Stephens's daily-changing menus, 'especially the freshly landed fish'. For instance, cod fillet, clam and bacon chowder, crispy kale. One hungry walker 'found the evening meals in both venues a bit ordinary'; 'a chewy pork chop, an indifferent crab cake, slightly small portions'. Breakfast, however, was 'excellent'. Eggs Benedict, smoked haddock, and scrambled tofu should satisfy the heartiest rambler. (MC, and others)

Cliff Road
Mullion Cove
Helston TR12 7EP

T: 01326 240328
E: enquiries@mullion-cove.co.uk
W: mullion-cove.co.uk

BEDROOMS: 30. Some on ground floor.
OPEN: all year.
FACILITIES: lift, 3 lounges, bar, restaurant, free Wi-Fi, in-room TV (Freeview), 1-acre garden, 10-metre heated outdoor swimming pool, public areas wheelchair accessible.
BACKGROUND MUSIC: at mealtimes and in bar.
LOCATION: on edge of village.
CHILDREN: all ages welcomed.
DOGS: allowed in some bedrooms, 1 lounge.
CREDIT CARDS: Amex, MC, Visa.
PRICES: per room B&B single £85–£320, double £100–£335, D,B&B double £170–£405. Set dinner £40, à la carte £33. 1-night bookings sometimes refused bank holiday Sat.

NEAR SAWREY Cumbria

MAP 4: inset C2

EES WYKE COUNTRY HOUSE

'Strongly endorsed by readers this year: 'The
exceptional ambience of this very fine hotel
reflects Richard Lee's personal, multi-talented
approach.' The Georgian country house
overlooking Esthwaite Water once welcomed
Beatrix Potter into its comfortable embrace.
So enamoured was she, that, after three family
holidays she bought a farmhouse nearby. Today,
Ees Wyke is liked just as well by visitors, as much
for its 'stunning location, lovely rooms and superb
food' as the 'excellent hospitality' provided by 'a
small but tremendously effective local team'. 'A
club-like atmosphere' pervades at dinner as 'guests
engage in polite, stimulating conversations (an
increasingly uncommon feature in many hotels)'
over dishes from Richard's daily-changing menu.
For instance: butterfly trout with lemon parsley
butter; slow-cooked local beef. The dining room
and the best bedrooms offer far-reaching lake
panoramas. 'Our light, comfortable room came
with a powerful en suite shower, fresh milk and
fantastic views.' A minor quibble: thieves' coat-
hangers. The award-winning breakfast includes
home-made pastries and marmalade, and local
sausages. (Stephen and Pauline Glover, J and IS)

25% DISCOUNT VOUCHERS

Near Sawrey
Ambleside LA22 0JZ

T: 015394 36393
E: mail@eeswyke.co.uk
W: eeswyke.co.uk

BEDROOMS: 9. 1 on ground floor,
7 en suite, 2 with separate private
bathroom.
OPEN: all year except Christmas.
FACILITIES: 2 lounges, restaurant,
free Wi-Fi, in-room TV (Freeview),
veranda, ½-acre garden, unsuitable
for disabled.
BACKGROUND MUSIC: none.
LOCATION: edge of village 2½ miles
SE of Hawkshead on B5285.
CHILDREN: not under 12.
DOGS: not allowed.
CREDIT CARDS: MC, Visa.
PRICES: per room B&B single £75–£127,
double £99–£190. Set dinner £38.
1-night bookings sometimes refused
weekends, bank holidays.

NETHER WESTCOTE Oxfordshire

THE FEATHERED NEST

♛ Previous César Winner

Award-winning chef Kuba Winkowski marks
his tenth year at Tony and Amanda Timmer's
'truly amazing' restaurant-with-rooms, in a
converted malthouse. Its garden overlooks the
Evenlode valley. A reader's one dilemma was how
to describe it – 'Hotel/pub/restaurant, call it what
you will.' And, yes, it is a local pub with a real
fire in the beamed bar, cask ales, 25 plus wines by
the glass. The bedrooms have pretty, cottage-style
decor, an espresso machine, bathrobes, Algotherm
toiletries. Three have a bath and walk-in shower;
Cockerel's Roost has just a shower. But it is Mr
Winkowski's cooking, honed in Raymond Blanc's
kitchen, that sets the place apart. Everything is
done on site, from baking to smoking, to curing,
churning, fermenting. Menus are presented as
a series of dishes, from charcuterie to cheeses
via such unusual offerings as hogget, hummus,
apricot, sumac; mussels, monk's beard, sea kale.
But courses are not delineated: please, pick
and mix. Meals are served 'in a pretty dining
room overlooking the Cotswold countryside'.
This exceptional chef is receiving the 'wider
recognition' for which Guide readers have long
been calling.

Nether Westcote
Chipping Norton OX7 6SD

T: 01993 833030
E: info@thefeatherednestinn.co.uk
W: thefeatherednestinn.co.uk

BEDROOMS: 4.
OPEN: closed 25 Dec, 2 weeks Jan,
Mon/Tues/Wed apart from special
trading days.
FACILITIES: 2 bars, small lounge,
dining room, free Wi-Fi, in-room
TV (Freeview), civil wedding licence,
45-acre grounds, restaurant and bar
wheelchair accessible, adapted toilet.
BACKGROUND MUSIC: in bar all day.
LOCATION: in hamlet, 5 miles S of
Stow-on-the-Wold.
CHILDREN: all ages welcomed.
DOGS: allowed in bar, not in bedrooms.
CREDIT CARDS: Amex, MC, Visa.
PRICES: per room B&B £295–£310,
D,B&B £390–£440. Set dinner 4-course
£70, 6-course £90.

NEW MILTON Hampshire

MAP 2:E2

CHEWTON GLEN

'My four-year-old loves Chewton as much as I do, it's always a struggle to leave.' 'We stayed to celebrate our 50th wedding anniversary, and it exceeded expectations.' After more than half a century, this country house hotel 'in beautiful grounds' close to a 'stunning, often deserted beach' continues to appeal to guests of all ages, growing and innovating but never losing sight of traditional values. This year brings a new Kids Club Treehouse, while afternoon tea is still served on the terrace. Children's menus, a kids' cookery course, bug hotel, and outdoor pool entertain little ones. Adult indulgences include hot tub suites, a tree-house hideaway suite, tennis courts, golf course. 'The spa was fantastic, the jet pool the best I've encountered.' Garden rooms have a balcony or terrace with views over parkland. Coach house suites, sleeping six, have a semi-private walled garden, a marble bathroom. Luke Matthews's menus, too, have broad appeal, with veggie dishes, classics such as sole meunière, more modern and exotic fare: 'I highly recommend the Thai crab risotto.' Staff are 'charming, dedicated, exceptional'. 'Expensive but good value.'
(M Moore, Dianna Tennant, and many others)

Christchurch Road
New Milton BH25 6QS

T: 01425 275341
E: reservations@chewtonglen.com
W: chewtonglen.com

BEDROOMS: 72. 14 on ground floor, 14 tree-house suites in grounds, 1 suitable for disabled.
OPEN: all year.
FACILITIES: lounges, bar, 2 restaurants, function rooms, free Wi-Fi, in-room TV (Sky), civil wedding licence, cookery school, spa, indoor pool, 130-acre grounds (heated pool, tennis, golf), public rooms (not spa) wheelchair accessible.
BACKGROUND MUSIC: 'subtle' in public areas.
LOCATION: on S edge of New Forest.
CHILDREN: all ages welcomed.
DOGS: allowed in tree-house suites, on terraces.
CREDIT CARDS: Amex, MC, Visa.
PRICES: per room B&B £370–£3,000, D,B&B £470–£3,120. À la carte £70. 1-night stays sometimes refused Sat.

NEW ROMNEY Kent

MAP 2:E5

ROMNEY BAY HOUSE

♛ Previous César Winner

'After a journey along the bumpy road, we were welcomed at the door by Lisa and Clinton, who took our cases up the rather steep stairs to a lovely room.' Readers enjoyed this year's stay at the Lovells' 'remote' 1920s house, built by Clough Williams-Ellis for Hollywood actress Hedda Hopper. It stands between golf links and brine, amid the wild beauty of Romney Marsh. 'It's a very personally run place,' say Guide inspectors who had 'one of the best sea-facing rooms', with 'lovely windows giving a glorious sunrise, a nice, big, wooden four-poster'. Small quibbles: dim lighting, no slippers, and 'the bathroom had a cold tiled floor'. Guests gather at 7.30 for drinks and 'delicious nibbles' by the lounge log fire, before 'the highlight of our stay, dinner', cooked by classically trained Mr Lovell. 'No choice, but we had corresponded about our requirements. We had smoked fish pâté, delicious cod – so fresh – and a selection of small, tasty puddings.' Breakfast brings 'nicely cooked bacon and sausages', 'specially baked croissants'. Praise for 'the very friendly, young staff.' Full marks to the 'caring, hard-working hostess' and her husband, 'a great chef'. (Peter Wainman, and others)

25% DISCOUNT VOUCHERS

Coast Road
Littlestone
New Romney TN28 8QY

T: 01797 364747
E: enquiries@romneybayhousehotel.
co.uk
W: romneybayhousehotel.co.uk

BEDROOMS: 10.
OPEN: all year except 2 weeks over Christmas and early Jan (open New Year), dining room open Tues/Wed/Fri/Sat evenings only.
FACILITIES: bar, sitting room, first-floor lounge with sea views, dining room, free Wi-Fi, in-room TV (Freeview), small function facilities, 1-acre garden, unsuitable for disabled.
BACKGROUND MUSIC: none.
LOCATION: 1½ miles from New Romney.
CHILDREN: 14 and upwards welcomed.
DOGS: only guide dogs allowed.
CREDIT CARDS: Amex, MC, Visa.
PRICES: per room B&B single £80–£95, double £110–£160. Set dinner £49. 1-night advance bookings refused weekends.

NEWBIGGIN-ON-LUNE Cumbria

MAP 4:C3

BROWNBER HALL

'As soon as we entered, we knew this was going to be special.' Readers offered high praise in 2019 after visiting Amanda and Peter Jaques-Walker's Victorian country house. 'We thoroughly enjoyed our stay,' report others. The owners, London escapees, are 'charming, attentive' hosts who run a 'luxurious, eclectically furnished' Dales property with interiors by a former Soho House architect. Prints, etchings and photos line the public rooms, while the 'tranquil', 'well-appointed' upstairs bedrooms have a 'comfortable' bed, and 'good attention to little details' from 100 Acres toiletries to the offer of fresh milk and mineral water. The best room, at the front, yields 'never-ending' green views to Howgill Fells. 'Clever touches' include individually adjustable bedside reading lights, the lounge's original 1950s honesty bar, a sideboard laden with cakes including 'delicious home-made banana and chocolate loaf'. New this year, Peter's stone-baked sourdough pizzas: 'the best we've ever tasted'. Morning brings an 'excellent, locally sourced' breakfast with 'perfectly cooked' dishes including scrambled eggs and spinach; waffles and streaky bacon. (Christina Voong, and others)

Newbiggin-on-Lune
Kirkby Stephen CA17 4NX

T: 015396 23208
E: enquiries@brownberhall.co.uk
W: brownberhall.co.uk

BEDROOMS: 8.
OPEN: all year except Christmas and New Year.
FACILITIES: 2 lounges (log fire, honesty bar), dining room, free Wi-Fi, in-room TV (Freeview), 1-acre garden, bicycle storage, unsuitable for disabled.
BACKGROUND MUSIC: all day in public rooms.
LOCATION: 6¼ miles SW of Kirkby Stephen – 'follow the hosts' clear directions, not satnav'.
CHILDREN: all ages welcomed.
DOGS: allowed in 2 bedrooms, public rooms.
CREDIT CARDS: MC, Visa.
PRICES: B&B single £70, double £100–£220. À la carte £30. 1-night bookings refused busy weekends.

NEWCASTLE UPON TYNE Tyne and Wear   MAP 4:B4

JESMOND DENE HOUSE

♔ Previous César Winner

'An oasis of calm in the northern suburbs of Newcastle', Peter Candler's mansion is named after the wooded valley in which it stands. Built for the city mayor in 1822 in Tudor style, and much altered (by Norman Shaw, among others), it impresses with its 'massive, rugged, dark stone facade'. In the past year, bedrooms and public areas have been refurbished, and a new chef has been appointed. Danny Parker brings experience in a Michelin-starred kitchen to his à la carte and set menus, with such dishes as Yorkshire pork, wild garlic, broccoli, morel, asparagus; roasted cauliflower, couscous, capers, raisins. An all-day menu offers club steak and bone marrow burger; cod and chips. Panelled lounges are hung with 'prints, cartoons, works by local artists'. Rooms are contemporary boutique style, some with both bath and walk-in shower. Two under-eaves suites have a roof terrace. All have Molton Brown toiletries, fresh milk, magazines. Breakfast in 'an attractive conservatory' brings 'good-quality' toast, freshly squeezed orange juice, fresh-baked pastries, avocado on sourdough, Craster kippers, Cumberland sausage. 'Staff greet one by name, with a smile: a very enjoyable stay.' (RG)

Jesmond Dene Road
Newcastle upon Tyne NE2 2EY

T: 0191 212 3000
E: info@jesmonddenehouse.co.uk
W: jesmonddenehouse.co.uk

BEDROOMS: 40. 8 in adjacent New House, 2 suitable for disabled.
OPEN: all year.
FACILITIES: lift, lounge, cocktail bar, billiard room, restaurant, conference/function facilities, terrace, free Wi-Fi, in-room TV (Sky), civil wedding licence, parking, 2-acre garden, public areas accessible by wheelchair.
BACKGROUND MUSIC: in public areas and restaurant.
LOCATION: 2 miles from city centre.
CHILDREN: all ages welcomed.
DOGS: allowed on restaurant terrace only.
CREDIT CARDS: Amex, MC, Visa.
PRICES: per room B&B £119–£299.
À la carte £45.

NEWMARKET Suffolk

MAP 2:B4

THE PACKHORSE INN

In a rural village overlooking a medieval packhorse bridge across the River Kennett, this 'revitalised' Victorian boozer was the first venture for Philip Turner's spreading Chestnut group. The once-brash polychrome-brick street front is now tastefully rendered, while interiors, styled by Mr Turner's wife, Amanda, 'look terrific'. Beyond a glassed-in corridor lie a bar and 'very smart' dining areas, with 'stripped floorboards, good-sized wood tables, a real fire burning in a dual-aspect fireplace'. Your dog-friendly bedroom might have a claw-foot in-room bath, a double-, king-, or super-king-size bed, or twins, a walk-in shower. Coach house rooms have under-floor heating and open on to a terrace. Dramatic Lark has oak furniture, oversized lamps, floor-to-ceiling windows. Regularly changing menus feature such dishes as Blythburgh pork belly, roasted apple purée, spinach, roast onion, creamed potato; chargrilled monkfish, pickled lime glaze, fennel salad, Suffolk new potatoes – as well as pub classics. Breakfast brings smoked salmon, eggs Benedict, the full Suffolk. Newmarket is three miles away: on race days expect to jockey for position at the bar for a pint of Woodforde's Wherry. (JB)

Bridge Street
Moulton
Newmarket CB8 8SP

T: 01638 751818
E: info@thepackhorseinn.com
W: thepackhorseinn.com

BEDROOMS: 8. 4 on ground floor in coach house, 3 suitable for disabled.
OPEN: all year.
FACILITIES: bar, restaurant, function room, free Wi-Fi, in-room TV (Freeview), courtyard, public areas wheelchair accessible, adapted toilet.
BACKGROUND MUSIC: in public rooms.
LOCATION: opposite green in Moulton village, 3 miles from Newmarket.
CHILDREN: all ages welcomed.
DOGS: allowed in courtyard rooms (£10 a night), restaurant and bar.
CREDIT CARDS: Amex, MC, Visa.
PRICES: per room B&B single £95–£275, double £110–£275. À la carte £40.

SEE ALSO SHORTLIST

NEWTON ABBOT Devon

MAP 1:D4

THE ROCK INN

At the centre of a row of quarrymen's cottages, built in 1820 of the same local granite, this 'charming hotel' is true to its motto, 'steadfastly traditional'. It is in the small village of Haytor Vale, 'just below the famous Haytor rocks' on the south-eastern edge of Dartmoor. The Graves family have owned it since 1983, 'long enough to know what people like', and a reader who has known it for years rates it 'eleven out of ten for cosiness'. Bedrooms have exposed beams, views over the garden or moors. They don't have all the latest gadgetry or swish bathroom fittings (a shower room was 'a miracle of turning a cupboard to greater use'), but a 'beautiful' room with oak four-poster had 'antique furniture, a delightful sitting area'. The highest praise is reserved for staff who 'really know what they are doing', and for 'seriously good cooking'. 'The food was top rate, the people were lovely.' You can eat in the bar (if you're over 14) or in one of the dining rooms, such dishes as Devonshire lamb rump, fondant potato, asparagus, pea purée, baby gem, red wine jus. There is a good children's menu and 'lots of wine by the glass – how sensible!' In short, 'Highly recommended!'

Haytor Vale
Newton Abbot TQ13 9XP

T: 01364 661305
E: enquiries@rock-inn.co.uk
W: rock-inn.co.uk

BEDROOMS: 9.
OPEN: all year except 25/26 Dec.
FACILITIES: bar, 3 dining rooms, lounge, free Wi-Fi, in-room TV (Freeview), ¼-acre garden, bar, dining rooms and lounge wheelchair accessible, no adapted toilet.
BACKGROUND MUSIC: none.
LOCATION: 3 miles W of Bovey Tracey.
CHILDREN: all ages welcomed, not under 14 in main bar area.
DOGS: allowed in some bedrooms, bar, 1 dining room.
CREDIT CARDS: MC, Visa.
PRICES: per room B&B £110–£170. À la carte £35 (fixed price £19.95–£24.95, for 2 or 3 coures, selected dishes from main menu). 1-night bookings sometimes refused.

NORTH WALSHAM Norfolk

BEECHWOOD HOTEL

There is no mystery to the appeal of Emma and Hugh Asher's 'comfortable, most welcoming', country hotel with strong Agatha Christie associations. Standing in 'beautiful gardens', near the north Norfolk coast, it is 'well liked by traditionalists', also by rock stars and petrolheads (past guests include Eric Clapton and Jeremy Clarkson). Bedrooms have dark furniture, heavy floral fabrics, some a carved four-poster, a Victorian-style bathroom with slipper bath and 'roomy, powerful' walk-in shower. Hotel photographs capture Christie staying here with doctor friends in the 1930s, talking plots and poisons, when this was The Shrubs. Evening drinks in the lounge can be 'a drawn-out affair', say readers in 2019. However, on the night of a big match, 'the kitchen kindly agreed to open early so we could eat and go to watch the football'. In the restaurant, with its Art Deco flourishes, Steven Norgate's locally sourced dishes include beef fillet, baby spring vegetables, potato pavé, green and pink peppercorn sauce. Vegetarians enjoy a separate menu. 'The food was very good, portions were huge.' Breakfast brings a 'lovely buffet, a decent cooked choice'. (Sara Price, MC)

25% DISCOUNT VOUCHERS

20 Cromer Road
North Walsham NR28 0HD

T: 01692 403231
E: info@beechwood-hotel.co.uk
W: beechwood-hotel.co.uk

BEDROOMS: 18. 4 on ground floor.
OPEN: all year except 27/28 Dec.
FACILITIES: bar, 2 lounges, restaurant, free Wi-Fi, in-room TV (Freeview), 100-metre landscaped garden (croquet).
BACKGROUND MUSIC: all day in public rooms.
LOCATION: near town centre.
CHILDREN: all ages welcomed.
DOGS: allowed, not in restaurant.
CREDIT CARDS: Amex, MC, Visa.
PRICES: per room B&B single £90, double £100–£175, D,B&B £140–£215. À la carte £40.

NORWICH Norfolk   MAP 2:B5

THE ASSEMBLY HOUSE

An opulent wedding venue, hotel, art gallery and cookery school in one, The Assembly House offers history and contemporary style in a Grade I listed city-centre location. The resplendent Georgian building's current incarnation is due to Iain Wilson and chef Richard Hughes, who added the 11 'luxuriously and tastefully' designed bedrooms in 2016. Housed in the east wing, rooms are a joyful mix of vintage and contemporary touches: a glass chandelier, perhaps, above a 'multi-coloured fabric headboard'. Most of the 'large and comfortable' bathrooms have a freestanding claw-footed bath; all have toiletries by Arran Aromatics and a drench shower. Lunch is 'excellent', while an early supper (5 pm–7 pm) is aimed at theatre-goers (the Theatre Royal is next door) and might include warm caramelised onion tart followed by herbed Cromer crab cake. Breakfast is a feast of hot dishes (eggs Benedict, kippers, veggie fry-up), plus cereal and baked goods; afternoon tea (from midday) includes the hotel's signature Gateau Assembly – layers of almond sponge, coffee buttercream and chocolate ganache. 'Ideally situated' for visitors to Norwich, 'whether on business or for pleasure'.

Theatre Street
Norwich NR2 1RQ

T: 01603 626402
E: admin@assemblyhousenorwich.
   co.uk
W: assemblyhousenorwich.co.uk

BEDROOMS: 11. All in St Mary's House extension, 6 with private garden, 1 suitable for disabled.
OPEN: all year.
FACILITIES: dining room, private dining and function rooms, civil wedding licence, free Wi-Fi, in-room TV (Sky, Freeview), 1-acre grounds, free permit parking, public rooms wheelchair accessible, adapted toilet.
BACKGROUND MUSIC: none.
LOCATION: central, car park permits for pay-and-display.
CHILDREN: all ages welcomed.
DOGS: not allowed.
CREDIT CARDS: Amex, MC, Visa.
PRICES: per room B&B £170–£270. À la carte £21.95.

SEE ALSO SHORTLIST

NORWICH Norfolk

MAP 2:B5

38 ST GILES

Built in 1700, and once home to the Lord Mayor of Norwich, this 'well-placed' luxury B&B is run 'with enthusiasm and commitment' by father and daughter Dennis and Holly Bacon. Medieval St Giles Church is at the end of the street (on Tuesday evenings the ringers practise their Plain Bob Majors in its soaring tower). Guests enter via a passage shared with a nursery, and are welcomed with tea and home-made cakes. Stylish bedrooms have a coffee machine, fresh milk, L'Occitane toiletries. The panelled Gurney Suite has a 'king-size bed, gold damask curtains, a lounge area with leather chesterfield sofa bed, and a good, small, bathroom with walk-in shower'. Most rooms have a monsoon shower, some a bath; the St Giles Suite has a freestanding bath and shower area. Book the two-bedroom apartment at No. 48, with drawing room and designer kitchen, and they'll deliver a continental breakfast and newspapers. At No. 38, breakfast, served in the 'elegant Georgian dining room', at tables 'beautifully laid with bone china', brings 'freshly squeezed juice, delicious yogurt with honey and berries', home-made granola, crème fraîche pancakes, smoked salmon, bacon. Service is by 'friendly young people'.

38 St Giles Street
Norwich NR2 1LL

T: 01603 662944
E: bookings@38stgiles.co.uk
W: 38stgiles.co.uk

BEDROOMS: 12. 1 on ground floor, 4 in apartment and town house.
OPEN: all year except 24–28 Dec.
FACILITIES: breakfast room, lounge, free Wi-Fi, in-room TV (Freeview), courtyard garden, unsuitable for disabled.
BACKGROUND MUSIC: at breakfast.
LOCATION: central, limited private parking (advance booking, £15 per day).
CHILDREN: all ages welcomed.
DOGS: not allowed.
CREDIT CARDS: MC, Visa.
PRICES: per room B&B single £105–£210, double £130–£260, town house (2 doubles) from £275, apartment (2 doubles) from £300.

SEE ALSO SHORTLIST

NOTTINGHAM Nottinghamshire

HART'S HOTEL

Built in 2003 on the old ramparts of the medieval castle, Tim and Stefa Hart's city hotel is a sister to their country house, Hambleton Hall, Hambleton (see entry). The look is contemporary and here, as at Hambleton, Mrs Hart has been responsible for the interior design. 'The central location makes it a clear choice for business travel and parents visiting offspring at university,' writes a trusted reader, but 'you wouldn't come here for spacious accommodation'. The bedrooms range from 'classic' to suites, but a superior double proved 'cramped', though with a comfortable bed and views across the city (classic rooms overlook an internal courtyard). Garden rooms, opening on to a private garden, have more sense of space. All rooms have a minibar, fresh milk, L'Occitane toiletries, king- or super-king-size bed. The restaurant, formerly in a separate building, has been brought in-house. Short, daily-changing menus include such dishes as wild mushroom and asparagus pasta, wild garlic; rump steak Diane, purple sprouting broccoli, green beans, mushrooms, radish. A buffet breakfast brings freshly squeezed orange juice, fruit salad, bread and muffins from the Harts' bakery; full English is £5 extra.

Standard Hill
Park Row
Nottingham NG1 6GN

T: 0115 988 1900
E: reception@hartshotel.co.uk
W: hartsnottingham.co.uk

BEDROOMS: 32. 2 suitable for disabled.
OPEN: all year, restaurant closed 1 Jan.
FACILITIES: lift, reception/lobby with seating, bar, restaurant, free Wi-Fi, in-room TV (Sky, Freeview), small exercise room, civil wedding licence, courtyard, private garden, secure car park (charges apply), restaurant wheelchair accessible, adapted toilet.
BACKGROUND MUSIC: 'light' in bar.
LOCATION: city centre.
CHILDREN: all ages welcomed.
DOGS: allowed in public rooms and bedrooms (not left unattended).
CREDIT CARDS: Amex, MC, Visa.
PRICES: room £139–£279. À la carte £35 (pre-theatre 2 courses £22 Mon–Thurs) plus 12.5% discretionary service charge.

OLD HUNSTANTON Norfolk

MAP 2:A5

THE NEPTUNE

A creeper-covered, former 18th-century coaching inn, The Neptune has been run as a 'most enjoyable restaurant-with-rooms' since 2007 by Kevin and Jacki Mangeolles – and has held its Michelin star since 2009. In a village on the west-facing tip of the north Norfolk coast, it is set apart from the resort of Hunstanton with its funfair, crazy golf and sea life centre. Kevin's menus are devised around a wealth of local produce – Brancaster mussels and lobsters, organic pork, game from surrounding estates. Readers praise the 'personal attention' shown to guests, the 'undimmed enthusiasm' of the owners for their operation, and their 'lack of complacency'. In the light and airy dining room, everything is just so, from the crisp white napery and 'elegant modern glass and china', to the 'execution and presentation' of such dishes as lemon sole, celeriac, polonaise, kale, pink fir apple; aged Dexter sirloin, braised oxtail, confit carrot, salsify, mash. Four 'spotless' white-and-cream bedrooms are supplied with an espresso machine, fresh milk, home-made biscuits. Breakfast brings home-baked croissants, good cooked dishes, setting you up for seal-watching or a round of golf. (BW)

85 Old Hunstanton Road
Old Hunstanton PE36 6HZ

T: 01485 532122
E: reservations@theneptune.co.uk
W: theneptune.co.uk

BEDROOMS: 4.
OPEN: all year, except Mon, and 26 Dec, 3 weeks Jan, 1 week May, 1 week Nov.
FACILITIES: bar area, restaurant, free Wi-Fi, in-room TV (Freeview), unsuitable for disabled.
BACKGROUND MUSIC: in restaurant in evening.
LOCATION: village centre, on A149.
CHILDREN: not under 10.
DOGS: not allowed.
CREDIT CARDS: Amex, MC, Visa.
PRICES: per room D,B&B £290–£320 (with tasting menu £320–£360). Set menus £47–£62, tasting menu £78. 1-night bookings sometimes refused Sat.

OLDSTEAD Yorkshire

THE BLACK SWAN AT OLDSTEAD

🏆 Previous César Winner

Tommy Banks was just 17 with dreams of a professional cricket career, when his dad bowled him a googly. Tommy's parents, Tom and Anne (farmers with deep roots in the Yorkshire soil), had taken on a failing 16th-century drovers' pub. While his brother, James, became front-of-house, Tommy entered the kitchen and headed towards Michelin stardom. At this now-famous gastronomic destination, Tommy and head chef Will Lockwood work with what the family grow, rear and forage. From a typical tasting menu: langoustine with dulse hollandaise, raw beef with Oldstead peppers; monkfish with fermented celeriac. Such fare benefits from 'professional, knowledgeable' serving staff. In an annexe wing, ground-floor bedrooms overlook the kitchen garden. Rooms in a nearby Georgian house have a feature bath and separate wet room. Some have a period fireplace, a four-poster, antiques; all have an unfussy style, a king-size bed. One reader found his 'a bit restaurant-with-rooms-ish', a touch impersonal. It's mostly about the food, however, and when they promise 'a proper breakfast' you know they mean it. (RC, BW)

Oldstead
York YO61 4BL

T: 01347 868387
E: enquiries@blackswanoldstead.co.uk
w: blackswanoldstead.co.uk

BEDROOMS: 9. 4, on ground floor in annexe wing, 5 in Ashberry House, 50 yds away.
OPEN: all year except 24–26 Dec.
FACILITIES: bar, restaurant, private dining room, free Wi-Fi, in-room TV (Freeview), garden, 2-acre kitchen garden and orchard.
BACKGROUND MUSIC: in restaurant.
LOCATION: in village 7 miles E of Thirsk.
CHILDREN: not under 18 overnight, over-10s only in restaurant.
DOGS: not allowed.
CREDIT CARDS: MC, Visa.
PRICES: per room D,B&B £390–£520. Tasting menu £98–£125.

ORFORD Suffolk

MAP 2:C6

THE CROWN AND CASTLE

♛ Previous César Winner

'We enjoyed our stay,' say trusted readers this year, returning to this much-loved Suffolk restaurant-with-rooms in a peaceful coastal town dominated by its castle. Now owned by the Small Hotel Folk group, and with experienced manager John Morrell at the helm, 'all is good'. 'Our terrace room was splendid, with a large bed, two good armchairs, an excellent modern bathroom with a spacious shower.' Another reader reported 'a few wobbles' (a malfunctioning TV in the bedroom and more weeds than desirable on the terrace) but was otherwise very positive. 'The bar, lounge and dining area are a delight, with cheerful furnishings and decorations. The staff, mainly young, were pleasant and helpful.' Chef Rob Walpole uses seasonal Suffolk ingredients with flair. 'The food is delicious', with 'lots of choice, and much local fish'. 'Superb' griddled asparagus; Felixstowe sprats and steak and kidney pie were especially enjoyable. It's worth visiting the castle, with one of the best-preserved keeps in England, or taking a boat trip to Orford Ness. Beaches and bird reserves are nearby. The acid test is, would one come again? The answer is 'Yes'. (Anthony Bradbury, Andy and Sylvia Aitken)

Market Hill
Orford
Woodbridge IP12 2LJ

T: 01394 450205
E: info@crownandcastle.co.uk
W: crownandcastle.co.uk

BEDROOMS: 21. 7 in main house, 10 (all on ground floor) in garden, 2 (on ground floor) in terrace, 1 in courtyard, 1 suite in stable block.
OPEN: all year, residents only 25, 26, 31 Dec, 1 Jan.
FACILITIES: bar, restaurant, free Wi-Fi, in-room TV (Freeview), parking, ¼-acre garden, restaurant wheelchair accessible, adapted toilet.
BACKGROUND MUSIC: none.
LOCATION: market square, about 100 yds from the castle.
CHILDREN: not under 8.
DOGS: allowed in 5 garden rooms, at one table in restaurant.
CREDIT CARDS: MC, Visa.
PRICES: per room B&B £140–£325, D,B&B £210–£385. À la carte £38. 1-night bookings usually refused Fri/Sat.

OSWESTRY Shropshire

MAP 3:B4

PEN-Y-DYFFRYN

'Our third visit. Most of the other guests were also returners. It isn't surprising.' Readers are drawn back time and again to this stone rectory in 'immaculate gardens' overlooking the Welsh hills. It is run as a hotel by owners Miles and Audrey Hunter with son Tommy and daughter Charlotte (sibling Henry has The Castle, Bishop's Castle, see entry). Bedrooms occupy the main house and coach house; some with warm, earthy hues, others with bright hits of colour. Four have a private patio where complimentary tea and cakes may be delivered by room service. Several rooms have a spa bath, a power shower. 'Everything is spotless, with good toiletries.' A 'wonderfully comprehensive information pack' includes walking routes, fishing on-site. Lounges have 'log fires, newspapers, big armchairs, bowls of fruit'. A late arriver, requesting supper, enjoyed 'a delicious, copious cold platter and home-made rolls'. David Braddick and Lewis Barton's three-course menus include vegetarian options and such dishes as Welsh Celtic Pride sirloin, short rib bonbon, celeriac purée, carrots, fondant potato, red wine jus. A morning newsletter accompanies an 'appetising' breakfast. (B and JH, and many others)

Rhydycroesau
Oswestry SY10 7JD

T: 01691 653700
E: stay@peny.co.uk
W: peny.co.uk

BEDROOMS: 12. 4, each with patio, in coach house, 1 on ground floor.
OPEN: all year except Christmas.
FACILITIES: 2 lounges, bar, restaurant, free Wi-Fi, in-room TV (Freeview), 5-acre grounds (summer house, dog-walking area, fly-fishing pool).
BACKGROUND MUSIC: in evening in bar and restaurant.
LOCATION: 3 miles W of Oswestry.
CHILDREN: not under 3.
DOGS: allowed in some bedrooms, not in public rooms after 6.30 pm.
CREDIT CARDS: MC, Visa.
PRICES: per person B&B £72–£107, D,B&B £99–£139, single occupancy £99–£120. Set menu £45. 1-night bookings occasionally refused Sat.

OXFORD Oxfordshire

MAP 2:C2

OLD BANK HOTEL

Ϣ Previous César Winner

Opposite the Bodleian Library, this contemporary
conversion of three stone buildings retains the
spacious feel of their Georgian origins. Artwork
from the private collection of owner Jeremy
Mogford (see also next entry) add to the light,
modern mood, despite puzzling some readers:
'We didn't know what to make of them, they
seemed to have no connection with Oxford.'
No such issues in the residents' library with its
sofas, elegant period windows and many books
dedicated to the city's history. On sunny days,
these might be enjoyed outside on the Italian
garden terrace. Many of the crisply up-to-date
bedrooms overlook the dreaming spires; the best
views are found in the rooftop room with floor-to-
ceiling windows and a private terrace overlooking
the Radcliffe Camera and All Souls College.
All rooms have a marble bathroom, art, tea and
coffee facilities. A former banking hall houses the
popular Quod brasserie where Rohan Kashid's
'very pleasant meals' include slow-cooked pork
belly, Pardina lentils, salsa verde. Guests can sleep
easy: breakfast (honey-baked ham-and-Cheddar
omelette, banana pancakes, eggs Royale) is served
until 11 am; then use the hotel bicycles to explore.

92–94 High Street
Oxford OX1 4BJ

T: 01865 799599
E: reception@oldbankhotel.co.uk
W: oldbankhotel.co.uk

BEDROOMS: 43. 1 suitable for disabled.
OPEN: all year.
FACILITIES: lift, residents' library/
bar, restaurant/bar, dining terrace,
2 meeting/private dining rooms,
free Wi-Fi, in-room TV (Freeview),
in-room spa treatments, small
garden, use of bicycles, restaurant, bar
wheelchair accessible, adapted toilet.
BACKGROUND MUSIC: in restaurant and
reception area.
LOCATION: central, car park.
CHILDREN: all ages welcomed.
DOGS: allowed on terrace only.
CREDIT CARDS: Amex, MC, Visa.
PRICES: per room B&B £210–£1,000. À
la carte £35 (plus 12½% discretionary
service charge). 1-night bookings
refused weekends in peak season.

SEE ALSO SHORTLIST

OXFORD Oxfordshire

MAP 2:C2

OLD PARSONAGE HOTEL

Beyond a walled terrace, an oak door leads into
a 17th-century house that now finds itself at the
edge of the city centre. It is run as an upmarket
hotel where owner Jeremy Mogford (see previous
entry) blends his passions for hospitality, literature
and art. In 'relatively small public rooms', an
'intimate, clubby' atmosphere prevails. The
dark-painted bar and restaurant sport many
'works from Jeremy Mogford's wonderful art
collection'. Upstairs is 'a conservatory-style library'
with outside terrace. The smart, contemporary
bedrooms have a marble bathroom, Noble Isle
toiletries and carefully chosen artwork. Some
have a bath and drench shower, a terrace or
Juliet balcony overlooking the garden. You
can eat all day, inside or out, starting with,
say, eggs Florentine, a kipper or honey-baked
ham omelette. At lunch and dinner, Allan
McLaughlin's 'very good' cooking includes such
dishes as grilled sea bream, roast fennel and
orange, rosemary butter sauce – for children,
lemonade-battered fish fingers. The young staff
'impress at every turn', the place looks appealing
and, as (alleged) former resident Oscar Wilde
opined, 'Only shallow people do not judge by
appearances.' (TM)

1 Banbury Road
Oxford OX2 6NN

T: 01865 310210
E: reception@oldparsonage-hotel.
   co.uk
W: oldparsonage-hotel.co.uk

BEDROOMS: 35. 10 on ground floor,
2 suitable for disabled.
OPEN: all year.
FACILITIES: lounge, library, bar/
restaurant, free Wi-Fi, in-room
TV (Freeview), civil wedding
licence, terrace, rear garden with
summerhouse, restaurant wheelchair
accessible.
BACKGROUND MUSIC: 'very light' in
restaurant and bar.
LOCATION: NE end of St Giles, small
car park.
CHILDREN: all ages welcomed.
DOGS: allowed on terrace only.
CREDIT CARDS: Amex, MC, Visa.
PRICES: per room B&B from £225,
D,B&B from £299. À la carte £40 (plus
12½% discretionary service charge).
1-night bookings sometimes refused
peak weekends.

SEE ALSO SHORTLIST

PADSTOW Cornwall

MAP 1:D2

PADSTOW TOWNHOUSE

Chef Paul Ainsworth's parents owned a Southampton guest house, where dinner might be dad's corned beef hash with Bisto gravy. His own enterprises are more high end, the rooms here complementing Michelin-starred Paul Ainsworth at No. 6 in downtown Padstow. The meticulously restored Georgian house has Tracey Emin artwork and suites lavishly styled by Paul's wife, Emma, and interior designer Eve Cullen-Cornes. Readers were 'blown away' by the level of service from the 'outstanding house team' led by manager Lucinda Bayne, the 'genuine, warm welcome' and scrupulous housekeeping. The pantry has everything from cakes to DIY cocktails. Each suite is unique. Ground-floor Popcorn has a king-size white French bed. Toffee Apple, inspired by the grounds of nearby Prideaux Place, has a double oak and copper bath. All suites have a double rain-head shower, coffee machine, minibar, fresh milk and more. They can lend you a bike, or shuttle you by electric car, to No. 6, where dishes might include Cornish hogget, red garlic ketchup, sweetbread, celeriac fricassée (no corned beef, no Bisto). Guests may eat more simply at sister restaurant Rojano's. 'Nothing fell short of expectations.' (K and VS)

16–18 High Street
Padstow PL28 8BB

T: 01841 550950
E: stay@padstowtownhouse.co.uk
W: paul-ainsworth.co.uk

BEDROOMS: 6. 2 on ground floor.
OPEN: all year except 24–26 Dec, 2 weeks Jan, open for New Year.
FACILITIES: honesty pantry, free Wi-Fi, in-room Smart TV, in-room spa treatments, electric car for guest transport, on-site car park.
BACKGROUND MUSIC: in reception and kitchen pantry area.
LOCATION: in old town, 5 mins' walk from harbour.
CHILDREN: not under 16.
DOGS: not allowed.
CREDIT CARDS: MC, Visa.
PRICES: per suite B&B £300–£380. À la carte (Paul Ainsworth at No. 6) £75, set menu £30–£34.

PADSTOW Cornwall   MAP 1:D2

THE SEAFOOD RESTAURANT

Rick and Jill Stein's boutique restaurant-with-rooms has been riding the crest of a wave since it opened more than four decades ago. Spawning a number of local businesses, from a cookery school to a fish and chip shop, this is the Stein flagship. Jill's bright and breezy coastal designs roll through the contemporary bedrooms, some of which have a private terrace and/or delightful views of the Camel estuary. Beds are 'comfy' with 'lots of pillows and cushions'. Home-from-home touches include novels by Cornish authors, tea- and coffee-making facilities with fresh milk and Stein biscuits, plus a generous supply of Jill's exclusive Porthdune toiletries. Dinner, served in the 'spectacular' restaurant, is prepared by chef Stéphane Delourme, who uses the finest local shellfish and fish to create simple, classic dishes from Rick's own recipes. Mussels with yellow kroeung (Cambodian spice paste), coconut milk and kaffir lime leaves, perhaps, or Padstow lobster, split and grilled, served in the shell with a shellfish reduction. Breakfast might include freshly squeezed orange juice and 'light' croissants, or maybe a 'fat and juicy' poached kipper or a dish of smoked haddock kedgeree.

Riverside
Padstow PL28 8BY

T: 01841 532700
E: reservations@rickstein.com
W: rickstein.com/stay/the-seafood-restaurant

BEDROOMS: 16.
OPEN: all year except 24–26 Dec.
FACILITIES: lift (to bedrooms), restaurant, free Wi-Fi, in-room TV (Freeview), restaurant and toilet wheelchair accessible.
BACKGROUND MUSIC: in restaurant.
LOCATION: town centre.
CHILDREN: all ages welcomed, not under 3 in restaurant.
DOGS: allowed in some bedrooms (dog-sitting service), in conservatory at breakfast.
CREDIT CARDS: Amex, MC, Visa.
PRICES: per room B&B £165–£350, D,B&B from £235. À la carte £45. 1-night bookings refused Sat.

PAINSWICK Gloucestershire

MAP 3:D5

THE PAINSWICK

In an 'idyllic' Cotswolds hillside village, this Palladian merchant's mansion with Arts and Crafts add-ons is part of the Calcot Collection (see Calcot, Tetbury). One of its glories is a wisteria-frilled, arched loggia from which to gaze and imagine you're in Tuscany. Interiors have 'a soft, contemporary look'. 'The decor is extremely tasteful, with two lovely sitting rooms, each with log fire.' A 'small but beautiful' Italianate garden with 'a lovely terrace' adjoins one of these. Bedrooms are 'luxurious', from the snuggest, under the eaves, and 'medium' in the garden wing, to 'big' in a chapel wing, 'bigger' in the main house, where George's Suite has its own balcony. All rooms have coffee machine, posh toiletries. In a 'tastefully decorated' dining room, 'ideal for romantic dinners', Jamie McCallum's menus, a little short on vegan options, include such dishes as Cotswold lamb rack and breast, brown butter, carrot. At breakfast there is home-made granola, kippers with lemon thyme butter, smashed avocado and dukkah on sourdough, the full English. You can borrow boots, hire a bike, visit charming Painswick Rococo Gardens. Sadly, the hotel's architecture doesn't allow wheelchair access to toilets in public areas.

Kemps Lane
Painswick GL6 6YB

T: 01452 813688
E: enquiries@thepainswick.co.uk
W: thepainswick.co.uk

BEDROOMS: 16. 7 in garden wing, 4 in chapel wing.
OPEN: all year.
FACILITIES: bar, lounge, restaurant, games room, private dining room, free Wi-Fi, in-room TV (Sky, Freeview), civil wedding licence, terrace, treatment rooms, ¾-acre garden, unsuitable for disabled.
BACKGROUND MUSIC: all day in public areas.
LOCATION: in village, 5 miles NE of Stroud.
CHILDREN: all ages welcomed.
DOGS: allowed by arrangement in some garden rooms, on terrace, in lounge, not in restaurant (£15 per night).
CREDIT CARDS: Amex, MC, Visa.
PRICES: per room B&B £195–£435. À la carte £43. 1-night bookings refused weekends.

PENRITH Cumbria

MAP 4: inset C2

ASKHAM HALL

'The warm welcome, beautiful setting and
delicious food' are 'truly exceptional' at Charles
Lowther's battlemented ancestral pile. A medieval
pele tower extended over centuries, this is a
child-friendly, dog-friendly family home, with
a 17th-century topiary garden, prolific kitchen
garden, rustic café, and animal-viewing area with
goats, pigs, ducks and shorthorn cattle. Public
lounges have a scuffed homeyness, real fires, an
honesty bar. Bedrooms are large, some huge,
some interconnecting. The dual-aspect Admiral's
Room was a favourite of the Duke of Edinburgh;
the duplex Train Room (once home to a model
railway) has a log-burner, a built-in four-poster;
Griffin has a stone fireplace and an oak-panelled
bathroom with antique roll-top bath. Chef
Richard Swale's 'creative dishes' are 'strongly
rooted in local, seasonal produce', garnered from
kitchen garden, orchard, farms, and moors, with
seasonal game. Typical dishes: home-reared goose,
celeriac, chicory and gizzard salad, sour cherry
sauce; skrei cod, maple-glazed carrots, artichoke,
roasted fish and hazelnut sauce. New this year in
Askham village is a 'health and well-being hub'.

25% DISCOUNT VOUCHERS

Askham
Penrith CA10 2PF

T: 01931 712350
E: enquiries@askhamhall.co.uk
W: askhamhall.co.uk

BEDROOMS: 18. 2 suitable for disabled.
OPEN: all year except Christmas, early
Jan to mid-Feb, Sun/Mon.
FACILITIES: drawing room, library,
billiard room, 3 dining rooms, free
Wi-Fi, in-room TV (Freeview), civil
wedding licence, 12-acre grounds, spa,
outdoor swimming pool, public areas
wheelchair accessible.
BACKGROUND MUSIC: in reception
rooms in evening.
LOCATION: 10 mins from Penrith and
junction 40 on M6.
CHILDREN: all ages welcomed.
DOGS: allowed in bedrooms and public
rooms, not in restaurant.
CREDIT CARDS: Amex, MC, Visa.
PRICES: per room B&B single
£138–£308, double £150–£320, D,B&B
£250–£420. Set menu £55, tasting
menu £70.

PENRITH Cumbria

THE HOUSE AT TEMPLE SOWERBY

NEW

'This will become our stop-over of choice on the way to west Scotland.' A full entry this year for Alison and Andi Sambrook's 'small, unpretentious hotel' opposite the green in a village bypassed by the A66. It occupies 'an 18th-century house with a 19th-century frontage'. Trusted readers received a 'friendly welcome' from the owners, who gave them a tour of the ground floor and carried up their bags. Bedrooms are traditionally styled. The larger ones, in main house and coach house, have an air-spa bath or walk-in hydrotherapy shower. The best are more contemporary with a super-king-size bed, an espresso machine. In the restaurant, Jack Bradley's short (some think too short) menus are long on ambition and include 'unusual ingredients'. For instance, silver hake, peas, potted Morecambe Bay shrimp, wood sorrel, puréed common sorrel, smoked hazelnut, all 'prepared with flair and great attention'. 'Guineafowl, halibut and hake were all very good with varied accompaniments, many new to me (hung yogurt??).' Breakfast brings 'softly textured scrambled egg, home-grown smoothies, granola'. 'They also do a very good packed lunch.' (Frances M Thomas, Robert Gower, and others)

25% DISCOUNT VOUCHERS

Temple Sowerby
Penrith CA10 1RZ

T: 017683 61578
E: stay@templesowerby.com
W: templesowerby.com

BEDROOMS: 12. 2 on ground floor, 4 in coach house.
OPEN: all year.
FACILITIES: 2 lounges, bar, restaurant, conference/function facilities, free Wi-Fi, in-room TV (Freeview), civil wedding licence, 1½-acre walled garden, public rooms wheelchair accessible, adapted toilet.
BACKGROUND MUSIC: 'carefully chosen' music in restaurant in the evening.
LOCATION: village centre.
CHILDREN: all ages welcomed.
DOGS: allowed in coach house rooms only (not unattended).
CREDIT CARDS: Amex, MC, Visa.
PRICES: per room B&B £100–£190, D,B&B £140–£270. Set dinner £35–£45.

PENRITH Cumbria

TEBAY SERVICES HOTEL

'How wonderful it would be if many service areas (and indeed motorway hotels) could be like this one.' Plentiful praise this year for this dog-friendly, child-friendly hotel, opened in 1976 by the ingenious Dunning family after the M6 sliced through their hill farm. Within an Alpine-inspired building, guests find 'a unique blend of modernity, informality, efficiency and cheerfulness'. The welcome is 'wonderfully warm, complete with a roaring fire in the open, comfortable area of the bar'. The bedrooms are 'truly restful – the motorway neither seen nor heard'. All rooms have home-made biscuits, Sedbergh Soap toiletries. Praise also for the good lighting and decor, the 'excellent bathroom'. Food is served in the bar, mezzanine and in the 'light and airy' restaurant, looking out to the fells beyond pond and waterfall. Special mention for herb-fed chicken croquette with smoked anchovies, five-spiced duck breast, new-season lamb, and local cheeses. After a buffet breakfast, the farm shop beckons. 'Our stops are always rather expensive once we've spent time at the cheese counter, the butcher, all the other distractions.' (Simon and Mithra Tonking, Jock and Jane Macdonald, and others)

Orton
Penrith CA10 3SB

T: 015396 24351
E: reservations@tebayserviceshotel.
com
W: tebayserviceshotel.com

BEDROOMS: 51. 1 suitable for disabled.
OPEN: all year except 24, 25 Dec.
FACILITIES: lounge with log fire, bar, mezzanine, restaurant, free Wi-Fi, in-room TV (Freeview), function/conference facilities, farm shop, restaurant, bar and lounge wheelchair accessible, adapted toilet.
BACKGROUND MUSIC: none.
LOCATION: 2½ miles SW of Orton.
CHILDREN: all ages welcomed (family rooms with bunk beds).
DOGS: allowed in some bedrooms (£10 per dog per night, max. 2 dogs), and in one area of lounge.
CREDIT CARDS: Amex, MC, Visa.
PRICES: per room B&B single £79–£119, double £109–£149, family room £137–£144. À la carte £30.

PENSFORD Somerset

MAP 2:D1

THE PIG NEAR BATH

There's nothing bland about a Pigling. 'We had a great time,' say Guide insiders after a 2019 visit to the third in Robin Hutson's burgeoning litter. 'They get the experience just right.' Taking a lead from mother Pig in Brockenhurst (see entry), this Georgian manor house with deer park has been tarted down in the shabby-chic style that is somehow so 'smart and classy'. Praise for the 'sheer enthusiasm of the young, well-trained staff'. A 'memorable meal' brought 'delicious grilled hispi cabbage', heritage carrots with aïoli, from the 'mostly picked this morning' section, 'gurnard and mussels, a chargrilled pork tomahawk – a massive but tender chop'. Wood-fired flatbreads on the terrace are an occasional summer treat. Breakfast brings 'pastries, home-made granola, big jugs of the freshest juice, compotes and fruit galore, eggs to boil from the estate chickens', many cooked dishes. All bedrooms have a monsoon shower; 'comfy-luxe' rooms have a freestanding bath, also. The two-storey Apple Store, a former shed in the kitchen garden (the heart of the operation) with wood-burning stove, monsoon shower and bath, is an absolute pippin. (Desmond and Jenny Balmer, LH and JF, and others)

Hunstrete House
Pensford BS39 4NS

T: 01761 490490
E: info@thepignearbath.com
W: thepighotel.com

BEDROOMS: 29. 5 in gardens, some on ground floor, 1 with wheelchair access and wet room.
OPEN: all year.
FACILITIES: 2 lounges, bar, restaurant, snug, private dining room, free Wi-Fi, in-room TV (Freeview), civil wedding licence, treatment room, kitchen garden, wild flower meadow, deer park, ground floor/garden areas wheelchair accessible.
BACKGROUND MUSIC: all day in public areas.
LOCATION: 7 miles SW of Bath.
CHILDREN: all ages welcomed.
DOGS: not allowed, except guide dogs.
CREDIT CARDS: Amex, MC, Visa.
PRICES: room £170–£340. Breakfast (continental) £12, (cooked) £16, à la carte £35. 1-night bookings refused weekends, Christmas/New Year.

PENTON Cumbria

PENTONBRIDGE INN

⚜ Previous César Winner

In the once lawless Debatable Lands, Gerald and Margo Smith have brought order to a former coaching inn-turned-contemporary hotel. Interiors evoke the surrounding landscape, with the use of timber, slate and stone, wool and tweeds. Bedrooms, each named after a clan of Borders reivers, have a state-of-the-art bathroom, home-baked biscuits, fresh flowers, Noble Isle toiletries. Trusted readers were shown to a room, up 'the imposing glass-walled staircase', with an espresso machine, good lighting, lovely views (though you had to sit down to appreciate them through the low windows). No sooner had the Guide awarded the place a coveted César for 2019, than the talented duo of chefs who launched it headed for the hills. Change upon change has followed, but with an enthusiastic new manager, David Hair, and chef, Chris Archer, things are settling down. The kitchen ethos is the same, with the use of locally farmed and foraged ingredients, vegetables from the kitchen garden of the Smiths' stately home, Netherby Hall. 'Despite its remoteness, it is not that far from the main Edinburgh–Carlisle road (A7) and Kielder Forest, with Hadrian's Wall to the south.' Reports, please.

25% DISCOUNT VOUCHERS

Penton CA6 5QB

T: 01228 586636
E: info@pentonbridgeinn.co.uk
W: pentonbridgeinn.co.uk

BEDROOMS: 9. 3 in converted barn, covered walkway from reception, 3 on ground floor.
OPEN: all year, restaurant closed Sun evening, Mon, Tues.
FACILITIES: bar, restaurant, conservatory, free Wi-Fi, in-room TV (Freeview), bar and conservatory wheelchair accessible (restaurant menu available), adapted toilet.
BACKGROUND MUSIC: in bar and conservatory.
LOCATION: rural, 10 mins from Longtown.
CHILDREN: all ages welcomed.
DOGS: allowed in 8 bedrooms, bar and conservatory, not in restaurant.
CREDIT CARDS: Amex, MC, Visa.
PRICES: per person B&B £100–£125. Pub menu of seasonal dishes £16–£28 per main-course dish.

PENZANCE Cornwall

MAP 1:E1

CHAPEL HOUSE

'Forget overcrowded St Ives – there's a real treat of a stay in Penzance.' Quirky character fills the 'beautifully restored' brick-and-granite former 18th-century admiral's house, but 'this inviting boutique hotel is all about the hostess, Susan Stuart'. 'Every requirement is looked after with professional charm.' Guests appreciated the 'exceptional' attention to detail, from the welcoming tea and cake, to an introduction to the local GP who runs nearby Tremenheere Sculpture Gardens, to the 'open house' approach. 'Even when we went out to dinner, we were welcomed into the kitchen for a complimentary glass of wine.' Throughout, there's a happy blend of contemporary and antique furniture, fresh flowers, and coastal hues. In the 'spacious' bedrooms, a huge handmade bed, an in-room bath, an iPad, panoramic harbour views. Above the open-plan landing is a retractable glass roof. Locally sourced, unfussy communal meals ('marvellous, impossibly good value') are a highlight, perhaps pan-fried brill with Cornish early potatoes and samphire. 'On our final morning, we enjoyed tea and cake with fresh raspberries and a glass of chilled Prosecco to wish us well on our journey.' (DS, and others)

Chapel Street
Penzance TR18 4AQ

T: 01736 362024
E: hello@chapelhousepz.co.uk
W: chapelhousepz.co.uk

BEDROOMS: 6.
OPEN: closed 24–29 Dec, kitchen closed for dinner Sun–Wed, but open for early-evening drinks all week.
FACILITIES: drawing room, open-plan kitchen/dining area, free Wi-Fi, in-room TV (Freeview), function facilities, terrace, garden, unsuitable for disabled.
BACKGROUND MUSIC: none.
LOCATION: town centre.
CHILDREN: all ages welcomed.
DOGS: allowed in bedrooms and public areas and in kitchen/dining area with consent of other guests.
CREDIT CARDS: MC, Visa.
PRICES: per room B&B single £125–£165, double £160–£220. Set dinner £27.50. 1-night bookings refused at bank holiday weekends (rooms 2, 4 and 6).

SEE ALSO SHORTLIST

PENZANCE Cornwall

MAP 1:E1

TREREIFE

This 'fantastic, large family home' was repurposed
a decade ago as a B&B and popular wedding
venue by its owners, the Le Grice family, who
have lived here for seven generations. The
splendid gardens are open for guided tours
(there's a new tea room this year), as is the house
– Elizabethan with Queen Anne additions – in
which there are four guest bedrooms, each named
after a 19th-century literary figure (associate of
the first family member to live here). Rooms
vary in size: Wordsworth and Coleridge on the
first floor are particularly spacious, with a rather
grand wall-canopied king- or super-king-size bed
and views over the garden. Coleridge also has a
roll-top bath. Hazlitt and Southey, both on the
ground floor with courtyard access, are simpler
and, in Hazlitt's case, smaller with no view. Two
courtyard self-catering apartments have been
created (breakfast available) and for glampers
there's a bell tent in the walled garden. A 'great
breakfast' – fruit salad followed by full English,
perhaps, or toast with Lizzie Le Grice's famous
medlar jelly – is eaten at a communal table. 'No
fancy touches but everything you need,' comments
more than one satisfied reviewer. (ME)

Penzance TR20 8TJ

T: 01736 362750
E: trereifepark@btconnect.com
W: trereifepark.co.uk

BEDROOMS: 4. 2 on ground floor, plus
2 self-catering apartments, and bell
tent for glamping.
OPEN: 1 March–end Nov.
FACILITIES: sitting room (honesty
bar), dining room, free Wi-Fi, in-
room TV (Freeview), civil wedding
licence, 5-acre grounds (parterres,
walled garden, woodland), parking,
unsuitable for disabled.
BACKGROUND MUSIC: none.
LOCATION: 1¼ miles SW of Penzance.
CHILDREN: all ages welcomed.
DOGS: allowed in ground-floor
bedrooms, not in public rooms (£15
per stay).
CREDIT CARDS: Amex, MC, Visa.
PRICES: per room B&B £80–£160.
Min. 2-night stay June–Sept and for
self-catering.

SEE ALSO SHORTLIST

PETWORTH Sussex

THE OLD RAILWAY STATION

Some grown men play with train sets. Gudmund Olafsson went further in 2005, when he bought one of Britain's most beautiful railway stations, renovating the property and the four Edwardian Pullman carriages on its disused line. The first-class B&B that Mr Olafsson ran here with Catherine Stormont has new owners, Jennie Hudson and Blair Humphry, and we trust everything is still on track. Two bedrooms occupy the original timber station building, opened in 1892 mainly to whisk the Prince of Wales to Goodwood. The lower colonial-style room has rattan chairs, slatted shutters, grey and white hues. The upper one, reached via a spiral staircase, is under the eaves, with a modern shower room. There are eight rooms in the carriages, 'charming, quirky spaces' with original mahogany fittings, period furniture, a 'surprisingly spacious' bathroom. The waiting room houses a cosy lounge and breakfast room, the walls adorned with brass lamps, black-and-white photographs, railway mementos. Afternoon teas are served here and under parasols on the platform. For dinner, cross the River Rother to a country inn, or take the short drive to The Halfway Bridge, Lodsworth (see entry). Reports, please.

Station Road
Petworth GU28 0JF

T: 01798 342346
E: info@old-station.co.uk
W: old-station.co.uk

BEDROOMS: 10. 8 in Pullman carriages. 1 room suitable for guests with slightly restricted mobility.
OPEN: all year except 23–26 Dec.
FACILITIES: lounge/bar/breakfast room, free Wi-Fi, in-room TV (Freeview), platform/terrace, 2-acre garden, public areas wheelchair accessible.
BACKGROUND MUSIC: 'soft '20s, '30s, '40s music' at breakfast.
LOCATION: 1½ miles S of Petworth.
CHILDREN: not under 10.
DOGS: not allowed.
CREDIT CARDS: MC, Visa.
PRICES: per room B&B double house £130–£170 (single-night premium rate Fri, Sat £204), Pullman £150–£210 (single-night premium rate Fri, Sat £228–£252), reduced rates for single occupancy 'sometimes offered'.

PICKERING Yorkshire

MAP 4:D4

THE WHITE SWAN

Occupying a prime spot in a moors-edge market town, this 'excellent hotel' has been a local hostelry for 450 years, though the Buchanan family has been at the helm for just 37 of those. Guests this year were impressed by the 'well-appointed rooms', the excellent meals and the 'pleasant, proactive staff'. Locals prop up the bar in the popular tap room, dogs lolling at their feet; it's an ideal spot for sampling real Yorkshire ales. The Bothy lounge, which occupies an old barn, has a well-stocked honesty bar and an inviting array of books and games, plus squashy sofas flanking the log-burning stove. Bedrooms are scattered across the main building and in converted stables ('extremely comfortable'). In the main building, traditional finishes are in keeping with the hotel's history, perhaps a four-poster or a chaise longue; in the outbuildings, it's decidedly more modern, with toasty under-floor heating. The cosy restaurant serves Darren Clemmit's seasonal 'short and simple' menu. 'I had a most enjoyable dinner of dressed crab, followed by half a lobster, new potatoes. The very well-presented breakfast was just as good, with a huge choice of hot dishes.' (Graham Child)

25% DISCOUNT VOUCHERS

Market Place
Pickering YO18 7AA

T: 01751 472288
E: welcome@white-swan.co.uk
W: white-swan.co.uk

BEDROOMS: 21. 9 in annexe, on ground floor.
OPEN: all year.
FACILITIES: lounge, bar, restaurant, private dining room, Bothy residents' lounge/event room, free Wi-Fi, in-room TV (Freeview), small terrace (alfresco meals), 3 electric charging points, restaurant, bar and lounge are wheelchair accessible, toilet not adapted.
BACKGROUND MUSIC: none.
LOCATION: central.
CHILDREN: all ages welcomed.
DOGS: allowed in some bedrooms, bar and lounge, not in restaurant (owners may dine with dogs in snug).
CREDIT CARDS: Amex, MC, Visa.
PRICES: per room B&B single £121–£215, double £151–£219, D,B&B double £219–£279. À la carte £36.

PORLOCK Somerset

MAP 1:B5

THE OAKS

This 'Edwardian gentleman's residence perched at the top of a steep hillside' is run as 'a first-class small hotel' by 'perfect hosts' Tim and Anne Riley. 'As you walk into the house,' write inspectors, 'you are enveloped by warmth. The place oozes serenity, good taste.' While Tim carried up the bags, Anne rustled up tea and cakes. A 'large, pleasant, airy' front bedroom afforded a 'fabulous view' over the hills and pretty village, where Exmoor national park meets the sea. It had 'leafy William Morris wallpaper, a huge bed', Portmeirion china on the tray, ground coffee, fresh milk. In a bathroom, with bath and shower, were Pecksniff's toiletries, fluffy towels on a 'piping hot' rail. There is the same lovely view from the dining room, where Anne Riley's menus include such dishes as cream of pear and watercress soup, hot smoked haddock mousse, Exmoor venison with port wine and redcurrant, a much-enjoyed raspberry sorbet with framboise. 'The plate would look less elegant if you allowed Tim to serve all the vegetables, but there was no questioning the great taste.' At night 'the silence is palpable'. Breakfast brings home-made bread, 'everything you could want'. (I and FW, M and JB)

Porlock TA24 8ES

T: 01643 862265
E: info@oakshotel.co.uk
W: oakshotel.co.uk

BEDROOMS: 7.
OPEN: Easter–end Oct.
FACILITIES: 2 lounges, bar, restaurant, free Wi-Fi, in-room TV (Freeview), 1-acre garden, patio, pebble beach 1 mile, unsuitable for disabled.
BACKGROUND MUSIC: occasionally classical in the dining room.
LOCATION: edge of village.
CHILDREN: not under 8.
DOGS: not allowed.
CREDIT CARDS: MC, Visa.
PRICES: per room D,B&B £260–£280.

PORTSCATHO Cornwall

MAP 1:E2

DRIFTWOOD HOTEL

You can order a picnic hamper and walk down to a private beach through lovely gardens at Paul and Fiona Robinson's New England-inspired hotel, or just relax on the deck, gazing across Gerrans Bay. The coastal path runs by. The Lost Gardens of Heligan are close. But once you've found your way to this sequestered spot, why leave? Bedrooms are contemporary with a breezy coastal mood; all but one overlook the ocean. One reader's 'very nice' room had a 'comfy' bed, seating area, a 'slightly small' bathroom. Another found a ground-floor room's layout 'idiosyncratic' and thought the place 'more a restaurant-with-rooms'. True, public areas are not huge, but there is a playroom, a lounge with driftwood lamps, a snug bar. And, anyway, what a restaurant! Chris Eden has held a Michelin star since 2012, for his 'superb' cooking of locally grown, fished and farmed ingredients, with 'tricksy bits'. Maybe roast cod, cauliflower, beurre noisette hollandaise, jus gras, pickled cucumber. Glad tidings about breakfast. It was 'excellent' with a good cooked choice, an adequate buffet. 'The home-made granola was a highlight. Smoked haddock with poached egg was a miniature delight.' (PA, and others)

Rosevine
Portscatho TR2 5EW

T: 01872 580644
E: info@driftwoodhotel.co.uk
W: driftwoodhotel.co.uk

BEDROOMS: 15. 4 accessed via courtyard, 2 in cabin (2 mins' walk).
OPEN: all year except 4–30 Jan.
FACILITIES: bar, restaurant, drawing room, snug, children's games room, free Wi-Fi, in-room TV (Freeview), 7-acre grounds (terraced gardens, private beach, safe bathing), unsuitable for disabled.
BACKGROUND MUSIC: all day in restaurant and bar.
LOCATION: 1½ miles N of Portscatho.
CHILDREN: all ages welcomed, no under-7s in restaurant in evening.
DOGS: not allowed.
CREDIT CARDS: Amex, MC, Visa.
PRICES: per room B&B £195–£300, D,B&B £260–£320. Tasting menus £85–£100, vegetarian £80, à la carte £70. 1-night bookings refused weekends.

RADNAGE Buckinghamshire

THE MASH INN

♛ Previous César Winner

Nick Mash has taken a step back to the future
in reinventing the 18th-century red brick
Three Horseshoes pub as a restaurant-with-
rooms. His family have farmed in the Chilterns
for generations and, in an age of molecular
gastronomy, he has favoured a more natural
culinary approach, with an open wood-fired grill
at the heart of the operation. In 'a semi-open
kitchen', chef Jon Parry works with whatever he
'forages from the woods, selects fresh from the
garden or draws from the family farm' on the day,
with fish delivered within 24 hours of landing.
Short daily menus offer such choices as chilled
wild garlic soup, Suffolk Cross lamb, white
sprouting broccoli, ewe's curd. Tasting menus are
more enigmatic: sea urchin; Norfolk asparagus
and bog butter; cheese and pontack (elderberry
sauce, since you ask). 'There is a cosy bar', a
dining area with 'splendid bespoke ash and oak
furniture'. Bedrooms have 'clean, modern decor';
two with a balcony overlook 'gardens with ponds,
seating areas, a beguiling view of fields, woodland
and hills'. Breakfast, in dining room or bedroom,
brings home-baked croissants, granola, turmeric
ginger beer tonic.

Horseshoe Road
Bennett End
Radnage HP14 4EB

T: 01494 482440
E: hello@themashinn.com
W: themashinn.com

BEDROOMS: 6.
OPEN: all year, closed Sun dinner, all
day Mon, Tues.
FACILITIES: snug bar and dining area,
semi-open-plan kitchen/dining room,
free Wi-Fi, 2½-acre garden, restaurant
wheelchair accessible, adapted toilet.
BACKGROUND MUSIC: in public areas.
LOCATION: in hamlet 7 miles NW of
High Wycombe.
CHILDREN: not under 16.
DOGS: allowed in bar.
CREDIT CARDS: MC, Visa.
PRICES: per room B&B £110–£250. Set
dinner menu £60, tasting menu £95,

RAMSGILL-IN-NIDDERDALE Yorkshire   MAP 4:D3

THE YORKE ARMS

A former 18th-century shooting lodge swathed in
Virginia creeper, this Michelin-starred restaurant-
with-rooms, with 'friendly service', enjoys an
'unsurpassed' location in the rolling Yorkshire
Dales. The prestigious star was won by the then
owner Frances Atkins in 2003. She sold up in
2018 but (much to everyone's relief) she remains in
the kitchen, conjuring up 'wonderful' flavour-
intense food that lures diners from far and wide
(sometimes by helicopter). Serious foodies plump
for the tasting menu: highlights include crab and
langoustine, tomato, nasturtium root, aubergine
custard or Laudale venison, bilberry, Douglas
fir pine. A short à la carte menu is offered in the
Little Dining Room, and might include Whitby
crab and smoked salmon, Nidderdale sirloin of
beef or grilled turbot. Bedrooms, in the main
building or in the courtyard, are 'comfortable'
and well appointed, decorated in country-chic
style with a touch of locational whimsy: the 'On
Yer Bike' wallpaper in the eponymously named
suite, for example, is a nod to the area's own Tour
de Nidderdale. Less ambitious cyclists can simply
enjoy the great cycling country that surrounds the
restaurant. (D and LH, and others)

Ramsgill-in-Nidderdale
Harrogate HG3 5RL

T: 01423 755243
E: enquiries@theyorkearms.co.uk
W: theyorkearms.co.uk

BEDROOMS: 18. 4 suites in courtyard,
1 suitable for disabled.
OPEN: all year except 25 Dec.
FACILITIES: lounge, bar, 2 dining
rooms, 1 private dining room, free
Wi-Fi in lounge and some bedrooms,
in-room TV (Freeview), function
facilities, 2-acre grounds.
BACKGROUND MUSIC: in public areas.
LOCATION: centre of village.
CHILDREN: not under 12.
DOGS: allowed in 1 bedroom and bar.
CREDIT CARDS: Amex, MC, Visa.
PRICES: per room D,B&B £375–£660.
À la carte £60, tasting menus
£75–£105.

RAVENSTONEDALE Cumbria

MAP 4:C3

THE BLACK SWAN

♛ Previous César Winner

'Our very special place, where we love to enjoy the peace and tranquillity of the countryside,' writes a reader this year, signing off with a smiley emoji. And there is much to smile about at Louise Dinnes's Victorian pub-with-rooms in an Eden valley conservation village. 'Fabulous individual accommodation' ranges from glamping tents to a four-poster suite with feature bathroom, double-ended roll-top bath, walk-in shower. Some rooms are cottage style, some contemporary; all have fresh milk, organic toiletries. Dog-friendly rooms have separate access. There is great praise for the 'welcoming, friendly and helpful staff', especially manager Selina Procter. You can relax in bars or lounge, with open fire, stuffed animals, clocks and curios, or drink cask ales in the riverside garden while watching the red squirrels. But the highlight is Scott Fairweather's 'most delicious' modern cooking, his skilful use of local ingredients in such dishes as rump and shoulder of lamb, white beans, beetroot, goat's curd, sage; cod loin, artichokes, mussel and almond vinaigrette; simple fish and chips. In the morning wake up to 'the best breakfast you could ever enjoy. We can't wait to visit again.'

25% DISCOUNT VOUCHERS

Ravenstonedale
Kirkby Stephen CA17 4NG

T: 015396 23204
E: enquiries@blackswanhotel.com
W: blackswanhotel.com

BEDROOMS: 16. 6 in annexe, 4 on ground floor, 3 suitable for disabled. Plus 3 'glamping' tents.
OPEN: all year.
FACILITIES: 2 bars, lounge, 2 dining rooms, free Wi-Fi, in-room TV (Freeview), Orange mobile signal only, beer garden in wooded grounds, tennis/golf in village, public rooms wheelchair accessible.
BACKGROUND MUSIC: in public areas all day, but optional.
LOCATION: in village 5 miles SW of Kirkby Stephen.
CHILDREN: all ages welcomed.
DOGS: max. 3 in each of 4 ground-floor annexe rooms, not in restaurant.
CREDIT CARDS: Amex, MC, Visa.
PRICES: per room B&B single from £95, double £85–£165. À la carte £36. 1-night bookings sometimes refused.

REEPHAM Norfolk

THE DIAL HOUSE

One of the Guide's most outré hotels occupies a
'handsome' red brick Georgian house overlooking
the market square of an attractive town. Owners
Hannah Springham and Andrew Jones took it
over in 2018, after launching their first restaurant
venture, in nearby Norwich, in 2017. Bedrooms
waft guests back to the age of exploration and
the Grand Tour. Choose Belle Époque Parisian
Garret; Natural History, with decked patio
and a bathroom behind a cabinet of curiosities;
pretty China, a celebration of Willow Pattern.
Each room has a marble bathroom, roll-top bath,
drench shower, a record-player and vinyl discs,
home-made biscuits. Public rooms are a constantly
changing 'cornucopia of delightful furnishings
and curios', every piece for sale. There is a cocktail
bar, small beauty spa, all-day lounge menu. In
the restaurant, Mr Jones, who has worked for
the likes of Richard Corrigan, creates such dishes
as roast cod, charred hispi cabbage, saffron and
mussel cream. At breakfast there are smoothies;
smashed avocado, field mushrooms and tomato
confit; the full English. You can order a picnic
hamper for a day on the Broads or the beaches of
the North Norfolk coast. Reports, please.

Market Place
Reepham
Norwich NR10 4JJ

T: 01603 879900
E: info@thedialhouse.org.uk
W: thedialhouse.org.uk

BEDROOMS: 8.
OPEN: all year.
FACILITIES: lounge, restaurant, private
dining rooms (chef's table, 'secret
room' and cellar), free Wi-Fi, in-room
TV (Sky), terrace, civil wedding
licence, public rooms wheelchair
accessible, adapted toilet.
BACKGROUND MUSIC: in public areas.
LOCATION: on main square.
CHILDREN: all ages welcomed.
DOGS: allowed in 1 bedroom, some
public rooms in part of restaurant.
CREDIT CARDS: Amex, MC, Visa.
PRICES: per room B&B single
£130–£175, double £165–210, D,B&B
£195–£240. À la carte £37. 1-night
bookings refused Christmas week.

RICHMOND Yorkshire

MAP 4:C3

THE COACH HOUSE AT MIDDLETON LODGE

♛ Previous César Winner

More tasteful developments this year among the potpourri of Georgian estate buildings that create James Allison's hotel 'in beautiful countryside a few miles from Scotch Corner'. The flair of architect partner Rebecca Tappin is evident in bedrooms (some for a family) in the newly restored dairy, some with an outdoor hot tub and private terrace. The serene suites blend creams, mellow wood and stand-alone baths – one a spectacular copper tub. Other rooms are laced through the coach house, potting sheds and a rustic-chic farmhouse, where guests enjoy a lounge with exposed brickwork, sofas and wood-burner. Readers tell us that the coach house's Tack room is 'amazing, double height with original beams and shutters, a comfortable bed', a bathroom 'almost as big'. Changes on the food front, too. To go with the relaxed all-day menu of the restaurant in former stables, a new fine-dining option, Forge, where Gareth Rayner uses produce grown in the estate's kitchen garden, foraged in its woods, or reared on nearby farms, perhaps Yorkshire duck, beetroot, grilled cabbage, elderberry vinegar. Breakfast is 'excellent'.

Kneeton Lane
Middleton Tyas
Richmond DL10 6NJ

T: 01325 377977
E: info@middletonlodge.co.uk
W: middletonlodge.co.uk

BEDROOMS: 29. 9 in coach house, 3 in Potting Shed, 11 in Dairy, 6 in farmhouse, 5 on ground floor, 1 suitable for disabled.
OPEN: all year, set package stays over Christmas/New Year.
FACILITIES: lounge, bar, snug, restaurant, free Wi-Fi, in-room TV (Sky), civil wedding licence, treatment rooms, courtyard, garden in 200-acre grounds, public rooms wheelchair accessible, adapted toilet.
BACKGROUND MUSIC: in public areas.
LOCATION: 1 mile N of village.
CHILDREN: all ages welcomed.
DOGS: allowed in some bedrooms, most public areas, one restaurant.
CREDIT CARDS: MC, Visa.
PRICES: per room B&B £160–£210, D,B&B £220–£330. À la carte £35.

SEE ALSO SHORTLIST

RICHMOND Yorkshire

MAP 4:C3

THE FRENCHGATE RESTAURANT & HOTEL

An 18th-century town house combines with its
17th-century neighbour as an atmospheric small
hotel, a stroll from a charming survivor of this
market town's Georgian heyday, the Theatre
Royal. There is theatre here, too, on cobbled
Frenchgate, in a bridal suite with ship's timber
beams, a Mouseman oak four-poster, a power
shower and spa bath with kinetic lighting. Some
bedrooms have a wet room, a Swedish power
shower, a Napoli 'egg bath', views of the River
Swale. Owners David and Luiza Todd 'ensure
this is a customer-centred business', wrote a
trusted reader, who was allowed to check in
an hour early. His single room (others can
accommodate a family) had 'modern furniture',
a monsoon shower. A guest lounge is furnished
in period style, while in the 'very small',
candlelit dining room, 'superb' chef Lisa Miller
demonstrates her skill with local produce in
such 'appetising' dishes as ballotine of pheasant,
truffle mash, pancetta, creamed cabbage, chestnut,
quince, bread terrine. Breakfast brings freshly
squeezed juice, naturally smoked haddock, local
sausages and bacon, free-range eggs. 'Service very
attentive and friendly.' (RG)

25% DISCOUNT VOUCHERS

59–61 Frenchgate
Richmond DL10 7AE

T: 01748 822087
E: info@thefrenchgate.co.uk
W: thefrenchgate.co.uk

BEDROOMS: 9, 1 on ground floor with
2 steps to en suite.
OPEN: all year.
FACILITIES: dining room, bar/terrace,
lounge, free Wi-Fi, in-room TV
(Freeview), civil wedding licence,
small garden, public rooms wheelchair
accessible, adapted toilet.
BACKGROUND MUSIC: soft jazz in public
rooms.
LOCATION: 200 yds NE of town square.
CHILDREN: all ages welcomed.
DOGS: not allowed.
CREDIT CARDS: Amex, MC, Visa.
PRICES: per room B&B single £80–£223,
double £138–£275, D,B&B double
£206–£318. À la carte set-price
menu £39.

SEE ALSO SHORTLIST

RICHMOND Yorkshire

MILLGATE HOUSE

♧ Previous César Winner

A trove of arts décoratifs is 'trustingly displayed'
in this Georgian town house, 'in a good situation
off the market square'. Tim Culkin and Austin
Lynch's eye for 'silver, china, glass, clocks, pictures
and more' has turned their 'nicely designed,
roomy, welcoming' B&B into a collector's paradise
– and a nightmare for fans of minimalism or
parents of young children. Individually decorated
with antiques (polished chests and wardrobes,
elegant dressing tables) and vintage prints, the
bedrooms might have a private sitting room
with an old fireplace and copious paperbacks;
a bathroom with cast iron bath and walk-in
shower; or dual-aspect windows gazing across the
'glorious' walled garden towards the River Swale.
Minor niggle: 'Our spacious, quiet room could
have done with more lighting and coat-hangers.'
To match the award-winning garden, which
teems with ferns, shrubs, roses and clematis, there
is an 'outstanding' breakfast: 'a generous buffet,
delicious home-made marmalade, toast and
croissant'. Burn it off with a 'lovely walk along the
river to Easby Abbey's romantic ruins' – the bare
12th-century stones are a counterpoint to the busy,
'wonderfully eccentric' B&B.

3 Millgate
Richmond DL10 4JN

T: 01748 823571
E: oztim@millgatehouse.demon.
   co.uk
W: millgatehouse.com

BEDROOMS: 6.
OPEN: all year.
FACILITIES: hall, drawing room, dining
room, free Wi-Fi, in-room digital
TV, ⅓-acre garden, unsuitable for
disabled.
BACKGROUND MUSIC: occasional soft
classical.
LOCATION: town centre.
CHILDREN: all ages welcomed.
DOGS: allowed in public rooms and
bedrooms (not unattended).
CREDIT CARDS: none.
PRICES: per room B&B £125–£165.

SEE ALSO SHORTLIST

RICHMOND-UPON-THAMES Surrey

MAP 2:D3

BINGHAM RIVERHOUSE

A change of both name and feel for Bingham
Riverhouse this year, its 'more traditional, opulent
style' replaced by 'something more informal and
friendly', say our inspectors. Set on the towpath
near Richmond Park, with a pretty riverside
garden and terrace, the hotel has been run by the
Trinder family for more than 30 years; Ruth and
Samantha Trinder are at the helm today. Our
inspectors were greeted warmly; their 'small and
cosy' double room had 'coffee and teas, fluffy
bathrobes, delicious home-made shortbread' and
a comfy bed with organic mattress. A peaceful
escape from the London hubbub. Rooms vary in
size – some have 'lovely river views'; many have
a copper bathtub. Food is 'at the heart' of the
hotel, with head chef Andy Cole masterminding
a 'seasonally focused menu', including good
vegetarian options; 'outstanding' chickpea chips
with swede, pickled celery, harissa and tahini
mayonnaise. Staff are 'particularly friendly,
relaxed and thoughtful'. A 'delicious' breakfast
includes plenty of hot cooked options, with eggs
Florentine 'cooked to perfection'. Guests have free
use of Samantha Trinder's wellness centre close
by, with massage and yoga classes.

25% DISCOUNT VOUCHERS

61–63 Petersham Road
Richmond-upon-Thames TW10 6UT

T: 020 8940 0902
E: be@binghamriverhouse.com
W: binghamriverhouse.com

BEDROOMS: 15.
OPEN: all year, restaurant closed Sun
evening.
FACILITIES: three drawing room/bar/
restaurant rooms, function room,
free Wi-Fi, in-room TV (Freeview),
civil wedding licence, terrace, ½-acre
garden, complimentary use of
nearby wellness centre, public rooms
wheelchair accessible, adapted toilet.
BACKGROUND MUSIC: in bar and
restaurant.
LOCATION: ½ mile S of centre.
CHILDREN: all ages welcomed.
DOGS: allowed in some bedrooms, in
public areas with prior permission.
CREDIT CARDS: MC, Visa.
PRICES: per room B&B £179–£339,
D,B&B £269–£429. Tasting menu £60,
fixed-price à la carte £37–£45. Check
hotel's website for latest offers/prices.

ROMALDKIRK Co. Durham

MAP 4:C3

THE ROSE & CROWN

'This hotel is amazing.' 'The perfect place for a break in the country.' A chorus of approval in 2019 for Cheryl and Thomas Robinson's 18th-century coaching inn beside the Saxon church in a 'charming, peaceful village'. 'The bar has a real log fire, flagged floors and a fine choice of drinks, with treats for four-legged companions.' Main house bedrooms have period features (beams, exposed stone), antique and locally made furniture. Courtyard rooms in a single-storey stone building are more contemporary, with outdoor seating area. 'Our courtyard room was fine, roomy, with an excellent bathroom.' Nice touches include Molton Brown toiletries, mineral water in reusable glass bottles. 'But the exceptional delight is the food' in the 'beautiful oak-panelled dining room'. The Robinsons, who also own Headlam Hall, Darlington (see Shortlist), have farmed in Teesdale for four generations; they are in tune with the seasons, committed to animal welfare. David Hunter's menus showcase local produce. 'Pan-fried loin of Teesdale lamb with crisp lamb bonbon, ratatouille, asparagus, aubergine was stunning.' Breakfast is 'to die for'. (Fran Walker, G Waters, Peter Anderson, and many others)

25% DISCOUNT VOUCHERS

Romaldkirk
Barnard Castle DL12 9EB

T: 01833 650213
E: hotel@rose-and-crown.co.uk
W: rose-and-crown.co.uk

BEDROOMS: 14. 2 in Monk's Cottage, 5 in rear courtyard, some on ground floor, 1 suitable for disabled.
OPEN: all year except 23–28 Dec, bar menu only Mon lunchtime.
FACILITIES: 2 lounges, bar, Crown Room (bar meals), restaurant, free Wi-Fi, in-room TV (Freeview), boot room, public rooms wheelchair accessible, no adapted toilet.
BACKGROUND MUSIC: in restaurant.
LOCATION: village centre, 6 miles W of Barnard Castle.
CHILDREN: all ages welcomed, no under-8s in restaurant after 8 pm.
DOGS: allowed in bedrooms and public rooms, except restaurant.
CREDIT CARDS: Amex, MC, Visa.
PRICES: per room B&B £120–£205, D,B&B £185–£270. À la carte £40.

ROSS-ON-WYE Herefordshire

WILTON COURT

A river runs through it. Originally a 16th-century courthouse, this mellow sandstone restaurant-with-rooms on the River Wye is 'steeped in history'. Kingfishers, swans, peregrine falcons, even the occasional otter, are regular visitors. 'The garden and patio areas make a wonderful place to relax.' Inside, the historic manor house is full of character, with 16th-century stone fireplaces, exposed beams and wood floors offset by richly coloured rugs and Far Eastern objets d'art collected by owners Helen and Roger Wynn on their travels. Upstairs, bedrooms have 'glorious' views of river or gardens. Each is individually decorated with William Morris or Sanderson wallpaper and fabrics, and has 'all the comforts' expected. There's a new chef in the Mulberry restaurant, Laura O'Brien, whose signature dishes, based on locally sourced ingredients, include pork tenderloin, fondant, sesame, carrot and ginger, radish, soy; fillet steak, dauphinoise, wild mushroom, purple sprouting broccoli jus. One reader found the house wines 'especially good value'. The market town of Ross-on-Wye is 15 minutes' walk away, and the beautiful Wye valley, Goodrich Castle and Symonds Yat are nearby. (B and JH)

25% DISCOUNT VOUCHERS

Wilton Lane
Ross-on-Wye HR9 6AQ

T: 01989 562569
E: info@wiltoncourthotel.com
W: wiltoncourthotel.com

BEDROOMS: 11. 1 on ground floor suitable for disabled.
OPEN: all year except first 2 weeks Jan.
FACILITIES: library, bar, restaurant, private dining room, Wi-Fi, in-room TV (Freeview), ½-acre grounds, bar area and restaurant wheelchair accessible.
BACKGROUND MUSIC: in restaurant.
LOCATION: ½ mile from centre.
CHILDREN: all ages welcomed (cots, high chairs).
DOGS: allowed in 9 bedrooms, public rooms, not in restaurant (£5 per dog per night).
CREDIT CARDS: Amex, MC, Visa.
PRICES: per room B&B single £110–£160, double £135–£195, D,B&B (min. 2 nights) double £185–£245. Set dinner £33, à la carte £45. 1-night bookings refused Sat in peak season.

ROWSLEY Derbyshire   MAP 3:A6

THE PEACOCK AT ROWSLEY

They get so much right at Lord and Lady
Manners's 17th-century manor house hotel.
Expect a 'friendly welcome', 'good ambience',
housekeeping 'beyond reproach' and 'interesting
old paintings', many of members of the owners'
family. Bedrooms, some with a handmade four-
poster, are reached 'along a maze of corridors'.
'Ours had a beautifully carved oak wardrobe, a
Regency chest of drawers, a new, very comfortable
bed,' writes a trusted reader this year. 'The tiny
bathroom was superb, with an excellent shower
over a deep bath.' But while 'the right balance
between classy antiques and ultra-modern
facilities' is struck, on a Sunday night, 'loud,
invasive' music played in public rooms, food
service was 'erratic', a burger shrivelled. The bar
menu offers fish of the day, pearl barley and wild
garlic risotto, braised lamb shoulder. In the dining
room, Dan Smith's locally sourced dishes include
Derbyshire beef fillet, ox cheek ravioli, wild garlic,
oyster mushrooms and red wine sauce; hake,
potted shrimps, cauliflower, spinach, rhubarb and
caper butter sauce. Breakfast brings 'much-liked'
Isle of Man kippers; 'the lightest and best croissant
I've ever eaten'. (Anthony Bradbury, and others)

Bakewell Road
Rowsley DE4 2EB

T: 01629 733518
E: reception@thepeacockatrowsley.
com
W: thepeacockatrowsley.com

BEDROOMS: 15.
OPEN: all year except 24–26 Dec,
2 weeks Jan.
FACILITIES: lounge, bar, 2 dining
rooms, private dining room, free
Wi-Fi, in-room TV (Freeview,
Apple), ½-acre garden on river,
fishing rights, public areas wheelchair
accessible.
BACKGROUND MUSIC: in public rooms.
LOCATION: village centre.
CHILDREN: not under 10 at weekends.
DOGS: allowed in bedrooms only, 'for
small supplement'.
CREDIT CARDS: Amex, MC, Visa.
PRICES: per room B&B single £135–
£150, double £215–£320, D,B&B single
£170–£185, double £295–£390. À la
carte, bar £34, restaurant (Mon–Sat)
£65, tasting menu (Fri and Sat) £75.
1-night bookings sometimes refused.

RYE Sussex

MAP 2:E5

THE GEORGE IN RYE

In a 'little, old, cobble-stoned, grass-grown, red-roofed town, on the summit of its mildly pyramidal hill' (as described by former Rye resident Henry James), the George presents the street front of a Georgian coaching inn. Within, it is an agglomeration of old buildings, some timber-framed and dating from the 1500s, around a central courtyard. Hence low, beamed ceilings, 17th-century panelling, a Georgian ballroom with older minstrels' gallery. Owners Alex and Katie Clarke have achieved 'the perfect mix of historic charm, with up-to-date style and decor'. Bedrooms are individually designed, some with a four-poster bed, perhaps hummingbird wallpaper, Venetian-style mirrored furniture, a private terrace, such 'quirky and fun touches' as a mustard-yellow roll-top bath inside a fireplace, a floor-to-ceiling toile bedhead, a tapestry of stormy seas, a sea captain's chest, plus 'lots of nice bath products' (by REN). There is all-day dining in the grill and tap room, with oysters every which way, charcoal-grilled steaks, wood-roasted Rye Bay scallops, Harvey's Ale-battered local cod and chips. Breakfast brings 'excellent eggs Florentine, tasty sausages, perfect poached eggs'.

98 High Street
Rye TN31 7JT

T: 01797 222114
E: stay@thegeorgeinrye.com
W: thegeorgeinrye.com

BEDROOMS: 34. 17 in annexe, some with private entrance.
OPEN: all year.
FACILITIES: bar, restaurant, guest lounge, function rooms, free Wi-Fi, in-room TV (Freeview), civil wedding licence, decked courtyard garden.
BACKGROUND MUSIC: in bar and restaurant.
LOCATION: town centre. Parking on street or in nearby public car park, £2.50 a day.
CHILDREN: all ages welcomed.
DOGS: allowed in bar only.
CREDIT CARDS: MC, Visa.
PRICES: per room B&B £125–£355. À la carte £40 (restaurant).

SEE ALSO SHORTLIST

RYE Sussex

MAP 2:E5

JEAKE'S HOUSE

A photogenic street of cobblestone and gently listing cross-beamed houses hosts this 'beautiful, comfortable and relaxing' B&B, once a haunt of Malcolm Lowry and Radclyffe Hall. A reader was made to 'feel special and very welcome' by owner Jenny Hadfield and her staff. While you can unload your car in front of the ivy-covered property, parking is a six-minute walk away ('straightforward once you got used to the route'). The atmospheric parlours of the former 17th-century wool storehouse have oil paintings, a blazing fire, antiques and clusters of seating, ideal for a drink from the honesty bar. Stairs, described by the owners as 'somewhat medieval', take visitors to the 'pretty, old-fashioned (but not tired) bedrooms'. The Elizabeth Fry room, where the prison reformer once slept, has an antique four-poster; the Conrad Aitken, the American novelist's former study, has a large bay window, four-poster and adjoining double room. Views are of Romney Marsh or Rye's rooftops; the 'well-equipped bathrooms' might have a roll-top bath. Mornings bring Richard Martin's 'exquisitely good breakfasts', served in the galleried former chapel, once the meeting place of the Rye Quakers. (A and CB)

Mermaid Street
Rye TN31 7ET

T: 01797 222828
E: stay@jeakeshouse.com
W: jeakeshouse.com

BEDROOMS: 11.
OPEN: all year.
FACILITIES: parlour, bar/library, breakfast room, free Wi-Fi, in-room TV (Freeview), unsuitable for disabled.
BACKGROUND MUSIC: chamber music in breakfast room.
LOCATION: central, private car park, 6 mins' walk away (charge for parking permit, advance booking).
CHILDREN: not under 8.
DOGS: allowed in bedrooms, public rooms, on leads and 'always supervised'.
CREDIT CARDS: MC, Visa.
PRICES: per room B&B £99–£155. 1-night bookings sometimes refused Fri/Sat.

SEE ALSO SHORTLIST

ST IVES Cornwall

MAP 1:D1

BLUE HAYES

After a day spent exploring the shops and galleries of St Ives, guests at Malcolm Herring's hilltop private hotel can relax on the seaward terrace with a Blue Hayes Colada and feel serenely above it all. Decorated in cool coastal blues and creams and set in palm-filled gardens, the hotel has just five 'very spacious' suites (and a single) with 'every possible comfort' (fresh milk, ground coffee, bone china, smart toiletries). 'Ours had a table and chairs in the window where meals could be taken.' Trelyon has a large roof terrace with fabulous views; all have a bath and walk-in shower. The 'well-trained' staff (many have been working here for years) are 'a joy'. For dining out, there are restaurants for all tastes and budgets, but guests staying put can order ahead from an 'amazing selection of cold supper dishes', served in the dining room or alfresco. Maybe a Cornish blue-cheese salad, lobster with saffron and dill mayonnaise, a seafood platter… A 'magnificent' breakfast brings kedgeree, berry pancakes with crème fraîche, a full English. The host is a visible presence front-of-house. 'Malcolm was happy to talk about the three years he took to convert the old tired building.'

Trelyon Avenue
St Ives TR26 2AD

T: 01736 797129
E: info@bluehayes.co.uk
W: bluehayes.co.uk

BEDROOMS: 6.
OPEN: Mar–Oct.
FACILITIES: 2 lounges, bar, dining room, free Wi-Fi, in-room TV (Freeview), small function facilities, room service, terrace, garden, parking, unsuitable for wheelchair.
BACKGROUND MUSIC: in bar and dining room only, at breakfast and supper.
LOCATION: ½ mile from centre of St Ives.
CHILDREN: not under 10.
DOGS: not allowed.
CREDIT CARDS: Amex, MC, Visa.
PRICES: per room B&B single £160–£252, double £160–£315. Supper from £17. Min. 2-night stay, but check availability.

SEE ALSO SHORTLIST

ST IVES Cornwall

MAP 1:D1

BOSKERRIS HOTEL

Built as a small hotel, this bright, airy property, 'halfway up the hill behind Carbis Bay beach', has been offering 'stunning sea views' since 1931. Supported by 'helpful staff with in-depth knowledge of the Penwith peninsula', owners Jonathan and Marianne Bassett blend a relaxed atmosphere with a pared-back, contemporary, coastal style – all bare boards and light hues, with splashes of ocean blue. The real wow factor comes on the large, sun-bleached deck with a widescreen panorama from Godrevy Lighthouse to St Ives harbour. Most of the bedrooms (some compact) exploit the view, and even non-ocean-facing rooms offer 'more than a glimpse of the sea'. 'Immaculate' rooms share the light Mediterranean style, along with super-king or king-size bed, a cafetière, proper coffee, fresh milk on request. They have waffle robes, slippers, White Company toiletries, A 'very good, promptly served' menu of 'bits and bites' includes beef carpaccio; hand-picked fresh Newlyn crab and aïoli; West Country cheeses. The locally sourced breakfast, with home-made muesli, oak-smoked salmon, a full Cornish, is fuel for a stroll along the Coast Path into St Ives.

Boskerris Road
Carbis Bay
St Ives TR26 2NQ

T: 01736 795295
E: reservations@boskerrishotel.co.uk
W: boskerrishotel.co.uk

BEDROOMS: 15. 1, on ground floor, suitable for disabled.
OPEN: mid-Feb to mid-Dec, restaurant closed Sun, Mon.
FACILITIES: lounge, bar, breakfast room, supper room, free Wi-Fi, in-room TV (Freeview), decked terrace, massage and reflexology treatment room, 1½-acre garden, parking, public rooms wheelchair accessible.
BACKGROUND MUSIC: in public rooms.
LOCATION: 1½ miles from centre (20 mins' walk), close to station.
CHILDREN: not under 10.
DOGS: not allowed.
CREDIT CARDS: Amex, MC, Visa.
PRICES: per room B&B single £120–£221, double £160–£295. À la carte £28. 1-night bookings usually refused in high season.

SEE ALSO SHORTLIST

ST MARY'S Isles of Scilly

MAP 1: inset C1

STAR CASTLE

With 'epic' views across to Tresco and Bryher, the Francis family's 'really good hotel' combines 'a great setting' with 'fabulous historic features'. A fortification from the age of Sir Francis Drake, it now welcomes guests with a range of 'wonderful comfy' bedrooms. Some, in the original 16th-century castle and ramparts, have a quirky shape, perhaps original beams, a half-tester bed. Most occupy two modern garden annexes with country cottage-style decor, some with sea views and a veranda. While 'nicely decorated, with extremely comfortable beds', one regular reader felt they 'lacked any wow factor'. Chef Billy Littlejohn's locally sourced, modern British menus, using lobster caught by the owner, and garden vegetables, are served in the vine-hung conservatory and the castle dining room, with wine from the hotel vineyard. A typical dish: local brill, samphire, garlic purée, caramelised onion tart, king oyster mushrooms, scallops, truffle butter sauce. Long-serving staff are 'friendly, highly professional'. The old stone-walled dungeon is now a bar. Outside, guests enjoy island-hopping, swimming with seals, and free access to 'the UK's loveliest golf course'. (AK-H, and others)

25% DISCOUNT VOUCHERS

The Garrison
St Mary's TR21 0JA

T: 01720 422317
E: info@star-castle.co.uk
W: star-castle.co.uk

BEDROOMS: 38. 27 in 2 garden wings.
OPEN: all year, B&B only Nov–mid-Feb, except Christmas–New Year (full service).
FACILITIES: lounge, bar, 2 restaurants, free Wi-Fi, in-room TV (Freeview), civil wedding licence, sun deck, 2-acre gardens, covered swimming pool (12 by 4 metres), vineyard, tennis, beach, golf nearby, unsuitable for disabled.
BACKGROUND MUSIC: none.
LOCATION: ¼ mile from town centre.
CHILDREN: all ages welcomed.
DOGS: allowed in garden rooms, lounge, bar, not in restaurants.
CREDIT CARDS: Amex, MC, Visa.
PRICES: per room B&B single £89–£165, double £179–£414, D,B&B double £200–£470. Set menu £37–£45, à la carte £42. 1-night bookings usually refused (but call to check).

SEE ALSO SHORTLIST

ST MAWES Cornwall

MAP 1:E2

THE IDLE ROCKS

'We found seats on the attractive terrace' with 'views across St Mawes harbour to Falmouth Bay', reports a visitor to Karen and David Richards's 'superb' hotel (Relais & Châteaux). It stands in an enviable situation right by the harbour wall of this fishing village on the Roseland peninsula. You could not do better than the dual-aspect sea-view room with emperor bed – though even cosy village-view rooms have charm. Each bedroom is individually styled in coastal colours, with Aromatherapy Associates toiletries. A top-floor room had 'a huge walk-in shower, a wonderfully comfortable bed' but minor irritations (no shaver point, shallow wardrobe). You can eat in the sea-facing dining room with floor-to-ceiling windows, or alfresco; a reader would have liked an alternative to 'the lunch menu at around £30'. Chef Guy Owen sources local produce for dishes 'of the highest quality'. Maybe curried Newlyn hake, cauliflower, sour grape, Israeli couscous, herb yogurt; pork belly, heritage carrot, anise, pear, watercress pesto; fish goujons or spaghetti for children. An 'excellent' breakfast brings freshly pressed juices, artisan breads, chia seed porridge, grilled kipper. (MW, and others)

Harbourside
St Mawes TR2 5AN

T: 01326 270270
E: reservations@idlerocks.co.uk
W: idlerocks.com

BEDROOMS: 19. 4 in adjacent cottage, 1 suitable for disabled.
OPEN: all year.
FACILITIES: lounge, restaurant, kids' room, boot room, free Wi-Fi, in-room TV (Sky), in-room treatments, waterside terrace, public areas wheelchair accessible, adapted toilet, small car park.
BACKGROUND MUSIC: all day in public areas.
LOCATION: central, on the harbour.
CHILDREN: all ages welcomed.
DOGS: allowed in 2 cottage bedrooms, not in main hotel.
CREDIT CARDS: Amex, MC, Visa.
PRICES: per room B&B double £150–£405, family £250–£380. Set price dinner menu £58, 5-course tasting menu £85. 2-night min. stay at weekends, 3 nights min. bank hols, 1 on D,B&B terms.

SEE ALSO SHORTLIST

ST MAWES Cornwall

MAP 1:E2

TRESANTON

'Expensive certainly, but it's worth paying for
quality,' a satisfied reader writes after visiting
Olga Polizzi's mix-and-match hillside cluster
of former yachting clubhouse and fishermen's
cottages with 'extraordinary views' across
Falmouth Bay. 'Perfect in every way,' writes
another. 'The decor shows excellent taste.'
That embraces a nautical palette with coastal
colours and original Cornish art. All but two
of the 'charming' bedrooms overlook the
brine, catching the seaside vibe with deckchair
stripes on 'comfortable' beds, alongside fresh
flowers and antiques. 'My splendid bathroom
had a bath and wonderfully powerful separate
shower.' Two minor wishes: 'A fridge; slightly
better soundproofing.' After a day at the
waterfront beach club, or on the hotel's vintage
yacht, appetites are sated in the light-washed
restaurant or on its terrace, where Paul Wadham's
Mediterranean-inflected dishes include garlicky
lobster, monkfish and olives. Breakfast is
'magnificent', with freshly squeezed juices,
smoothies, 'delicious' cooked fare. The hardy
might enjoy the steep ascent to the car park but
help is available. Hotel Endsleigh, Milton Abbot
(see entry), is a sister. (TL, SK, and others)

27 Lower Castle Road
St Mawes TR2 5DR

T: 01326 270055
E: info@tresanton.com
W: tresanton.com

BEDROOMS: 30. In 5 houses.
OPEN: all year.
FACILITIES: 2 lounges, bar, restaurant,
cinema, playroom, conference
facilities, free Wi-Fi, in-room TV
(Freeview), civil wedding licence,
terrace, ¼-acre garden, beach club
(May–Sept), 48-foot yacht, only
restaurant wheelchair accessible.
BACKGROUND MUSIC: none.
LOCATION: on seafront, valet parking
(car park up hill).
CHILDREN: all ages welcomed.
DOGS: allowed in some bedrooms and
in dogs' bar.
CREDIT CARDS: Amex, MC, Visa.
PRICES: per room B&B £225–£775.
À la carte £46. Min. 2-night bookings
at weekends, 3-night bookings on
bank holidays.

SEE ALSO SHORTLIST

ST TUDY Cornwall

THE ST TUDY INN   [NEW]

With 'a blissful location in a chocolate box village' close to Bodmin Moor, the Camel Trail and the Padstow/Rock coast, this 17th-century inn turned gastropub-with-rooms is 'in every sense charming', writes a Guide inspector in 2019. It is owned by wine-producer Mark Hellyar and chef/director Emily Scott. Bedrooms, in a converted barn, are decorated in soft Farrow & Ball greys, with 'carefully chosen fabrics', a king-size bed. Extras include 'lovely Bramley toiletries, a coffee machine, fresh milk, mini-meringues'. A shower room was snug but well designed. It is Ms Scott's cooking, though, that is the big draw. 'This is a smart pub, basically', but the food, in bar and dining areas, is more 'restaurant standard', from a 'nicely varied menu using local and foraged ingredients'. Maybe risotto, nettle, wild garlic, Parmesan, mustard frills; fish stew, haddock, gurnard, mussels, saffron aïoli. Portions were perfectly formed but small. Flavours on the night lacked a wow factor, but 'the waiter took the time to talk us through each dish'. 'Breakfast was lovely – avocado on sourdough, eggs and asparagus', though the buffet was a bit sparse. 'I would definitely go back.'

St Tudy
Bodmin PL30 3NN

T: 01208 850656
E: sttudyinn@gmail.com
W: sttudyinn.com

BEDROOMS: 4. In converted barn annexe, 2 on ground floor.
OPEN: bar and dining room closed Sun pm, Mon.
FACILITIES: bar, dining room, terrace, free Wi-Fi, in-room TV, wheelchair accessible, adapted toilet.
BACKGROUND MUSIC: in restaurant.
LOCATION: centre of village.
CHILDREN: all ages welcomed.
DOGS: allowed by arrangement in 1 bedroom, bar, not dining room.
CREDIT CARDS: Amex, MC, Visa.
PRICES: per room B&B £150–£165, D,B&B £210–£225. À la carte £30. 2-night min. stay at weekends.

SALCOMBE Devon

SOAR MILL COVE HOTEL

♛ Previous César Winner

'We rate this very highly in almost every respect.'
Praise from a reader for Keith Makepeace's
much-loved, family-run, family-friendly, dog-
friendly hotel in a 'gorgeous' coastal setting.
'Comfortable, well-appointed' bedrooms have
views of sea or rolling National Trust countryside;
floor-to-ceiling glass doors lead on to a private
patio. 'The lounge is a beautiful room enhanced
by interesting abstract paintings.' The staff are
'without exception, pleasant and helpful'. You
can take lunch in the restaurant, on the terrace, or
in Castaways, the 'barefoot café', serving coffees,
cream teas, light bites; a chowder of 'the freshest
fish'; a sharing board of Salcombe crab, crevettes,
smoked salmon; char-grilled steak; veggie options.
At night, chef Ian MacDonald's 'imaginative'
menus feature such dishes as hake, Parmesan and
herb crunch, creamed potatoes, wilted greens,
salsa verde. A Devonshire breakfast sets guests
up for a ramble along the South West Coast Path,
or a gentle stroll to the beautiful, secluded beach
below. 'We were very taken with the amazing
wild flowers. A group of red deer hinds was
seen on the slope opposite the hotel.' (John Saul,
D and JB)

Soar Mill Cove
Salcombe TQ7 3DS

T: 01548 561566
E: info@soarmillcove.co.uk
W: soarmillcove.co.uk

BEDROOMS: 22. 21 on ground floor.
OPEN: all year, except Jan (open
Christmas/New Year).
FACILITIES: lounge, bar, restaurant,
coffee shop, free Wi-Fi, in-room
TV (Freeview), indoor spring-fed
swimming pool, spa, gym, civil
wedding licence, 10-acre grounds,
public rooms wheelchair accessible,
adapted toilet.
BACKGROUND MUSIC: in public areas.
LOCATION: 3 miles SW of Salcombe.
CHILDREN: all ages welcomed.
DOGS: allowed in all but 1 bedroom,
bar, coffee shop.
CREDIT CARDS: Amex, MC, Visa.
PRICES: per room B&B £199–£359,
D,B&B £277–£437. À la carte £39.
1-night bookings refused holiday
weekends.

SEE ALSO SHORTLIST

SANDWICH Kent

MAP 2:D5

THE SALUTATION

♦Previous César Winner

'We had an absolutely lovely stay.' 'Such a graceful house' in 'one of England's best preserved medieval towns.' Guide readers in 2019 joined fans in feeling 'truly cosseted' at this Queen Anne-style house. The 'lovingly' restored building, designed by Sir Edwin Lutyens, is the project of John and Dorothy Fothergill, who have imbued it with 'space and indulgence'. 'Plush, comfortable' bedrooms are spread across the main house, the former gatehouse and two cottages; ask for a room overlooking the 'truly special' and (rumoured-to-be) Gertrude Jekyll-designed gardens. 'We stayed in William, in the main house, which has a huge bed, a proper bath; big windows opening on to the garden.' Henry, named after one of the Farrers who commissioned the house, has a super-king-size canopy bed, a double bath in the 'vast bathroom' with Penhaligon soap. 'We awoke to the lowing of neighbouring cows.' Preprandials and dinner are 'flawlessly served'; chef Shane Hughes delights in smoked rainbow trout, citrus salad; seared langoustine, smoked bisque, celeriac lasagne. Breakfast has cooked options galore. Walmer Castle, Canterbury and some rather good golf courses are nearby. (Sybille Raphael)

25% DISCOUNT VOUCHERS

Knightrider Street
Sandwich CT13 9EW

T: 01304 619919
E: enquiries@the-salutation.com
W: the-salutation.com

BEDROOMS: 17. 8 in main house, 9 in three cottages.
OPEN: all year.
FACILITIES: drawing room, bar, 3 dining rooms, shop and café, free Wi-Fi, in-room TV (Freeview), civil wedding licence, 3½-acre gardens, unsuitable for disabled.
BACKGROUND MUSIC: in public areas.
LOCATION: town centre, walking distance from train station.
CHILDREN: all ages welcomed.
DOGS: allowed in 2 cottages, gardens and café.
CREDIT CARDS: Amex, MC, Visa.
PRICES: per room B&B £200–£345, D,B&B £335–£435. Tasting menu £75, à la carte £54. Min. 2-night bookings at Christmas.

SEAHAM Co. Durham

MAP 4:B4

SEAHAM HALL

Readers 'felt they had done their very best to look after us', after a week-long stay at this Georgian mansion. It stands in landscaped gardens overlooking the North Sea. It has been lavishly made over in a style that some find 'bizarre', but 'that's a matter of taste'. A Garden Suite, although 'really a large room whose windows open on to an external seating area' (with hot tub), had an 'enormous, very comfortable bed', lighting controls so sophisticated that 'in a week we barely mastered them' (but did get decent reading light). The Ada Lovelace Suite, with twin slipper baths in the window, nods to the hall once hosting the wedding of her parents, Lord Byron and Anne Isabella Millbanke. A portrait of Byron in Albanian dress hangs on the dining room wall, where Damian Broom's appealing menus include poached day-boat fish, girolles, broad beans, shrimps, elderflower. Near the spa, guests can eat Ozone's pan-Asian dishes, 'mainly curries and stir-fries, done very competently'. 'We were the only customers not in bathrobe and slippers.' Breakfast brings a 'wide, imaginative' choice. The young staff manifest 'infectious enthusiasm, a genuine desire to please'. (Andrew Wardrop)

Lord Byron's Walk
Seaham SR7 7AG

T: 0191 516 1400
E: reservations@seaham-hall.com
W: seaham-hall.co.uk

BEDROOMS: 21. 1 suitable for disabled.
OPEN: all year.
FACILITIES: lift, 2 lounges, bar, 2 restaurants, private dining room, conference facilities, in-room TV (Sky, BT), free Wi-Fi, civil wedding licence, spa (treatment rooms, outdoor hot tubs, sun terrace, fitness suite, 20-metre heated swimming pool), 37-acre grounds (terraces, putting green), public areas wheelchair accessible, adapted toilet.
BACKGROUND MUSIC: all day in public areas.
LOCATION: 5 miles S of Sunderland.
CHILDREN: all ages welcomed.
DOGS: not allowed.
CREDIT CARDS: Amex, MC, Visa.
PRICES: per room B&B £209–£425, D,B&B £299–£510. Set menu £30, à la carte £50.

SEAHOUSES Northumberland

ST AIDAN HOTEL & BISTRO

'We really rated this friendly little hotel,' wrote a Guide reader of Robin and Tegan Tait's B&B and bistro, 'right on the seafront' with 'stunning views' to the Farne Islands and Holy Island (binoculars provided). The bedrooms are decorated in a coastal palette of pale blues and greens, with pine furniture. Brownsman, on the ground floor, with separate access, is named after the island once home to Grace Darling, now to puffin and guillemot, razorbill and tern. The views are variously of islands, village, harbour and dramatically sited Bamburgh Castle. 'The bar and dining room are similarly comfortable and relaxed, with stunning views.' The bistro operates three nights a week, when chef James Ash cooks such locally sourced dishes as coq au Riesling; Northumbrian beef bourguignon; roasted hake or a vegetarian option. This is not a grand or boutique place, but inexpensive, and located on a starkly beautiful stretch of coast with unspoilt sandy beaches. A perfect base for exploring the islands, and for castle visits, maybe to Alnwick with its lovely garden and associations with two famous Harrys – Shakespeare's 'hare-brained Hotspur' and the boy magician Potter. (ST)

1 St Aidan's
Seahouses NE68 7SR

T: 01665 720355
E: info@staidanhotel.co.uk
W: staidanhotel.co.uk

BEDROOMS: 9. 2 in annexe.
OPEN: all year except 7 days over Christmas, 2 Jan–2nd weekend Feb, bistro open Thurs–Sat dinner.
FACILITIES: breakfast room/bistro, bar area (honesty bar), free Wi-Fi, in-room TV (Freeview), front lawn (picnic tables), unsuitable for disabled.
BACKGROUND MUSIC: chilled acoustic in public rooms.
LOCATION: 300 yds from harbour, on north side of village, with views towards Bamburgh.
CHILDREN: not under 12.
DOGS: allowed in annexe rooms, 1 area of breakfast room, not in bistro.
CREDIT CARDS: none (debit cards accepted).
PRICES: per room B&B £95–£145. À la carte £28.

SEAHOUSES Northumberland

MAP 4:A4

ST CUTHBERT'S HOUSE

♥ Previous César Winner

On the edge of this seaside town, a 'lovingly
converted' Presbyterian chapel dedicated to
Northumberland's patron saint is run as a 'superb'
B&B and occasional music venue by enthusiastic
owners and 'great hosts' Jeff and Jill Sutheran.
The 'very comfortable and stylish' bedrooms,
some rather snug, have a super-king-size bed,
blackout curtains, an espresso machine, robes
and slippers. Dual-aspect Aidan and Columba
each have an original arched window. Both
have a great shower, but with a narrow access
door, while Brigid has a bath – and a glimpse,
across the rooftops, of mighty Bamburgh Castle.
Accessible ground-floor Bede has a wet room.
The pulpit gallery overlooks the former sanctuary,
which serves as a guest lounge, with honesty bar
and harmonium. At breakfast they pull out all
the stops. There is porridge with Lindisfarne
mead, kedgeree, locally smoked kippers with
horseradish, award-winning sausages, bubble and
squeak, bread from the bakery and Jill's home-
made marmalade. 'A perfect base for exploring':
take a trip to see the seals on the Farne Islands.
(Helge Rubinstein)

25% DISCOUNT VOUCHERS

192 Main Street
Seahouses NE68 7UB

T: 01665 720456
E: stay@stcuthbertshouse.com
W: stcuthbertshouse.com

BEDROOMS: 6. 2 on ground floor,
1 suitable for disabled.
OPEN: all year except 'holiday periods
in winter'.
FACILITIES: lounge, dining area, free
Wi-Fi, in-room TV (Freeview), public
rooms wheelchair accessible.
BACKGROUND MUSIC: instrumental at
breakfast.
LOCATION: under 1 mile from harbour
and village centre.
CHILDREN: 12 and upwards welcomed.
DOGS: assistance dogs only.
CREDIT CARDS: MC, Visa.
PRICES: per room B&B single £110–
£130, double £130. 1-night bookings
occasionally refused in high season.

SHAFTESBURY Dorset

MAP 2:D1

LA FLEUR DE LYS

Personal attention from the owners won high praise from readers this year, after a stay at this restaurant-with-rooms overlooking Blackmore Vale. 'David looked after us well in every way,' wrote Guide regulars celebrating their ruby wedding anniversary. 'It is thoroughly worthy of its entry.' Since its 1991 launch in a market town familiar from the old 'boy and bike' Hovis ad, it has remained a welcoming, traditional place, defined by its 'friendly and helpful hosts', Mary and David Griffin-Shepherd and Marc Preston. Bedrooms, each named after a grape variety, are not in any way boutique, and snug Sauvignon, though 'clean and comfortable', was judged by another guest to be 'a one-night only room'. Longer stays might merit a four-poster bedroom. All contain such considerate touches as fresh coffee, milk in a fridge, home-made biscuits. At dinner, David and Marc's cooking is 'well worth a (long) detour', with modern dishes like grilled fillets of South Coast sole, langoustines, asparagus, lemon-infused butter; seared sika venison, parsnip, apple, swede and tomato ratatouille, dark rosemary sauce. Breakfast brings fresh juice, a good cooked choice. (Geoffrey Bignell, and others)

25% DISCOUNT VOUCHERS

Bleke Street
Shaftesbury SP7 8AW

T: 01747 853717
E: info@lafleurdelys.co.uk
W: lafleurdelys.co.uk

BEDROOMS: 8. 1, on ground floor, suitable for disabled.
OPEN: all year, restaurant closed Sun, lunchtime Mon and Tues.
FACILITIES: lounge, bar, dining room, conference room, free Wi-Fi, in-room TV (Freeview), courtyard garden; bar and restaurant wheelchair accessible.
BACKGROUND MUSIC: none, but some live music events.
LOCATION: N edge of historic town centre.
CHILDREN: all ages welcomed.
DOGS: not allowed.
CREDIT CARDS: Amex, MC, Visa.
PRICES: per room B&B single £90–£115, double £110–£160. Set dinner £31–£40, 5-course tasting menu (for whole table only) £48. 1-night bookings sometimes refused weekends in summer.

SHAFTESBURY Dorset

MAP 2:D1

THE GROSVENOR ARMS NEW

There has been an inn on this spot since the 1500s, a stone's throw from Shaftesbury's famous and historic Gold Hill. This may well be the inn's most successful incarnation, with 'top-notch' staff, 'stunning' rooms and a 'first-class' restaurant. Recent inspectors found Room 5, on the first floor, 'light and bright', with 'floor-to-ceiling windows overlooking the square', a 'comfortable bed' and traffic noise 'not at all intrusive'. Bathrobes and full-size bottles of Bramley toiletries in the 'smart' bathroom were appreciated. Food, by executive chef Tom Blake, is an all-day affair, served in the 'bustling' bar, conservatory or restaurant, the last an 'elegant' room with 'well-spaced tables and comfortable chairs'. The cauliflower soup with home-made crusty bread is 'very good'; the 'whole Cornish plaice with brown shrimps', 'first class'. Breakfast comprises a buffet with a 'standard selection' of fruit juices, cereals, croissants and pastries plus a good choice of cooked dishes: 'smoked salmon from Severn and Wye with avocado and poached eggs', perhaps, or the scrambled eggs served on 'super sourdough bread'. 'Recommended without hesitation.' (RB, and others)

The Commons
Shaftesbury SP7 8JA

T: 01747 850580
E: reception@grosvenorarms.co.uk
W: grosvenorarms.co.uk

BEDROOMS: 16, 2 first-floor rooms accessible by lift with no further steps.
OPEN: all year.
FACILITIES: lift, bar, lounge, restaurant, conservatory, private dining room, ballroom, free Wi-Fi, in-room Smart TV (Freeview), courtyard garden, bar and restaurant wheelchair accessible, adapted toilet.
BACKGROUND MUSIC: in the bar.
LOCATION: town centre, a stone's throw from Gold Hill.
CHILDREN: all ages welcomed.
DOGS: allowed in bedrooms (£10 per dog), bar, conservatory, not in restaurant.
CREDIT CARDS: Amex, MC, Visa.
PRICES: per room B&B £95–£220, D,B&B £130–£255. À la carte £37.

SHEFFIELD Yorkshire

MAP 4:E4

BROCCO ON THE PARK

♛ Previous César Winner

'A beacon of how to do things properly: metropolitan style with Yorkshire substance.' Generous praise from a regular reader this year for this 'smart, sophisticated' hotel on the edge of Sheffield's student quarter. The blend of warm northern hospitality and Scandinavian pared-back style is courtesy of owner Tiina Carr, born in nearby Doncaster but with a Finnish family. The 'immaculately presented, stylishly furnished' bedrooms, all white, greys, earth tones and occasional splashes of colour, might have an in-room copper slipper bath, contemporary four-poster or fireplace (with candle, of course). All have a wooden floor, rugs, robes, a Nespresso machine, 'an exceptional range of tea and coffee'. 'Luxurious' bathrooms provide a 'fantastic' walk-in monsoon shower and organic toiletries. In the 'outstanding' bistro-style restaurant, with central kitchen, Leslie Buddington's 'superb' modern British dishes with a Nordic twist include crispy squid with garlic aïoli; halloumi fritters, spring onion jam, herb pesto. An 'interesting and varied breakfast' includes 'some of the best grilled bacon I've ever tasted, even the baked beans had a bespoke quality'. (Mike Craddock, and others)

92 Brocco Bank
Sheffield S11 8RS

T: 0114 266 1233
E: hello@brocco.co.uk
W: brocco.co.uk

BEDROOMS: 8. 1 suitable for disabled.
OPEN: all year, restaurant closed Sun 6 pm and Christmas Day.
FACILITIES: reception area with sofas, 2 restaurants (1 with bar), free Wi-Fi, in-room Smart TV, terrace (barbecue, seating), bicycle hire, restaurant wheelchair accessible, adapted toilet.
BACKGROUND MUSIC: in restaurant, plus Sunday jazz afternoons.
LOCATION: 1½ miles W of city centre.
CHILDREN: all ages welcomed (under-3s free).
DOGS: allowed only on terrace.
CREDIT CARDS: Amex, MC, Visa.
PRICES: room only £115–£245. Breakfast items from £5, full English £11, à la carte £45. Min. 2-night stay at Christmas.

SIDLESHAM Sussex   MAP 2:E3

THE CRAB & LOBSTER

'We enjoyed the waterside location,' write
trusted readers this year, drawn back for a third
stay at Sam and Janet Bakose's 350-year-old inn
overlooking Pagham Harbour with its reserve
of mudflats and salt marsh. A sister to The
Halfway Bridge, Lodsworth (see entry), it has
four bedrooms decorated in pastels and earthy
hues, echoing the surroundings. A dual-aspect
deluxe room was 'spacious and comfortable',
with a 'big bed, separate seating area', a modern
bathroom with a 'powerful' monsoon over-bath
shower. The odd creaking floorboard might be
heard from above. In the smart bar/dining room,
with its mix of old and new decor, or alfresco in
the sunshine, fish-lovers are 'spoilt for choice' by
Clyde Hollett's locally sourced dishes including
whole lemon sole, Jersey Royals, samphire,
brown-shrimp butter. Expect meaty options too,
a veggie dish, sandwiches, salads. The manager,
Mark Vincent, and his team provide 'exceptional
personal service'. After a 'fine' breakfast with
'interesting cooked items', perhaps visit Church
Norton beach, where, 90 years ago, Eric Coates
was moved to pen By the Sleepy Lagoon, which
still today heralds Desert Island Discs. (Michael
Gwinnell, PA)

Mill Lane
Sidlesham PO20 7NB

T: 01243 641233
E: enquiries@crab-lobster.co.uk
W: crab-lobster.co.uk

BEDROOMS: 4. 2 in adjacent self-
catering Crab Cottage.
OPEN: all year.
FACILITIES: bar/dining room/snug,
free Wi-Fi, in-room TV (Freeview),
terrace, small beer garden, bar and
restaurant wheelchair accessible.
BACKGROUND MUSIC: 'quiet' in
restaurant and bar.
LOCATION: 6 miles S of Chichester.
CHILDREN: all ages welcomed.
DOGS: allowed in garden area.
CREDIT CARDS: Amex, MC, Visa.
PRICES: per room B&B single £115–
£135, double £190–£320. À la carte
£38. 2-night min. stay at weekends.

SIDMOUTH Devon

HOTEL RIVIERA

Elizabeth Barrett (not yet Browning) would have known this 'charming, traditional' white stucco seafront hotel when she moved to Sidmouth in 1832 for the balmy climate. Behind a 'very impressive facade', the interiors today would not faze her. Owner Peter Wharton does not pursue change for its own sake, say readers approvingly. 'The decor is old-fashioned but in keeping with the hotel style' and public rooms are air-conditioned. A bow-fronted, sea-view room was 'excellent', the bed 'very comfortable'. 'The hotel was beautifully clean, and our bathroom modern with everything working well.' Robes and flowers are pleasing touches. On some nights a pianist plays in the refurbished cocktail bar. In the 'convivial' dining room Martin Osedo cooks classics with a modern twist – for instance, seared lemon sole fillet, new potato and spring onion salad, crispy leeks, avocado and tomato beurre noisette. 'The meal was excellent and served with style. It was a pleasure to see staff dressed traditionally.' There is table service at breakfast, which brings freshly squeezed orange and grapefruit juice, smoked haddock, omelettes, hash browns. 'In all a lovely experience.' (John Barnes, ML)

The Esplanade
Sidmouth EX10 8AY

T: 01395 515201
E: enquiries@hotelriviera.co.uk
W: hotelriviera.co.uk

BEDROOMS: 26. None on ground floor.
OPEN: all year.
FACILITIES: Small lift (not suitable for large wheelchairs), foyer, lounge, bar, restaurant, function facilities, free Wi-Fi, in-room TV (Freeview), terrace, opposite beach (safe bathing), public rooms wheelchair accessible.
BACKGROUND MUSIC: in bar and restaurant, occasional live piano music in bar.
LOCATION: central, on the esplanade.
CHILDREN: all ages welcomed.
DOGS: small dogs allowed in some bedrooms, not in public rooms except foyer.
CREDIT CARDS: Amex, MC, Visa.
PRICES: per person B&B £118–£239, D,B&B £139–£260. Set dinner £42–£46, à la carte £46.

SNETTISHAM Norfolk

MAP 2:A4

THE ROSE & CROWN

'We had a wonderful stay. It's a fabulous pub in a gorgeous village, and just a couple of miles from the sea.' Readers lavished praise this year on the whitewashed 14th-century pub-with-rooms, run with boundless enthusiasm by owners Jeannette and Anthony Goodrich. 'It has bags of history and character in the front and back bars, further comfortable eating areas and a large beer garden, once the village bowling green.' A 'spacious and very comfortable' bedroom had a bathroom with 'bath and a big walk-in power shower' and '101 dogs and a cat cartoon on the wall'. All rooms have books, magazines, Molton Brown toiletries. It's not the Ritz; the style is simple and contemporary, with touches of humour. There has been much updating since last year, and a new chef, Neil Austin, is now in the kitchen, cooking such locally sourced pub classics as rib-eye steaks, beer-battered fish and chunky chips, alongside more ambitious dishes (pan-fried sea trout, roast tomato, chorizo, mussel meat, white bean cassoulet). There are veggie options, a children's menu. Breakfasts were 'really superb'. Tellingly, the 'capable, universally friendly staff genuinely seem to enjoy working here'. (Steve Jack)

Old Church Road
Snettisham PE31 7LX

T: 01485 541382
E: info@roseandcrownsnettisham.
    co.uk
W: roseandcrownsnettisham.co.uk

BEDROOMS: 16. 2 on ground floor, 1 suitable for disabled.
OPEN: all year.
FACILITIES: 3 bar areas, 2 restaurant rooms, garden room, free Wi-Fi, in-room TV (Freeview), large walled garden (children's play area, climbing frame).
BACKGROUND MUSIC: low-key, mainly soft jazz in dining areas.
LOCATION: in village centre, 5 miles S of Hunstanton.
CHILDREN: all ages welcomed.
DOGS: well-behaved dogs allowed in bedrooms, bars and garden room, not in dining areas.
CREDIT CARDS: Amex, MC, Visa.
PRICES: per room B&B single £100, double £120. À la carte £30.

SOMERTON Somerset

MAP 1:C6

THE LYNCH COUNTRY HOUSE

Lynne Vincent is the perfect hostess and a mine of information at Roy Copeland's Grade II listed Georgian country house B&B on the edge of a market town, a former capital of Wessex. It has 'lots of character', views across the Somerset countryside from the belvedere. The coach house, with its own separate entrance, has ground-level rooms, while those in the main house range from Goldington, with antique oak four-poster, to snug Alderly, under the eaves, with starlight windows, a roll-top bath and hand-held shower. You can wander in the 'lovely grounds', where ducks and black swans glide on the lake, specimen trees cast their shade, and a rill runs through. Breakfast, served in an orangery flooded with light through tall Venetian arched windows, includes freshly squeezed orange juice, dry-cured Wiltshire bacon, Clonakilty black and white pudding, and Loch Fyne smoked salmon, roasted tomatoes, fluffy scrambled eggs. It is all 'very comfy' and they are flexible about timing. A grand piano and jazz memorabilia recall Mr Copeland's career as a jazz saxophonist. And if the look and fittings are here and there a bit dated, so what? 'A very good B&B.' (M M-D)

4 Behind Berry
Somerton TA11 7PD

T: 01458 272316
E: enquiries@thelynchcountryhouse.co.uk
W: thelynchcountryhouse.co.uk

BEDROOMS: 9. 4, in coach house, on ground floor.
OPEN: all year, only coach house rooms at Christmas and New Year, no breakfast 25/26 Dec, 1 Jan.
FACILITIES: breakfast room, small sitting area, free Wi-Fi, in-room TV (Freeview), ¾-acre grounds (lake), unsuitable for disabled.
BACKGROUND MUSIC: none.
LOCATION: edge of town.
CHILDREN: all ages welcomed.
DOGS: allowed (not unattended) in 1 coach house room, not in public rooms.
CREDIT CARDS: Amex, MC, Visa.
PRICES: per room B&B single £70–£95. double £80–£125.

SEE ALSO SHORTLIST

SOUTH BRENT Devon

MAP 1:D4

GLAZEBROOK HOUSE

NEW

Welcome to Wonderland. On the edge of
Dartmoor national park, Fran and Pieter
Hamman's Alice-themed hotel has been styled in
the manner of a 19th-century collector's mansion.
'There are chandeliers everywhere – at least two
in each bedroom,' relate Guide insiders. You look
around, wide-eyed, at 'skeletons of a horse and
emu, a collection of plates adorning the dining-
room wall', hats hanging outside the Cheshire Cat
room. Curiouser and curiouser, the Mad Hatter
room has wall-mounted doll's houses, sunny
Tweedle Deez has twin four-posters. All rooms
have handmade furniture, 'beautiful bespoke
wardrobes from China, shiny patterned tiles on
heated bathroom floors', luxury fittings. Cigar
aficionados may smoke in the humidor. At lunch
and dinner, Josh Ackland uses local produce,
herbs from the herb garden, in such dishes as
pan-roasted lamb rack, peas à la française, thyme
dauphine, asparagus; sage gnocchi, truffled
Dawlish mushrooms, Parmesan velouté. In the
morning, take a stroll in the wonderful grounds,
or join one of the hotel's guided walking tours
to work off breakfast of chilli avocado on artisan
bread, American pancakes, eggs Benedict.

25% DISCOUNT VOUCHERS

Glazebrook
South Brent
Totnes TQ10 9JE

T: 01364 73322
E: enquiries@glazebrookhouse.com
W: glazebrookhouse.com

BEDROOMS: 9. 1, on ground floor,
suitable for disabled.
OPEN: all year.
FACILITIES: reception lobby, drawing
room, bar/library, whisky/gin tasting
room, restaurant, Chef's Kitchen
patio, Wi-Fi, in-room TV (Freeview),
civil wedding licence, 3½-acre garden,
parking, public rooms wheelchair
accessible, adapted toilet.
BACKGROUND MUSIC: in public areas,
not library or tasting room.
LOCATION: 1 mile SW of town centre.
CHILDREN: over-15s welcomed in hotel,
children over 5 in restaurant with
responsible adults.
DOGS: not allowed.
CREDIT CARDS: Amex, MC, Visa.
PRICES: per room B&B £199–£324.
À la carte £45, tasting menus £50
(6 courses), £64 (8 courses).

SOUTH DALTON Yorkshire

MAP 4:D5

♀ THE PIPE AND GLASS INN

César award: inn of the year

'Brilliant, my favourite hotel.' A trusted reader raves about James and Kate Mackenzie's former coaching inn with Michelin-starred cooking. Five 'very comfortable, well-equipped' bedrooms, with striking contemporary decor, have a 'spectacular bathroom' or wet room with underfloor heating, private patio or terrace and garden. Lovage has toile de Jouy fabrics, a twin-shower wet room, lovely views over Dalton Park. 'But the real draw is the food.' You can eat in the cosy, beamed bar, perhaps a ploughman's, or superior pork sausages and bubble-and-squeak, with a pint of their own Two Chefs ale. The light-filled restaurant is more formal, with Kate front-of-house. There are tables, also, in the recently designed garden where, astonishingly, everything they have planted, from roses to rosemary, is edible. A classic James Mackenzie dish: Barnsley chop, devilled kidneys, lamb belly boulangère, mint sauce, butter-braised Chantenay carrot. 'It's difficult to select an outstanding dish. Everything was perfect. Even if you're not vegetarian, it's worth having a look at the vegetarian menu.' 'The staff are brilliant, too.' Breakfast brings home-baked bread, the full works. (Peter Anderson)

West End
South Dalton HU17 7PN

T: 01430 810246
E: email@pipeandglass.co.uk
W: pipeandglass.co.uk

BEDROOMS: 5. All on ground floor in garden, 1 suitable for disabled, 4 more scheduled in annexe 500 yards away.
OPEN: all year except 2 weeks in Jan, no room reservations Sun and Mon.
FACILITIES: lounge, conservatory, bar, restaurant, private dining room, free Wi-Fi, in-room TV (Freeview), patio (alfresco dining), garden (herbarium, kitchen garden), public rooms wheelchair accessible, adapted toilet.
BACKGROUND MUSIC: in bar and restaurant.
LOCATION: 7 miles NW of Beverley.
CHILDREN: all ages welcomed (own menu).
DOGS: not allowed.
CREDIT CARDS: Amex, MC, Visa.
PRICES: per room B&B single £170–£210, double £200–£260. À la carte £60.

SOUTH LEIGH Oxfordshire   MAP 3:E6

ARTIST RESIDENCE
OXFORDSHIRE

The Cotswolds outpost of Justin and Charlotte
Salisbury's small boutique hotel collection, this
16th-century hub-of-the-village pub-with-rooms
is now a charming, bohemian bolt-hole. Public
spaces have the Salisburys' signature blend:
rough-hewn walls, bold neon art, William
Morris-influenced wallpaper, kilim cushions, open
fireplaces, flagstones and creaking floorboards.
Any outward eccentricity is matched by 'textbook'
service, say Guide inspectors. The bedrooms
('splendid') include the Loft rooms above the pub
and a set in outbuildings; a third option is the
Shepherd's Hut, perfumed by the adjacent herb
garden. Farmhouse Loft rooms, full of vintage
finds and reclaimed treasures, have a large high
bed, copper bathtub, rainfall shower. The 'well-
stocked, upmarket' refreshments, gowns and
slippers are pleasing extras. New chef Fernao
Namura serves wholesome comfort food in the
restaurant, Mason Arms (a nod to the inn's former
name); perhaps onglet steaks, roasted shallot,
BBQ broccoli, bone marrow sauce. At breakfast:
pancakes, bacon, maple syrup; boiled egg and
soldiers; 'fine leaf tea and strong coffee'. Ideal fuel
for a tour of picture-perfect Cotswold villages.

Station Road
South Leigh OX29 6XN

T: 01993 656220
E: oxford@artistresidence.co.uk
W: artistresidence.co.uk/our-hotels/
   oxford

BEDROOMS: 9, 1 bedroom and 2 suites
in outbuildings, Shepherd's Hut in
garden.
OPEN: all year.
FACILITIES: bar, restaurant (2 dining
areas, closed Sun eve), free Wi-Fi,
in-room TV (Freeview), large beer
garden, unsuitable for disabled.
BACKGROUND MUSIC: in pub and
restaurant.
LOCATION: countryside, 10 miles from
Oxford, 3 miles from Witney centre.
CHILDREN: all ages welcomed.
DOGS: allowed in some rooms and
public rooms (£20 per dog per night,
dog beds provided).
CREDIT CARDS: Amex, MC, Visa.
PRICES: room only £130–£425.
Breakfast from around £10.50,
à la carte £32. Min. 2-night stay at
weekends.

SOUTHAMPTON Hampshire

MAP 2:E2

THE PIG IN THE WALL

A Georgian house 'charmingly set into the ancient city wall', this little Piggy is wee, wee, wee – at least, compared with its country cousins. The second in Robin Hutson's expanding collection of concept hotels, it has only 12 bedrooms, no restaurant, no kitchen garden, but it is no less a Pig for that. Entering the deli bar you find the signature, 'very stylish' eclectic interiors: 'pots of growing herbs' on scuffed tables, mismatched armchairs, fireplaces, trophy heads. Bedrooms, styled by Judy Hutson, might have a beamed ceiling, an original fireplace or shutters. Bigger rooms have a freestanding in-room bath and a walk-in monsoon shower that 'makes no retro concessions to efficiency'. 'Our super-king-size bed with four spiralling posts was comfortable, with crisp white linen.' Smaller comfy rooms have just the shower. The Snug is tucked into the attic. All rooms have a larder of snacks to buy. At night, guests receive a Land Rover lift to dinner at The Pig in the Forest, Brockenhurst (see entry). Back in the wall, staff are 'young, efficient, enthusiastic'. Breakfast is a 'buffet affair, nothing hot', make your own toast, with 'a nice selection'. In all, 'a lovely experience'.

8 Western Esplanade
Southampton SO14 2AZ

T: 02380 636900
E: reception@thepiginthewall.com
W: thepighotel.com

BEDROOMS: 12. 2 on ground floor, 1 with wet room and wheelchair access via side door.
OPEN: all year.
FACILITIES: open-plan lounge/bar/deli counter, free Wi-Fi, in-room TV (Freeview), car park (£10 a night), public rooms wheelchair accessible.
BACKGROUND MUSIC: in public areas.
LOCATION: close to city centre.
CHILDREN: all ages welcomed.
DOGS: not allowed.
CREDIT CARDS: Amex, MC, Visa.
PRICES: room £140–£195. Breakfast £10.

SEE ALSO SHORTLIST

STAMFORD Lincolnshire

MAP 2:B3

THE GEORGE OF STAMFORD

'Another excellent stay,' reports a Guide regular this year, after returning to Lawrence Hoskins's 'very traditional' town-centre hotel, once a coaching inn on the old Great North Road. Her single room was upgraded at no extra cost. A friend was similarly 'impressed' by the 'small but beautifully arranged garden', and the lounges with 'imposing fireplaces and age-crinkled wood panelling'. Over the centuries, the bedrooms, some snug, some large with half-tester bed, leather sofa and mullioned windows, have hosted royalty, nobility and gamblers, perhaps attracted by 'the world's finest cockpit', built in 1725. Another visitor wrote of a room 'straight out of Agatha Christie, with four-poster, blankets and heavy curtains but a cracking modern bathroom'. Male guests must wear a jacket to dine in the Oak Room which serves Paul Nicholls's classic English fare including sirloin carved at a silver-domed wagon; pan-roasted venison; roasted partridge. In the informal Garden Room, dishes include a Grand Brittany seafood platter; antipasti; and a 'very good lobster spaghetti'. Staff are 'helpful, extremely pleasant'. Breakfast 'has lots of choice'. (Helen Ann Davies, IB, and others)

71 St Martins
Stamford PE9 2LB

T: 01780 750750
E: reservations@
    georgehotelofstamford.com
W: georgehotelofstamford.com

BEDROOMS: 45.
OPEN: all year.
FACILITIES: 2 lounges, 2 bars, 2 restaurants, 2 private dining rooms, business centre, free Wi-Fi, in-room TV (Sky, Freeview), civil wedding licence, 2-acre grounds (courtyard, gardens), public rooms wheelchair accessible, adapted toilet.
BACKGROUND MUSIC: none.
LOCATION: ¼ mile from centre.
CHILDREN: all ages welcomed.
DOGS: allowed, not unattended in bedrooms, only guide dogs in restaurants.
CREDIT CARDS: Amex, MC, Visa.
PRICES: per room B&B single from £135, double £225–£400. À la carte £65. 1-night bookings refused during Burghley Horse Trials.

SEE ALSO SHORTLIST

STANTON WICK Somerset

MAP 1:B6

THE CARPENTERS ARMS

Flower decked without, welcoming within, this 'excellent' village pub, contrived from three former miners' cottages, is liked by readers flying out of nearby Bristol Airport. Forget bland airport hotels. Here are low, beamed ceilings, stone walls, a cosy bar with log-burner. The public areas have been refurbished since last year. The bedrooms are modestly priced, cottage style, 'very comfortable'. Bright fabrics are offset by neutral decor. Fresh milk is provided for tea or coffee. Bathrooms have a shower or bath with shower over. Eat where you choose – in the bar, the lounge, either of two dining rooms, or the garden. Christian Wragg's menus range from pub classics (Brixham fish and chips, West Country beef-and-ale pie), to such ambitious dishes as herb-crusted lamb rump, sweet potato mash, confit leek, mint jus. Vegetarian choices might include nut roast, Thai vegetable curry. 'When we returned from a busy day, although it was before the restaurant opened, the chef produced warm bread, olive oil and balsamic, eaten by a roaring fire.' 'A good choice of wines by the glass is appreciated.' 'Very tasty' breakfasts are cooked to order. 'Everyone is so obliging and helpful.' (JB)

Wick Lane
Stanton Wick
Pensford BS39 4BX

T: 01761 490202
E: carpenters@buccaneer.co.uk
W: the-carpenters-arms.co.uk

BEDROOMS: 13.
OPEN: all year except evenings 25/26 Dec, 1 Jan.
FACILITIES: bar, snug, lounge, 2 restaurants, function room, free Wi-Fi, in-room TV (Freeview), patio, secure parking, public areas wheelchair accessible, adapted toilet.
BACKGROUND MUSIC: in some areas.
LOCATION: 8 miles S of Bristol, 8 miles W of Bath.
CHILDREN: all ages welcomed (under-12s free, children's menu, high chairs, changing facilities available).
DOGS: allowed in bar, snug and outside areas.
CREDIT CARDS: Amex, MC, Visa.
PRICES: per room B&B single £70–£107, double £100–£180. À la carte £37.

STOKE BY NAYLAND Suffolk   MAP 2:C5

THE CROWN

In landscaped gardens that gently melt into
Constable country, with tables for alfresco
drinking and dining, 'one of Suffolk's oldest
pubs has been renovated very smartly' under the
ownership of Richard Sunderland. Bedrooms
are in a 'beautifully presented' annexe at the rear.
Some executive rooms have French windows on
to a private terrace overlooking lawns, fields and
woodland. Inside, 'a sofa, armchairs, a spacious
bathroom with large walk-in shower and double-
ended bath'. There was cafetière coffee, fresh milk
and 'excellent pillows'. The Guide inspectors'
standard room had just one armchair ('they did
ask if we would like another'), glossy magazines,
a rainforest shower. Within the open bar and
dining room, a wine shop offers a range of bottles
to drink with dinner or to take out, and more
than 30 wines by the glass. Nick Beavan's menus
change every five weeks, with ingredients sourced
as locally as possible for such dishes as roasted
rainbow trout, cavolo nero, toasted almonds, baby
capers, thick-cut chips. In the morning, there is
table service, with 'excellent fresh orange juice'
from 'one of the best breakfast menus we've seen
in a long time'. (MG, and others)

Park Street
Stoke by Nayland CO6 4SE

T: 01206 262001
E: info@crowninn.net
W: crowninn.net

BEDROOMS: 11. In separate annexe, 7 on
ground floor, 1 suitable for disabled.
OPEN: all year except 25/26 Dec.
FACILITIES: bar, restaurant, snug area,
reception area with seating, terrace,
wine shop, free Wi-Fi, in-room TV
(BT, Freeview), garden, parking,
public rooms wheelchair accessible,
adapted toilet.
BACKGROUND MUSIC: none.
LOCATION: village centre.
CHILDREN: all ages welcomed.
DOGS: allowed in parts of restaurant,
not in bedrooms.
CREDIT CARDS: Amex, MC, Visa.
PRICES: per room B&B single
£110–£210, double £145–£295.
À la carte £35.

STUDLAND Dorset

MAP 2:E2

THE PIG ON THE BEACH

♛ Previous César Winner

With rooms in thatched dovecotes, a shepherd's hut and an 'eccentric' Victorian villa, Robin Hutson's 'whimsical' seaside hotel is 'wonderfully located' and 'very welcoming'. The main house, 'a Gothic blend of Hansel and Gretel and Hammer House of Horror', displays the group's trademark artfully mismatched interiors: squashy sofas, stuffed birds, old portraits, red brocade lamps, a large coat of arms – a movie prop from Pirates of the Caribbean. The 'comfy' bedrooms range from 'quite snug but beautifully designed', to generous, with a super-king-size bed and freestanding in-room bath, via eaves rooms that suit a family. One contains a 17th-century woodcarving from a Portuguese palace. All have a monsoon shower, Roberts radio and 'the best-stocked minibar I've ever encountered'. Staff are 'attentive and charming'. In the relaxed conservatory restaurant, the locally sourced and home-grown 25-mile menu includes the likes of Fowey River mussels, Purbeck sirloin steak, pollack with Portland crab sauce. Wood-fired flatbreads are served on the terrace, spa treatments in a garden hut, sea views to Old Harry Rocks from the 'lovely grounds'. 'We will go back.' (J and GM, IB, and others)

Manor House
Manor Road
Studland BH19 3AU

T: 01929 450288
E: info@thepigonthebeach.com
W: thepighotel.com

BEDROOMS: 23. Some on ground floor, 2 Dovecot hideaways, Harry's Hut and Pig Hut in grounds, 1 suitable for disabled.
OPEN: all year.
FACILITIES: bar, lounge, snug, restaurant, private dining room, free Wi-Fi, in-room TV (Freeview), civil wedding licence, 2 treatment cabins, garden, ground-floor public rooms and part of gardens wheelchair accessible.
BACKGROUND MUSIC: all day in public areas.
LOCATION: above Studland beach.
CHILDREN: all ages welcomed.
DOGS: not allowed.
CREDIT CARDS: Amex, MC, Visa.
PRICES: room only £160–£360. Breakfast £12–£16, à la carte £35. 1-night bookings refused weekends, Christmas, New Year.

STURMINSTER NEWTON Dorset

MAP 2:E1

PLUMBER MANOR

'There is a timeless feel and magic about the setting' of this Jacobean manor house. It stands in 'immaculate gardens', in Thomas Hardy's 'vale of little dairies'. It has been in the same family since it was built, and is run by Richard Prideaux-Brune, with his wife, Alison, front-of-house, while his brother Brian cooks with head chef Louis Haskell. It is, then, a real family affair, dog-friendly, child-friendly, hung with portraits of near ancestors. The ambience is informal, log fires blaze in bar and restaurants, guests feel 'cosseted and cared for' by the 'lovely staff'. Main house bedrooms have been newly refurbished but have largely resisted the boutique treatment in favour of a penchant for stripes, spots, sprigs. Two large rooms have a big Victorian bath, a walk-in shower. However, a 2019 guest staying in a courtyard room was unhappy with its 'grimy curtains and ancient carpet'. Raconteur Richard mixes cocktails and chats before a dinner of such 'good, honest fare' as roasted loin of pork with celeriac and pea mash; vegetable Wellington with Madeira sauce; a fish of the day. On summer days you can play croquet, tennis, or just relax in a deckchair.

25% DISCOUNT VOUCHERS

Sturminster Newton DT10 2AF

T: 01258 472507
E: book@plumbermanor.com
W: plumbermanor.co.uk

BEDROOMS: 16. 10 on ground floor in courtyard, 2 suitable for disabled.
OPEN: all year except Feb.
FACILITIES: snug, bar, dining room, gallery, free Wi-Fi, in-room TV (Freeview), 1-acre grounds (garden, tennis, croquet, stream), restaurant, lounge and toilet wheelchair accessible.
BACKGROUND MUSIC: none.
LOCATION: 2½ miles SW of Sturminster Newton.
CHILDREN: all ages welcomed.
DOGS: allowed in 4 courtyard bedrooms, not in public rooms.
CREDIT CARDS: Amex, MC, Visa.
PRICES: per room B&B single £120–£150, double £160–£240. Set dinner £33–£40.

SWAFFHAM Norfolk

MAP 2:B5

STRATTONS

A tiny lane just off the High Street in a bustling market town leads to a striking Palladian villa set by a circular courtyard of hornbeam trees. Les and Vanessa Scott have created a 'playful, welcoming' retreat that's eco-aware to boot. Hannah and Dominic Hughes, the owners' daughter and husband, manage day to day. Filled with eclectic pieces, the villa blends 'imaginative' decor with practical amenities. The 'comfortable' bedrooms, in the main building and converted outbuildings, may have a deep antique bath before a cinema screen; a mural of angels and nymphs flitting above your baroque bedhead; a bed with a gilt mirror at one end, a copper stand-alone tub at the other, a red velvet chesterfield sofa. Opium, which perhaps inspired the design, has an elaborately carved oriental bedhead. The Scotts' eco credentials are particularly evident in the award-winning restaurant with rustic white stone walls and gold-hued furniture, where Dan Freear's modern British locally sourced dishes include produce from the hosts' kitchen garden. Breakfast is served in the popular CoCoes deli, before its acclaimed fishcakes ('crisp outside, light inside') appear at lunch.

4 Ash Close
Swaffham PE37 7NH

T: 01760 723845
E: enquiries@strattonshotel.com
W: strattonshotel.com

BEDROOMS: 14. 6 in annexes, 1 on ground floor.
OPEN: all year except 1 week at Christmas.
FACILITIES: drawing room, reading room, restaurant, free Wi-Fi, in-room TV (Freeview), terrace, café/deli, 1-acre garden, café wheelchair accessible.
BACKGROUND MUSIC: all day in public areas.
LOCATION: central, parking.
CHILDREN: all ages welcomed.
DOGS: allowed in some bedrooms (£10 per day), lounges, not in restaurant.
CREDIT CARDS: Amex, MC, Visa.
PRICES: per room B&B single £96–£234, double £100–£256. À la carte £30. 1-night bookings refused weekends, 3-night min. bank holidays.

SWALLOWCLIFFE Wiltshire

THE ROYAL OAK

Previous César Winner

The whitewashed, thatched exterior of this former tannery-turned-ale house does little to betray its 'stunning, modern' interiors, nor the 'warmth and charm' that welcome visitors and locals. The once derelict early 18th-century building was saved by a group of villagers determined to recreate it as the hub of local life. The result: 'The most elegant, comfortable pub we have ever visited.' The airy bar and dining areas brim with squashy sofas, modern art and wooden furniture handmade by a local artisan. 'Everything has been chosen with flair and perfect taste.' Chef Jonny Sutcliffe serves seasonal fare in the oak-beamed conservatory ('the jewel in the crown'); perhaps stalkers' pie, seasonal vegetables; ricotta dumplings, rocket pesto, plus a glass from the 'well-judged' wine list. Away from the bustle, 'wonderfully restful' bedrooms are 'faultlessly appointed'. In each, proper coffee, fluffy towels and 'excellent lighting' are de rigueur. Win Green, framed by dual-aspect windows and a beamed ceiling, can be twinned with Wardour to create a generous family suite. Comfortable Cranborne is dog-friendly. Breakfast includes home-made granola, a home-baked bacon bap, a full English.

Swallowcliffe SP3 5PA

T: 01747 870211
E: hello@royaloakswallowcliffe.com
W: royaloakswallowcliffe.com

BEDROOMS: 6. 1 suitable for disabled.
OPEN: all year, but no accommodation 25 Dec evening.
FACILITIES: lift, bar, dining room, Oak Room, free Wi-Fi, in-room TV (Freeview), garden with outdoor seating, public rooms wheelchair accessible.
BACKGROUND MUSIC: none.
LOCATION: 2 miles SE of Tisbury.
CHILDREN: all ages welcomed.
DOGS: 'friendly, well-behaved' dogs allowed in 1 bedroom, public rooms except Oak Room (treats, towels provided).
CREDIT CARDS: Amex, MC, Visa.
PRICES: per room B&B £100–£150. À la carte £33.

TALLAND-BY-LOOE Cornwall   MAP 1:D3

TALLAND BAY HOTEL

'One of our favourite hotels,' enthuses a reader about Teresa and Kevin O'Sullivan's quirky and luxurious cliff-top hideaway in this south Cornish seaside hamlet. The O'Sullivans took over in 2015, preserving the previous owner's playful decor – 'entertainment in its own right' – and adding to it with a table cut into the wall here or a lion coffee table there. But there's nothing whimsical about the service or the staff, who are welcoming and 'very kind', particularly if you're accompanied by a four-legged friend in this 'most dog-friendly hotel'. Each bedroom is unique, some have views of sea, some of garden with private patio. Beds, of various styles and sizes, are 'very comfortable'. Chef Nick Hawke's 'wonderful' dishes make the most of fresh Cornish produce. Looe Bay John Dory or roasted Cornish scallops, say, followed by West Country spring lamb or matured Moorland Cross beef. Eat on the terrace in warm weather, or gaze at the sea from a reclining chair in the sub-tropical gardens. Breakfast is a feast with 'everything' from cereal and stewed fruit to smashed avocado and eggs Royale. 'We left with the overarching feeling that nothing is too much trouble.' (JM, and others)

Porthallow
Talland-by-Looe PL13 2JB

T: 01503 272667
E: info@tallandbayhotel.com
W: tallandbayhotel.co.uk

BEDROOMS: 23. 4 in cottages, 6 on ground floor.
OPEN: all year.
FACILITIES: lounge, bar, restaurant, brasserie/conservatory, free Wi-Fi, in-room TV (Freeview), civil wedding licence, terrace, outside seating, 2-acre garden, public rooms wheelchair accessible.
BACKGROUND MUSIC: in bar and restaurant.
LOCATION: 2½ miles SW of Looe.
CHILDREN: all ages welcomed.
DOGS: in bedrooms and brasserie, not in restaurant (£12.50 per dog per night includes sausage breakfast, chicken dinner).
CREDIT CARDS: Amex, MC, Visa.
PRICES: per room B&B £160–£350, D,B&B £240–£430. À la carte £45–£55. 1-night bookings refused weekends in peak season.

TAPLOW Berkshire

CLIVEDEN HOUSE

Meghan Markle spent the night before her wedding at this 'magnificent' Italianate mansion in 'glorious' National Trust grounds on a bluff above the Thames. Built by Sir Charles (Palace of Westminster) Barry, its rollcall of past guests includes Queen Victoria, Kipling, Nancy Astor, the Beatles… A luxury hotel since 1985, now on top form, 'sublime', 'a very special place', 'eccentric but fabulous', 'the definitive country house'. Even the cheapest club rooms, in the garden wing, with views over the acclaimed spa's garden, have antique furniture, a private terrace with hot tub. Junior suites are replete with original features, paintings, fine furniture, perhaps a rococo fireplace. In a 'flawless' dining room dripping with chandeliers, Paul O'Neill's 'exquisite' cooking includes such dishes as wild halibut, cèpe, artichoke, chestnut; loin of roe deer Wellington. There are separate menus for vegans and vegetarians; also for children, who are welcomed if not so actively catered to as at sister hotel Chewton Glen, New Milton (see entry). In the Astor Grill in the old stables, an all-day menu offers steaks, burgers, beer-battered fish of the day. Overall, 'expensive but worth every penny'. (MC)

Cliveden Road
Taplow SL6 0JF

T: 01628 668561
E: reservations@clivedenhouse.co.uk
W: clivedenhouse.co.uk

BEDROOMS: 47. Some on ground floor, 1 suitable for disabled.
OPEN: all year.
FACILITIES: Great Hall, bar/lounge, library, 2 restaurants, private dining rooms, free Wi-Fi, in-room TV (Freeview), civil wedding licence, spa, swimming pools, 376-acre National Trust estate, public areas wheelchair accessible.
BACKGROUND MUSIC: all day in public areas.
LOCATION: 20 mins from Heathrow, 40 mins Central London.
CHILDREN: all ages welcomed.
DOGS: allowed in bedrooms, public areas (excl. 1 restaurant, spa, parts of garden).
CREDIT CARDS: Amex, MC, Visa.
PRICES: per room B&B £445–£1,535. Tasting menu £98, à la carte £73. 1-night bookings sometimes refused.

TAVISTOCK Devon

MAP 1:D4

THE HORN OF PLENTY

What do Jennifer Saunders and David Bowie have in common? Both have stayed at this 'superbly relaxing', dog-friendly spot overlooking the Tamar valley. The well-tended grounds and sweeping lawns must have been an attraction – the late singer was a keen gardener. As must the 'fabulous location'. The former Victorian mine captain's house sits on a sheltered hillside on the Devon/Cornwall border. This year is the tenth anniversary of Julie Leivers and Damien Pease taking the helm. An air of calm continuity fills the attractive lounge which has a log fire, shelves of books and board games. 'Very comfy' bedrooms are spread across the main house, the original coach house and a cosy annexe. Zesty splashes of colour (and the occasional original feature in the main house) brighten the rooms; each has a minibar and fresh milk; most enjoy lovely views from a balcony, terrace or full-height window. In the dining room Ashley Wright's locally sourced seasonal fare includes the likes of Brixham gurnard, lobster ravioli, heritage carrots, sea herbs. 'A bit "nouvelle" for my taste, but beautifully prepared and presented.' 'Breakfasts were great.' This 'wonderful place is in my top five hotels'. (PA, and others)

Gulworthy
Tavistock PL19 8JD

T: 01822 832528
E: enquiries@thehornofplenty.co.uk
W: thehornofplenty.co.uk

BEDROOMS: 16. 12 in old and new coach houses (1–2 mins' walk), 7 on ground floor, 1 suitable for disabled.
OPEN: all year.
FACILITIES: lounge/bar, library, drawing room, restaurant, free Wi-Fi, in-room TV (Freeview), civil wedding licence, 5-acre grounds, ground-floor public areas wheelchair accessible.
BACKGROUND MUSIC: occasional background music in restaurant only, 'when it's quiet'.
LOCATION: 3 miles SW of Tavistock.
CHILDREN: all ages welcomed.
DOGS: allowed in most bedrooms and library, not in restaurant or drawing room (£10 per dog per night).
CREDIT CARDS: MC, Visa.
PRICES: per room B&B single £120–£265, double £130–£275, D,B&B £210–£355. Dinner £53, tasting menu £70.

SEE ALSO SHORTLIST

TEFFONT EVIAS Wiltshire

HOWARD'S HOUSE

'Such a romantic spot.' Deep in the Nadder valley, amid narrow country lanes that are 'a pleasure to get lost in', this 17th-century house is owned by Grahame and Prue Senior and Simon and Charlotte Greenwood. Stealing the spotlight: chef Andy Britton's 'tremendous' daily-changing menu turns locally sourced produce (much of it from the kitchen garden) into 'innovative, delicious haute cuisine'. 'Our perfect feast had many unexpected details: chocolate sauce with lamb, a hay-and-oat topping.' The 'artistically presented' meal was served in the dining room, where ivy-fringed windows overlook 'a beautiful garden' whose blooms perfume the 'light-filled' sitting room. Well-designed bedrooms, upstairs, might have a four-poster, or comfy seating area; in each, crisp linens, a capsule machine, 'lovely' REN toiletries in the bathroom. 'Our capacious room, with more than enough space for us and our toddlers, overlooked the road, but all was silent. We slept like tops.' Some communication issues this year over a broken boiler on a cold day left one reader dissatisfied. A 'superb' breakfast of 'succulent mushrooms, super sausages and excellent coffee' was a 'great' start to the morning.

25% DISCOUNT VOUCHERS

Teffont Evias
Salisbury SP3 5RJ

T: 01722 716392
E: enq@howardshousehotel.co.uk
W: howardshousehotel.co.uk

BEDROOMS: 9.
OPEN: all year except 23–27 Dec.
FACILITIES: lounge, snug, restaurant, function facilities in coach house, free Wi-Fi, in-room TV (Freeview), 2-acre grounds, restaurant wheelchair accessible.
BACKGROUND MUSIC: in dining room.
LOCATION: 10 miles W of Salisbury.
CHILDREN: all ages welcomed (cot, high chair).
DOGS: allowed (£15 charge) in bedrooms, in public rooms except restaurant.
CREDIT CARDS: Amex, MC, Visa.
PRICES: per room B&B single £85–£120, double £150–£225. Tasting menu £80, à la carte £45.

TETBURY Gloucestershire

MAP 3:E5

CALCOT

Families have 'a grand time' at this 16th-century manor house with spa, in 'lovely manicured grounds'. Part of the Calcot Collection (see Barnsley House, Barnsley; The Lord Crewe Arms, Blanchland; The Painswick, Painswick), it is 'top of the tree', a little birdie tells us this year. The style is 'light, bright, informal, clean, modern, not posh'. Bedrooms have an espresso machine, mini-fridge, fresh fruit, home-made shortbread, Aromatherapy Associates toiletries. There are duplex family suites, some with private garden. Other rooms accommodate an extra bed or cot. 'Children were happy in the Playzone (for under-eights) and the Mez (over-eights), staffed by responsible nursery nurses – and in the playground. Meanwhile adults could unwind in the excellent spa.' The Conservatory restaurant serves such dishes as line-caught cod, sweetcorn and clam chowder, lemon-scented mash; also good veggie options. Gastropub fare is served in the Gumstool Inn – fishcakes, burger, steaks, fish with chips cooked in goose fat, 'the best I've ever had! I would return for those alone!' After a 'very good breakfast', you can play tennis, or borrow bikes to cycle a 'trim trail' in the grounds. (Jane and Martin Bailey, RF)

Tetbury GL8 8YJ

T: 01666 890391
E: reservations@calcot.co
W: calcot.co

BEDROOMS: 35. 10 (for families) in cottage, 13 around courtyard, on ground floor, some suitable for disabled.
OPEN: all year.
FACILITIES: lounge, 2 bars, 2 restaurants, crèche, free Wi-Fi, in-room TV (Sky, Freeview), civil wedding licence, 220-acre grounds (tennis, heated swimming pool), spa (with pool), public areas wheelchair accessible, adapted toilet.
BACKGROUND MUSIC: in restaurants.
LOCATION: 3 miles W of Tetbury.
CHILDREN: all ages welcomed.
DOGS: allowed in courtyard bedrooms, not in public rooms.
CREDIT CARDS: Amex, MC, Visa.
PRICES: per room B&B double £219–£459. À la carte (Conservatory) £50, (Gumstool Inn) £35.

TETBURY Gloucestershire   MAP 3:E5

THE HARE AND HOUNDS

'It is impossible to criticise this hotel,' wrote a
reader, praising everything from the service to the
'delicious food' at this mellow stone hotel. Owned
by the Cotswold Inns and Hotels group (see also
The Lamb Inn, Burford), it stands in woodland
and gardens, close to the National Arboretum.
'They frequently upgrade us,' another Guide (and
hotel) regular reports – as they do the rooms, most
recently the large modern bedrooms in Silkwood
Court. Main house and coach house rooms
blend country house and contemporary style; the
Magnolia suite has a private garden terrace and
hot tub. All rooms have 'every facility', along
with robes, Molton Brown toiletries. The hare
motif crops up everywhere, in fabrics, pictures,
ornaments, even in Jack Hare's bar, where you
can eat simply by the open fire. In the Beaufort
restaurant, Pete Lias's 'very good', imaginative
locally sourced dishes include braised venison
and root vegetable casserole, grain mustard
dumplings. A minor grumble from a reader,
who 'did not like' the buffet-style breakfast, but,
happily, silver service has been restored for the
likes of oak-smoked salmon, scrambled eggs;
a kipper or full English. (MC)

Bath Road
Westonbirt
Tetbury GL8 8QL

T: 01666 881000
E: reception@hareandhoundshotel.
com
W: cotswold-inns-hotels.co.uk

BEDROOMS: 42. 2 suitable for disabled,
3 in coach house, 5 in garden
cottage, 12 in Silkwood Court, 1 in
gamekeeper's cottage.
OPEN: all year.
FACILITIES: drawing room, lounges,
library, bar, restaurant, private dining
room, free Wi-Fi, in-room TV
(Freeview), civil wedding licence,
gardens, woodland.
BACKGROUND MUSIC: in lounge and bar.
LOCATION: 3 miles SW of Tetbury.
CHILDREN: all ages welcomed.
DOGS: allowed in some bedrooms, bar,
garden, not in restaurant.
CREDIT CARDS: Amex, MC, Visa.
PRICES: per room B&B £120–£230,
D,B&B £180–£290. À la carte £36.

TETBURY Gloucestershire

MAP 3:E5

THE ROYAL OAK   NEW

'This is indeed a lively community pub,' write
trusted readers, urging a promotion from the
Shortlist for Kate Lewis and Chris York's popular
pub-with-rooms. An inn since 1781, it 'has been
recently refurbished out of Farrow and Ball's
catalogue'. At ground level, 'lovely window
boxes brim with flowers'. Bedrooms in soothing
browns, creams and greens occupy 'an oldish
but beautifully refurbished building just across a
path leading to the garden'. A spectacular luxury
suite has a super-king-size bed, a living room
and mezzanine twin beds, an in-room roll-top
bath, an en suite walk-in shower. The smallest
room was, yes, small, 'but had a very cute en suite
shower room', Bramley toiletries, 'everything
needed for a two-night stay'. Food is served in the
beamed, wood-floored restaurant and the bar with
upcycled furniture, a piano and vintage jukebox.
A 'tsunami' of locals overwhelmed the service on
one night, but 'the very good staff kept smiling
and chatting through the turmoil'. A 'well-cooked
burger' and a 'simply lovely rump steak' were
better liked than pan-fried hake with wild garlic
pesto. At breakfast there was 'wonderful eggs
Benedict', 'proper' local ham. (David Birnie)

25% DISCOUNT VOUCHERS

1 Cirencester Road
Tetbury GL8 8EY

T: 01666 500021
E: stay@theroyaloaktetbury.co.uk
W: theroyaloaktetbury.co.uk

BEDROOMS: 6, 1 suitable for disabled.
OPEN: all year except 1 week Jan.
FACILITIES: bar, restaurant, private
dining/meeting room, free Wi-Fi,
in-room TV (Freeview), large garden,
boules, bicycle storage, bar and garden
wheelchair accessible, adapted toilet.
BACKGROUND MUSIC: in bar and
restaurant, monthly live music
sessions.
LOCATION: a few mins' walk up the
hill from the town centre.
CHILDREN: all ages welcomed.
DOGS: allowed (no charge).
CREDIT CARDS: Amex, MC, Visa.
PRICES: per room B&B £90–£190.
À la carte £30. 1-night bookings
usually refused Fri and Sat.

THORPE MARKET Norfolk

MAP 2:A5

THE GUNTON ARMS

'One of the most unusual hotels we've ever visited.' Guide inspectors were left reeling by art dealer Ivor Braka's pub-with-rooms in the deer park of Gunton Hall. It is filled with 'fascinating furniture, vintage artefacts, and antiques'. The cosy lounges have roaring fires, prints, photographs, gilt-framed paintings; here Julian Opie, there Gilbert and George, 'in the ladies' loo a Damien Hirst'. Bedrooms are designer rustic, with exposed beams. One recalls Lillie Langtry, who stayed when the Prince of Wales visited the Hall. Its marble bathroom was salvaged from a derelict mansion in Alexandria; no TV, but a Roberts radio. Simone Tattershall is front-of-house, while her husband, Stuart, is the (Mark Hix-trained) chef. In the Elk Room, crowned like a cuckold with giant elk antlers, Blythburgh pork chops, steaks and other manly, meaty things are flamed on the fire. The eclectic menu runs from fish fingers and chips to Gunton venison stew with herb-baked dumplings. Service was 'impeccable, jolly, helpful'. Eat in any of three dining rooms. You won't be hungry or bored. 'Trust me' reads a neon sign by Tracey Emin. Trust us: this place is 'a delight'.

Cromer Road
Thorpe Market NR11 8TZ

T: 01263 832010
E: office@theguntonarms.co.uk
W: theguntonarms.co.uk

BEDROOMS: 16. 4 in coach house on ground floor, 4 suites in converted barn house, 1 suitable for disabled.
OPEN: all year except 25 Dec, half day 31 Dec.
FACILITIES: 3 restaurants, 3 lounges, bar, free Wi-Fi, TVs in bar and lounges, set in privately owned 1,000-acre game estate, public rooms wheelchair accessible, adapted toilet.
BACKGROUND MUSIC: in bar area.
LOCATION: 5 miles from Cromer, 4 miles from North Walsham.
CHILDREN: all ages welcomed.
DOGS: allowed in 5 bedrooms, public rooms, not in Elk Room.
CREDIT CARDS: Amex, MC, Visa.
PRICES: per room B&B single £85–£310, double £95–£320. À la carte from £35. Min. 2-night stays on Sat.

TIMBLE Yorkshire

MAP 4:D3

THE TIMBLE INN

A 'friendly and cosseting atmosphere' awaits at this smartly turned-out gastropub, in the beautiful Washburn valley. Run by the Stainsby family, the former 18th-century coaching inn mixes period character – flagstone floors, exposed beams, open fires – with more contemporary country style. Our 'superior room lived up to its name', reports a regular reader, 'large, with places to sit and write' and a 'really comfortable' bed. Rooms at the front have views of the surrounding countryside; those at the back overlook the garden. Downstairs, the bar is 'bright and cheery' while the restaurant is 'smartly laid out', with well-spaced tables. Musak was promptly turned down on request. The 'excellent' food is Modern British with a Yorkshire twist: maybe confit duck terrine, pear purée and pickles followed by roast cod loin, creamed savoy cabbage, baby leeks, mussel and parsley butter – all was 'attractively presented and delicious'. Service is 'crisp, cheerful and efficient'. Not so the patchy Wi-Fi signal but, say readers, it's a small price to pay for the superb location and the warm atmosphere. 'An ideal sanctuary from which to explore the Yorkshire Dales.' (Simon and Mithra Tonking)

Timble
Harrogate LS21 2NN

T: 01943 880530
E: info@thetimbleinn.co.uk
W: thetimbleinn.co.uk

BEDROOMS: 9. 2 in cottages, 4 with own private entrance, 2 on ground floor.
OPEN: all year, restaurant closed Mon (lunch and dinner) and Tues (dinner), except by prior arrangement.
FACILITIES: bar, restaurant, residents' lounge, free Wi-Fi, in-room TV (Freeview), garden, public rooms wheelchair accessible.
BACKGROUND MUSIC: at meal times in public areas.
LOCATION: centre of village, 10 miles west of Harrogate.
CHILDREN: all ages welcomed.
DOGS: allowed in public rooms (from midday to 4 pm only), 2 bedrooms (£20 per dog per night).
CREDIT CARDS: MC, Visa.
PRICES: per room B&B £150–£240. À la carte £45.

TISBURY Wiltshire   MAP 2:D1

THE BECKFORD ARMS

Deep in rural Wiltshire, on the edge of the
Fonthill Estate and Cranborne Chase, this 'lovely
old Georgian inn' is Dan Brod and Charlie
Luxton's sophisticated take on a country pub.
'Bright, light' country-chic bedrooms vary in
size; as do the en suite bathrooms, with Bramley
toiletries made by Charlie's wife, Chloë. Two are
a 15-minute walk across the estate. Inspectors in
2019 found on their 'Welcome Tray' 'a small bag
with "Treat" written on it and, inside, a lovely
piece of chocolate cake'. After an aperitif in the
'bustling bar' came dinner in the restaurant
where 'well-spaced' tables have 'views of terraced
gardens'. Food, using 'local ingredients and
suppliers', is 'top quality', says another recent
visitor, who had 'charred mackerel, smoked
beetroot purée, baby fennel' followed by 'sea
bream with New Forest asparagus, Jersey Royal
and Keta caviar'. The wine list, drawn from the
pub's extensive cellars, is 'a delight'. Breakfast is
'good' though one visitor's scrambled eggs, served
by an 'uninterested' waitress, were 'tepid'. But
this was the only flaw in otherwise 'excellent'
service from 'an enthusiastic team'. 'We loved the
artwork, the atmosphere, the surroundings.'

Fonthill Gifford
Tisbury SP3 6PX

T: 01747 870385
E: info@beckfordarms.com
W: beckfordarms.com

BEDROOMS: 10. 2 in lodges on the
Fonthill Estate.
OPEN: all year except 25 Dec.
FACILITIES: sitting room (sometimes
Sunday classic-movie nights), bar,
restaurant, private dining room,
free Wi-Fi, in-room TV (Freeview),
function facilities, 1-acre garden.
BACKGROUND MUSIC: in public areas
all day.
LOCATION: in village, 1 mile N of
Tisbury.
CHILDREN: all ages welcomed, no
children in lodges.
DOGS: allowed in 1 bedroom and
public areas.
CREDIT CARDS: MC, Visa.
PRICES: per room B&B £95–£195,
D,B&B £155–£255. À la carte £40.
1-night bookings usually refused
weekends.

SEE ALSO SHORTLIST

TITCHWELL Norfolk

MAP 2:A5

TITCHWELL MANOR

'A log fire was burning in a small sitting room' when our inspectors arrived on a rainy night, at Eric Snaith's Victorian farmhouse hotel overlooking field and marsh to the sea. After a swift check-in, in a 'cheery foyer with alluring mermaid-print wallpaper', they were shown to one of the 'utterly quiet' annexe bedrooms surrounding the herb garden. It had stone floor tiles, white walls, a comfortable bed, 'spacious, warm' bathroom. 'I was surprised how plain it was.' Main house rooms are jazzier, with bold colours, patterned wallpaper, vintage furniture. The Potting Shed has a log-burner, fridge, coffee machine, roll-top bath and double shower. You can dine in the Eating Rooms with floor-to-ceiling windows, or the more formal Conservatory overlooking the walled garden. Mr Snaith and head chef Chris Mann's menus range from modern tapas and classics (fish and chips cooked in dripping) to such dishes as salt-aged goose roasted on the crown, confit leg, orange sauce, golden beetroot, thyme. The staff are 'young and affable'. Breakfast brings 'moreish granolas, thick yogurt with tangy berry compote'; 'dark yellow scrambled egg' and smoked salmon. Birdwatchers are in their element.

25% DISCOUNT VOUCHERS

Titchwell
Brancaster PE31 8BB

T: 01485 210221
E: info@titchwellmanor.com
W: titchwellmanor.com

BEDROOMS: 26. 12 in herb garden, 3 in stables, 1 in Potting Shed, 18 on ground floor, 2 suitable for disabled.
OPEN: all year.
FACILITIES: lounge, bar, conservatory, restaurant, free Wi-Fi, in-room TV (Freeview), civil wedding licence, in-room treatments, ¼-acre walled garden, public rooms wheelchair accessible, adapted toilet.
BACKGROUND MUSIC: in restaurant and bar (at mealtimes).
LOCATION: off A149 between Burnham Market and Hunstanton.
CHILDREN: all ages welcomed.
DOGS: allowed in some rooms, bar, not lounge or restaurant (£15 per dog, per night).
CREDIT CARDS: Amex, MC, Visa.
PRICES: per room B&B £110–£325. À la carte £42. 1-night bookings occasionally refused.

TITLEY Herefordshire   MAP 3:C4

THE STAGG INN

♤ Previous César Winner

After 20 years at the helm, Steve and Nicola
Reynolds continue to offer a heady brew of cosy
pub, 'wonderful' food and 'professional, friendly
service'. Rooms are spread between the inn and
the Grade II listed, 'tastefully decorated' Vicarage,
a few minutes' walk away. Those bringing dogs
should opt for the former, with canine-friendly
bedrooms (one has direct outside access). Those
seeking peace and quiet might prefer the latter,
where the guest sitting room and large garden
give the feel of a family home. All bedrooms
are spacious, with a 'comfortable bed', tea- and
coffee-making facilities, fresh milk and a well-
stocked minibar (pub prices). Dinner is the
main event, cooked by Steve and showcasing
the finest local ingredients: 28-day dry-aged
Herefordshire rump steak with pepper sauce, say,
or rump and slow-cooked shoulder of local lamb
with Jerusalem artichokes, spring cabbage and
potato dauphinoise. Bar snacks are outstanding.
Breakfast, cooked to order, is no less of a feast: full
English, kippers, free-range eggs, freshly baked
bread. 'The best breakfast ever,' declared one
reviewer – with 'friendly service'. (KMcM)

25% DISCOUNT VOUCHERS

Titley
Kington HR5 3RL

T: 01544 230221
E: reservations@thestagg.co.uk
W: thestagg.co.uk

BEDROOMS: 6. 3 at The Vicarage
(300 yds).
OPEN: all year except 24–26 Dec, 1 Jan,
restaurant closed Sun eve, Mon, Tues,
check website for dates of holiday
closures.
FACILITIES: sitting room (Old
Vicarage), bar, dining room, small
outside seating area (pub), free Wi-Fi,
in-room TV (Freeview), 1½-acre
garden (Old Vicarage).
BACKGROUND MUSIC: none.
LOCATION: on B4355 between Kington
and Presteigne.
CHILDREN: all ages welcomed.
DOGS: allowed in pub bedrooms,
public rooms.
CREDIT CARDS: Amex, MC, Visa.
PRICES: per room B&B £100–£140.
À la carte £35. 1-night bookings
occasionally refused bank holiday
weekends.

TUDDENHAM Suffolk

MAP 2:B5

TUDDENHAM MILL

Otters frolic on the banks as guests frolic in an outdoor hot tub at this old mill by a stream. A white-painted clapboard and brick structure, its chimney cutting 'a striking silhouette', it is run as a hotel by chef/patron Lee Bye. There are three bedrooms in the main mill, others in 'good-looking buildings' across the car park or along a path by the stream, as well as loft suites and chalet-style 'meadow nooks'. All are 'impressive', with maybe a double-ended stone bath, a real-flame fire, a terrace. 'Modern and minimalist' bathrooms (some too minimalist for the bashful – ask when booking) have ESPA toiletries but little shelving for soaps or washbag. 'An enormous bed, velvet easy chairs, a mini-fridge with milk and freshly squeezed orange juice' were appreciated. In the bar, 'the waterwheel is a dramatic feature'. In the 'characterful' dining room, 'fetching views over the millstream', and Mr Bye's 'inspired combinations of ingredients'. Perhaps Sika deer 'Argyle', spelt, green sauce, roots, honey porter; for vegans, roasted artichoke, Clem's carrot, wild honey, coastal herbs. Breakfast brings home-made jam, smoothies, Dingley Dell sausages. 'A wholly enjoyable experience.'

25% DISCOUNT VOUCHERS

High Street
Tuddenham
Newmarket IP28 6SQ

T: 01638 713552
E: info@tuddenhammill.co.uk
W: tuddenhammill.co.uk

BEDROOMS: 21. 18 in 2 separate buildings, 12 on ground floor, 6 in 'Meadow Nooks' in meadow, 2 with hot tub, 1 suitable for disabled.
OPEN: all year.
FACILITIES: bar/snug, restaurant, function rooms, free Wi-Fi, in-room TV (Freeview), civil wedding licence, treatment room, 12-acre meadow.
BACKGROUND MUSIC: in bar, reception and restaurant.
LOCATION: in village, 8 miles NE of Newmarket.
CHILDREN: all ages welcomed.
DOGS: allowed in some bedrooms (£15 a night), and in bar.
CREDIT CARDS: MC, Visa.
PRICES: per room B&B £150–£415. À la carte £47, early dining (Sun–Fri 6.30–7.30 pm) £23, tasting menu £70. 2-night min. stay at weekends.

TWO BRIDGES Devon   MAP 1:D4

PRINCE HALL

In 'an amazing situation' amid 'bleak and
beautiful Dartmoor', Chris Daly's 18th-century
manor house-turned-hotel is 'truly special' with
'lovely staff', say Guide readers. Regular returnees
come for the 'friendly and lived-in feel, which is
why we love it'. 'Spacious and warm' bedrooms.
mainly in white or cream, mix period and
contemporary furnishings. Houndtor bedroom
has 'two large bay windows, a gorgeous fireplace'.
Arthur Conan Doyle is thought to have stayed
here and been inspired to pen The Hound of
the Baskervilles. More lovable pooches than that
hellish hound are welcome everywhere but in
the dining room, and may join owners for meals
in the bistro or on the terrace. Chef Luke Daly,
Chris's son, cooks a seasonally changing menu of
such dishes as fishcakes, venison sausages with
horseradish mash, chargrilled rib-eye steak. 'The
menu stayed the same for five nights but Luke did
special evenings for us, one night pizza, the next
the most amazing Chinese dish! The food was
delicious, all locally sourced.' In sum, 'a complete
escape from reality; if you are looking for a top-of-
the-range hotel with a fast internet signal, it is not
for you.' (Sybille Raphael, Ross Westcott)

Two Bridges
Dartmoor PL20 6SA

T: 01822 890403
E: info@princehall.co.uk
W: princehall.co.uk

BEDROOMS: 9.
OPEN: all year.
FACILITIES: lobby, bar, lounge, dining
room, free Wi-Fi in some rooms and
bar/bistro, in-room TV (Freeview),
terrace, 5-acre grounds, public rooms
wheelchair accessible.
BACKGROUND MUSIC: none:
LOCATION: 3 miles E of Princetown.
CHILDREN: all ages welcomed.
DOGS: 'very much' allowed (treats,
facilities for food storage and dog
washing, pet-friendly garden and
grounds), not in restaurant, but same
menu available in bistro for owners
with dogs.
CREDIT CARDS: MC, Visa.
PRICES: per room B&B single £85,
double £176–£220. À la carte £35.

ULLSWATER Cumbria

MAP 4: inset C2

HOWTOWN HOTEL

Bong, bong! It is dinner time at this ancient farmhouse-turned-hotel in grounds bordering Lake Ullswater, where the gong still summons guests to table. 'So retro it's almost trendy', it has been owned by the Baldry family for some 120 years. Log fires crackle in a parlour adorned with horse brasses, Toby jugs, long-case clock and chintz. Bedrooms have an electric blanket, no door key. Switch on the wireless and you half expect it to be tuned to the Light Programme for Mrs Dale's Diary. There is limited Wi-Fi, a TV room with, by now, even, maybe, a colour set. It is old-fashioned, yes, but that does not mean frowsy: 'Everything is done just so.' It's a perfect place for dog-owners, walkers, climbers. Scrub up with the Imperial Leather and head down to the duck-egg-blue dining room, where respected chef Colin Akrigg cooks locally sourced dishes with 'pitch-perfect flavours' – maybe duck pâté, liver and bacon, trifle. Off the hallway, with warming pans and umbrella stand, daylight filters through stained glass into a plush residents' bar. Lunches, scones, cakes and coffees are served in the tea room, ales in the walkers' bar. Your 8 am wake-up call comes with tea and biscuits. (ST)

Ullswater
Penrith CA10 2ND

T: 017684 86514
E: editor@goodhotelguide.com
W: howtown-hotel.co.uk

BEDROOMS: 15. 2 in annexe, plus 4 self-catering cottages.
OPEN: 22 Mar–3 Nov.
FACILITIES: 3 lounges, TV room, 2 bars, dining room, tea room, Wi-Fi in cottages and tea room only, 2-acre grounds, 200 yds from lake (private foreshore, fishing), walking, sailing, climbing, riding, golf nearby, restaurant wheelchair accessible, toilet not adapted.
BACKGROUND MUSIC: none.
LOCATION: 4 miles S of Pooley Bridge, bus from Penrith station 9 miles.
CHILDREN: all ages welcomed.
DOGS: allowed in some bedrooms (£4 per night charge), not in public rooms.
CREDIT CARDS: MC, Visa.
PRICES: per person B&B £67–£75, D,B&B £104–£108, dinner £37.

UPPER SLAUGHTER Gloucestershire

LORDS OF THE MANOR

🏅Previous César Winner

A golden stone Carolean manor-turned-rectory in an 'idyllic setting' is run as a 'welcoming, comfortable and relaxing' hotel, under highly experienced manager Michael Obray. Portraits of past rectors gaze down from walls. You can enjoy 'a refreshing cup of tea by the fire' with former incumbent Francis Edward Witts, or at least with his Diary of a Cotswold Parson (1837–42). Bedrooms in the barn and granary are country style, those in the main house more glamorous, with maybe a colonial four-poster, an in-room bath. First-floor Witts is 'large, with a splendid view' over the gardens. Recent changes include the creation of a walled herb garden, while this year brings more dining options. In the new Atrium, Charles Smith's 'spectacularly lovely' tasting menus continue to showcase Cotswold ingredients, Cornish fish, responsibly reared Lake District meat, seasonal game. For instance: fallow deer, hispi cabbage, young beetroots, violet mustard; olive oil-poached stone bass, heritage carrot, mussel and saffron cream. You can now eat less formally and for less from the restaurant's à la carte menu. 'A most magnificent place,' say readers, who were 'looked after beautifully'. (RM)

Upper Slaughter GL54 2JD

T: 01451 820243
E: reservations@lordsofthemanor.
   com
W: lordsofthemanor.com

BEDROOMS: 26. 16 in granary and stables, 1 on ground floor.
OPEN: all year.
FACILITIES: lounges, bar, 2 restaurants, library, games room, free Wi-Fi, in-room TV (Freeview), civil wedding licence, terrace, 8-acre grounds, some public rooms wheelchair accessible, no adapted toilet.
BACKGROUND MUSIC: in lounge bar and restaurant.
LOCATION: in village, 2 miles N of Bourton-on-the-Water.
CHILDREN: all ages welcomed.
DOGS: allowed in some bedrooms, public rooms, not restaurant (£30 a night).
CREDIT CARDS: Amex, MC, Visa.
PRICES: per room B&B £155–£510, D,B&B £280–£640. À la carte £45, tasting menu £95. 1-night bookings refused mid-summer Sat.

UPPINGHAM Rutland

MAP 2:B3

LAKE ISLE

'The real break we had hoped for.' 'We haven't had a bad meal here in over 30 years.' High praise from readers in 2019, suggesting this small restaurant-with-rooms was right to name itself after Yeats's ode to tranquillity and relaxation. Owned by Richard and Janine Burton, the 17th-century property sits in the oldest part of a 'charming' Rutland market town. Its rooms, some cosy, occupy the main house and two cottages. Some have a whirlpool bath, all mix a dash of contemporary style, be it earth tones or bright wallpapers, with a 'really comfy' bed. 'Our cottage bedroom was smallish but it didn't matter as there was a sitting room, and large bathroom.' But, as other readers stress: 'You come for the food. It's brilliant.' The man to thank is Stuart Mead, whose locally sourced seasonal dishes include pan-roasted venison, braised red cabbage, celeriac dauphinoise. Breakfast doesn't drop the bar, with freshly squeezed juices; a full Rutland; home-baked croissant, scrambled egg and smoked salmon. 'We really enjoyed being waited on. Each delicious, beautifully presented course was brought to our table. We very much look forward to returning.' (Catherine Held, CH)

16 High Street East
Uppingham LE15 9PZ

T: 01572 822951
E: info@lakeisle.co.uk
W: lakeisle.co.uk

BEDROOMS: 12. 2 in cottages.
OPEN: all year, restaurant closed Sun night, Mon lunch, bank holidays.
FACILITIES: bar, restaurant, free Wi-Fi, in-room TV (Freeview), small car park, unsuitable for disabled.
BACKGROUND MUSIC: in restaurant.
LOCATION: town centre.
CHILDREN: all ages welcomed.
DOGS: allowed in courtyard bedrooms, not in public areas.
CREDIT CARDS: MC, Visa.
PRICES: per room B&B single £75–£85, double £90–£120, D,B&B single £114–£124, double £167–£197. À la carte £38.

VENTNOR Isle of Wight

HILLSIDE

'As we pulled up at Hillside, Gert shot out to meet us, greeted us warmly, gathered up our baggage and took us to our room.' Guide insiders had a great stay at Gert Bach's late Georgian thatched villa on wooded, south-facing slopes above town. Invited to come down for tea (rooms have no hospitality tray), they found themselves instead sipping champagne. Other trusted readers were 'greeted like long-lost cousins' whenever they returned from a sortie. Interiors are Scandinavian style, stripped down, pale, with bare floors or woollen carpets, 'spotless white rugs'; 'colour comes from the abstract artwork'. A 'very simple' bedroom had a 'fabulous view over town to the sea'. Drinks, including the house ale, are served in the conservatory or on the terrace. From 3 to 8 pm the brasserie has unambitious fare (perhaps 'a tasty chicken pie with salad, a rich chocolate brownie with cream'), all ingredients locally sourced, or from the garden and greenhouse. Gert happily recommends local eateries for a 'proper' dinner. 'The breakfast buffet offers an excellent spread of fresher-than-fresh options made on the premises', honey from the hives, free-range eggs from the hens. (D and JB, F and IW)

151 Mitchell Avenue
Ventnor PO38 1DR

T: 01983 852271
E: mail@hillsideventnor.co.uk
W: hillsideventnor.co.uk

BEDROOMS: 12. Plus self-catering apartment.
OPEN: all year.
FACILITIES: restaurant, 2 lounges, conservatory, free Wi-Fi, in-room TV, terrace, 5-acre garden (vegetable garden, sheep, beehives), close to tennis club, golf, unsuitable for disabled.
BACKGROUND MUSIC: in restaurant in evening.
LOCATION: above village centre.
CHILDREN: not under 12.
DOGS: not allowed.
CREDIT CARDS: MC, Visa.
PRICES: per room B&B single £78–£143, double £108–£236. Brasserie, 2 courses £15. Min. 2-night bookings preferred.

VENTNOR Isle of Wight

THE ROYAL HOTEL

You can take afternoon tea, as Queen Victoria did, at this 'VERY good hotel', perhaps on the Geranium Terrace, 'the whole length adorned with superb pink geraniums'. Sub-tropical gardens roll out before you, with views past the pool to the bay. Established in 1832, the former Fisher Hotel, now owned by William Bailey, attracted the Mayfair set, keen to swap London smog for sea-bathing and clean air. A reader this year praises the 'high-quality accommodation', the 'personal, friendly service', the advice given when choosing a room. These range from small to family, some in contemporary style, some with a country house feel. Another reader found Room 20 'spacious, well equipped, very comfortable, with two large windows facing the gardens and sea'. Lunch can be taken in the brasserie, bar, conservatory – or, in summer, from a hamper on the Riviera Terrace. Dinner is served under chandeliers in an opulent dining room. Chef Jon-Paul Charlo 'aims high and delivers', with such dishes as south coast crab with hand-rolled linguine, chilli, lime, coriander; lamb sausages, creamed potatoes, local greens, crispy onion, lamb sauce. Cooked breakfasts are 'excellent', too. (Graham Angel, MW)

Belgrave Road
Ventnor PO38 1JJ

T: 01983 852186
E: enquiries@royalhoteliow.co.uk
W: royalhoteliow.co.uk

BEDROOMS: 51. 1 suitable for disabled.
OPEN: all year.
FACILITIES: lift, lounge, bar, 2 restaurants, conservatory, function rooms, free Wi-Fi, in-room TV, civil wedding licence, spa treatment rooms, terrace, 2-acre grounds, outdoor heated pool, public areas/toilet wheelchair accessible.
BACKGROUND MUSIC: in public areas, pianist on peak-season weekends.
LOCATION: short walk from centre.
CHILDREN: all ages welcomed.
DOGS: allowed in some bedrooms, not in restaurants.
CREDIT CARDS: Amex, MC, Visa.
PRICES: per room B&B single £100–£115, double £195–£305, D,B&B add £35 per person. Dinner £40, tasting menu £50. 2-night min. on peak weekends.

VERYAN-IN-ROSELAND Cornwall   MAP 1:D2

THE NARE

♛Previous César Winner

'The views are glorious,' writes a Guide regular,
after a visit to Toby Ashworth's hotel above Carne
Beach. 'Each night I fell asleep to the sound of
waves.' The widescreen panorama of Gerrans
Bay is fully exploited by 'beautifully maintained'
gardens with 'many spaces to sit and gaze across
to Nare Head, and a deliciously warm outdoor
pool'. It's a vista shared by many of the 'spacious'
rooms with balcony or terrace. All are supplied
with those country house essentials: armchairs,
books, magazines, fresh blooms. Readers also
praise the 'super-soft' towels, 'good linen', fresh
milk at turn-down, overnight shoe cleaning. 'It's
difficult to imagine being as comfortable away
from home.' Service is 'faultless'. In the relaxed
Quarterdeck, and the more formal silver-service
restaurant, Brett Camborne-Paynter's menus,
with much seafood and daily lobsters, offer
'fantastic quality and taste'. One guest enjoyed the
dessert trolley in particular, and having 'venison
or bananas flambéed at your table'. There's a
top-notch afternoon tea, acclaimed artwork,
an elegant motor launch, espionage games for
younger guests, a spa for older ones. 'I wish we
could visit more often.' (TS, and others)

Carne Beach
Veryan-in-Roseland TR2 5PF

T: 01872 501111
E: stay@narehotel.co.uk
W: narehotel.co.uk

BEDROOMS: 37. Some on ground floor,
1 in adjacent cottage, 5 suitable for
disabled.
OPEN: all year.
FACILITIES: lift, lounge, drawing room,
sun lounge, gallery, study, bar, library,
light lunch room, 2 restaurants,
conservatory, free Wi-Fi, in-room
TV (Sky, Freeview), gym, indoor
and outdoor swimming pools, 2-acre
grounds, 2 boats, tennis, public rooms
wheelchair accessible, adapted toilet.
BACKGROUND MUSIC: none.
LOCATION: S of Veryan.
CHILDREN: all ages welcomed.
DOGS: allowed in bedrooms, gardens,
not in public areas (except assistance
dogs).
CREDIT CARDS: Amex, MC, Visa.
PRICES: per room B&B £299–£845,
D,B&B £319–£887. Set dinner £50,
à la carte £50. Min. 2-night bookings
at Christmas, New Year.

WAREHAM Dorset

MAP 2:E1

THE PRIORY

'This hotel is amazingly charming.' A reader was delighted this year by a stay at this 16th-century priory-turned-hotel, 'in a beautiful location' beside the church and the River Frome. The main house's 'steep, narrow' stairs lead to individually styled bedrooms, but there are ground-floor rooms too (and in the Boathouse). A junior suite was 'quite large, well furnished in a rather old-fashioned way', with fresh milk in the minibar, an 'excellent walk-in shower'. The main house's Purbeck Suite has a walk-in shower and a high-sided copper bath judged a triumph of style over substance. Tea is served by 'polite, helpful' staff on the terrace or in a 'large, beamed drawing room with log fire' and comfy seating. In the much-admired 'light, modern' Garden restaurant, 'overlooking the attractive garden and river', Stephan Guinebault's 'truly excellent' set menus include such locally sourced dishes as West Country duck, blackcurrant mustard cream potato, roasted fig, sugar snap peas, red wine jus. 'The Grand Marnier soufflé was so good I had it two days running.' Breakfast brings freshly squeezed juices, kippers, smoked salmon. 'We just have to go back.' (John GP Barnes, Bill Bennett)

25% DISCOUNT VOUCHERS

Church Green
Wareham BH20 4ND

T: 01929 551666
E: admin@theprioryhotel.co.uk
W: theprioryhotel.co.uk

BEDROOMS: 17. Some on ground floor, 4 suites in Boathouse, 1 suitable for disabled.
OPEN: all year.
FACILITIES: sitting room, drawing room, snug bar, 2 dining rooms, free Wi-Fi, in-room TV (Freeview), spa treatments, 4½-acre gardens (croquet, river frontage, moorings, fishing), restaurant wheelchair accessible.
BACKGROUND MUSIC: pianist in drawing room Sat evenings 'and special occasions'.
LOCATION: town centre.
CHILDREN: not under 14.
DOGS: not allowed.
CREDIT CARDS: Amex, MC, Visa.
PRICES: per room B&B single £176–£304, double £220–£380, D,B&B double £295–£455. Set dinner £53. 1-night bookings refused high season, peak weekends.

WELLS Somerset

STOBERRY HOUSE

Previous César Winner

'Fabulous views' over the cathedral and the Vale of Avalon to Glastonbury Tor await at Frances and Tim Meeres Young's 18th-century coach house, run as a 'faultless' B&B. 'The site is beautiful', in gardens and parkland, with wildlife ponds and water features, rose garden, acer glades, a fernery, a potager, 'wonderful, huge trees'. Bedrooms are lavishly furnished, Lady Hamilton has a four-poster and an Italian-tiled bathroom, Black Orchid modern styling, an espresso machine. The Studio, in a gravel courtyard, beside car parking, was 'very nice, with table and chairs on a small patio', a reader reports. Tea and cake are offered on arrival. Toiletries are cruelty free, locally made. Guests have use of a sitting room with a pantry. Give notice to dine in, either a light supper or full silver service. A 'vast and impressive continental breakfast' in the orangery brings freshly baked breads and pastries, home-made jams. Cooked dishes, with an extra charge, must be ordered the night before. 'I don't eat meat but was given a vegetarian Scotch egg and delicious pear and Stilton pâté.' It is a happy ship. 'The staff said how much they loved working there.' (Diana Goodey, Sally Mehalko)

25% DISCOUNT VOUCHERS

Stoberry Park
Wells BA5 3LD

T: 01749 672906
E: stay@stoberry-park.co.uk
W: stoberryhouse.co.uk

BEDROOMS: 7. 1 in studio cottage, 2 in the gatehouse cottage.
OPEN: all year except 2 weeks over Christmas and New Year.
FACILITIES: 3 sitting rooms (1 with pantry), breakfast room/orangery, free Wi-Fi, in-room TV (Freeview), 6½-acre garden in 25 acres of parkland.
BACKGROUND MUSIC: none.
LOCATION: outskirts of Wells.
CHILDREN: allowed for parties that occupy the whole house, if children are old enough to have their own room.
DOGS: not allowed.
CREDIT CARDS: Amex, MC, Visa.
PRICES: per room B&B (continental) single £85, double £95–£157. À la carte £28–£43 (pre-ordered). 1-night bookings sometimes refused weekends during high season.

WEST HOATHLY Sussex

MAP 2:E4

THE CAT INN

♀ Previous César Winner

'From the warm greeting on arrival to the friendly farewell, we had a thoroughly enjoyable stay.' More plaudits in 2019 for Andrew Russell's tile-hung, 16th-century pub-with-rooms in a Wealden village close to Gravetye Manor, East Grinstead (see entry), where he cut his teeth. The popular locals bar has blazing log fires, low beams hung with pewter mugs. Upstairs, 'Room 1 was large and comfortable, with a charming view over the church, underfloor heating in the bathroom.' All have fresh milk, an espresso machine. In bar and restaurant, Alex Jacquemin's cooking is 'varied and delicious', from pub classics (Trenchmore Farm burger, beer-battered fish and chips), to roasted hake fillet, Apache potato, purple sprouting broccoli, caper and seaweed butter; duck breast, parsnip, mushrooms, rainbow chard, red wine sauce. It is served by 'knowledgeable and helpful' staff. Breakfasts are 'stylish – pottery dishes of yogurt, fruits and cereal on each table; home-made bread, and everything, including cooked dishes, as one hopes'. It's quality fuel for a day walking the High Weald or Ashdown Forest. 'A great spot from which to explore.' (Embry Rucker, Joan MacLean, and others)

25% DISCOUNT VOUCHERS

North Lane
West Hoathly RH19 4PP

T: 01342 810369
E: thecatinn@googlemail.com
W: catinn.co.uk

BEDROOMS: 4.
OPEN: all year except Christmas, restaurant open New Year's Day for lunch only.
FACILITIES: bar, 3 dining areas, free Wi-Fi, in-room TV (Freeview), terrace (alfresco meals), restaurant wheelchair accessible.
BACKGROUND MUSIC: none.
LOCATION: in village.
CHILDREN: not under 7 (unless 'well-behaved').
DOGS: allowed in bedrooms, bar, specific dining area.
CREDIT CARDS: MC, Visa.
PRICES: per room B&B single £90–£115, double £130–£165. À la carte £28.

WHASHTON Yorkshire

MAP 4:C3

THE HACK & SPADE

There is Yorkshire hospitality with tea and cakes
for arrivals at Jane Ratcliffe's B&B in a hamlet
five miles from Scotch Corner. Originally the
Oddfellows, a small ale house, it was extended to
quench thirsty quarrymen, evolving as a parlour
pub, then restaurant, before taking on its present
form eight years ago. The outward appearance
is of 'a somewhat unprepossessing, stone-faced,
early 19th-century country inn', reported a Guide
insider, unafraid to call a spade a spade. But the
welcome was 'friendly and informal'. The interior
was simple, comfortable, 'tastefully appointed'.
The bedrooms are individually styled, with
contemporary furnishings, earthy or neutral tones.
A 'compact and domestic' room had a queen-size
bed, two upright chairs, a 'spotless' and apparently
new bathroom, with walk-in monsoon shower.
In the beamed dining room, with its display
of fishing rods, adjoining a 'small lounge', a
breakfast cooked by the owner includes the full
Yorkshire, smoked haddock with poached eggs.
Ms Ratcliffe is a sociable but not pushy hostess,
and has many returning guests. For dinner try the
Frenchgate, Richmond (see entry). 'A convenient
stop-over for a drive to Scotland.' (RG)

Whashton
Richmond DL11 7JL

T: 01748 823721
E: jane@hackandspade.com
W: hackandspade.com

BEDROOMS: 5.
OPEN: all year except Christmas/New
Year, last 2 weeks Jan.
FACILITIES: small lounge and bar,
breakfast room, free Wi-Fi, in-room
TV (Freeview), garden, unsuitable
for disabled.
BACKGROUND MUSIC: 'quiet spa-type
music' in the mornings.
LOCATION: 4 miles NW of Richmond.
CHILDREN: not under 7.
DOGS: not allowed.
CREDIT CARDS: MC, Visa.
PRICES: per room B&B £125–£140.

WHITEWELL Lancashire

MAP 4:D3

THE INN AT WHITEWELL

'Conjuring up an image of a heartier England, with hunting, idiosyncratic aristocracy and solid home comforts', this 'great inn' continued to delight readers this year. In 'a stunningly beautiful location on the banks of the River Hodder', in the care of third-generation owner Charles Bowman, it has 'grand, eccentric decor', blazing fires, antiques, paintings. Every bedroom has something special – a four-poster, a peat fire, a grandfather clock, a modern wet room or Victorian cabinet bath and vintage weighing scales. The views are 'some of the best in England', with 'the Forest of Bowland fells folding into the distance'. A refurbished Room 7, with Savoir bed, 'looked smarter, and its bathroom, with an epic-sized bath and cabinet shower, remained as majestically luxurious as ever'. Hearty bar meals include the 'deservedly famous Whitewell fish pie', while in the restaurant, Jamie Cadman's menus bring such dishes as roast rack of salt marsh lamb, crushed minted peas, rosemary tomatoes, lemon and mint jelly. A less good breakfast ('overcooked bacon, no freshly squeezed juice') was not enough to take off the shine. 'The place never fails to impress.' (Mike Craddock, RM, ML)

Whitewell
Clitheroe BB7 3AT

T: 01200 448222
E: reception@innatwhitewell.com
W: innatwhitewell.com

BEDROOMS: 23. 4 in coach house, 150 yds, 2 on ground floor.
OPEN: all year.
FACILITIES: 3 bars, restaurant, boardroom, private dining room, in-house wine shop, spa treatments, free Wi-Fi, in-room TV (Freeview), civil wedding licence, 5-acre grounds (wild flower meadow, large river terrace with tables), 7 miles fishing (ghillie available), main bar, hall, reception wheelchair accessible, adapted toilet.
BACKGROUND MUSIC: none.
LOCATION: 6 miles NW of Clitheroe.
CHILDREN: all ages welcomed.
DOGS: allowed in bedrooms, not in dining room.
CREDIT CARDS: MC, Visa.
PRICES: per room B&B single £99–£225, double £137–£278. À la carte £40.

WILMINGTON Sussex

MAP 2:E4

CROSSWAYS HOTEL

David Stott and Clive James 'nurture an
atmosphere of repose and tranquillity, along
with informality, laughter and the friendliest of
welcomes' at their restaurant-with-rooms beneath
the South Downs. So writes a trusted reader
this year who has often stayed when attending
Glyndebourne opera. Within the whitewashed
house, once home to Elizabeth David's parents,
there is no residents' lounge, but 'two gazebos in
the garden are a haven for reading or enjoying
drinks'. 'The personal service from the proprietors
is admirable.' A 'home from home' atmosphere
includes a 'china teapot collection in the dining
room, wooden ducks, floral wallpapers' (a slight
'time warp', said one visitor). Individually styled
bedrooms have a fridge, fresh milk, earplugs to
cut road noise, a recently updated bathroom. At
dinner, David's 'impressive, richly varied' menu
uses locally sourced and home-grown ingredients
in such dishes as roast rack of lamb, shallot soubise
sauce, 'always plenty of vegetables', 'wonderful
damson sorbet'. Breakfast is 'as much a joy as
dinner', with 'uniquely wonderful bacon', perfect
scrambled eggs, 'home-made marmalade, slabs of
butter'. (Ann Lawson Lucas, Carol Jackson, RP)

25% DISCOUNT VOUCHERS

Lewes Road
Wilmington BN26 5SG

T: 01323 482455
E: stay@crosswayshotel.co.uk
W: crosswayshotel.co.uk

BEDROOMS: 7. Plus self-catering cottage
and apartment.
OPEN: all year except 21 Dec–late Jan,
restaurant closed Sun/Mon.
FACILITIES: breakfast room, restaurant,
free Wi-Fi, in-room TV (Freeview),
2-acre grounds (duck pond).
BACKGROUND MUSIC: occasionally, in
dining areas.
LOCATION: 2 miles W of Polegate on
A27.
CHILDREN: not under 12.
DOGS: not allowed.
CREDIT CARDS: Amex, MC, Visa.
PRICES: per room B&B single £85,
double £150–£175, D,B&B £220–£250.
Set dinner £43.

WINCHESTER Hampshire

MAP 2:D2

THE OLD VINE

A vine indeed grows up the Georgian frontage of Ashton Gray's pub-with-rooms, behind which lies an older building – with a 14th-century tavern in the cellar. Nowadays, the 'beautifully decorated' bedrooms have fabrics and wallpapers by named designers, but the Osborne and Little room gives some sense of the property's history, with Georgian plaster panelling, a mahogany four-poster, a carved Jacobean overmantel. Zoffany, with sleigh bed, overlooks the cathedral green. 'The inn is wonderfully situated, and the cathedral view from our eyrie suite was a delight,' a reader reported. All rooms have a mini-fridge, fresh milk, Noble Isle toiletries. Snacks and cream teas are served in the bar by 'young, enthusiastic staff'. In the restaurant the food is pub and bistro fare – sandwiches, beer-battered fish and chips, steak and chips, miso-glazed salmon with sesame seeds, wasabi horseradish mash, edamame beans, spinach, dashi broth; vegan and veggie options. The 'excellent' breakfast includes free-range eggs, fresh-baked bread, Hampshire sausages and preserves. Parking permits are available, but a reader urges: 'Go by train as we did – Winchester streets are a nightmare.' (S and JM, KS)

8 Great Minster Street
Winchester SO23 9HA

T: 01962 854616
E: reservations@oldvinewinchester.com
W: oldvinewinchester.com

BEDROOMS: 6. Self-contained 2-bed apartment, with garage, in annexe.
OPEN: all year except Christmas Day.
FACILITIES: bar, restaurant, free Wi-Fi, in-room TV (Freeview), restaurant and bar wheelchair accessible, but not toilets.
BACKGROUND MUSIC: in bar.
LOCATION: town centre, permits supplied for on-street parking.
CHILDREN: all ages welcomed, no under-6s in restaurant or in bar at night.
DOGS: only in bar.
CREDIT CARDS: Amex, MC, Visa.
PRICES: per room B&B single £120–£160, double £140–£200. Set menu (2/3 courses) £25 residents only, à la carte £30.

SEE ALSO SHORTLIST

WINDERMERE Cumbria

MAP 4: inset C2

CEDAR MANOR

'A true gem in the Lake District.' Readers this year had a 'thoroughly enjoyable' stay at Caroline and Jonathan Kaye's 'fabulous' small hotel. 'Without being intrusive, the owners made us feel welcome.' The 'exceptional and quiet' bedrooms have 'lovely touches, from REN toiletries and fine bedlinen to thick robes and chocolates'. Each is individually decorated (some are snug), one has a hand-crafted canopy bed, others fine, ecclesiastical windows overlooking the Lebanese cedar that lends its name. 'Our small bathroom was well organised, with reasonable storage space, a decent bath, an effective heated towel rail.' Many guests praise chef Roger Pergl-Wilson's 'excellent, well-presented' modern British dishes, perhaps crab and salmon fishcakes, coriander and red onion yogurt sauce, baby vegetables, saffron potatoes. One reader, however, while enjoying the pork medallions and lamb rump, was underwhelmed by both fish dishes, and the restaurant's 'intrusive' background music. Come morning, a hearty Cumbrian grill, smoked salmon and scrambled eggs, toast with home-made marmalade, hit the spot. 'We would happily stay here again.' (Peter Anderson, Margaret Daniel, D Berrington)

25% DISCOUNT VOUCHERS

Ambleside Road
Windermere LA23 1AX

T: 015394 43192
E: info@cedarmanor.co.uk
W: cedarmanor.co.uk

BEDROOMS: 10. 1 split-level suite in coach house.
OPEN: all year except 17–26 Dec, 3–26 Jan.
FACILITIES: 2 lounges, restaurant, free Wi-Fi, in-room TV (Freeview), patio, ¼-acre garden, unsuitable for disabled.
BACKGROUND MUSIC: 'very quiet', at mealtimes, in lounge and restaurant.
LOCATION: 5-min. walk from town centre.
CHILDREN: not under 10.
DOGS: not allowed.
CREDIT CARDS: MC, Visa.
PRICES: per room B&B single £125–£425, double £145–£475, D,B&B double £235–£565. Set dinner £35–£45, à la carte £45. 2-night min. stay at weekends and bank holidays.

WINDERMERE Cumbria

MAP 4: inset C2

GILPIN HOTEL AND LAKE HOUSE

'Nothing compares' with the Cunliffes' 'really special' country house hotel and its glamorous satellite, Lake House, with spa, half a mile away. Begun in 1988, it is a family operation, with its own 'very creative' in-house architects, Ben and Rachael, overseeing constant additions, such as the single-storey junior suites – large, light-washed rooms with a patio, spa bath and walk-in shower. Even the cheapest classic rooms are spacious, with a lovely bathroom. Garden suites have a feature fireplace, decked gardens, a hot tub, while each of the detached cedar-clad spa lodges has a fresh contemporary style, and a treatment area, steam room, outdoor sauna, hydrotherapy tub and walled garden. All have Lakeland views. 'They have rooms for all ages' and food for differing tastes. In HRiSHi restaurant, Michelin-starred Hrishikesh Desai cooks such modern British dishes as rolled braised belly of Huntsham Farm pork with five-spice sauce, while in the cheaper, 'funky, very modern Asian' Gilpin Spice, tapas-style pan-Asian dishes include Thai green curry of Morecambe seafood, Herdwick lamb with nizami masala. 'It's expensive but has a great reputation.' (ST, and others)

Crook Road
Windermere LA23 3NE

T: 015394 88818
E: hotel@thegilpin.co.uk
W: thegilpin.co.uk

BEDROOMS: 31. 6 in orchard wing, 5 in spa lodges, 6 in Lake House (½ mile from main house), 1 room suitable for disabled.
OPEN: all year.
FACILITIES: Gilpin Hotel: bar, lounge, 2 restaurants, gardens, 22-acre grounds; Lake House: lounge, conservatory, spa (20-metre heated pool), 100-acre grounds; free Wi-Fi, in-room TV (Sky), civil wedding licence.
BACKGROUND MUSIC: in restaurants.
LOCATION: on B5284, 2 miles SE of Windermere.
CHILDREN: not under 7.
DOGS: allowed in 2 bedrooms, not in public rooms.
CREDIT CARDS: Amex, MC, Visa.
PRICES: per room B&B £285–£635, D,B&B £375–£725. Set dinner £70, tasting menu (HRiSHi) £90, (Gilpin Spice) £40.

WINGHAM Kent

THE DOG AT WINGHAM   NEW

Who says you can't teach an old dog new
tricks? Under enthusiastic owner Marc Bridgen
this ancient pub is today 'less a local than a
comfortable lounge bar' and canine-friendly
restaurant-with-rooms. The timber-frame
building, 'outside a pretty village', enters the
Guide this year after an inspection by our sleuth-
hounds. Their bedroom, styled by Marc's interior
designer mother, Marilyn, was 'comfortably sized',
with 'glitzy touches, a huge, gold velvet-framed
bedhead, gold and orange tub chairs, a sunburst
mirror, light grey walls with one painted lovat
green; a neatly designed shower room'. Some
noise was heard from the room above. In the
beamed bar, 'comfortable tweedy chairs, all with
a sheepskin draped over', a log-burner and 'lots of
dog pictures'. In the dining room 'the quality and
style' of Samuel McClurkin's cooking impressed,
especially 'honeyed carrots, a revelation; lobster
ravioli and bisque, very good; feta and mushroom
Wellington, deserved praise'. Breakfast, in the
conservatory, was 'somewhat mixed'. Orange
juice wasn't fresh, 'perfect poached eggs and
hollandaise but overcooked bacon'. Overall:
'Winning value for money.' (Joanna Crossley,
Vicky Cox, and others)

25% DISCOUNT VOUCHERS

Canterbury Road
Wingham
Canterbury CT3 1BB

T: 01227 720339
E: info@thedog.co.uk
W: thedog.co.uk

BEDROOMS: 8.
OPEN: all year.
FACILITIES: lounge bar, restaurant bar,
dining room, garden room, terrace
(alfresco dining), free Wi-Fi, in-room
TV (Freeview), civil wedding licence,
golf packages, monthly dining club,
unsuitable for disabled.
BACKGROUND MUSIC: in bar and
restaurant, live music events.
LOCATION: in village 7 miles E of
Canterbury.
CHILDREN: all ages welcomed.
DOGS: welcomed throughout.
CREDIT CARDS: Amex, MC, Visa.
PRICES: per room B&B single £65–£280,
double £80–£280. À la carte £40 (vegan
£38, 24 hours' notice).

WOLD NEWTON Yorkshire

MAP 4:D5

THE WOLD COTTAGE

Not a cottage at all but an elegant Georgian
manor house once owned by playwright and
newspaper proprietor Major Edward Topham,
now run as a B&B by Katrina and Derek
Gray. Everyone is welcomed with 'warmth
and kindness', and shown to one of six well-
appointed rooms, four in the main house and
two in an adjacent barn. Each is named after
a former resident; all have a slightly different
feel. The Major Topham Suite has a rather
grand four-poster bed; the JB Bird Suite is more
contemporary, with a stylish oversized headboard.
Bathrooms are 'spotless' with a bath and overhead
shower or separate walk-in shower, Cole & Lewis
toiletries and home-made lavender soap. A hearty
breakfast has a distinctly Yorkshire flavour:
Yorkshire black pudding with the full English;
locally smoked kippers, or perhaps Filey Bay
crab and boiled egg, washed down with a cup of
Yorkshire tea (other teas, plus coffee, available).
Surrounded by farmland with the glorious
Yorkshire Wolds beyond, this is the ideal spot for
walking, birdwatching, croquet in the garden, or
a visit to a certain column commemorating Major
Topham's discovery here, in 1795, of a meteorite.
(DL, and others)

25% DISCOUNT VOUCHERS

Wold Newton
Driffield YO25 3HL

T: 01262 470696
E: katrina@woldcottage.com
W: woldcottage.co.uk

BEDROOMS: 6. 2 in converted barn, 1 on
ground floor, 2 self-catering cottages.
OPEN: all year.
FACILITIES: lounge, dining room, free
Wi-Fi, in-room TV (Freeview), 3-acre
gardens (croquet) in 240-acre grounds
(farmland, woodland), public rooms
wheelchair accessible.
BACKGROUND MUSIC: at breakfast in
dining room.
LOCATION: just outside village.
CHILDREN: all ages welcomed.
DOGS: not allowed.
CREDIT CARDS: MC, Visa.
PRICES: per person B&B £55–£90,
family room £135–£200. 1-night
bookings refused weekends in
summer.

WOOTTON COURTENAY Somerset   MAP 1:B5

DUNKERY BEACON COUNTRY HOUSE

An Edwardian hunting lodge, rumoured to
have been a 1960s MI6 training centre, is today
a welcoming country house hotel where guests
wake to glorious views over Exmoor. It doesn't
take a spook to reveal that its success is due to
'caring and friendly' hosts John and Jane Bradley.
'They encourage a degree of informality,' writes
a reader, whose walking group stays every year,
'but there is nothing casual about the way they
run the hotel.' Traditionally styled and furnished
bedrooms include two dog-friendly suites (one
with four-poster) with a separate lounge. All
rooms have fresh milk, a cafetière or espresso
machine, luxury toiletries. In the Coleridge
restaurant, with view to the Coleridge Way, John's
'outstanding' regularly changing menus with
nightly twists bring such 'memorable dishes' as
'wild boar terrine, quince jam, toasted ciabatta;
Exmoor honey-roasted duck breast, truffle mash,
raspberry infused red cabbage'; 'a tiramisu to die
for'. Wines are supplied by prestigious merchant
Berry Bros. & Rudd, where Jane worked for 15
years. Devotees will be sad to hear that at the time
of the Guide going to press, the hotel was on the
market. (Andrew Butterworth, JA, MC)

25% DISCOUNT VOUCHERS

Wootton Courtenay TA24 8RH

T: 01643 841241
E: info@dunkerybeacon
    accommodation.co.uk
W: dunkerybeacon
    accommodation.co.uk

BEDROOMS: 8. 1 on ground floor.
OPEN: mid-Feb–27 Dec, restaurant
closed Sun/Mon/Tues.
FACILITIES: lounge, restaurant,
breakfast room, free Wi-Fi in public
areas and some bedrooms, in-room
TV (Freeview), limited mobile phone
reception, ¾-acre garden, unsuitable
for disabled.
BACKGROUND MUSIC: in restaurant in
evening.
LOCATION: 4 miles SW of Dunster.
CHILDREN: not under 10.
DOGS: allowed in 2 suites (£5 per night,
max. 2 dogs), not in public rooms.
CREDIT CARDS: MC, Visa.
PRICES: per room B&B £85–£170,
D,B&B £147–£232. À la carte £37.
1-night bookings refused Fri/Sat and
on all stays in peak season (but check
for late availability).

YARM Yorkshire

MAP 4:C4

JUDGES

♔ Previous César Winner

'Everything about Judges smacked of class and excellence.' Readers this year loved this smart hotel on the edge of the North Yorkshire moors. Built as a family residence in 1881, and surrounded by mature gardens, it served in the 1970s as lodgings for circuit judges. Today it is run for the Downs family by the 'charming, humorous' manager, Tim Howard, and his 'attentive, friendly, courteous' staff. 'We particularly liked the way the receptionist came to the door when we got back each evening, to welcome us "home".' Afternoon tea is served by the fire in the elegant lounge. Bedrooms, some with whirlpool bath, have a sleigh bed or four-poster, rich fabrics, complimentary fruit and sherry. New chef David McBride uses produce from local suppliers and the walled kitchen garden in such 'sensational' dishes as Yorkshire lamb rump, pommes purée, garden peas, anchovy, salsa verde, cherry tomatoes, rosemary jus. There are also vegan and vegetarian menus, and one with simpler fare (salads, pastas, burgers). 'Lunch, dinner and breakfast were delicious.' 'Our stay was sublime.' (Robert Senior, Glynne Davies, Anne Cooling)

Kirklevington Hall
Kirklevington
Yarm TS15 9LW

T: 01642 789000
E: reception@judgeshotel.co.uk
W: judgeshotel.co.uk

BEDROOMS: 21. Some on ground floor.
OPEN: all year.
FACILITIES: lounge, bar, restaurant, private dining room, free Wi-Fi, in-room TV (Freeview), function facilities, business centre, civil wedding licence, 36-acre grounds (paths, running routes), access to local spa and sports club, unsuitable for disabled.
BACKGROUND MUSIC: Radio 4 at breakfast, classical background music in restaurant.
LOCATION: 1½ miles S of centre.
CHILDREN: all ages welcomed.
DOGS: guide dogs only.
CREDIT CARDS: Amex, MC, Visa.
PRICES: per room B&B single £99–£205, double £145–£225, D,B&B double £220–£300. À la carte £50.

YORK Yorkshire

MAP 4:D4

MIDDLETHORPE HALL & SPA

Handy for the racecourse, this William and
Mary mansion, built for Sheffield cutler Thomas
Barlow 'in the Italian mode', operates as a hotel
and spa, 'ideal for those seeking individual
attention and pampering'. After years of neglect
and a stint as Brummels nightclub, it is now in
the hands of the National Trust. Public rooms,
with period furniture, 'imposing portraits' and tall
windows, overlook gardens with a lake, croquet
lawn and ha-ha. A trusted reader found 'deep
sofas' in a lounge 'warmed by a roaring fire'.
His bedroom was 'small and functional, with a
comfortable bed, a somewhat vintage bedside
radio'. Far grander suites include the Duke of
York with fireplace and coronet king-size bed,
named after a visit by Prince Andrew, or the Lady
Mary, recalling the diarist and former resident,
Lady Mary Wortley Montagu. In the panelled
dining room, chef Ashley Binder uses produce
from the walled garden in 'very good' seasonal
dishes. Our man enjoyed 'duck and salmon
canapés, a pumpkin panna cotta, grouse with
haggis'. Breakfast brings freshly squeezed orange
juice, 'exemplary' scrambled eggs. 'Tis indeed 'a
very pritty place', as Lady Mary noted. (RG)

Bishopthorpe Road
York YO23 2GB

T: 01904 641241
E: info@middlethorpe.com
W: www.middlethorpe.com

BEDROOMS: 29. 17 in courtyard, 2 in
cottage, 1 suite with wheelchair access.
OPEN: all year.
FACILITIES: drawing room, sitting
rooms, library, bar, restaurant,
2 private dining rooms, free Wi-Fi,
in-room TV (Freeview), civil wedding
licence, 20-acre grounds, spa (10 by
6 metre indoor swimming pool),
public rooms wheelchair accessible, no
adapted toilet.
BACKGROUND MUSIC: none.
LOCATION: 1½ miles S of centre.
CHILDREN: not under 6.
DOGS: allowed in garden suites and
cottage only, by prior arrangement.
CREDIT CARDS: Amex, MC, Visa.
PRICES: per room B&B £149–£569,
D,B&B from £219. 6-course tasting
menu £75, à la carte £60.

SEE ALSO SHORTLIST

ZENNOR Cornwall

MAP 1:D1

THE GURNARD'S HEAD

'It never fails to please,' write Guide regulars in 2019 after a return visit to Charles and Edmund Inkin's dining pub-with-rooms. 'We highly recommend the accommodation and the food.' Sitting close to the Coast Path above the Atlantic, it has a relaxed air enhanced by shabby-chic interiors with mix-and-match furniture, well-thumbed paperbacks and local artwork. Bedrooms have a Roberts radio, Bramley toiletries, fresh flowers, views of sheep-grazed moor or ocean. 'To say the food is very good is a serious understatement,' continue the readers. 'You would expect fish this close to the ocean but the meat and vegetarian dishes are splendid.' Take a bow, Max Wilson. The chef moved here in 2016 from the Inkins' first venture, The Felin Fach Griffin, Felin Fach, Wales (see entry), and he looks to local farmers, fishers and foragers for such dishes as rump of beef, wild garlic, broccoli, crispy tongue; gurnard, creamed leeks, pancetta, chives. Praise also for the restaurant's 'smiling, professional and attentive staff' from readers who dined here while staying at sister hotel, The Old Coastguard, Mousehole (see entry). Eat alfresco when the sun shines. (Chris and Erika Savory, Sue and John Jenkinson, RM)

25% DISCOUNT VOUCHERS

Treen
Zennor
St Ives TR26 3DE

T: 01736 796928
E: enquiries@gurnardshead.co.uk
W: gurnardshead.co.uk

BEDROOMS: 7.
OPEN: all year except 24/25 Dec.
FACILITIES: bar, restaurant, lounge area, free Wi-Fi, 3-acre garden (alfresco dining), public areas wheelchair accessible.
BACKGROUND MUSIC: Radio 4 at breakfast, selected music at other times, in bar and restaurant.
LOCATION: 7 miles SW of St Ives, on B3306.
CHILDREN: all ages welcomed.
DOGS: allowed (water bowls, towels and biscuits provided).
CREDIT CARDS: MC, Visa.
PRICES: per room B&B single £110–£150, double £130–£195. Set menus £22–£28, à la carte £28. 1-night bookings refused weekends occasionally.

SCOTLAND

Isle of Skye

ALYTH Perth and Kinross   MAP 5:D2

TIGH NA LEIGH

The name means 'house of the doctor', and this double-fronted Victorian stone villa was just that, though today it is run as a guest house with smart contemporary interiors. It stands 'on the main street into the village' – in fact, a small town on the Alyth burn. Behind is a 'surprisingly large and pretty' landscaped garden with pond, overlooked by a conservatory breakfast/dining room. New owners Graham and Karen Smith continue the hospitable tradition of their predecessors. 'There are two sizeable lounges', one with television, though bedrooms have their own, and all but one has a spa bath. The largest has an emperor-size four-poster; another room has a separate lounge. One is on the ground floor, another tucked away under the eaves. You can order ahead to eat in, from a limited-choice menu of locally sourced, modern British dishes such as rack of lamb, sweet potato, rosemary and red chilli mash; pan-seared salmon fillet, hollandaise. At breakfast there are home-made jams and compotes, brioche French toast with crispy bacon, smoked salmon, feta or smashed avocado on sourdough. 'A beautiful project with such design style, such a beautiful site.' (J and EG)

22–24 Airlie Street
Alyth PH11 8AJ

T: 01828 632372
E: book@tighnaleigh.com
W: tighnaleigh.com

BEDROOMS: 6. 1 on ground floor, 1 up steep stairs.
OPEN: 7 Feb–25 Nov, dining room evenings Wed–Sat Feb–end Mar, Sept–Nov, Mon–Sat Apr–Aug.
FACILITIES: lounge, TV room, conservatory sitting/dining room, free Wi-Fi, in-room TV (Freeview), ½-acre landscaped garden with pond, parking, unsuitable for disabled.
BACKGROUND MUSIC: in dining room/conservatory.
LOCATION: close to town centre.
CHILDREN: not under 12.
DOGS: allowed in bedrooms, in public rooms except dining room.
CREDIT CARDS: Amex, MC, Visa.
PRICES: per room B&B single £60–£90, double/suites £92–£115. À la carte £28. 1-night stay refused high season weekends if guest is not dining.

ARDUAINE Argyll and Bute

LOCH MELFORT HOTEL

A 'warm' welcome for pooches and their human companions can be expected at Calum and Rachel Ross's 'peaceful' retreat on the Argyll coast. The former late Victorian merchant family's house takes full advantage of its 'magical' location: from every window are views that stretch along the Craignish peninsula on one side, and across to the islands of Shuna, Scarba and Jura on the other. The only public room that doesn't gaze across the sea is the wood-panelled library. 'Clean, well-kept' bedrooms in the main house and an annexe sport a muted palette and splashes of cheerful colour; in each a 'comfortable' bed; plenty of hot water and Sea Kelp toiletries in the bathroom. All annexe rooms have a private balcony or terrace offering 'stunning sea views'. In the dining room, chef Roger Brown's locally sourced seasonal menus offer everything from catch of the day to wild boar or Argyll lamb or Angus beef. There is one report of disappointing bar meals. After a leisurely breakfast, perhaps a smoked Scottish haddock, the dazzling variety of Arduaine Garden's 20 acres beckons. Clean towels and treats for the four-legged visitors await upon your return. (J and H T-P, and others)

25% DISCOUNT VOUCHERS

Arduaine
Oban PA34 4XG

T: 01852 200233
E: reception@lochmelfort.co.uk
W: lochmelfort.co.uk

BEDROOMS: 30. 20 in annexe with 10 on ground floor, 8 and 2 suites in main house, 2 rooms suitable for disabled.
OPEN: all year except Mon–Wed Nov–Mar, 3 weeks Dec/Jan, open Christmas/New Year.
FACILITIES: sitting room, library, bar/bistro, restaurant, free Wi-Fi, in-room TV (terrestrial), wedding facilities, 17-acre grounds (National Trust for Scotland's Arduaine Garden next door), public rooms wheelchair accessible.
BACKGROUND MUSIC: in restaurant and bistro.
LOCATION: 19 miles S of Oban.
CHILDREN: all ages welcomed.
DOGS: allowed in 6 bedrooms (£10 per dog per night), not in public rooms, except bistro.
CREDIT CARDS: Amex, MC, Visa.
PRICES: per room B&B £160–£294, D,B&B £232–£366. Set dinner £42.

AUCHENCAIRN Dumfries and Galloway   MAP 5:E2

BALCARY BAY HOTEL

In a 'wonderful setting' on the shores of the
Solway Firth, Graeme Lamb's hotel affords
spectacular views across the water to Hestan Isle
and the peaks of the Lake District. The original
17th-century building, now much extended, is
said to have been used by smugglers and built
over a vault for stashing brandy for the parson,
'baccy for the clerk'. Today's guests are wholly
respectable, 'mostly retirees like us, who return
year after year'. The accommodation is 'first
class', contemporary and comfortable. The rooms
to choose, of course, are those with a bay view,
although you could do worse than gaze out at
the mature gardens. There is casual dining in the
bar and the light-filled conservatory (sandwiches,
salads, fish and chips). Don best bib and tucker
for the formal dining room, 'no denim jeans,
shorts, trainers/walking boots'. Chef Craig
McWilliam's daily-changing menus, including
such dishes as fillet of Galloway beef, creamed
potato, red cabbage, onion purée, red wine sauce,
are bookended by 'canapés, petits fours and good
coffee'. 'The hotel's restaurants are well spoken
of throughout Galloway.' Breakfast brings a
full Scottish with local haggis, or a buttered
Arbroath smokie.

Shore Road
Auchencairn DG7 1QZ

T: 01556 640217
E: reservations@balcary-bay-hotel.
   co.uk
W: balcary-bay-hotel.co.uk

BEDROOMS: 20. 3 on ground floor.
1 suitable for disabled.
OPEN: 7 Feb–29 Nov.
FACILITIES: 2 lounges, cocktail bar,
conservatory, restaurant, free Wi-Fi
in reception area, in-room TV
(Freeview), 3-acre grounds, public
areas wheelchair accessible.
BACKGROUND MUSIC: none.
LOCATION: 2 miles SW of village.
CHILDREN: all ages welcomed.
DOGS: allowed in bedrooms, not in
public rooms (max. 2 small or 1 large
dog per room).
CREDIT CARDS: MC, Visa.
PRICES: per person B&B £80–£96,
D,B&B £95–£130 (min. 2 nights).
Set dinner £37–£48, à la carte
(conservatory and bar) £30. 1-night
bookings usually refused weekends.

AULDEARN Highland

BOATH HOUSE

⚜ Previous César Winner

'A beautiful hotel with wonderful food and lovely young staff.' Readers this year loved their stay at Don and Wendy Matheson's Georgian mansion in gardens and parkland. 'The interior is decorated in a country house style with contemporary accents', and provides gallery space for local artists. The original master bedroom has twin slipper baths by the window. A basement room has a conservatory. A front-facing room was 'attractive and comfortable', with coffee machine, 'delicious shortbread', Molton Brown toiletries. 'We slept with the window open and enjoyed the wind in the oaks and birches.' In the lofty dining room, with lake views through French windows, Craig Munro's 'wonderful' three-course menus exploit local, home-grown and foraged produce. Praise this year for heritage tomato salad, gnocchi, 'soft, succulent venison with peas and pancetta'. You can eat more simply, indoors or alfresco, at the café in the walled garden, which has a wood-fired pizza oven. A breakfast of 'freshly squeezed orange juice, strawberry yogurt and muesli, an exquisite smoked haddock omelette with Connage Dunlop cheese and wilted greens' fuelled our reader's visit to Cawdor Castle. (David Birnie)

Auldearn
Nairn IV12 5TE

T: 01667 454896
E: info@boath-house.com
W: boath-house.com

BEDROOMS: 9. 2 in cottages (50 yds), 1 suitable for disabled. Plus 2 in separate B&B at owners' house.
OPEN: all year.
FACILITIES: 2 lounges, whisky bar/library, restaurant, private dining room, free Wi-Fi, in-room TV (Freeview), civil wedding licence, 22-acre grounds (woods, walled garden, meadow, streams, trout lake, café), public rooms wheelchair accessible, step up to toilet.
BACKGROUND MUSIC: soft in dining room.
LOCATION: 2 miles E of Nairn.
CHILDREN: all ages welcomed.
DOGS: allowed in some bedrooms, not in public rooms.
CREDIT CARDS: Amex, MC, Visa.
PRICES: per room B&B single £190–£260, double £295–£365. Set dinner £45.

BALLANTRAE Ayrshire

GLENAPP CASTLE

Beyond 'splendid wrought iron gates', a 'beautifully wooded half-mile drive' leads to Paul and Poppy Szkiler's towered and turreted Victorian pile, with a fountain 'dominating the forecourt'. Our inspector was met by a battalion of staff ('never have I seen so many waiting to assist') and shown to a room with 'a wonderful view of mature trees shielding lush gardens', a chandelier, 'five gracious table lamps'. A 'large period bathroom' had a bath with monsoon shower over. Each lavish bedroom has a sea or garden view, antique furniture, Penhaligon toiletries. New this year, a penthouse apartment with sauna and roof terrace. Downstairs, a 'spacious divided lounge' has 'Corinthian columns, wonderful stucco ceilings'. If a fellow guest murders Mozart on the Bösendorfer grand, escape to the 'small, panelled library'. In the dining room, with sunset views to Ailsa Craig and the Mull of Kintyre, David Alexander uses produce from kitchen garden and glasshouses in such dishes as roast loin of Galloway Forest deer, celeriac purée, girolles, haggis bonbon, blackberry and port reduction. Breakfast brings Ayrshire bacon, haggis, tatty scones. 'We had a lovely stay.' (Carol Bulloch, and others)

Ballantrae KA26 0NZ

T: 01465 831212
E: info@glenappcastle.com
W: glenappcastle.com

BEDROOMS: 17. 7 on ground floor, 1 suitable for disabled.
OPEN: all year.
FACILITIES: lift, drawing room, library, 2 dining rooms, wedding facilities, free Wi-Fi, in-room TV (Freeview), 36-acre grounds (walled gardens, woodland, lake, tennis, croquet), boat for charter, access to local spa, public rooms wheelchair accessible.
BACKGROUND MUSIC: occasional piano during meals and tea.
LOCATION: 2 miles S of Ballantrae.
CHILDREN: all ages welcomed.
DOGS: allowed in some bedrooms, not in public rooms.
CREDIT CARDS: Amex, MC, Visa.
PRICES: per room B&B £395–£675, D,B&B £525–£795. Set menu £53–£73.

BLAIRGOWRIE Perth and Kinross   MAP 5:D2

KINLOCH HOUSE

'Our stay was a treat from start to finish.' 'We cannot speak too highly of it.' Our readers are impressed by the hospitality at the Allen family's traditional Scottish country house hotel set amid woods and parkland. An oak staircase leads up from a panelled hall with fireplace and seating, to bedrooms ranging from quite generous in size to positively spacious. The large rooms have chairs, a settee and everything one would expect from a Relais & Châteaux member. Extras include chocolates, fresh flowers, Arran Aromatics toiletries. A junior suite has a four-poster bed, and views over the gently rolling countryside. Other rooms overlook parkland grazed by Highland cattle. Lounges sport open fires, gilt-framed oil paintings, acres of comfy seating. In the dining room, chef Steve MacCallum's 'excellent' daily-changing seasonal menus exploit local game, wild salmon and seafood, Scottish meat, produce from the garden, and the area's abundant fruit. A typical dish: loin of Perthshire lamb, gratin potatoes, mashed swede and carrot, roast garlic, broad beans, rosemary sauce. Breakfast does not disappoint: everything from bread and jams to sausages made in the kitchen. (RGW, BW)

Dunkeld Road
Blairgowrie PH10 6SG

T: 01250 884237
E: reception@kinlochhouse.com
W: kinlochhouse.com

BEDROOMS: 15. 4 on ground floor.
OPEN: all year except 2 weeks from mid-Dec, open for New Year.
FACILITIES: bar, lounge, drawing room, conservatory, dining room, private dining room, free Wi-Fi, in-room TV (Freeview), civil wedding licence, 28-acre grounds, public areas on ground floor wheelchair accessible, toilet not adapted.
BACKGROUND MUSIC: none.
LOCATION: 3 miles W of Blairgowrie, on A923.
CHILDREN: all ages welcomed, not under 6 in restaurant at dinner.
DOGS: not allowed.
CREDIT CARDS: Amex, MC, Visa.
PRICES: per room B&B £210–£360, D,B&B £300–£470. Set dinner £55. 1-night bookings refused busy periods.

BRIDGEND Argyll and Bute

BRIDGEND HOTEL

There is whisky galore on the Inner Hebrides island of Islay; bonhomie in the bar of this friendly hotel. It was first mentioned in 1849, when it hosted the Morrison family: they liked it so much, they bought the island. Manager Alison Gray and her staff 'have clearly thought through their guests' comfort'. Rooms blend contemporary and traditional style, neutral decor with tartan and floral fabrics. They are supplied with local toiletries and tablet (the fudgy confection, not a device). Chef Scott Chance has a passion for local produce – game from Islay estates, vegetables from the community garden, Argyll meat, freshly landed seafood. The restaurant's daily-changing menu includes such imaginative dishes as medallion and faggot of venison, truffle croquette, woodland mushroom, parsnip, berry sauce; vegetable linguine. Readers so loved the soft local background music that they 'downloaded it, and still sing along'. You'll find more casual dining in the public bar, Morrison tartan underfoot in a lounge warmed by a blazing fire. After a breakfast kipper, you can set out to spot seal and sea eagle, visit distilleries, or 'follow a stream through woods and farms to a local craft centre'.

Bridgend
Isle of Islay PA44 7PJ

T: 01496 810212
E: info@bridgend-hotel.com
W: bridgend-hotel.com

BEDROOMS: 11. 1 family room with bunk bed.
OPEN: all year except 25 Dec and 1 Jan.
FACILITIES: lounge bar, public bar, restaurant, free Wi-Fi, in-room TV (Freeview), wedding facilities, terrace, garden, drying room, half-acre grounds, parking, public areas wheelchair accessible, adapted toilet.
BACKGROUND MUSIC: in public areas.
LOCATION: centre of small village.
CHILDREN: all ages welcomed.
DOGS: well-behaved dogs allowed in bedrooms, bar.
CREDIT CARDS: Amex, MC, Visa.
PRICES: per room B&B £120–£250. À la carte £30. 1-night bookings sometimes refused during Islay Festival end of May.

CHIRNSIDE Scottish Borders

CHIRNSIDE HALL

Whether you come to bag birds, fish for salmon, or visit historic Borders castles and houses, Christian Korsten's mansion is a fine place to hang your tweed hat. Built in 1834 for an Edinburgh businessman, with views of the Cheviots, it is 'clean and well maintained', with blazing fires in comfy lounges, where you can sink into a sofa and leaf through copies of The Field. Walls are hung with pictures, stags' heads and antlers. Some bedrooms (not all) are 'large and airy', with perhaps a four-poster, an original fireplace. They mix traditional and vintage furnishings, plain decor, smart plaid fabrics, wool carpets and modern bathrooms with posh toiletries. At dinner, Mark Harvey's daily-changing four-course menus are 'always enjoyed'. Typical dishes, roast line-caught cod, crushed peas, langoustine tortelloni, potato rösti, chive beurre blanc; for veggies maybe beetroot and goat's cheese risotto, chive crème fraîche. If you can, book the table in the bay window – it's the best. Breakfast brings 'an excellent kipper'. Floors ('Flurs') Castle, with lovely walled garden, is a 40-minute drive, Sir Walter Scott's Abbotsford, 50 minutes. Or walk the estate, spotting deer, hares, raptors.

Chirnside
Duns TD11 3LD

T: 01890 818219
E: reception@chirnsidehallhotel.com
W: chirnsidehallhotel.com

BEDROOMS: 10.
OPEN: all year.
FACILITIES: 2 lounges, dining room, private dining room/library/conference rooms, free Wi-Fi, in-room TV (Freeview), billiard room, wedding facilities, 1½-acre grounds, lounge and restaurant wheelchair accessible.
BACKGROUND MUSIC: 'easy listening' in public areas.
LOCATION: 1½ miles E of Chirnside, NE of Duns.
CHILDREN: all ages welcomed.
DOGS: allowed in some bedrooms, not in public rooms.
CREDIT CARDS: Amex, MC, Visa.
PRICES: per room B&B single £100, double £180, D,B&B single £135, double £240. À la carte £40.

COLINTRAIVE Argyll and Bute

THE COLINTRAIVE HOTEL

In a small coastal village from where cattle were once swum across to the Isle of Bute, Patricia Watt's former shooting lodge turned pub-with-rooms-with-moorings wins more reader approval. 'What a gem! Our bedroom was large, overlooking the Kyles of Bute.' That would have been the Bute Room, or dual-aspect Attenborough, favoured by the late Sir Richard, who had a farmhouse on the island. Ardentraive (sleeping four) and Cala have country views. Each is individually styled, with a mix of contemporary and antique pieces, work by local artists. 'Staff are very friendly, and the bar is used by locals, who chat to the guests, giving the hotel a warm buzz.' The restaurant has views of grazing cattle at the water's edge. The 'engaging, enthusiastic' hostess not only runs the next-door post office/store but, with David Cummings, cooks 'bistro-style' food; langoustine from the bay, freshly caught crayfish and prawns, hand-dived scallops, steak-and-Guinness pie. 'We enjoyed linguine with prawns and mussels, home-made steak pie, fish and chips. After breakfast, Tricia made a point of chatting to new guests. . . We thoroughly enjoyed ourselves and will definitely return.' (GC)

Colintraive PA22 3AS

T: 01700 841207
E: enquiries@colintraivehotel.com
W: colintraivehotel.com

BEDROOMS: 4.
OPEN: all year (residents only, 25 Dec).
FACILITIES: lounge, bar, restaurant, free Wi-Fi in reception, in-room TV (Freeview), wedding facilities, small beer garden, yacht moorings, public rooms on ground floor wheelchair accessible, no adapted toilet.
BACKGROUND MUSIC: in public areas; occasional live music.
LOCATION: in village, 20 miles W of Dunoon.
CHILDREN: all ages welcomed.
DOGS: allowed in bedrooms, public rooms, not in restaurant.
CREDIT CARDS: MC, Visa.
PRICES: per room B&B single £85–£140, double £99–£185. À la carte £35.

COLONSAY Argyll and Bute

MAP 5:D1

THE COLONSAY

You can take the ferry from Oban, or hop across on a twin-propeller plane, to discover Jane and Alex Howard's 18th-century inn, bar and village hub, on a hillside overlooking the harbour. Guide inspectors were 'very taken' with the 'relaxed hotel' and the island (population 135), host to an annual April book festival, and to the rare corncrake, kittiwake, shag, seal and porpoise. The new manager, Zoe Butler, is in charge of front-of-house with its relaxed contemporary mood, open fires, squashy sofas and 'seaside feel'. Bedrooms are simple but not plain. The largest, Ardskenish, has Designers Guild fabrics, a bath with shower over, views towards the harbour. Pigs Paradise, comprising adjoining single and double rooms, has a westerly view of hills, fabrics by Vanessa Arbuthnott. The single room, Port Lobh, has a bathroom down the corridor. Eat where you like – in bar, conservatory or restaurant – though a restaurant table 'in a prime position by the window' is hard to beat. There is a new chef, too. Anthony Orr's dishes include Aberdeen Angus rib-eye steak, pepper sauce, chips; West Coast scallops, cauliflower and dill purée, vegetable risotto, house ice cream with Colonsay honey.

Colonsay PA61 7YU

T: 01951 200316
E: cottages@colonsayholidays.co.uk
W: colonsayholidays.co.uk

BEDROOMS: 9.
OPEN: mid-Mar–1 Nov, Christmas, New Year.
FACILITIES: conservatory, 2 lounges, log room, bar, restaurant, free Wi-Fi on ground floor, in-room TV (Sky), 1-acre grounds, ground-floor public rooms and toilet wheelchair accessible.
BACKGROUND MUSIC: in bar sometimes.
LOCATION: 400 yds W of harbour.
CHILDREN: all ages welcomed.
DOGS: allowed in 2 bedrooms, public rooms except restaurant.
CREDIT CARDS: MC, Visa.
PRICES: per room B&B single £85–£90, double £115–£170. Pre-ferry set menus £17–£20 Mon, Thurs, Fri, Sat, à la carte £30.

CONTIN Highland

MAP 5:C2

COUL HOUSE

'A comfortable and friendly base,' writes a
trusted Guide reader and first-time visitor to
Susannah and Stuart Macpherson's 'really lovely'
Highlands hotel. Built for Sir George Steuart
Mackenzie in 1821, the 'rambling, wonderful'
building is swaddled by 'magnificent' gardens
with rhododendrons and mature trees including
two giant sequoia. The ground-floor public
rooms sport vintage hunting paintings hung
beneath ornate plasterwork ceilings – a key
element in Coul's listed status. It all adds up to 'a
very pleasant atmosphere'. A room at the back
had 'superb' views, a 'restful green-grey' palette,
generous storage, good lighting. Some rooms have
a smart sofa that converts into a bed for children;
one has a four-poster and a bathroom with a
double-ended, roll-top tub. In the octagonal
dining room with its dramatic red curtains, chef
Garry Kenley's 'inventive' locally sourced dishes
include slow-roasted pork belly, mashed potato,
savoury cabbage, barbecue sauce, butternut squash
chutney. More varied menus would have been
appreciated. Your pet won't care about that. Dogs
are welcome. 'Ours was fussed over by the staff.
The grounds were great for first and last exercise.'
(MK Webster)

Contin
Strathpeffer IV14 9ES

T: 01997 421487
E: stay@coulhouse.com
W: coulhousehotel.com

BEDROOMS: 21. 4 on ground floor,
1 suitable for disabled.
OPEN: all year except 23–26 Dec.
FACILITIES: lounge bar, drawing room,
hall, restaurant, free Wi-Fi, in-room
Smart TV, conference/wedding
facilities, 8-acre grounds (children's
play area, 9-hole pitch and putt).
BACKGROUND MUSIC: in lounge bar and
restaurant.
LOCATION: 17 miles NW of Inverness.
CHILDREN: all ages welcomed.
DOGS: allowed in some bedrooms, all
public rooms except restaurant (£7.50
per dog per night).
CREDIT CARDS: Amex, MC, Visa.
PRICES: per room B&B single £75–£110,
double £95–£325. À la carte £39.
1-night bookings refused New Year.

CRAIGHOUSE Argyll and Bute

MAP 5:D1

JURA HOTEL

'A friendly, comfortable place to stay in an enchanting part of the country.' Warm praise for the McCallum family's hotel overlooking the Sound of Jura on one of Scotland's 'wildest islands'. Guests on a shoestring may camp on their field (with shower and toilet block), but the bedrooms are affordable, with an appropriate and pleasing simplicity. Some may be snug, say readers whose premium double had an 'excellent king-size bed, plenty of storage space, unbelievable views' over the sea, beside which a seal was seen to bask as otters fished. Two rooms interconnect for a family of four. In the restaurant, where 'background music was a minor niggle', chef Stuart Russell's locally sourced dishes include 'delicious venison fillet from wild Jura red deer; fish pie, scampi, home made from monkfish', Islay crab. There is a TV lounge, a jolly locals bar with pub fare. You can visit the nearby distillery, catch a boat to Corryvreckan Whirlpool, which nearly swallowed George Orwell before he could finish Nineteen Eighty-Four. Sadly Jura's spectacular new Ardfin golf club may be out of reach. At the time of writing it seems membership will cost more than the average local house. (A and EW)

Craighouse
Isle of Jura PA60 7XU

T: 01496 820243
E: hello@jurahotel.co.uk
W: jurahotel.co.uk

BEDROOMS: 17. 15 en suite, 2 with private bathroom.
OPEN: all year except Christmas and New Year.
FACILITIES: bar, TV lounge, restaurant, outdoor eating area, free Wi-Fi (in bedrooms only), picnic benches, wedding facilities (events shack), public areas wheelchair accessible, no adapted toilet.
BACKGROUND MUSIC: all day in bar and restaurant.
LOCATION: in village, opposite Small Isles Bay, 300 yds from passenger ferry terminal, 7 miles from car ferry terminal.
CHILDREN: all ages welcomed.
DOGS: allowed in pub only.
CREDIT CARDS: MC, Visa.
PRICES: per room B&B single £70, double £105–£135. À la carte £35.

DUNVEGAN Highland   MAP 5:C1

THE THREE CHIMNEYS AND THE HOUSE OVER-BY

Lang may the lums reek at this remote restaurant-with-rooms on the shores of Loch Dunvegan. After 34 years, Shirley and Eddie Spear have moved on, but all is well. The new owner is experienced hotelier Gordon Campbell Gray (see also The Pierhouse, Port Appin), and guests can still expect a welcome with tea and scones, 'delicious food and wine', 'excellent service'. Scott Davies continues in the kitchen of the restaurant in a whitewashed stone crofter's cottage, working with the best produce from 'Skye, Land and Sea', in such dishes as scorched langoustine tails, pickled beetroot, oyster mousse, puffed wild rice; wood-fired Skye red deer, salsify, faggot; with tasting menus for omnivores and vegetarians. In the adjacent House Over-By, suites have a sea view and direct garden access, a king-size bed, minibar, coffee machine, a double-ended bath and 'beautiful, hot shower'. Five are split-level; one is suitable for a wheelchair-user or family (no charge for a child under eight, sharing). Extras include fresh fruit, milk, home-baked goodies, Temple Spa toiletries. In the morning you might spot porpoises as you breakfast on grilled kipper with seaweed butter, haggis or the full Scottish.

Colbost
Dunvegan
Isle of Skye IV55 8ZT

T: 01470 511258
E: eatandstay@threechimneys.co.uk
W: threechimneys.co.uk

BEDROOMS: 6. All on ground floor (5 split-level) in separate building, 1 suitable for disabled.
OPEN: all year except 16 Dec–16 Jan.
FACILITIES: lounge/breakfast room (House Over-By), restaurant, free Wi-Fi, in-room TV (Freeview), wedding facilities, garden on loch, restaurant and lounge wheelchair accessible, adapted toilet.
BACKGROUND MUSIC: in lounge and restaurant, 'for different moods and times of day'.
LOCATION: 5 miles W of Dunvegan.
CHILDREN: all ages welcomed.
DOGS: not allowed.
CREDIT CARDS: Amex, MC, Visa.
PRICES: per room B&B double £360, triple £460. Dinner menu £69, tasting menu £98 (vegetarian £88), kitchen table dinner £110.

EDINBURGH

94DR

NEW

'From the moment I made the inquiry and spoke to Paul, I knew this was going to be a very special place.' A ringing endorsement from a fellow Guide hotelier after a 2019 visit to Paul Lightfoot and John MacEwan's Victorian town house B&B near Holyrood Park. 'On arrival we were greeted by Paul, who gave us a lovely introduction to Edinburgh, how to get around, things to do.' A Guide inspector had a similarly warm welcome, 'with arms round the shoulder and patted back, very personable and helpful'. An entrance hall with 'beautiful period tiles' leads to a lounge with library and honesty bar. A bay-windowed bedroom had a marble fireplace and 'tasteful furnishing scheme', abstract paintings; in the bathroom, underfloor heating, smart toiletries, robes. Front rooms look towards Salisbury Crags, rear ones to the Pentland hills. Breakfast, served in the orangery by the 'very friendly' John, was, continues our reader, 'the best we've had anywhere. Paul makes his own granola every day, with different twists. He comes to the table to explain what he can cook for you.' Our inspector opted for 'avocado, tomato, grilled bacon and poached egg – a great start to the day'. (Richard Burton)

94 Dalkeith Road
Edinburgh EH16 5AF

T: 0131 662 9265
E: stay@94dr.com
W: 94dr.co.uk

BEDROOMS: 6.
OPEN: all year except Christmas Day, 2 weeks in Jan.
FACILITIES: lounge, drawing room, breakfast room, free Wi-Fi, in-room TV (Freeview, Netflix), walled garden, bicycles available to borrow, pop-up dining event twice a month.
BACKGROUND MUSIC: during the day in guest lounge.
LOCATION: A 20-min. walk or a 10-min. bus journey to all amenities.
CHILDREN: 3 and upwards welcomed.
DOGS: not allowed.
CREDIT CARDS: MC, Visa.
PRICES: per room B&B £150–£225. 2-night min. stay weekends Mar–Oct, 4-night min. at New Year.

SEE ALSO SHORTLIST

EDINBURGH

MAP 5:D2

PRESTONFIELD

'Dr Johnson and Mr James Boswell dine here tomorrow – which they did and I gave Mr Johnson rhubarb seeds and some melon.' Here is Sir Alexander Dick, Laird of Prestonfield, writing of visitors to his 17th-century mansion at the foot of Arthur's Seat. A pioneer of rhubarb cultivation, he established the hospitable traditions observed today. In 'grounds with peacocks and Highland cattle', this hotel is owner James Thomson's riposte to corporate blandness. Opulence abounds, with Mortlake tapestries, ancestral portraits, gilded antiques, a sitting room panelled with Cordoban leather. 'Wonderful bedrooms' look over parkland, with views variously of golf course, Royal Holyrood Park, ruined Craigmillar Castle. Each has a mosaic-lined bathroom. Some recall illustrious past guests. The Allan Ramsay suite has a four-poster, silk toile walls, 17th-century furniture. Dick championed rhubarb's medicinal properties. In Rhubarb restaurant it appears in a crumble with ginger ice cream, after, say, breast and pithivier of guineafowl, chard, spiced pear, thyme confit potato. Breakfast brings free-range eggs, kedgeree, hot-smoked salmon. See also The Witchery by the Castle, Edinburgh (Shortlist).

Priestfield Road
Edinburgh EH16 5UT

T: 0131 225 7800
E: reservations@prestonfield.com
W: prestonfield.com

BEDROOMS: 23. 1, on ground floor, suitable for disabled.
OPEN: all year.
FACILITIES: lift, 2 drawing rooms, sitting room, library, whisky bar, restaurant, private dining rooms, free Wi-Fi, in-room TV (Sky), wedding facilities, terraces, tea house, 20-acre grounds, public rooms wheelchair accessible, adapted toilet.
BACKGROUND MUSIC: 'when suitable' in public areas.
LOCATION: next to Royal Holyrood Park.
CHILDREN: all ages welcomed.
DOGS: allowed in bedrooms, public rooms and park, not in restaurant (£25 per dog per night).
CREDIT CARDS: Amex, MC, Visa.
PRICES: per room B&B £345–£575, D,B&B £405–£635. Set dinner £38, à la carte £55.

SEE ALSO SHORTLIST

EDINBURGH

MAP 5:D2

23 MAYFIELD

NEW

A Victorian house on the south side of the
city, built 'to the highest specification' for a tea
merchant and run as a B&B, proved to be precisely
our inspector's cup of Rosie Lee. A 'warm and
friendly' welcome from owner Ross Birnie was
followed by 'a tour of the ground floor, and good
advice on sourcing an evening meal'. 'Tastefully
appointed' bedrooms have a solid, carved
mahogany bed, framed Punch cartoons from
the 1830s, a fridge, a bathroom with underfloor
heating, rain shower. Extras included 'a flagon
of (home-grown) rosemary water, slabs of fudge
made by Ross's mother', Noble Isle toiletries.
Within its smart dark walls, the lounge has a
Georgian chess table, 'plenty of interesting books,
leather seating, newspapers, an honesty bar,
laptop and printer for guest use'. In the morning
the breakfast room was 'a striking scene, with
a candle placed on each table, silver deer-head
napkin rings'. You tick boxes the night before
to order from a menu including 'yogurt topped
with granola, blueberries and whisky-infused
honey, plum tomatoes glazed with thyme, rare
breed Stranraer sausage, beautifully textured
Stornoway black pudding'. Overall verdict: 'Quite
outstanding.'

Mayfield Gardens
Edinburgh EH9 2BX

T: 0131 667 5806
E: info@23mayfield.co.uk
W: 23mayfield.co.uk

BEDROOMS: 7, 1 on ground floor.
OPEN: all year except Christmas.
FACILITIES: club room, breakfast
room, free Wi-Fi, in-room smart TV
(Freeview), terrace, garden, parking.
BACKGROUND MUSIC: at breakfast.
LOCATION: 1 mile S of city centre.
CHILDREN: aged 3 and over welcomed.
DOGS: not allowed.
CREDIT CARDS: MC, Visa.
PRICES: per room B&B £120–£230.
Usually 2-night min. stay but check
availability.

SEE ALSO SHORTLIST

ELIE Fife

MAP 5:D3

THE SHIP INN

NEW

Guide inspectors in 2019 were bowled over by this village pub overlooking the Firth of Forth, with, uniquely, its own beach cricket team. Standing 'right on the beach, on a no-through road', it has been remodelled by Rachel and Graham Bucknall (see also The Bridge Inn at Ratho) and is promoted from the Shortlist. The best bedroom is Admiral, at the top, with sea views, roll-top bath and walk-in shower. Dog-friendly Sir Walter Raleigh, on the ground floor, had 'a clear view of the beach', and was furnished in 'a simple but attractive way', with 'an enormous, comfortable bed' taking most of the space. The 'spotless bathroom' had a 'very efficient walk-in shower, Siabann bath products'. Downstairs, the bar was 'humming'. You can eat here, in an adjoining dining room, and sometimes alfresco – perhaps Cullen skink, Arbroath smokie pâté, fish and chips, plenty for veggies and children. In the upstairs restaurant, Marc Wohner's 'wonderful' menus are strong on local produce. Maybe hake, boulangère potato, confit shallots, asparagus, garlic chive cream. At breakfast fish was off the menu – 'until the fish man arrived at the door'. The staff are 'keen to make sure you are happy'.

The Toft
Elie KY9 1DT

T: 01333 330246
E: info@shipinn.scot
W: shipinn.scot

BEDROOMS: 6.
OPEN: all year, except Christmas Day.
FACILITIES: bar, restaurant, beach bar, free Wi-Fi, in-room TV (Freeview), beer garden/terrace.
BACKGROUND MUSIC: in public areas.
LOCATION: in town, on the bay.
CHILDREN: all ages welcomed.
DOGS: in bar, downstairs restaurant, 2 bedrooms (£15 per stay).
CREDIT CARDS: MC, Visa.
PRICES: per person B&B £110–£185. À la carte £35 (vegetarian/vegan £27).

GAIRLOCH Highland

MAP 5:B1

SHIELDAIG LODGE

Stone eagles mark your arrival at the gates of
Nick and Charlotte Dent's 'impressive' Victorian
hunting lodge, down a single-track road, its
lawns lapped by Loch Gairloch. Beyond the
oak-panelled vestibule, Guide inspectors found
a 'rich and comfortable' ambience, 'deep leather
sofas, crackling fires, an intimate bar stocking
300 whiskies and smelling peatily of Scotch'.
Bedrooms are furnished with antiques. Superior
rooms have stunning loch views; the suite has an
in-room roll-top bath. 'Our room had tweed-
covered armchairs, a table in the window alcove
from which to gaze at starlight', plus fresh milk
and home-made shortbread. A 'handsome'
panelled bathroom was 'beautifully fitted', with
two tall, shuttered windows. In a dining room
with 'gorgeous loch views', Jerome Prodanu's
short menus are devised around locally reared
meat, loch fish and shellfish, home-grown
vegetables. For instance, pan-seared Ardgay estate
pheasant breasts, fondant potato, celeriac, red
cabbage, mustard jus. 'Our meal was good,' writes
a reader, though a promised anniversary cake had
been forgotten. A 'near-perfect breakfast' brings
porridge with maple syrup, vegetarian haggis, the
full Scottish.

Badachro
Gairloch IV21 2AN

T: 01445 741333
E: reservations@shieldaiglodge.com
W: shieldaiglodge.com

BEDROOMS: 12.
OPEN: all year.
FACILITIES: lounge, library, bar,
restaurant, snooker/private dining
room, free Wi-Fi, in-room TV
(Freeview), wedding facilities, garden,
26,000-acre estate (tennis, fishing,
red deer stalking, falconry centre,
motor boat for charter), public areas
wheelchair accessible.
BACKGROUND MUSIC: in lounge, bar and
restaurant.
LOCATION: 4¼ miles S of Gairloch.
CHILDREN: all ages welcomed.
DOGS: not allowed.
CREDIT CARDS: Amex, MC, Visa.
PRICES: per room B&B single £160,
double £220–£320, family £360–£380.
Set dinner £39, tasting menu (on
request) £59.

GLASGOW

MAP 5:D2

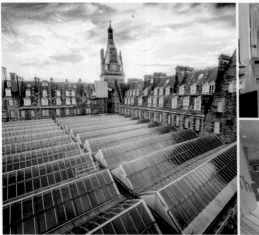

GRASSHOPPERS

Just a hop from Glasgow's cultural attractions, with views across the glass roof of Central Station, Barrie Munn's budget hotel occupies the penthouse floor of a 1905 office building. A trusted reader, having buzzed the intercom and punched in a code, passed through an 'unprepossessing' street door and took the lift. On arrival he received 'a warm welcome from a Scottish hostess', and found 'a small seating area' at one end of a 'brightly lit' corridor. At the other end was The Kitchen, where meals are served, and the day's treats were 'free cakes, mulled wine and ice cream'. His bedroom was 'pod-like but clean, with a wooden floor, a desk with a lamp, a plastic chair'. A shower room, occupying a corner, had a 'sliding door, Villeroy & Boch fittings, Arran Aromatics toiletries'. Another reader, staying in summer, found his room too hot without air conditioning. You should order supper in advance, from a buffet (maybe soup, salads, chicken pie, lamb curry). Our reader ate out, but breakfast was a 'delicious hot buffet, served by a friendly Glaswegian waitress'. Verdict: 'Basic, but clean, modern and superbly located for travellers either staying in or passing through the city.'

25% DISCOUNT VOUCHERS

87 Union Street
Glasgow G1 3TA

T: 0141 222 2666
E: info@grasshoppersglasgow.com
W: grasshoppersglasgow.com

BEDROOMS: 29.
OPEN: all year except 4 days Christmas.
FACILITIES: breakfast/supper room, sitting room with small bar, free Wi-Fi, in-room TV (Sky).
BACKGROUND MUSIC: none.
LOCATION: by Central Station.
CHILDREN: all ages welcomed, cots and extra beds (request at time of booking).
DOGS: allowed.
CREDIT CARDS: Amex, MC, Visa.
PRICES: per room B&B single £68–£108, double £85–£138. À la carte £17.

SEE ALSO SHORTLIST

GLENFINNAN Highland

MAP 5:C1

GLENFINNAN HOUSE HOTEL

In one of the most dramatic settings of any UK hotel, Jane MacFarlane's 18th-century-cum-Victorian mansion stands against a backdrop of woodland and mountain, overlooking Loch Shiel. Since 2002, Manja and Duncan Gibson have been manager and chef. 'Warmth and comfort' pervade public rooms filled with antique and traditional furniture. Oil paintings share a Jacobite theme (the house was built for a bloodied survivor of Culloden). Loch-facing bedrooms have views of the Glenfinnan Monument and distant Ben Nevis. Some rooms have a four-poster or sleigh bed, perhaps an 'enormous' spa bath. For families there are suites and interconnecting rooms. Fresh flowers and fruit are a nice touch. In a bar sprigged with antlers, food choices include nibbles and sandwiches. In the dining room, Duncan's menus include chargrilled steaks, chicken and salmon, maybe home-made venison sausages with sautéed mushrooms, red wine and onion gravy; pumpkin ravioli, minced garlic, Scottish rapeseed oil, rocket leaves. Young fans of Harry Potter might opt for a burger, pasta, fish and chips before heading out to ride the steam train over Robert (Concrete Bob) McAlpine's soaring viaduct. Wizard!

Glenfinnan
Fort William PH37 4LT

T: 01397 722235
E: availability@glenfinnanhouse.com
W: glenfinnanhouse.com

BEDROOMS: 14.
OPEN: 27 Mar–1 Nov.
FACILITIES: drawing room, bar/lounge, playroom, restaurant, wedding facilities, free Wi-Fi, 1-acre grounds (play area), unsuitable for disabled.
BACKGROUND MUSIC: Scottish in bar and restaurant.
LOCATION: 15 miles NW of Fort William.
CHILDREN: all ages welcomed.
DOGS: allowed in bedrooms and some public rooms, not in restaurant or drawing room.
CREDIT CARDS: Amex, MC, Visa.
PRICES: per room B&B single £125–£225, double £145–£245. À la carte £25–£40.

GLENFINNAN Highland

MAP 5:C1

THE PRINCE'S HOUSE

A 17th-century coaching inn at the head of
Loch Shiel is run as a hotel and well-regarded
restaurant by Ina and Kieron Kelly. Bedrooms
are traditionally furnished. Superior doubles have
a king-size bed, mahogany furniture, 'a good
bathroom', Arran Aromatics toiletries. A room
with Jacobean four-poster comes with extras –
bathrobes, fresh flowers, chocolates, whisky mac.
Book ahead to dine in the panelled restaurant
in the oldest part of the house, hung with
paintings by French and Scottish artists. 'Chef par
excellence' Kieron's five-course menus are devised
daily according to what is available from local
suppliers. Typical dishes: organic dry-cured ham
with Strathdon blue cheese, walnuts, trinity of
beets, soft herbs; roast best end of hill lamb, gratin
dauphinoise, Madeira and thyme jus; raspberry,
iced mascarpone, orange. Simpler fare is found
in the Stage House Bistro, a 1980s extension
overlooking a burn, where a blackboard lists such
dishes as grilled hake, lemon, caper and herb
butter sauce; Highland venison steak with Islay
malt whisky and honey glaze. 'I cannot believe
you will get a friendlier welcome or more attentive
service than you do here.' Reports, please.

Glenfinnan
Fort William PH37 4LT

T: 01397 722246
E: princeshouse@glenfinnan.co.uk
W: glenfinnan.co.uk

BEDROOMS: 9.
OPEN: hotel and bistro mid-Mar–end
Oct, 27 Dec–early Jan, restaurant
Easter–end Sept.
FACILITIES: restaurant, bistro/bar, free
Wi-Fi, in-room TV (Freeview), small
front lawn, unsuitable for disabled.
BACKGROUND MUSIC: in bar, bistro, at
breakfast and dinner in restaurant.
LOCATION: 17 miles NW of Fort
William, 330 yards from Glenfinnan
station.
CHILDREN: all ages welcomed.
DOGS: not allowed.
CREDIT CARDS: Amex, MC, Visa.
PRICES: per room B&B single £80–£110,
double £150–£260. Set menu (in
restaurant) 5 courses £55, à la carte (in
bistro) £30.

GRANTOWN-ON-SPEY Highland   MAP 5:C2

CULDEARN HOUSE

'Our stay at William and Sonia Marshall's delightful small country house could not have been bettered,' write Guide regulars. 'We so enjoyed their warm, personal service.' The Victorian villa, built in 1860 for Lord Seafield's daughter, retains the atmosphere of a family home, with open fire, paintings, photographs. Bedrooms are individually styled with a mix of antique and contemporary furniture. Dual-aspect Craigievar has views of the hills of Cromdale and local woodland, a double-ended bath and separate shower. Dunnottar, writes another reader, 'is a lovely room with attractive, soft, blue-patterned wallpaper, not large, but it felt roomy enough'. At 7 pm guests gather for drinks. 'Mr Marshall was there to chat. We had a local gin and tonic with delicious little treats on savoury biscuits.' Sonia Marshall's short menus showcase local produce. 'We had Cullen skink, venison and lamb, cooked to perfection, and for dessert a pavlova with raspberries and passion fruit.' Whisky aficionados are in Scotch heaven. In the morning, 'the breakfast menu offered a wide choice including Scottish favourites such as haggis. . . We picked a winner!' (G and CF, J T-P, and others)

Woodlands Terrace
Grantown-on-Spey PH26 3JU

T: 01479 872106
E: enquiries@culdearn.com
W: culdearn.com

BEDROOMS: 6. 1 on ground floor, with wet room, suitable for disabled.
OPEN: all year except Feb.
FACILITIES: drawing room, dining room, free Wi-Fi, in-room TV (Freeview), ¾-acre garden, public rooms wheelchair accessible.
BACKGROUND MUSIC: none.
LOCATION: edge of town (within walking distance).
CHILDREN: 10 and upwards welcomed, younger children by arrangement.
DOGS: not allowed, except for guide dogs.
CREDIT CARDS: Amex, MC, Visa.
PRICES: per person B&B single £125–£170, double £80–£90, D,B&B £110–£170. À la carte £48.

GRANTOWN-ON-SPEY Highland

MAP 5:C2

THE DULAIG

Some retirees get a gold watch. The Countess
of Seafield did her estate manager, John Smith,
rather better, commissioning this handsome house
for him in 1910. It was designed by Alexander
Marshall Mackenzie, architect of London's
Waldorf Astoria – a smart hotel, indeed, but
lacking in that personal touch which Carol and
Gordon Bulloch bring to their 'idyllic' B&B.
Home comforts include tea and scones by the
fire, home-baked treats delivered daily to guest
rooms. There are 'so many lovely amenities',
write readers, citing 'luxury bedding, heated
bathroom floor and towel racks'. Bedrooms, each
named after an Arts and Crafts designer, have a
handmade bed. Taylor has furniture designed by
Ernest Taylor, a contemporary of Charles Rennie
Mackintosh, Benson has Art Nouveau pieces. All
rooms have a silent mini-fridge, ground coffee,
chocolates, still and sparkling water, Scottish
toiletries. In the garden, red squirrels play and
hens lay eggs for an award-winning breakfast that
includes porridge with heather honey, cream and
malt whisky, local sausages and haggis, potato
scones, scrambled eggs with Glenfeshie hot-
smoked salmon. 'You should go out of your way
to stay.' (NI)

Seafield Avenue
Grantown-on-Spey PH26 3JF

T: 01479 872065
E: enquiries@thedulaig.com
W: thedulaig.com

BEDROOMS: 3.
OPEN: all year except Christmas, New
Year.
FACILITIES: drawing room, dining
room, free Wi-Fi, computer available,
in-room TV (Freesat), 1½-acre garden
(pond, summer house), veranda,
parking (garage for motorbikes and
bicycles), not suitable for disabled.
BACKGROUND MUSIC: quiet Scottish
music at breakfast 'with guests'
permission'.
LOCATION: 600 yards from Grantown-
on-Spey.
CHILDREN: not under 12.
DOGS: only assistance dogs allowed.
CREDIT CARDS: Amex, MC, Visa.
PRICES: per room B&B single
£145–£155, double £185–£195.

GULLANE East Lothian

MAP 5:D3

THE BONNIE BADGER [NEW]

Michelin-starred and Bibbed Edinburgh chef Tom
Kitchin and wife, Michaela, have transformed
the old Golf Inn in this coastal village into a
cutting-edge gastropub-with-rooms. Bedrooms,
in colours reflecting the East Lothian landscape,
have striking wallpaper by artist Mairi Helena, a
coffee machine, marble bathroom with walk-in
shower, bespoke handmade toiletries, perhaps an
in-room bath, an original fireplace. 'The attention
to detail on every account was outstanding,'
writes a reader in 2019. 'We were welcomed with
afternoon tea. To find chocolate and macaroons
when we went to bed was a real surprise.' Public
rooms are a blend of Scottish and Scandi style. In
the Stables dining room, with its dramatic, high-
beamed ceiling, exposed stone walls and towering
fireplace, locally sourced seasonal produce appears
in nature-to-plate modern pub classics – grass-fed
Highland Wagyu burger, spelt and lentil burger,
fish pie, ham, egg and chips, steak pie and bone
marrow. Local man Matthew Budge heads the
kitchen. There is a children's menu, an outdoor
wood-fired oven. Muirfield (and several other golf
courses) and fine Firth of Forth beaches are a tee
shot away. (Lynn Annette Middleton)

Main Street
Gullane EH31 2AB

T: 01620 621111
E: info@bonniebadger.com
W: bonniebadger.com

BEDROOMS: 13. 5 in adjacent cottages.
OPEN: all year except 25 Dec (but
check).
FACILITIES: bar, restaurant, outside
dining room, garden room, private
dining room, garden area, free Wi-Fi,
in-room TV (Sky), wedding facilities,
bar and restaurant wheelchair
accessible, adapted toilet.
BACKGROUND MUSIC: in public areas.
LOCATION: centre of village.
CHILDREN: all ages welcomed.
DOGS: allowed in superior rooms
(£25 a night), in restaurant and pub
area.
CREDIT CARDS: Amex, MC, Visa.
PRICES: per room B&B £195–£470
(£225–£595 around key golf event
days). À la carte £45.

GULLANE East Lothian

MAP 5:D3

GREYWALLS

NEW

'Why is it only on the Shortlist?' asks a reader this year, commending the Weaver family's Edwardian country house hotel with views to the sparkling Firth of Forth across Muirfield golf course. Why indeed? And in our fair way, we've upgraded it. The house, designed by Sir Edwin Lutyens, sits amid 'outstanding' gardens attributed to Gertrude Jekyll, with croquet lawn, tennis court, putting green, lavender border, herb garden and glasshouses. A stay here is 'excellent in every way, from reception to departure'. Bedrooms (some in cottages at the end of the drive) are presented in period style, with antiques, rich hues, harmonious prints; some with views through dual-aspect windows. 'Our ground-floor room was perfect for our accompanying dog.' Public rooms are 'beautifully furnished'. In Chez Roux restaurant, rising culinary star Ryan McCutcheon cooks such dishes as Highland venison, broccoli purée, blue cheese gnocchi, almond skirlie; from the veggie menu, lemon and rosemary gnocchi, seasonal vegetables, butter sauce. Golfers are in heaven, with ten courses within five miles. There are stunning, unspoilt beaches, and all this just a half-hour drive from Edinburgh. (Mrs EA Smith)

Muirfield
Gullane EH31 2EG

T: 01620 842144
E: enquiries@greywalls.co.uk
W: greywalls.co.uk

BEDROOMS: 23, 4 on ground floor, 6 in cottages 100 yards from main house.
OPEN: all year.
FACILITIES: bar/lounge, drawing room, library, restaurant, free Wi-Fi, in-room TV (Freeview), wedding/function facilities, spa treatments, 6-acre garden, tennis court.
BACKGROUND MUSIC: none, pianist on Fri, Sat pm.
LOCATION: 20 miles E of Edinburgh.
CHILDREN: all ages welcomed.
DOGS: allowed in cottage bedrooms, not in public rooms.
CREDIT CARDS: Amex, MC, Visa.
PRICES: per room B&B single £95–£410, double £300–£430. Set dinner £45, à la carte £55.

INVERKEILOR Angus

GORDON'S

'We spent three nights at Gordon's. Maria Watson made us feel as if we were staying in her home.' 'They treated us like old friends, offering superb hospitality.' Glowing reports this year from readers, on this restaurant-with-rooms in a Victorian terrace house in a hamlet close to glorious Lunan Bay. It was opened in 1986 by Maria and her husband, Gordon. They were joined by son Garry, who worked with his father, assuming the chef's toque on Gordon's death in 2016. It is 'a family business in name and substance', with Maria a charming presence front-of-house. Some bedrooms are small, but all are super-stylish, with bold wallpapers and fabrics. Courtyard, a suite with ground-floor access, stand-alone bath and separate shower room, is 'immaculate and spacious'. But: 'The highlight was the food. Each five-course dinner had a different menu and was exquisitely prepared.' Scottish produce figures large in such dishes as Skye scallops, pea purée, duck ham, curry dressing; Angus Scotch beef fillet, artichoke and truffle ravioli, bacon jam, hay-baked celeriac, Rioja jus. And in the morning: 'Needless to say, breakfast was perfect.' (Joan and John Nicholson, Sally and Andy Mehalko)

Main Street
Inverkeilor DD11 5RN

T: 01241 830364
E: gordonsrest@aol.com
W: gordonsrestaurant.co.uk

BEDROOMS: 5. 1 on ground floor in courtyard annexe.
OPEN: all year except Jan.
FACILITIES: lounge, restaurant, free Wi-Fi, in-room TV (terrestrial), small garden and patio, only restaurant wheelchair accessible.
BACKGROUND MUSIC: in restaurant.
LOCATION: in hamlet, 6 miles NE of Arbroath.
CHILDREN: over-12s welcomed (no family rooms).
DOGS: not allowed.
CREDIT CARDS: MC, Visa.
PRICES: per room B&B £110–£165. Set dinner £65.

IONA Argyll and Bute

MAP 5:D1

ARGYLL HOTEL

'Being here makes even a committed atheist feel holy,' wrote a reader after a visit to Iona and a stay at this hotel, occupying a row of crofters' cottages. Or, as Dr Johnson put it, 'That man is little to be envied. . . whose piety would not grow warmer among the ruins of Iona.' It is a magic place, and the Argyll is 'amazing' that same reader avers. Hosts Wendy and Rob MacManaway and Katy and Dafydd Russon create a 'warm, informal' ambience. Bedrooms come in all shapes and sizes, some looking out over the Sound of Iona. One has its own log-burner. For another reader, to sit with a glass of wine, watching the boats at sunset, in 'lawned gardens going down to the rocky shoreline', was 'heavenly'. 'The restaurant prides itself on the use of organic and local ingredients', sustainably landed fish, vegetables home grown and from local crofts. Dinner might bring dill-cured fillet of line-caught mackerel, celeriac and shaved fennel salad; Iona crab, garden herb pâté, rocket, chive oil; loin of hogget, rainbow chard, dauphinoise, roast mooli, parsley and anchovy dressing. More reports, please.

25% DISCOUNT VOUCHERS

Isle of Iona PA76 6SJ

T: 01681 700334
E: reception@argyllhoteliona.co.uk
W: argyllhoteliona.co.uk

BEDROOMS: 17. 7 in linked extension.
OPEN: 27 Mar–23 Oct.
FACILITIES: 3 lounges (1 with TV), conservatory, dining room, free Wi-Fi in public areas, wedding facilities, seafront lawn, organic vegetable garden, lounges/dining room wheelchair accessible, unadapted toilet, one step up.
BACKGROUND MUSIC: modern Scottish, 'gentle' jazz, country music in dining room.
LOCATION: village centre.
CHILDREN: all ages welcomed, under-4s free.
DOGS: max. 2 allowed in bedrooms, not in dining room, sun lounge.
CREDIT CARDS: MC, Visa.
PRICES: per room B&B single £80–£85, double £100–£215. À la carte £35. 1-night bookings often refused (call to check).

KILBERRY Argyll and Bute

KILBERRY INN

'Our 11th yearly visit; David greeted us as old friends.' This restaurant-with-rooms, in a tin-roofed former croft on a single-track road on the Knapdale peninsula, draws devotees back like a magnet. 'A young French couple were there for their third year.' Kilberry Inn is owned by Clare Johnson and David Wilson, she a chef, he a waiter – and also a personable host, who showed our readers to their 'large bedroom'. Occupying single-storey cottages set around a courtyard with raised herb beds, rooms are 'decorated in different, bright colours, and spotlessly clean'. Each has a walk-in shower, fresh milk, home-made shortbread, robes, slippers. Their pleasing simplicity is reflected in the 'high-quality menus', offered in a dining room with rough stone walls and blazing fire. Typical dishes: crab and radicchio gratin; king scallops, cauliflower, hazelnuts, golden sultanas, capers; lamb tajine. Breakfast includes home-made granola, Kintyre eggs, Isle of Ewe smoked salmon, Stornoway black pudding. Let them know if you want to bring your dog, for scenic walks on empty beaches. 'Our location is pretty special,' they say with modest understatement. (GC)

Kilberry
Tarbert PA29 6YD

T: 01880 770223
E: relax@kilberryinn.com
W: kilberryinn.com

BEDROOMS: 5. All on ground floor.
OPEN: Tues–Sun, mid-Mar–end Oct; Fri–Sun, Nov–Dec.
FACILITIES: restaurant, snug (wood-burning stove), variable Wi-Fi (Kilberry is a Wi-Fi 'not-spot'), in-room TV (Freeview), small garden.
BACKGROUND MUSIC: in restaurant at dinner.
LOCATION: 16 miles NW of Tarbert, on B8024.
CHILDREN: not under 12.
DOGS: allowed by arrangement in 2 bedrooms, not in public rooms.
CREDIT CARDS: MC, Visa.
PRICES: per room D,B&B £245. À la carte £37. 1-night bookings sometimes refused holiday weekends.

KILLIECRANKIE Perth and Kinross

KILLIECRANKIE HOTEL

♛ Previous Cesar Winner

'Strongly endorsed' by trusted readers on a return visit, this 'wonderful' whitewashed 1840s dower house at the end of a tree-lined drive displays 'impressive, unchanging excellence'. Guests relax at the hands of an 'attentive team of tartan-clad staff', under the 'personal, hands-on' host Henrietta Fergusson. 'It's always a joy,' say guests this year, 'to watch the great variety of birds which can be seen from windows of the breakfast room and bar.' In winter, such cosy scenes are enhanced in the lounge by a blazing fire and an expansive whisky menu. Bedrooms are 'well-furnished' retreats, handsomely decorated with antique pieces, thick woollen blankets, fresh flowers, and supplied with 'proper wooden' coat-hangers. 'The recently refurbished bathroom takes the bedroom into "wow factor" territory.' In the dining room with its 'rich tasteful colours and sumptuous curtains', Mark Easton's daily-changing menu teems with Rannoch-smoked venison, Perthshire lamb, locally cured gravadlax and crayfish, so benefiting from Killiecrankie's situation at the gateway to the Highlands. The 'nicely tended' garden awaits for a preprandial stroll. (Pauline and Stephen Glover, MK Webster)

25% DISCOUNT VOUCHERS

Killiecrankie
Pitlochry PH16 5LG

T: 01796 473220
E: enquiries@killiecrankiehotel.co.uk
W: killiecrankiehotel.co.uk

BEDROOMS: 10. 2 on ground floor.
OPEN: 23 Mar–3 Jan.
FACILITIES: sitting room, bar with conservatory, dining room, breakfast conservatory, free Wi-Fi, in-room TV (Freeview), 4½-acre grounds (gardens, woodland), public areas wheelchair accessible.
BACKGROUND MUSIC: none.
LOCATION: in hamlet 3 miles W of Pitlochry.
CHILDREN: all ages welcomed.
DOGS: allowed in bar and some bedrooms (not unattended), not in sitting or dining rooms.
CREDIT CARDS: Amex, MC, Visa.
PRICES: per room B&B £135–£250, D,B&B £170–£350. Set dinner £45. 1-night bookings sometimes refused weekends.

KINCLAVEN Perth and Kinross

MAP 5:D2

BALLATHIE HOUSE

A Victorian ghost, a Russian grand duke and a former Prince of Wales have all graced this 'lovely' Scottish country house in a 'delightful position' on the River Tay. It once enjoyed a private stop on a major railway route. Run by the Milligan family since 2005, the turreted and gabled pile certainly doesn't rest on its historical laurels. Roaring fires, inviting sofas and 'numerous monster salmon in glass cases' – a nod to the days when it was famed for Scotland's best autumn fishing – grace the public rooms and wood-panelled bar. Bedrooms, spread across the main house, riverside annexe and lodge, blend traditional grandeur with modern comfort. Those in the house might have an Art Deco bathroom, four-poster, antiques; in the outbuildings, perhaps a patio or balcony. Tay views spill into the elegant dining room (with hand-painted birds and vines on the walls), where the farm-to-fork ethos underpins Scott Scorer's 'skilfully prepared' seasonal modern Scottish dishes: say, Perthshire lamb racks, mint and parsley salsa, aubergine purée; chargrilled Hebridean salmon, lemon and dill butter. Breakfast brings porridge, a kipper, Stornoway black pudding, local sausages.

Kinclaven
Stanley PH1 4QN

T: 01250 883268
E: email@ballathiehousehotel.com
W: ballathiehousehotel.com

BEDROOMS: 53. 14 in riverside building, 11 in Sportsman's Lodge, some on ground floor, 1 suitable for disabled.
OPEN: all year.
FACILITIES: lounge, morning room, bar, restaurant, terrace room, private dining rooms, free Wi-Fi, in-room TV (Freeview), wedding/function facilities, 11-acre estate (golf, fishing, shooting), public rooms wheelchair accessible, adapted toilet.
BACKGROUND MUSIC: none.
LOCATION: 1½ miles SW of Kinclaven.
CHILDREN: all ages welcomed.
DOGS: allowed in some bedrooms (not unattended), not in public rooms.
CREDIT CARDS: MC, Visa.
PRICES: per person B&B single £117–£162, double £82–£127, D,B&B £122–£168. Set dinner £55.

KINGUSSIE Highland

MAP 5:C2

THE CROSS AT KINGUSSIE

♀ Previous Cesar Winner

'Derek and Celia are skilled and charming hosts.
We cannot speak too highly of them.' Warm
approval this year from a Guide reader, for
the Kitchingmans' restaurant-with-rooms in a
converted Victorian tweed mill. Bedrooms are
'very well equipped', supplied with fresh coffee,
biscuits, Arran Aromatics toiletries. 'Our room
had a lovely view over the Gynack Burn, with
the soothing sound of mountain water rattling
over stones.' Pine furniture seemed a little passé,
pictures and ornaments almost too numerous;
'But I quibble; it was very comfortable.' The
dining room has beams, stone walls, an open
fire. 'Delicious canapés arrived with our drinks.'
Chef David Skiggs displays impressive skill. A
'beautifully cooked' quail and foie gras starter
was followed by 'perfectly cooked' halibut, a
'wonderfully tender' steak, strawberry cheesecake
with a 'fantastic' sorbet. Breakfast brought freshly
squeezed orange juice, 'good pain au chocolat',
'faultless' smoked haddock with poached egg.
Sit on the terrace by the burn and you might spot
herons, red squirrel, roe deer. 'The location is
beautiful and one is unaware that the hotel is in a
town.' (David Birnie)

Ardbroilach Road
Kingussie PH21 1LB

T: 01540 661166
E: relax@thecross.co.uk
W: thecross.co.uk

BEDROOMS: 8.
OPEN: closed Christmas and Jan,
except Hogmanay, Sun and Mon.
FACILITIES: 2 lounges, restaurant, free
Wi-Fi, in-room TV (Freeview), 4-acre
grounds (terraced garden, woodland),
restaurant wheelchair accessible.
BACKGROUND MUSIC: none.
LOCATION: 440 yds from village centre.
CHILDREN: all ages welcomed.
DOGS: not allowed.
CREDIT CARDS: Amex, MC, Visa.
PRICES: per room B&B £100–£200,
D,B&B £200–£280. Set 3-course
dinner £55, 6-course tasting menu
£65. À la carte £55.

KIRKBEAN Dumfries and Galloway

MAP 5:E2

CAVENS

'A rare combination of relaxed professionalism, with high standards from Angus and Jane Fordyce, made us feel very cared for.' Readers this year recall a stay at this Georgian country house hotel, built in 1752 for the Oswald family, who planted the yews and giant rhododendrons in the landscaped grounds. Rabbie Burns visited and penned the insulting ode to Mrs Oswald displayed in Oswald bedroom, with its wall of windows. She may indeed have been an old skinflint; the Fordyces could not be more generous. All bedrooms are lavishly furnished. Ground-floor Solway and dual-aspect Criffel are huge. 'The decor is Scottish Country House, with good paintings and interesting objects'; log fires, oriental rugs. Angus Fordyce draws on local suppliers for his short menus, which might include pan-fried sole with caper sauce; grilled sirloin of Galloway beef. 'Five nights somewhat challenge the menu but we especially enjoyed the very fresh plaice and the crunchy lemon brûlée.' There are interesting wines, but half bottles and more by the glass would be welcome. At breakfast, there are locally made sausages, local bacon. 'We hae meat and we can eat, so let the Lord be thanket!' (Frances and David Thomas)

Kirkbeans DG2 8AA

T: 01387 880234
E: enquiries@cavens.com
W: cavens.com

BEDROOMS: 6. 1 on ground floor.
OPEN: Mar–Nov, exclusive use by groups at New Year.
FACILITIES: 2 sitting rooms, dining room, wine cellar, meeting facilities, free Wi-Fi, in-room TV (Freeview), 10-acre grounds.
BACKGROUND MUSIC: light classical all day in 1 sitting room, dining room.
LOCATION: in village.
CHILDREN: all ages welcomed.
DOGS: allowed by arrangement, not in public rooms or unattended in bedrooms.
CREDIT CARDS: MC, Visa.
PRICES: per room D,B&B £200–£3,300. 1-night bookings refused Easter, bank holidays.

KYLESKU Highland

MAP 5:B2

KYLESKU HOTEL

♲ Previous Cesar Winner

Sit on the decking at this former 17th-century
coaching inn overlooking Loch Glendhu, and
watch basking seals – or supper being landed on
the old ferry slipway. Owners Tanja Lister and
Sonia Virechauveix are 'wonderful, charming,
full of energy, completely focused on keeping the
hotel's edge', writes a regular visitor this year.
The staff are 'clearly part of a large family with
shared values and a focus on guests'. The interior
has a stripped-down look, 'almost Scandinavian
in style', bare floorboards, wood-burners, loch
views through big windows. Most bedrooms are
in the main house, but the best are the four in
the annexe, Willie's Hoose – one that can sleep
four, one with wheelchair access, all facing the
loch. Limited Wi-Fi is a fair trade-off for vast,
empty beaches and a star-filled dark sky. Jo
Christison's food has a simplicity which allows
ingredients to shine. 'They work closely with local
suppliers – the pigs are exercised on a beach, and
so on.' Lobsters, langoustines and crabs are creel
caught, mussels rope grown, scallops hand dived.
A 'magnificent shellfish bisque' was enjoyed at
lunch. 'We are keen to return for a longer stay.'
(Robert Gower, and others)

Kylesku IV27 4HW

T: 01971 502231
E: info@kyleskuhotel.co.uk
W: kyleskuhotel.co.uk

BEDROOMS: 11. 4 in annexe, 1 suitable
for disabled.
OPEN: mid-Feb–end Nov.
FACILITIES: lounge, bar, restaurant,
free Wi-Fi in bar and lounge, in-room
TV (Freeview), small garden (tables
for outside eating), area of lounge and
dining room wheelchair accessible,
toilet not adapted.
BACKGROUND MUSIC: from 10 am, in
bar and half the dining area.
LOCATION: 10 miles S of Scourie.
CHILDREN: all ages welcomed.
DOGS: allowed (£10 a night to a max.
£40 a stay), but not unattended in
bedrooms.
CREDIT CARDS: MC, Visa.
PRICES: per room B&B single £79–£120,
double £120–£190. À la carte £45.

LOCHEPORT Western Isles

MAP 5: inset A1

LANGASS LODGE

On an island of long, white-sand beaches, lochs, peat bogs and tidal strands, Amanda and Niall Leveson Gower run their 'handsome' white-painted sporting lodge as a family-friendly hotel. Lodge bedrooms are snug and traditional. There are larger ones in a 'slightly barn-like' annexe built into the hillside. Readers found theirs 'stylishly furnished', with rugs on bare floorboards, French windows on to a little terrace. There was a large shower, a rather small bath, 'very powerful radiators'. Off the 'cosy bar', the conservatory has 'big sofas and tables'. You can eat here, à la carte, or from a daily-changing menu in the restaurant, with 'fabulous views over the pretty little garden, across Loch Eport to Ben Eaval'. Chef Mike MacDonald uses locally fished, foraged, dived and hunted produce in such dishes as pan-fried hake, pea purée, creamy mashed potato, butter peas; seafood platter; a mixed grill of venison, rolled lamb flank, wood pigeon, pig's trotter croquette, braised red cabbage, broccoli, hazelnut polenta, game jus. North Uist is 'a paradise for wildlife', where you will spot otter and seal, hear the rasp of the corncrake. Amanda is a fount of knowledge on the best walks.

Locheport
Isle of North Uist HS6 5HA

T: 01876 580285
E: langasslodge@btconnect.com
W: langasslodge.co.uk

BEDROOMS: 11. Some in extension, 1 suitable for disabled.
OPEN: Apr–end Oct.
FACILITIES: conservatory, bar, restaurant, free Wi-Fi, in-room TV (Freeview), 11-acre garden in 200-acre grounds, bar and restaurant wheelchair accessible, adapted toilet.
BACKGROUND MUSIC: in public rooms.
LOCATION: 7½ miles SW of Lochmaddy.
CHILDREN: all ages welcomed (2 family rooms, extra beds, children's menu).
DOGS: allowed in bedrooms and public rooms, not in restaurant.
CREDIT CARDS: MC, Visa.
PRICES: per room B&B single £95–£130, double £105–£165, family room £150–£240. À la carte (bar) £34, set menu (restaurant) £35–£40.

MUIR OF ORD Highland   MAP 5:C2

THE DOWER HOUSE

A former dowager's residence owned by the
Mackenzies of Highfield, this enchanting
stone cottage-orné is a 'gem' of a B&B run by
'lovely' owners Robyn and Mena Aitchison.
Wisteria scrambles over the slate roof. Every
room has fresh-cut flowers from the brimming
garden, which has a large pond and 'benches
everywhere'. The interior is a treasure trove of
objets, clocks and candlesticks. In the sitting room
winged armchairs are drawn up to a log-burner.
Bookshelves are jam-packed. Bedrooms have
antiques, paintings, original features, personality.
Bathrooms have a roll-top, claw-footed Victorian
bath, Arran Aromatics toiletries. The hosts no
longer offer an evening meal, but Coul House,
Contin (see entry), is only 15 minutes' drive
away. A first-rate breakfast includes eggs from
the resident free-range hens. Four-times prime
minister William Ewart Gladstone used the
property as a shooting lodge (who knows if it was
here that he shot a finger off?). Today's guests
come for the salmon fishing, to play golf, to hit the
Whisky Trail, go dolphin and whale spotting, or
just to soak up the serene beauty of the Highlands.

Highfield
Muir of Ord IV6 7XN

T: 01463 870090
E: info@thedowerhouse.co.uk
W: thedowerhouse.co.uk

BEDROOMS: 3. All on ground floor, plus
small self-contained 2-bed flat.
OPEN: Apr–Oct.
FACILITIES: lounge, dining room, snug/
TV room, free Wi-Fi, in-room TV
(Freeview), 5-acre grounds.
BACKGROUND MUSIC: none.
LOCATION: 14 miles NW of Inverness.
CHILDREN: all ages welcomed.
DOGS: maximum 2 allowed in
bedrooms (not on bed or furniture),
not in public rooms.
CREDIT CARDS: MC, Visa.
PRICES: per room B&B single
£120–£135, double £145–£165.

MUTHILL Perth and Kinross

MAP 5:D2

BARLEY BREE

Chef/patron Fabrice Bouteloup loves working with game at this coaching inn-turned-restaurant-with-rooms in the rural village of 'Mew-thil'. Bag a bird and he'll cook it for you. His wife, Alison, is a wine expert. Concise three-course menus reveal a passion for seasonal, locally raised, grown, caught or shot produce. Typical dishes: guineafowl supreme, lemon and parsley, chorizo, cannellini beans, little gem; halibut fillet, salsify, wilted spinach, Vitelotte potato, tarragon beurre blanc; always an apple tarte Tatin. From amuse-bouche to dessert, everything is 'very tasty, and attractively presented'. Bread, ice cream, anything that can be, is home made. There are menus for vegetarians and children. To stump up a £2.25 supplement for extra gravy might be pushing the boat out. Still, readers praise the 'superb welcome and service', the 'cosy bar and restaurant, with real fires'. Bedrooms, 'decorated in neutral colours', are 'spotlessly clean, and inviting'. Most have a shower; one has an original fireplace, a sofa, roll-top bath, separate shower. At breakfast there is 'the usual buffet', French toast with bacon, smoked salmon and more. 'We very much enjoyed our visit.' (RL)

25% DISCOUNT VOUCHERS

6 Willoughby Street
Muthill PH5 2AB

T: 01764 681451
E: info@barleybree.com
W: barleybree.com

BEDROOMS: 6.
OPEN: all year except 24–26 Dec, various dates throughout year (see website), restaurant closed Mon, Tues.
FACILITIES: lounge bar, restaurant, free Wi-Fi, in-room TV (Freeview), small terrace and lawn, drying facilities, restaurant wheelchair accessible, toilet not adapted.
BACKGROUND MUSIC: none.
LOCATION: village centre.
CHILDREN: all ages welcomed.
DOGS: assistance dogs only.
CREDIT CARDS: MC, Visa.
PRICES: per room B&B £99–£160. À la carte £48.

OBAN Argyll and Bute

MAP 5:D1

THE MANOR HOUSE

With 'wonderful views from the terrace, and handy for the ferry terminal', Leslie and Margaret Crane's hotel looks out across Oban Bay to the isles of Lismore and Mull. It was from Mull that Dr Johnson and Boswell sailed in 1773, sitting on the ferry floor, to find in Oban a 'tolerable inn'. They would do better today. The stone manor house, built in 1780 for the Duke of Argyll, has cosy period interiors, a lounge replete with comfy sofas. Bedrooms, on the snug side, display a warmly traditional style, some with antiques. Posh toiletries and binoculars are supplied. One of two larger sea-view rooms would be first choice. Guests can lunch in Nelson's bar, on West Coast fish pie, deep-fried haddock, pea and mint risotto. At dinner, items from the five-course fixed-price menu can be ordered individually. Award-winning chef Gerard McCluskey uses local meat and game, freshly landed fish, organic fruit and vegetables, in such dishes as pepper-crusted Argyll venison, mixed vegetable pearls, consommé, red chard and pommes purée; squid ink tagliatelle, mixed seafood in creamy mussel sauce. A 'hearty' breakfast brings oak-smoked salmon and Inverawe kippers. (C and PB)

Gallanach Road
Oban PA34 4LS

T: 01631 562087
E: info@manorhouseoban.com
W: manorhouseoban.com

BEDROOMS: 11. 1 on ground floor.
OPEN: all year except 24–26 Dec.
FACILITIES: lounge, bar, restaurant, free Wi-Fi, in-room TV (Freeview), wedding facilities, 1½-acre grounds, private car park, deep water mooring, access to nearby gym and golf.
BACKGROUND MUSIC: traditional in bar and restaurant.
LOCATION: ½ mile from centre.
CHILDREN: not under 12.
DOGS: allowed in bedroom by arrangement, not unattended, not in public rooms.
CREDIT CARDS: Amex, MC, Visa.
PRICES: per room B&B £140–£295, D,B&B £230–£393. Set dinner £49, all dishes available à la carte.

SEE ALSO SHORTLIST

PEAT INN Fife   MAP 5:D3

THE PEAT INN

In the middle of nowhere, this 18th-century coaching inn-turned-gastronomic destination defines the village to which it gives its name. Awarded Scotland's first Michelin star in 1987, it has been owned by Katherine and Geoffrey Smeddle since 2006, regaining the star, in 2010, which it retains to this day. It's a 'very special' place, with light, contemporary decor and splashes of colour, along with 'a warm welcome' for new arrivals. The bedroom suites are in the Residence, a separate building with a 'big window' overlooking the 'well-tended' garden. All but one room is split level: steps lead down to a 'very comfortable' bedroom and 'well-equipped' bathroom; up to a sitting room, where you can take breakfast. At the front of the restaurant is a lounge with padded banquette seats and an open fire. Mr Smeddle's style is modern Scottish, showcasing the country's finest seasonal ingredients in such dishes as herb-roasted breast of guineafowl, Anster and potato gratin, scarlet elf cap mushrooms, glazed baby shallots, cider and thyme velouté. 'Everything is served looking beautiful.' The ambience is 'unhurried', service 'impeccable'. 'Not cheap but very luxurious.'

Peat Inn
Cupar KY15 5LH

T: 01334 840206
E: stay@thepeatinn.co.uk
W: thepeatinn.co.uk

BEDROOMS: 8. All suites, on ground floor in annexe, 7 split-level, 1 suitable for disabled.
OPEN: all year except 1 week Christmas, 1 week Jan, open from 28 Dec for Hogmanay, restaurant closed Sun/Mon.
FACILITIES: lounge in restaurant, Wi-Fi, in-room TV (terrestrial), ½-acre garden, restaurant wheelchair accessible, adapted toilet.
BACKGROUND MUSIC: in restaurant.
LOCATION: 6 miles SW of St Andrews.
CHILDREN: all ages welcomed, no under-7s at dinner, no under-14s unaccompanied in suite.
DOGS: not allowed.
CREDIT CARDS: Amex, MC, Visa.
PRICES: per room B&B single £215, double £235–£260. Set dinner £58, à la carte £65, tasting menu £78.

PITLOCHRY Perth and Kinross

DALSHIAN HOUSE

You can tour the Edradour distillery in bustling
Pitlochry – but why bother? Guests staying at
Martin and Heather Walls's 'blissfully remote'
Georgian house B&B can start the day with a nip
of the whisky in their porridge, or sip a tot while
relaxing with a book by the wood-burning stove.
In this Victorian town, something is always afoot,
from Winter Words at the Festival Theatre and
the March into Pitlochry music jamboree, to the
annual Highland Games. Golf and fishing await
nearby but here, so near and yet so far from town,
utter peace prevails. This is no boutique hotel.
Everything, from the comfy lounge with sink-
into sofas, a tartan carpet and magazines, to the
bedrooms, has the feel of a private home: a 'warm,
friendly' mix of the traditional and contemporary.
There is shortbread on the hospitality tray, and
you can ask for a packed lunch before setting off
to explore, or simply relax in gardens surrounded
by woodland, spotting birds and red squirrels. An
'outstanding' breakfast brings Earl Grey-infused
figs, organic free-range eggs, Dunkeld smoked
salmon, tattie scones. For dinner try the Green
Park (next entry), as you pat your pockets and
contemplate what you saved on B&B.

Old Perth Road
Pitlochry PH16 5TD

T: 01796 472173
E: dalshian@btconnect.com
W: dalshian.co.uk

BEDROOMS: 7.
OPEN: all year except Christmas.
FACILITIES: lounge, dining room, free
Wi-Fi, in-room TV (Freeview), 1-acre
garden, unsuitable for disabled.
BACKGROUND MUSIC: none.
LOCATION: 1 mile S of centre.
CHILDREN: all ages welcomed.
DOGS: allowed by arrangement, not in
public rooms.
CREDIT CARDS: MC, Visa.
PRICES: per person B&B £37–£45, single
occupancy £60, 1-night bookings
refused New Year.

SEE ALSO SHORTLIST

PITLOCHRY Perth and Kinross

MAP 5:D2

THE GREEN PARK

Previous César Winner

Bright gardens, dotted with sculptures, and a sweep of lawns tumble down to a private lochside terrace from this Victorian country house, where many thoughtful touches 'set the hotel apart'. 'On a scorching day, iced water was on constant offer.' The multigenerational McMenemie family, helped by 'warm, friendly staff', treat visitors 'like royalty'. The many returning guests especially appreciate the little details: the guide to British birds and the binoculars in the book-filled lounge, 'and as much sherry as one likes before dinner'. Spread across the main house and separate wings, corridors are hung with 'quality watercolours', and the 'spacious, immaculately clean' bedrooms have a well-equipped drinks tray, a fridge, local organic handmade toiletries. Balcony bedrooms have lovely loch views from the two deckchairs and table on an iron-railed balcony. In the dining room, 'we enjoyed succulent salmon' from Chris Tamblin's modern Franco-Scottish 'good-value' menu. Minor dissent: the all-day coffee was in a Thermos and accompanied by 'tired-looking cakes', and the public rooms 'could do with an upgrade. There is inconsistency in the striving for excellence.' (PG, JT, and others)

Clunie Bridge Road
Pitlochry PH16 5JY

T: 01796 473248
E: bookings@thegreenpark.co.uk
W: thegreenpark.co.uk

BEDROOMS: 51. 16 on ground floor, 1 suitable for disabled.
OPEN: all year except Christmas.
FACILITIES: 2 lifts, lounge bar, main lounge, sun lounge, free Wi-Fi, in-room TV (BT, Freeview), 3-acre garden, public areas wheelchair accessible.
BACKGROUND MUSIC: none.
LOCATION: ½ mile N of town centre.
CHILDREN: all ages welcomed.
DOGS: allowed in bedrooms, not in public rooms.
CREDIT CARDS: MC, Visa.
PRICES: per person B&B £89–£99, D,B&B £101–£128. Set dinner £30. No supplement for singles.

SEE ALSO SHORTLIST

PITLOCHRY Perth and Kinross   MAP 5:D2

KNOCKENDARROCH HOTEL

♥ Previous César Winner

'A real centre of hospitality.' Trusted Guide
readers visiting Struan and Louise Lothian's small
hotel were impressed this year by the 'attentive
but never intrusive service and the superb meals'.
The 'good-humoured' hotel team went the extra
mile. 'When our car slipped on the icy drive, we
were immediately rescued by a staff member.
Next morning, while surrounding roads were
snowy, the drive was immaculate.' Two fires
burn in the 'inviting' lounges with a whisky
cabinet, shelves of books, well-matched sofas and
leather armchairs. A 'comfortable without being
luxurious' premium room had 'a sofa, attractive
bedside lamps, thick full-length curtains, a small
bathroom with Scottish Fine Soaps toiletries'.
A balcony and binoculars exploit widescreen
views from the top-floor bedrooms; a vista of
Ben Vrackie can be seen from those at the front.
Come evening, promoted chef Nick Imrie's
daily-changing menus earn high praise. 'The
outstandingly delicious pecan cheesecake trifle
was worth the calories. Equally fine was a crab
cake, followed by a perfectly cooked rack of lamb.'
Breakfast was 'just as good', although 'no freshly
squeezed juice'. (Robert Gower, GF)

Higher Oakfield
Pitlochry PH16 5HT

T: 01796 473473
E: bookings@knockendarroch.co.uk
W: knockendarroch.co.uk

BEDROOMS: 14. 2 on ground floor.
OPEN: Feb–15 Dec.
FACILITIES: 2 lounges, restaurant,
free Wi-Fi, in-room TV (Freeview),
2-acre wooded garden, bicycle storage,
unsuitable for disabled.
BACKGROUND MUSIC: in restaurant in
evening.
LOCATION: central.
CHILDREN: not under 10.
DOGS: not allowed.
CREDIT CARDS: Amex, MC, Visa.
PRICES: per room B&B £155–£305,
D,B&B £205–£355. Set dinner
£46. 1-night bookings sometimes
refused Sat.

SEE ALSO SHORTLIST

PITLOCHRY Perth and Kinross

MAP 5:D2

RIVERWOOD

A contemporary Arts and Crafts-style house, in large grounds on the edge of a conservation village, is home to Ann and Alf Berry's 'tranquil' B&B. Fringed by the silvery Tay river, on which you can fly-fish for brown trout, it has 'beautiful' natural gardens including a forest with oaks, bluebells and wild garlic. Inside 'it's all very relaxing', helped by log fires and a smart lounge with chocolate-hued sofas and book-lined cabinets; the hosts' no-outdoor-shoes preference keeps it pristine. Comfort is equally important. A white-and-dove palette marks the 'spacious', crisply contemporary bedrooms. Alongside river views, each has a Nespresso machine and mini-fridge; a bathroom with Arran Aromatics toiletries, robes, underfloor heating. Suites, each named after a local Victorian building, include one with a private hallway, lounge and walk-in dressing room; others have a garden patio. 'The food is superb.' Locally sourced dinners are served on certain nights. Every morning the 'ever-attentive' Alf delivers Ann's 'wonderful breakfast', from griddled pancakes to Dunkeld smoked salmon, and French toast with crispy bacon. Pitlochry's theatres are a 12-minute drive away.

Strathtay
Pitlochry PH9 0PG

T: 01887 840751
E: info@riverwoodstrathtay.com
W: riverwoodstrathtay.com

BEDROOMS: 7. 4 suites on ground floor.
OPEN: 6 Feb–14 Dec, dinner available on selected days (check website).
FACILITIES: lounge/dining room, library, free Wi-Fi, in-room TV (Freeview), 4½-acre grounds (lawns, woodland, fishing), complimentary access to nearby golf course.
BACKGROUND MUSIC: 'easy listening' in dining room at mealtimes.
LOCATION: in village, 9½ miles SW of Pitlochry.
CHILDREN: not under 12.
DOGS: not allowed.
CREDIT CARDS: MC, Visa.
PRICES: per room B&B £110–£155, D,B&B (on selected nights) £180–£215. À la carte £35. 1-night bookings sometimes refused in peak season.

SEE ALSO SHORTLIST

POOLEWE Highland

POOL HOUSE

For over 30 years, the Harrison family has greeted visitors to their former 18th-century fishing lodge with 'genuine warmth and interest'. The house brims with antiques and curios (a suit of armour; century-old family snaps), open fires and 'a terrific library', now with a cinema area. Sisters Elizabeth and Mhairi ensconce arriving guests in the drawing room for 'a marvellous afternoon tea – just right after a long drive'. The Harrison pater takes over hosting duties in the evening, serving anecdotes with preprandial cocktails. Dinner, in the formal dining room, 'which catches the light of the setting sun' through huge picture windows, includes 'perfectly portioned' dishes. Perhaps 'delicious falafels', roasted venison with sweet-and-sour parsnips, 'a fresh-tasting Granny Smith apple sorbet'. 'We were perfectly comfortable in our enormous suite. The bed was a dream, while the handsome Edwardian bathroom was bigger than some London flats. Otter-spotting with the room's binoculars was an unexpected delight.' Come morning, 'excellent coffee' and 'a delicious full Scottish', ordered the night before, provided 'plentiful fuel for a wander through Inverewe Garden across Loch Ewe'.

25% DISCOUNT VOUCHERS

by Inverewe Garden
Poolewe IV22 2LD

T: 01445 781272
E: enquiries@pool-house.co.uk
w: pool-house.co.uk

BEDROOMS: 3 suites.
OPEN: Apr–Oct, closed Mon except bank holidays, dining room closed Sun–Tues and Thurs (soup and sandwiches available).
FACILITIES: reception room, drawing room/library, dining room, private dining room, billiard/whisky room, free Wi-Fi in public areas, in-room TV (Freeview), ½-acre garden, unsuitable for disabled.
BACKGROUND MUSIC: none.
LOCATION: in village 6 miles NE of Gairloch.
CHILDREN: not under 14.
DOGS: not allowed.
CREDIT CARDS: Amex, MC, Visa.
PRICES: per room B&B £225–£325. Set menu £48. 1-night bookings refused weekends.

PORT APPIN Argyll and Bute

MAP 5:D1

♥THE AIRDS HOTEL

César award: Scottish luxury hotel of the year

'A real star, we enjoyed our stay,' enthuse Guide regulars, who visited several hotels on either side of this year's Scottish cruise. 'It was by far our favourite.' High praise for Shaun and Jenny McKivragan's hotel beside Loch Linnhe with views to the Morvern mountains. What started life as an early 18th-century ferry inn is today a chic gourmet destination (Relais & Châteaux). Individually designed, 'clean and comfortable' bedrooms have designer fabrics and wallpaper, Frette linen, Bulgari toiletries, robes, slippers, whisky mac. Most have a loch view, two a balcony, one a suntrap patio. This is a family-friendly place, with high tea for under-eights. 'Everything is so personal.' Guests can take a cream tea by the fire in one of the lounges, or alfresco. The restaurant's 'really talented chef', Chris Stanley, exploits West Coast and home-grown produce. 'The freshest fish and shellfish we've ever had.' Typical dishes: pan-seared monkfish, cauliflower, leeks, pommes galette; fillet of Scottish beef, pommes Anna, wild garlic. Breakfast delivers freshly squeezed juices, bannocks, Ayrshire bacon, Finnan haddock, free-range eggs. 'Would certainly return.' (Barbara Watkinson, FM, SS)

Port Appin PA38 4DF

T: 01631 730236
E: airds@airds-hotel.com
W: airds-hotel.com

BEDROOMS: 11. 2 on ground floor, plus 2 self-catering cottages.
OPEN: all year, restaurant closed Mon/Tues Nov–end Jan (open Christmas and New Year).
FACILITIES: 2 lounges, conservatory, whisky bar, restaurant, wedding facilities, free Wi-Fi, in-room TV (Freeview), spa treatments, ½-acre garden, unsuitable for disabled.
BACKGROUND MUSIC: none.
LOCATION: 20 miles N of Oban.
CHILDREN: all ages welcomed, no under-8s in dining room in evening (children's high tea).
DOGS: allowed in bedrooms (not unattended) and conservatory.
CREDIT CARDS: MC, Visa.
PRICES: per room D,B&B single £285–£515, double £320–£550. Set dinner £60.

PORT APPIN Argyll and Bute   MAP 5:D1

THE PIERHOUSE

'In the most beautiful position, with sea, islands
and mountains in full view', this former Victorian
piermaster's house stands 'right on the shores of
Loch Linnhe'. New owner Gordon Campbell
Gray has made a few tweaks (some new carpets,
lamps, artwork in the restaurant), but the ethos
remains 'relaxed and friendly' as ever, with
'welcoming' staff. All bedrooms, from a double-
aspect sea-view room, to those with a cliff view,
have a super-comfortable bed, shortbread,
sparkling and still water, Arran Aromatics
toiletries. Our inspector's room, 'decorated
in cream and beige', had 'two armchairs, a
small bathroom with tiny but efficient shower.
Everything was clean and well maintained.'
There is 'a real buzz' in the restaurant, where
Sergejs Savickis's menus are strong on fish and
seafood, perhaps 'delicious Cullen skink', a large
shellfish platter ('getting through it was quite an
adventure'), and such vegan choices as pea and
truffle risotto. A reader 'enjoyed the snug in the
evenings, with stove and a glass of malt'. Breakfast
brings fresh-baked croissants, kippers, Inverawe
smoked salmon, home-made jams. 'We loved our
stay.' (Michael and Patricia Blanchard, and others)

Port Appin PA38 4DE

T: 01631 730302
E: reservations@pierhousehotel.co.uk
W: pierhousehotel.co.uk

BEDROOMS: 12.
OPEN: all year except 24–26 Dec.
FACILITIES: residents' snug, lounge,
bar, restaurant, private dining room,
free Wi-Fi, in-room TV (Freeview),
wedding facilities, sauna, in-room spa
treatments, terrace, yacht moorings,
unsuitable for disabled.
BACKGROUND MUSIC: in bar and
restaurant.
LOCATION: in village, 20 miles N of
Oban.
CHILDREN: all ages welcomed (cots,
high chairs).
DOGS: well-behaved dogs allowed in
3 bedrooms (not unattended), not in
public rooms (£15 per night).
CREDIT CARDS: Amex, MC, Visa.
PRICES: per room B&B £125–£295
(single occupancy of cliff-facing room,
Sun–Thurs, Nov–Mar, £85). À la carte
£35–£40.

PORTPATRICK Dumfries and Galloway   MAP 5:E1

KNOCKINAAM LODGE

'A very special place,' say guests in 2019, of Sian
and David Ibbotson's Victorian hunting lodge
overlooking the Irish Sea. 'The accommodating
hosts went out of their way, more than once, to
ensure we had a terrific time.' Reached by a long
driveway through wooded cliffs, the house made
a discreet retreat for Churchill and Eisenhower's
D-Day planning in 1944 – an old radar station
nearby is called Hush Hush. It's still 'fabulously
tranquil' today. The country-style lounge is the
spot for leaf tea and 'the finest scones I have
tasted'; evenings are for sampling some of the
120-plus single malts in the bar with its fire and
leather wingback chairs. In the restaurant, Tony
Pierce's modern Scottish fare, including slow-
roast Angus beef, shallot purée, potato terrine,
wild mushrooms, port and thyme reduction, is
'delicate, well judged, perfectly executed'. Rooms
have a warm, traditional style, bathrobes and
upmarket Scottish toiletries. Whin has widescreen
sea views through triple-aspect windows;
Churchill, where the PM stayed, has a super-king-
size sleigh bed, original fireplace and century-old
enamelled concrete tub. 'I can't recommend it
highly enough.' (Deborah Loveluck)

25% DISCOUNT VOUCHERS

Portpatrick DG9 9AD

T: 01776 810471
E: reservations@knockinaamlodge.
com
W: knockinaamlodge.com

BEDROOMS: 10.
OPEN: all year, speciality weekends at
Christmas and New Year.
FACILITIES: 2 lounges, bar, restaurant,
Wi-Fi, in-room TV (Freeview),
wedding facilities, 20-acre grounds,
public areas wheelchair accessible.
BACKGROUND MUSIC: 'easy listening'/
classical in restaurant in evening.
LOCATION: 3 miles S of Portpatrick.
CHILDREN: all ages welcomed, no
under-12s in dining room, children's
high tea provided.
DOGS: allowed in some bedrooms,
grounds, not in public rooms.
CREDIT CARDS: Amex, MC, Visa.
PRICES: per person D,B&B single £190–
£330, double £155–£230. Set lunch
£40. 1-night bookings refused certain
weekends, Christmas, New Year.

PORTREE Highland

MAP 5:C1

VIEWFIELD HOUSE

Set within a comfortable expanse of wooded acreage, the Macdonalds' 'fabulous' country house is run in 'an efficient but relaxing way'. The family is at the heart of everything, with Iona Macdonald the latest generation to extend a 'warm welcome', while her father, Hugh, the former doyen, weaves yarns and exchanges stories with guests (who should ask about his Garden Collective project). The property, a Georgian house extended in Victorian times, holds a rich collection of antiques and colonial memorabilia collected over 150 years, the hall sporting trophy heads and horns alongside taxidermy. Some guests may find it a little dated, but it all adds to the unstuffy atmosphere of an ongoing house party. The 'excellent, comfortably appointed' bedrooms, including two in newly converted stables, might have a fireplace, brass bedstead, period writing desk, or a window seat gazing out to sea or over woodland. Dinners, ordered in the morning at breakfast and served at 7.30 pm, include an 'especially good' parsnip and cumin soup, and duck breast in plum sauce, alongside a 'very reasonably priced wine list'. 'We thoroughly enjoyed our stay and hope to visit again.' (A and EW, and others)

Viewfield Road
Portree
Isle of Skye IV51 9EU

T: 01478 612217
E: info@viewfieldhouse.com
W: viewfieldhouse.com

BEDROOMS: 13. 1 on ground floor, 2 in adjacent converted stables, 1 suitable for disabled.
OPEN: Apr–Oct.
FACILITIES: drawing room, morning/TV room, dining room, free Wi-Fi, 20-acre grounds (croquet, swings), public rooms wheelchair accessible.
BACKGROUND MUSIC: none.
LOCATION: S side of Portree.
CHILDREN: all ages welcomed.
DOGS: allowed in bedrooms, not in public rooms.
CREDIT CARDS: MC, Visa.
PRICES: per person B&B £73–£100, D,B&B £98–£125. Set dinner from £25. 1-night bookings only on application in high season.

SEE ALSO SHORTLIST

RANNOCH STATION Perth and Kinross   MAP 5:D2

MOOR OF RANNOCH
RESTAURANT & ROOMS

Previous César Winner

'The very-much-in-evidence hosts, Scott and
Stephanie Meikle, have transformed this remote
property' into a 'very well equipped and designed'
restaurant-with-rooms. Admirers this year
were enchanted by this 'excellent, small, remote
hotel' surrounded by uninhabited moorland
and peat bog, where service is 'professional and
unobtrusive'. The hosts usher guests in with a
warm welcome, 'even extending dinner for an
hour when my train was delayed'. A 'modern,
well-appointed bedroom' had a king-size bed,
fresh milk in the fridge and binoculars for wildlife
viewing; also 'a small decanter of local malt
whisky, chocolates and Steph's oatmeal biscuits'.
In the 'comfortable, airy and characterful public
rooms', guests enjoy a small Munro of books
and board games. Dinner is 'exceptional and
reasonably priced'. The hostess/chef's daily-
changing menus include seared Gartmorn duck,
duck croquette, asparagus; almond cream, peach
relish. A 'generous' breakfast is similarly 'impressive'.
Walkers setting out in the morning can ask for a
packed lunch. 'A special stay in a special place.'
(Stephen and Pauline Glover, Geoffrey Bignell)

Rannoch Station PH17 2QA

T: 01882 633238
E: info@moorofrannoch.co.uk
W: moorofrannoch.co.uk

BEDROOMS: 5.
OPEN: 2nd week Feb–end Oct.
FACILITIES: lounge, bar, conservatory
dining room, no Wi-Fi or TV,
unsuitable for disabled.
BACKGROUND MUSIC: none.
LOCATION: on a single-track, dead-end
road, 40 miles W of Pitlochry.
CHILDREN: all ages welcomed.
DOGS: welcomed in all areas of the
hotel.
CREDIT CARDS: Amex, MC, Visa.
PRICES: per room B&B single £125,
double £180. Set meal £42.

RATHO Midlothian

THE BRIDGE INN AT RATHO

Guide stalwarts received 'a most genial welcome from Chris the barman' on arrival at Graham and Rachel Bucknall's pub-with-rooms beside a bridge over the Union Canal. Addressed as 'you guys', they were shown to a seriously snug but 'warm, clean room with a shower, luxury Scottish toiletries'. Baird is the largest room, with a king-size double bed, a slipper bath with hand-held shower. Bonnington has a mahogany four-poster and antique chandelier. All four have a canal view. The Bucknalls have brought the same restrained taste to the interiors as to sister hotel The Ship Inn, Elie (see entry). Fires burn in a bar popular with locals. Since last year chef Ben Watson has become general manager, and sous-chef Ross Traill is now head chef. He uses local produce, home-grown vegetables and home-reared pork in a wide-ranging menu of pub classics (fish and chips, pie of the day, sausage and mash, Mull Cheddar macaroni) and more elaborate dishes (roast rump, rack and slow-cooked shoulder of lamb, spring greens, potato gratin, jus). Breakfast brings rare breed sausages, new-laid hen and duck eggs from Ratho Hall, fuel for a seven-mile walk down the towpath to Edinburgh. (Jock and Jane Macdonald)

27 Baird Road
Ratho EH28 8RA

T: 0131 333 1320
E: info@bridgeinn.com
W: www.bridgeinn.com

BEDROOMS: 4.
OPEN: all year except 25 Dec.
FACILITIES: 2 bars, restaurant, free Wi-Fi, in-room TV (Freeview), wedding facilities, terrace (beer garden, boat shed), bar and restaurant wheelchair accessible, adapted toilet.
BACKGROUND MUSIC: 'relaxed' all day, monthly live music nights.
LOCATION: in village, 7 miles W of Edinburgh.
CHILDREN: all ages welcomed.
DOGS: allowed in main bar only.
CREDIT CARDS: MC, Visa.
PRICES: per room £105–£175, cot £15, extra bed for child under 12 £25, bed for older child/adult £50.
À la carte £35.

ST OLA Orkney Islands

MAP 5:A3

THE FOVERAN

'What a delightful place!' Surrounded by a widescreen landscape washed with ever-changing light, this thoroughly Orcadian, 'extremely welcoming' restaurant-with-rooms is run by the hands-on Doull family. You're never far from a sea view, but the best are found in the restaurant, a popular venue for locals, where huge windows take in Scapa Flow and the southern Orkney islands. Here, the bounty of Orkney's larder shapes Paul Doull and Roddy Belford's innovative monthly menus, in particular the freshest-of-fresh seafood. Typical dishes: smoked haddock and pea risotto; pan-seared Orkney scallops, red wine and pear relish; Gressingham duck breast, plum and Orkney-distilled Aurora gin sauce. While the focus is food (and there's no check-in before 4.30 pm), the unfussy, 'comfortable' rooms are well appointed, spotlessly tidy and supplied with sustainable Duck Island toiletries. Come morning, free-range eggs, local sausages, home-made bread, bannocks and preserves lay solid foundations for island walks. The 'young, local, very helpful' staff can advise on local routes and history. 'We have recommended the Foveran to friends.' More reports, please.

Kirkwall
St Ola KW15 1SF

T: 01856 872389
E: info@thefoveran.com
W: thefoveran.com

BEDROOMS: 8. All on ground floor, 1 single with private bathroom across hall.
OPEN: Apr–early Oct, by arrangement at other times, restaurant closed variable times Apr, Oct.
FACILITIES: lounge, restaurant, free Wi-Fi, in-room TV, 12-acre grounds (private rock beach), restaurant wheelchair accessible.
BACKGROUND MUSIC: local/Scottish traditional in restaurant.
LOCATION: 3 miles SW of Kirkwall.
CHILDREN: all ages welcomed.
DOGS: not allowed.
CREDIT CARDS: MC, Visa.
PRICES: per room B&B single from £85, double from £125, D,B&B (for dinner up to £30) single from £113, double from £180. À la carte £35. 1-night bookings refused May–Sept (phone to check).

SANQUHAR Dumfries and Galloway   MAP 5:E2

BLACKADDIE HOUSE   **NEW**

25% DISCOUNT VOUCHERS

Sweet flows Rabbie Burns's beloved River Nith, past the garden of an old manse that the poet knew well. Owned by Jane and Ian McAndrew, it is swept up from the Shortlist on a wave of reader approval. Traditional bedrooms are supplied with home-made shortbread and tablet. The River Suite's French doors open on to a patio above the water; Grouse has a super-king-size four-poster, spa bath and monsoon shower. 'We were more than happy with our accommodation, but the real star was the food.' Ian McAndrew trained under Anton Mosimann at the Dorchester, and in 1980 became the youngest British chef to hold a Michelin star. His five-course menu (with either/or choices) and tasting menu highlight fine Scottish produce. Typical dishes: halibut, black rice, brown shrimps, sea purslane, spinach; seared roe deer loin, acidulated chocolate, braised red cabbage, burnt onion, braised walnuts, millefeuille potatoes, lightly pickled raspberries. Guests, too, can be lightly pickled from a tempting wine list. 'Dinner was simply wonderful.' 'Ian and Jane could not have been more welcoming.' A breakfast of smoked haddock and poached egg 'was simply divine'. (Mr and Mrs Murray, Michael Asquith, PK)

Blackaddie Road
Sanquhar DG4 6JJ

T: 01659 50270
E: ian@blackaddiehotel.co.uk
W: blackaddiehotel.co.uk

BEDROOMS: 7, plus two 2-bed self-catering cottages, 1 suitable for disabled (from Autumn 2019).
OPEN: all year.
FACILITIES: bar, restaurant, breakfast/function room, library, conservatory, free Wi-Fi, in-room TV (Freeview), wedding/function facilities, 2-acre grounds, cookery school, fishing, parking, public rooms wheelchair accessible.
BACKGROUND MUSIC: in public areas.
LOCATION: outskirts of village.
CHILDREN: all ages welcomed.
DOGS: allowed in most bedrooms (£10 per night), public rooms, not in restaurant.
CREDIT CARDS: Amex, MC, Visa.
PRICES: per room B&B single £105–£230, double £125–£250. Set menu £63, tasting menu £80.

SCARISTA Western Isles

SCARISTA HOUSE

♛ Previous César Winner

'Excellent food' and a 'lovely' welcome await visitors to Tim and Patricia Martin and Neil King's former manse overlooking the Maldivian-blue seas and sugar-white sands of a bite-shaped cove. 'You'd never guess you were in the Outer Hebrides.' Arriving guests are treated to a delicious afternoon tea of 'tasty vegan scones (with advance notice)', 'scrumptious' Victoria sponge and proper leaf tea, served in the library by 'delightful' local staff. Squashy sofas and walls of books and photos fill this 'homey' room and the drawing room upstairs. Bedrooms have a similar mix of antiques and modern furniture, 'good bedside lighting', well-stocked hospitality tray. 'Ours, in the converted outbuildings, had glorious sea views and a powerful shower. All that could be heard at night was the muted sound of the sea.' Dinner, cooked by Patricia, using organic, foraged and home-made produce, is 'pleasingly inventive and utterly delicious'. Garlicky Harris langoustine; spinach-beetroot dumplings; cinnamon ice cream. The cooked breakfast is 'almost as good', with the addition of a 'tasty' buffet ('excellent home-made granola') and 'good strong coffee'.

Scarista
Isle of Harris HS3 3HX

T: 01859 550238
E: bookings@scaristahouse.com
W: scaristahouse.com

BEDROOMS: 6. 3 in annexe.
OPEN: 3 Apr–23 Oct.
FACILITIES: drawing room, library, 2 dining rooms, free Wi-Fi in most bedrooms and all public areas, wedding facilities, 1-acre garden, unsuitable for disabled.
BACKGROUND MUSIC: none.
LOCATION: 15 miles SW of Tarbert.
CHILDREN: all ages welcomed.
DOGS: allowed in bedrooms and 1 public room.
CREDIT CARDS: Amex, MC, Visa.
PRICES: per room B&B single £165–£180, double £230–£248. Set dinner £50. Advance 1-night bookings refused.

SCOURIE Highland

MAP 5:B2

EDDRACHILLES HOTEL   NEW

'In a superb position overlooking Badcall Bay',
this 18th-century church manse-turned-hotel
gains a full entry at the urging of readers and a
Guide inspector. Fiona and Richard Trevor have
been refurbishing and upgrading their 'wonderful
retreat' since taking over in 2016. Fiona, the
perfect hostess, 'radiates energy, and is happy to
pass the time of day'. Alongside a well-stocked
library, a sun lounge has 'intriguing views of
passing weather fronts'. At 4 pm, attention
switches to complimentary home-made cakes.
A 'basically' but pleasingly furnished first-floor
room had 'a comfortable super-king-size bed'.
Six rooms overlook the bay; four the courtyard
garden. All have a bath or shower, upmarket
Scottish toiletries. Chef Ian Godfrey's 'first-rate'
daily-changing menus, served in two smallish
dining rooms, showcase shellfish from the bay,
produce from local crofts. celeriac soup, a beetroot
and goat curd salad; 'beautifully cooked scallops';
chicken supreme, and 'indulgent raspberry
cranachan' all hit the spot. 'A breakfast buffet
included first-class fruit compote; sizeable hot
dishes arrived swiftly; good black pudding and
tattie scones.' (Mr and Mrs Edward Knowles, and
others)

Badcall Bay
Scourie IV27 4TH

T: 01971 502080
E: info@eddrachilles.com
W: eddrachilles.com

BEDROOMS: 10, 4 ground-floor rooms.
OPEN: mid-Mar–mid-Nov, exclusive
use over Christmas and New Year.
FACILITIES: large reception, bar/
lounge, sun lounge, restaurant, free
(slow) Wi-Fi in public areas, in-room
TV (Freeview), wedding facilities,
3-acre grounds, parking, public rooms
wheelchair accessible.
BACKGROUND MUSIC: in public areas
3–10.30 pm, not in sun lounge.
LOCATION: 2 miles S of Scourie, on the
North Coast 500 route.
CHILDREN: all ages welcomed.
DOGS: well-behaved dogs allowed in
bedrooms, some public areas.
CREDIT CARDS: MC, Visa.
PRICES: per room B&B single £80–£125,
double £120–£165. Set dinner £33–£39.

SLEAT Highland

KINLOCH LODGE

♔ Previous César Winner

'The welcome was superb, the setting magical, the staff were friendly and helpful,' writes a reader in 2019, of Lord and Lady Macdonald's former hunting lodge on the shores of Loch Na Dal. It owes much of its charm to the Macdonalds' daughter, Isabella, the long-time manager. 'Luxurious' bedrooms, in the main house and extension, have a colour palette that reflects the Isle of Skye landscape; antiques and original artwork. Most look over the loch or towards Kinloch hill. The house 'still has very much the feel of a home, with family portraits and photographs'. Roux-trained Marcello Tully's creative, locally sourced dishes include Shetland cod, Harris gin and citrus sauce; Black Isle lamb fillet, cashew and black olive, dauphinoise potatoes. One reader this year found the first meal 'superb', but would have liked the menu to vary more thereafter. But 'the magnificent cheeseboard was a real delight'. The 'excellent' breakfast brings home-stewed prunes and apricots with crème fraîche; scrambled Armadale eggs with South Uist hot-smoked salmon; Lochalsh sausages and Mallaig kippers. A ghillie organises all manner of outdoor activities. (David Ganz, and others)

Sleat
Isle of Skye IV43 8QY

T: 01471 833333
E: reservations@kinloch-lodge.co.uk
W: kinloch-lodge.co.uk

BEDROOMS: 19. 10 in North Lodge, 9 in South Lodge. 3 on ground floor, 1 suitable for disabled.
OPEN: all year.
FACILITIES: 3 drawing rooms, whisky bar, dining room, free Wi-Fi, in-room TV (Sky), wedding facilities, cookery courses, 'huge' grounds on edge of loch, public rooms wheelchair accessible.
BACKGROUND MUSIC: gentle classical in dining room.
LOCATION: on shore of Loch Na Dal on east coast of Skye, not far off A851.
CHILDREN: all ages welcomed.
DOGS: in bedrooms only, and not unattended.
CREDIT CARDS: MC, Visa.
PRICES: per person, B&B £130–£210, D,B&B £150–£250. Set dinner (5 courses) £85, tasting menu (7 courses) £95.

SPEAN BRIDGE Highland

MAP 5:C2

SMIDDY HOUSE

NEW

'The moment you walk in it is obvious that care, interest and real flair have been shown in the decoration. We loved the unusual clocks and knick-knacks.' A rise to a full entry this year after inspectors visited Robert Bryson and Glen Russell's restaurant-with-rooms in a former village smithy. 'Robert greeted us warmly and took us to our beautiful front bedroom.' It was snug, 'restful and welcoming', with 'wonderful bluebird wallpaper, a soft blue carpet'. Among blue cushions on the bed sat 'a teddy bear from Australia'. The property stands at a crossroads, but 'double glazing makes it warm and quiet'. Invited down to the lounge for tea and 'delicious iced ginger cake', they were struck by the hosts' consideration for their guests. Drinks in the sun lounge were followed by 'a wonderful dinner in the quirky dining room', aka Russell's. Top marks for 'delicious celery, apple and almond soup; one of the best venison dishes I've ever had, in a lovely sauce'. Glen Russell's menus exploit local produce: Mull scallops, Arisaig prawns, Wester Ross salmon, Highland meats. In the morning 'a lovely breakfast, with a good choice'. Altogether 'a great place to stay'.

25% DISCOUNT VOUCHERS

Roy Bridge Road
Spean Bridge PH34 4EU

T: 01397 712335
E: enquiry@smiddyhouse.com
W: smiddyhouse.com

BEDROOMS: 5, 1 suite in adjacent cottage.
OPEN: all year except 25/26, 31 Dec, restaurant closed Mon all year, Tues, Wed, Jan–Mar.
FACILITIES: garden room, restaurant, free Wi-Fi, in-room TV (Freeview), parking.
BACKGROUND MUSIC: in restaurant.
LOCATION: 9 miles N of Fort William.
CHILDREN: not under 7.
DOGS: not allowed.
CREDIT CARDS: MC, Visa.
PRICES: per room B&B single £105, double £120–£195, D,B&B single from £145, double £200–£290. À la carte £40.

STRACHUR Argyll and Bute

THE CREGGANS INN

Once owned by Sir Fitzroy Maclean, the likely inspiration for James Bond, this 'marvellously positioned' 19th-century whitewashed inn is now a tranquil retreat with far-reaching Loch Fyne views. Hosts Gill and Archie MacLellan and their 'affable' team 'warmly welcome' guests with tea and cake. In the cosy bar, you'll find a crackling fire, trophies won by the area's shinty team, and a range of single malts including MacPhunn, developed by the same real-life 007. 'Very comfortable' superior bedrooms have designer wallpaper and fabrics, king-size bed, loch views; standard rooms are warm, traditional and unfussy, overlooking woodland or garden. All have tea- and coffee-making facilities, Sea Kelp toiletries. Light sleepers may prefer a room not directly on to the road. In the 'lovely restaurant with fantastic views' and in the bistro, where one reader ate cheek by jowl with other diners (a seating thing, not the day's special), chef Irvine McArthur's seasonal, locally sourced dishes include Highland 'Coo' beef steak and ale pie, mash seasonal vegetables; salmon, samphire, pea and mint fricassée, roasted fennel. Breakfast includes potato scones, Loch Fyne kippers. 'A very comfortable place to stay.'

Strachur PA27 8BX

T: 01369 860279
E: info@creggans-inn.co.uk
W: creggans-inn.co.uk

BEDROOMS: 14.
OPEN: all year, except Christmas.
FACILITIES: 2 lounges, bar, dining room, bistro, free Wi-Fi, in-room TV (Freeview), 2-acre grounds, moorings for guests arriving by boat.
BACKGROUND MUSIC: all day in bar.
LOCATION: in village.
CHILDREN: all ages welcomed.
DOGS: allowed in bar, bedrooms (not unattended).
CREDIT CARDS: Amex, MC, Visa.
PRICES: per room B&B £130–£200.
À la carte £30.

STRATHTUMMEL Perth and Kinross   MAP 5:D2

THE INN AT LOCH TUMMEL

'An ideal place to relax,' writes a reader after a 2019 visit to Alice and Jade Calliva 18th-century coaching inn turned rustic-chic hotel with a 'wonderful lochside setting.' The owners swapped Soho's fleshpots for Perthshire's forested hills, to give the property a stylish make-over. Outside, the old rugged facade; inside, bedrooms with designer fabrics, a power shower, shortbread and whisky. The bar has polished wood floors, settles, red-velvet chairs. In the snug, resident pooches Maggie and Mabel snooze by a blazing log fire. Upstairs, the library/breakfast room and more distinctive design: deep blue stone walls, bookshelves and sofas. You can eat and drink at picnic tables on the grass above the loch, or on a terrace with wood-fired oven. Darren Simpson's short menus, including Shetland steamed mussels, garlic, white wine and cream; pork cheek, crackling, dauphinoise potatoes, butternut squash purée, cider jus, are served by 'friendly, helpful staff'. Breakfast brings American-style pancakes with maple syrup, Ayrshire bacon, smoked salmon, eggs Benedict. 'Both breakfast and dinner were very good. We were glad to find such a welcoming and calming place.' (David Ganz)

Queens View
Strathtummel
Pitlochry PH16 5RP

T: 01882 634317
E: info@theinnatlochtummel.com
w: theinnatlochtummel.com

BEDROOMS: 6. 2, on ground floor, suitable for disabled.
OPEN: all year, but closed Christmas and Jan (except the few days before New Year), Sun evening, all day Mon.
FACILITIES: snug, bar, library, breakfast room, free Wi-Fi in communal areas, large garden and patio (alfresco meals and drinks), wedding facilities, ground floor bar and snug wheelchair accessible, no adapted toilet.
BACKGROUND MUSIC: in bar/restaurant and library.
LOCATION: 10 miles W of Pitlochry.
CHILDREN: not under 5.
DOGS: allowed throughout, £10 per dog per night.
CREDIT CARDS: MC, Visa.
PRICES: per room £105–£140. À la carte £27. 1-night bookings refused peak weekends.

STRONTIAN Highland

MAP 5:C1

KILCAMB LODGE

'They make you feel welcome and at home' at Sally and David Ruthven-Fox's dog-friendly hotel 'by the shores of Loch Sunart, surrounded by hills'. A whitewashed 18th-century house bookended by Victorian stone extensions, it stands in extensive grounds of woodland and meadow, where your fellow visitors include deer, red squirrels and golden eagles. Within, 'everything is beautifully presented', with blazing fires, 'comfy sofas, pictures, maps; fresh flowers everywhere'. Bedrooms range from small and contemporary to spacious, in country house style. The best might have a balcony, a half-tester bed, a separate bath and shower. All bathrooms have underfloor heating, 'lovely' toiletries, robes and 'plentiful fluffy towels'. You can eat informally in the brasserie, or do yourself very well in the restaurant, where Gary Phillips's menus include such dishes as roast loin of Highland venison, wild mushroom and truffle boudin, fondant turnip, bourguignon sauce; West Coast seafood; braised feather blade of Highland beef. The service is 'impeccable'. Breakfast brings porridge with whisky and cream, free-range pork sausages, Stornoway black pudding, smoked haddock omelette.

25% DISCOUNT VOUCHERS

Strontian PH36 4HY

T: 01967 402257
E: enquiries@kilcamblodge.co.uk
W: kilcamblodge.co.uk

BEDROOMS: 11.
OPEN: all year, 'some closures in Nov, Dec, Jan', restaurant closed Mon, Tues Nov–Jan.
FACILITIES: drawing room, lounge/bar, restaurant, brasserie, free Wi-Fi, in-room TV (Freeview), wedding facilities, 22-acre grounds, bar, brasserie, restaurant wheelchair accessible, toilet not adapted.
BACKGROUND MUSIC: at dinner.
LOCATION: edge of village.
CHILDREN: all ages welcomed.
DOGS: allowed in 5 bedrooms, not in public rooms, from £12 per dog per night.
CREDIT CARDS: MC, Visa.
PRICES: per room B&B single £185–£225, double £245–£330, D,B&B £295–£470. Tasting menu £78, à la carte £55. 1-night bookings refused Christmas, New Year, Easter.

TARLAND Aberdeenshire

DOUNESIDE HOUSE

'Top of the range in every respect.' Much praise from a Guide stalwart after this year's visit to the MacRobert Trust's 'wonderful' hotel bordering the Cairngorms national park. The family expanded the property in the early 1900s; more recently, it received a 'tasteful, high-quality' facelift. The result is a graceful mix of antique heirlooms, wood panelling, and comfortable groups of low armchairs, warming fires and a grand piano. Some things are little changed: the library has, perhaps, a few more volumes; the view of the Grampians remains 'spectacular'. Stone paths lace 'beautifully landscaped and maintained grounds'. At dinner, in the conservatory, local produce (much from the walled garden) fuels David Butters's 'outstanding' Scottish dishes, perhaps belly and loin of Fife pork, sprouting broccoli, potato mousseline, fermented apple, thyme jus. Afterwards, a solid night's sleep. 'Our well-equipped room, though not large, had all the necessary extra comforts, ground coffee, good art, plenty of bathroom shelf space.' The day starts with 'perfect haggis, scrambled egg, potato scone, good coffee, all promptly and courteously served'. (Robert Gower, and others)

Tarland AB34 4UL

T: 01339 881230
E: manager@dounesidehouse.co.uk
W: dounesidehouse.co.uk

BEDROOMS: 23. 9 in cottages, plus 4 apartments in Casa Memoria, 2 cottages suitable for disabled.
OPEN: all year.
FACILITIES: bar, wine bar, piano lounge, library, restaurant, free Wi-Fi, in-room Smart TV (Freeview), wedding facilities, health centre (indoor swimming pool, all-weather tennis court), 17-acre grounds, public areas wheelchair accessible, adapted toilet.
BACKGROUND MUSIC: in bar and restaurant.
LOCATION: 7 miles NW of Aboyne.
CHILDREN: all ages welcomed.
DOGS: allowed in cottages and apartments, not in public rooms.
CREDIT CARDS: MC, Visa.
PRICES: per room B&B from £174, D,B&B from £250. Set dinner £35–£45, tasting menu £80.

TIRORAN Argyll and Bute

MAP 5:D1

TIRORAN HOUSE

'A wonderful and special place from which to explore this magical island,' a trusted reader, wrote after 'a very relaxing, enjoyable stay' at this Victorian country house overlooking Loch Scridain. It stands in 56 acres with a burn running through. The 'warm, friendly' hosts, Laurence and Katie Mackay, 'generate a relaxed country house feel' ('a glass of champagne welcomes guests on arrival'). Loch-facing bedrooms are the most sought after; others overlook orchard and hills. All are traditionally furnished, supplied with White Company toiletries. 'Dinner was relaxed (just come when you want to).' Katie cooks seasonal Scottish produce 'simply but with flair', maybe Argyll beef sirloin; West Coast smoked haddock fishcake; local venison cottage pie. 'A nice touch was a board of Scottish cheeses with grapes from the vine that grows over the dining room roof.' A light Sunday supper brought 'wonderful lasagne'. An 'excellent breakfast' includes 'poached kippers – so much nicer than grilled', porridge, croissants, 'a good fruit bowl'. Wildlife spotters are in heaven: 'We saw whitetail and golden eagles, buzzards, seals, otters and red deer.' 'An exemplary hotel of its type.' (DB, CT)

25% DISCOUNT VOUCHERS

Tiroran
Isle of Mull PA69 6ES

T: 01681 705232
E: info@tiroran.com
W: tiroran.com

BEDROOMS: 7. 2 on ground floor. 4 self-catering cottages. 1 suitable for disabled.
OPEN: 'seldom closed', special breaks and events in winter, restaurant closed Sun pm.
FACILITIES: lounge, breakfast room, dining conservatory, dining/bar area, free Wi-Fi, in-room TV (Freeview), 17½-acre gardens in 56-acre grounds, beach with mooring, wedding facilities, coffee shop, public rooms wheelchair accessible.
BACKGROUND MUSIC: sometimes in bar/dining area.
LOCATION: N side of Loch Scridain.
CHILDREN: all ages welcomed.
DOGS: allowed in 2 bedrooms.
CREDIT CARDS: MC, Visa.
PRICES: per room B&B single £75–£160, double £185–£245. À la carte £25–£50.

ULLAPOOL Highland

MAP 5:B1

THE CEILIDH PLACE

'As ever, very enjoyable, and three minutes from
the ferry terminal.' The Urquhart family's 'busy,
buzzy' café/bar, bookshop, hotel and cultural
hub hits all the right notes. It began in 1970
when the late character actor Robert Urquhart
opened a café in a boatshed in this fishing village,
invited musicians to play, and fed them. In time
it expanded into adjoining cottages, to create a
'warren of rooms' that somehow feels 'open and
spacious'. Music events and art exhibitions are a
staple, yet it is 'a haven of peace'. Simple, pretty
bedrooms have a Roberts radio, well-chosen
books. Guests can take tea and coffee in the
beamed first-floor parlour with its armchairs,
library, honesty bar, pantry and piano. If you're on
a tight budget, take a bunk in the Clubhouse. 'A
lovely log-burner' blazes in the restaurant which
looks on to the garden. Scott Morrison cooks
fine bistro fare. 'We enjoyed smoked haddock
chowder; grilled mackerel with apple coleslaw;
beef and boar olives, spinach, grain mustard
mash.' Breakfast brings porridge, a kipper, a full
Scottish or full veggie. Jock Urquhart is manager;
'bantering' with staff, 'doing everything with a
smile'. (Christine and Philip Bright, GC)

25% DISCOUNT VOUCHERS

12–14 West Argyle Street
Ullapool IV26 2TY

T: 01854 612103
E: stay@theceilidhplace.com
W: theceilidhplace.com

BEDROOMS: 13. 10 with facilities
en suite, plus 11 in Clubhouse across
car park.
OPEN: all year except from 3 Jan for
three weeks.
FACILITIES: bar, lounge, café/restaurant,
bookshop, conference/function
facilities, free Wi-Fi, wedding
facilities, 2-acre garden, public areas
wheelchair accessible.
BACKGROUND MUSIC: 'eclectic' in public
areas.
LOCATION: village centre (large car
park).
CHILDREN: all ages welcomed.
DOGS: allowed throughout (not
unattended in bedroom), £12 per dog
per stay.
CREDIT CARDS: MC, Visa.
PRICES: per room B&B £132–£180
(rooms in Bunkhouse £24–£32 per
person). À la carte £26.

WALKERBURN Scottish Borders

MAP 5:E2

WINDLESTRAW

'Stunning hotel, stunning views.' A reader
this year endorses John and Sylvia Matthews's
restaurant-with-rooms in an Edwardian manor
house overlooking the Tweed valley. Bedrooms
are done in period style. An inspector's deluxe
room was 'simply furnished', with 'tasteful
willow-green decor', an 'extremely comfortable
king-size bed', an espresso machine. The 'warm
and inviting' bathroom had a monsoon shower
and slipper bath. One room has an original
Edwardian tub. All rooms have White Company
toiletries, espresso machine. Open fires burn in
public rooms where family memorabilia and soft
lighting 'create a peaceful, domestic ambience'. A
bay window frames a pastoral river view. Former
chef and wine merchant Mr Matthews is a genial
host 'with an eye for detail'. In the panelled dining
room, Stu Waterston uses kitchen garden and
seasonal Borders ingredients in such 'first-rate'
dishes as Gressingham duck breast, roast pear
and Calvados jus, Stornoway black pudding;
turbot, fresh peas, watercress purée, lemon curd.
Breakfast brought our reader 'the best omelette
I have ever had. I highly recommend this hotel.'
Abbotsford, Walter Scott's 'Conundrum Castle', is
nearby. (RG, and others)

25% DISCOUNT VOUCHERS

Galashiels Road
Tweed Valley
Walkerburn EH43 6AA

T: 01896 870636
E: stay@windlestraw.co.uk
W: windlestraw.co.uk

BEDROOMS: 6.
OPEN: all year except mid-Dec to Feb.
FACILITIES: bar, sunroom, lounge/
restaurant, free Wi-Fi in reception,
in-room TV (Freeview), wedding
facilities, 2-acre landscaped garden,
parking.
BACKGROUND MUSIC: none.
LOCATION: in Walkerburn, 8 miles east
of Peebles.
CHILDREN: all ages welcomed.
DOGS: allowed in bedrooms (not
unattended), public rooms, not
restaurant, £10 per dog per night.
CREDIT CARDS: MC, Visa.
PRICES: per room B&B single
£175–£265, double £200–£290, D,B&B
£320–£410. 4-course set menu £60,
à la carte £45.

WALLS Shetland

BURRASTOW HOUSE

♀Previous César Winner

In a beautiful location overlooking the Sound of Vaila, on Shetland's remote west coast, this 18th-century laird's house, altered and extended, offers a home-from-home experience. Belgian owner Pierre Dupont describes it as a 'pension', suggesting the unpretentious ambience that most visitors love. 'Pierre is keen to give you exactly what you want,' reported one reader, while the welcome with tea in the conservatory, with 'gorgeous orange cake', made a great start for others. Choose your room carefully: ideally go for the 'splendid and spacious' Laird's Room with tester bed and uplifting turquoise hues. It has 'stunning views on two sides', and it is Ring of Bright Water before your very eyes, as otters dive for fish and cavort on shore. Pierre cooks a nightly hanging menu of 'straightforward, uncomplicated fare', using locally caught fish and shellfish (turbot, halibut, crab and lobster, sea trout), heather-fed lamb. 'Don't be shocked,' guests are urged, if afterwards you are asked for your 'breakfast desires'. 'Pierre simply wants to please you.' Such temptation! 'I could not resist the kipper on two occasions.'

Walls ZE2 9PD

T: 01595 809307
E: info@burrastowhouse.co.uk
W: burrastowhouse.co.uk

BEDROOMS: 7. 3 in extension, 2 on ground floor.
OPEN: Apr–Oct.
FACILITIES: sitting room, library, dining room, conservatory, free Wi-Fi in reception and library, in-room TV (Freeview), 'weak mobile phone signal', grounds, wedding facilities, unsuitable for disabled.
BACKGROUND MUSIC: none.
LOCATION: 2 miles from Walls, 27 miles NW of Lerwick.
CHILDREN: all ages welcomed (under-13s half price).
DOGS: not allowed.
CREDIT CARDS: MC, Visa.
PRICES: per person B&B £55–£65, D,B&B £90–£100. Set menu £35.

WALES

ABERAERON Ceredigion   MAP 3:C2

HARBOURMASTER HOTEL

'An old favourite, a lovely place for a calm and
grown-up break.' It proved a happy return for
readers to Glyn and Menna Heulyn's vivid blue
former harbourmaster's house on the Georgian
quayside. 'Aberaeron itself is part of the charm,
with its rainbow-coloured houses and the boats
bobbing in the harbour, and the hotel makes
the most of the setting.' There's no residents'
lounge, and the bar is 'heaving' in the evenings,
but there is plenty of comfy seating. The inn
rooms, up the spiral staircase, have harbour
views, bold colours, unfussy boutique chic. All
are supplied with Molton Brown toiletries,
gowns and slippers. Some have an exposed
stone wall, fun artwork. Rooms in a converted
warehouse have lift access, sofa, minibar, a stylish
contemporary bathroom. Aeron Queen has a zinc
roll-top bath. Chef Ludo Dieumegard uses local
produce, especially locally landed fish and seafood
(Cardigan Bay crab, bream, hake, bass), Welsh
lamb, organic vegetables. Bread is home baked,
and the breakfast menu includes American-style
pancakes, porridge with figs, locally cured bacon,
beans with chorizo, a full Welsh with laver bread.
'We will go back again and again.' (FT)

Pen Cei
Aberaeron SA46 0BT

T: 01545 570755
E: info@harbour-master.com
W: harbour-master.com

BEDROOMS: 13. 4 in warehouse, 2 in
cottage, 1 suitable for disabled.
OPEN: all year except 24 (6 pm)–26
Dec, drinks only (from 2 pm) on
Boxing Day.
FACILITIES: lift (in warehouse), bar,
restaurant, free Wi-Fi, in-room TV
(Freeview), small terrace, restaurant
and bar wheelchair accessible.
BACKGROUND MUSIC: all day in bar.
LOCATION: central, on the harbour.
CHILDREN: 5 and upwards welcomed,
must have own room.
DOGS: only guide dogs.
CREDIT CARDS: Amex, MC, Visa.
PRICES: per room B&B single
£110–£255, double £120–£265, D,B&B
double £180–£325. Set dinner £27.50–
£35, à la carte £35. 1-night bookings
refused most weekends, min. 2-night
stay for D,B&B rate.

ABERDOVEY Gwynedd

MAP 3:C3

TREFEDDIAN HOTEL

'It was fabulous to gaze across the dunes and golf course to the sea, with the sunset,' writes a reader who 'much enjoyed' this year's break at the Cave family's hotel. Overlooking Cardigan Bay, Trefeddian has an all-year, all-weather holiday vibe. On wet days, the lounges, library, 'great playroom, table tennis, pool tables' and indoor pool come into their own. When the sun shines, tennis courts, putting green and 'huge, wonderful sandy beach' beckon. You must cross road, railway line and dunes to get there, but it's worth it, and you can take a packed lunch. Bedrooms include some with a sea-facing balcony, others a view of hills. Family rooms are generous; all are bright and modern. 'Impeccable' housekeeping and a sense of efficiency extends to the dining room, where 'we deduced everything was prepared, cooked, ready to go'. Not fine dining, then, but 'very acceptable' fare – 'duck, pollack, lamb shank, syrup sponge and custard… extremely quickly served'. An all-day lounge menu and children's supper allow flexible eating. In sum, 'very well run, perhaps not suiting someone who wanted something more intimate or individual'. (Carol Jackson, S and JM, and others)

Tywyn Road
Aberdovey LL35 0SB

T: 01654 767213
E: info@trefwales.com
W: trefwales.com

BEDROOMS: 59. 1 suitable for disabled.
OPEN: all year except 8 Dec–12 Jan.
FACILITIES: lift, lounge bar, study, family lounge, adult lounge, restaurant, games room (snooker, table tennis), free Wi-Fi, in-room TV (Freeview), indoor swimming pool, beauty salon, 15-acre grounds (lawns, sun terrace, tennis, putting green), most public rooms wheelchair accessible.
BACKGROUND MUSIC: none.
LOCATION: ¼ mile N of Aberdovey.
CHILDREN: all ages welcomed.
DOGS: allowed in 1 lounge, some bedrooms.
CREDIT CARDS: MC, Visa.
PRICES: per person B&B £75–£95, D,B&B £98–£151. Set dinner £33. 2-night min. stay preferred (but check for 1-night availability).

ABERGAVENNY Monmouthshire   MAP 3:D4

♛THE ANGEL HOTEL

César award: Welsh hotel of the year
'Thank you for guiding me to this ideal hotel in
the heart of the Welsh market town,' writes a
reader who chose William Griffiths's family-run
establishment for a celebratory 70th birthday stay
this year. 'Everything was spot on.' As was service
from 'exceptionally helpful, cheery staff'. Most
bedrooms are in the main building, a Georgian
coaching inn. Some are in the former mews,
a Victorian lodge within the castle grounds,
and two cottages. Hotel and mews bedrooms
have upmarket fabrics, 'proper coat-hangers',
bathrooms with toiletries. Public rooms display
original artwork chosen by William's gallery-
owner mother. The award-laden afternoon tea
showcases 'feather-light scones, perfect pastries
and cakes' from the hotel's bakery next door. For
main meals try the Foxhunter bar or Oak Room
restaurant – or head out to the Walnut Tree, a
Michelin-starred sister enterprise. In the Oak
Room, Paul Brown and Wesley Hammond's
menus cater to all comers, vegetarian, vegan,
gluten intolerant… Perhaps butternut squash and
aubergine Penang curry, or roast loin of venison.
Breakfast brings a full English and smoked
Bloody Mary. (David Sefton, VAA)

15 Cross Street
Abergavenny NP7 5EN

T: 01873 857121
E: info@angelabergavenny.com
W: angelabergavenny.com

BEDROOMS: 35. 2 in adjacent mews,
plus 2-bedroom lodge and 2 cottages.
OPEN: all year except 24–27 Dec.
FACILITIES: lift, lounge, bar, tea room,
restaurant, private function rooms,
bakery, free Wi-Fi, in-room TV
(Freeview), civil wedding licence,
courtyard, public rooms wheelchair
accessible.
BACKGROUND MUSIC: in restaurant and
tea room.
LOCATION: town centre.
CHILDREN: all ages welcomed.
DOGS: allowed in the Foxhunter bar
and courtyard.
CREDIT CARDS: Amex, MC, Visa.
PRICES: per room B&B £109–£259,
Set dinner £32, à la carte £40. 1-night
bookings sometimes refused.

SEE ALSO SHORTLIST

ABERSOCH Gwynedd

MAP 3:B2

PORTH TOCYN HOTEL

There is a deceptively 'wacky' quality to the
Fletcher-Brewers' 'lovely' hotel overlooking
Cardigan Bay, a casual vibe that belies the
professionalism of the operation. It has been
in the family since 1948, when it had just five
guest bedrooms. Today, there are 17, as well as a
cosy shepherd's hut named Ty Cwtch ('Cuddle
House'). Nick Fletcher-Brewer is the jovial host.
His wife, Louise, with Darren Shenton-Morris,
is chef. Now son Henry and his wife, Kelly, have
come on board, so continuity is assured. After
'a very friendly welcome', guests are shown to a
traditionally styled room, with perhaps a sea view.
Doubles have a super-king-size bed, bathrooms
a bath with power shower over. The hotel is
avowedly family friendly. There are 'several
lounges and sitting areas with fresh flowers,
books, magazines'. The set-price dinner includes
such elaborate dishes as grilled sea bass on a
spiced vegetable stir fry, roast plum, curry-infused
potato, crisp noodles, chilli glaze. Or you can eat
more simply from the Comfort Supper menu.
Thumbs up for breakfast, with 'tasty sausages',
smoked haddock, home-made preserves,
'delicious local yogurts'. 'Excellent, attentive
service' seals the deal.

Bwlchtocyn
Abersoch LL53 7BU

T: 01758 713303
E: bookings@porthtocynhotel.co.uk
W: porthtocynhotel.co.uk

BEDROOMS: 17. 3 on ground floor,
1 shepherd's hut, 1 self-catering
cottage in grounds sleeping 6.
OPEN: 2 weeks before Easter–early
Nov.
FACILITIES: sitting rooms, children's
snug, small bar, dining room, free
Wi-Fi, in-room TV (Freeview),
20-acre grounds (outdoor swimming
pool, 10 by 6 metres, heated May–end
Sept, tennis), call to discuss wheelchair
access.
BACKGROUND MUSIC: none.
LOCATION: 2 miles outside village.
CHILDREN: all ages welcomed, no
under-6s at dinner (high tea provided).
DOGS: allowed in bedrooms, not in
restaurant or some public rooms.
CREDIT CARDS: MC, Visa.
PRICES: per room B&B single from
£87, double £123–£205. À la carte £49.
1-night bookings occasionally refused.

ABERYSTWYTH Ceredigion   MAP 3:C3

GWESTY CYMRU

On the Victorian promenade of this university
town, Huw and Beth Roberts's small hotel is
fronted by a small lawn with outdoor tables and
seating – 'a fine place to be on a sunny evening',
says a Guide insider. A reader this year praises the
'immaculately furnished and decorated bedrooms'
and tells a tale of two rooms – one, at the back,
'compact', with 'efficient, silent air conditioning',
'looked out over a tangle of rooftops'; the other,
at the front, was spacious, 'with a glorious sea
view from the bay window', and armchairs to
watch the sunset. A rear-facing room is, of course,
cheaper so you pays your money and you takes
your choice. All rooms have handmade Welsh
furniture, modern oil paintings inspired by the
landscape. The best have a bath and separate
shower. The staff are bilingual and welcoming.
In the basement restaurant – rated 'excellent' by
some readers ('a beautifully cooked lamb rump'),
'OK' by others – the eclectic, bistro-style fare
includes pan-fried cod, garlic and Parmesan mash;
mushroom, hazelnut and feta linguine, pea shoots
and truffle oil. Parking is an issue; come by train if
you can. (Alan and Edwina Williams, and others)

19 Marine Terrace
Aberystwyth SY23 2AZ

T: 01970 612252
E: info@gwestycymru.co.uk
W: gwestycymru.com

BEDROOMS: 8. 2 on ground floor.
OPEN: all year except 22 Dec–4 Jan,
restaurant closed for lunch Tues.
FACILITIES: small bar area, restaurant,
seafront terrace, free Wi-Fi, in-room
TV (Freeview), unsuitable for
disabled.
BACKGROUND MUSIC: 'easy listening' all
day in reception and restaurant.
LOCATION: central, on seafront.
CHILDREN: no under-5s, all ages
welcomed at lunch.
DOGS: not allowed.
CREDIT CARDS: MC, Visa.
PRICES: per room B&B single £70–£80,
double £90–£155. À la carte £35.

BARMOUTH Gwynedd

MAP 3:B3

COES FAEN

Coes Faen means 'leg of stone', bringing to mind Shelley's Ozymandias, but there is no vainglory at Sara and Richard Parry-Jones's adults-only hotel overlooking the Mawddach estuary. Our inspector's jaw dropped at first sight of the 'stunning' entrance, with an 'incredible glass staircase in the hillside'. A 'tunnel, trickling water', led to gardens with woodland walks, stone benches, views of Cader Idris. It is 'all fabulous', not least the 'strikingly designed' and 'well-lit' bedrooms, each with unique features – an ash-wood bath on slate plinth, a cedar hot tub, a cedar-and-slate steam room, an Italian marble bathroom with seashell-tiled rain shower, a widescreen cinema. On four nights, chef Wayne Scarlet's 'excellent' Tuscan-inspired dinner, served in the stone dining room, may include local lemon sole fillet, olive oil, lemon and herb sauce, steamed green beans; roasted aubergines, Taleggio cheese, tomato sauce, mushrooms. In the morning a 'most impressive' breakfast brings smoked black pudding, hot-smoked salmon, crisp pancetta, smoothies. There are stables where you can board your horse, and good dogs can hit the hay. 'A brilliant project. We loved it!' (P and JT)

25% DISCOUNT VOUCHERS

Barmouth LL42 1TE

T: 01341 281632
E: croeso@coesfaen.co.uk
W: coesfaen.co.uk

BEDROOMS: 6. 1, on ground floor with patio, suitable for disabled.
OPEN: all year except Christmas, Jan, dinner served Wed–Sat.
FACILITIES: entrance hall, snug, dining room, free Wi-Fi, in-room TV (Freeview), 15-acre grounds (woodland garden), stable, restaurant and bar wheelchair accessible.
BACKGROUND MUSIC: in public areas.
LOCATION: 1 mile E of town centre.
CHILDREN: not under 18.
DOGS: 'clean, well-behaved dogs (no puppies)' allowed in 1 bedroom and stables by arrangement, not in public rooms, dog-sitting available.
CREDIT CARDS: Amex, MC, Visa.
PRICES: per room B&B single £165–£255, double £185–£275. Set dinner £35–£55.

BARMOUTH Gwynedd

MAP 3:B3

LLWYNDU FARMHOUSE

In 'the most fabulous location', at the foot of the Rhinog mountains, overlooking Cardigan Bay, Peter and Paula Thompson's guest house is 'full of character'. The hosts, writes a reader, are 'most obliging and welcoming'. Quirky bedrooms are in a 16th-century farmhouse, an 18th-century granary and a converted hay barn. There are beamed ceilings, bare stone walls. One room has a sea view through the mullion window of a walk-in wardrobe. Two sea-view rooms in the main house have a four-poster. 'The family room is small but beautifully appointed and warm as toast.' Drinks are served in a lounge with wood-burner, before a 'delicious' candlelit dinner in the dining room, cooked with local ingredients (pigeon breasts from Shropshire, freshly landed fish and shellfish, salt marsh lamb), true to the principles of the Slow Food Movement. The daily-changing menu offers four choices at each course. A typical dish, Welsh Black beef rib-eye steak, red onion and crab apple marmalade. Breakfast on award-winning sausages, dry-cured smoked bacon, smoked salmon. Afterwards there are 'castles and ruins to explore... As long as the weather is as glorious, I'm not sure why you'd go anywhere else.'

25% DISCOUNT VOUCHERS

Llanaber
Barmouth LL42 1RR

T: 01341 280144
E: intouch@llwyndu-farmhouse.co.uk
W: llwyndu-farmhouse.co.uk

BEDROOMS: 6. 3 in granary, 1 on ground floor.
OPEN: all year except Christmas, restaurant closed Sun and Wed.
FACILITIES: lounge, restaurant, free Wi-Fi, in-room TV (Freeview), ¼-acre garden in 4-acre grounds.
BACKGROUND MUSIC: 'occasionally and on demand' in dining room.
LOCATION: 2 miles N of Barmouth.
CHILDREN: all ages welcomed.
DOGS: not allowed.
CREDIT CARDS: MC, Visa.
PRICES: per room B&B £98–£124. Set dinner £25–£30 (2 or 3 courses). 1-night bookings sometimes refused July/Aug.

BEAUMARIS Anglesey

MAP 3:A3

THE BULL BEAUMARIS

A Georgian front belies the history of this ancient coaching inn, part of its fabric dating from the 1500s, in a town at the eastern entrance to the Menai Strait. Owned by David Robertson, it is a 'well-run' hotel with bedrooms in the original inn and adjoining Townhouse. Some have exposed beams, all have Welsh toiletries and biscuits, a Nespresso machine, room service. The open-plan Bull Suite has a free-standing bath and walk-in shower. Townhouse rooms have a bold, contemporary style with striking cylindrical seating; Clementine sports flamboyant wallpaper. After an 'efficient, friendly check-in', a reader was shown to a 'clean, comfortable' Townhouse room with a 'spotless bathroom', though the upholstery needed refreshing. The cosy bar has an open fire, walls adorned with weaponry. In the Coach restaurant and alfresco, new chef Darren Taylor's seasonal menus include such locally sourced dishes as chargrilled Welsh rib-eye, dauphinoise potato, caramelised mushroom and onion, red wine jus. One regular reader in 2019 would have liked to see a similar passion for Welsh produce in the breakfast. Don't leave town without visiting one of Wales's most beautiful castles.

Castle Street
Beaumaris LL58 8AP

T: 01248 810329
E: info@bullsheadinn.co.uk
W: bullsheadinn.co.uk

BEDROOMS: 25. 2 on ground floor, 1 in courtyard, 13 in Townhouse, some rooms wheelchair accessible.
OPEN: all year (limited opening over Christmas period).
FACILITIES: lift (in Townhouse), lounge, bar, restaurant, free Wi-Fi, in-room TV (Freeview), courtyard (alfresco dining), restaurant wheelchair accessible.
BACKGROUND MUSIC: in Coach restaurant at mealtimes.
LOCATION: central.
CHILDREN: all ages welcomed, no children in bar after 9 pm.
DOGS: allowed in 2 bedrooms, bar.
CREDIT CARDS: Amex, MC, Visa.
PRICES: per room B&B single £85–£125, double £95–£190, D,B&B double £145–£230. À la carte (Coach) £29.

BRECHFA Carmarthenshire

MAP 3:D2

TY MAWR

♔ Previous Cesar Winner

The River Marlais runs by the garden of Annabel and Stephen Thomas's 16th-century country house in a village on the edge of Brechfa Forest. Bring your mountain bike. Bring your dog and book an 'ideal' large and 'beautifully warm' ground-floor room with outdoor access. A Guide inspector found serviceable pine furniture, 'normal tea/coffee/water provisions, pump-tub toiletries, thin waffle robes'. Not chic, then, but a super-king-size bed was super-comfortable, and the hotel is justly popular: 'A glance at the guest register confirmed it is much in demand.' Annabel welcomes new arrivals with tea and cake, in a residents' lounge with wood-burner. 'Her ability to generate a spirit of relaxation and revival amongst her guests keeps the place running very successfully.' At night, in a dining room with a large stone fireplace, 'she acted as our warm and always punctilious waitress'. Stephen, meanwhile, cooks 'outstanding, well-presented' locally sourced dishes, including griddled Llansawel Croft Farm lamb chops on wilted Ty Mawr wild garlic and cavolo nero. Breakfast sets you up for a forest foray – free-range eggs, local sausages, dry-cured ham or smoked salmon.

25% DISCOUNT VOUCHERS

Brechfa SA32 7RA

T: 01267 202332
E: info@wales-country-hotel.co.uk
W: wales-country-hotel.co.uk

BEDROOMS: 6. 2 on ground floor, 1 with private access.
OPEN: all year.
FACILITIES: sitting room, bar, breakfast room, restaurant, free Wi-Fi, in-room TV (Freeview), 1-acre grounds.
BACKGROUND MUSIC: classical in restaurant during dinner.
LOCATION: village centre.
CHILDREN: 10 and upwards welcomed.
DOGS: allowed in bedrooms, sitting room and bar, not in restaurant or breakfast room (no extra charge), biscuits, bowls, and information on local walks provided.
CREDIT CARDS: Amex, MC, Visa.
PRICES: per room B&B single £80–£100, double £115–£130, D,B&B double £160–£175. Set dinner £25–£30.
1-night bookings occasionally refused.

BRECON Powys

MAP 3:D3

THE COACH HOUSE

NEW

'We and four other regulars, staying for the Brecon Baroque Music Festival, consider this the best accommodation in the town; we book from year to year.' Guide stalwarts, on a fifth visit, again found everything pitch perfect at this former Georgian coach house, run today as a smart, contemporary B&B by Kayt and Hugh Cooper. 'Tea and coffee on arrival is very welcome, and Hugh helped carry our luggage upstairs.' The bedrooms, in restful, natural shades, are supplied with plenty of towels and fresh milk on request. Most have an en-suite shower room; Dwynwen has a bath with shower over. A mini-suite with 'plenty of space for reading, making tea/coffee or having a drink' is equipped with a minibar fridge, robes and slippers, and has a bathroom with separate shower. Breakfast involves a 'substantial menu'. As well as the full Welsh and a vegetarian version, there are omelettes, Welsh rarebit, pikelets, scrambled eggs with smoked salmon and laver bread. You can order a packed lunch the night before, for a day's walking in the Brecon Beacons national park – or come in October for the food festival and spend the day grazing. (Jill and Mike Bennett)

25% DISCOUNT VOUCHERS

12 Orchard Street
Brecon LD3 8AN

T: 01874 640089
E: reservations@coachhousebrecon.
   com
W: coachhousebrecon.com

BEDROOMS: 6.
OPEN: all year except 1 week over Christmas.
FACILITIES: reading room, breakfast room, lounge (with drink service), free Wi-Fi, in-room TV (Freeview), garden, drying room, secure bicycle storage, unsuitable for disabled.
BACKGROUND MUSIC: classical or Welsh harp music in breakfast room.
LOCATION: ½ mile from town centre.
CHILDREN: 15 and upwards welcomed.
DOGS: not allowed.
CREDIT CARDS: MC, Visa.
PRICES: per room B&B single £74–£155, double £79–£160, 1-night bookings usually refused Fri and Sat Mar–Oct.

CAERNARFON Gwynedd   MAP 3:A2

PLAS DINAS COUNTRY HOUSE `NEW`

'An absolute gem!' wrote a reader, of Neil Baines and Marco Soares's 'stunning country house', the former home of the Armstrong-Jones family, with views to the Menai Strait and Snowdonia on the doorstep. It is promoted from the Shortlist with a nod from an inspector. 'Part 17th-century, mostly Victorian', it stands in 'attractive grounds at the end of a potholed drive' and is 'full of family and royal memorabilia'. Bedrooms vary from the 'compact' Butler's Room, 'reached by steep stairs', to four-poster Princess Margaret, with a bathroom TV, an ice bucket for the fizz. 'Lady Armstrong-Jones was my favourite, in gentle greys and yellows, with a four-poster, countryside views', a 'tiny' bathroom. Guests are encouraged to gather for drinks in the sitting room, with grand piano, open fire, a cacophony of competing patterns, before dinner in the Gun Room, cooked by Daniel ap Geraint, served by white-gloved waiters. Perhaps wild mushroom risotto, pickled celeriac, crispy sage, truffle oil; braised pork cheek, malted cauliflower, apple and caper; 'excellent' sirloin of Welsh beef. Breakfast was the proverbial curate's egg, but 'the hits outweigh the misses'. (Tom Challinor, and others)

Bontnewydd
Caernarfon LL54 7YF

T: 01286 830214
E: info@plasdinas.co.uk
w: plasdinas.co.uk

BEDROOMS: 10, 1 on ground floor.
OPEN: all year except Christmas, restaurant closed Sun, Mon.
FACILITIES: drawing room, restaurant, private dining room, free Wi-Fi, in-room TV (Freeview), civil wedding licence, 15-acre grounds, parking.
BACKGROUND MUSIC: in drawing room and dining room.
LOCATION: 5-min. drive S of town.
CHILDREN: over-12s welcomed.
DOGS: small, well-behaved dogs allowed in 2 bedrooms, by arrangement (£10 per night).
CREDIT CARDS: Amex, MC, Visa.
PRICES: per room B&B £99–£199. Set dinner £36–£46. 2-night min. stay at weekends.

CARDIGAN Ceredigion

MAP 3:D2

CAEMORGAN MANSION

'This a place to which we would happily return,' write trusted (and exacting) readers, after a visit to David and Beverley Harrison-Wood's 19th-century mansion turned eco-friendly guest house. It stands on a quiet road five minutes' drive from Cardigan, 'approached by a short drive, and set in grounds of pasture rather than lawns'. A 'spacious, newly carpeted' bedroom had a walk-in wardrobe, under-floor biomass heating, a coffee machine, but cold LED lighting. A 'very trendy, narrow, slate-tiled en suite had a 'shower complete with all-singing, all-dancing body jets'. A bar with comfy seating led to a dining room divided by a central wood-burning stove. 'Competent' cooking produced smoked salmon with avocado; pork tenderloin and chicken breast. Limoncello panna cotta was 'rated highly'. At breakfast there was 'a sizeable buffet, with rich, tart fruit compote, decanters of chilled (not freshly squeezed) juice, yogurt, poached eggs with laver bread, Welsh rarebit', served on good china with linen napkins. 'A warm farewell from our hosts' left a good impression. (RG)

Caemorgan Road
Cardigan SA43 1QU

T: 01239 613297
E: guest@caemorgan.com
W: caemorgan.com

BEDROOMS: 5.
OPEN: all year except Christmas and New Year, restaurant closed Sun.
FACILITIES: bar and restaurant (for residents only), free Wi-Fi, in-room TV (Freeview), function facilities, 2-acre gardens.
BACKGROUND MUSIC: in restaurant.
LOCATION: ½ mile N of town centre.
CHILDREN: not under 15.
DOGS: assistance dogs only.
CREDIT CARDS: MC, Visa.
PRICES: per room B&B £94–£130.
À la carte £35. 1-night bookings often refused peak weekends.

CRICKHOWELL Powys

MAP 3:D4

GLIFFAES

'An amazing mansion set in equally amazing gardens.' Praise from Guide readers this year, for this former Victorian vicar's house high above the River Usk. The Italianate property is run by Peta Brabner and Susie and James Suter, the second and third generation of the same family owners, supported by 'very friendly and helpful' staff. The rose-coloured drawing room with its magnificent fireplace cossets with flowers, books and sink-into sofas, to the gentle sound of clinking croquet balls on the lawn. Afternoon tea, taken in the conservatory or on the terrace with 'fabulous' river views, 'could set you up for the day'. Bedrooms have a period country house style; a Delft-tiled fireplace, an antique desk or a balcony. All have a Roberts radio, bathrobes. Some guests liked their 'large, comfortable' bedroom but found a steamy bathroom (no extractor fan) and slippery bath without grab rails a hazardous combination. Chef Karl Cheetham's 'imaginative, so tasty' Welsh dishes include sea bream, crab ravioli, vegetable linguini, crushed butter beans. Many guests raved, others found the menu 'static'. Fishing along a private beat is minutes away. (Jill and Mike Bennett, ML, and others)

25% DISCOUNT VOUCHERS

Gliffaes Road
Crickhowell NP8 1RH

T: 01874 730371
E: calls@gliffaeshotel.com
W: gliffaeshotel.com

BEDROOMS: 23. 4 in cottage, 1 on ground floor suitable for disabled.
OPEN: all year except Jan and New Year.
FACILITIES: 2 sitting rooms, conservatory, bar, dining room, free Wi-Fi, in-room TV, civil wedding licence, 33-acre garden (tennis, croquet, private fishing on River Usk), public rooms wheelchair accessible.
BACKGROUND MUSIC: in bar in the evening.
LOCATION: 3 miles W of Crickhowell.
CHILDREN: all ages welcomed.
DOGS: not allowed indoors (free kennels available).
CREDIT CARDS: Amex, MC, Visa.
PRICES: per room B&B single £135–£173, double £149–£315, D,B&B double £225–£389. À la carte £38–£40. 1-night bookings refused high-season weekends.

DOLFOR Powys

MAP 3:C4

THE OLD VICARAGE

In the Cambrian mountains, set back from the A483, this red brick former Victorian vicarage-turned-B&B has been praised for its 'atmosphere of heart-warming hospitality'. Guests are 'warmly greeted with tea and cakes'. Helen and Tim Withers are 'charming, helpful hosts', 'dedicated to sustainability' (come by electric car and you'll find a charging point). Bedrooms, each named after a nearby river, have antiques, a king- or super-king-size bed (which can be set up as twins), perhaps toile de Jouy wallpaper. Severn has two bedrooms, separated by a shared bathroom with shower over bath. Teme, with a view of Glog mountain, can accommodate an additional single bed. In the evening you can choose a meze plate of home-grown salads, meat, cheese, hot-smoked salmon, or a three-course dinner, served at 7 pm by prior arrangement, from Monday to Saturday. Dishes might include sea bream plaki, Jersey Royals, fennel salad; organic Caerphilly cheese soufflé. Breakfast is from 7.30 to 8.30 am (9 am at weekends, still a little early for some) and brings free-range eggs from the hens in the large garden. Afterwards, Powis Castle, with its baroque gardens and deer park, awaits.

Dolfor
Newtown SY16 4BN

T: 01686 629051
E: mail@theoldvicaragedolfor.co.uk
W: theoldvicaragedolfor.co.uk

BEDROOMS: 4.
OPEN: all year except last 3 weeks Dec, dining room closed Sun.
FACILITIES: drawing room, dining room, free Wi-Fi, in-room TV (Freeview), 1½-acre garden, unsuitable for disabled.
BACKGROUND MUSIC: none.
LOCATION: 3 miles S of Newtown.
CHILDREN: all ages welcomed, under-2s free.
DOGS: not allowed.
CREDIT CARDS: Amex, MC, Visa.
PRICES: per room B&B single £70–£90, double £95–£120 (family £150, cot £10), D,B&B double £145–£170. Set dinner £25, meze plate £12. 1-night bookings sometimes refused bank holidays.

DOLGELLAU Gwynedd

MAP 3:B3

FFYNNON

Up a 'testing' country lane beneath Cader Idris, this quirky bolt-hole is run by the 'impressive' Angela and Bernhard Lanz, who 'could not be more friendly or obliging'. While built of Snowdonia's grey stone, the former Victorian rectory has been 'imaginatively' converted by an interior designer. Among the guest rooms, Sydney boasts a huge, decorative wooden bedhead and an in-room, freestanding bath; Emily contains a chaise longue, see-through chair and spectacular bathroom; Annis has an oriental theme likened to 'a Mikado stage set. I found it disorientating in a very Welsh town but suspect younger guests will find it stimulating. The sheets were Egyptian cotton, the lighting was superb, there were no noises offstage.' All rooms offer glorious views. The many walks into the national park are matched by numerous spots to unwind, from an elegant book-strewn lounge with piano and honesty bar, to an outdoor hot tub. Evenings bring Bernhard's 'excellent' modern Welsh dishes, perhaps honey, mustard and herb-crusted rack of Welsh lamb, leek and potato gratin, blackberry reduction. An extensive breakfast includes a full Welsh, porridge, a Ffynnon potato cake with smoked salmon. (S and TT)

Love Lane
Dolgellau LL40 1RR

T: 01341 421774
E: info@ffynnontownhouse.com
W: ffynnontownhouse.com

BEDROOMS: 6.
OPEN: all year except Christmas, restaurant closed Sun–Wed.
FACILITIES: sitting room, dining room, study/hall, butler's pantry, free Wi-Fi, in-room TV (Freeview), 'reasonably sized' garden (secluded outdoor hot tub).
BACKGROUND MUSIC: all day in sitting room and dining room.
LOCATION: town centre.
CHILDREN: all ages welcomed
DOGS: not allowed.
CREDIT CARDS: MC, Visa.
PRICES: per room B&B single £110–£160, double £160–£220. Set dinner £28–£50, à la carte £35. 2-night min. stay at weekends and bank holidays.

SEE ALSO SHORTLIST

DOLYDD Gwynedd

MAP 3:A3

Y GOEDEN EIRIN

The promised welcome in the vales is extended
by Eluned Rowlands at this converted granite
cowshed-turned-characterful B&B with views to
Snowdonia and the Menai estuary. It is infused
with a love of things Welsh – slate and timber,
wool blankets, fleeces, dresser, art and books.
A portrait by Sir Kyffin Williams in the dining
room is of the late John Gwilym Jones, a personal
friend, whose short story collection Y Goeden
Eirin (The Plum Tree) inspired the house name.
Up 'a broad staircase lined with prints' by the
same artist, a reader's bedroom was 'almost a
bedsit' with a dressing room between bedroom
and bathroom, 'prints of real artistic merit', and
'many interesting objects, including rugged carved
wooden animals surrounding the bath'. The bed,
though more 'princess-size' than the hoped-for
super-king, made for a dreamy night's sleep. The
hostess is 'evangelically green', with many eco
credentials: in-room recycling instructions, solar
panels. Ingredients for an Aga-cooked breakfast
are organic and mainly local – not the juicing
oranges, obviously, but bacon, sausages, lamb's
kidneys, free-range eggs, home-made preserves.
'Eluned Rowlands is a loving lady.' (S and TT)

Dolydd
Caernarfon LL54 7EF

T: 01286 830942
E: eluned.rowlands@tiscali.co.uk
W: ygoedeneirin.co.uk

BEDROOMS: 3. 2 in annexe 3 yds from
house.
OPEN: all year except Christmas/New
Year.
FACILITIES: breakfast room, lounge,
free Wi-Fi in bedrooms and dining
room, in-room TV (Freeview), 20-
acre pastureland, electric car charging
point.
BACKGROUND MUSIC: none.
LOCATION: 3 miles S of Caernarfon.
CHILDREN: not under 10.
DOGS: by prior arrangement only –
ring to discuss.
CREDIT CARDS: none, cash or cheque
payment requested on arrival.
PRICES: per room B&B single from £65,
double £90–£100. 1-night bookings
refused peak summertime.

EGLWYSWRW Pembrokeshire

MAP 3:D2

AEL Y BRYN

♀ Previous Cesar Winner

'From the moment we arrived, we knew this was special'; 'the hospitality is outstanding'; 'Robert and Arwel are perfect hosts'. Another year, another trove of praise for Robert Smith and Arwel Hughes's 'delightful B&B'. Peering out at the Preseli hills, the white-painted bungalow is 'full of comfort and charm': 'everything is designed to make visitors relax'. The hosts exude 'generosity and warmth', stocking each 'palatial, spotlessly clean' room with 'everything one could want: real coffee, fresh milk at the door each morning, HUGE chocolate biscuits', plus 'crisp bedlinen'. Such 'impressive attention to detail' extends to the vaulted sitting room, book-stuffed library and cosy conservatory, which overlook 'magnificent gardens, strewn with sculptures', and a pond hopping with wildlife. 'Lovingly prepared, high-standard' communal dinners (prior notice required) include lamb chumps or 'lovely casseroles'; puddings are 'wonderful'. Breakfasts are just as highly rated. Before you succumb to the Sand Man, go outside and look up: the Milky Way glitters in a deep dark sky. 'We hope to return very soon.' (Mabel Tannahill, Penelope Johnson, Kerry King, and others)

25% DISCOUNT VOUCHERS

Eglwyswrw
Crymych SA41 3UL

T: 01239 891411
E: stay@aelybrynpembrokeshire.co.uk
W: aelybrynpembrokeshire.co.uk

BEDROOMS: 4. All on ground floor.
OPEN: all year except Christmas/New Year.
FACILITIES: library, music room, dining room, conservatory (telescope), free Wi-Fi, in-room TV (Freeview), courtyard, 2½-acre garden (wildlife pond, stream, bowls court), public rooms wheelchair accessible.
BACKGROUND MUSIC: none.
LOCATION: ½ mile N of Eglwyswrw.
CHILDREN: not under 16.
DOGS: not allowed.
CREDIT CARDS: Amex, MC, Visa.
PRICES: per room B&B single £90–£120, double £110–£150. Set dinner £26–£30. 1-night bookings refused bank holidays.

FELIN FACH Powys

MAP 3:D4

THE FELIN FACH GRIFFIN

♥ Previous César Winner

Brothers Charles and Edmund Inkin invite you
to eat, drink, sleep. Pray and love, too, by all
means: there is a free-and-easy vibe at this dining
pub, 'a truly wonderful place'. Set in a beautiful
landscape of rivers and mountains, it was the
first of a trio that includes The Old Coastguard,
Mousehole, and The Gurnard's Head, Zennor,
England (see entries), and established the style,
with shabby-chic dining areas (the tack room,
library, Aga room, locals bar), and an all-round,
'happy-making atmosphere'. The bedrooms have
a comfortable bed, ground coffee, fresh milk,
'lovely' shortbread, cut flowers, Bramley toiletries.
There's no TV but a Roberts radio, 'plenty of
magazines', and new improved broadband access.
The cooking has a similar elegant simplicity, with
extensive use of home-grown fruit and vegetables,
from heritage tomatoes to pink rhubarb. A day's
menu might include lamb belly, peas, courgette,
fondant potato; sea trout, fregola, little gem.
'The food was really good, the staff were very
welcoming to our dog.' If you're staying more
than two days, they say, and if there is something
you especially fancy to eat, let them know. 'I'd
happily stay here again.' (SH, CS)

Felin Fach
Brecon LD3 0UB

T: 01874 620111
E: enquiries@felinfachgriffin.co.uk
W: felinfachgriffin.co.uk

BEDROOMS: 7.
OPEN: all year except 24/25 Dec.
FACILITIES: bar, dining rooms, free
Wi-Fi, limited mobile signal, 3-acre
garden (stream, kitchen garden,
alfresco dining), bar/dining room
wheelchair accessible.
BACKGROUND MUSIC: Radio 4 at
breakfast, 'selected music' afternoon
and evening.
LOCATION: 4 miles NE of Brecon, in
village on A470.
CHILDREN: all ages welcomed.
DOGS: allowed in bedrooms (not on
bed), in bar and tack room, but not
in restaurant (no additional charge),
bowls, towels, biscuits supplied.
CREDIT CARDS: MC, Visa.
PRICES: per room B&B £140–£180,
D,B&B £197–£238. À la carte £33, set
supper £29.

FISHGUARD Pembrokeshire

MAP 3:D1

THE MANOR TOWN HOUSE

In a market town by the Preseli hills, this
'superbly located' B&B in a powder-blue Georgian
town house delighted readers again this year. 'An
exceptional establishment. Every need we had was
happily met.' The curatorial owners, Helen and
Chris Sheldon, display the works of Welsh artists
and photographers in two lounges, alongside a
harmonious blend of wood floors, earthy hues,
antiques and a wood-burning stove – a perfect
spot for the hosts' home-made cakes and cream
teas. Come sunshine, eat in the terraced gardens
alongside views of Cardigan Bay. Individually
decorated, the 'immaculate, welcoming bedrooms'
mix antique and contemporary finds, with bold
colour; two have an original fireplace; four gaze
across the brine. All have a generous bed (even
the 'single' has a double), woollen blankets, comfy
seating, a pod coffee machine, robes. 'First-class'
breakfasts include organic free-range eggs, locally
made breads, a cooked daily special. Bicycle
hire and packed lunches can be arranged: the
Pembrokeshire Coastal Path runs through the
valley below the rear garden terrace. The hosts
have great advice on nearby dining. 'Our only
regret was not staying longer.' (Julia Spotswood)

11 Main Street
Fishguard SA65 9HG

T: 01348 873260
E: info@manortownhouse.com
W: manortownhouse.com

BEDROOMS: 6.
OPEN: all year except 23–28 Dec.
FACILITIES: 2 lounges, breakfast room,
free Wi-Fi, in-room TV (Freeview),
small walled garden, unsuitable for
disabled.
BACKGROUND MUSIC: classical in
breakfast room.
LOCATION: town centre.
CHILDREN: all ages welcomed.
DOGS: not allowed.
CREDIT CARDS: MC, Visa.
PRICES: per room B&B single £80–£105,
double £105–£150. 1-night bookings
sometimes refused peak weekends.

GLYNARTHEN Ceredigion

MAP 3:D2

PENBONTBREN

♛ Previous César Winner

Leave the West Wales coast road, head down a country lane, and you've suddenly arrived at this 'superb' B&B, a former Victorian farm among 'delightful grounds' in 'complete silence'. Owners and 'charming hosts' Richard Morgan-Price and Huw Thomas show 'wonderful attention to detail'. Visitors choose between a garden room with a pergola, and individually designed, self-contained suites, converted from the stables, threshing barn and granary. In the suites, the sitting room has a hospitality tray with daily fresh milk and tasty Welsh cakes, while the bedroom sports cheerily patterned wallpaper, woollen blankets, a king-size bed. Each has a fridge, minibar, capsule coffee machine and private patio overlooking the gardens: 'an ideal spot to sip a glass of wine'. Breakfast, 'beautifully cooked' by Richard Morgan-Price, starts the day with a 'great choice, and home-made bread'. For all other meals, an ever-updated list of local eateries is supplied, with Richard keen to receive feedback. If you can't bear the thought of venturing out, a 'marvellous' farm shop at the top of the lane has ample provisions. 'I fully recommend it to anyone who enjoys the good life.' (JA, and others)

25% DISCOUNT VOUCHERS

Glynarthen
Llandysul SA44 6PE

T: 01239 810248
E: contact@penbontbren.com
W: penbontbren.com

BEDROOMS: 6. 5 in annexe, 1 in garden, 3 on ground floor, 1 family suite, 1 suitable for disabled.
OPEN: all year except Christmas.
FACILITIES: breakfast room, free Wi-Fi, in-room TV (Freeview), 7-acre grounds, public rooms wheelchair accessible, adapted toilet.
BACKGROUND MUSIC: none.
LOCATION: 5 miles N of Newcastle Emlyn.
CHILDREN: all ages welcomed.
DOGS: allowed in some bedrooms, not in breakfast room.
CREDIT CARDS: MC, Visa.
PRICES: per room B&B single £85–£110, double £95–£140. 1-night bookings sometimes refused weekends.

HARLECH Gwynedd

MAP 3:B3

CASTLE COTTAGE

Spread across two of Harlech's oldest houses, Glyn and Jacqueline Roberts's restaurant-with-rooms won approval from Guide regulars this year, with 'an excellent room, and lovely dinner on both nights'. High praise – and a high location, above the town's 12th-century castle, reached by a steep street. 'We could just spot the castle behind the house opposite,' say inspectors, who were warmly greeted by chef/patron Mr Roberts, an 'efficient, intelligent, affable' host. Most of the bedrooms in the 400-year-old cottage and adjacent former inn have a beamed ceiling. Room No. 7 has especially fine timbers. All have modern fittings, oak furniture, neutral decor, a large, comfortable bed. Some have a sea view. 'We were provided with fresh milk, butternut crunch biscuits, Evian water, an extraordinary range of teas, fluffy towels.' After 'imaginative' canapés in the bar/lounge, locally sourced menus, served in the dining room, include such dishes as boned and rolled sucking pig, red cabbage, sage potatoes, black pudding, apple sauce, Calvados jus; line-caught sea bass on buttered linguine, asparagus, white wine and cream sauce. Breakfast is 'outstanding'. (Sally Mehalko, T and ST)

25% DISCOUNT VOUCHERS

Y Llech
Harlech LL46 2YL

T: 01766 780479
E: glyn@castlecottageharlech.co.uk
W: castlecottageharlech.co.uk

BEDROOMS: 7. 4 in annexe, 2 on ground floor.
OPEN: all year except 3 weeks Nov, Christmas and New Year, restaurant closed Sun–Wed in winter months, Sun–Tues in summer.
FACILITIES: bar/lounge, restaurant, free Wi-Fi, in-room TV (Freeview), unsuitable for disabled.
BACKGROUND MUSIC: in bar and restaurant at mealtimes.
LOCATION: town centre.
CHILDREN: all ages welcomed.
DOGS: not allowed.
CREDIT CARDS: MC, Visa.
PRICES: per room B&B single £85–£125, double £130–£175. Set menus £39–£42, tasting menu £45.

LAMPETER Ceredigion

MAP 3:D3

THE FALCONDALE

At the end of a long drive, Chris and Lisa Sutton's 'welcoming' Italianate villa stands 'in stunning grounds', a mile outside Lampeter. Guests this year declared the dog-friendly spot 'definitely worth its entry'. The 'comfortable public rooms' have a classic country house feel, all crackling fires, polished wood, inviting sofas. 'The entire place has a welcoming, cosy vibe about it,' wrote a delighted bride after the hotel hosted her 'relaxed, glorious day'. 'Every member of staff was warm and professional.' The lounge and many bedrooms offer 'magnificent views' over gardens abounding with rhododendrons and azaleas. Some of the uncluttered rooms have a four-poster, some a Juliet balcony overlooking the Teifi valley; all are 'classically styled' with Farrow and Ball-inspired colour schemes, antiques, bathroom with Temple Spa toiletries. Seasonal Ceredigion produce takes centre stage in Tony Schum's modern Welsh menus. 'We enjoyed delicious cauliflower panna cotta and a very generous sharing fish platter.' Come morning, the full Welsh; local charcuterie and cheese; bacon with cockles and laver bread are among several 'interesting' options. (Robert Gower, PM)

25% DISCOUNT VOUCHERS

Falcondale Drive
Lampeter SA48 7RX

T: 01570 422910
E: info@thefalcondale.co.uk
W: thefalcondale.co.uk

BEDROOMS: 17.
OPEN: all year.
FACILITIES: lift (does not access all bedrooms), bar, 3 lounges, conservatory, restaurant, free Wi-Fi, in-room TV (Freeview), civil wedding licence, beauty treatment room, terrace, 14-acre grounds (lawns, woodland), restaurant and ground floor wheelchair accessible, adapted toilet.
BACKGROUND MUSIC: in restaurant and lounges.
LOCATION: 1 mile N of Lampeter.
CHILDREN: all ages welcomed.
DOGS: allowed (£10 per night) in bedrooms, public areas except restaurant.
CREDIT CARDS: MC, Visa.
PRICES: per room B&B single £100–£205, double £135–£230, D,B&B double (min. 2 nights) £225–£320. À la carte £50.

LLANDRILLO Denbighshire

MAP 3:B4

TYDDYN LLAN

'Not quite the back of beyond', but this restaurant-with-rooms 'in a very pleasant, quiet, rural location' is well worth the trek, according to trusted Guide readers. 'Food is the main event' at Susan and Bryan Webb's Michelin-starred retreat, 'and the menu makes you want to stay longer to try more of his cooking'. Backed by 'spot-on' service from 'professional, friendly' staff, the chef marries crab and langoustine with avocado salsa, calves' sweetbreads with bubble and squeak, panna cotta with blood orange and grappa, taking advantage of seasonal Welsh produce. Away from the epicurean delights, the 'sympathetically extended' Georgian property has 'tastefully decorated' guest rooms. 'There was plenty of storage, two armchairs, a very comfortable bed. Our bathroom had great towels, a walk-in shower and freestanding bath, but no shaving mirror or soap dish in the shower. Minor irritations.' Overseeing everything is Susan Webb, who is 'very much in evidence', ensuring that events runs like clockwork. Breakfast brings 'good coffee', several 'freshly cooked' options. Perhaps, mused one guest, the excellent bread served at dinner could be used for morning toast. (DH, and others)

25% DISCOUNT VOUCHERS

Llandrillo
Corwen LL21 0ST

T: 01490 440264
E: info@tyddynllan.co.uk
W: www.tyddynllan.co.uk

BEDROOMS: 13. 3 with separate entrance, 1, on ground floor (garden suite), suitable for disabled.
OPEN: all year except Mon/Tues, and last 2 weeks Jan, restaurant closed Wed/Thurs lunch.
FACILITIES: 2 lounges, bar, 2 dining rooms, free Wi-Fi, in-room TV (Freeview), civil wedding licence, 3-acre garden, public rooms wheelchair accessible.
BACKGROUND MUSIC: none.
LOCATION: 5 miles SW of Corwen.
CHILDREN: all ages welcomed.
DOGS: allowed in some bedrooms (£10 per night), not in public rooms.
CREDIT CARDS: Amex, MC, Visa.
PRICES: per room B&B £180–£250, D,B&B £320–£430. Set dinner £70, tasting menus £85–£95, à la carte £70. 1-night bookings refused Christmas.

LLANDUDNO Conwy

MAP 3:A3

BODYSGALLEN HALL AND SPA

'A highlight of our journey. It was everything one could expect, in a historic setting.' A reader on a hotel tour this year was impressed by this Grade I listed Elizabethan mansion-turned-hotel-and-spa, in parkland with views of Snowdonia and Conwy Castle. In the care of the National Trust, it is 'reminiscent of an earlier age', with 'staff in plaid waistcoats carrying your bags and bringing tea'. But the ethos is relaxed: 'They went above what could be expected, providing a simple lunch when we arrived early, and letting us take an early breakfast to make a golf tee time nearby.' A 'huge, well-furnished' suite had 'a small sitting room, a bathroom with bath and separate shower room', views over the Arts and Crafts gardens. In the fine-dining restaurant, John Williams cooks such elaborate dishes as poached and grilled saddle of venison, celeriac cannelloni, herb gnocchi, tarragon jus. There are vegan options; plain grilled fish or steak on request. 'Our Bulgarian waitresses were excellent, funny, efficient and anxious to look after us.' 'We recommend this to anyone who is in the area, even if you need to go out of your way to get there.' (Sally Mehalko, DH)

The Royal Welsh Way
Llandudno LL30 1RS

T: 01492 584466
E: info@bodysgallen.com
W: bodysgallen.com

BEDROOMS: 31. 16 in cottages, 1 suitable for disabled.
OPEN: all year, restaurant closed Mon and Tues lunch.
FACILITIES: hall, drawing room, library, bar, dining room, free Wi-Fi, in-room TV (Sky, Freeview), civil wedding licence, 220-acre park (gardens, tennis, croquet), spa (swimming pool), ground floor wheelchair accessible.
BACKGROUND MUSIC: none.
LOCATION: 2 miles S of Llandudno and Conwy.
CHILDREN: no under-6s in hotel, or under-8s in spa.
DOGS: allowed in some cottages.
CREDIT CARDS: Amex, MC, Visa.
PRICES: per room B&B single £180–£430, double £200–£490, D,B&B double £280–£580. À la carte £63. 1-night bookings sometimes refused.

SEE ALSO SHORTLIST

LLANDUDNO Conwy

MAP 3:A3

OSBORNE HOUSE

If you do like to be beside the seaside, you'll be beside yourself with glee at this opulent small hotel on the promenade of a quintessential Victorian coastal resort. This is not a place for minimalists; the Maddocks and Waddy families have furnished it throughout in full-blown 1850s style. Six sea-facing suites have a comfy sitting room, 'table lamps everywhere', a marble bathroom with bath and walk-in shower, perhaps a four-poster with diaphanous drapes, a working gas fire in a marble fireplace. Public rooms are lavish, with acres of seating, gilded mirrors, oil paintings, chandeliers. Readers praise the 'gorgeous surroundings', and advise choosing a second-floor room for the best views. Food is served all day in the bistro where Michael Waddy's menus draw on local produce for such dishes as lamb shank with rosemary jus; seared scallops, fish and chips. There is a continental breakfast – if you want a full Welsh you can go round to the sister hotel, The Empire, where you also have use of spa and gym. Don't miss a ride on the funicular tramway to the top of Llandudno's Great Orme mini-mountain to see the feral Kashmir goats – and be sure to send us a postcard describing your stay.

17 North Parade
Llandudno LL30 2LP

T: 01492 860330
E: sales@empirehotel.co.uk
W: osbornehouse.co.uk

BEDROOMS: 7.
OPEN: all year, except 15–27 Dec.
FACILITIES: sitting room, bar, café/bistro, small patio, in-room TV (Freeview), free Wi-Fi, unsuitable for wheelchair users.
BACKGROUND MUSIC: in public rooms.
LOCATION: on promenade.
CHILDREN: not under 14.
DOGS: not allowed.
CREDIT CARDS: Amex, MC, Visa.
PRICES: per room B&B £135–£195, D,B&B £160–£225. À la carte £25.
1-night bookings refused weekends.

SEE ALSO SHORTLIST

LLANGAMMARCH WELLS Powys

MAP 3:D3

THE LAKE

'In a beautiful setting' in wooded grounds, with trout lake and the River Irfon running through it, Jean-Pierre Mifsud's hotel is especially praised for its 'location, ambience and welcoming staff'. It began life in 1840 as a fishing and hunting lodge, later remodelled to create an odd mix of mock Tudor and Colonial; but within, all is harmony with log-burners, lots of comfortable seating. There are country-house style bedrooms in the main house, with antique pieces. 'Our corner suite, with lovely views, was well furnished.' Suites in the purpose-built lodge are more contemporary with an open-plan sitting room, bath and walk-in shower, and will suit a family. One reader felt the main house would benefit from a little updating. The 'very good' spa harks back to 1912 when Germany's Kaiser Wilhelm visited to take the waters. In the dining room, Mike Evans's 'beautifully cooked and prepared' dishes include duck breast, apricot chutney, beetroot, roast cauliflower, port wine jus; pan-fried hake, herb mash, tenderstem broccoli, lemon butter. Breakfast brings smoked haddock, kippers, free-range eggs Florentine; fuel for a spot of golf or a day's fishing. (Paul Hogarth, and others)

25% DISCOUNT VOUCHERS

Llangammarch Wells LD4 4BS

T: 01591 620202
E: info@lakecountryhouse.co.uk
W: lakecountryhouse.co.uk

BEDROOMS: 32. 12 suites in adjacent lodge, 7 on ground floor, 1 suitable for disabled.
OPEN: all year.
FACILITIES: lounge, bar, restaurant, breakfast room, free Wi-Fi, in-room TV (Freeview), spa (15-metre swimming pool), civil wedding licence, 50-acre grounds (tennis, trout lake, 9-hole golf course), public rooms wheelchair accessible.
BACKGROUND MUSIC: none.
LOCATION: 8 miles SW of Builth Wells.
CHILDREN: all ages welcomed.
DOGS: allowed (£15 per dog per night), not in main lounge, dining room, spa.
CREDIT CARDS: Amex, MC, Visa.
PRICES: per room B&B single from £115, double £125–£260, D,B&B (min. 2 nights) £195–£340. Set dinner £45.

LLANTHONY Monmouthshire   MAP 3:D4

LLANTHONY PRIORY HOTEL

In the beautiful landscape of the Welsh Borders',
in the Vale of Ewyas, and within the precincts of
a ruined Augustinian abbey, Victoria and Geoff
Neal's hotel incorporates a Grade I listed medieval
tower. The main building may have been the
prior's lodgings. In the early 1800s it belonged to
eccentric poet Walter Savage Landor, who waxed
lyrical about nightingales and glow-worms but
fell out with the locals. In a later incarnation, as
the Abbey Hotel, it was frankly spartan. Even
now, four bedrooms in the tower, reached by a
stone spiral staircase, share two first-floor shower
rooms. Two further bedrooms share a bathroom.
All have been done in 'a tasteful and restful way',
furnished with antiques, perhaps a four-poster
or half-tester bed. Come for the history, the
atmosphere, the views of the Black mountains,
the dark sky, the peace (no TV, no Wi-Fi, no
phone signal). There's a lounge with an open fire,
a snug little bar in the undercroft serving real
ales. Walkers returning hungry from the Offa's
Dyke Path can tuck into abbot's casserole, turkey
Caerphilly, nut roast with capsicum sauce, or spicy
bean goulash, in the vaulted dining room in the
crypt, before compline.

Llanthony
Abergavenny NP7 7NN

T: 01873 890487
E: llanthonypriory@btconnect.com
W: llanthonyprioryhotel.co.uk

BEDROOMS: 7. All with shared showers/
bathrooms.
OPEN: Fri–Sun (Nov–Mar), Tues–Sun
(Apr–Oct), 27 Dec–1 Jan, closed Mon
except bank holidays.
FACILITIES: lounge, bar, dining room,
no Wi-Fi or TV, extensive grounds
(including priory ruins), unsuitable
for disabled.
BACKGROUND MUSIC: none.
LOCATION: 10 miles N of Abergavenny.
CHILDREN: over-4s welcomed in family
rooms.
DOGS: not allowed.
CREDIT CARDS: MC, Visa.
PRICES: per room B&B single £75–£80,
double £95–£100.

LLYSWEN Powys

LLANGOED HALL

A 'fabulous' art collection still adorns this Jacobean mansion, which was opened as a hotel by the late Sir Bernard Ashley in 1990. The building was redesigned in 1912 by Clough Williams-Ellis, before he got to work on Portmeirion. A trusted reader visiting at Christmas found the halls 'beautifully' decked, staff 'in plentiful supply, attentive, friendly, efficient'. The 'spacious, lovely' bedrooms are filled with antiques. Some have a four-poster, original Laura Ashley fabrics and decor. All have fresh fruit, Noble Isle toiletries. You can eat simply from the lounge menu, or hold back on the 'delicious scones for cream tea' and succumb to Nick Brodie's tasting menu. Ingredients are sourced locally and from the kitchen garden, for such dishes as scallop, buttermilk, kohlrabi, caviar, yuzu; beef tartare, taramasalata, nasturtium; duck, red leaves, bramble, foie gras. 'We enjoyed the fine dining, and the special food was enhanced by elegant glassware and china.' Breakfast brings new-laid eggs from the ducks and hens, home-smoked salmon, a full Welsh with laver bread cake, smashed avocado on sourdough toast. 'A really grand, most welcoming country house.' (Mary Coles)

Llyswen
Brecon LD3 0YP

T: 01874 754525
E: reception@llangoedhall.com
W: llangoedhall.com

BEDROOMS: 23.
OPEN: all year.
FACILITIES: great hall, morning room, library, bar/lounge, restaurant, billiard room, function rooms, free Wi-Fi, in-room TV (Freeview), civil wedding licence, 17-acre gardens and parkland, unsuitable for disabled.
BACKGROUND MUSIC: during functions, pianist on special occasions.
LOCATION: 12 miles NE of Brecon.
CHILDREN: all ages welcomed.
DOGS: allowed in 2 bedrooms, £25 per night, not in public rooms, heated kennels (no charge) available.
CREDIT CARDS: MC, Visa.
PRICES: per room B&B £150–£950, D,B&B £250–£1,050. À la carte £55, six-course tasting menu £60, nine-course £90.

NARBERTH Pembrokeshire

MAP 3:D2

THE GROVE

♛ Previous César Winner

In a grove, indeed, surrounded by flower gardens, kitchen garden, meadows, with views to the Preseli hills, Neil and Zoë Kedward's hotel is 'a real haven'. A 17th-century house, remodelled in the 1870s, with Arts and Crafts Gothic interiors, it has 'lovely public rooms and grounds', writes a reader this year. Bedrooms are in the main house and cottages, including a 15th-century longhouse. They are of a high order, stylish, with original artwork, contemporary touches. Sage, in Herb Cottage, was 'very comfortable with its own garden'. You can take tea on the lawn or by the fire in a panelled lounge, dine in the relaxed atmosphere of the Artisan Rooms (perhaps a plate of Welsh cheeses, a steak, roasted hake, risotto). The big change this year is the appointment of new head chef Douglas Balish, with a Michelin star under his belt, to preside over the fine-dining Fernery restaurant; we expect great things. In a report preceding his arrival, a reader described how the dining room service almost stalled one night. However, 'housekeeping was good. Reception staff are cheery and helpful.' You can order a hamper or rucksack picnic; the coast is a 12-minute drive away. (SH, PJ, and others)

Molleston
Narberth SA67 8BX

T: 01834 860915
E: reservations@grovenarberth.co.uk
W: thegrove-narberth.co.uk

BEDROOMS: 26. 12 in cottages in grounds, 1 suitable for disabled.
OPEN: all year.
FACILITIES: 3 lounges, bar, 4 restaurant rooms, free Wi-Fi, in-room TV (Sky), in-room spa treatments, civil wedding licence, 26-acre grounds, ground floor wheelchair accessible.
BACKGROUND MUSIC: in public areas.
LOCATION: 1 mile S of Narberth.
CHILDREN: all ages welcomed, no under-12s in Fernery.
DOGS: allowed in some bedrooms and lounge, the Snug dining room.
CREDIT CARDS: Amex, MC, Visa.
PRICES: per room B&B £240–£650, D,B&B £368–£778. Tasting menu £94, set dinner £69, à la carte (Artisan Rooms) £40. 1-night bookings refused peak times.

SEE ALSO SHORTLIST

NEWPORT Pembrokeshire

CNAPAN

'Hospitality of the highest quality lies behind the front door of this outstanding B&B.' A Guide inspector had 'a most rewarding stay' at this pink-washed, Grade II listed Georgian house in a conservation area. Second-generation owners Judith and Michael Cooper run it with their son, Oliver. 'Judith's energy, enthusiasm and kindness radiate, while Michael provides friendly, cultured support, with Oliver carrying on in the welcoming style.' New arrivals enjoy tea and Welsh cake in a lounge with log-burner or in the secluded garden. Bedrooms have restful decor, contemporary styling, a super-king-size bed that can be made up as twins, smart toiletries, books, maps. 'Our good-sized bedroom had a comfortable bed, high-quality linen, a small en suite shower (very efficient).' Front rooms, overlooking the street, may have some traffic noise, but afford views of the Norman castle and distant Carningli mountain. 'Breakfast comprised a simple buffet, very good home-made mango and lime yogurt, followed by vegetarian sausages.' There are kippers, smoked salmon, the full Welsh with local bacon, 'everything piping hot'. The Pembrokeshire Coast national park awaits explorers.

East Street
Newport SA42 0SY

T: 01239 820575
E: enquiry@cnapan.co.uk
W: cnapan.co.uk

BEDROOMS: 5. Includes 1 family room. Plus self-catering cottage.
OPEN: all year except Christmas and holiday in Feb and early March (ring or check website for dates).
FACILITIES: sitting room, bar, free Wi-Fi, in-room TV (Freeview), small garden.
BACKGROUND MUSIC: none.
LOCATION: town centre.
CHILDREN: all ages welcomed.
DOGS: not allowed.
CREDIT CARDS: MC, Visa.
PRICES: per room B&B single £60–£75, double £80–£98, family room (sleeps 3) £100–£115. Dinner for parties of 18 or more by arrangement. 1-night bookings sometimes refused weekends at peak times.

NEWPORT Pembrokeshire

MAP 3:D1

LLYS MEDDYG

♀ Previous César Winner

'You sense that hospitality comes naturally to the owners and their team.' A Guide insider was impressed by Edward and Louise Sykes's 'personable', family-run restaurant-with-rooms inside the Pembrokeshire Coast national park. Occupying a Georgian house once owned by a local doctor, it overlooks a village street, although the background noise is the 'gentle sloshing' of a brook. Bedrooms have contemporary styling, local artwork, a king-size bed, minibar, fresh milk, Conscious Skincare products. A top-floor room was 'compact but well organised, with a modern-rustic look and an enormous, smart bathroom'. Food is served in the cosy cellar bar and formal dining room or, on sunny days, in the kitchen garden. A new chef is awaited as we go to press, but the sous-chef does sterling work with fresh, local produce, some foraged by Ed from shore and hedgerow, Menus include such dishes as sirloin and cheek of Dexter beef, burnt shallot, garlic cabbage, preserved damsons. A children's menu is unusually imaginative. Breakfast brings freshly squeezed orange juice, 'lovely blueberry jam and marmalade made by Ed's brother'. 'We would return at any time.' (CS, AS)

East Street
Newport SA42 0SY

T: 01239 820008
E: info@llysmeddyg.com
W: llysmeddyg.com

BEDROOMS: 8. 1 on ground floor, 3 in mews annexe, plus a cottage.
OPEN: all year, restaurant closed Mon, Tues (Nov–Apr).
FACILITIES: bar, lounge, restaurant, kitchen garden dining area (open in summer holidays), free Wi-Fi, in-room TV (Freeview), civil wedding licence, garden, unsuitable for disabled.
BACKGROUND MUSIC: in bar and dining room.
LOCATION: central.
CHILDREN: all ages welcomed.
DOGS: allowed in 3 annexe bedrooms, bar, on lead in garden.
CREDIT CARDS: MC, Visa.
PRICES: per room B&B single £80–£145, double £100–£160. D,B&B double £150–£220. À la carte £35.

PENARTH Vale of Glamorgan   MAP 3:E4

RESTAURANT JAMES SOMMERIN
♀ Previous César Winner

In a 'lovely location on the quiet seafront', with views over the Severn estuary and the pier pavilion, James Sommerin and family run this acclaimed restaurant-with-rooms. Behind the quaint, balconied, brick-and-timber exterior lies a modern dining room styled in tones of brown and turquoise, the tables laid with crisp white linen. Big windows overlook the esplanade, while through the long serving hatch you can watch Michelin-starred chef James and his team, including daughter Georgia, at work in the kitchen. His wife, Louise, is in charge front-of-house. The cooking is 'wonderful, the menus are as short on hyperbole as they are long on promise'. For instance, corn-fed chicken, celeriac, thyme, girolles; monkfish, salsify, kale, spices; root vegetable, tomato, basil. 'The tasting menu was beautifully presented and efficiently served,' writes a reader this year. The 'attractive if functional' bedrooms, most with sea view, are smart and contemporary, with seaside colours of aquamarine and wet sand, floor-to-ceiling windows, luxury toiletries. Breakfast brings 'a wide choice'. 'A good if pricey experience.' (Geoffrey Bignell, CT, PK)

The Esplanade
Penarth CF64 3AU

T: 029 2070 6559
E: info@jamessommerinrestaurant.co.uk
W: jamessommerinrestaurant.co.uk

BEDROOMS: 9. 1 suitable for disabled.
OPEN: all year except Mon, Tues, 24–26 Dec, 1 Jan, restaurant closed 26 Dec, 1 Jan.
FACILITIES: bar, restaurant, private dining room, free Wi-Fi, in-room Smart TV (Freeview), restaurant and bar wheelchair accessible, adapted toilet.
BACKGROUND MUSIC: in bar and restaurant.
LOCATION: on the esplanade.
CHILDREN: all ages welcomed.
DOGS: not allowed.
CREDIT CARDS: Amex, MC, Visa.
PRICES: per room B&B £150–£170, D,B&B £240–£260. Tasting menus £75–£95, à la carte £50 (not Fri or Sat).

SEE ALSO SHORTLIST

PWLLHELI Gwynedd

MAP 3:B2

THE OLD RECTORY

'Lindsay is one of the most welcoming people I've ever met; the breakfasts, all freshly cooked by Gary, are delicious.' Praise this year for the Ashcrofts, your hosts at this Georgian rectory on the beautiful Llyn peninsula. Four miles outside the market town of Pwllheli with its Blue Flag beaches. the B&B stands 'in stunning grounds' with mature trees, lawns, and banks of flowers bordering a drive that sweeps up to the front door. Within, the house is 'nicely decorated throughout'. Squashy leather sofas emit a contented sigh when you sink down by the wood-burning stove in a lounge with windows on to the front and back gardens. Upstairs, past the landing's rocking horse, the 'roomy' bedrooms have nice touches, sherry, chocolates, plenty of toiletries, an informative welcome pack. 'Beds provide a comfortable, cosy night's sleep.' The rooms have garden views, proper en suite facilities (Room 3 has a particularly good bathroom). Breakfast, served at a long table in a dining room, brings locally sourced fish and meat, free-range eggs, home-made bread and preserves. 'A lovely break in a beautiful area.' (Sharon Warn)

25% DISCOUNT VOUCHERS

Boduan
Pwllheli LL53 6DT

T: 01758 721519
E: theashcrofts@theoldrectory.net
W: theoldrectory.net

BEDROOMS: 4. Plus a self-catering cottage and lodge.
OPEN: all year except Christmas and New Year.
FACILITIES: drawing room, breakfast/dining room, free Wi-Fi, in-room TV (Freeview), aromatherapy treatments, 3-acre grounds, beach hut in season, unsuitable for disabled.
BACKGROUND MUSIC: none.
LOCATION: 4 miles NW of Pwllheli.
CHILDREN: all ages welcomed.
DOGS: only assistance dogs allowed.
CREDIT CARDS: MC, Visa.
PRICES: per room B&B single £85–£95, double £100–£120. 1-night bookings refused some weekends, high season and bank holidays.

ST DAVID'S Pembrokeshire

MAP 3:D1

TWR Y FELIN HOTEL

We don't wish to blow our own trumpet, but we like to think the Guide played a small part in the runaway success of Wales's first contemporary art hotel. One of our top discoveries of 2019, the architect-owned and redesigned Edwardian hotel, built around a Georgian windmill, is set to add 20 new bedrooms by March 2020. It is 'pristine, immaculately furnished, in beautifully landscaped grounds', writes a trusted reader this year. 'They have thought of everything.' Spacious, chocolate-and-cream bedrooms are hypoallergenic (no dogs), with terrace or balcony, espresso machine, mini-fridge, bath, shower, aromatherapy toiletries. 'The bathroom was the best we've experienced.' The Tower Suite has a spiral staircase to the belvedere overlooking the St David's peninsula. Staff are 'attentive and welcoming'. Many of the paintings on display are by local street artists. Sous-chef Sam Owen has now stepped up as head chef, creating such dishes as malt-glazed halibut, scallop tortellini, pea, pancetta, from prime Welsh ingredients. 'The extensive breakfast menu' includes freshly squeezed orange juice, freshly baked pastries, home-made preserves, 'well-cooked' hot dishes. (Mary Coles, RC)

25% DISCOUNT VOUCHERS

Caerfai Road
St David's SA62 6QT

T: 01437 725555
E: stay@twryfelinhotel.com
W: twryfelinhotel.com

BEDROOMS: 21. Some on ground floor, some in separate wing, 1 suitable for disabled, more are planned.
OPEN: all year.
FACILITIES: bar, restaurant, lounge, free Wi-Fi, in-room TV (Sky), landscaped grounds, civil wedding licence, public areas wheelchair accessible.
BACKGROUND MUSIC: in public areas.
LOCATION: a few hundred yards from centre of St David's.
CHILDREN: not under 12.
DOGS: not allowed.
CREDIT CARDS: Amex, MC, Visa.
PRICES: per room B&B £180–£400, D,B&B £250–£470. À la carte £35. Normally 2-night min. stay Fri and Sat, but check for 1-night availability.

SEE ALSO SHORTLIST

SAUNDERSFOOT Pembrokeshire   MAP 3:D2

ST BRIDES SPA HOTEL

'An example of what a British seaside hotel can
do.' Trusted readers were impressed by Lindsey
and Andrew Evans's coastal property, created
with an 'ambition, vision and style one might
associate with California or Australia'. Sitting
above Carmarthen Bay, it has 'exceptional views'.
Light floods in through floor-to-ceiling windows,
ocean air through glass doors. 'Very pleasant,
stylish' bedrooms, with breezy nautical hues, are
rated 'good', 'better', 'best', the cheapest being
'quite small', though 'some have a balcony'. All
rooms are supplied with robes, slippers, VOYA
toiletries, a fridge and milk. Residents get a
90-minute session in the spa's hydro pool. The
ethos was 'rather corporate; we'd have liked
a warmer welcome'. But 'service was good'.
Dine in the Cliff restaurant, the Gallery bar, or
on the terrace. Daniel Retter's locally sourced
dishes include salmon tempura oyster, pak choi,
curried mussel sauce. A fish and chips outlet and
beach barbecue are offshoots. Children get their
own menu. Breakfast brings smoked haddock,
mushrooms and laver bread on toasted muffins.

St Brides Hill
Saundersfoot SA69 9NH

T: 01834 812304
E: reservations@stbridesspahotel.com
W: stbridesspahotel.com

BEDROOMS: 34. 1 suitable for disabled.
Plus six 2-bed apartments in grounds,
12 self-catering in village.
OPEN: all year.
FACILITIES: lift, lounge, bar, restaurant,
Gallery dining area, meeting/
function rooms, Wi-Fi, in-room TV
(Freeview), civil wedding licence,
terraces, art gallery, spa (treatments,
infinity pool), public areas wheelchair
accessible, adapted toilet.
BACKGROUND MUSIC: all day.
LOCATION: 3 mins' walk to village.
CHILDREN: all ages welcomed.
DOGS: allowed in some apartments.
CREDIT CARDS: Amex, MC, Visa.
PRICES: per room B&B single
£145–£230, double £190–£350, D,B&B
double £210–£430 (at limited times of
year). À la carte £40.

SKENFRITH Monmouthshire

MAP 3:D4

THE BELL AT SKENFRITH

'In a lovely location', Richard Ireton and Sarah Hudson's restored coaching inn on the banks of the River Monnow continues to delight readers. Rooms at the back of the 300-year-old, oak-beamed building look on to 'the gardens and surrounding hills', while those at the front enjoy tranquil views of the river (there's paddling in summer) and the humpback bridge that spans it. A visitor this year found her room to be 'generously proportioned and comfortable', with 'a huge, high bed'. The 'homey and luxurious feel' comes courtesy of cosy Welsh blankets, Noble Isle toiletries and home-made shortbread. Some of the bathrooms have a 'large freestanding bath'. Food, created by Welsh chef Joseph Colman, is 'excellent and simple' using locally sourced produce as well as vegetables and fruit from the hotel's kitchen garden: choice might include 'deliciously tender roast lamb with fondant potatoes and steamed broccoli' or 'fantastic chicken liver pâté'. In summer, meals can be served outside on the terrace. After such epicurean treats, one guest found the cooked breakfast 'underwhelming', but there is nothing lacklustre about the staff, who are 'unfailingly kind and friendly'. (ANR)

25% DISCOUNT VOUCHERS

Skenfrith NP7 8UH

T: 01600 750235
E: reception@skenfrith.co.uk
W: skenfrith.co.uk

BEDROOMS: 11.
OPEN: all year.
FACILITIES: bar, restaurant, Wine Room (for reading, relaxing, private dining), Dog and Boot bar, free Wi-Fi, in-room TV (BT, Freeview), 2-acre grounds (terrace, garden), restaurant, bar and terrace wheelchair accessible, adapted toilet.
BACKGROUND MUSIC: 'intermittently' in bar and restaurant.
LOCATION: 9 miles W of Ross-on-Wye.
CHILDREN: all ages welcomed.
DOGS: well-behaved dogs allowed in bedrooms and Dog and Boot bar, Pooch Parlour dog shower in garden with towels.
CREDIT CARDS: MC, Visa.
PRICES: per room B&B £150–£250, D,B&B £190–£290. À la carte £36. 1-night bookings refused Sat.

TYWYN Gwynedd

DOLFFANOG FAWR

'Alex and Lorraine's 18th-century farmhouse offers a level of hospitality to rival many of the best small hotels in the UK.' Readers are taken with Alex Yorke and Lorraine Hinkins's Snowdonia guest house with views over Tal-y-llyn lake to Cader Idris. 'They achieve their aim of offering good value for money, and minimising food miles.' Simply furnished bedrooms, each named after a local river, have comfortable bed, local art, Melin Tregwynt throws, upmarket toiletries. Front-facing Mawddach, with views to the Dyfi and Tarren hills, was 'well appointed' with a corner bath and shower over in 'an excellent en suite'. The others enjoy a lake view, and Wnion has windows to the front and back. Three nights a week, Lorraine cooks a meal taken communally around the oak table. 'We enjoyed eating with other visitors, exchanging tales of our day's activities.' The menu, inspired by the seasons, might feature roast Tal-y-llyn lamb or wild sea trout. 'The breakfast choice is excellent', with award-winning sausages, dry-cured bacon, free-range eggs, organic home-baked bread, home-made jam, fish options; all setting you up for a long walk. The garden's hot tub awaits your return. (B and JH)

Tal-y-llyn
Tywyn LL36 9AJ

T: 01654 761247
E: info@dolffanogfawr.co.uk
W: dolffanogfawr.co.uk

BEDROOMS: 4. 1 reached by covered walkway.
OPEN: Mar–Oct, dinner served Thurs–Sat.
FACILITIES: lounge, dining room, free Wi-Fi, in-room TV (Freeview), 1-acre garden (hot tub), unsuitable for disabled.
BACKGROUND MUSIC: none.
LOCATION: by lake, 10 miles E of Tywyn.
CHILDREN: not under 10.
DOGS: allowed by arrangement, in bedrooms (not unattended) and lounge 'if other guests don't mind', not in dining room.
CREDIT CARDS: MC, Visa.
PRICES: per room B&B single £90–£120, double £100–£120. À la carte £28 (2% surcharge if paying by credit card). 1-night bookings often refused.

WHITEBROOK Monmouthshire

MAP 3:D4

THE WHITEBROOK

Some forest findings with your roast Jerusalem artichokes? Estuary greens with the scallops? Nature's wild bounty features prominently at this lauded restaurant-with-rooms owned by Michelin-starred chef Chris Harrod and his wife, Kirsty. Set above a single-track road in a sequestered hamlet, deep in the Wye valley, it is hard to find. 'Our satnav decided we needed to drive across a snow-covered field,' related a reader. Persistence was repaid with a warm welcome and 'meltingly delicious Welsh cake'. An unfussy, 'well-equipped' bedroom nailed the basics: a queen-size bed with 'good-quality bedding', a bathroom 'with a proper window, organic toiletries, an enormous bath and a walk-in shower'. The food is the highlight, however. A protégé of Raymond Blanc, Mr Harrod draws on local producers, fish from Cornwall and ingredients he and forager Henry Ashby garner from forest and hedgerow. Typical dishes: roasted cauliflower, pine, blackened onions, crispy kales, hedge bedstraw; grey mullet, potato purée, purple sprouting broccoli, brown shrimp, three-cornered garlic. 'A great meal. I urge you to go,' writes our reader, who was lucky (or unlucky) not to have been snowed in. (DH)

Whitebrook NP25 4TX

T: 01600 860254
E: info@thewhitebrook.co.uk
W: thewhitebrook.co.uk

BEDROOMS: 8.
OPEN: all year, except 24–26 Dec (rooms), 2 weeks Jan, restaurant closed Mon, and Tues lunch, 26 Dec.
FACILITIES: lounge/bar, restaurant, free Wi-Fi, in-room TV (Freeview), terrace, 2-acre garden, restaurant and women's toilet wheelchair accessible.
BACKGROUND MUSIC: 'chill-out' in restaurant and lounge.
LOCATION: 6 miles S of Monmouth.
CHILDREN: all ages welcomed, over-8s only in restaurant on weekdays, over-16s only at weekends.
DOGS: only guide dogs allowed.
CREDIT CARDS: Amex, MC, Visa.
PRICES: per room B&B £140–£235, D,B&B £279–£405. 7-course dinner £85, set lunch £42–£55.

CHANNEL ISLANDS

Elizabeth Castle, Jersey

HERM

THE WHITE HOUSE

The ferry from Guernsey brings guests to this
tiny, car-free island; the one and only hotel sends a
tractor for their bags. Surrounded by sub-tropical
gardens, with memorable views across to a beach
of white sand, it's 'a great place for kids', says
a reader who returns every year – and they're
moving with the times! 'There are now clocks
on the radios in the bedrooms', though still no
telephone or TV. A minor issue of some supplies
drying up, hinting at logistical problems, in no
way ruined 'a good stay enjoyed by all the family'.
Some bedrooms have a balcony, some have French
doors to the pool. All can accommodate a cot
or child's bed. In the Conservatory restaurant
new chef Krzysztof Janiak (whose CV includes
catering for royal banquets and a UN officers'
mess) cooks modern British dishes with German
and French influences. For instance, 'inspired
by Jackson Pollock', duck brined with juniper
berries, Silesian dumplings, spinach and
watercress purée, preserved and fresh redcurrant.
You can eat more simple, brasserie fare in
the turquoise-painted Ship Inn. With just 60
permanent human residents plus colonies of
seals and puffins, Herm offers a complete escape.
(Jane Thornton)

Herm GY1 3HR

T: 01481 750075
E: hotel@herm.com
W: herm.com

BEDROOMS: 40. 23 in cottages, some on
ground floor.
OPEN: early Apr–end Oct.
FACILITIES: 3 lounges, 2 bars,
2 restaurants, conference room, free
Wi-Fi, 1-acre gardens (tennis, croquet),
7-metre solar-heated swimming pool,
wheelchair access to island difficult.
BACKGROUND MUSIC: background in
the Ship Inn.
LOCATION: by harbour, ferry from
Guernsey (20 mins).
CHILDREN: all ages welcomed.
DOGS: allowed in 2 bedrooms (£20
per dog per night), reception lounge,
garden bars, with restrictions.
CREDIT CARDS: MC, Visa.
PRICES: per person B&B single
£70–£224, double £145–£270, D,B&B
single from £95, double £195–£370.
Set dinner £38, à la carte £29.

LITTLE SARK Sark

MAP 1: inset E6

LA SABLONNERIE

'Wonderful as ever,' writes a reader this year, a regular returnee to Elizabeth Perrée's 16th-century, whitewashed stone farmhouse in a beautiful part of this car-free island. A horse-drawn carriage awaits guests arriving by ferry from Guernsey. The hotel is unabashedly old-fashioned – 'the distilled essence of Sark', as another reader put it. Bedrooms, in the main house and surrounding cottages, are pretty and traditional, simple but not skimped. Guests tend to gather for an aperitif – perhaps the house sloe gin – before dinner, a formal affair served in the restaurant or in the rose-filled garden. Chef Colin Day 'continues to delight' with his daily-changing menu strong on freshly landed fish and seafood and locally farmed and home-grown produce. For instance, scallops with garlic butter, Sark lobster Thermidor; beef fillet with wild mushrooms; for vegetarians maybe a herb risotto. Far from the distractions of modern life, you can swim in the natural Venus pool, scuba-dive, cycle, take fishing trips, spot oystercatchers and puffins, explore caves, visit gardens or, like our mathematician reader, brush up on Galois theory. (John Barnes, and others)

Little Sark GY10 1SD

T: 01481 832061
E: reservations@sablonneriesark.com
W: sablonneriesark.com

BEDROOMS: 22. Some in nearby cottages.
OPEN: mid-Apr–Oct.
FACILITIES: 3 lounges, 2 bars, restaurant, Wi-Fi by arrangement, civil wedding licence, 1-acre garden (tea garden/bar, croquet), unsuitable for disabled.
BACKGROUND MUSIC: classical/piano in bar.
LOCATION: Little Sark, via boat from Guernsey (guests will be met at the harbour on arrival).
CHILDREN: all ages welcomed.
DOGS: allowed at hotel's discretion in some bedrooms, not in public rooms.
CREDIT CARDS: MC, Visa.
PRICES: per room B&B £98-£166, D,B&B £137–£196. Set menus £31, à la carte £51.

ST BRELADE Jersey

MAP 1: inset E6

THE ATLANTIC HOTEL

It's a golden anniversary year for Patrick Burke's sleek ocean liner of a hotel in mature landscaped gardens overlooking St Ouen's Bay. It was opened in 1970 by Patrick's father, Henry, whose first Jersey venture, the Penguin, was – bingo! – scooped up by Billy Butlins. So Patrick has hotel-keeping in his blood and, year on year here, 'all is great'. Bedrooms, with marble bathroom, are contemporary in style and 'spotless'. They aren't all huge, but ocean-view rooms with glass doors and balcony have a great sense of space. Rooms facing La Moye Golf Course are also 'beautifully appointed', and though lacking the vista, should suit golf nuts to a tee. In the 'quite wonderful' Ocean restaurant Michelin-starred chef Will Holland cooks a daily-changing market menu. Or dine à la carte on such 'lovely, sometimes innovative' dishes as grilled John Dory fillet, confit fennel, clams, potato purée, caper and olive oil dressing. There are vegetarian options, a children's menu, refined dining in The Tasting Room, lighter lounge fare. Staff are 'always about but not intrusive'. A health club, flower-decked terrace and pool round things off. 'It deserves to be in the Guide. We will return.'

Le Mont de la Pulente
St Brelade JE3 8HE

T: 01534 744101
E: info@theatlantichotel.com
W: theatlantichotel.com

BEDROOMS: 50. Some on ground floor.
OPEN: all year except 2 Jan–7 Feb.
FACILITIES: lift, lounge, library, cocktail bar, restaurant, private dining room, fitness centre, free Wi-Fi, in-room TV (Sky), civil wedding licence, 6-acre garden (tennis, indoor and outdoor heated swimming pools, 10 by 5 metres), public rooms wheelchair accessible.
BACKGROUND MUSIC: in restaurant, lounge and cocktail bar in evenings.
LOCATION: 5 miles W of St Helier.
CHILDREN: all ages welcomed.
DOGS: guide dogs only.
CREDIT CARDS: Amex, MC, Visa.
PRICES: per room B&B single £130–£450, double £150–£470. Set dinner £55, tasting menu £87, à la carte £68.

SEE ALSO SHORTLIST

ST PETER Jersey

MAP 1: inset E6

GREENHILLS COUNTRY HOUSE HOTEL

In 'a lovely location in a quiet rural spot' within Jersey's network of Green Lanes, this hotel centres on an 'elegant and attractive' building dating from 1674. A recent £1.2 million renovation by family owners Seymour Hotels (founded in 1919) saw the addition of 11 new bedrooms. Three wings enclose a flower-filled patio garden with 'a small pool, chairs and loungers'. Guests take afternoon tea alfresco – or sink into a chair by the fire in a beamed lounge. Bedrooms range from 'standard' to 'superior plus' with sofa, espresso machine, fridge, bath, walk-in shower, French doors on to the garden. The styling is contemporary country house, the presentation 'first class – the standard and quality cannot be faulted'. The top-floor Killiecrankie Suite has a separate lounge and dining area, a bath and walk-in shower. All rooms are supplied with home-made biscuits and White Company toiletries. In the dining room, chef Lukasz Pietrasz's menus highlight fine local produce, from a bowl of moules marinière to Grouville Bay oysters, vanilla, sherry, shallots; turbot fillet, herb gnocchi, crab tortellini, brunoise summer vegetables. 'We could not find any negatives, which is rare.'

Mont de l'École
St Peter JE3 7EL

T: 08458 005555
E: reservations@greenhillshotel.com
W: seymourhotels.com

BEDROOMS: 33. 10 on ground floor, 1 suitable for disabled.
OPEN: all year except 23 Dec–mid-Feb.
FACILITIES: 2 lounges, bar, restaurant, garden, terrace, free Wi-Fi, in-room TV, civil wedding licence, outdoor heated swimming pool, access to leisure club at sister hotel, public rooms wheelchair accessible.
BACKGROUND MUSIC: in public areas.
LOCATION: 8 miles NW of St Helier.
CHILDREN: all ages welcomed.
DOGS: allowed in 4 ground-floor bedrooms (£10 per dog per night), not in public areas, but assistance dogs 'always welcome'.
CREDIT CARDS: Amex, MC, Visa.
PRICES: per room B&B £109–£224. Set dinner £40, à la carte £50.

ST PETER PORT Guernsey

MAP 1: inset E5

LA FREGATE

High above St Peter's Port harbour, this elegant,
extended 18th-century town house allows guests
to awake to 'fantastic views' across rooftops
and a sea frescoed with boats, to neighbouring
islands. The original property initially takes
centre stage with a thick stone entrance, and
a bar-cum-lounge sporting beams, exposed
brickwork and plush sofas. It opens on to the
sun-soaked terrace above the old granite wall,
'just the spot for a refreshing drink on a hot day'.
Huge windows exploit the hilltop position in
the bedrooms, four of them newly refurbished,
with a sand, aqua and peach palette inspired by
the island setting. Many in the new wing have
a balcony or terrace designed to catch the early
morning sun; each comes with fluffy robes, crisp
bedlinen, turn-down. In a dining room washed
with ocean light, freshly landed seafood stars on
Tony Leck's seasonal menu. For instance, Herm
Island oysters, champagne butter; Guernsey brill,
champ potatoes, asparagus, lobster beurre blanc.
The well-considered vegetarian dishes include
Guernsey smoked Cheddar beignets; asparagus,
poached hen's egg. Breakfast has 'much choice'.
A pretty path drops from the hotel garden into
the town centre.

Beauregard Lane
Les Cotils
St Peter Port GY1 1UT

T: 01481 724624
E: enquiries@lafregatehotel.com
W: lafregatehotel.com

BEDROOMS: 22.
OPEN: all year.
FACILITIES: lounge/bar, restaurant,
lift, private dining/function rooms,
free Wi-Fi, in-room TV (Freeview),
terrace (alfresco dining), ½-acre
terraced garden, unsuitable for
disabled.
BACKGROUND MUSIC: in bar.
LOCATION: hilltop, 5 mins' walk from
centre.
CHILDREN: all ages welcomed.
DOGS: guide dogs only.
CREDIT CARDS: Amex, MC, Visa
PRICES: per room B&B single £100,
double £205–£260. À la carte £50.

SEE ALSO SHORTLIST

ST SAVIOUR Jersey

MAP 1: inset E6

LONGUEVILLE MANOR

Behind a 16th-century facade festooned with
wisteria in springtime, this manor house hotel
(Relais & Châteaux), in its own wooded valley,
abounds in modern five-star comfort. Its
third-generation owners, Malcolm and Patricia
Lewis, have 'a personal touch', helped by 'plenty
of smiles' from the 'professional, attentive'
staff. Rooms are a mix of the traditional and
contemporary, perhaps with a four-poster, a
patio, an in-room bath and a wet room. One suite
has beams from the Spanish Armada; another,
in a turret, has a stone bath, oversized shower,
garden access. You can dine in the original Great
Hall, partly panelled with broken-up oak chests.
Chef Andrew Baird's locally sourced menus use
produce from the kitchen garden, honey from the
hives. Typical dishes: slow-roast belly pork, Jersey
bean crock, glazed apples; délice of sole, grilled
tiger prawn, scallop shumai, Asian broth. More
casual options include a kebab from the pool-side
barbecue. Tastings are held in a state-of-the-art
wine cellar of more than 4,000 bottles. Grounds
landscaped by a Victorian clergyman, a former
resident, offer lovely forest walks. Small guests
enjoy nature trails, tennis or cookery classes.

Longueville Road
St Saviour JE2 7WF

T: 01534 725501
E: info@longuevillemanor.com
W: longuevillemanor.com

BEDROOMS: 30. 8 on ground floor, suite
in cottage.
OPEN: all year except part of Jan, call
to check.
FACILITIES: lift, 2 lounges, cocktail bar,
2 dining rooms, free Wi-Fi, in-room
Smart TV, conference facilities, civil
wedding licence, spa, 18-acre grounds
(croquet, tennis, outdoor heated pool),
public areas wheelchair accessible.
BACKGROUND MUSIC: in bar and
restaurant.
LOCATION: 1½ miles E of St Helier.
CHILDREN: all ages welcomed.
DOGS: allowed, not in restaurant.
CREDIT CARDS: Amex, MC, Visa.
PRICES: per room B&B £200–£575,
D,B&B £310–£685. Set dinner £55.
tasting menu £92, à la carte £70.
1-night bookings refused weekends,
bank holidays.

IRELAND

Rural Ireland

BAGENALSTOWN Co. Carlow

MAP 6:C6

LORUM OLD RECTORY

♛ Previous César Winner

Bobbie Smith is the welcoming heart and soul
of this B&B in a former 19th-century rectory,
which she runs with her daughter. It's a 'hidden
gem', say readers, with 'tasteful and fine decor
and furniture', 'exemplary comfort and service'.
A homey atmosphere is to be expected: Bobbie
grew up here, and rooms are filled with personal
possessions, antique clocks, paintings and
ornaments. You can take tea in a drawing room
with upright piano, deep sofas, a blazing peat
or log fire; curl up with a book in the study.
Bedrooms are furnished with solid antiques,
perhaps a four-poster, a crammed bookcase,
and are supplied with home-made biscuits. All
overlook the Blackstairs mountains. The dining
room's deep-crimson walls are hung with hunting
prints, silhouettes and orientalist portraits. At
night, candlelight reflects in polished mahogany,
as guests enjoy a 'delicious' convivial five-course
dinner – starter, soup, sorbet, main course, dessert
– cooked by the hostess, using local, seasonal and
organic ingredients. In the morning, a hearty,
'expertly cooked' breakfast sets you up for a day's
walking, fishing, or horse riding courtesy of the
local equestrian centre.

25% DISCOUNT VOUCHERS

Kilgreaney
Bagenalstown R21 RD45

T: 00 353 59 977 5282
E: bobbie@lorum.com
W: lorum.com

BEDROOMS: 4.
OPEN: Feb–end Nov.
FACILITIES: drawing room, study,
dining room, snug, free Wi-Fi, 1-acre
garden (croquet) in 18-acre grounds,
wedding facilities, unsuitable for
disabled.
BACKGROUND MUSIC: none.
LOCATION: 4 miles S of Bagenalstown
on R705 to Borris.
CHILDREN: aged 16 and over
welcomed.
DOGS: by arrangement, not on
furniture or in dining room.
CREDIT CARDS: MC, Visa.
PRICES: per room B&B single
€120–€130, double €180–€190. Set
dinner €50.

BALLINGARRY Co. Limerick

MAP 6:D5

THE MUSTARD SEED AT ECHO LODGE

'We were charmed by the hotel and its attentive staff.' Guide regulars declared John Edward Joyce's country house hotel 'in a class of its own' in 2019, with praise for the man himself: 'Mr Joyce has a gift for hospitality.' The Victorian property is 'the perfect place to unwind, with beautiful gardens to wander round, flower-filled public rooms, lovely valley views'. Guests are personally welcomed with tea and home-made biscuits. Traditionally styled bedrooms, with antiques and vintage prints, include 'thoughtful touches that make it seem more a private house than a hotel'. One room has a four-poster, another an original fireplace; the best rooms, in the older part of the house, have dual-aspect countryside views. In the 'graciously proportioned' dining rooms, Angel Pirev's 'delightful' four-course menus include venison, coffee, Szechuan pepper, Béarnaise sauce, turnip, shortbread; 'effortlessly served on a busy night', it 'richly deserves its excellent reputation'. Come morning, feast on soda bread, perhaps 'smoked salmon and potato farls'. 'Pretty Adare is nearby, but why stir when you can happily while away the hours in a shady spot in the terraced gardens?' (Helena Shaw, JH)

Ballingarry

T: 00 353 69 68508
E: mustard@indigo.ie
W: mustardseed.ie

BEDROOMS: 16. 1, on ground floor, suitable for disabled.
OPEN: all year except 24–26 Dec.
FACILITIES: entrance hall, library, restaurant, sunroom, free Wi-Fi, in-room TV (terrestrial), wedding facilities, 12-acre grounds, restaurant and public rooms wheelchair accessible.
BACKGROUND MUSIC: in restaurant.
LOCATION: in village, 18 miles SW of Limerick.
CHILDREN: all ages welcomed.
DOGS: 'well-behaved' pets welcome, in designated bedrooms (not unattended), not in public rooms.
CREDIT CARDS: Amex, MC, Visa.
PRICES: per person B&B €90–€160, D,B&B €129–€195. Set menus €49–€64.

BALLYCASTLE Co. Mayo

MAP 6:B4

STELLA MARIS

In a 'dramatically beautiful' setting, overlooking Bunatrahir Bay on the Wild Atlantic Way, Frances Kelly-McSweeney's hotel was built for its stellar sea views. Dating from the mid-1800s, it was designed as a coast guard's fortress, complete with gun turrets. But times change; all is now 'totally tranquil', and these days only binoculars are trained on the ocean, from the 100-foot sunroom that runs the length of the building, in the hope of spotting cavorting dolphins. Almost all of the 'comfortable, individually furnished' bedrooms face the ocean. Traditionally styled public rooms en enfilade are warmed by open fires. At night, the hostess dons her toque to cook a short, daily menu of contemporary Irish dishes, 'fresh, simple and local'. Maybe oak-smoked salmon; slow-braised Ballycastle lamb with rosemary and red wine jus, herbed parsnip mash; fish from the day boats; organic leaves from the garden. A reader especially appreciates the 'laid-back' atmosphere (no house-party ethos, no pressure to join in), with 'books scattered around'. Days might be spent on coastal walks, whale-watching, on the links at Enniscrone, or on the lush fairways of Ballina, a leisurely drive away.

Ballycastle

T: 00 353 96 43322
E: info@stellamarisireland.com
W: stellamarisireland.com

BEDROOMS: 11. 1, on ground floor, suitable for disabled.
OPEN: 1 May–30 Sept, restaurant closed Mon evening.
FACILITIES: lounge, bar, restaurant, conservatory, free Wi-Fi ('most dependable in public areas'), in-room TV (Freeview), 2-acre grounds, public rooms wheelchair accessible.
BACKGROUND MUSIC: none.
LOCATION: 1½ miles W of Ballycastle.
CHILDREN: not under 5.
DOGS: not allowed.
CREDIT CARDS: MC, Visa.
PRICES: per room B&B single €90–€110, double €150–€195. À la carte €40.

BALLYMOTE Co. Sligo

MAP 6:B5

TEMPLE HOUSE

A half-mile avenue meanders through parkland to Roderick and Helena Perceval's classical mansion overlooking the ivy-clad ruins of a Knights Templar castle on a lake. There have been Percevals here since 1665, though the present house dates from 1825 and was remodelled in 1862. From the main foyer, a 'wide-sweeping staircase' leads to bedrooms sporting antiques and paintings. Twins Room has two of everything, including matching half-tester beds, a 'large, modern bathroom with excellent water pressure in the shower'. Porch has parkland views, a half-tester bed, a 14-foot wardrobe. Doors lock from the inside only ('this is a house party, you're among friends!'). The drawing room has 'lots of easy chairs, family photos, books and guides'. In the dining room, where a portrait of Roderick's great-great-great-grandfather hangs above the fireplace, guests sit down at a mahogany table to a dinner cooked by new chef Dave Mullan. His locally sourced dishes might include asparagus velouté, smoked salmon tartare, braised Temple House lamb. Breakfast brings a full Irish with sausages, bacon, 'excellent black and white pudding', setting outdoor types up for a day's coarse fishing on the lake.

Temple House Demesne
Ballymote F56 NN50

T: 00 353 71 918 3329
E: stay@templehouse.ie
W: templehouse.ie

BEDROOMS: 6.
OPEN: Apr–mid-Nov.
FACILITIES: morning room, dining room, vestibule, table tennis room, free Wi-Fi, wedding facilities, 1½-acre garden on 1,000-acre estate, water sports on site.
BACKGROUND MUSIC: none.
LOCATION: 12 miles S of Sligo.
CHILDREN: all ages welcomed.
DOGS: not allowed.
CREDIT CARDS: MC, Visa.
PRICES: per room B&B single €115–€145, double €175–€220. Set dinner €55.

BALLYVAUGHAN Co. Clare

MAP 6:C4

GREGANS CASTLE HOTEL

♛ Previous César Winner

'Country house luxury' abounds in this Georgian mansion, run by owners Simon Haden and Frederieke McMurray as a luxury hotel. It stands at the foot of Corkscrew Hill, across from a 15th-century tower house built for the chief of the O'Lochlainns, 'Prince of the Burren', that otherworldly 'place of stone'. Bedrooms are a stylish blend of the contemporary and the antique, with views of gardens, Galway Bay and mountain; some have a private garden area. Robes and organic toiletries are supplied. In the dining room, tables are 'beautifully set', the staff are 'friendly and helpful', chef Robbie McCauley's cooking is 'stunning in intensity of flavour and visual impact. It's a question of whether to eat the main course or paint it.' Dinner begins with an 'exquisite' amuse-bouche, and proceeds with such dishes as 'cod with lobster mousse and artichoke, wood pigeon with polychrome carrots'. On a night when the restaurant was closed, 'I ate in the bar, a relatively simpler meal, but one that would have graced a good many fine restaurants'. At breakfast there is organic porridge, poached smoked haddock, the full Irish with wild boar puddings, pancakes with organic apple syrup. (RP)

Gragan East
Ballyvaughan H91 CF60

T: 00 353 65 707 7005
E: stay@gregans.ie
W: gregans.ie

BEDROOMS: 21. 7 on ground floor, 1 suitable for disabled.
OPEN: mid-Feb–early Dec, restaurant closed Mon, Thurs (bistro fare available).
FACILITIES: drawing room, bar, dining room, free Wi-Fi (not in restaurant), 15-acre grounds (ornamental pool, croquet), wedding facilities, public areas wheelchair accessible, no adapted toilet.
BACKGROUND MUSIC: all day in bar, mealtimes in dining room.
LOCATION: 3½ miles SW of Ballyvaughan.
CHILDREN: all ages welcomed.
DOGS: allowed in some ground-floor bedrooms, not in public rooms.
CREDIT CARDS: Amex, MC, Visa.
PRICES: per room B&B €295–€515, D,B&B €389–€655. Set menu and à la carte €75, tasting menu €100. 1-night bookings sometimes refused Sat, bank holidays.

CASTLEHILL Co. Mayo

MAP 6:B4

ENNISCOE HOUSE

It's 'something of a mystery tour' getting to this 'fine-looking' pale-pink Georgian house, 'but utterly worth it', says a Guide inspector. 'Welcoming' Susan Kellett and her son, DJ, are liked for their 'combination of affable hospitality and attention to detail'. The well-kept grounds are 'ideal for a tramp before afternoon tea', with a woodland path revealing the lake and views of Mount Nephin. A roaring peat fire and 'antiques, colourful rugs and curio upon curio' fill a comfortable sitting room; a more formal one has French pastels, plush fabrics and gilt-framed oil paintings. Upstairs, each high-ceilinged room is different, a canopy bed here, an enormous Victorian bathtub there; 'to comment on the "original" fireplace is moot – it's all original, collected over 350 years of family occupation'. One bedroom has a 'new' carpet this year – a 'heritage' item from an aunt; another has a revamped bathroom. After preprandials in the former library, dinner in the wood-panelled dining room is cooked by Susan ('think young Martha Stewart: just delightful'). Everything is fished, foraged and grown locally, some at Enniscoe. 'Breakfast was wonderful; the mushrooms were especially good.'

25% DISCOUNT VOUCHERS

Castlehill
Ballina F26 EA34

T: 00 353 96 31112
E: mail@enniscoe.com
W: enniscoe.com

BEDROOMS: 6. Plus self-catering units behind house.
OPEN: Apr–Oct, New Year.
FACILITIES: 2 sitting rooms, dining room, free Wi-Fi (in public rooms, some bedrooms), wedding facilities, 3-acre garden in 30-acre grounds.
BACKGROUND MUSIC: occasionally in public areas.
LOCATION: 2 miles S of Crossmolina, 12 miles SW of Ballina.
CHILDREN: all ages welcomed.
DOGS: allowed in certain bedrooms, public rooms, not dining room.
CREDIT CARDS: MC, Visa.
PRICES: per person B&B single €100–€140, double €90–€130, D,B&B double €130–€170. Set menus €50.

CASTLELYONS Co. Cork   MAP 6:D5

BALLYVOLANE HOUSE

With a seven-a-side soccer pitch, glamping tents,
Bertha's Revenge Gin distilled in a converted
cattle shed, and breakfast served until noon,
this is no run-of-the-mill hotel. A Georgian
mansion, it stands in 'beautifully maintained
grounds' with a lake and woodland trails. Within,
it is 'magnificently furnished', yet obviously a
family home. Owners Jenny and Justin Green
run the place house-party style, creating a
'relaxed, informal' atmosphere. Bedrooms have
a Nespresso machine, home-made blackcurrant
cordial and cookies. The views are of parkland,
lakes and distant mountains. A typical bedroom
had a marble fireplace, 'a vintage portable radio',
an antique bath 'approached by varnished steps',
with an enamel jug for a makeshift shower. At
night, chef Steven Mercer plans his menus around
artisan produce, rare breed pigs, ducks and hens
raised on the estate, wild salmon, game in season,
fruit and vegetables from the walled garden,
foraged berries, plants and sea vegetables. Perhaps
nettle soup with Pernod; a 'beautifully rare' steak
Béarnaise, walled-garden kale, potato dauphinoise
or wild garlic mash. At breakfast there are new-
laid eggs, home-baked bread, the full Irish. (RG)

Castlelyons
Fermoy P61 FP70

T: 00 353 25 36349
E: info@ballyvolanehouse.ie
W: ballyvolanehouse.ie

BEDROOMS: 6. Plus 'glamping' tents
May–Sept.
OPEN: all year except Christmas/New
Year (self-catering only).
FACILITIES: hall, drawing room,
honesty bar, dining room, free Wi-Fi,
wedding facilities, 80-acre grounds
(15-acre garden, croquet, tennis,
3 trout lakes, woodland, fields),
unsuitable for disabled.
BACKGROUND MUSIC: none.
LOCATION: 22 miles NE of Cork.
CHILDREN: all ages welcomed (tree
house, farm animals, games, high tea).
DOGS: allowed, but kept on lead
during shooting season July–Jan.
CREDIT CARDS: MC, Visa.
PRICES: per room B&B single €200,
double €200–€260, glamping
€160–€185. Set dinner €65.

CLIFDEN Co. Galway

MAP 6:C4

♛ THE QUAY HOUSE

César award: Irish B&B of the year

In a small harbour town between the foothills of the Twelve Bens and the Owenglin river where it meets the Atlantic, Julia and Paddy Foyle run their B&B with 'generosity of spirit'. They are 'delightful, tactile hosts' front-of-house; son Toby is in the kitchen. The property centres on the 19th-century harbourmaster's house and 'is spread across four houses, knocked through'. An inspector's eye was immediately caught by a top-hatted cupid – 'the Foyles are enthusiastic auction hoppers' – while sitting rooms are filled with quirky 'antique, vintage and reproduction' furniture, zebra stripes, regency stripes, 'curio upon curio', and yet 'it all works'. The bedrooms are (very) individually furnished, with maybe a four-poster, vintage luggage, 'a broken Marie Antoinette clock', a bust of Napoleon, his portrait over the bed. Each has a terrace or balcony, most have harbour views. Beds have an orthopaedic mattress ('We slept like tops'). Breakfast, in a 'lovely conservatory with a vine-hung ceiling', brings 'freshly squeezed orange juice, perfect poached eggs', home-baked bread, cheeses, cold cuts, 'two unexpected breakfast cakes – "Go on, treat yourself", read the sign alongside.'

Beach Road
Clifden H71 XF76

T: 00 353 95 21369
E: thequay@iol.ie
W: thequayhouse.com

BEDROOMS: 16. 3 on ground floor, 1 suitable for disabled, 7 studios (6 with kitchenette) in annexe.
OPEN: end Mar–end Oct.
FACILITIES: 2 sitting rooms, breakfast conservatory, free Wi-Fi, in-room TV (Freeview), small garden, fishing, sailing, golf, riding nearby, breakfast room and public areas wheelchair accessible.
BACKGROUND MUSIC: none.
LOCATION: on harbour, 8 mins' walk from centre.
CHILDREN: all ages welcomed.
DOGS: not allowed.
CREDIT CARDS: MC, Visa.
PRICES: per room B&B single €100–€120, double €165–€175.

SEE ALSO SHORTLIST

CLIFDEN Co. Galway

MAP 6:C4

SEA MIST HOUSE

Sheila Griffin is the innately welcoming hostess at this Georgian house near the foot of the Sky Road, 'a gorgeous route around the coast and up the Wild Atlantic Way'. Her grandfather bought the property in around 1920, her parents ran it as a B&B before her, and today she 'does all the cooking while running front-of-house', always with 'warmth and charm'. From the cherry-red front door to the chickens that 'gossip' in the flower-filled, sloping back garden, everything lifts the spirit. This is 'a comfortable, lived-in home', with 'pictures of old Clifden, china displayed in cabinets, art on the walls in every room, up the stairs and down the corridors'. On chilly days a peat fire burns in a 'cheery yellow' sitting room with 'dangerous sofas' ('you don't want to leave'). A twin bedroom overlooking the street had 'a comfortable armchair, lovely little window seat, well-equipped bathroom' with 'narrow walk-in shower'. Breakfast is a generous affair, served in a room looking on to that dazzling garden, with eggs from the hens, honey from the bees, 'excellent spiced stewed fruit, well-cooked scrambled eggs, flavourful soda bread'. Overall, 'an excellent stay; good value for money'.

Seaview
Clifden H71 NV63

T: 00 353 95 21441
E: sheila@seamisthouse.com
W: seamisthouse.com

BEDROOMS: 4.
OPEN: mid-Mar–end Oct.
FACILITIES: 2 sitting rooms, conservatory dining room, mini-library, free Wi-Fi, ¾-acre garden, unsuitable for disabled.
BACKGROUND MUSIC: none.
LOCATION: just down from the main square, on the edge of town.
CHILDREN: not under 4.
DOGS: not allowed.
CREDIT CARDS: Amex, MC, Visa.
PRICES: per room B&B €90–€120.

SEE ALSO SHORTLIST

CLONES Co. Monaghan

MAP 6:B6

HILTON PARK

Reached by a mile-long drive, Fred and Joanna Madden's grand Italianate country house stands in 'an estate of great beauty', with working farm, golf, lakes for fishing and wild swimming. Built in 1734 – and rebuilt after a fire in the 1800s, when it acquired a stunning porte cochère – it has passed down through ten generations. 'A very warm welcome' includes tea and home-made cake. Reception rooms are filled with 'flower arrangements, stacks of books, portraits, documents, photos'. Some bedrooms have a half-tester or four-poster bed. A Guide inspector's looked down on immaculate topiary, 'the mirror-like, still waters' of a lake. It had 'an abundance of period furniture and reading material', a bathroom with freestanding bath, Neal's Yard toiletries. Cocktails usher in a four-course dinner cooked by trained chef Fred. Typical dishes might include roast duck breast, damson jus, balsamic radicchio; pan-fried John Dory, almond and caper butter. Breakfast chef Joanna rustles up 'delicious stewed fruit, home-made bread with strawberry and lavender marmalade, perfectly judged eggs'. Guests have free use of the 18-hole golf course; lessons available. 'An outstanding venue.'

Clones H23 C582

T: 00 353 47 56007
E: mail@hiltonpark.ie
W: hiltonpark.ie

BEDROOMS: 6.
OPEN: Mar–mid-Dec, groups only at Christmas/New Year.
FACILITIES: 3 drawing rooms, study, breakfast room, dining room, games room, billiard room, free Wi-Fi (in public areas), wedding facilities, 600-acre grounds (3 lakes for fishing and wild swimming, golf course, croquet).
BACKGROUND MUSIC: occasionally in dining room.
LOCATION: 4 miles S of Clones.
CHILDREN: all ages welcomed, children's high tea.
DOGS: not allowed in house.
CREDIT CARDS: Amex, MC, Visa.
PRICES: per room B&B €210–€280, extra bed €40–€50 (under-3s stay free). Set dinner €65.

DRINAGH Co. Wexford   MAP 6:D6

KILLIANE CASTLE COUNTRY HOUSE AND FARM

A stone farmhouse abutting a 15th-century castle, at the heart of a working dairy farm, is run as a guest house by Jack and Kathleen Mernagh. It is very much a family enterprise, and this year marks a centenary: Jack's father bought the property in 1920, and today the Mernaghs' son Paul is manager, while Paul's wife, Patrycja, cooks. Readers write of 'a beautiful place', of 'great hosts', a warm welcome from Kathleen, with tea and home-baked biscuits. The house is filled with antique furniture, cosy sofas, china and ornaments. The 'beautifully decorated' bedrooms are traditionally styled, supplied with magazines, electric blankets, spring water from the artesian well. From June until the end of August, Patrycja cooks a three-course evening meal with meat from the farm, and home-grown salads. A 'lovely breakfast menu' includes home-made soda bread and yogurt, farm free-range eggs, bacon and sausages, perhaps Duncannon smoked salmon, pancakes with maple syrup. Guests may explore the castle, admire the view from the top of the tower, walk through an old beech grove, visit a holy well in the grounds. There is a pitch-and-putt course, a tennis court and a croquet lawn.

Drinagh Y35 E1NC

T: 00 353 53 915 8885
E: info@killianecastle.com
W: killianecastle.com

BEDROOMS: 10. 2 in former stable block.
OPEN: mid-Feb–mid-Dec.
FACILITIES: lounge (honesty bar), snug, dining room, free Wi-Fi, in-room TV (Freeview), garden, grounds (nature trail, tennis, croquet, pitch and putt, 300-metre driving range), 230-acre dairy farm, unsuitable for disabled.
BACKGROUND MUSIC: in dining room and reception.
LOCATION: 1½ miles S of Drinagh.
CHILDREN: all ages welcomed.
DOGS: allowed in grounds, not indoors.
CREDIT CARDS: MC, Visa.
PRICES: per room B&B single €85–€95, double €125–€155, D,B&B double €190–€225. Set dinner €40.

GLASLOUGH Co. Monaghan

MAP 6:B6

CASTLE LESLIE

A 'splendidly labyrinthine' Victorian pile overlooking a lake, this castle in name only is Ireland's brilliant riposte to the corporate blandness of many modern hotels. In the care of Samantha Leslie, it goes from strength to strength (self-catering cottages in the estate village were added this year). Castle rooms come with a story. Sir John's, reclaimed from the cellars by the late Sir Jack Leslie, fourth baronet, has a glitter ball in the bathroom. Shane's Room has a Gothic bath in a curtained alcove. Theatrical Aggie's room, with four-poster and in-room bath, recalls wartime secret agent and cabaret star Agnes Bernelle, 'Ireland's oldest punk'. 'Very smart' Lodge rooms have a boutique feel. Public rooms are a feast for the eyes, with panelling, oil portraits, a grand piano. Locals and residents chat in Conor's bar with its brick arches and open fire, where 'simple country fare' includes beef and Guinness casserole; fish and chips. In Snaffles restaurant Philip Brazil creates such dishes as roast loin of estate venison, venison burger, crispy kale, celeriac, chestnuts, fermented blackberries. The service is 'polite and attentive'; breakfast is as lavish as everything else.

Glaslough H18 FY04

T: 00 353 47 88100
E: info@castleleslie.com
W: castleleslie.com

BEDROOMS: 50 bedrooms. 29 in Lodge (2 suitable for disabled); self-catering cottages, mews.
OPEN: all year except 16–27 Dec.
FACILITIES: drawing rooms, bar, breakfast room, restaurant, conservatory, billiard room, library, cinema, free Wi-Fi, some in-room TV, wedding facilities, spa, equestrian centre, 14-acre gardens on 1,000-acre estate, public areas wheelchair accessible.
BACKGROUND MUSIC: in public areas of Lodge.
LOCATION: 7 miles NE of Monaghan.
CHILDREN: all ages welcomed.
DOGS: allowed on estate, not in Castle, Lodge.
CREDIT CARDS: Amex, MC, Visa.
PRICES: per room B&B €140–€290. Set dinner €65. 1-night bookings sometimes refused.

GOREY Co. Wexford   MAP 6:D6

MARLFIELD HOUSE

Approached through 40 acres of manicured grounds embracing woodland, lake and lawns, the Bowe family's 'ambitious, guest-centred hotel' occupies an 'imposing Regency house with a sympathetic modern addition'. An entrance with classical statuary, columns and topiary sets a 'stylish' tone. Guide regulars were met by a grand piano in the hall, and a 'unique triple chandelier' suspended in the stairwell. Two 'inviting' lounges mix antiques, 'gilt-framed artwork' and sumptuous swags and drapes with fresh flowers. The 'very pleasant' bedrooms range from cosy standard to classic with garden and courtyard views, to grand state rooms, one with French doors overlooking the lake, a king-size four-poster and a marble bathroom with freestanding tub, separate shower and peephole on to the parterre. 'A firm mattress and soft pillows provided a most restful sleep.' In the fine-dining Conservatory restaurant, Ruadhan Furlong's 'tempting' modern Irish dishes include grilled turbot, white bean, crab, Gubbeen chorizo. In the less formal Duck restaurant, perhaps slow-cooked Wexford lamb shank, cocoa bean and vegetable cassoulet. 'We could have happily eaten our way through the entire menu.'

25% DISCOUNT VOUCHERS

Courtown Road
Gorey Y25 DK23

T: 00 353 53 942 1124
E: reservation@marlfieldhouse.ie
W: marlfieldhouse.com

BEDROOMS: 19. 8 on ground floor.
OPEN: 2 Feb–2 Jan, hotel and Duck except Mon/Tues Oct–Easter; Conservatory Wed–Sun July–Aug, except Mon/Tues all year; ring hotel for other opening times.
FACILITIES: reception hall, drawing room, library/bar, 2 restaurants, free Wi-Fi, in-room TV (Freeview), wedding facilities, 36-acre grounds (tennis, croquet).
BACKGROUND MUSIC: in library/bar, Duck.
LOCATION: 1 mile E of Gorey.
CHILDREN: all ages welcomed.
DOGS: allowed ('always on a lead') by prior arrangement, not in public rooms.
CREDIT CARDS: Amex, MC, Visa.
PRICES: per room B&B €224–€700, D,B&B €278–€728. Set dinner €66, à la carte €45.

HOLYWOOD Co. Down

MAP 6:B6

RAYANNE HOUSE

NEW

'There is a magnificent view over Belfast lough' from Conor and Bernie McClelland's Victorian merchant's house in large gardens close to Holywood Golf Club. It was from this lough that the Titanic sailed for Southampton in 1912. Hence Conor's occasional Titanic Menu, a recreation of dinner served to first-class passengers. 'Not for those who prefer understatement or minimalism in food and decor, Rayanne House offers a wholehearted, endearing combination of old-fashioned lavishness and contemporary standards.' 'A riot of stained glass, chintz, porcelain and cushions in public rooms prepares guests for the colourful and comfortable bedrooms', each with a 'luxurious bathroom'. The Rory McIlroy Room has a golf-themed bathroom with grass-effect floor tiles, one of McIlroy's clubs repurposed as a grab bar. This is really a B&B (there are good brasseries nearby), but roughly twice a month, guests can sign up for a multi-course evening meal, either the Titanic menu, or a fresh seasonal menu. Book well ahead; dates on the website. An 'astonishingly varied and delicious breakfast menu' includes chilled porridge with raspberry purée, home-made pork and prune sausages.

60 Demesne Road
Holywood BT18 9EX

T: 028 9042 5859
E: info@rayannehouse.com
W: rayannehouse.com

BEDROOMS: 10. 1, on ground floor, suitable for disabled.
OPEN: all year, 'limited service' Christmas/New Year.
FACILITIES: 2 lounges, dining room, free Wi-Fi, conference facilities, 1-acre grounds, public rooms wheelchair accessible, adapted toilet.
BACKGROUND MUSIC: light jazz in dining room.
LOCATION: ½ mile from Holywood town centre, 6 miles NE of Belfast.
CHILDREN: all ages welcomed.
DOGS: not allowed.
CREDIT CARDS: Amex, MC, Visa.
PRICES: per room B&B single £100–£120, double £140–£160, family £160–£165. Dinner, 9-course tasting menu £65 (10% service added).

KENMARE Co. Kerry   MAP 6:D4

BROOK LANE HOTEL

In a pretty town between the wild and wonderful
Ring of Beara and the spectacular Ring of Kerry,
this 'attractively priced' hotel exudes 'a genuine
sense of hospitality', thanks to the 'warm, helpful,
friendly' staff – and to hosts Una and Dermot
Brennan. 'It transpired that our waitress was the
owner, a delightful, articulate woman.' There
are inviting public spaces with 'leather sofas in
alcoves', curtains pooling on the floor, the walls
hung with 'good modern art'. Bedrooms have
contemporary and reproduction furniture, comfy
seating, room service (teas and coffees arrive with
home-baked biscuits). Bathrooms, some with bath
and walk-in shower, have under-floor heating,
'spotless modern fittings', smart toiletries. All
rooms have bottled water, a yoga mat for your
downward dog. Dinner in Casey's bar brings local
produce, some from the Brennans' own farm.
Typical dishes: Kerry lamb tagine, rare breed
sausage and Sneem black pudding with white
bean cassoulet; Killarney beer-battered fish and
chips. Sister restaurant No. 35 is 15 minutes' walk
away. Breakfast might include home-made bread,
pastries, award-winning sausages, organic eggs,
potato cake, porridge with a slug of Jameson.

Sneem Road
Kenmare V93 T289

T: 00 353 64 664 2077
E: info@brooklanehotel.com
W: brooklanehotel.com

BEDROOMS: 22. 9 on ground floor,
1 suitable for disabled.
OPEN: all year except 24–26 Dec.
FACILITIES: lift, bar/restaurant, library,
reception area (seating, open fire),
free Wi-Fi, in-room TV, wedding
facilities, parking, public areas
wheelchair accessible, adapted toilet.
BACKGROUND MUSIC: in public areas,
live music events in Casey's bar.
LOCATION: 5-min. walk from town
centre.
CHILDREN: all ages welcomed, cots,
beds, children's menus.
DOGS: not allowed.
CREDIT CARDS: MC, Visa.
PRICES: per room B&B single €85–€140,
double €105–€185. À la carte €35
(Casey's bar).

KINSALE Co. Cork

MAP 6:D5

THE OLD PRESBYTERY

Even in this fishing town known for its brightly coloured shops, Philip and Noreen McEvoy's scarlet front door and vivid plantings catch the eye. Built in 1750 for a Spanish merchant, the house has been run as a B&B by these 'charming' hosts for more than two decades, yet it retains the feel of a family home. In the sitting room, an upright piano, book-lined shelves, leather sofas and a wind-up gramophone; in the hall, hunting horns, old maps, a barometer. Steep, narrow stairs lead to bedrooms with an iron or brass bed and mellow pine furniture. Two have a balcony, one a roof garden, another a velvet sofa, some a spa bath. All are supplied with robes, slippers, distilled water, books and DVDs. Guests have the use of a small patio and parking. The gesture of serving afternoon cheese and wine as well as tea and coffee is 'a novel, much appreciated touch'. Green credentials include solar panels, organic and Fairtrade food and drinks. Breakfast chef Philip varies the menu, which might include, alongside a full Irish, smoked salmon; bagels, eggs and bacon; a hot fruit crêpe with maple syrup; eggs Benedict. Local restaurants are many and varied. 'Not a cheap B&B but good value for money.'

43 Cork Street
Kinsale P17 AE80

T: 00 353 21 477 2027
E: info@oldpres.com
W: oldpres.com

BEDROOMS: 6. Plus 3 apartments (continental breakfast available).
OPEN: Mar–Oct.
FACILITIES: sitting room, dining room, free Wi-Fi, in-room TV (Freeview), patio with seating, secure parking, unsuitable for disabled.
BACKGROUND MUSIC: in dining room at breakfast.
LOCATION: town centre.
CHILDREN: all ages welcomed.
DOGS: not allowed.
CREDIT CARDS: MC, Visa.
PRICES: per room B&B single €100–€190, double €125–€220. 1-night bookings sometimes refused May–Sept.

LAHINCH Co. Clare   MAP 6:C4

MOY HOUSE   NEW

In a 'stunning location' overlooking Lahinch Bay,
Antoin O'Looney's small hotel is upgraded from
the Shortlist this year, on the urging of a reader
who delighted in all that she found. Built for Sir
Augustine Fitzgerald, the quite singular Georgian
house is filled with antiques – a huge grandfather
clock, carved oak chairs and chest. The bedrooms
– some with sea view – are traditionally styled.
The ocean-facing Well Room is a contemporary
suite with private conservatory lounge, a large
bathroom with freestanding bath and original
well. All are 'meticulously furnished, with
luxurious bedlinens, bathrobes and slippers'. In
contrast to the 'cosy' drawing room and library,
the orangery dining room floods with natural
light. Chef Matthew Strefford uses produce
from the hotel's farm and kitchen garden in his
'excellent', daily-changing supper menu and
six-course tasting menu. For instance, Atlantic
salmon, beurre blanc, creamy mash, garden
vegetables. 'The helpful and knowledgeable staff
make the hotel truly special.' A 'superb' breakfast
includes home-made bread, pastries and granola,
'silky scrambled eggs, and smoked salmon with
perfectly poached eggs'. (Patricia Higgins, TC)

Lahinch

T: 00 353 65 708 2800
E: info@moyhouse.com
W: moyhouse.com

BEDROOMS: 9, 4 on ground floor.
OPEN: Apr–Oct, restaurant. closed
Sun, Mon.
FACILITIES: drawing room, library,
restaurant, free Wi-Fi, computer
provided, in-room TV (Freeview),
wedding facilities, 15-acre grounds,
unsuitable for disabled.
BACKGROUND MUSIC: in restaurant at
mealtimes.
LOCATION: 2 miles outside Lahinch.
CHILDREN: all ages welcomed.
DOGS: not allowed.
CREDIT CARDS: Amex, MC, Visa.
PRICES: per room B&B €165–€395,
D,B&B €290–€525. À la carte €40,
tasting menu (Tues–Sat) €65.

LETTERFRACK Co. Galway

MAP 6:C4

ROSLEAGUE MANOR

Much loved by a loyal following, this 'very special', creeper-clad pink Georgian county house is a beacon of hospitality in wild Connemara. Third-generation owner Mark Foyle keeps up the family's 50-year tradition, welcoming guests with 'endless, easy-going enthusiasm'. Surrounded by 'glorious' grounds including an impressive kitchen garden, it offers an informal, lived-in-and-loved atmosphere. Gilt-framed mirrors, rugs and old artwork decorate the drawing rooms; a sonorous grandfather clock stands in the hall. 'Convivial conversation is there if you want it, but you can always just sit quietly by the turf fire.' Spread across the original house and a newer wing, well-used antiques, sumptuous four-poster or brass beds, and 'eclectic' family keepsakes decorate the 'spacious, comfortable' bedrooms, perhaps with a slipper bath or patio. The best overlook mountains and bay. In the 'magnificent' dining room, Emmanuel Neu's locally sourced, home-grown dishes include Connemara lamb rack, herb crust, ratatouille, rosemary jus; Killary lobster, seasonal leaves, lemon herb butter. Breakfast brings all the usuals plus garden rhubarb or berries, devilled kidneys, freshly caught mackerel.

Letterfrack

T: 00 353 95 41101
E: info@rosleague.com
W: rosleague.com

BEDROOMS: 21. 2 on ground floor.
OPEN: mid-Mar–mid-Nov.
FACILITIES: 2 drawing rooms, conservatory/bar, dining room, free Wi-Fi, in-room TV (Freeview), wedding facilities, 25-acre grounds (tennis).
BACKGROUND MUSIC: none.
LOCATION: 7 miles NE of Clifden.
CHILDREN: all ages welcomed.
DOGS: 'well-behaved' dogs allowed.
CREDIT CARDS: MC, Visa.
PRICES: per room B&B single from €117, double €147–€216, D,B&B double from €217. Set dinner €36–€55, à la carte €42. Min. 2-night stay at bank holiday weekends.

LIMERICK Co. Limerick   MAP 6:D5

NO. 1 PERY SQUARE

In the city's Georgian quarter, a grand terrace town house overlooking the People's Park is owned and run by Patricia Roberts as a chic hotel with a spa 'in the vaults'. Until 2003 it was a youth hostel – out went 65 bunk beds, in came chandeliers! The reception is round the corner, with 15 snug, contemporary 'club rooms' and a top-floor suite. The spacious, elegant town house bedrooms enjoy views of park or kitchen garden and terrace, a handmade brass and gilt bed. All have a bathroom with roll-top tubs, separate monsoon shower and VOYA toiletries. A reader was greeted by 'porters in smart Irish tweed waistcoats' and shown to 'very roomy' Vanderkiste. Tea and home-made biscuits 'were brought up to the room promptly'. In the first-floor Sash restaurant, 'a very pleasant environment from which to watch the world go by', chef Timothy Harris's 'excellent' dishes include slow-cooked beef cheek, bourguignon, colcannon, parsnip crisps. An all-day menu in the ground-floor Park Room offers fish and chips, cheese and charcuterie plates. The orange juice at breakfast is freshly squeezed, the porridge organic, the eggs are free-range, the kippers served with rocket, mustard and lemon. (DB)

Georgian Quarter
1 Pery Square
Limerick

T: 00 353 61 402402
E: info@oneperysquare.com
W: oneperysquare.com

BEDROOMS: 20. 3 suitable for disabled.
OPEN: all year except 24–27 Dec.
FACILITIES: lift, lounge, drawing room, restaurant, private dining room, free Wi-Fi, in-room TV (Freeview), wedding facilities, small kitchen garden, terrace, basement spa, deli/wine shop, public rooms wheelchair accessible.
BACKGROUND MUSIC: in restaurant and lounge.
LOCATION: central.
CHILDREN: all ages welcomed.
DOGS: not allowed.
CREDIT CARDS: Amex, MC, Visa.
PRICES: per room B&B single from €135, double from €195. Set dinner (Sash restaurant) €49, à la carte (Park Room) €30.

LISDOONVARNA Co. Clare   MAP 6:C4

SHEEDY'S

On the crest of a hill overlooking the Burren, this
18th-century mansion is a cheerful landmark on
the Lisdoonvarna townscape, from its yellow-
painted facade to its front path lined with blooms.
As the fourth generation of the same family
to run the show, Martina and John Sheedy are
'gifted hosts, whose genuine warmth creates a
welcoming atmosphere, to a backdrop of the
discreet bustle of a well-ordered staff'. There are
two open-plan seating areas in lieu of a lounge,
and a 'comfortable, well-stocked bar'. 'Martina
Sheedy expertly directed our preprandial drinks
to two heavenly G&Ts, both using artisan Irish
gins.' John Sheedy rules in the kitchen, sending
'succulent' vegetarian cassolet or garlicky
Garrihy's crab claws to tables in the atmospheric
bar or restaurant, where guests dine by firelight.
Upstairs, 'cosseting, silent' bedrooms, 'filled with
thoughtful extras', all but guarantee a good night's
sleep. Morning brings a pick of Irish classics, from
porridge served with compote, to a 'lovely' full
Irish, dark coffee and 'wonderfully tart, freshly
pressed apple juice'. 'A pot of dairy-free spread
for the vegan among us was delivered with toast, a
really thoughtful touch.'

Lisdoonvarna V95 NH22

т: 00 353 65 707 4026
E: info@sheedys.com
w: sheedys.com

BEDROOMS: 11. 5 on ground floor.
OPEN: Easter–Sept, closed Mon/Tues
in Apr, restaurant closed Sun evening
May–Sept.
FACILITIES: sitting room/library, sun
lounge, bar, restaurant, free Wi-Fi,
in-room TV (Freeview), ½-acre
garden, restaurant wheelchair
accessible, adapted toilet.
BACKGROUND MUSIC: 'easy listening' at
breakfast, light jazz at dinner.
LOCATION: 20 miles SW of Galway.
CHILDREN: over-11s welcomed.
DOGS: not allowed.
CREDIT CARDS: MC, Visa.
PRICES: per room B&B €160–€200,
D,B&B €220–€280. À la carte €55.
1-night bookings refused weekends
in Sept.

LONGFORD Co. Longford   MAP 6:C5

VIEWMOUNT HOUSE

♻ Previous César Winner

In 'beautifully maintained' grounds, from orchards to a Japanese garden, Beryl and James Kearney's early 17th-century mansion is 'memorable for all the right reasons', reports a Guide stalwart in 2019. 'The warm welcome, the quality of the accommodation, the exquisite meal and the setting all score the highest marks.' The reader's ground-floor suite had rugs, period furniture and antique mirrors, and a staircase leading up to a seating area with a 'comfortable sofa, books and magazines'. An 'immaculate bathroom had a whirlpool bath and a powerful shower'. All bedrooms, some in an extension, have bottled water, cut flowers, handmade toiletries. At dusk, a garden stroll and 'all was peaceful, the only sound birdsong'. Newly promoted chef Marcio Laan's seasonal dishes, served by candlelight in VM restaurant, included a 'perfectly presented crab starter, the most tender and gorgeous lamb rump I've ever tasted', an 'absolutely scrumptious' chocolate pudding. The young staff were 'cheerful, faultless, clearly well trained'. Breakfast brings 'potato cake with poached eggs and delicious smoked bacon. What a pity I was staying only one night.' (Trevor Lockwood)

25% DISCOUNT VOUCHERS

Dublin Road
Longford N39 N2X6

T: 00 353 43 334 1919
E: info@viewmounthouse.com
W: viewmounthouse.com

BEDROOMS: 12. 7 in modern extension, some on ground floor, 1 suitable for disabled.
OPEN: all year except 26 Oct–4 Nov, restaurant open Wed–Sat for dinner, Sun lunch, closed 24–27 Dec.
FACILITIES: reception room, library, sitting room, breakfast room, restaurant, free Wi-Fi, in-room TV, wedding facilities, 4-acre grounds, breakfast room and restaurant wheelchair accessible, adapted toilet.
BACKGROUND MUSIC: in restaurant.
LOCATION: 1 mile E of town centre.
CHILDREN: all ages welcomed.
DOGS: not allowed.
CREDIT CARDS: Amex, MC, Visa.
PRICES: per room B&B €170–€190. Set dinner €65 (early bird dinner €38).

MAGHERALIN Co. Armagh

MAP 6:B6

NEWFORGE HOUSE

Ⓠ Previous César Winner

It was surely the 'star quality' noted by Guide inspectors that saw John Mathers recognised in the 2018 Queen's Birthday Honours List for Service to Hospitality and Tourism. He and his wife, Louise, welcome guests to their Georgian mansion with unstinting generosity. Rooms are filled with antiques and paintings bearing witness to six generations of family life here. Bedrooms are supplied with fresh milk, shortbread, toiletries. Beaumont has a half-tester bed, and Hanna has a four-poster. The best views, through floor-to-ceiling windows, are of the grounds, with woodland, rose garden and wild-flower meadow. At night, John uses local ingredients, and produce from the garden, in such creative dishes as roast butternut squash, baby kale, walnuts, Corleggy goat's cheese; dry-aged rib-eye beef, garlic and herb butter. Lou, the queen of puddings, might make streusel with home-grown rhubarb, Bramley apple and caramel ice cream. Cockerel Henry will give a wake-up call in time for a 'superb' Ulster fry, with freshly squeezed orange juice, home-made soda bread, hand-churned butter, eggs from the orchard's hens. Verdict: 'Absolutely first rate.'

58 Newforge Road
Magheralin BT67 0QL

T: 028 9261 1255
E: enquiries@newforgehouse.com
W: newforgehouse.com

BEDROOMS: 6.
OPEN: Feb–14 Dec, restaurant closed Sun/Mon evenings.
FACILITIES: drawing room, dining room, free Wi-Fi, in-room TV (Freeview), wedding facilities, 2-acre gardens (vegetable garden, wild-flower meadow, orchard, woodland) in 50 acres of pastureland, unsuitable for disabled.
BACKGROUND MUSIC: in dining room.
LOCATION: edge of village, 20 miles SW of Belfast.
CHILDREN: 10 and over welcomed.
DOGS: not allowed.
CREDIT CARDS: MC, Visa.
PRICES: per room B&B single £95–£140, double £135–£210, D,B&B double £229–£304. À la carte £47.

MOUNTRATH Co. Laois

ROUNDWOOD HOUSE

A library in the stables, dedicated to the history of the evolution of civilisation, is a unique selling point, but there is much more to enjoy at Paddy and Hannah Flynn's Georgian mansion in parkland beneath the Slieve Bloom mountains. From a double-height hallway overlooked by curved balconies, stairs lead up to bedrooms furnished in period style, their walls painted in heritage colours and hung with an eclectic mix of drawings, paintings, prints – on the floor perhaps a frayed carpet, on a child's bed a teddy. Four rooms are in the adjacent Yellow House, thought to date from the 1600s. A passionate cook, Paddy rustles up award-winning five-course dinners, 'beautifully presented', eaten communally or not, and he happily caters for children and special diets. Typical dishes, roast beef striploin, horseradish mash, caramelised baby heirloom carrots, beans almandine, beetroot purée, sweet potato crisps; raspberry lemon pie, gin and meringue ice cream. This is a family home, not a sterile corporate hotel. The chatty hosts create a warm, inclusive atmosphere. People drive out from Dublin for 'a relaxing stay with superb food', country air and the craic around a crackling fire. (JB)

25% DISCOUNT VOUCHERS

Mountrath R32 TK79

T: 00 353 57 873 2120
E: info@roundwoodhouse.com
W: roundwoodhouse.com

BEDROOMS: 10. 4 in Yellow House.
OPEN: all year except 24–26 Dec.
FACILITIES: drawing room, dining room, study, library, free Wi-Fi, wedding facilities, 18-acre grounds, parking, unsuitable for disabled.
BACKGROUND MUSIC: none.
LOCATION: 3 miles N of village.
CHILDREN: all ages welcomed, under-5s sharing with parents free, travel cots, children's supper.
DOGS: not allowed.
CREDIT CARDS: Amex, MC, Visa.
PRICES: per room B&B single €110, double €170. Set dinner (3 courses, Sun–Wed) €45, (5 courses, all week) €60, children's supper €15.

MULTYFARNHAM Co. Westmeath

MAP 6:C5

MORNINGTON HOUSE

It's a glorious drive through rolling countryside to Anne and Warwick O'Hara's manor house, where guests are welcomed with tea and 'a delicious variety' of home-made cakes. Original furniture, china and the Victorian drawing-room wallpaper attest to long family occupation. The house we see is the remodelling of an earlier one, in 1869, for Warwick's grandparents, by church architect WH Byrne. The dual-aspect drawing room has 'photos on the grand piano, pictures, attractive flower arrangements'. Bedrooms are spacious and elegant, with comfy seating, views of gardens and parkland. In the evening guests gather for sherry before dining by candlelight at the oak table at 7.30 pm. Anne uses local and home-grown ingredients – fruit and vegetables from the kitchen garden, apples from the trees – in her four-course menu. Perhaps a blue cheese soufflé, mushroom soup, herbed chicken or salmon with fennel sauce, raspberry ice cream, apple tart. In the morning Warwick prepares and serves breakfast, with home-made jam and stewed fruit on the buffet, cooked dishes ordered the night before. Afterwards, guests can wander the grounds, visit donkeys Holly and Noddy or fly-fish in nearby loughs.

25% DISCOUNT VOUCHERS

Multyfarnham N91 NX92

T: 00 353 44 937 2191
E: stay@mornington.ie
W: mornington.ie

BEDROOMS: 4.
OPEN: 19 Apr–31 Oct (and for groups in Nov).
FACILITIES: drawing room, dining room, free Wi-Fi in reception and some bedrooms, 50-acre grounds (¾-acre garden, croquet, bicycle hire), unsuitable for disabled.
BACKGROUND MUSIC: none.
LOCATION: 9 miles NW of Mullingar.
CHILDREN: welcomed by arrangement only.
DOGS: not allowed.
CREDIT CARDS: Amex, MC, Visa.
PRICES: per room B&B single €105, double €160. Set dinner €48.

OUGHTERARD Co. Galway

MAP 6:C4

CURRAREVAGH HOUSE

Opened as a sporting lodge by owner Henry
Hodgson's great grandfather in 1890, this
Victorian country house is surely Ireland's
longest-standing hotel under family ownership.
Devotees return year after year to inhale the 'cosy,
undemanding atmosphere', to wander wooded
grounds and parkland, to fish in Lough Corrib, or
just to gaze at the 'wonderful views'. All receive
the proverbial 'O'Kelly welcome': the house-
party ethos, with 'easy-going, warm hospitality'.
Bedrooms are large, with a traditional country
house style and views of lough or mountain.
Doubles have a super-king-size bed. There are
no door keys, no TV – except for a set in the
study, with 400 channels (pass the remote!). A
gong summons guests to dinner at 8 pm, cooked
by Henry's wife, Lucy, who trained under Prue
Leith. Her daily four-course menu includes such
dishes as loin of Connemara lamb marinated
in port and honey, with 'attractive garniture'
(chargrilled courgette, sautéed potatoes, tomato
and anise chutney). There are Irish cheeses, a
'good, affordable wine list'. After 'an excellent
breakfast', you can order a picnic and drive to
the otherworldly Burren, or cast a fly for Corrib's
wild brown trout. (RP)

Oughterard

T: 00 353 91 552312
E: rooms@currarevagh.com
W: currarevagh.com

BEDROOMS: 12.
OPEN: 12 Mar–30 Nov.
FACILITIES: sitting room/library,
drawing room, dining room, free
Wi-Fi, 180-acre grounds (lakeshore,
fishing, ghillies available, boating,
tennis, croquet), golf, riding nearby,
unsuitable for disabled.
BACKGROUND MUSIC: none.
LOCATION: 4 miles NW of Oughterard.
CHILDREN: aged 6 and upwards
welcomed.
DOGS: allowed in 1 bedroom, not in
public rooms.
CREDIT CARDS: MC, Visa.
PRICES: per person B&B single
occupancy €100–€120, double €80–€95,
D,B&B (double) €120–€140, Set
dinner €50.

RATHMULLAN Co. Donegal

MAP 6:B5

RATHMULLAN HOUSE

More a professional operation, less an intimate Irish country house experience, Mark and Mary Wheeler's hotel on the shore of Lough Swilly, in 'wild and wonderful' Donegal, has something for everyone. A Georgian house, built for a bishop and much extended over time, it has cosy lounges with lough views and blazing turf fires, a splendid bar, walls adorned with china plates, 'portraits of former owners, botanical prints'. There is an indoor pool, a playroom, a croquet lawn and a 'spectacular' sandy beach. Bedrooms, including interconnecting family suites, are individually and traditionally furnished. Those in the Regency wing, which was added in 2004, are more contemporary, with balcony or patio. Some of the bathrooms have a freestanding bath. You can enjoy stone-baked pizzas in the Tap Room or try the Cook & Gardener restaurant, where locally raised, fished or foraged ingredients, and produce from the 'incredible' walled garden, grace weekly-updated menus. For instance, roast Slaney valley lamb, gratin potato, confit carrot, pea purée, rosemary jus. 'Breakfast is a delightful buffet with surprises from the kitchen garden. Scrumptious and all home made.' (L and PS)

Rathmullan F92 YA0F

T: 00 353 74 915 8188
E: reception@rathmullanhouse.com
W: rathmullanhouse.com

BEDROOMS: 34. Some on ground floor.
OPEN: open all year except 24–27 Dec, 6 Jan–6 Feb.
FACILITIES: bar, 2 lounges, library, TV room, playroom, cellar bar/pizza parlour, restaurant, free Wi-Fi, in-room TV (terrestrial), wedding facilities, 15-metre heated indoor swimming pool, 7-acre grounds (tranquillity garden, walled kitchen garden, croquet), restaurant wheelchair accessible.
BACKGROUND MUSIC: none.
LOCATION: ½ mile N of village.
CHILDREN: all ages welcomed.
DOGS: allowed in bedrooms, not in public rooms.
CREDIT CARDS: Amex, MC, Visa.
PRICES: per person B&B €80–€145. À la carte €50. 1-night bookings refused Sat and public holidays.

RIVERSTOWN Co. Sligo

COOPERSHILL

Approached through rolling deer-nibbled pastureland, 'gracious', welcoming Simon and Christina O'Hara provide an 'immensely enjoyable' slice of Irish country house living at their Georgian pile in Yeats country. Expect a warm greeting from the hosts, their Collie, Juno, and the efficient staff ('mostly called Mary', joke the owners). In this family home for seven generations, guests are encouraged to 'feel they are visiting old friends'. Although all bedrooms sport antiques, freshly cut garden blooms and views of the Sligo countryside, each is different. One has a king-size canopy bed; another is huge with two period four-posters; another is dual aspect with a Victorian roll-top bath and separate shower. All are supplied with Penhaligon toiletries, robes and slippers, tap water from the estate's spring; there's 'a blissful' absence of TV and radio. In the dining room, beneath portraits of past O'Haras, Christina's daily-changing limited menu exploits home-grown and local produce. For instance, Coopershill venison, juniper sauce; Donegal monkfish, tomato and parsley sauce. Breakfast brings the neighbour's eggs, home-made potato bread, Ballaghaderreen black and white pudding.

Riverstown F52 EC52

T: 00 353 71 916 5108
E: reservations@coopershill.com
W: coopershill.com

BEDROOMS: 7.
OPEN: Apr–Oct, off-season house parties by arrangement.
FACILITIES: front hall, drawing room, dining room, snooker room, free Wi-Fi, wedding facilities, 500-acre estate (garden, tennis, croquet, woods, farmland, river with trout fishing), unsuitable for disabled.
BACKGROUND MUSIC: none.
LOCATION: 11 miles SE of Sligo.
CHILDREN: all ages welcomed.
DOGS: not allowed.
CREDIT CARDS: MC, Visa.
PRICES: per person B&B single occupancy €151–€175, double €101–€125, D,B&B double €158–€182. Set dinner €57.

SHANAGARRY Co. Cork

MAP 6:D5

BALLYMALOE HOUSE

'Utter comfort – a fire lit after breakfast in the drawing room, drinks from the bar when needed.' An endorsement from a regular visitor, following another stay at this family-run hotel. A wisteria-draped Georgian house grafted on to what remains of a 15th-century castle, it began life in 1964 as a restaurant, opened by a farmer's wife, the late Myrtle Allen, and has blossomed to include a kitchen shop, café, events venue, cookery school and more. 'Still great', it 'gets all the important things right', report other return visitors in 2019. Main house rooms have an understated elegance, some lovely views across fields. There are newer garden rooms at the back, with river views; and further accommodation in a farm building. All have fresh-cut flowers, paintings and ceramics by Irish artists. At dinner, Dervilla O'Flynn's menus showcase all that is local or home grown and raised. Perhaps Ballymaloe Farm pork braised in Normandy cider sauce, glazed apples, Ballyhoura mushrooms; 'superb beef cooked rare as requested'. 'The breakfast cold table is outstanding, with lots of home-grown compotes, honeycomb, porridge and so on. Cooked things as you would expect in Ireland.' (RP)

Shanagarry P25 Y070

T: 00 353 21 465 2531
E: res@ballymaloe.ie
W: ballymaloe.ie

BEDROOMS: 30. 10 in adjacent building, 4 on ground floor with wheelchair access.
OPEN: all year, except 24–26 Dec, Jan.
FACILITIES: drawing room, bar, 2 sitting/TV rooms, conservatory, restaurant, private dining, free Wi-Fi, wedding facilities, 6-acre gardens, farm, tennis, 9-hole golf course, outdoor swimming pool (10 by 4 metres), cookery school, café/kitchen shop, restaurant wheelchair accessible.
BACKGROUND MUSIC: none.
LOCATION: 20 miles E of Cork.
CHILDREN: all ages welcomed.
DOGS: not allowed.
CREDIT CARDS: Amex, MC, Visa.
PRICES: per room B&B €280–€400. Set dinner, 3 courses (Mon–Thurs) €65, 5 courses (Fri/Sat) €80, Sun buffet €70.

SHORTLIST

Palé Hall, Gwynedd, Wales

LONDON
BATTY LANGLEY'S

Novelists, politicians, silk merchants as well as
the petty thieves, tarts and vagabonds of the area
are commemorated in this eccentric hotel in
gentrified Spitalfields. In two artfully restored
18th-century buildings Peter McKay and Douglas
Blain fuse Georgian 'Grand Taste' and sybaritic
comforts. A wood-panelled sitting room, with
plush sofas, cosy nooks and honesty bar, offers
a tranquil escape from nearby bustling Brick
Lane and the City. In the bedrooms, crushed
velvet bedspreads and goose down-filled pillows
sit comfortably with quirky details – bathrooms
might have a loo behind a bookcase, or a 'bathing
machine'. Breakfast, delivered to the room, has
yogurt, fruit, granola, fresh pastries, bagels.
(Underground: Liverpool Street)

MAP 2:D4
12 Folgate Street
London E1 6BX
T: 020 7377 4390
W: battylangleys.com

BEDROOMS: 29. 1 suitable for disabled.
OPEN: all year.
FACILITIES: lift, library, parlour, lounge,
meeting rooms, free Wi-Fi, in-room
TV, small courtyard.
BACKGROUND MUSIC: none.
LOCATION: 5 mins' walk from
Liverpool Street station.
CHILDREN: all ages welcomed (under-
12s free of charge, by arrangement).
DOGS: assistance dogs only.
CREDIT CARDS: Amex, MC, Visa.
PRICES: per room £250–£350.
Breakfast £11.

LONDON
BERMONDSEY SQUARE HOTEL

Buzzy Bermondsey is home to trendsetting
London culture, and this youthful hotel offers
good-value, comfortable accommodation in
a bright, modern setting. Snappily designed
bedrooms vary in size. Spacious top-floor suites
have expansive views stretching to The Shard,
and private terraces, one with a large hot tub;
on lower levels, some rooms share a terrace.
Freelancers, students, office workers meet in
the book-lined lounge/restaurant for an all-
day British menu; a patio on the square opens
for dining in fine weather. The hotel is alcohol
free; glasses are provided for guests who bring
their own, to have in their room. Breakfast
has smoothies and burritos. (Underground:
Bermondsey, London Bridge)

MAP 2:D4
Bermondsey Square
London SE1 3UN
T: 020 7378 2450
W: bermondseysquarehotel.co.uk

BEDROOMS: 90. 4 suitable for disabled.
OPEN: all year.
FACILITIES: lift, open-plan lounge/
restaurant/co-working space, free
Wi-Fi, in-room TV (Freeview),
meeting rooms, terrace.
BACKGROUND MUSIC: in public spaces.
LOCATION: near Bermondsey Station,
London Bridge Station.
CHILDREN: all ages welcomed.
DOGS: allowed (boutique dog beds).
CREDIT CARDS: Amex, MC, Visa.
PRICES: per room B&B from £206.
À la carte from £35.

LONDON

CHARLOTTE STREET HOTEL

Just north of Soho and the West End theatres, the zesty embrace of art and colour confirms this hotel as one in the Firmdale group. Public spaces are light, with cosy log-burning fires and modern British art (the hotel's design was inspired by the Bloomsbury set); a well-stocked honesty bar tempts. Bedrooms are bright and bold; varying in size, some can be connected to accommodate a group. Younger guests are warmly welcomed with a gift, mini-bathrobe, milk and cookies at bedtime. The lively restaurant serves chef Bradd Johns's modern British classics, perhaps John Dory saltimbocca, crushed new potatoes, salsa verde, capers, olives and tomato, as well as pastas, salads and grills. (Underground: Goodge Street)

MAP 2:D4
15–17 Charlotte Street
London W1T 1RJ
T: 020 7806 2000
W: firmdalehotels.com

BEDROOMS: 52. 1 suitable for disabled.
OPEN: all year.
FACILITIES: bar/restaurant, drawing room, library, free Wi-Fi, in-room TV (Freeview), civil wedding licence, cinema, gym.
BACKGROUND MUSIC: in restaurant and bar.
LOCATION: 1 min. N of Soho.
CHILDREN: all ages welcomed.
DOGS: not allowed.
CREDIT CARDS: Amex, MC, Visa.
PRICES: per room from £288. Breakfast £18, set menu (2 courses) £22.50, (3 courses) £25, à la carte £45.

LONDON

CITIZENM BANKSIDE

Style-conscious, budget-friendly and well located – a winning combination for this 'excellent-value' hotel within easy reach of the financial and cultural quarters. Part of a Dutch chain, it has a cool, international atmosphere and gets the basics right: sleep, shower, welcoming spaces for work, rest and play. Guests check themselves in; 'friendly and helpful' 'ambassadors' are there if required. Highlights of the bright, modular bedrooms: a huge bed, blackout blinds, cutting-edge technology (a touch-screen tablet controls lighting, room temperature, window blinds and on-demand TV). Breakfast on pastries or a full English feast and 'truly excellent' coffee. See CitizenM Tower of London, next entry. (Underground: London Bridge, Southwark)

MAP 2:D4
20 Lavington Street
London SE1 0NZ
T: 020 3519 1680
W: citizenm.com/destinations/london/london-bankside-hotel

BEDROOMS: 192. 12 suitable for disabled.
OPEN: all year.
FACILITIES: lift, open-plan lobby/bar/deli, work stations, meeting rooms, free Wi-Fi, in-room TV.
BACKGROUND MUSIC: in public spaces.
LOCATION: Bankside, close to Tate Modern.
CHILDREN: all ages welcomed.
DOGS: not allowed.
CREDIT CARDS: Amex, MC, Visa.
PRICES: per room from £125. Breakfast from £14.50. Registered 'Citizens' receive the best available rate and a complimentary drink on arrival.

LONDON

CITIZENM TOWER OF LONDON

Above Tower Hill Underground station, this Dutch-owned modern hotel has breathtaking views, and delivers good value with bundles of style. A super-cool interior, a tech-lover's dream, you check yourself in (multilingual staff are on hand when needed). In the buzzy living room-cum-lobby: jaunty furnishings, iMac-adorned work stations, a library of design, fashion and travel books. The open-kitchen canteen serves breakfasts, light lunches and simple dinners. Snug, state-of-the-art bedrooms have a large bed, a free minibar; a touch-screen tablet to control lighting, temperature and TV. Some have a picture window facing the Tower of London. On the top floor, a residents-only bar gazes across the capital old and new. (Underground: Tower Hill)

MAP 2:D4
40 Trinity Square
London EC3N 4DJ
T: 020 3519 4830
W: citizenm.com/destinations/london/
tower-of-london-hotel

BEDROOMS: 370. Some suitable for disabled.
OPEN: all year.
FACILITIES: lift, residents' bar, open-plan lobby/canteen/workspace, meeting rooms, free Wi-Fi, in-room TV, courtyard.
BACKGROUND MUSIC: in public spaces.
LOCATION: by Tower Hill Underground station.
CHILDREN: all ages welcomed.
DOGS: not allowed.
CREDIT CARDS: Amex, MC, Visa.
PRICES: room from £125. Breakfast £14.50. Registered 'Citizens' receive the best available rate.

LONDON

COVENT GARDEN HOTEL

A calm oasis in buzzy surroundings, Kit Kemp's signature modern English style surges through this swanky West End hotel. The wood-panelled drawing room and characterful bedrooms display sassy wallpapers, elegantly mismatched furnishings, embroidered fabrics, vintage prints. Bedrooms are utterly individual, with theatrical bursts of colour; some have a deep bathtub in a granite-and-oak bathroom. Connecting rooms are ideal for families. Staff are attentive and enthusiastic. A modern menu, available in Brasserie Max or in the rooms, includes such dishes as grilled salmon, white radish, seaweed, lime, sesame wasabi dressing. Breakfast includes vegan and vegetarian options. (Underground: Covent Garden, Leicester Square)

MAP 2:D4
10 Monmouth Street
London WC2H 9HB
T: 020 7806 1000
W: firmdalehotels.com

BEDROOMS: 58.
OPEN: all year.
FACILITIES: bar, drawing room, library, restaurant, meeting room, free Wi-Fi, in-room TV (Freeview), cinema, spa room, gym, civil wedding licence.
BACKGROUND MUSIC: in public areas.
LOCATION: in Covent Garden.
CHILDREN: all ages welcomed (amenities, treats, activities).
DOGS: small dogs allowed, by arrangement.
CREDIT CARDS: Amex, MC, Visa.
PRICES: per room from £300. Breakfast £16–£28.50, à la carte £42.

LONDON

ECCLESTON SQUARE HOTEL

High-spec technology meets 'domesticated heaven' at this sophisticated Pimlico hotel on a tranquil garden square, within easy reach of a major travel hub. The 'super-friendly staff' at the Georgian building maintain an 'impeccable' standard. The 'comfortable rooms' (some small, some with a balcony) have a monochrome palette and high-tech-but-intuitive features: a 'digital concierge' on an iPad; smart-glass shower walls; an adjustable bed with massage settings. Rooms have a do-it-yourself capsule coffee machine, and genteel pots of tea are delivered on request. Guests are also given a smartphone loaded with local information and free mobile Internet. Neighbourhood eateries abound; deliveries can be arranged. (Underground: Victoria)

MAP 2:D4
37 Eccleston Square
London SW1V 1PB
T: 020 3503 0692
W: ecclestonsquarehotel.com

BEDROOMS: 39. Plus 2-bedroom Town House with patio garden.
OPEN: all year.
FACILITIES: drawing room, cocktail lounge, free Wi-Fi, in-room TV (Sky), parking discounts.
BACKGROUND MUSIC: in public areas.
LOCATION: 5 mins' walk from Victoria train and tube station.
CHILDREN: over-13s welcomed.
DOGS: not allowed.
CREDIT CARDS: Amex, MC, Visa.
PRICES: per room B&B from £180.

LONDON

THE FIELDING

'Simple, ideally located and representing good value', this small hotel with a pretty, plant-decked Georgian exterior is 'remarkably quiet' considering its prime position in bustling Covent Garden. Henry Fielding, the novelist and one-time local magistrate, lends his name. Audience and cast members of the nearby Royal Opera House like it for its well-turned-out but modest bedrooms and reliable staff. Each room has a comfortable bed, clean, well-equipped bathroom (only two have a bath), 'excellent lighting', tea- and coffee-making facilities, slippers and an eye mask. There's no breakfast, but there's plenty of choice in the surrounding neighbourhood – just ask the 'helpful staff' at reception. (Underground: Covent Garden)

MAP 2:D4
4 Broad Court
London WC2B 5QZ
T: 020 7836 8305
W: thefieldinghotel.co.uk

BEDROOMS: 25. Some on ground floor.
OPEN: all year.
FACILITIES: free Wi-Fi, in-room TV (Freeview), free access to nearby spa and fitness centre.
BACKGROUND MUSIC: none.
LOCATION: Covent Garden.
CHILDREN: all ages welcomed.
DOGS: not allowed.
CREDIT CARDS: Amex, MC, Visa.
PRICES: per room single £108–£120, double £168–£192.

NEW

LONDON

54 QUEEN'S GATE

Steps away from museums, the Royal Albert Hall
and Hyde Park, an intimate hotel in a Grade II
listed South Kensington town house. Its modern
interior blends geometric patterns with subtle
blues, green and tawny shades. Serene bedrooms
are made comforting with air conditioning,
dressing gowns, USB sockets, a safe, coffee
machine, complimentary minibar. Renowned
Londoners who have lived in the area are recalled
with a photo on the wall and a book. (Front-
facing rooms may hear traffic noise.) Breakfast is
taken in a light, airy dining room; a full English
is freshly cooked. After a day's outing, the
lounge, bar and terrace offer lulling retreats. No
on-site restaurant, but plentiful choices nearby.
(Underground: South Kensington)

MAP 2:D4
54 Queen's Gate
London SW7 5JW
T: 020 7761 4000
W: 54queensgate.com

BEDROOMS: 24.
OPEN: all year.
FACILITIES: bar, lounge, terrace, free
Wi-Fi, in-room TV.
BACKGROUND MUSIC: none.
LOCATION: South Kensington.
CHILDREN: not under 16.
DOGS: not allowed.
CREDIT CARDS: Amex, MC, Visa.
PRICES: room from £168.

LONDON

GOOD HOTEL

Tied up in Royal Victoria Dock, a floating hotel
'with a cause'. The charitable business channels
profits into social initiatives, including on-the-job
training for long-term-unemployed locals. The
'great, spacious' open-plan industrial-style living
room has freelancers and budding entrepreneurs
in mind (communal tables, work stations),
balanced by cosy, cushion-filled nooks. iPads
are provided for guests' use. All-day breakfast
and light bites are served in the living room, and
on the AstroTurfed rooftop garden. Minimalist
bedrooms have original artwork and tea-making
facilities; picture windows look across the water
to the city. ExCel London is nearby; the O2 arena
is a ten-minute cable-car ride away. (DLR: Royal
Victoria)

MAP 2:D4
Western Gateway
London E16 1FA
T: 020 3637 7401
W: goodhotellondon.com

BEDROOMS: 148.
OPEN: all year.
FACILITIES: bar, lounge, library,
restaurant, meeting rooms, free Wi-Fi,
lift, terrace, 24-hour concierge service,
bicycle hire.
BACKGROUND MUSIC: in public spaces.
LOCATION: near City Airport.
CHILDREN: all ages welcomed.
DOGS: assistance dogs only in
bedrooms, other dogs on lead in
public areas.
CREDIT CARDS: Amex, MC, Visa.
PRICES: per room B&B from £169.
À la carte £29.

LONDON

HAM YARD HOTEL

Guests are bowled over by this tranquil hotel in Soho, with sweeping views over the London skyline. A Tony Cragg sculpture greets visitors in the courtyard; inside, the latest from an international roster of artists, vibrant fabrics and quirky furniture displaying Kit Kemp's Firmdale Hotels signature look. The elegant bedrooms have city or courtyard views through floor-to-ceiling windows. There's top-to-bottom allure from a beehive-lined residents' roof terrace to a neon lady diver overlooking the basement bar; in between, the well-stocked library and the vast restaurant serve teas and leisurely meals. A cinema, a spa and an original 1950s bowling alley are striking features. (Underground: Piccadilly Circus)

MAP 2:D4
1 Ham Yard
London W1D 7DT
T: 020 3642 2000
W: firmdalehotels.com

BEDROOMS: 91. 6 suitable for disabled.
OPEN: all year.
FACILITIES: lift, bar, restaurant, drawing room, library, meeting rooms, spa, gym, free Wi-Fi, in-room TV (Freeview), civil wedding licence, rooftop terrace and garden, valet parking (charge).
BACKGROUND MUSIC: in bar.
LOCATION: Soho.
CHILDREN: all ages welcomed.
DOGS: allowed 'on a case-by-case basis'.
CREDIT CARDS: Amex, MC, Visa.
PRICES: per room £480. Breakfast from £15, à la carte £42, pre-theatre menu £24 (3 courses).

LONDON

HAYMARKET HOTEL

A gleeful mix of vintage furnishings and striking artwork defines this 'beautiful, very quiet hotel' ideally situated for Theatreland. The vibrant library and the buzzy conservatory are made for relaxation; in the basement, a 'beautiful' heated indoor pool; made-to-order cocktails are rustled up at an eye-catching bar. The 'lovely, characterful' bedrooms have 'a very comfortable bed', sofa, a granite-and-oak bathroom. Town house rooms have their own front door and direct access to the main hotel. Brumus restaurant serves modern bistro dishes – taken on the terrace when the weather's fine. 'Breakfast is top quality': 'wonderful granola', sweetcorn chilli fritters with avocado, tomato and lime salsa, are highlights. (Underground: Green Park, Piccadilly Circus)

MAP 2:D4
1 Suffolk Place
London SW1Y 4HX
T: 020 7470 4000
W: firmdalehotels.com

BEDROOMS: 50. Plus 5-bed town house, some suitable for disabled.
OPEN: all year.
FACILITIES: lift, lobby, library, conservatory, bar, restaurant, free Wi-Fi, in-room TV, civil wedding licence, indoor swimming pool, gym.
BACKGROUND MUSIC: in bar and restaurant.
LOCATION: in the heart of London's theatre district.
CHILDREN: all ages welcomed.
DOGS: allowed 'on a case-by-case basis'.
CREDIT CARDS: Amex, MC, Visa.
PRICES: per room B&B from £324. Breakfast from £17.

LONDON

HENRIETTA HOTEL

A Gallic oasis off busy Covent Garden Piazza
created by four Parisians (Experimental group),
this small hotel occupies a couple of red brick
Victorian town houses with a literary past as the
former offices of Victor Gollancz. Soft curves
soften strong colours and marble skirtings in chic,
Italianate-styled bedrooms, while beds sport a
signature multi-layered headboard; one room at
the top has views across to the London Eye from
a petite balcony. The long, quirkily designed
restaurant and bar has a mezzanine floor for
intimate dining. The bistro is run by chef Sylvain
Roucayrol, whose south-west France and Basque
dishes include Ibaïama pork balls with tomato
sauce and quail egg; Basque breakfasts too.
(Underground: Covent Garden)

MAP 2:D4
14–15 Henrietta Street
London WC2E 8QH
T: 020 3794 5313
W: henriettahotel.com

BEDROOMS: 18.
OPEN: all year.
FACILITIES: lift, bar, restaurant, free
Wi-Fi, in-room TV, room service.
BACKGROUND MUSIC: none.
LOCATION: Covent Garden.
CHILDREN: all ages welcomed.
DOGS: assistance dogs allowed.
CREDIT CARDS: Amex, MC, Visa.
PRICES: per room B&B from £440.
Breakfast from £15.

LONDON

HOTEL 41

Front-facing rooms peep into The Royal Mews
from the fifth floor of this historic building,
overlooking Buckingham Palace. Discreet,
luxurious, this Red Carnation group hotel gets
to know its guests before arrival, the better to
anticipate their whims: a questionnaire safeguards
personal preferences (pillow firmness, a
humidifier, yoga mat, etc) in the distinctive black-
and-white bedrooms; home-made treats, season-
specific bathrobes are among the thoughtful
extras. Pampering is bolstered by a personal butler
and an invitation to 'plunder the pantry' in the
clubby lounge. Sister hotel The Rubens (within
the same building) takes care of lunch and dinner.
On Sundays, a leisurely start: breakfast is served
until 1 pm. (Underground: Victoria)

MAP 2:D4
41 Buckingham Palace Road
London SW1W 0PS
T: 020 7300 0041
W: 41hotel.com

BEDROOMS: 30. Some suitable for
disabled if requested.
OPEN: all year.
FACILITIES: lounge, free Wi-Fi,
in-room TV (Sky), room service,
butler and chauffeur service, free
access to nearby spa and gym.
BACKGROUND MUSIC: in public areas.
LOCATION: near Victoria station.
CHILDREN: all ages welcomed.
DOGS: allowed in bedrooms, public
spaces (concierge, welcome hamper,
bed).
CREDIT CARDS: Amex, MC, Visa.
PRICES: per room B&B from £365.

LONDON

THE HOXTON HOLBORN

A lively vibe attracts bright young things to
this former office block-turned-cool hotel.
The cavernous lobby is the antithesis of a dull
office, with communal tables, conveniently
placed sockets and complimentary newspapers
encouraging casual meetings between
entrepreneurial types. Stylish bedrooms
('Shoebox' and 'Snug' are no exaggeration) have
nifty under-bed storage, a flip-lid desk and
thoughtful touches (blackout curtains, a Roberts
radio, a map of local hot spots). Eateries abound:
all-day Brooklyn-style Hubbard & Bell; spit-
roasted birds at the Chicken Shop. Breakfast bags
left on the door handle at night are, by morning,
filled with a granola pot, fruit and a bottle of
orange juice. (Underground: Holborn)

MAP 2:D4
199–206 High Holborn
London WC1V 7BD
T: 020 7661 3000
W: thehoxton.com

BEDROOMS: 174. Some suitable for
disabled.
OPEN: all year.
FACILITIES: lift, open-plan lobby/
lounge/co-working space, café/bar,
2 restaurants, free Wi-Fi, meeting/
function rooms.
BACKGROUND MUSIC: live DJ nights.
LOCATION: Holborn.
CHILDREN: all ages welcomed.
DOGS: allowed.
CREDIT CARDS: Amex, MC, Visa.
PRICES: per room B&B from £219.

LONDON

THE HOXTON SHOREDITCH

'Intensely stylish', this good-value hotel
welcomes visitors with a playful blend of slick
architecture and arcade-game nostalgia. Design
aficionados appreciate the industrially chic
lobby/lounge, where remote workers busily
tap away at computers. Shrewd use of space in
'cool' bedrooms packs in a huge circular mirror,
desk, comfortable bed, 'splendid' bathrooms
with powerful shower. Larger, eclectically
styled Concept rooms are designed by local
artists. Standard for all guests: a neighbourhood
guidebook; an hour of free international calls.
The Hoxton Grill with its exposed brick walls
serves American-style grub all day. Mornings,
a breakfast bag is delivered to the door (fruit,
granola, orange juice). (Underground: Old Street)

MAP 2:D4
81 Great Eastern Street
London EC2A 3HU
T: 020 7550 1000
W: thehoxton.com

BEDROOMS: 210. 11 suitable for
disabled.
OPEN: all year.
FACILITIES: lift, lounge, shop, free
Wi-Fi, in-room TV (Freeview),
courtyard, meeting rooms.
BACKGROUND MUSIC: in public spaces.
LOCATION: Shoreditch.
CHILDREN: all ages welcomed.
DOGS: assistance dogs allowed.
CREDIT CARDS: Amex, MC, Visa.
PRICES: per room B&B from £109.

LONDON
H10 LONDON WATERLOO

A complimentary glass of cava – a nod to the hotel group's Spanish origins – welcomes guests to this good-value hotel within walking distance of the National Theatre and the South Bank. Later, wonder at London's skyline over a cocktail in the eighth-floor Waterloo Sky bar. Floor-to-ceiling windows in the understated modern bedrooms (some small) have 'good double glazing' to protect from outside noises; some offer panoramas of the city. Newspapers and magazines are available in the lounge. 'Excellent cooked dishes' and a 'considerable breakfast buffet' kick-start the day, while the first-floor restaurant serves Mediterranean fare with a Spanish flourish. (Underground: Waterloo)

MAP 2:D4
284–302 Waterloo Road
London SE1 8RQ
T: 020 7928 4062
W: h10hotels.com/en/london-hotels/
   h10-london-waterloo

BEDROOMS: 177. Some suitable for disabled.
OPEN: all year.
FACILITIES: lifts, 2 bars, restaurant, free Wi-Fi, in-room TV, public areas wheelchair accessible, adapted toilet.
BACKGROUND MUSIC: in public areas.
LOCATION: Waterloo.
CHILDREN: all ages welcomed.
DOGS: assistance dogs allowed.
CREDIT CARDS: Amex, MC, Visa.
PRICES: per room B&B £119–£550, D,B&B £141–£580. À la carte £30.

LONDON
KNIGHTSBRIDGE HOTEL

All is serene at this handsome 1860s town house hotel (Firmdale group) just minutes from Hyde Park. Co-owner Kit Kemp combines statement pieces, antique prints and earthy tones in its cosy sitting areas. A striking oversized headboard and good bedside lighting feature in the bright, spacious bedrooms. Each has a powerful shower; front rooms overlook verdant Beaufort Gardens. A short all-day room-service menu stands in lieu of a restaurant, offering the likes of crab and chilli spaghetti. For young guests, a special menu, London activity book and milk and cookies at bedtime. Those exhausted by the museums and crowds in nearby South Kensington can recover with cocktails and in-room beauty treatments. (Underground: Knightsbridge)

MAP 2:D4
10 Beaufort Gardens
London SW3 1PT
T: 020 7584 6300
W: firmdalehotels.com

BEDROOMS: 44.
OPEN: all year.
FACILITIES: drawing room, library, free Wi-Fi, in-room TV (Freeview), room service.
BACKGROUND MUSIC: in public areas.
LOCATION: Knightsbridge.
CHILDREN: all ages welcomed.
DOGS: small dogs allowed by arrangement.
CREDIT CARDS: Amex, MC, Visa.
PRICES: per room from £318. Breakfast £18.

NEW

MAP 2:D4
181 Tooley Street
London SE1 2JR
T: 020 3765 0000
W: thelalit.com

LONDON
THE LALIT

In a former grammar school for boys near Tower Bridge, Victorian grandeur has been overlaid with Indian opulence to make a classy hotel. One of a large privately owned portfolio, the neoclassical building's panelled walls, large windows and stone fireplaces are embellished with blue chandeliers, carved screens, displays of exotic flowers; more privilege than penance, enter the Headmaster's Room for champagne or cognac, and sight of a spectacular moulded ceiling. Richly embroidered headboards adorn ochre- and sand-coloured bedrooms; many were classrooms and retain soaring ceilings. Baluchi restaurant serves contemporary Indian cuisine in the majestic assembly hall. Eastern and Western therapies in the spa. Underground: London Bridge

BEDROOMS: 70. 4 suitable for disabled.
OPEN: all year.
FACILITIES: bar, lounge, restaurant, The Naan'ery, tea lounge, free Wi-Fi, in-room TV, terrace, gym, spa,
BACKGROUND MUSIC: low level, in restaurant, public spaces.
LOCATION: London Bridge, Tower Bridge.
CHILDREN: all ages welcomed.
DOGS: assistance dogs only.
CREDIT CARDS: Amex, MC, Visa.
PRICES: per room from £331. Breakfast £20.

MAP 2:D4
8 Pembridge Gardens
London W2 4DU
T: 020 7792 6688
W: living-rooms.co.uk

LONDON
THE LASLETT

Named after Rhaune Laslett, a community activist and co-founder of the area's annual carnival, this vibrant hotel occupies a row of five white stucco Victorian houses and draws inspiration from its eclectic locality. Public spaces (part art gallery showcasing collaborations with designers and artists, part coffee house, part drinking hole) offer the relaxed vibe of a popular neighbourhood hang-out. Penguin classics, artwork and vintage curios are found in the chic, homely bedrooms; two are mezzanine; all are air conditioned, with well-equipped bathroom providing bathrobes and high-end toiletries. Healthy brunches are served till 4 pm; all-day small plates, large plates, sweets and nibbles. (Underground: Notting Hill Gate)

BEDROOMS: 51. 2 are mezzanine, 5 suitable for disabled.
OPEN: all year.
FACILITIES: lift, bar/restaurant, front terrace, free Wi-Fi, in-room TV (Sky), room service, complimentary passes to local gym, discounts at nearby restaurants.
BACKGROUND MUSIC: all day in public areas.
LOCATION: next to Notting Hill Gate tube station.
CHILDREN: all ages welcomed.
DOGS: small dogs allowed by arrangement.
CREDIT CARDS: Amex, MC, Visa.
PRICES: per room from £239. Breakfast £22–£25, à la carte from £42.

LONDON
LIME TREE HOTEL

Bright modernity filters through this smart,
surprisingly affordable Belgravia B&B within
walking distance of some of London's most iconic
sights. Run by Charlotte and Matt Goodsall, staff
are always on hand to help carry luggage up the
many flights of stairs across the two Georgian
town houses. Uncluttered bedrooms have their
original high ceiling, cornicing and fireplace, sash
windows and the occasional creaky floorboard.
They vary in size (those in the eaves are smallest),
but all have the necessary basics – tea- and coffee-
making facilities, a bathroom with good toiletries,
a safe, a wide-screen TV. A small sitting area has
guidebooks and magazines; the neat rear garden
is scented with lavender and roses in the summer.
(Underground: Victoria)

MAP 2:D4
135–137 Ebury Street
London SW1W 9QU
T: 020 7730 8191
w: limetreehotel.co.uk

BEDROOMS: 28.
OPEN: all year.
FACILITIES: snug, breakfast room,
free Wi-Fi, in-room TV (Freeview),
meeting facilities, garden.
BACKGROUND MUSIC: none.
LOCATION: Belgravia.
CHILDREN: not under 5.
DOGS: not allowed.
CREDIT CARDS: Amex, MC, Visa.
PRICES: per room B&B £105–£250.
1-night bookings sometimes refused
Sat and peak periods.

LONDON
THE MAIN HOUSE

Visitors can live like a local at this eclectic
Victorian house in chic yet quirky Notting Hill.
Each spacious, uncluttered suite occupies an entire
floor and has a tasteful mix of mellow wood,
white walls, antique furnishing and artwork.
Independent travellers are well supplied with the
essentials for city exploration: guidebooks, maps,
purified water, umbrella, hairdryer, secure, fast
Wi-Fi, fridge and organic tea and coffee in the
room. The day starts with tea or coffee brought
to the room, then breakfast at the nearby deli or
artisan bakery, where discounts (and at other local
eateries) are available. Guests can also entertain
visitors – a special doorbell is just for that
purpose. Use of a private health club is included.
(Underground: Notting Hill Gate)

MAP 2:D4
6 Colville Road
London W11 2BP
T: 020 7221 9691
w: themainhouse.co.uk

BEDROOMS: 4.
OPEN: all year.
FACILITIES: fast secure internet,
in-room TV (Freeview), roof terrace,
airport chauffeur service, DVD
library, use of pool, gym at private
club.
BACKGROUND MUSIC: none.
LOCATION: 1 mile W of London's
West End.
CHILDREN: well-behaved, on request.
DOGS: not allowed.
CREDIT CARDS: MC, Visa.
PRICES: per room £130–£150 (3-night
min. stay), discounts at local
restaurants.

LONDON

THE PILGRM

A ticket toss from the station, three meticulously restored Victorian town houses in a Paddington side street have been reinvented as 'an affordable boutique hotel'. Check-in is by laptop in the coffee shop lobby (open to everyone). A digital key system accesses pared-back rooms with wood flooring and cast iron radiators, books and magazines; 'on the small side' but with 'all the essentials': a safe under the bed, hanging space for clothes, natural toiletries. A 'compact spotless' bathroom had a 'large shower head, amazing water pressure'. On each floor, a pantry with filtered water and complimentary hot drinks. Room service is ordered by text. An all-day menu is served in the stylishly updated first-floor lounge. (Underground: Paddington)

MAP 2:D4
25 London Street
London W2 1HH
T: 020 7667 6000
W: thepilgrm.com

BEDROOMS: 73.
OPEN: all year.
FACILITIES: lift, coffee shop, lounge, free-Wi-Fi, in-room TV.
BACKGROUND MUSIC: in public spaces.
LOCATION: Paddington.
CHILDREN: all ages welcomed (cots).
DOGS: not allowed.
CREDIT CARDS: MC, Visa.
PRICES: per room B&B £129–£220.

LONDON

ROSEATE HOUSE

Not far from Hyde Park and Marble Arch, an elegant hotel spread over three mid-19th century townhouses with a comfortable, homely atmosphere. Managed by Parvez Unmar with helpful, courteous staff, classically decorated public spaces have period furnishings and oil paintings; traditional bedrooms look on to the tree-lined street or a private mews. The rooms vary in size – a four-poster suite has its own sitting room – but all have an antique desk, an easy chair; a well-supplied limestone shower or bathroom with bathrobes, slippers, high-end toiletries. In the bar: cocktails, a large selection of whiskies and small plates. Breakfast can be taken in the bedroom. (Underground: Paddington, Lancaster Gate)

MAP 2:D4
3 Westbourne Terrace
London W2 3UL
T: 020 7479 6600
W: roseatehotels.com/london/
    roseatehouse

BEDROOMS: 48.
OPEN: all year.
FACILITIES: lift, bar, restaurant, free Wi-Fi, in-room TV, business/function facilities, terrace, garden, parking.
BACKGROUND MUSIC: in reception, bar and restaurant during the day.
LOCATION: Hyde Park.
CHILDREN: all ages welcomed.
DOGS: allowed in bedrooms only.
CREDIT CARDS: Amex, MC, Visa.
PRICES: per room B&B from £179. Breakfast from £15.

LONDON

ST JAMES'S HOTEL AND CLUB

In a quiet spot, this Mayfair hotel (Althoff collection) in a former diplomats' club has a secret shortcut on to Green Park. Silkily decorated bedrooms display a Murano glass chandelier and black lacquered furniture. Natural stone bathrooms come with spoiling toiletries; two suites have sweeping London views from a private terrace. Old-style service is complemented with slick technology (including free international calls from provided smartphones). In the Michelin-starred restaurant, Seven Park Place, chef William Drabble's French-inspired menu caters for pre- and post-theatre supper crowds. A themed afternoon tea transports tastes back to the Victorian era with rediscovered recipes like 'tipsy' cake. Underground: Green Park

MAP 2:D4
7–8 Park Place
London SW1A 1LS
T: 020 7316 1600
W: stjameshotelandclub.com

BEDROOMS: 60. 2 on ground floor.
OPEN: all year.
FACILITIES: lounge, bar, bistro, restaurant (closed Sun, Mon), 4 private dining rooms, free Wi-Fi, in-room TV, civil wedding licence, function rooms.
BACKGROUND MUSIC: in public areas.
LOCATION: near Mayfair, Buckingham Palace and St James's Palace.
CHILDREN: all ages welcomed.
DOGS: not allowed.
CREDIT CARDS: Amex, MC, Visa.
PRICES: per room B&B from £340, D,B&B from £449. À la carte lunch £32.50, dinner £78.

LONDON

ST PAUL'S HOTEL

A smart hotel in a former boys' school between Olympia London exhibition centre and Hammersmith. Designed by Alfred Waterhouse, architect of the Natural History Museum, the scaled-down building shares some of its grand Romanesque details in arches and terracotta brickwork. Trim, modern bedrooms combine tastefully muted hues with period features; some have an original fireplace; each has a marble bathroom, a minibar, tea and coffee facilities, a safe. Afternoon tea is a bubbly affair; European dishes feature in the elegant Melody restaurant, perhaps gently cooked pork cheek with smoked potato mash, piquillo peppers, caviar jus and thyme sand. (Underground: Hammersmith, Kensington Olympia, Barons Court)

MAP 2:D4
153 Hammersmith Road
London W14 0QL
T: 020 8846 9119
W: stpaulhotel.co.uk

BEDROOMS: 35. 1 suitable for disabled.
OPEN: all year.
FACILITIES: lift, bar, restaurant, free Wi-Fi, in-room TV, wedding/business facilities, garden, limited parking.
BACKGROUND MUSIC: in public spaces.
LOCATION: Hammersmith.
CHILDREN: all ages welcomed.
DOGS: not allowed.
CREDIT CARDS: Amex, MC, Visa.
PRICES: per room single from £208, double from £212. Continental breakfast £12.50–£19.50, à la carte from £36.50.

LONDON

THE SOHO HOTEL

Sculptor Fernando Botero's ten-foot-high bronze cat cheekily pokes its tongue out at guests in the lobby of this creatively designed hotel. Surrounded by some of the capital's most vibrant nightlife, it has the witty flourishes and vivid English contemporary look favoured by Kit Kemp, of Firmdale Hotels. Throughout are zingy colour schemes, bold artwork and masses of fresh flowers. Delightfully individual bedrooms have a flamboyant padded headboard, huge warehouse-style windows, a modern bath- or shower room. Interconnecting suites are ideal for a family; younger guests are showered with books, board games, a mini-bathrobe, bedtime milk and cookies. Refuel restaurant caters for every taste. (Underground: Leicester Square)

MAP 2:D4
4 Richmond Mews (off Dean Street)
London W1D 3DH
T: 020 7559 3000
W: firmdalehotels.com

BEDROOMS: 96. 4 suitable for disabled, plus 4 apartments.
OPEN: all year.
FACILITIES: lift, bar, drawing room, library, restaurant, 4 private dining rooms, free Wi-Fi, in-room TV (Freeview), civil wedding licence.
BACKGROUND MUSIC: in public spaces.
LOCATION: between Dean and Wardour streets.
CHILDREN: all ages welcomed.
DOGS: small dogs allowed by arrangement.
CREDIT CARDS: Amex, MC, Visa.
PRICES: room only from £312. Breakfast £26, set dinner £23–£25, à la carte £46.

LONDON

SOUTH PLACE HOTEL

'Distinctly cool' luxury combines with 'exceptional value' in this City hotel designed with playful flair by Terence Conran. An after-work haunt of business types, buzzing at weekends, it's liked for its 'friendly staff', 'beautiful rooms' and 'tasty breakfasts'. Venue choices offer cocktails and snacks, or sophisticated seafood in the Michelin-starred Angler restaurant on the roof-top terrace; updated British classics in the ground-floor Chop House. 'Truly relaxing, quiet rooms' have original artwork, bespoke furniture; well-equipped bathrooms have a deep tub or walk-in slate shower. A morning paper arrives with breakfast: perhaps pastries, fruit compote, cooked dishes. 'Recommended 100 per cent.' (Underground: Liverpool Street, Moorgate)

MAP 2:D4
3 South Place
London EC2M 2AF
T: 020 3503 0000
W: southplacehotel.com

BEDROOMS: 80. 4 suitable for disabled.
OPEN: all year, restaurant closed Sat lunch, Sun.
FACILITIES: lift, 4 bars, 2 restaurants, residents' lounge room, gym, spa, free Wi-Fi, in-room TV (Sky, Freeview), meeting rooms, garden, civil wedding licence.
BACKGROUND MUSIC: in public areas, live DJ weekends in bars.
LOCATION: Bishopsgate.
CHILDREN: all ages welcomed.
DOGS: small-/medium-size dogs allowed in rooms, bars, assistance dogs in restaurant.
CREDIT CARDS: Amex, MC, Visa.
PRICES: per room B&B from £250. Set menu from £55; tasting menu £70–£100 (Angler restaurant), from £23.50 (Chop House).

LONDON

THE STAFFORD

Discreetly tucked away from the hustle and
bustle of the West End, a calm town house
hotel with an intriguing history. In the 17th
century, underground tunnels provided a safe
link between its 380-year-old wine cellars and St
James's Palace. During WW2 bombing raids, the
subterranean labyrinth provided shelter, while
servicemen found solace in the famous American
bar that still displays wartime mementos. Plush
rooms in the main house retain a period feel,
while those in mews and carriage houses have
country house comfort. In the Game Bird
restaurant, the seasonal menu might include
guineafowl, broad beans, morels, wild garlic
velouté. Indulgent breakfasts offer waffles with a
choice of topping. (Underground: Green Park)

MAP 2:D4
16–18 St James's Place
London SW1A 1NJ
T: 020 7493 0111
W: thestaffordlondon.com

BEDROOMS: 107. Some suitable for
disabled.
OPEN: all year.
FACILITIES: lift, lounge, bar, restaurant,
free Wi-Fi, in-room TV, civil wedding
licence, function facilities, courtyard,
parking.
BACKGROUND MUSIC: in public areas.
LOCATION: St James's.
CHILDREN: all ages welcomed.
DOGS: not allowed.
CREDIT CARDS: Amex, MC, Visa.
PRICES: per room from £355. Breakfast
£26–£32.

LONDON

THE VICTORIA INN

Cushty! This transformed former Victorian
public house has been part of the landscape since
1878. Local history is captured in old photographs
and modern art. Behind the handsomely
restored bar: Victorian tiling and traditional
mirroring; in front: locals and residents, dark
leather banquettes, mismatched tables and
chairs. Craft beers and artisan spirits are served
alongside inspired gastropub dishes including
IPA beer-battered haddock, pea purée. Scandi-
style bedrooms upstairs are well kitted out; some
suitable for a family. Each has a large bed, a
capsule coffee machine, Bluetooth sound system;
useful technology including independently
controlled air conditioning. Breakfast is as hearty
as you like. (Overground: Peckham Rye)

MAP 2:D4
77 Choumert Road
London SE15 4AR
T: 020 7639 5052
W: www.victoriainnpeckham.com

BEDROOMS: 15.
OPEN: all year.
FACILITIES: bar, dining room, private
function room, free Wi-Fi, in-room
TV (Freeview), small beer garden.
BACKGROUND MUSIC: in public spaces.
LOCATION: Peckham, 15 mins by train
to central London.
CHILDREN: all ages welcomed.
DOGS: not allowed.
CREDIT CARDS: Amex, MC, Visa.
PRICES: per room B&B from £100.
À la carte £35.

ABBERLEY Worcestershire

THE ELMS

'A place for relaxing weekends and special occasions', a country house hotel in a 'beautifully' proportioned Queen Anne mansion. A grand staircase leads off the impressive entrance hall; at the top a stunning stained-glass half-dome. The lounge area has a homely feel, with a warming fire, soft throws and cushions on deep armchairs and sofas. Spacious bedrooms (some need updating) are spread across the main house and an annexe nearby; most enjoy expansive views of the gardens and the Teme valley. Light meals and snacks are available in the bar, made 'clubby' with old books and interesting objects, or on the terrace. For fine dining, Brookes restaurant serves 'inventive' three-course menus. In extensive grounds: tennis, croquet, a luxury spa.

MAP 3:C5
Stockton Road
Abberley WR6 6AT
T: 01299 896666
w: theelmshotel.co.uk

BEDROOMS: 23. 6 within coach house annexe, 1 suitable for disabled.
OPEN: all year.
FACILITIES: drawing room, bar, café, dining room, free Wi-Fi, in-room TV (Freeview), civil wedding licence, spa, swimming pool (12-metre), 10-acre gardens (tennis, croquet).
BACKGROUND MUSIC: all day in front hall, bar, restaurant, café and spa.
LOCATION: 11 miles SW of Kidderminster.
CHILDREN: all ages welcomed, no under-10s in restaurant in evening.
DOGS: allowed in coach house annexe rooms (£15 per night), on lead in bar and lounge.
CREDIT CARDS: Amex, MC, Visa.
PRICES: per room B&B single £100–£360, double £115–£375, D,B&B £191–£451. À la carte £43. 1-night bookings refused peak weekends.

ALFRISTON Sussex

DEANS PLACE

'A hidden treasure.' On the banks of the Cuckmere river, this handsome, extensively enlarged old farmhouse is run 'with the highest standards of hospitality'. Comfortable bedrooms (many with a refurbished bathroom) may be snug, but feel expansive, thanks to views over 'beautifully cared-for' gardens. A 'small but well-balanced menu' of 'exceptional' modern British dishes is served in the refined restaurant or more informally by a log fire in the bar. In fine weather, afternoon tea and alfresco meals are enjoyed in the Victorian garden. Terraces have plenty of seating. At the foot of the South Downs national park, outdoor exploration beckons, sustained by 'enormous' portions of 'good traditional stuff' at breakfast.

25% DISCOUNT VOUCHERS

MAP 2:E4
Seaford Road
Alfriston BN26 5TW
T: 01323 870248
w: deansplacehotel.co.uk

BEDROOMS: 36. 1 suitable for disabled.
OPEN: all year, pre-bookings only over Christmas, New Year.
FACILITIES: bar, restaurant, function rooms, free Wi-Fi, in-room TV (Freeview), civil wedding licence, terrace, 4-acre garden, heated outdoor swimming pool (May–Sept).
BACKGROUND MUSIC: in dining room, occasional live jazz at Sunday lunch.
LOCATION: Alfriston village, 3 miles from the coast and walking distance of South Downs.
CHILDREN: all ages welcomed.
DOGS: allowed in some bedrooms, public rooms.
CREDIT CARDS: MC, Visa.
PRICES: per room B&B single £75–£135, D,B&B £170–£290. À la carte £38.

ALFRISTON Sussex

WINGROVE HOUSE

A colonial-style veranda wraps round this
'charming' 19th-century restaurant-with-
rooms in a picturesque village. Friendly staff
create a relaxing atmosphere, helped by a cosy,
'well-decorated' lounge, with an open fire,
and the house's heated, all-weather terraces.
Chic bedrooms (some in an ancient malthouse
conversion) mix neutral hues, tweedy fabrics,
soft throws, dark wood; most have verdant
views. Footfall from above may be noticeable.
Chef Mathew Comben's 'top-quality' modern
European dishes are served in the bright, spacious
restaurant, candlelit at night. Local and seasonal,
menus might include port and orange marinated
rump of lamb, roasted garlic mashed potato,
buttered spinach and carrot purée.

MAP 2:E4
High Street
Alfriston BN26 5TD
T: 01323 870276
W: wingrovehousealfriston.com

BEDROOMS: 16, 3 on ground floor. Plus
3-bedroom cottage (pet-friendly).
OPEN: all year.
FACILITIES: lounge/bar, restaurant,
private dining room, free Wi-Fi,
in-room TV (Freeview), terrace,
walled garden, restaurant wheelchair
accessible.
BACKGROUND MUSIC: in restaurant.
LOCATION: at the end of the village
High Street, 20 mins' drive from
Glyndebourne.
CHILDREN: not under 2 (no family
rooms).
DOGS: not in bedrooms, 'well-behaved
dogs are welcome on the terrace'.
CREDIT CARDS: MC, Visa.
PRICES: per room B&B £100–£210. Set
dinner £34.

ALNWICK Northumberland

THE COOKIE JAR

A former convent opposite Alnwick Castle has
received a heavenly make-over into a luxurious
boutique hotel. Owned by Debbie Cook, the
striking sandstone property is washed with
natural light, highlighting Wedgwood-blue
hues and quirky original features. Handsome
bedrooms (six with castle views) have comfy
seating, well-chosen coffee and teas, home-made
biscuits from the cookie jar. A dramatic suite in
the former chapel retains a high ceiling, stained-
glass windows. Afternoon tea, 'small plates'
during the day, scrummy dinners (Friday and
Saturday) are served in the bistro. Shooting parties
and their dogs are welcome. The hidden garden
cigar shack is a place of sanctuary.

MAP 4:A4
12 Bailiffgate
Alnwick NE66 1LU
T: 01665 510465
W: cookiejaralnwick.com

BEDROOMS: 11. Some suitable for
disabled.
OPEN: all year, bistro open all day
Tues–Sat, Fri evening.
FACILITIES: lounge, bistro, drying
room, secure gun room, free Wi-Fi,
in-room TV (Freeview), terrace with
fire pit, garden.
BACKGROUND MUSIC: in public spaces.
LOCATION: near town centre.
CHILDREN: all ages welcomed.
DOGS: in some bedrooms, not in public
areas, 5 kennels for gun dogs.
CREDIT CARDS: MC, Visa.
PRICES: per room £160–£335. Set
3-course dinner £42.50.

AMBLESIDE Cumbria

THE ELTERMERE INN

Enfolded within verdant gardens, an 18th-century
country house with 'stunning views' across to the
Langdale Pikes. Many walks start and end in the
cosy bar, which is stocked with quality wines,
locally produced spirits and beers. Bedrooms
are spread along short corridors, up steep steps
– 'but worth the effort'. Each is different, with a
modern bathroom and shower. 'We particularly
like the top-floor room with a roll-top bath and
long views.' In the bright restaurant overlooking
the lake and garden, chef Derek Peart's 'very
well-presented' menu includes pan-roasted pork
fillet, herb consommé, spring cabbage, Chinese
dumplings filled with wild mushroom, leeks,
shallots. Guests have complimentary access to
The Langdale Spa, 5 minutes' drive away.

MAP 4: inset C2
Ambleside LA22 9HY
T: 01539 437207
W: eltermere.co.uk

BEDROOMS: 12.
OPEN: all year except 24–27 Dec.
FACILITIES: 2 lounges, bar, restaurant,
free Wi-Fi (in public areas), 3-acre
garden, terrace, complimentary passes
for Langdale Hotel spa.
BACKGROUND MUSIC: contemporary in
public spaces.
LOCATION: 4½ miles from Ambleside.
CHILDREN: all ages welcomed.
DOGS: allowed in 3 bedrooms, bar,
garden.
CREDIT CARDS: Amex, MC, Visa.
PRICES: per room B&B £145–£250. À la
carte £40. 2-night min. stay weekends.

AMBLESIDE Cumbria

NANNY BROW

In six acres of grounds and woodland, Sue and
Peter Robinson's 'sympathetically restored'
Arts and Crafts stone house overlooks walkers'
paradise Brathay valley. A private gate at the
back leads on to National Trust land, and a
network of public footpaths; maps are provided
on request. Varying in size, the individually styled
bedrooms are a well-chosen mishmash of antiques
and contemporary pieces. Displays of drawings,
photographs and paintings acknowledge the
property's original architect, Francis Whitwell.
Breakfast ('good cafetière coffee; good black
pudding'), served in the original dining room, has
a 20-mile-radius farm-to-plate ethos. Booking
advisable for local restaurants.

MAP 4: inset C2
Ambleside LA22 9NF
T: 015394 33232
W: nannybrow.co.uk

BEDROOMS: 14. 2 in annexe, sharing
a lounge.
OPEN: all year.
FACILITIES: lounge, bar, breakfast
room, free Wi-Fi, in-room TV
(Freeview), 6-acre grounds. unsuitable
for disabled.
BACKGROUND MUSIC: 'at low volume' in
breakfast room and bar.
LOCATION: 1½ miles W of Ambleside.
CHILDREN: not under 12.
DOGS: not allowed.
CREDIT CARDS: Amex, MC, Visa.
PRICES: per room B&B single
£115–£285, double £130–£300. 1-night
bookings refused weekends.

NEW

ANGMERING Sussex

THE LAMB INN

In a village on the edge of the South Downs
national park, the Newbon family has given
a new lease of life to a run-down West Sussex
pub. Expanded and restored, the Grade II listed
building has half-timbered walls, oak flooring;
ancient fireplaces and characterful brickwork in
the 'lively' bar. In the smart, informal restaurant
executive chef Richard Cook's gastropub dishes
are 'delicious and reasonably priced', served by
'unfailingly smiley staff'. 'The shellfish bisque was
particularly flavoursome.' Sunday roasts for both
lunch and dinner. Softly coloured, plain-walled
rooms (one with its own entrance) have space for a
large bed, vintage furnishing, well-placed sockets,
a coffee machine. A peaceful terrace has views
across St Nicholas Gardens.

MAP 2:E3
The Square
Angmering BN16 4EQ
T: 01903 774300
w: thelamb-angmering.com

BEDROOMS: 8.
OPEN: all year, restaurant closed
25 Dec.
FACILITIES: bar, restaurant, free Wi-Fi,
in-room TV, terrace, garden.
BACKGROUND MUSIC: 'quiet', in public
spaces.
LOCATION: in Angmering village.
CHILDREN: all ages welcomed; not in
bar area after 9 pm.
DOGS: in pub.
CREDIT CARDS: MC, Visa.
PRICES: per room B&B from £115.
À la carte £35.

ARMSCOTE Warwickshire

FUZZY DUCK

A local hot spot for real ales, signature cocktails
and zesty pub classics, the Slater siblings have
got country comfort down to a fine art at their
stylish 18th-century coaching inn. 'It was good
value and the food was extremely good.' Typical
fare: pan-fried sea bass fillet, Cornish crab cake,
celeriac, samphire, orange and rosemary butter.
Above the restaurant, 'minimalist' bedrooms,
named after types of duck, have high-quality
linens; bathrooms are supplied with robes and
complimentary goodies from the owners' beauty
company, Baylis & Harding. Some rooms, ideal
for a family, have a loft bed tucked in above the
bathroom, and a dress-up box for younger guests.
Breakfast is cooked to order. Borrow guidebooks
and wellies for a countryside ramble.

MAP 3:D6
Ilmington Road
Armscote CV37 8DD
T: 01608 682635
w: fuzzyduckarmscote.com

BEDROOMS: 4.
OPEN: all year, except Sun evening
from 5 pm, all day Mon.
FACILITIES: bar, restaurant, snug, free
Wi-Fi, in-room smart TV (Freeview),
civil wedding licence, 1-acre garden.
BACKGROUND MUSIC: in public areas.
LOCATION: 7 miles from Stratford-
upon-Avon.
CHILDREN: all ages welcomed.
DOGS: allowed (welcome pack,
home-made dog biscuits and snacks
in the bar).
CREDIT CARDS: Amex, MC, Visa.
PRICES: per room B&B from £110.
À la carte £32.

ARNSIDE Cumbria

NUMBER 43

Lesley Hornsby's modern B&B in a tall Victorian
house gazes across the Kent estuary to the
Lakeland fells – and provides binoculars to take
it all in. The bay window of the bright, airy, art-
hung sitting room is a tranquil spot to savour the
view, along with a tipple from the dining room's
honesty bar. Pretty bedrooms provide homely
comforts: biscuits, posh teas and freshly ground
coffee; milk in the mini-fridge; spoiling toiletries.
Suite Two has a sofa, atmospheric landscape
photographs, a widescreen panorama. Breakfast,
fresh and local, is a feast: home-made. A suntrap,
in the afternoon and evening, the terrace affords
astounding views.

MAP 4: inset C2
The Promenade
Arnside LA5 0AA
T: 01524 762119
W: no43.org.uk

BEDROOMS: 5.
OPEN: all year.
FACILITIES: lounge, dining room,
free Wi-Fi, in-room TV (Freeview),
terrace.
BACKGROUND MUSIC: at breakfast.
LOCATION: village centre, on The
Promenade.
CHILDREN: not under 5.
DOGS: not allowed.
CREDIT CARDS: MC, Visa.
PRICES: per room B&B £125–£195.
2-night min. stay weekends and bank
holidays.

ASTHALL Oxfordshire

THE MAYTIME INN

A 'delightful, friendly place', this 'extraordinarily
good-value' 17th-century mellow stone coaching
inn has recently been refreshed, yet retains its
authentic country air. In its popular bar, exposed
17th-century stonework, old timbers and a 'good
selection of gins', ales and ciders. The kitchen
sends a hearty roast to the table on Sundays;
local and seasonal rustic dishes and pub classics
on other days, perhaps lamb rump, Parmesan
risotto, spinach, roasted shallots, wild mushrooms.
'Comfortable, beautifully converted' bedrooms,
in the main building and around the courtyard,
have mellow wood, light decor, and a serenade of
the burbling Windrush stream. Two rooms have a
stand-alone bath and walk-in shower. Breakfast is
'imaginative, top-notch'.

25% DISCOUNT VOUCHERS

MAP 2:C2
Asthall
Burford OX18 4HW
T: 01993 822068
W: themaytime.com

BEDROOMS: 6. All on ground floor.
OPEN: all year, except 25 Dec.
FACILITIES: bar, restaurant, free Wi-Fi,
in-room TV (Freeview), large terrace,
garden with outdoor bar, boules pitch.
BACKGROUND MUSIC: in bar and
restaurant areas.
LOCATION: 2 miles from Burford.
CHILDREN: all ages welcomed (under-
18s must be accompanied by an adult).
DOGS: allowed in public areas, not in
bedrooms.
CREDIT CARDS: MC, Visa.
PRICES: per room B&B single,
£85–£160, double £95–£160, D,B&B
£135–£200. À la carte £30.

NEW

MAP 1:C5
Lyme Road
Axminster EX13 5SW
T: 01297 792763
W: oldparkhall.co.uk

AXMINSTER Devon
OLD PARK HALL

In a picturesque setting on the Devon/Dorset border, a surprising exuberance bounds through this Grade II listed Georgian building remodelled in Scottish Baronial style. Bold colours and carefully chosen vintage and modern pieces decorate the wood-floored sitting room, warmed by a crackling fire; in the laid-back snug, games, an honesty bar and a large screen for watching movies. Uniquely decorated bedrooms have furs, throws, and cushions made for wallowing. For breakfast, home-made granola, jams and compotes, smoothies or a full English; a continental breakfast basket can be brought to the room. Pre-arranged picnic hampers, afternoon tea and suppers. The Jurassic Coast is on the doorstep.

BEDROOMS: 4.
OPEN: all year.
FACILITIES: sitting room, snug (honesty bar), dining room, free Wi-Fi, in-room TV, games room, treatments, garden.
BACKGROUND MUSIC: none.
LOCATION: off the A35, close to Bridport, Lyme Regis.
CHILDREN: not under 12.
DOGS: welcomed (£25 per night).
CREDIT CARDS: MC, Visa.
PRICES: per room B&B from £160. Packed lunch £10, supper (hearty main, dessert with a complimentary glass of wine) £25.

25% DISCOUNT VOUCHERS

MAP 4:C3
Aysgarth
Leyburn DL8 3SR
T: 01969 663635
W: stowhouse.co.uk

AYSGARTH Yorkshire
STOW HOUSE

At this playful, welcoming B&B in a solidly Victorian former rectory, owners Phil and Sarah Bucknall claim to 'eschew chintz, embrace eclecticism'. They have filled their house with contemporary art, books and the crackling fire of several wood-burners. Cheeky touches in the bedrooms include a wall-mounted kangaroo; a burnished-orange chaise longue; a papier-mâché badger overlooking a claw-footed bath. There are pieces of period furniture, exposed timbers and fabulous views of Wensleydale. The hostess's made-to-order cocktails are the perfect pick-me-up after hiking – Bolton Castle is a four-mile yomp from the front door. At breakfast, local produce is transformed into hearty fare, including home-made sausages from the local butcher.

BEDROOMS: 7. 1 on ground floor.
OPEN: all year, except 23–28 Dec.
FACILITIES: sitting room, snug, dining room, free Wi-Fi, in-room TV (Freeview), 2-acre grounds.
BACKGROUND MUSIC: none.
LOCATION: 7 miles from Leyburn, 9 miles from Hawes.
CHILDREN: all ages welcomed.
DOGS: well-behaved dogs allowed in 5 bedrooms.
CREDIT CARDS: MC, Visa.
PRICES: per room B&B £110–£175. 2-night min. stay weekends May–Sept.

BAINBRIDGE Yorkshire
YOREBRIDGE HOUSE

No cause for truancy at this revamped former Victorian school and headmaster's house, in a pretty Dales village on the River Ure. Owners Charlotte and David Reilly have adorned indulgent bedrooms with items collected from their foreign travels; a bedhead fashioned from an antique Moroccan window; Caribbean seashells; rooms with a private terrace and a hot tub worthy of California, alongside contemporary earth tones and exposed timbers. All rooms have fabulous views, posh smellies, fluffy robes. Afternoon tea is worth the trip to the Master's Room, while in the shamelessly romantic, candlelit dining room chef Dan Shotton's seasonal, fare includes Yorkshire venison, blackberry and beetroot; wild halibut, with onion and langoustine bisque.

MAP 4:C3
Bainbridge
Leyburn DL8 3EE
T: 01969 652060
W: yorebridgehouse.co.uk

BEDROOMS: 12. Some on ground floor suitable for disabled, 4 in schoolhouse, plus The Barn suite in village, 5 mins' walk.
OPEN: all year.
FACILITIES: lounge, bar, garden room, restaurant, free Wi-Fi in public areas, in-room TV (Sky), civil wedding licence, 5-acre grounds.
BACKGROUND MUSIC: all day in public areas.
LOCATION: outskirts of Bainbridge.
CHILDREN: all ages welcomed.
DOGS: allowed (in 2 rooms, by arrangement).
CREDIT CARDS: MC, Visa.
PRICES: per room B&B from £220, D,B&B from £340. À la carte £60.

BAINTON Yorkshire
WOLDS VILLAGE

An imaginative take on traditional Yorkshire Wolds accommodation, Sally and Chris Brealey, along with Maureen Holmes, Sally's mother, have created an intriguing destination, where rooms and restaurant are joined by a tea shop, gift shops and an art gallery on their Georgian farmstead. The surrounding woods contain several bear sculptures, part of a whimsical art collection along a meandering forest trail. A barn, traditionally built using reclaimed materials, houses comfortable, soundproofed bedrooms. Decor in each heralds a different historic period, from Tudor to Art Deco; tea-/coffee-making facilities are provided. The restaurant and tea room serve locally sourced country classics (ploughman's, salads, pies, vegetarian options).

25% DISCOUNT VOUCHERS

MAP 4:D5
Manor Farm
Bainton YO25 9EF
T: 01377 217698
W: woldsvillage.co.uk

BEDROOMS: 7. 3 on ground floor, 1 suitable for disabled.
OPEN: all year, except 2 weeks from 28 Dec.
FACILITIES: lounge, bar, restaurant, free Wi-Fi, in-room TV (Freeview), art gallery, 6-acre grounds.
BACKGROUND MUSIC: in restaurant.
LOCATION: 6 miles W of Driffield.
CHILDREN: all ages welcomed.
DOGS: allowed in outside courtyard.
CREDIT CARDS: Amex, MC, Visa.
PRICES: per room B&B single from £70, double from £100, D,B&B double from £140. À la carte £25.

BARNSLEY Gloucestershire

THE VILLAGE PUB

The hub of a pretty Cotswolds village, this mellow stone pub-with-rooms (Calcot Collection) is liked for its stylish accommodation and relaxed nature. Ranging from snug to capacious, spruce bedrooms (separate entrance) might have a high four-poster bed, a claw-footed bath, exposed beams. Some visitors suggest that light sleepers request a room away from the road. In the pub seasonal classics include chicken Kiev, truffle mashed potato, mushrooms, green beans. Cotswold breakfast in the morning: apple juice; home-made jam, home-baked bread; scrambled Burford Brown eggs. Guests receive complimentary access to the nearby grounds of sister hotel Barnsley House (see main entry), designed by gardening doyenne Rosemary Verey.

MAP 3:E6
Barnsley GL7 5EF
T: 01285 740421
W: thevillagepub.co.uk

BEDROOMS: 6.
OPEN: all year.
FACILITIES: bar, restaurant, free Wi-Fi, in-room TV (Freeview).
BACKGROUND MUSIC: in bar and restaurant.
LOCATION: on the B4425 Cirencester to Bibury road, 4 miles NE of Cirencester town.
CHILDREN: all ages welcomed.
DOGS: allowed.
CREDIT CARDS: Amex, MC, Visa.
PRICES: per room B&B from £109, D,B&B from £169. À la carte from £35.

BARNSTAPLE Devon

BROOMHILL ART HOTEL

Weird, wonderful, full of colour: Rinus and Aniet van de Sande's well-liked, 'quirky', late Victorian hotel receives praise for its confluence of art, culture and hospitality. Ringed by woodland, it stands amid a well-curated contemporary sculpture garden – one of the south-west's largest permanent collections. The 'interesting' display continues in the large ground-floor art gallery and spacious, contemporary bedrooms; bathrooms are smallish but smart. Mediterranean 'slow food' and tapas take centre stage in the award-winning Terra Madre restaurant, with such dishes as lamb ragout with merguez sausage. After breakfast (home-baked breads, organic local bacon, smoked trout), view the sculpture in the extensive grounds.

MAP 1:B4
Muddiford Road
Barnstaple EX31 4EX
T: 01271 850262
W: broomhillart.co.uk

BEDROOMS: 6.
OPEN: all year, except 21 Dec–8 Jan, restaurant closed Sun evening.
FACILITIES: bar, restaurant, library, lounge, art gallery, free Wi-Fi, in-room TV, civil wedding licence, 10-acre grounds including terrace.
BACKGROUND MUSIC: none.
LOCATION: 4 miles N of Barnstaple.
CHILDREN: all ages welcomed.
DOGS: allowed in bedrooms, in garden by arrangement.
CREDIT CARDS: MC, Visa.
PRICES: per room B&B single from £75, double £85–£145, D,B&B double (Wed–Sat) £145–£185.

BATH Somerset

GRAYS

A tranquil atmosphere and glorious city skyline views are offered at this fresh boutique B&B in a Victorian villa with manicured gardens. Inside, soft colours rest against crisp whites; framed Audubon-reminiscent prints, pastoral fabrics, fresh flowers and Provençal-style furniture induce a serene atmosphere. Bright bedrooms are individually styled: one has a triple-aspect window gazing across to the Royal Crescent; a blue-hued attic room has a breezy vibe. Most of the bathrooms have a deep tub; all offer natural toiletries, towelling robes. Breakfast, served in the light-filled conservatory, has a help-yourself spread (cereals, yogurts, compotes, preserves); meaty and vegetarian options cooked to order. On-site parking is a major perk in Bath.

MAP 2:D1
9 Upper Oldfield Park
Bath BA2 3JX
T: 01225 403020
W: graysbath.co.uk

BEDROOMS: 12. 4 on ground floor.
OPEN: all year except 3 days over Christmas.
FACILITIES: lounge, breakfast room, free Wi-Fi, in-room TV (Freeview), garden, parking.
BACKGROUND MUSIC: none.
LOCATION: Upper Oldfield Park.
CHILDREN: not under 12.
DOGS: not allowed.
CREDIT CARDS: Amex, MC, Visa.
PRICES: per room B&B £110–£245.
2-night min. stay weekends preferred.

BATH Somerset

GROVE LODGE

Flamboyantly colourful, Mary and Giovanni Baiano's Georgian villa interweaves old-world charm, expert interior design and high-spec technology. There are crystal chandeliers, velvet sofas, and whimsical wallpaper including chinoiserie. Spacious suites, spread over the first and second floors, have an original fireplace, moulded covings, a Bose speaker, coffee machine, home-made biscotti and fudge; each has a private drawing room where breakfast (granola; yogurt; potato cakes; the full English) arrives on a polished tray. Large windows overlook the verdant front garden and countryside. The hospitable Anglo-Italian owners offer a complimentary pick-up service (by arrangement) for guests arriving by train or bus.

25% DISCOUNT VOUCHERS

MAP 2:D1
11 Lambridge
Bath BA1 6BJ
T: 01225 310860
W: grovelodgebath.co.uk

BEDROOMS: 3 suites.
OPEN: Feb–Dec.
FACILITIES: free Wi-Fi, in-room TV (Freeview), large front garden.
BACKGROUND MUSIC: none.
LOCATION: 1.7 miles from Bath Spa station. A scenic 20-min. walk along the canal to city centre.
CHILDREN: 12 and over.
DOGS: not allowed.
CREDIT CARDS: Amex, MC, Visa.
PRICES: per room B&B £140–£195.
1-night bookings sometimes refused at weekends.

BATH Somerset

HARINGTON'S HOTEL

Through a classical arch, on a narrow central lane, this boutique city hotel has bags of character and a genial atmosphere. Well-equipped bedrooms are spread across the three upper floors – no lift, but friendly staff help with luggage. Each room, some compact, all with vividly patterned wallpaper, has great basics (tea- and coffee-making facilities; oversized towels, a power shower), plus quirky touches (stag-head wall hook, a Bakelite telephone). Light meals, hot drinks are served in the lounge; in the bar, Bath ales and hand-mixed cocktails. Breakfast has bacon butties, pancakes, leaf teas. The secluded courtyard offers a contemporary take on the thermal baths – a private hot tub (extra charge).

MAP 2:D1
8–10 Queen Street
Bath BA1 1HE
T: 01225 461728
W: haringtonshotel.co.uk/
    hotel-overview.html

BEDROOMS: 13. Plus self-catering town house and apartments.
OPEN: all year, except 25/26 Dec.
FACILITIES: lounge, breakfast room, café/bar, free Wi-Fi, in-room TV (Freeview), room service, conference room, small courtyard, secure parking nearby (extra charge).
BACKGROUND MUSIC: in public areas.
LOCATION: city centre.
CHILDREN: all ages welcomed.
DOGS: assistance dogs only.
CREDIT CARDS: Amex, MC, Visa.
PRICES: per room B&B £70–£198.
2-night min. stay some weekends.

BATH Somerset

PARADISE HOUSE

A slim stretch of the River Avon separates the city from David and Annie Lanz's peaceful B&B, set in a half-acre award-winning walled garden. A 'good-value option at a good address', it receives praise for its 'top-notch breakfasts', 'most comfortable' bedrooms and 'willing, laid-back staff'. The elegant Georgian drawing room has floor-to-ceiling windows, an open fire, fine city views – the perfect spot for afternoon tea or a preprandial drink. A choice of period- or modern-styled bedrooms: each has 'an excellent bed', 'a powerful shower' in a handsome bathroom, which 'could perhaps do with more storage space'. Breakfast has an 'extensive' menu with good vegetarian options.

MAP 2:D1
86–88 Holloway
Bath BA2 4PX
T: 01225 317723
W: paradise-house.co.uk

BEDROOMS: 12. 4 on ground floor, 3 in annexe.
OPEN: all year, except 3 days over Christmas.
FACILITIES: drawing room, breakfast room, free Wi-Fi, in-room TV (Freeview), ½-acre garden, parking.
BACKGROUND MUSIC: in public areas ('Classic FM').
LOCATION: 15 mins' downhill walk to the centre.
CHILDREN: all ages welcomed.
DOGS: not allowed.
CREDIT CARDS: Amex, MC, Visa.
PRICES: per room B&B £140–£220.
2-night min. stay weekends.

BATH Somerset

THE ROSEATE VILLA

A peaceful villa formed from two Victorian houses 'within walking distance of everything' – but guests might not want to leave. The hotel (part of Bird Group) stands in 'pretty gardens' and overlooks the seven acres of Henrietta Park. On arrival, visitors receive 'a friendly welcome' from 'delightful' managers Caroline Browning and Jean-Luc Bouchereau (and dog, Muttley), along with 'a generous tea' including home-baked cakes. All around, well-chosen antiques and interesting prints. Individually decorated bedrooms have home-made shortbread and fresh milk. Breakfast brings a complimentary Buck's Fizz, paired with, perhaps, yogurt compotes, croissants, 'proper kippers'. The hosts offer informed dinner recommendations in the centre of Bath.

MAP 2:D1
Henrietta Road
Bath BA2 6LX
T: 01225 466329
W: roseatehotels.com/bath/
    theroseatevilla

BEDROOMS: 21. 2-room suite on lower ground floor.
OPEN: all year.
FACILITIES: bar, breakfast/dining room, free Wi-Fi, in-room TV, small garden, terrace, parking.
BACKGROUND MUSIC: 'soft' radio in breakfast room.
LOCATION: 3 mins' walk from the city centre, by Henrietta Park.
CHILDREN: all ages welcomed.
DOGS: allowed (not under 10 months, £15 charge).
CREDIT CARDS: Amex, MC, Visa.
PRICES: per room B&B £150–£495.

BATH Somerset

THREE ABBEY GREEN

Central Bath is on the doorstep of Nici and Alan Jones's good-value B&B on a cobbled Georgian square, a toga drape away from the Abbey and Roman baths. Accommodation sprawls comfortably across two well-restored town houses with parts dating back to 1689. Each room has its own extra feature, perhaps clever eaves storage, a fireplace in the bathroom, a huge four-poster bed and enormous windows overlooking the leafy square. Pale hues and a springy mattress in the Jane Austen wing, up narrow, winding stairs, would be familiar to her heroines. Breakfast has plentiful cooked options, home-made preserves. Any queries about the locale are readily answered by the friendly hosts.

MAP 2:D1
3 Abbey Green
Bath BA1 1NW
T: 01225 428558
W: threeabbeygreen.com

BEDROOMS: 10. 3 in adjoining building, 2 on ground floor suitable for disabled, plus 1-bedroom apartment.
OPEN: all year except 24–26 Dec.
FACILITIES: dining room, free Wi-Fi, in-room TV (Freeview).
BACKGROUND MUSIC: in breakfast room.
LOCATION: city centre.
CHILDREN: all ages welcomed.
DOGS: not allowed.
CREDIT CARDS: MC, Visa.
PRICES: per room B&B single £81–£216, double £90–£240. 2-night min. stay at weekends.

BELPER Derbyshire

DANNAH FARM

On a 150-acre working farm, clucking hens are
the only neighbours at Joan and Martin Slack's
'charming, welcoming' B&B in the Derbyshire
Dales. Spacious bedrooms are decked out 'with all
the luxury trimmings'; some have a baronial-style
bed forged from old timbers, or a four-poster.
Split-level suites have a deck and hot tub, as
does a contemporary cabin (available for private
use) in its own walled garden. Supper platters
(meats, cheeses, fish, salads, home-made bread
and puddings) can be arranged; the hosts can
recommend local eateries too (and will arrange
transport if needed). The 'plentiful' breakfast is a
'delicious' start to the day, including just-plucked
farmyard eggs, thickly cut home-made bread.

25% DISCOUNT VOUCHERS

MAP 2:A2
Bowmans Lane
Belper DE56 2DR
T: 01773 550273
W: dannah.co.uk

BEDROOMS: 8. 4 in adjoining converted
barn, 3 on ground floor.
OPEN: all year except Christmas.
FACILITIES: 2 sitting rooms, dining
room, meeting room, free Wi-Fi,
in-room TV (Freeview), large walled
garden, parking.
BACKGROUND MUSIC: none.
LOCATION: 2 miles from Belper.
CHILDREN: all ages welcomed.
DOGS: allowed (in certain rooms).
CREDIT CARDS: MC, Visa.
PRICES: per room B&B single £95–£110,
double £165–£295. Supper platter
£18.95. 2-night min. stay Fri, Sat.

BEXHILL-ON-SEA Sussex

COAST

Piero and Lucia Mazzoni bring 'warm' Italian
hospitality to the British seaside at their
'impeccably decorated' B&B. A new take on the
old world wafts through the Edwardian villa:
dusky wood floors, a minimalist grey and white
palette, against which there are occasional colour
pops: red wingback chairs, clusters of yellow
flowers. Genteel, recently refurbished bedrooms
(some compact) have little luxuries: biscuits, a
capsule coffee machine and a silent fridge; a
cascade shower; fluffy towels on a heated rail;
under-floor heating in the bathroom; high-end
toiletries. The best room has a whirlpool bath on
its own balcony with sea views. Breakfast includes
pancakes with crème fraîche and maple syrup,
fresh fruit, home-baked bread.

MAP 2:E4
58 Sea Road
Bexhill-on-Sea TN40 1JP
T: 01424 225260
W: coastbexhill.co.uk

BEDROOMS: 5.
OPEN: all year.
FACILITIES: lounge, breakfast room,
free Wi-Fi, in-room TV (Freeview,
Sky), secure bicycle storage.
BACKGROUND MUSIC: none.
LOCATION: town centre, 100 yds from
the seafront.
CHILDREN: not under 5.
DOGS: not allowed.
CREDIT CARDS: Amex, MC, Visa.
PRICES: per room B&B single £80–£100,
double £90–£135. 1-night bookings
sometimes refused weekends and
high season.

NEW

MAP 2:E4
40 Sackville Road
Bexhill-on-Sea TN39 3JE
T: 01424 732584
W: thedriftwoodbexhill.co.uk

BEXHILL-ON-SEA Sussex

THE DRIFTWOOD

A few paces from the modernist De La Warr pavilion and seafront lies a small, well-designed hotel and restaurant in a Victorian building in the heart of this ancient town. The interior is styled throughout with natural timbers, exposed brick walls, olive- and dark-toned leather. Asian-influenced dishes such as Malaysian beef rendang, chicken in black bean sauce, green and red peppers, jasmine rice are prepared in an open kitchen in the ground-floor restaurant. Upstairs, bedrooms in heritage colours have peppy throws on large beds, and a fully tiled bathroom with walk-in shower. Pleasing extras: bathrobes and slippers, a coffee machine, iron and board, a mini-fridge with fresh milk, water and beer. Leisurely traditional breakfasts are cooked to order.

BEDROOMS: 6.
OPEN: all year.
FACILITIES: restaurant, free Wi-Fi, radio.
BACKGROUND MUSIC: none.
LOCATION: in town centre.
CHILDREN: all ages welcomed.
DOGS: not allowed.
CREDIT CARDS: Amex, MC, Visa.
PRICES: per room B&B from £99. 1-night bookings not accepted weekends.

BIBURY Gloucestershire

THE SWAN

'What a setting!' On the banks of the River Coln, a busy former 17th-century coaching inn (Cotswold Inns and Hotels), in a quaint village William Morris described as the most beautiful in England. Rolling meadow views pour into light, country-style bedrooms supplied with high-quality toiletries and a coffee machine. The pretty garden's cottage suites (one with a hot tub) are ideal for larger groups. Gastropub fare is served in the bar and courtyard; modern European cooking in the brasserie, perhaps the hotel speciality: poached Bibury trout. Breakfast brings freshly squeezed juice, home-made marmalade, local organic preserves. Across the lane, a trickling stream, summer house, deckchairs in the hotel's delightful riverside gardens.

25% DISCOUNT VOUCHERS

MAP 3:E6
Bibury GL7 5NW
T: 01285 740695
W: cotswold-inns-hotels.co.uk/
    the-swan-hotel

BEDROOMS: 22. Some on ground floor, 4 in adjacent garden cottages.
OPEN: all year.
FACILITIES: lift, lounge, bar (wood-burning stove), brasserie, free Wi-Fi, in-room TV (Freeview), ½-acre garden, civil wedding licence, functions.
BACKGROUND MUSIC: in public spaces ('subtle').
LOCATION: village centre.
CHILDREN: all ages welcomed.
DOGS: well-behaved dogs allowed in bar, lounge, garden, some bedrooms.
CREDIT CARDS: Amex, MC, Visa.
PRICES: per person B&B £160–£405, D,B&B £230–£475. À la carte (brasserie) £36.

BIRMINGHAM Warwickshire

THE HIGH FIELD TOWN HOUSE

Run in conjunction with The High Field gastropub (a Peach pub) next door, this white-fronted Victorian villa in upmarket Edgbaston has the feel of a 'boutique country house'. Its welcoming sitting room sets a homely scene with vases of fresh flowers, complimentary newspapers and a capsule coffee machine. Something a little stronger is found in the honesty bar or in the gastropub, alongside seasonal British fare including Cornish lamb pavé, braised breast, warm quinoa salad and mint jus and 28-day dry-aged steaks. Well-chosen antiques and retro furnishings fill the creative bedrooms (some large enough to suit a family). The peaceful area has shops and restaurants nearby, and is just five minutes from the city centre.

MAP 3:C6
23 Highfield Road
Birmingham B15 3DP
T: 0121 647 6466
w: highfieldtownhouse.co.uk

BEDROOMS: 12. Some suitable for disabled.
OPEN: all year, except 24/25 Dec.
FACILITIES: sitting room, bar, restaurant in adjacent building, free Wi-Fi, in-room TV (Freeview), private dining, terrace, garden, parking.
BACKGROUND MUSIC: in sitting room.
LOCATION: 5 mins from city centre.
CHILDREN: all ages welcomed.
DOGS: allowed.
CREDIT CARDS: Amex, MC, Visa.
PRICES: per room B&B from £110. À la carte £35.

BISHOPSTONE Wiltshire

HELEN BROWNING'S ROYAL OAK

On a working organic farm, this quirky, affable pub-with-rooms reflects the vision of food ethics pioneer Helen Browning. The well-established pub (Arkell's Brewery) is loved for the real ales, organic wines and generous meals (meat, nuts, fruit, milk and honey from the farm). Set around a sunny courtyard, appealingly rustic bedrooms have their own front door, woollen throws, a comfy bed. Each is named after a field on the farm (immortalized by a giant photo). The residents' lounge, with books, hot drinks, a record-player (and Helen's partner Tim's old LPs) is made for 'wallowing in'. From the pub, circular walks take in woodland, orchards and the farm's pigs, sheep and cattle.

25% DISCOUNT VOUCHERS

MAP 3:E6
Cues Lane
Bishopstone SN6 8PP
T: 01793 790481
w: helenbrowningsorganic.co.uk

BEDROOMS: 12. All in annexe, 100 yds from pub, 1 suitable for disabled.
OPEN: all year.
FACILITIES: lounge, pub, meeting/function room, free Wi-Fi, in-room TV (Freeview), ½-acre garden (rope swing, Wendy house, 'flighty hens'), parking, some public areas wheelchair accessible, adapted toilet.
BACKGROUND MUSIC: occasional, in public spaces.
LOCATION: on an organic farm, in village, 7 miles E of Swindon, 10 miles from Marlborough.
CHILDREN: all ages welcomed.
DOGS: allowed in 3 bedrooms, public rooms.
CREDIT CARDS: MC, Visa.
PRICES: per room B&B £90–£145. À la carte £32.

BLACKPOOL Lancashire

NUMBER ONE ST LUKE'S

A three-minute amble from the famous promenade and Pleasure Beach, Mark and Claire Smith's South Shore B&B offers comfy, good-value, contemporary accommodation in a handsome detached house. Spotless bedrooms, decorated in a fresh, modern style, have a king-size bed and make-yourself-at-home extras (including a large TV screen and a games console for nights in); cosseting bathrooms have a power shower, a spa bath, plus wall-mounted TV and a music system. Breakfast specials include a 'full Blackpool'. A large conservatory overlooks the garden; the putting green, hot tub and sun loungers entice outside. A universal electric car charging point is for guests' use. (See also sister hotel Number One South Beach, next entry.)

MAP 4:D2
1 St Luke's Road
Blackpool FY4 2EL
T: 01253 343901
W: numberoneblackpool.com

BEDROOMS: 3.
OPEN: all year.
FACILITIES: dining room, conservatory, free Wi-Fi, in-room TV (Freeview), garden, parking.
BACKGROUND MUSIC: none.
LOCATION: 2 miles S of town centre.
CHILDREN: not under 4.
DOGS: not allowed.
CREDIT CARDS: Amex, MC, Visa.
PRICES: per room B&B from £110–£140. 1-night bookings occasionally refused weekends.

BLACKPOOL Lancashire

NUMBER ONE SOUTH BEACH

Modern, personal accommodation is found minutes from Blackpool's Pleasure Beach at this cheery hotel by the sea. Janet and Graham Oxley, and Claire and Mark Smith, are the enthusiastic owners (see also Number One St Luke's, previous entry). Individually decorated bedrooms, many with a bright, mood-lifting palate, enjoy smart technological touches: remote-controlled lighting, a waterproof TV by the spa bath, a walk-in power shower; the best have a balcony with sea views; some a contemporary four-poster, all have a king-size bed. The games room has an indoor golf simulator for wet days. Dinner, perhaps grilled sea bass, tarragon, white wine sauce, requires advance notice. Breakfast, featuring all the favourites, uses local produce.

25% DISCOUNT VOUCHERS

MAP 4:D2
4 Harrowside West
Blackpool FY4 1NW
T: 01253 343900
W: numberonesouthbeach.com

BEDROOMS: 14. Some suitable for disabled.
OPEN: all year except 26–31 Dec.
FACILITIES: lounge, bar, restaurant, games room, lift, free Wi-Fi, in-room TV (Freeview), meeting/conference facilities, parking.
BACKGROUND MUSIC: quiet classical music in bar and lounge.
LOCATION: 2½ miles S of Blackpool town centre.
CHILDREN: not under 5.
DOGS: assistance dogs only.
CREDIT CARDS: Amex, MC, Visa.
PRICES: per room B&B £85–£174. À la carte £25.85–£29.85. 2-night min. stay at weekends in high season.

NEW

BORROWDALE Cumbria
THE ROYAL OAK

'A really classic walkers' delight', the former 18th-century farmhouse and one-time miners' tavern continues its century-old tradition of providing accommodation for visitors and hikers, and the Downey family's inn now provides food too. The cosy spot serves straightforward British classics (and a few fusion favourites) in the traditionally styled dining room; perhaps crispy duck spring rolls; sausage and mash with cider apple chutney. The narrow bar is propped up by locals and visitors quenching thirsts with Thwaites' cask ales and a good wine list, while dogs lap happily from a water bowl. Pretty bedrooms, in the main hotel and outbuildings, have an alpine sensibility. Breakfast is plentiful fuel for walks in the surrounding fells.

MAP 4: inset C2
Rosthwaite
Borrowdale CA12 5XB
T: 017687 77214
W: royaloakhotel.co.uk

BEDROOMS: 8. Some in annexe.
OPEN: all year.
FACILITIES: restaurant, garden, free Wi-Fi, in-room TV.
BACKGROUND MUSIC: none.
LOCATION: in town.
CHILDREN: all ages welcomed.
DOGS: allowed.
CREDIT CARDS: Amex, MC, Visa.
PRICES: per person D,B&B £72–£76.

BOURNEMOUTH Dorset
THE GREEN HOUSE

Ethical hospitality is a priority at this hotel in a handsome Victorian villa close to the seafront. The garden is eco-aware, the roof sports solar panels and beehives – fuelling breakfast in more ways than one. In the smart bedrooms, some snug, there are harmonious earth tones and eco prints. Organic bedlinen and natural materials are cossetingly cool and contemporary. The best rooms have a reclaimed Victorian tub; all bathrooms have a stone basin, a walk-in shower. The Arbor restaurant is open all day from breakfast through to dinner. Naturally, chef Andy Hilton uses organic, Fairtrade and locally sourced ingredients for his unfussy, modern menus.

MAP 2:E2
4 Grove Road
Bournemouth BH1 3AX
T: 01202 498900
W: thegreenhousehotel.co.uk

BEDROOMS: 32. 1 suitable for disabled.
OPEN: all year.
FACILITIES: lift, bar, restaurant, free Wi-Fi, in-room TV (Freeview), civil wedding licence, 1-acre garden, terrace, parking.
BACKGROUND MUSIC: in public areas.
LOCATION: short walks to town centre and to beach.
CHILDREN: all ages welcomed.
DOGS: not allowed.
CREDIT CARDS: Amex, MC, Visa.
PRICES: per room B&B from £119, D,B&B from £179. À la carte £35. 1-night bookings refused Sat at peak times.

BOWNESS-ON-WINDERMERE Cumbria

LINDETH HOWE

The verdant surrounds of this Victorian country house above Lake Windermere make an inspiring setting. Beatrix Potter once lived here, and the connection is highlighted in public areas downstairs. Recently refurbished throughout, country-style bedrooms (tweeds, vintage photographs, floral curtains) overlook the sweeping gardens and fells; three ground-floor rooms have direct garden access. The morning room has books and board games for inclement days, although intrepid walkers will venture forth, rain or shine. In the dining room, with its huge panoramic windows, chef Chris Davis serves innovative British dishes including Barbary duck, sweet potato mash, pine nuts, marmalade glaze, beetroot, redcurrant and juniper jus.

MAP 4: inset C2
Lindeth Drive
Bowness-on-Windermere LA23 3JF
T: 01539 445759
w: lindeth-howe.co.uk

BEDROOMS: 35. 3 suitable for disabled.
OPEN: all year.
FACILITIES: morning room, lounge, bar, restaurant, free Wi-Fi, in-room TV (Freeview), civil wedding licence, sun terrace, 6-acre grounds, electric car charging point, electric bicycles for hire, public areas wheelchair accessible.
BACKGROUND MUSIC: in bar and restaurant.
LOCATION: 1 mile from Bowness Pier.
CHILDREN: all ages welcomed, not under 7 in restaurant in evening.
DOGS: allowed (in some bedrooms, morning room).
CREDIT CARDS: Amex, MC, Visa.
PRICES: per room B&B £210–£390, D,B&B £284–£484. À la carte £48. 1-night bookings sometimes refused.

BOWNESS-ON-WINDERMERE Cumbria

THE RYEBECK

A gabled Arts and Crafts country house in extensive grounds with 'tantalising' views of Lake Windermere and Coniston Fells. Informal and pooch-friendly, several of the hotel's bright, spacious bedrooms are on the ground floor, with patio access to the garden. Cotton bedlinen, home-made biscuits, tea and coffee from a local merchant, Cumbria-made toiletries are found in all. Served in the glass-walled restaurant, chef Nick Edgar's 'inventive' dishes use Lakeland produce. A visitor in 2019 disliked 'the mishmash of unappealing vegetables'. OS maps for fell walks from the door are available to borrow – the less rugged might prefer a leisurely stroll in the grounds. Sister hotels: Hipping Hall, Cowan Bridge, and Forest Side, Grasmere (see main entries).

MAP 4: inset C2
Lyth Valley Road
Bowness-on-Windermere LA23 3JP
T: 01539 488195
w: ryebeck.com

BEDROOMS: 26.
OPEN: all year.
FACILITIES: bar, lounge, restaurant, free Wi-Fi, in-room TV (Freeview), civil wedding licence, portable ramp, 5-acre grounds, bicycle storage, parking.
BACKGROUND MUSIC: in bar, restaurant.
LOCATION: on the Lyth Valley Road, 10-min. walk from Bowness-on-Windermere centre.
CHILDREN: all ages welcomed.
DOGS: allowed in 6 bedrooms, public rooms (dog bed, 2 dog bowls for water and food, tasty treats), guests may dine with their pets in the lounge by prior arrangement, £20 per day charge.
CREDIT CARDS: Amex, MC, Visa.
PRICES: per room B&B £159–£279, D,B&B £229–£329. À la carte £37.

BRADFORD-ON-AVON Wiltshire

TIMBRELL'S YARD

By the footpath skirting the Avon, this popular
bar/restaurant-with-rooms occupies a Grade II
listed building in a 'delightful little town'. Owned
by the Stay Original Company, its 'excellent' bar
has a 'great selection' of craft spirits, local ales,
West Country ciders. Throughout the day, snacks,
small plates, refined pub food and dry-aged
steaks are plied in the industrial-style dining
areas. Outdoor seating in the courtyard 'is a plus'.
Along a maze of stairs and corridors, voguish
bedrooms (many facing the river) have modern
textiles ranged across reclaimed furniture, timber
cladding and wonky floors: split-level suites
('steep, polished steps') have deep window seats.
See also The Swan, Wedmore, and The White
Hart, Somerton (Shortlist entries).

MAP 2:D1
49 Saint Margaret's Street
Bradford-on-Avon BA15 1DE
T: 01225 869492
w: timbrellsyard.com

BEDROOMS: 17.
OPEN: all year.
FACILITIES: bar, restaurant, private
dining room, free Wi-Fi, in-room
TV (Freeview), river-facing terrace.
BACKGROUND MUSIC: in public spaces
'to suit time and ambience'.
LOCATION: centre of Bradford-on-
Avon, 3-min. walk from railway
station.
CHILDREN: all ages welcomed.
DOGS: allowed in all rooms (£10 per
dog per stay).
CREDIT CARDS: MC, Visa.
PRICES: per room B&B £85–£145.
À la carte £30.

BREEDON ON THE-HILL Leicestershire

BREEDON HALL

Bags of style and a splendid walled garden make
Charles and Charlotte Meynell's B&B a charming
stop-over. Not far from the M1, the listed
Georgian manor house has a grand entrance and a
welcoming country house atmosphere; in the fire-
warmed drawing room guests are offered tea and
biscuits, or can help themselves to a drink from
the honesty bar. Some of the spacious bedrooms,
each named after a local hunt, have elegant sash
windows, others have exposed timbers; all have
oodles of character. Plentiful breakfasts include
fresh fruit, home-made granola and eggs from the
Meynells' hens. Local pub grub is as near as the
end of the drive.

25% DISCOUNT VOUCHERS

MAP 2:A2
Breedon on the Hill DE73 8AN
T: 01332 864935
w: breedonhall.co.uk

BEDROOMS: 5. Plus 3 self-catering
cottages.
OPEN: closed Sundays, Christmas and
New Year.
FACILITIES: drawing room, dining
room, snug, free Wi-Fi, in-room
TV (Freeview), 1-acre grounds, civil
wedding licence, parking.
BACKGROUND MUSIC: none.
LOCATION: Calke Abbey, Staunton
Harold Church, Donington Park
Race Track and National Forest are
close by.
CHILDREN: all ages welcomed.
DOGS: well-behaved dogs allowed
(resident dog) in bedrooms, public
rooms.
CREDIT CARDS: MC, Visa.
PRICES: per room B&B from £85.

BRIGHTON Sussex

PASKINS

An Art Deco theme runs through this characterful B&B within the East Cliff conservation area. Run by the Marlowe family, it has long been a bastion of sustainable practices and high-quality, locally sourced organic food. Forged from twin 19th-century stucco houses in Kemp Town, it has an Art Nouveau reception with a vintage typewriter and Bakelite telephone. 'Comfortable' bedrooms, their bathroom stocked with certified cruelty-free toiletries, are colourful and eclectic. A creative, international flair takes over breakfast, with iced gold whisky added to organic porridge (for those who prove Scottish heritage); Cajun vegan sausages; warm croissants; 'Pavilion' rarebit; meat and fish dishes are also available. Parking permits can be provided.

MAP 2:E4
18–19 Charlotte Street
Brighton BN2 1AG
T: 01273 601203
W: paskins.co.uk

BEDROOMS: 19.
OPEN: all year except 23–26 Dec.
FACILITIES: dining room, free Wi-Fi, in-room TV (Freeview), parking vouchers (£10 for 24 hours).
BACKGROUND MUSIC: 1920s/1930s music at breakfast.
LOCATION: 10 mins' walk from centre.
CHILDREN: all ages welcomed.
DOGS: allowed (not unattended) in some bedrooms, by arrangement.
CREDIT CARDS: Amex, MC, Visa.
PRICES: per room B&B £60–£190. Discounts for Vegetarian Society, Vegan Society and Amnesty International members. Parking permits: £10 for 24 hours.

BRIGHTON Sussex

A ROOM WITH A VIEW

Steps from the beach in arty Kemp Town, this 'immaculately presented' Regency house is a 'small but so comfortable' B&B. The 'cheerful, friendly' spot has an appealing, unfussy decor, with pictures of the town by local artists. Bedrooms, each 'light, airy and clean', have their own style; a 'comfy bed', 'thoughtful' comforts (earplugs in the bedside drawer, biscuits and a capsule coffee machine, mini-fridge, 'fluffy towels and dressing gowns'), perhaps a walk-in wet room or a freestanding tub in the bathroom. Almost all look over the sea and down to Palace Pier. The highlight is the 'excellent' breakfast: blueberry pancakes, 'highly recommended double eggs Benedict'. Free parking can be pre-arranged.

MAP 2:E4
41 Marine Parade
Brighton BN2 1PE
T: 01273 682885
W: aroomwithaviewbrighton.com

BEDROOMS: 9.
OPEN: all year.
FACILITIES: lounge, breakfast room, free Wi-Fi, in-room TV, parking.
BACKGROUND MUSIC: 'gentle' in breakfast room.
LOCATION: in Kemp Town.
CHILDREN: not under 12.
DOGS: not allowed.
CREDIT CARDS: Amex, MC, Visa.
PRICES: per room B&B single from £80, double £110–£270.

BROADWAY Worcestershire

THE OLIVE BRANCH

'Beautifully appointed', a B&B in a Grade II
listed late 16th-century building overlooking a
Cotswold high street of mellow stone houses.
It is run by Pam Talboys, a friendly, 'perfect'
host. The country cottage-style bedrooms are
well equipped with 'a comfy bed, beautiful linen
and towels, decent storage space, a small but
lavishly provisioned bathroom'. The enclosed rear
garden is a serene spot to enjoy a tipple from the
honesty bar in the homely sitting room. 'First-
rate breakfasts', taken in the front parlour with
its original stone flags, are stocked with home-
baked cakes and breads, local jam, marmalade
and honey, and smoothies; the breakfast menu is
available in Japanese.

25% DISCOUNT VOUCHERS

MAP 3:D6
78 High Street
Broadway WR12 7AJ
T: 01386 853440
W: theolivebranch-broadway.com

BEDROOMS: 7. Some on ground floor,
1 suitable for disabled.
OPEN: all year.
FACILITIES: lounge, breakfast room,
free Wi-Fi, in-room TV, ¼-acre
garden, gazebo, 'easy parking',
dining room and lounge wheelchair
accessible.
BACKGROUND MUSIC: in lounge,
breakfast room.
LOCATION: in village centre.
CHILDREN: all ages welcomed.
DOGS: not allowed.
CREDIT CARDS: MC, Visa.
PRICES: per room B&B single £90–£115,
double £125–£145.

BROCKENHURST Hampshire

DAISYBANK COTTAGE

New Forest trails lead to a gingerbread Arts
and Crafts house, the home and B&B of 'perfect
hosts' Ciaran and Cheryl Maher. Freshly baked
cupcakes appear on guests' arrival, perhaps with
a pick-me-up from the well-stocked honesty bar.
'Spacious, beautifully decorated' bedrooms, in the
main house and a prettily converted cottage, have
a wide bed, plantation shutters; a well-appointed
bathroom or wet room; a Nespresso machine;
hand-made chocolates. Cottage suites have their
own patio with garden access; the shepherd's hut
has a wood-burner. Breakfast orders, placed in the
flowerpot outside at night, are transformed into
'fantastic' Aga-fresh fare: home-baked soda bread,
artisan jams and honey, eggs, bacon, sausages
from a nearby farm.

25% DISCOUNT VOUCHERS

MAP 2:E2
Sway Road
Brockenhurst SO42 7SG
T: 01590 622086
W: bedandbreakfast-newforest.co.uk

BEDROOMS: 8. 2 in Gardener's Cottage,
all on ground floor, plus 1-bed
shepherd's hut available Apr–Sept,
some suitable for disabled but not
fully adapted.
OPEN: all year, except 1 week over
Christmas.
FACILITIES: 2 sitting rooms, breakfast
room, free Wi-Fi, in-room TV
(Freeview), ½-acre garden, parking.
BACKGROUND MUSIC: in breakfast area.
CHILDREN: over-8s welcomed.
DOGS: not allowed.
CREDIT CARDS: MC, Visa.
PRICES: per room B&B £110–£160.
2-night min. stay preferred weekends.

BUCKDEN Cambridgeshire
THE GEORGE

In a 'quaint village' just off the Great North Road, Anne and Richard Furbank's 19th-century coaching inn is done up with a dash of good humour. Each of the bedrooms is named after a famous (or infamous) George – Eliot, Orwell, Best, etc. Plain and traditional, they all have a 'clean, modern bathroom', with a drench shower, spoiling toiletries. 'Dedicated young staff' extend a 'warm welcome'. Downstairs, in the 'popular, family-friendly restaurant', chef El Akil Benaissa's 'truly excellent' modern British dishes might include medallions of local venison, sautéed potatoes, parsnip purée, baby leeks, green peppercorn and Marsala jus. Breakfast brings 'perfectly poached eggs' and 'excellent' coffee.

MAP 2:B4
High Street
Buckden PE19 5XA
T: 01480 812300
w: thegeorgebuckden.com

BEDROOMS: 12. 3 suitable for disabled.
OPEN: all year.
FACILITIES: lift, bar, lounge, restaurant, private dining rooms, free Wi-Fi, in-room TV (Freeview), civil wedding licence, courtyard.
BACKGROUND MUSIC: in public areas.
LOCATION: ¼ mile from centre.
CHILDREN: all ages welcomed.
DOGS: allowed, not unattended in bedrooms, only guide dogs in restaurants.
CREDIT CARDS: Amex, MC, Visa.
PRICES: per room B&B £95–£150, D,B&B £155–£210. À la carte £50.

BUCKFASTLEIGH Devon
KILBURY MANOR

Just up from the River Dart, Julia and Martin Blundell's peaceful countryside B&B occupies a characterful Devonshire longhouse dating back to the 17th century. Homely bedrooms, spread across the main house and converted barn, have oodles of character; the loft room has a vaulted beamed ceiling; all have a generous hospitality tray, aromatic toiletries. Served in the pretty dining room with wood-burning stove, a well-presented breakfast brings home-made preserves and compotes, devilled tomatoes on granary toast, English muffin with locally smoked salmon. Dietary requirements are catered for with advance notice. The hosts have dining recommendations for the evening. Great walks virtually from the door.

MAP 1:D4
Colston Road
Buckfastleigh TQ11 0LN
T: 01364 644079
w: kilburymanor.co.uk

BEDROOMS: 4. 2 in converted stone barn across the courtyard, plus a 1-bedroom cottage.
OPEN: all year.
FACILITIES: breakfast room, free Wi-Fi, in-room TV (Freeview), 4-acre garden, courtyard, bicycle and canoe storage.
BACKGROUND MUSIC: none.
LOCATION: 1 mile from Buckfastleigh centre.
CHILDREN: over-8s welcomed.
DOGS: not allowed.
CREDIT CARDS: none accepted.
PRICES: per room B&B single from £65, double £80–£99. 2-night min. booking Apr–Sept.

BURFORD Oxfordshire

BAY TREE HOTEL

A wisteria-festooned arch frames the entry to
this prettily refurbished hotel, in a hilly Cotswold
town. Forged from a row of 17th-century
honey-stone houses, the hotel (Cotswold Inns
and Hotels) has flagstone floors, ancient beams, a
galleried staircase and huge open fireplaces. The
country-contemporary bedrooms (some compact)
have their own style, with a mix of florals, checks,
tweeds, hunting-themed fabrics. All have fluffy
robes, upmarket toiletries, a Nespresso machine.
For canine travellers, there are garden rooms with
direct outdoor access. In the bar, board games,
local ales, ciders and light meals; in the restaurant,
well-crafted modern British cuisine including
crisp lamb shoulder, lamb cutlet, dauphinoise
potato, baby gem, heritage carrots.

25% DISCOUNT VOUCHERS

MAP 3:D6
Sheep Street
Burford OX18 4LW
T: 01993 822791
W: cotswold-inns-hotels.co.uk/
the-bay-tree-hotel

BEDROOMS: 21. 2 adjoining garden
rooms on ground floor.
OPEN: all year.
FACILITIES: library, bar, restaurant, free
Wi-Fi, in-room TV (Freeview), civil
wedding licence, function facilities,
patio, walled garden.
BACKGROUND MUSIC: in public areas
('subtle').
LOCATION: 5 mins' walk from Burford
High Street.
CHILDREN: all ages welcomed.
DOGS: well-behaved dogs allowed in
some bedrooms, public rooms except
restaurant.
CREDIT CARDS: Amex, MC, Visa.
PRICES: per room B&B £130–£310,
D,B&B £190–£370. À la carte £38.

NEW

BURLEY Hampshire

BURLEY MANOR

A New Forest Victorian verderer's manor house
overlooking a deer park is today a restful hotel
with a popular restaurant at its heart. Bedrooms
range from 'snug' to suites, perhaps with
four-poster and in-room bath. Our inspector's
'spacious' garden suite had a super-king-size
bed, a private terrace, 'steps down to lawn and
swimming pool'. All have a Hypnos bed, a
cafetière and biscuits. An 'unusual, eclectic' menu
brings tapas and sharing plates – kale, hazelnut
and halloumi borek, wood-roasted octopus. Main
dishes might include seared sea trout, za'atar leek,
wild garlic. 'The quality of food and wine was
excellent.' Breakfast, too, was good, 'with extra
points for adding hollandaise, on request, to the
poached eggs'.

MAP 2:E2
Ringwood Road
Burley BH24 4BS
T: 01425 403522
W: burleymanor.com

BEDROOMS: 40. Some in garden wing,
2 suitable for disabled.
OPEN: all year.
FACILITIES: entrance hall, drawing
room, lounge/bar, 3 dining rooms
(1 conservatory), conference facilities,
free Wi-Fi, in-room TV, civil wedding
licence, treatment rooms, 8-acre
grounds, heated outdoor pool (July–
Sept), parking.
BACKGROUND MUSIC: in public rooms.
LOCATION: 7-min. walk N of Burley
village.
CHILDREN: children welcome at lunch,
no under-13s overnight.
DOGS: allowed in most bedrooms,
public rooms, not in restaurant
(£30 a night, £45 for 2).
CREDIT CARDS: MC, Visa.
PRICES: per room B&B £109–£263.
Tapas £4.50–£7.50, main dishes
£15–£21, sharing plates £33–£55.

BURRINGTON Devon

NORTHCOTE MANOR HOTEL & SPA

'A very welcoming place.' Deep in the Taw valley, Jean-Pierre Mifsud's wisteria-hung 18th-century manor house is a characterful 'high standard' hideaway, surrounded by orchards and woodlands. 'Accommodating' staff are attentive and polite. The lounge ('very comfortable') is 'tastefully furnished'; stacks of books to borrow line the 'great log stove'. Snug or spacious, traditional or modern, with terrace or garden views, bedrooms have 'all the necessities'. 'Housekeeping was excellent', as were Chef Richie Herkes's menus. The gourmet tasting menu with accompanying wines is 'unmissable'. A luxury spa opened in May 2019. Sister hotel to The Lake, Llangammarch Wells (see main entry).

MAP 1:C4
Burrington EX37 9LZ
T: 01769 560501
W: northcotemanor.co.uk

BEDROOMS: 16. 5 in extension, 1 suitable for disabled.
OPEN: all year.
FACILITIES: bar, snug, restaurant, free Wi-Fi, in-room TV (Freeview), civil wedding licence, spa with steam room, sauna, hot tub, swimming pool (12.5 metres), gym, treatment rooms, lounge and café area, 20-acre grounds.
BACKGROUND MUSIC: classical in public areas after midday.
LOCATION: 3 miles S of Umberleigh.
CHILDREN: all ages welcomed; no under-9s in restaurant at dinner.
DOGS: allowed in some bedrooms, not in 1 lounge or restaurant.
CREDIT CARDS: Amex, MC, Visa.
PRICES: per room B&B £180, D,B&B £355. À la carte £49.50, gourmet menu with wines £95. 1-night bookings refused at Christmas, New Year.

BURY ST EDMUNDS Suffolk

THE NORTHGATE

Moments from Bury's ancient abbey, two Victorian town houses have been transformed into a smart spot in the town. Owned by the small Chestnut Inns group, the red brick building has spacious, 'nicely furnished' bedrooms in a muted palette, Provençal furniture, modern bathroom with stylishly retro fittings. Some have a fireplace, an in-room bath; those facing the garden are quietest. Cocktails, ordered from a vast selection in the slick, contemporary bar, have a preprandial zing before 'ambitious' menus in the handsome restaurant. Perhaps Loomswood farm duck, local sweet onions, heritage carrots and blackberries. The large terrace makes 'an excellent venue'. Sister hotel The Packhorse Inn is in Newmarket (see main entry).

MAP 2:B5
Northgate Street
Bury St Edmunds IP33 1HP
T: 01284 339604
W: thenorthgate.com

BEDROOMS: 10.
OPEN: all year.
FACILITIES: bar/lounge, restaurant, private function room, free Wi-Fi, in-room TV (Freeview), garden, terrace, parking.
BACKGROUND MUSIC: in public areas.
LOCATION: 6-min. walk into town.
CHILDREN: all ages welcomed.
DOGS: allowed in 1 bedroom, in public rooms except chef's table.
CREDIT CARDS: Amex, MC, Visa.
PRICES: per person B&B single £115–£140, double £140–£280. À la carte £35, 5-course tasting menu £45.

CAMBRIDGE Cambridgeshire

GONVILLE HOTEL

Overlooking verdant Parker's Piece, this large, family-owned hotel is a short walk to colleges, shops and cafés. It is liked for its 'delightful, helpful staff'. A cheerful air floats throughout the dapper public spaces. Bedrooms range from simply plain to sumptuous floral-themed rooms in Gresham House Wellness spa, within the grounds; all have a pillow menu, in-room valet via an iPad, air conditioning; an evening turn-down service. 'Tasty' meals are served in the Atrium brasserie; fine dining, courtesy of Master Chef Hans Schweitzer, in Cotto restaurant. Breakfast had an 'enormous buffet', made-to-order cooked dishes. On-site parking (paid) is a bonus; bicycle hire is complimentary. City tours, pick-ups, drop-offs in the hotel's Bentley can be pre-arranged.

MAP 2:B4
Gonville Place
Cambridge CB1 1LY
T: 01223 366611
W: gonvillehotel.co.uk

BEDROOMS: 84. Some on ground floor, some suitable for disabled, 8 in Gresham House within the grounds.
OPEN: all year.
FACILITIES: lift, bar, lounge, 2 restaurants, free Wi-Fi, in-room TV (Freeview), parking (£15 council charge), bicycles to borrow.
BACKGROUND MUSIC: in public areas.
LOCATION: in centre.
CHILDREN: all ages welcomed (under-12s free).
DOGS: allowed in some bedrooms, reception area.
CREDIT CARDS: Amex, MC, Visa.
PRICES: per room B&B from £192. Set dinner (Cotto) £70–£75, à la carte (Atrium brasserie) £50.

CAMBRIDGE Cambridgeshire

QUY MILL HOTEL & SPA

A modern spa hotel, staffed by a friendly, welcoming team, in a 19th-century watermill in lovely surroundings five miles from the city centre. Stylish rooms in the original building have long views over the well-maintained gardens or river; some have a four-poster, a fireplace; larger rooms (some with private patio, exposed timbers) are in converted barns across the courtyard. Served in the garden-facing Mill House restaurant, or on the patio, chef Gavin Murphy's modern British and European dishes use locally sourced ingredients. All-day light bites are served in the lounge/bar. The hardest decision is picking from over 50 malt whiskies for a nightcap. The spa has a sauna, treatment rooms, a mud chamber and indoor pool.

MAP 2:B4
Church Road
Cambridge CB25 9AF
T: 01223 293383
W: cambridgequymill.co.uk

BEDROOMS: 51. Some in converted barns across courtyard, 1 suitable for disabled.
OPEN: all year, no food served on Christmas Day.
FACILITIES: bar/lounge, restaurant, free Wi-Fi, in-room TV (Freeview), civil wedding licence, conference facilities, leisure centre, 2-acre grounds, parking.
BACKGROUND MUSIC: in public spaces.
LOCATION: 5 miles NE of Cambridge city centre.
CHILDREN: all ages welcomed.
DOGS: not allowed.
CREDIT CARDS: Amex, MC, Visa.
PRICES: per room B&B £100–£300, D,B&B £170–£400. À la carte £45. 1-night stay sometimes refused at busy periods.

CAMBRIDGE Cambridgeshire

THE VARSITY HOTEL & SPA

Balmy evenings are made for celebrating the 'wonderful views' of Jesus Green and nearby campuses over cocktails on the roof terrace of this modern hotel. Between St John's and Magdalene colleges, top marks are awarded for its 'very convenient location' and 'helpful staff'. Campus memorabilia lines the corridors; contemporary bedrooms (some with a four-poster, extra seating or an inspiring outlook) have air conditioning, quirky artwork, tablets loaded with newspapers and magazines. River bar serves a classic surf and turf menu by the waterside; brasserie-style fare is available all day on the sixth floor. Extra-curricular activities? A spa (sauna, steam room, treatments), a gym with daily fitness classes; complimentary bicycles for touring the city.

MAP 2:B4
Thompson's Lane
Cambridge CB5 8AQ
T: 01223 306030
w: thevarsityhotel.co.uk

BEDROOMS: 48. 3 suitable for disabled.
OPEN: all year except Christmas.
FACILITIES: lift, bar, 2 restaurants, roof terrace, health club and spa, free Wi-Fi, in-room TV, civil wedding licence, conference facilities, valet parking service (charge).
BACKGROUND MUSIC: in restaurants.
LOCATION: by the Cam, in the centre.
CHILDREN: all ages welcomed.
DOGS: not allowed.
CREDIT CARDS: Amex, MC, Visa.
PRICES: per room B&B (continental) from £199.

CANTERBURY Kent

CANTERBURY CATHEDRAL LODGE

Within an architect-designed complex, this contemporary hotel enjoys a 'prime position' in the 'serene grounds' of the World Heritage site. Run by 'cheerful staff', it offers free admission to the cathedral and its precincts. 'Comfortable' bedrooms are uncluttered linear, with a good shower room. Cathedral-facing options have 'blissful' views. Books on the area and ecclesiastical tomes line the library/sitting room, which has complimentary newspapers and a computer for guests' use. At breakfast in the busy refectory or on the terrace, a 'small buffet' and 'well-served' hot dishes lay heavenly foundations for the day. Guests have discounts at local restaurants, 'many within easy walking distance'.

MAP 2:D5
The Precincts
Canterbury CT1 2EH
T: 01227 865350
w: canterburycathedrallodge.org

BEDROOMS: 35. 1 suitable for disabled.
OPEN: all year.
FACILITIES: lift, sitting room, breakfast room, free Wi-Fi, in-room TV (Freeview), Campanile garden, meeting/function facilities, limited parking (pre-booking required).
BACKGROUND MUSIC: none.
LOCATION: in the cathedral grounds.
CHILDREN: all ages welcomed.
DOGS: not allowed.
CREDIT CARDS: Amex, MC, Visa.
PRICES: per room B&B single from £91, double from £100.

CHATTON Northumberland

CHATTON PARK HOUSE

Peace and tranquillity reign at Paul and Michelle Mattinson's 'most welcoming' Georgian house, where well-manicured gardens stretch towards magnificent Northumberland countryside. A child-free spot, it has plenty of space to recharge. The large, airy sitting room has cosy armchairs for reading a borrowed book or a newspaper; the grounds are ideal for restful strolls. Recently refurbished, well-equipped, capacious bedrooms, all garden-facing, have thoughtful extras (tea-/coffee-making facilities, USB connectivity, a mini-fridge, fluffy bathrobes, good toiletries); two have a separate lounge. Ordered in advance, breakfasts are generous (oak-smoked local kippers, locally made jams). The owners offer knowledgeable advice about the numerous attractions in the area.

25% DISCOUNT VOUCHERS

MAP 4:A3
New Road
Chatton NE66 5RA
T: 01668 215507
W: chattonpark.com

BEDROOMS: 4. Plus 2-bed self-catering lodge with private garden.
OPEN: Mar–Nov.
FACILITIES: sitting room, breakfast room, free Wi-Fi, in-room TV (Freeview), 4-acre grounds, parking.
BACKGROUND MUSIC: none.
LOCATION: ½ mile from Chatton.
CHILDREN: not under 17.
DOGS: not allowed.
CREDIT CARDS: Amex, MC, Visa.
PRICES: per person B&B single £54–£119, double £139–£249. 1-night bookings sometimes refused.

CHELTENHAM Gloucestershire

BEAUMONT HOUSE

Close to the centre of this Regency town (with a 'spacious' car park), Fiona Burke's white-painted Victorian villa B&B is a good base during festivals, races and celebrations and gatherings in between. Staff are 'friendly and obliging'. 'Very clean and well maintained', the fetching bedrooms (some snug) are individually designed. Spacious suites, including one with an Africa theme, another Asia, have a spa bath in the 'super' bathroom and high-end toiletries. In all rooms: tea-/coffee-making facilities, bottled water, biscuits. The neat lawn and well-maintained garden are worth a visit with a little something from the honesty bar. On offer at breakfast ('a disappointment') is a simple, self-serve continental buffet.

MAP 3:D5
56 Shurdington Road
Cheltenham GL53 0JE
T: 01242 223311
W: willowboutiquehotels.com

BEDROOMS: 16.
OPEN: all year.
FACILITIES: lounge, breakfast room, free Wi-Fi, in-room TV (Sky, Freeview), garden, parking.
BACKGROUND MUSIC: in breakfast room.
LOCATION: 1 mile S of town centre.
CHILDREN: all ages welcomed.
DOGS: not allowed.
CREDIT CARDS: Amex, MC, Visa.
PRICES: per room B&B (continental) £60–£220. 2-night min. stay on Sat night, during festivals and Cheltenham Gold Cup.

NEW

CHELTENHAM Gloucestershire

THE BRADLEY

Bounteous offerings, elegant surroundings and friendly staff converge in this Georgian town house in the fashionable Montpellier district. Restored by the de Savary family, the boutique B&B brims with period features, paintings and objets d'art. In the spacious lounge, a complimentary G&T is appreciated along with fresh flowers, home-made cakes, and a plentiful supply of books, newspapers and board games. Treats, too, in the individually designed bedrooms – sloe gin, nibbles, fresh milk, robes and fine toiletries; some rooms have under-floor heating in the modern bathroom; three have a terrace or patio. The peaceful garden entices on sunny days. Shops, restaurants and railway station are all nearby. Parking permits can be arranged.

MAP 3:D5
19 Royal Parade
Cheltenham GL50 3AY
T: 01242 519077
W: thebradleyhotel.co.uk

BEDROOMS: 10.
OPEN: all year.
FACILITIES: bar, lounge, dining room, conservatory, free Wi-Fi, in-room TV (Freeview), garden.
BACKGROUND MUSIC: none.
LOCATION: in Montpellier area of Cheltenham.
CHILDREN: not under 16.
DOGS: welcomed (dog bed, bowl, treats, £15 per night).
CREDIT CARDS: Amex, MC, Visa.
PRICES: per room B&B from £145.

CHELTENHAM Gloucestershire

BUTLERS

'Exceptional service' is nothing less than might be expected at Paul Smyth and Shaun Bailey's butler-themed B&B. 'Enjoyable, quirky and good value', it occupies a former 19th-century gentleman's residence. Alongside Edwardian paraphernalia and curios, the lounge's bookshelves make it 'a tempting place to lose time in'. 'Elegant, capacious bedrooms' each bear the name of a famous butler (Jeeves, Hudson, Brabinger, etc); inside, a 'very comfortable bed, pleasing antiques; a gleaming bathroom' with a powerful shower; some rooms offer views of the distant Malvern hills. Breakfast can be taken on the roof terrace. The 'quiet, well-located spot' is 'an easy walk' from the centre.

MAP 3:D5
Western Road
Cheltenham GL50 3RN
T: 01242 570771
W: butlers-hotel.co.uk

BEDROOMS: 8.
OPEN: all year except Christmas.
FACILITIES: drawing room, breakfast room, free Wi-Fi, in-room TV (Freeview), ¼-acre garden, parking.
BACKGROUND MUSIC: quiet radio in the morning.
LOCATION: 10 mins' stroll to the promenade or Montpellier.
CHILDREN: over-9s welcomed.
DOGS: not allowed.
CREDIT CARDS: MC, Visa.
PRICES: per room B&B single from £80, double from £99. 2-night min. stay during weekends and festivals.

CHELTENHAM Gloucestershire
NO. 131

Across from Imperial Gardens, this well-restored Georgian villa has heightened its metropolitan allure with fun spaces and further accommodation in The House, next door. Spacious lounges have squashy sofas, tables groaning with magazines, striking modern art from the likes of David Hockney, Banksy, Peter Blake. Voguish bedrooms (some grand, some snug hideaways) have a 'great bed'; a decadent bathroom, sometimes accessed by steps, with a hook on the deep tub for a wine glass. An all-day brunch venue becomes the place to party at weekends, with inspired cocktails; 350 gins. The restaurant's locally sourced dishes include serious steaks. Guests can soak up the evening sun on one of several terraces. Part of The Lucky Onion group.

MAP 3:D5
131 Promenade
Cheltenham GL50 1NW
T: 01242 822939
W: no131.com

BEDROOMS: 19. Split between No. 131 and The House, 17 more planned in an additional building.
OPEN: all year.
FACILITIES: drawing room, lounge, bar, snug, restaurant, private dining rooms, cheese and wine room, juice bar, games room, free Wi-Fi, in-room Apple TV (Sky), terraces, parking.
BACKGROUND MUSIC: all day in public areas.
LOCATION: in town centre.
CHILDREN: all ages welcomed.
DOGS: allowed on terraces only.
CREDIT CARDS: Amex, MC, Visa.
PRICES: per room B&B from £180, D,B&B from £240. À la carte £35.

CHELTENHAM Gloucestershire
NO. 38 THE PARK

A spicy addition to this Georgian town house, renowned restaurant Prithvi relocated here from its previous spot in town. Well-presented, gastronomic Indian cuisine is served on spotless white tablecloths in the chicly rustic restaurant. (Booking recommended.) Easy-going cool seeps through the hotel's public spaces, which are styled with re-purposed furniture, modern lighting, interesting artwork by British artists; deep sofas in the lounge are made for curling up with a drink and a biscuit from the help-yourself cookie jar. Modish bedrooms (some snug) set their own tone, a claw-footed bath here, a vivid mohair blanket or original fireplace there. All have king-size beds, decent robes, good toiletries and a Nespresso machine. Part of The Lucky Onion group.

25% DISCOUNT VOUCHERS

MAP 3:D5
38 Evesham Road
Cheltenham GL52 2AH
T: 01242 822929
W: theluckyonion.com/property/no-38-the-park

BEDROOMS: 13. 1, on ground floor, suitable for disabled.
OPEN: all year.
FACILITIES: sitting room, open-plan kitchen/restaurant, private dining room, free Wi-Fi, in-room Apple TV (Sky), small courtyard garden, limited parking.
BACKGROUND MUSIC: all day in public areas.
LOCATION: 10 mins' walk from Cheltenham town centre.
CHILDREN: all ages welcomed, not in restaurant.
DOGS: allowed in bedrooms, public rooms except restaurant.
CREDIT CARDS: Amex, MC, Visa.
PRICES: per room B&B £110–£400. À la carte £94.

CHESTER Cheshire

THE CHESTER GROSVENOR

Grand from every direction, this 'very smart' Grade II listed hotel (Bespoke Hotels) is 'a very good place to stay, peopled with polite, cheerful staff'. Bedrooms are up 'the wide staircase, past the huge, dramatic chandelier'. Some are modern, some traditional; all have a comfortable bed and 'every amenity' (air conditioning, double glazing, a marble bathroom with 'piping hot water'). In the light-filled brasserie, classic modern dishes; in chef Simon Radley's Michelin-starred restaurant, perhaps Pyrenean mountain lamb, sweet and wild garlic, morel mushrooms, crispy curds and faggot gravy, or the 8-course tasting menu. A wide choice at breakfast ('ample, excellent'). Centrally located, the hotel is ideal for exploring the city.

MAP 3:A4
Eastgate
Chester CH1 1LT
T: 01244 324024
W: chestergrosvenor.com

BEDROOMS: 80. 1 suitable for disabled.
OPEN: all year except Christmas Eve and Day.
FACILITIES: lift, drawing room, lounge, bar, brasserie, restaurant, meeting/private dining rooms, free Wi-Fi, in-room TV (Sky, Freeview), civil wedding licence, function facilities, spa, parking.
BACKGROUND MUSIC: in public areas.
LOCATION: in city centre.
CHILDREN: all ages welcomed (over-11s only in restaurant).
DOGS: not allowed.
CREDIT CARDS: Amex, MC, Visa.
PRICES: per room B&B from £155. Tasting menu (restaurant) £69 or £99, à la carte (brasserie) £45.

CHESTER Cheshire

ODDFELLOWS

The former meeting place of an altruistic society of misfits and artists (the Odd Fellows), so rumour has it, this 'great' neoclassical hotel redefines 'quirky' through and through. Wickerwork boxing hares; typewriters chasing up the walls; a colourful zaniness bounds through the restaurant and bar and out on to the AstroTurfed terrace, popular with lively gatherings and weddings. The bedrooms, in the main house and a modern annexe, are just as comfortably eccentric: perhaps a circular bed, Randolph Caldecott illustrations, two roll-top baths. Tempting cocktails and imaginative, uncomplicated dishes are served in the 'secret garden', the flamboyant lounge bar and the mural-decorated restaurant.

MAP 3:A4
20 Lower Bridge Street
Chester CH1 1RS
T: 01244 345454
W: oddfellowschester.com

BEDROOMS: 18. 14 in annexe, 1 suitable for disabled, plus self-catering apartments nearby.
OPEN: all year except Christmas Day.
FACILITIES: bar, lobby, restaurant, private dining room, free Wi-Fi, in-room TV, civil wedding licence, terrace, garden.
BACKGROUND MUSIC: in public spaces.
LOCATION: in city centre.
CHILDREN: all ages welcomed.
DOGS: not allowed.
CREDIT CARDS: Amex, MC, Visa.
PRICES: per room B&B from £129.50. À la carte £28, tasting menu £45.

CHICHESTER Sussex

CHICHESTER HARBOUR HOTEL

Priory Park, where W G Grace once wore whites, is a cricket ball throw from this Georgian hotel inside the city's Roman walls. Within the Grade II* listed building, a cheery design melds with well-maintained original features (grand staircase, marble fireplaces, large sash windows). Colourful bedrooms are individually done, with an oversized headboard, velvet cushions, bold wallpaper and leafy or cathedral views. The marble-topped bar with its Art Deco vibe attracts locals for pre-dinner drinks and cocktail masterclasses, before settling in the Jetty restaurant for brasserie dishes (seafood, grills and salads). Underneath, the subterranean spa has a hydro pool and many treatments (small extra charge). In the Harbour Hotels collection.

25% DISCOUNT VOUCHERS

MAP 2:E3
North Street
Chichester PO19 1NH
T: 01243 778000
w: harbourhotels.co.uk/hotels/chichester

BEDROOMS: 36. Plus 1-bedroom cottage.
OPEN: all year.
FACILITIES: bar, restaurant, orangery, private dining room, free Wi-Fi, in-room TV, lift, terrace, spa, gym, civil wedding licence, business facilities, limited parking.
BACKGROUND MUSIC: in public areas.
LOCATION: within the city walls.
CHILDREN: all ages welcomed (cots, extra beds, over-3s £25).
DOGS: assistance dogs allowed.
CREDIT CARDS: Amex, MC, Visa.
PRICES: per room B&B from £155, D,B&B from £205. Set dinner £12.75, à la carte £30. 2-night min. stay preferred.

CHIDDINGFOLD Surrey

THE CROWN INN

On the corner of the village green, a 'lovely' country inn which has been offering hospitality to pilgrims and travellers for centuries. Constructed in 1441, the timber-framed building is full of 'traditional character'; in the popular bar, local tipples are served amid medieval carvings, 'massive beams', stained-glass windows and inglenook fireplaces. In the oak-panelled restaurant, pub grub is attentively served to well-scrubbed tables. Characterful well-appointed bedrooms, all sloping floors and antique furnishings, have chic toiletries, a digital radio; some feature a barley twist four-poster bed. Across the courtyard, two rooms open on to a private garden. Breakfast has a buffet of morning-baked pastries, good cooked choices.

MAP 2:D3
The Green
Chiddingfold GU8 4TX
T: 01428 682255
w: thecrownchiddingfold.com

BEDROOMS: 8.
OPEN: all year.
FACILITIES: bar, snug, restaurant, free Wi-Fi, in-room TV (Sky, Freeview), private dining, 2 small courtyard gardens, large terrace, parking, public rooms wheelchair accessible.
BACKGROUND MUSIC: in public spaces.
LOCATION: 20 mins from Guildford.
CHILDREN: all ages welcomed.
DOGS: allowed in bar and lounge, not in bedrooms.
CREDIT CARDS: Amex, MC, Visa.
PRICES: per room B&B £90–£215, D,B&B £120–£275. À la carte £27.50.

CHILGROVE Sussex

THE WHITE HORSE

Chic and rustic, this 'simply lovely' spot, in the foothills of the South Downs, is a country inn through and through. In the bar, mellow old wood, vintage pictures, the odd fox's head; in the restaurant, 'simple but satisfying meals' exploiting local produce, including foraged fare, freshly caught trout from nearby rivers; pigeon and rabbit from local estates. Expansive views of the South Downs pour in through the large picture windows of the 'comfortable' courtyard bedrooms, where a cosy style is complete with woolly blankets, sheepskin rugs and exposed beams; some rooms have a private patio, and an outdoor hot tub. For tea and coffee drinkers, fresh milk is delivered to the door each morning. Dogs are made welcome with their own bed and bowl.

MAP 2:E3
1 High Street
Chilgrove PO18 9HX
T: 01243 519444
W: thewhitehorse.co.uk

BEDROOMS: 15. All on ground floor, 13 in rear annexe.
OPEN: all year.
FACILITIES: bar, restaurant, private dining room, free Wi-Fi, in-room TV, function facilities, 2 patios, garden, croquet, parking, helipad.
BACKGROUND MUSIC: 'soft' in public areas, live jazz on Sun afternoons.
LOCATION: 6 miles from Chichester.
CHILDREN: all ages welcomed.
DOGS: allowed (£15 per night).
CREDIT CARDS: Amex, MC, Visa.
PRICES: per room B&B from £95. À la carte £30.

CHURCH STRETTON Shropshire

VICTORIA HOUSE

'Splendid all round', Diane Chadwick offers 'well-priced, comfortable and convenient accommodation, with superb breakfasts' at her town-centre B&B. The 'wonderfully energetic, helpful' hostess has a careful eye for detail, much appreciated by guests. The homely bedrooms are 'tastefully done', with a comfortable bed, original artwork and a well-supplied hospitality tray (biscuits, hot chocolate, complimentary sherry). In a pretty room overlooking the garden, the breakfast buffet is chock full of fruit compotes, organic yogurt, and organic muesli from a nearby farm; hot dishes include egg and soldiers, bacon from locally reared pigs. Return from tramping the Shropshire hills to a home-cooked lunch or afternoon tea in Jemima's Kitchen.

25% DISCOUNT VOUCHERS

MAP 3:C4
48 High Street
Church Stretton SY6 6BX
T: 01694 723823
W: victoriahouse-shropshire.co.uk

BEDROOMS: 6.
OPEN: all year.
FACILITIES: seating area, breakfast room, café/tea room (open 9.30 am to 4 pm Wed–Sun), free Wi-Fi, in-room TV (Freeview), walled garden, pay-and-display parking (deducted from hotel bill or permits supplied).
BACKGROUND MUSIC: in breakfast room.
LOCATION: in town centre.
CHILDREN: all ages welcomed.
DOGS: allowed in some bedrooms and in the café.
CREDIT CARDS: Amex, MC, Visa.
PRICES: per room B&B single £64–£82, double £85–£102.

COLEFORD Gloucestershire

FOREST HOUSE

Barbara and Simon Andersen 'get almost everything right' at their small hotel in a market town in the Wye valley, a friendly, affordable base for exploring the Forest of Dean. Dating back to the 1790s, the former home of pioneering metallurgist David Mushet has been extended and modernised. Immaculate bedrooms have pine furniture, armchairs, 'good lighting', tea, coffee and biscuits; bathrooms have a power shower, good-quality toiletries. The bar provides complimentary coffee refills. The restaurant's wide-ranging options include fish and seafood dishes such as salmon, leek, spinach and mascarpone parcel; slow-cooked meats. 'Both our dinners were delicious.' Breakfast brings smoked haddock; eggs all ways; a Forest House full English.

MAP 3:D4
Cinder Hill
Coleford GL16 8HQ
T: 01594 832424
W: forest-house.co.uk

BEDROOMS: 8.
OPEN: 22 Dec–10 Jan.
FACILITIES: bar/lounge, restaurant, small dining room, lawned front garden, rear car park, secure bicycle storage, free Wi-Fi, in-room TV (Freeview), restaurant wheelchair accessible.
BACKGROUND MUSIC: in bar and restaurant.
LOCATION: in town centre.
CHILDREN: all ages welcomed.
DOGS: not allowed.
CREDIT CARDS: Amex, MC, Visa.
PRICES: per room B&B single £80–£95, double £95–£120. À la carte £30. Min. 2-night stay preferred bank holiday weekends.

NEW

COLERNE Wiltshire

LUCKNAM PARK

Fortune from wealthy families helped create this honey-toned 18th-century mansion on a large Wiltshire estate; fortunate visitors nowadays arrive to a wealth of additional delights. There's an arboretum and rose garden to wander through; parkland trails to explore, on horseback if desired; fun-filled cookery classes catering for all tastes. In a walled garden, the wood, glass and marble spa has pools and treatments galore. Young visitors can retreat to the Hideaway, packed with games and activities. Refined bedrooms decorated with subtle florals or stripes have antique furniture, a TV/DVD-iPod docking station, a safe. Elegant fine dining is in Executive Chef Hywel Jones's eponymous Michelin-starred restaurant; the Brasserie is a casual affair.

MAP 2:D1
Colerne SN14 8AZ
T: 01225 742777
W: lucknampark.co.uk

BEDROOMS: 42. Some in courtyard, plus a 3-bedroom and a 4-bedroom cottage.
OPEN: all year, restaurant closed Mon, Tues.
FACILITIES: drawing room, library, restaurant, brasseries, room service, free Wi-Fi, in-room TV, civil wedding licence, spa, indoor pools, outdoor hydrotherapy and saltwater plunge pool, terrace, tennis, croquet, football pitch, equestrian centre, 5-acre grounds within 500 acres of parkland.
BACKGROUND MUSIC: in public spaces.
LOCATION: on a 500-acre estate close to Chippenham.
CHILDREN: all ages welcomed.
DOGS: allowed in 4 bedrooms, part of Brasserie, by arrangement (beds, bowls, food, £25 per night).
CREDIT CARDS: Amex, MC, Visa.
PRICES: per room B&B from £384.

CONSTANTINE Cornwall

TRENGILLY WARTHA INN

Surrounded by farms and woodland, the gardens of Will and Lisa Lea's family-friendly pub-with-rooms are verdant with giant ferns and tiny orchids and contain a lake, an arboretum and wildlife areas. Locals flock to the lively bar, with its piano, settles, wood-burner and beams covered in beer mats, for its real ales and ciders, occasional folk music evenings and classic farmhouse cooking. Chef Nick Tyler's award-winning fare may also be eaten in the bistro or conservatory. Many of the country cottage-style bedrooms have uninterrupted valley or garden views; one might have a hand-crafted bedhead, another its own private, covered deck area. Unique accommodation is also offered in two 'tree-top' safari tents. A full Cornish breakfast fuels the day.

MAP 1:E2
Nancenoy
Constantine TR11 5RP
T: 01326 340332
W: trengilly.co.uk

BEDROOMS: 12. 2 in garden annexe.
OPEN: all year except Christmas.
FACILITIES: bar, restaurant, conservatory, private dining room, games room, free Wi-Fi, in-room TV (Freeview), terrace, 6-acre garden, public rooms wheelchair accessible.
BACKGROUND MUSIC: live music in bar 'now and again'.
LOCATION: 15 mins' drive from Falmouth.
CHILDREN: all ages welcomed.
DOGS: allowed.
CREDIT CARDS: Amex, MC, Visa.
PRICES: per room B&B single from £77, double £84–£130. À la carte £25.

CORNWORTHY Devon

KERSWELL FARMHOUSE

Named after the wells and cress beds fed by nearby springs, Nichola and Graham Hawkins's B&B is enfolded by their small working farm. Throughout the well-renovated 400-year-old longhouse, antiques blend with farmhouse furnishings, fresh-cut flowers spill from vases, and myriad contemporary artwork hang on walls and decorate crannies. The old milking parlour, as well as housing the honesty bar, exhibits the work of contemporary ceramicists, glassmakers, painters and photographers. Spacious bedrooms have all the essentials, plus thoughtful extras (teas and ground coffee, fluffy bathrobes, novels and magazines). At breakfast, farm-fresh produce appears on the plate: sausages from home-reared pigs; eggs from free-range hens.

MAP 1:D4
Cornworthy
Totnes TQ9 7HH
T: 01803 732013
W: www.kerswellfarmhouse.co.uk

BEDROOMS: 5. 1 in adjacent barn, 1 on ground floor.
OPEN: Mar–end Oct.
FACILITIES: 2 dining rooms, sitting room, art gallery, free Wi-Fi, in-room TV (Freeview), 14-acre grounds, parking.
BACKGROUND MUSIC: none.
LOCATION: 4 miles S of Totnes, 4 miles N of Dartmouth.
CHILDREN: not under 12.
DOGS: not allowed.
CREDIT CARDS: none accepted
PRICES: per room B&B single £90–£125, double £120–£160. 2-night min. stay preferred.

CORSHAM Wiltshire
THE METHUEN ARMS

MAP 2:D1
2 High Street
Corsham SN13 0HB
T: 01249 717060
W: themethuenarms.com

Handsome and historic, this buzzy pub-with-rooms (owned by Butcombe Brewing) has character to spare. The conscientiously restored Georgian coaching inn, down the High Street from Corsham Court of Poldark fame, has a voguish appeal, with tweed cushions, heritage hues and botanical prints hanging above plush sofas. Alongside craft brews, chef Leigh Evans's acclaimed Italian-influenced dishes (perhaps game and suet pudding, parsnips, mash); alfresco, in pretty gardens, is an option. Bedrooms are neatly designed (some snug), each with tall Georgian windows, an armchair, fridge, tea-/coffee-making facilities; a Roberts radio. Some have a four-poster. At breakfast, interesting cooked options, plus freshly baked pastries, home-made granola.

BEDROOMS: 19. 5 in annexe.
OPEN: all year.
FACILITIES: bar, restaurant, private dining rooms, free Wi-Fi, in-room TV (Freeview), garden, courtyard, parking.
BACKGROUND MUSIC: in private dining areas and bar.
LOCATION: 8 miles NE of Bath.
CHILDREN: all ages welcomed.
DOGS: allowed in 2 bedrooms, bars, casual dining area, courtyard (£15 per night).
CREDIT CARDS: Amex, MC, Visa.
PRICES: per room B&B £120–£220. À la carte £35.

MAP 3:C6
Shilton Lane
Coventry CV7 9LH
T: 02476 612629
W: barnaclehall.co.uk

COVENTRY Warwickshire
BARNACLE HALL

BEDROOMS: 3.
OPEN: all year except Christmas, New Year.
FACILITIES: sitting room, dining room, free Wi-Fi, in-room TV (Freeview), patio, garden.
BACKGROUND MUSIC: none.
LOCATION: 20 mins NE of Coventry, SE of Nuneaton.
CHILDREN: all ages welcomed.
DOGS: assistance dogs accepted.
CREDIT CARDS: none accepted.
PRICES: per room B&B single £45–£55, double £75–£85.

Beyond the old oak door of this 16th-century farmhouse lies a tranquil haven – three miles from the M6, a 20-minute drive from Coventry, and a world away from both. Standing within lush gardens swaddled by surrounding fields, the house is full of character. It has low doorways, nooks and crannies. Steps of varying heights betray its age, but the spacious, traditionally decorated bedrooms have all the modern essentials: a flat-screen TV, a radio alarm, individually controlled central heating. They also come with a generous hospitality tray and fresh flowers. Breakfast caters for all, with fresh fruit and cereal, as well as hot dishes cooked to order.

COVENTRY Warwickshire
COOMBE ABBEY

Traces of its past as a 12th-century Cistercian abbey drift through this atmospheric hotel, which combines 'character, eccentricity and individuality at its best'. It stands amid a 'well-maintained' country park and 'superb' formal gardens. The 'stunning' building's grand interiors include a carved stone pulpit, antique armchairs, a series of confessional booths in the high-vaulted lobby. Glorious 'bed chambers' may have a canopy bed, original moulding or mullion windows, while the well-designed bathrooms sport such features as a Victorian bath or a richly tiled waterfall shower; some are hidden behind a bookcase. Indulgent afternoon teas and menus with a modern take on British cooking are served in the conservatory, candlelit at night. A popular events venue.

MAP 3:C6
Brinklow Road
Coventry CV3 2AB
T: 02476 450450
W: coombeabbey.com

BEDROOMS: 119.
OPEN: all year.
FACILITIES: bar, restaurant, private dining rooms, free Wi-Fi, in-room TV, wedding/conference facilities, terrace, 500-acre grounds, parking (£5 per day).
BACKGROUND MUSIC: in public spaces.
LOCATION: just outside city, in Coombe Country Park.
CHILDREN: all ages welcomed.
DOGS: not allowed.
CREDIT CARDS: Amex, MC, Visa.
PRICES: per room B&B from £89, D,B&B from £149. À la carte £48.

COVERACK Cornwall
THE BAY HOTEL

In an unspoilt fishing village, stepped lawns are all that separates this 'welcoming, relaxed hotel' from the sea. Coastal-cool bedrooms (some snug) have been given Cornish colours, tongue-and-groove panelling and a powerful shower in the bathroom. Huge windows in nearly all the bedrooms offer horizon views; the best rooms have a balcony, or a private terrace, accessed through pretty French doors. Bay-landed lobster, and chefs Chris Conboye and Ric House's 'excellent' daily-changing menus, are served in the candlelit restaurant overlooking the harbour. Full Cornish breakfasts. A Coastal Path and dog-friendly beach are just outside.

MAP 1:E2
North Corner
Coverack TR12 6TF
T: 01326 280464
W: thebayhotel.co.uk

BEDROOMS: 14. 1, on ground floor, suitable for disabled.
OPEN: mid-Mar–27 Dec.
FACILITIES: lounge, bar/restaurant, conservatory, free Wi-Fi, in-room TV (Freeview), 2 tiered gardens, large sun terrace, parking.
BACKGROUND MUSIC: quiet classical music or blues in bar and restaurant.
LOCATION: village centre, 9 miles SE of Helston.
CHILDREN: all ages welcomed ('we are not suitable for babies or very young children').
DOGS: allowed in bedrooms and on lead in grounds, not in public rooms.
CREDIT CARDS: MC, Visa.
PRICES: per room B&B single £108–£195, double £150–£295, D,B&B £190–£335. Set dinner £28.50 (2 courses),£35 (3 courses). 1-night bookings sometimes refused.

CRAYKE Yorkshire

THE DURHAM OX

For three centuries Michael and Sasha Ibbotson's village pub-with-rooms has hosted visitors following an ancient Celtic trail to York, and has been family-owned for two decades. Today, modern comforts sit alongside stone flags, wood panelling, inglenook fireplaces. The L-shaped bar offers well-pulled pints and an 'interesting, varied' blackboard menu of pub classics and daily specials (including vegetarian and gluten-free options), perhaps slow-cooked confit shoulder of Dales lamb, mashed potato and seasonal greens. The old outbuildings are now roomy country-style bedrooms. In each: a large bed, a spot to sit with a cuppa from the hospitality tray. On clear days, panoramic views stretch all the way to York Minster. Walks from the door; guides available.

MAP 4:D4
Westway
Crayke YO61 4TE
T: 01347 821506
W: thedurhamox.com

BEDROOMS: 6. 1 suite accessed via external stairs, plus 3-bed self-catering cottage in village.
OPEN: all year.
FACILITIES: 3 bars, restaurant, private dining room, free Wi-Fi, in-room TV (Freeview), function facilities, 2-acre grounds, parking.
BACKGROUND MUSIC: in pub and restaurant.
LOCATION: 3 miles E of Easingwold town centre.
CHILDREN: all ages welcomed.
DOGS: allowed in public areas, some bedrooms.
CREDIT CARDS: Amex, MC, Visa.
PRICES: per room B&B single £100–£150, double £120–£150, D,B&B £175–£205. À la carte £30.

DARLINGTON Co. Durham

HEADLAM HALL

Girdled by walled gardens, with farmland sprawling beyond, the Robinson family's stately 17th-century property has an intimate, 'country house feel' running through its smart, contemporary public spaces. The panelled sitting room is scattered with squashy seating, its walls hung with serene pastoral scenes. Uncluttered chic-rustic bedrooms (in the main house, and in converted outbuildings and mews cottages) have harmonious heathery and pale hues; some have lovely views over the grounds. Fresh fruit and vegetables from the Hall's own garden are used for the modern British/French menus. 'The whole stay was wonderful.' Along with spa treatments, and a golf course, bicycles and classic cars (extra charge) are available to borrow.

25% DISCOUNT VOUCHERS

MAP 4:C4
Darlington DL2 3HA
T: 01325 730238
W: headlamhall.co.uk

BEDROOMS: 38. 9 in coach house, 6 in mews, 7 in spa, 2 suitable for disabled.
OPEN: all year except 24–27 Dec.
FACILITIES: lift, bar, brasserie, lounge, drawing room, library, private dining rooms, free Wi-Fi, in-room TV (Freeview), civil wedding licence, function facilities, 4-acre garden, spa, tennis, 9-hole golf course.
BACKGROUND MUSIC: all day in bar, restaurant.
LOCATION: 8 miles W of Darlington.
CHILDREN: all ages welcomed.
DOGS: allowed in bedrooms, public rooms.
CREDIT CARDS: Amex, MC, Visa.
PRICES: per room B&B single £115–£205, double £145–£235, D,B&B double £215–£305. À la carte £35.

DARTMOUTH Devon

STRETE BARTON HOUSE

The Far East meets the South West at Stuart Litster and Kevin Hooper's 'beautiful' B&B in a South Hams coastal village. Uncluttered, contemporary bedrooms in their Jacobean manor house have silks, tassels, Buddha sculptures and Chinese calligraphy, to go with 'pristine bedding', fresh flowers, magazines, biscuits and a beverage tray. With three large sofas, there is generous space in the cosy lounge to enjoy the hosts' good cheer and slice of welcome cake – and marvel at the widescreen views across Start Bay. Fresh fruit, local yogurts, Devon sausages at breakfast. With the Coastal Path directly outside, there are good walks from the front door. The sheltered, pine-fringed bay around Blackpool Sands is an area of outstanding natural beauty.

25% DISCOUNT VOUCHERS

MAP 1:D4
Totnes Road
Dartmouth TQ6 0RU
T: 01803 770364
W: stretebarton.co.uk

BEDROOMS: 6. 1 in cottage annexe.
OPEN: all year.
FACILITIES: sitting room, breakfast room, free Wi-Fi, in-room TV (Freeview), ⅓-acre garden.
BACKGROUND MUSIC: none.
LOCATION: 5 miles W of Dartmouth.
CHILDREN: not under 8.
DOGS: allowed in cottage suite.
CREDIT CARDS: Amex, MC, Visa.
PRICES: per room B&B £105–£175. 1-night bookings sometimes refused in high season.

DELPH Lancashire

THE OLD BELL INN

'Quite an appearance.' A well-illuminated display of gin bottles on glass shelves greets visitors to Philip Whiteman's 'well-kept, traditional' inn in a scenic village outside Manchester. The Gin Emporium, a Guinness World Record holder, has over 1000 types. Occupying an 18th-century coaching house, there's a busy bar ('all polished brass, shiny bottles, hard-working staff'), an informal brasserie serving 'excellent meals, freshly prepared, full of flavour' and a cosy restaurant, popular for its imaginative menus – daily specials, prime steaks. 'Clean, workaday bedrooms' are well equipped (quieter ones at the rear). To escape the throng, overnight guests may use a first-floor conservatory lounge. At breakfast, hearty cooked options, freshly squeezed orange juice, pastries.

MAP 4:E3
Huddersfield Road
Delph OL3 5EG
T: 01457 870130
W: theoldbellinn.co.uk

BEDROOMS: 18.
OPEN: all year.
FACILITIES: bar, lounge, brasserie, restaurant, free Wi-Fi, in-room TV (Freeview), function facilities, terrace, parking.
BACKGROUND MUSIC: in public areas.
LOCATION: 5 miles from Oldham.
CHILDREN: all ages welcomed.
DOGS: not allowed.
CREDIT CARDS: Amex, MC, Visa.
PRICES: per room B&B £69–£145. À la carte £32.

DERBY Derbyshire

THE COACH HOUSE

Vibrantly colourful inside, Rob and Roberta
Aitken's handsome Victorian B&B occupies a
historic mill village near Darley Abbey. Help-
yourself home-made brownies and books galore
add allure to plush seating in the vivid blue snug;
all around, something to catch the eye: playful
animal-themed curios, a large tiled fireplace, a
wooden bar. B&B guests stay in simple, grey-
toned bedrooms or in spacious, design-led rooms
(feature wallpaper, bright cushions, soft fabrics) in
the stable annexe; one has a Juliet balcony, another
access to the charming garden. 'Rustic' breakfast,
in a calming green-hued room, includes fresh
juice, 'creamy yogurt, delicious warmed red berry
coulis'. In sum, 'Plenty of style, a very useful place
for Derby.'

MAP 2:A2
185A Duffield Road
Derby DE22 1JB
T: 01332 554423
w: coachhousederby.com

BEDROOMS: 7. 3 in annexe.
OPEN: all year.
FACILITIES: snug, restaurant, free
Wi-Fi, in-room TV (Freeview), small
garden.
BACKGROUND MUSIC: in snug.
LOCATION: 2 miles from Derby station.
CHILDREN: all ages welcomed.
DOGS: allowed, except in 1 room.
CREDIT CARDS: Amex, MC, Visa.
PRICES: per room B&B single from £50,
double from £65.

NEW

DEREHAM Norfolk

THE BRISLEY BELL

Very much a local, 'full of character and characters',
Amelia Nicholson and Marcus Seaman's revival
and expansion of a 17th-century pub on the edge
of the village is well pitched. On Friday nights,
cricket matches, including a ladies' team, are
held on the lovely common opposite. Inside,
inglenook fireplaces warm the large oak-floored
bar and beamed snug on cold days. A book-lined
room looks out on to a covered patio and garden.
Converted barns house chic bedrooms supplied
with a decanter of local liquor and home-made
biscuits. French chef Hervé Stouvenel tweaks
British favourites with Caribbean flavours:
seafood bouchée à la reine (scallops, crayfish,
prawns in cream sauce) to start, rounded off with,
maybe, banana and saffron crème brûlée.

MAP 2:B5
The Green
Dereham NR20 5DW
T: 01362 705024
w: thebrisleybell.co.uk

BEDROOMS: 6. All on ground floor
in converted barns, 1 suitable for
disabled.
OPEN: all year, except for
accommodation, food on 25/26 Dec.
FACILITIES: bar, snug, restaurant
(closed Mon), garden room, free
Wi-Fi, in-room TV (Freeview), 2-acre
garden, croquet lawn.
BACKGROUND MUSIC: none, except for
live music events.
LOCATION: just outside village.
CHILDREN: all ages welcomed.
DOGS: welcomed in 2 bedrooms, bar,
snug, garden.
CREDIT CARDS: Amex, MC, Visa.
PRICES: per room B&B £88–£182.
À la carte £30–£35.

NEW

DIDMARTON Gloucestershire
THE KING'S ARMS
Embracing its rural roots, a cosy, traditional
inn deep in the Cotswold countryside. There
are hunting trophies on the walls, comfortable
leather armchairs beside a log fire, and dark-
hued, individually decorated bedrooms named
after prize-winning hounds from the local hunt.
Visiting dogs are warmly welcomed with a bowl,
a bed and a sausage for breakfast. Split between
the main pub building and a renovated stable,
rooms have quality bedding, handmade toiletries,
vintage-style mugs, shortbread from a local
bakery. The restaurant's British dishes feature
game sourced from neighbouring estates, plus
daily blackboard specials; bread and ice cream is
home-made. In summer, pizzas are cooked in a
wood-fired oven in the garden.

MAP 3:E5
The Street
Didmarton GL9 1DT
T: 01454 238245
W: kingsarmsdidmarton.co.uk

BEDROOMS: 6. Plus 2 self-catering
cottages.
OPEN: all year.
FACILITIES: 2 bars, restaurant, free
Wi-Fi, private dining room, garden,
boules.
BACKGROUND MUSIC: in pub.
LOCATION: in village.
CHILDREN: all ages welcomed.
DOGS: welcomed (£15 charge).
CREDIT CARDS: MC, Visa.
PRICES: per room B&B £70–£260.
À la carte £33.

NEW

DODDINGTON Kent
THE OLD VICARAGE
With spectacular views over rolling countryside,
Claire Finley's elegant, white-painted Georgian
guest house stands in well-maintained gardens.
The Grade II listed house, recently renovated,
balances a modern country-house aesthetic
(squashy sofas, original art, statement flower
arrangements, the occasional antique) while
retaining core period features dating back to
1656. Large suites overlook the garden or 11th-
century churchyard next door; one has a roll-top
bath, another a French-style brass bed-frame.
Breakfast, served in a bright, airy room, is locally
sourced whenever available. Ask for restaurant
recommendations – the hosts are happy to share
their local knowledge of the many good country
pubs and Michelin-starred eateries nearby.

MAP 2:D5
Church Hill
Doddington ME9 0BD
T: 01795 886136
W: oldvicaragedoddington.co.uk

BEDROOMS: 5 suites, 2 in adjacent
cottage.
OPEN: closed 22 Dec–5 Jan.
FACILITIES: entrance hall, drawing
room, breakfast room, free Wi-Fi,
in-room TV, ¼-acre garden.
BACKGROUND MUSIC: none.
LOCATION: on the edge of the village,
6 miles from Sittingbourne railway
station.
CHILDREN: over-3s welcomed.
DOGS: not allowed.
CREDIT CARDS: MC, Visa.
PRICES: per room B&B single from £75,
double from £105.

DONNINGTON Sussex

THE BLACKSMITHS

Steeped with Scandinavian cool, Mariella and William Fleming's village pub-with-rooms is a stylishly spot near the Chichester canal towpath. A blazing fire entices visitors into the bar as does the strong list of local ales and organic wines, including bubbly from the nearby Tinwood Estate. Tools of the blacksmith's trade are displayed on a rail on the wall. Chic, minimalist bedrooms have a large bed, plump armchairs; two have an original fireplace, a roll-top bathtub. A seating area on the landing with books and a hospitality tray has space for relaxing. Pub classics and more modern dishes are served in the snug, rustic dining room or the walled terrace with wicker seating, parasols, a fire pit and country views. The chicken flock supplies breakfast.

MAP 2:E3
Selsey Road
Donnington PO20 7PR
T: 01243 785578
W: the-blacksmiths.co.uk

BEDROOMS: 3.
OPEN: all year except Christmas Day, New Year's Eve.
FACILITIES: bar, restaurant, free Wi-Fi, in-room TV (Freeview), patio garden, parking.
BACKGROUND MUSIC: in public areas; occasional live music events.
LOCATION: 2 miles S of Chichester
CHILDREN: all ages welcomed.
DOGS: allowed.
CREDIT CARDS: MC, Visa.
PRICES: per room B&B £120–£150.

DULVERTON Somerset

THREE ACRES COUNTRY HOUSE

Attention to detail, peaceful surroundings and cheerful hospitality make Julie and Edward Christian's 'beautifully furnished' B&B 'a special place'. At the end of a curving tree-lined lane, the 1930s house overlooks Exmoor national park from secluded grounds. Light suppers (home-made soups, sandwiches), ordered in advance, may be taken in the traditional bar/lounge. Thoughtful extras in the individually decorated bedrooms include ground coffee, fresh milk, Exmoor spring water, a silent-tick alarm clock. Please note: As we went to press, it was announced that Three Acres Country House has been sold, and it will no longer operate as a B&B.

25% DISCOUNT VOUCHERS

MAP 1:B5
Ellersdown Lane
Dulverton TA22 9AR
T: 01398 323730
W: threeacresexmoor.co.uk

BEDROOMS: 6. 1 on ground floor, 1 family suite in small annexe.
OPEN: all year.
FACILITIES: bar, lounge, breakfast room, free Wi-Fi, in-room TV (Freeview), sun terrace, 2-acre grounds.
BACKGROUND MUSIC: none.
LOCATION: outskirts of village.
CHILDREN: all ages welcomed.
DOGS: not allowed in the house.
CREDIT CARDS: Amex, MC, Visa.
PRICES: per person B&B £45–£75. 2-night min. stay preferred.

DUNWICH Suffolk

THE SHIP AT DUNWICH

Once a smugglers' haunt, the creeper-covered red brick building has become a great base for twitchers, outdoorsy types and their dogs. 'Unpretentious and friendly', the inn (part of Agellus hotels) is close to the beach and the RSPB reserves at Dingle Marshes and Minsmere. The cosy bar with wood-burner is popular for its real ales; the wood-floored restaurant for 'generous portions' of such dishes as home-made turkey and leek pie. The sheltered courtyard and 'lovely garden' are ideal suntraps. The traditionally decorated bedrooms are each different (some snug); the best have expansive marsh views; family rooms have a TV in both rooms; others, in converted outbuildings, are 'perfect for dogs'. Breakfast has 'excellent choice'.

MAP 2:B6
St James Street
Dunwich IP17 3DT
T: 01728 648219
W: shipatdunwich.co.uk

BEDROOMS: 16. 4 on ground floor in converted stables, 1 suitable for disabled.
OPEN: all year.
FACILITIES: bar, restaurant, courtyard, free Wi-Fi, in-room TV (Freeview, smart TV in family rooms), garden.
BACKGROUND MUSIC: none.
LOCATION: a few hundred yards from Dunwich beach.
CHILDREN: all ages welcomed.
DOGS: warmly welcomed inside and out.
CREDIT CARDS: MC, Visa.
PRICES: per room B&B £95–£165, D,B&B £125–£185. À la carte £25. Min. 2-night stay weekends in peak season.

DURHAM Co. Durham

FORTY WINKS GUEST HOUSE & RESIDENCE

Brimful with curiosities, Debbie and Nigel Gadd's opulent Edwardian house is on a quiet cobbled street a short walk from the town centre and castle. Spread over four floors, its 'entertaining if slightly overcrowded' public rooms display wall trophies, a diving helmet, a penny-farthing, life-size giraffe, taxidermy specimens, sporting a hat maybe. The up-to-date bedrooms have 'excellent lighting, instant hot water, and extremely comfortable beds; a clever use of space'. Rooms at the front gaze across woods and the river to the cathedral and castle; churchyard views at the back. 'Breakfast was all one could wish for. The eggs were absolutely fresh, a rich orange, the fruit bowl was ample, the coffee excellent.'

MAP 4:B4
40 South Street
Durham DH1 4QP
T: 0191 386 8217
W: fortywinksdurham.co.uk

BEDROOMS: 8.
OPEN: all year, except 24–27 Dec.
FACILITIES: dining room, study, free Wi-Fi, in-room TV (Freeview), courtyard, public parking (charge).
BACKGROUND MUSIC: 'classical music' at breakfast.
LOCATION: a short walk from the city centre.
CHILDREN: over-16s welcomed.
DOGS: not allowed.
CREDIT CARDS: Amex, MC, Visa.
PRICES: per room B&B £110–£195.

EAST WITTON Yorkshire

THE BLUE LION

Across a cobbled driveway, Paul and Helen
Klein's 'sophisticated' 18th-century inn is an
'utterly authentic' slice of rural Wensleydale
hospitality. The former coaching house is liked for
its 'good atmosphere' and 'outstanding service'.
Within, crackling log fires, settles, 'pleasant,
knowledgeable staff', and many locals (whose
dogs get a bowl of water) enjoying hand-pumped
ales. In the bar and candlelit restaurant, 'well-
executed comfort food': cassoulet of Yorkshire
duck confit, Morteau sausage, roasted tomato
and white beans, served with sourdough and
sauerkraut. Provençal-style bedrooms, 'spotlessly
clean and comfortable', occupy the main building
and converted outbuildings. Breakfast will see
you through to lunch.

MAP 4:C4
East Witton DL8 4SN
T: 01969 624273
W: thebluelion.co.uk

BEDROOMS: 15. 9 in courtyard annexe.
OPEN: all year.
FACILITIES: 2 bars, 2 dining areas,
private dining room, free Wi-Fi,
in-room TV (Freeview), 1-acre
garden, parking, restaurant, bar
wheelchair accessible.
BACKGROUND MUSIC: none.
LOCATION: in village.
CHILDREN: all ages welcomed (under-
2s free).
DOGS: allowed in bar, some bedrooms.
CREDIT CARDS: MC, Visa.
PRICES: per room B&B £99–£155,
D,B&B £145–£195. Lunch (Mon–Sat)
2 courses £22, 3 courses £28, à la carte
£39.50.

EDENBRIDGE Kent

HEVER CASTLE B&B

Double-moated 13th-century Hever Castle, the
childhood home of ill-fated Anne Boleyn, is now
home to a sumptuous B&B. Bedrooms are in two
Tudor-style Edwardian additions, the Aster and
Anne Boleyn wings. Each room blends Tudor-
inspired features and comforts fit for a queen:
a gold-coloured chaise longue, a four-poster,
spoiling toiletries in a decadent bathroom of
limestone or marble. Moulded ceilings, grand
chimney pieces and rich tapestries heighten the
grandeur. Breakfast, a lavish affair, is served
in each wing's own dining room. Residents are
granted complimentary open-hours access to
the castle and grounds and, after hours, to the
peaceful gardens. A beautiful courtyard has wild
flower plantings and outdoor furniture.

MAP 2:D4
Edenbridge TN8 7NG
T: 01732 861800
W: hevercastle.co.uk

BEDROOMS: 28. Some on ground floor,
some suitable for disabled, plus self-
catering Medley Court cottage.
OPEN: all year except 25 and 31 Dec,
1–15 Jan, 20–22 Jan, 27–29 Jan, 3–5
Feb, 11–12 Feb.
FACILITIES: lounge, billiard room, free
Wi-Fi, in-room TV (Sky, Freeview),
680-acre grounds, parking.
BACKGROUND MUSIC: none.
LOCATION: 1½ miles from Hever
station.
CHILDREN: all ages welcomed.
DOGS: not allowed.
CREDIT CARDS: Amex, MC, Visa.
PRICES: per room B&B £175–£325.
Dine and stay events on select dates
throughout the year.

EDINGTON Wiltshire

THE THREE DAGGERS

The hub of the village, within trotting distance of the iconic white horse, this 'impressive' pub-with-rooms has much going on. A buzzy on-site microbrewery calls to craft-beer lovers; the well-stocked farm shop and 'well-populated' dining room entice epicures; a take-one-leave-one library beguiles bookworms. 'Splendid' bedrooms have fresh flowers, fluffy towels and a cool, rustic flair. In the kitchen, seasonal food exploits ingredients from the pub's own Priory Farm nearby; in the garden, pizzas arrive courtesy of the wood-fired oven. Away from it all, the comfy residents' lounge has a generous stash of tea, coffee and biscuits – and, befitting the many muddy trails from the door, there are wellies to borrow.

MAP 2:D1
47 Westbury Road
Edington BA13 4PG
T: 01380 830940
W: threedaggers.co.uk

BEDROOMS: 3.
OPEN: all year.
FACILITIES: bar, dining area, private dining room, free Wi-Fi, in-room TV (Freeview), civil wedding licence, garden, microbrewery, farm shop.
BACKGROUND MUSIC: in public spaces.
LOCATION: 10 mins' drive from Westbury.
CHILDREN: all ages welcomed.
DOGS: welcomed.
CREDIT CARDS: Amex, MC, Visa.
PRICES: per person B&B from £99. À la carte £25.

EGHAM Surrey

THE RUNNYMEDE ON THAMES HOTEL AND SPA

An idyllic spot, this Thames-side hotel and spa is 'so very relaxing'. The 1970s building may be uninspiring but the attractive interiors have myriad quirky touches (retro decor, oversized deckchairs, toy ducks in the lounge). Modern clean-lined bedrooms (some confined) have 'every amenity'; those facing the river have 'spectacular' views. Quieter rooms are away from the road. Choose to eat buffet-style overlooking the water, or sample 'excellent' traditional dishes in The Lock Bar & Kitchen, all light wood, pale hues and monochrome photographs. 'The made-to-order breakfast is spectacular.' The spa provides 'endless treatment opportunities'. Hiking trails lead to Windsor Park.

MAP 2:D3
Windsor Road
Egham TW20 0AG
T: 01784 220946
W: runnymedehotel.com

BEDROOMS: 180. Some suitable for disabled.
OPEN: all year.
FACILITIES: lounge, 2 restaurants, free Wi-Fi, in-room TV (Freeview), civil wedding licence, indoor and outdoor pools, 12-acre grounds, parking.
BACKGROUND MUSIC: in public areas.
LOCATION: close to Windsor Castle, Windsor Great Park and Legoland.
CHILDREN: all ages welcomed.
DOGS: allowed in some bedrooms, by prior arrangement, not in public areas.
CREDIT CARDS: Amex, MC, Visa.
PRICES: per room B&B £145–£380, D,B&B £165–£430. Set menus £24–£29, à la carte £32.

EXETER Devon
THE CITY GATE

Abutting the Roman city walls, this style-savvy red brick old coaching inn (Young's Brewery) has a lively atmosphere. Inside, a host of interesting curios including a vintage sewing machine, a ship's masthead, and splashes of colour lend a quirky yet unpretentious vibe. 'Boutiquey' bedrooms are themed (water, wool, cotton); all are supplied with a capsule coffee machine, various teas, complimentary port and Devon fudge with little 'Eat Me Drink Me' signs (and who are we to resist?); a glossy metro-tiled bathroom. Microbrewed drinks and traditional pub classics are served all day in the buzzy restaurant (half-panelled walls, mismatched chairs). In balmy weather, diners spill on to the large beer garden.

MAP 1:C5
Iron Bridge
Exeter EX4 3RB
T: 01392 495811
W: citygatehotel.com

BEDROOMS: 15.
OPEN: all year.
FACILITIES: 2 bars, snug, restaurant, conservatory, free Wi-Fi, in-room TV (Sky), function facilities, large beer garden, limited parking, bar and garden wheelchair accessible.
BACKGROUND MUSIC: in public spaces.
LOCATION: central.
CHILDREN: all ages welcomed.
DOGS: allowed in public areas.
CREDIT CARDS: Amex, MC, Visa.
PRICES: per person B&B from £105. À la carte £30.

FAIRFORD Gloucestershire
THE BULL HOTEL

Facing the market square, a stone-built 15th-century building which has variously hosted a monks' chanting-house, a post office and a coaching inn (now part of Barkby group). Its cosy bar has exposed stonework and an impressively horned bull's head over the crackling fire. The multi-level dining areas are given depth with strong colours, timber features and burnished metal artefacts. Mediterranean-influenced menus highlight Italian regional cuisines. Serene bedrooms are filled with well-chosen vintage finds and pure wool throws; toiletries are locally made. The town's church, St Mary's, is renowned for its pre-Reformation stained-glass windows. Fishing enthusiasts will appreciate the hotel's private stretch of the River Coln.

25% DISCOUNT VOUCHERS

MAP 3:E6
Market Place
Fairford GL7 4AA
T: 01285 712535
W: thebullhotelfairford.co.uk

BEDROOMS: 21.
OPEN: all year.
FACILITIES: bar, lounge, morning room, function room, 3 dining rooms, free Wi-Fi, in-room TV (Freeview), terraces, private fishing rights.
BACKGROUND MUSIC: in bar, dining rooms.
LOCATION: in village centre.
CHILDREN: all ages welcomed (cots, Z-beds).
DOGS: in 1 bedroom and bar.
CREDIT CARDS: Amex, MC, Visa.
PRICES: per person B&B £75–£220, D,B&B £90–£220. À la carte £30.

NEW

FALMOUTH Cornwall
THE GREENBANK

Soothing sounds of the sea, boats bobbing
on the water, 'magnificent' vistas across the
harbour – life on the water's edge doesn't come
much closer. The large hotel is an amalgam of
modern additions to the oldest hotel in Falmouth.
Florence Nightingale stayed here; her name
can still be seen in the guest book displayed in
reception. Light floods in to contemporary public
spaces, toned to match the colours of sea and sky.
Luxurious bedrooms have harbour-facing seating,
statement wallpaper, splashes of vivid blue.
Throughout the day, menus are served in the
Water's Edge restaurant: shellfish lasagne with
pan-fried brill; seared lamb striploin with lamb
croquette and port jus. Guests can step straight on
to the water, into a boat from the hotel's pontoons.

MAP 1:E2
Harbourside
Falmouth TR11 2SR
T: 01326 312440
W: greenbank-hotel.co.uk

BEDROOMS: 61.
OPEN: all year.
FACILITIES: lift, bar, pub, restaurant,
lounge, free Wi-Fi, in-room TV,
ramps, civil wedding licence, spa
treatments.
BACKGROUND MUSIC: in bar, restaurant.
LOCATION: Falmouth harbour.
CHILDREN: all ages welcomed.
DOGS: allowed in 9 dog-friendly
rooms, pub, not restaurant, bar.
CREDIT CARDS: Amex, MC, Visa.
PRICES: per room B&B £109–£359,
D,B&B £159–£409. 1-night stays
sometimes refused.

FALMOUTH Cornwall
HIGHCLIFFE

'Beautifully decorated, a little quirky,
scrupulously clean', Vanessa and Simon Clark's
'highly recommended' Victorian town house lies
between the town and the seafront. Inside, the
B&B brims with interesting features and lively
colours. High-ceilinged, imaginatively designed
bedrooms share a hip, 'boutiquey' look and
thoughtful amenities; some offer sweeping views
of the sun rising over the harbour and estuary. In
the breakfast room with its multicoloured chairs,
guests enjoy freshly squeezed juices; many daily
specials (wilted spinach and garlic mushrooms on
organic bread; home-made rösti with a poached
egg, dry-cured streaky bacon and seaweed).
'Superb hosts', the Clarks offer helpful advice on
where to eat, drink and visit.

MAP 1:E2
22 Melvill Road
Falmouth TR11 4AR
T: 01326 314466
W: highcliffefalmouth.com

BEDROOMS: 8.
OPEN: 8 Jan–early Dec.
FACILITIES: lounge, breakfast room,
free Wi-Fi, in-room TV (Freeview),
parking.
BACKGROUND MUSIC: occasionally in
dining room.
LOCATION: centrally located.
CHILDREN: not under 8 (no family
rooms).
DOGS: not allowed.
CREDIT CARDS: MC, Visa.
PRICES: per room B&B £50–£160.
1-night bookings sometimes refused.

FALMOUTH Cornwall
THE ROSEMARY

'Great for a relaxing time', Lynda and Malcolm Cook's 'delightful' B&B has 'fabulous' views stretching across Falmouth Bay. The 'friendly' hosts welcome guests with a drink and lemon drizzle cake and provide tips on what to see and do in the area. 'Shipshape' bedrooms of the Edwardian town house are well supplied (fresh milk for hot drinks, filtered water, biscuits, spoiling toiletries, fluffy bathrobes); binoculars in sea-view rooms. Panoramas can be enjoyed in the lounge over a Cornish cream tea. The 'beautiful' garden at the back has a sun deck. Guests wanting to explore might ask for a picnic hamper, before embarking on a coastal ramble or trip to the beach. Breakfast has 'first-class' choices: home-made preserves, honey, fresh fruit or a Cornish cooked.

MAP 1:E2
22 Gyllyngvase Terrace
Falmouth TR11 4DL
T: 01326 314669
W: therosemary.co.uk

BEDROOMS: 8.
OPEN: 4 Jan–end Dec (advisable to call for winter availability).
FACILITIES: lounge, bar, breakfast room, free Wi-Fi, in-room TV (Freeview), garden, sun deck.
BACKGROUND MUSIC: none.
LOCATION: beach and seafront are 200 yds away, town 10 mins' walk.
CHILDREN: all ages welcomed.
DOGS: allowed in some bedrooms by arrangement (not unattended), lounge, bar, garden on a lead.
CREDIT CARDS: MC, Visa.
PRICES: per room B&B single £60–£75, double £80–£115. 2-night min. stay preferred in high season.

FAR SAWREY Cumbria
CUCKOO BROW INN

Atop a hill in a pretty village between Lake Windermere and Hawkshead, an unpretentious 18th-century inn offers fuss-free hospitality. Muddy dogs and walkers join the throng in the convivial bar (wood-burning stove, garlands of hops) and dining room, for local ales and hearty pub fare. Most of the modern, simply decorated bedrooms are in an annexe attached to the main building; family rooms have a screened-off area for children; superior rooms have a roll-top bath in a smartly refurbished bathroom. Come evening, the old stables' squashy sofas, games and log-burning stove create a cosy retreat. The beautiful scenery that inspired Beatrix Potter can be viewed from the area's many walking and cycling trails. Hill Top, her farmhouse home (NT) is nearby.

MAP 4: inset C2
Far Sawrey LA22 0LQ
T: 01539 443425
W: cuckoobrow.co.uk

BEDROOMS: 14. Some on ground floor.
OPEN: all year.
FACILITIES: bar, lobby, dining room, lounge/games room, free Wi-Fi, in-room TV (Freeview), terrace, small garden.
BACKGROUND MUSIC: in bar, lounge, games room.
LOCATION: in the centre of a small village.
CHILDREN: all ages welcomed.
DOGS: in bedrooms and public rooms (£10 per night).
CREDIT CARDS: MC, Visa.
PRICES: per room B&B from £130, D,B&B from £170.

FERRENSBY Yorkshire

THE GENERAL TARLETON

'Just the place to break up trips across the border.'
Chef/patron John Topham and his wife, Claire's
restaurant-with-rooms is not far from the road
to Scotland. The 18th-century coaching inn
with views across open countryside is 'great at
what it does: fantastic service, excellent food
and comfortable rooms'. It also represents 'great
value for money'. After a drink by the fire in the
comfortable cocktail lounge, 'first-rate' dishes are
served in the stone-walled restaurant; perhaps
Wensleydale cheese soufflé with roast hazelnuts,
fennel, apple, rocket; glazed Goosnargh duckling,
black pudding, rhubarb and foie gras. Modern
bedrooms have warm, rich hues, home-made
biscuits and luxury smellies. Harrogate, York and
the Dales are an easy drive away.

MAP 4:D4
Boroughbridge Road
Ferrensby HG5 0PZ
T: 01423 340284
w: generaltarleton.co.uk

BEDROOMS: 13.
OPEN: all year, no accommodation
24–26 Dec, 1 Jan.
FACILITIES: bar, cocktail lounge,
atrium, restaurant, private dining
room, free Wi-Fi, in-room TV
(Freeview), parking.
BACKGROUND MUSIC: in public areas.
LOCATION: 4 miles from
Knaresborough.
CHILDREN: all ages welcomed.
DOGS: not allowed.
CREDIT CARDS: Amex, MC, Visa.
PRICES: per room B&B single from £75,
double from £129. À la carte £35.

FOLKESTONE Kent

ROCKSALT

Assertive and stylish, the dark-timber-and-glass,
purpose-built restaurant cantilevers over the
harbour, offering striking Channel views. Owned
by Mark Sargeant (a Gordon Ramsay alumnus)
and Josh de Haan, its 'imaginative' menu uses fish
caught off the south-east coast, served to the long
leather banquette, or on the deck on balmy days.
The day's haul might include gilt-head bream,
served with white beans, marinated tomatoes,
green sauce. One minute away, in the converted
Smokehouse above a sister restaurant, bedrooms
look out at the water (binoculars provided);
stripped-back brick walls, antique beds, a trim
wet room, and a Provençal palette prove a chic
formula. A continental breakfast hamper is
delivered to the room in the morning.

MAP 2:E5
4–5 Fish Market
Folkestone CT19 6AA
T: 01303 212070
w: rocksaltfolkestone.co.uk

BEDROOMS: 4.
OPEN: closed Mon Oct–Mar, restaurant
closed Sun, Mon Oct–Mar.
FACILITIES: bar, restaurant, terrace, free
Wi-Fi, in-room TV (BT), on-street
parking.
BACKGROUND MUSIC: in restaurant.
LOCATION: by the harbour.
CHILDREN: all ages welcomed.
DOGS: not allowed.
CREDIT CARDS: Amex, MC, Visa.
PRICES: per room B&B £85–£140.
À la carte £40, cooked breakfast £10.

FONTMELL MAGNA Dorset
THE FONTMELL

Carefully restored, with an abundance of quirky details – a stream separates the dining room from bar – this well-designed roadside inn is a social media hit. Upstairs, appealing, eclectic bedrooms might have exposed beams, a bay-window reading nook, a squashy sofa, a roll-top bath on a wooden dais. Downstairs, the appealing bar lures in (and rewards) locals with craft beers and weekly-changing guest ales. In the bookshelf-lined dining room, chef/patron Tom Shaw uses locally sourced produce on menus that range from British to Asian cuisine, including bacon, sausages and pork dishes made from their own rare breed Old Spot pigs. On weekend summer evenings the garden's wood-fired oven delivers fresh pizza.

MAP 2:E1
Crown Hill
Fontmell Magna SP7 0PA
T: 01747 811441
W: thefontmell.co.uk

BEDROOMS: 6.
OPEN: all year.
FACILITIES: bar, restaurant, free Wi-Fi, in-room TV (Freeview), large garden, DVD library.
BACKGROUND MUSIC: in public areas.
LOCATION: 5 miles S of Shaftesbury.
CHILDREN: all ages welcomed.
DOGS: allowed in some bedrooms, public rooms.
CREDIT CARDS: Amex, MC, Visa.
PRICES: per room B&B £75–£190. À la carte £30.

FOWEY Cornwall
THE OLD QUAY HOUSE

Once the refuge of seamen, this 'marvellously situated' Victorian building has transformed into a stylish quayside hotel with dazzling estuary views. Public spaces, overseen by 'exceptionally friendly, helpful' staff, have been 'tastefully rejuvenated'. Classic British fare with a Cornish twist, perhaps sea bass, button mushroom beignet, brown shrimp, shallot and pancetta, is served in the informal restaurant or out on the 'beautiful terrace'. Thoughtful touches abound in the 'clean, fresh, contemporary' bedrooms: biscuits and bottled water, books and DVDs, local guides, umbrellas and raincoats. A fridge on the landing has little jugs of fresh milk. Expect a wake-up call of seagulls and lapping sea. Breakfast is in the sun-drenched restaurant.

25% DISCOUNT VOUCHERS

MAP 1:D3
28 Fore Street
Fowey PL23 1AQ
T: 01726 833302
W: theoldquayhouse.com

BEDROOMS: 13.
OPEN: all year.
FACILITIES: open-plan lounge, bar, restaurant, free Wi-Fi, in-room TV (Freeview), civil wedding licence, terrace, parking permits supplied.
BACKGROUND MUSIC: 'relaxed' at mealtimes.
LOCATION: central location within the town of Fowey.
CHILDREN: not under 12.
DOGS: not allowed.
CREDIT CARDS: Amex, MC, Visa.
PRICES: per room B&B single £120–£320, double £150–£350. Set dinner £37.50 (2 courses), £45 (3 courses).

GILSLAND Cumbria

THE HILL ON THE WALL

Protected from the border's lawless raiders by
a 16th-century 'bastle', Elaine Packer's 'superb'
Georgian farmhouse overlooking Hadrian's Wall
near Birdoswald, is full of 'every comfort'. Proper
tea and home-made cake, taken by the drawing
room fire or in the 'beautiful' walled garden,
welcome arriving guests. Shutters at the windows
promise a sound night in the traditionally
decorated bedrooms; 'sumptuously styled',
each is well supplied with glossy magazines,
cafetière coffee, a biscuit barrel and chocolates.
'So peaceful.' Ordered the night before, breakfast
features 'delicious' home-cooked Northumbrian
fare; the 'gigantic portions' are just the thing for
hikers and bikers setting off for the day. Packed
lunches available (£6).

MAP 4:B3
The Hill
Gilsland CA8 7DA
T: 01977 47214
W: hillonthewall.co.uk

BEDROOMS: 3. 1 on ground floor.
OPEN: Mar–Oct.
FACILITIES: lounge, breakfast room,
free Wi-Fi, in-room TV (Freeview),
1-acre garden, terrace, parking, secure
bicycle storage.
BACKGROUND MUSIC: none.
LOCATION: 1 mile W of Gilsland on
the B6318.
CHILDREN: not under 10.
DOGS: not allowed.
CREDIT CARDS: MC, Visa.
PRICES: per room B&B from £90.

GILSLAND Cumbria

WILLOWFORD FARM

Roman history doesn't come much closer than
at Liam McNulty and Lauren Harrison's rustic
B&B. The longest unbroken stretch of Hadrian's
Wall cuts through the yard of their organic sheep
and cattle farm. Cosy bedrooms, in the converted
byre, gaze upon the remains of a bridge and two
turrets. Spacious, clutter-free and full of character,
the energy-efficient rooms have exposed wood
beams, antique furniture, a heated floor of
local Westmorland slate; each is supplied with
Fairtrade tea and coffee. The nearby Samson
Inn, under the same management (lifts cheerfully
offered), uses the farm's produce. Breakfast options
include porridge, pastries, smoked trout with
scrambled eggs. Packed lunches available (£6).

MAP 4:B3
Gilsland CA8 7AA
T: 01977 47962
W: willowford.co.uk

BEDROOMS: 5. All on ground floor in
converted barn, 1 suitable for disabled.
4 bedrooms in sister pub, The Samson
Inn.
OPEN: Mar–Nov, Fri, Sat, Sun,
Christmas, New Year.
FACILITIES: lounge/breakfast room, free
Wi-Fi, in-room TV (Freeview).
BACKGROUND MUSIC: none.
LOCATION: ½ mile W of Gilsland,
between Gilsland village and
Birdoswald Roman fort.
CHILDREN: all ages welcomed.
DOGS: well-behaved dogs allowed
by arrangement in bedrooms, not in
public rooms (£5 charge, chickens and
sheep on farm).
CREDIT CARDS: MC, Visa.
PRICES: per room B&B single £75–£80,
double £95–£100.

GOATHLAND Yorkshire

FAIRHAVEN COUNTRY GUEST HOUSE

Head straight out on to beautiful moorland from the doorstep of Peter and Sarah Garnett's 'very comfortable' Edwardian guest house in a scenic village. Return by steam locomotive to Goathland station – a stand-in for Hogsmeade in the Harry Potter films. The hosts provide a welcoming pot of tea and home-made cake in the large lounge with its open fire, games, books and TV. Traditionally furnished bedrooms have fine views, seating, well-stocked trays; fresh milk and filtered water in the dining-room fridge. 'Superb' breakfasts include daily specials such as baked spiced plums with home-made granola, a kipper with poached egg. A lawned back garden and front terrace catch the sunset.

MAP 4:C5
The Common
Goathland Y022 5AN
T: 01947 896361
w: fairhavencountryguesthouse.co.uk

BEDROOMS: 9. 1 with separate private bathroom.
OPEN: all year except 1 week Christmas.
FACILITIES: lounge, dining room, front terrace, in-room TV (Freeview), free Wi-Fi, large garden, parking, secure bicycle storage, dinner available on certain evenings in winter, all year for parties of 6 or more.
BACKGROUND MUSIC: during breakfast.
LOCATION: close to the North Yorkshire Moors Steam Railway, 8 miles from Whitby.
CHILDREN: all ages welcomed.
DOGS: not allowed.
CREDIT CARDS: MC, Visa.
PRICES: per room B&B single £42–£79, double £90–£110.

NEW

GRANGE-IN-BORROWDALE Cumbria

BORROWDALE GATES

Hugged by wooded grounds, a peaceful atmosphere, broad views and walks from the doorstep draw guests back to this comfortable Lakeland hotel. On inclement days, the lounge's large picture windows provide immersive views over the Borrowdale valley without your moving a muscle. 'Tranquil, well-appointed' bedrooms make the most of the scenery; many have a balcony or patio access to the garden; all have a refreshment tray, bathrobes, a Digital Library of magazines and newspapers via a smartphone or tablet; modern bathrooms. A showcase for Cumbrian produce, 'superb food for all including vegetarians', is created by head chef Christopher Standhaven and team. 'Breakfast was designed to sustain fell walkers through a long day.'

MAP 4: inset C2
Grange-in-Borrowdale CA12 5UQ
T: 01768 777204
w: borrowdale-gates.com

BEDROOMS: 25.
OPEN: all year, except Jan.
FACILITIES: open-plan bar, dining room and lounge (log fire), reading room, free Wi-Fi, in-room TV, 2-acre grounds, terrace (alfresco drinks), wedding facilities (exclusive use only), lift.
BACKGROUND MUSIC: none.
LOCATION: 5 miles from Keswick in the heart of the Borrowdale valley.
CHILDREN: all ages welcomed (special rates for under-12s).
DOGS: allowed in 3 rooms, not in dining room, bar, lounge (£7 per night).
CREDIT CARDS: MC, Visa.
PRICES: per person B&B from £106. À la carte from £43.

GRANGE-OVER-SANDS Cumbria
CLARE HOUSE

'Marvellous stay.' The Read family's 'wonderfully old-fashioned' hotel draws back regular guests for the 'wonderful food and very friendly staff'. The comfortably furnished Victorian house has well-appointed rooms, 'equally good' bathrooms. Morning coffee, light lunches and afternoon tea can be enjoyed in the lounges which have open fires and views of the bay, or in the 'well-tended' garden. Andrew Read and Mark Johnston's 'beautifully presented' dishes might include roast loin of lamb, fondant potato, braised barley, red cabbage, caramelised parsnips, rosemary jus; perhaps raspberry Cranachan, fresh raspberries, toasted oats, honey, whipped cream and whisky to follow. In the morning, an 'excellent', innovative breakfast is served at table.

25% DISCOUNT VOUCHERS

MAP 4: inset C2
Park Road
Grange-over-Sands LA11 7HQ
T: 015395 33026
W: clarehousehotel.co.uk

BEDROOMS: 18. 1 on ground floor suitable for disabled.
OPEN: mid-Mar–mid-Dec.
FACILITIES: 2 lounges, dining room, free Wi-Fi, in-room TV (Freeview), 1-acre grounds, parking.
BACKGROUND MUSIC: none.
LOCATION: in village.
CHILDREN: all ages welcomed.
DOGS: assistance dogs accepted.
CREDIT CARDS: MC, Visa.
PRICES: per person B&B £81–£90, D,B&B £101–£110. À la carte £40.

GREAT LANGDALE Cumbria
THE OLD DUNGEON GHYLL

Fell walkers, climbers – including some of Britain's greatest mountaineers – and sleepy travellers have sought this unpretentious, dog-friendly inn, in a 'glorious setting', for more than 300 years. Standing at the head of the Great Langdale valley, the inn is managed for the National Trust by Jane and Neil Walmsley. Visitors like the 'willing, helpful staff' and 'reasonably priced accommodation'. Home-baked treats are an indulgent addition to morning coffee or afternoon tea, served in the residents' lounge. Most of the 'quite basic', 'country-style' rooms have dramatic, uninterrupted views of the fells. The popular Hikers' bar (one-time cow stalls) dishes up 'straightforward pub food'. Just ask about walking routes and packed lunches.

MAP 4: inset C2
Great Langdale LA22 9JY
T: 015394 37272
W: odg.co.uk

BEDROOMS: 12.
OPEN: all year except 24–26 Dec.
FACILITIES: residents' bar and lounge, dining room, bar, free Wi-Fi in public areas and some bedrooms, 1-acre garden, drying room, parking.
BACKGROUND MUSIC: live music on first Wed of every month.
LOCATION: 5 miles from Hawkshead.
CHILDREN: all ages welcomed.
DOGS: allowed (£5 per night).
CREDIT CARDS: MC, Visa.
PRICES: per room B&B from £58. À la carte £25. 2-night min. stay weekends.

HALIFAX Yorkshire
SHIBDEN MILL INN

Opposite Red Beck, the stream that once powered its machinery, a former mill in the wooded Shibden valley draws locals and visitors to its enfolding comforts. Simon and Caitlin Heaton's refurbished 17th-century inn might run on different fuel, but it's still packed with original features including the oak beams and fireplace in the bustling bar, where guests sample Shibden Mill's own brew. Jolly bedrooms are individually styled, a soaring ceiling in one; a stone archway in another, leading to a freestanding bath. All are supplied with teas and coffee, robes, a DVD-player. Chef Will Webster's imaginative menus have surprises: cured chalk stream trout, fennel pollen crème fraîche, beetroot cubes, sesame seed tuile, treacle dressing; alfresco grub from the Shack.

MAP 4:D3
Shibden Mill Fold
Halifax HX3 7UL
T: 01422 365840
W: shibdenmillinn.com

BEDROOMS: 11.
OPEN: all year except 25/26 Dec, 1 Jan.
FACILITIES: bar, lounge, restaurant, private dining room, free Wi-Fi, in-room TV (Freeview), small conference facilities, patio, 2-acre garden, parking, complimentary access to local health club.
BACKGROUND MUSIC: in main bar and restaurant.
LOCATION: 2 miles from Halifax town centre.
CHILDREN: all ages welcomed.
DOGS: allowed in bar.
CREDIT CARDS: Amex, MC, Visa.
PRICES: per room B&B single £95–£220, double £100–£265, D,B&B £188–£259. À la carte £35.

NEW

HAMPTON-IN-ARDEN West Midlands
HAMPTON MANOR

The austere Tudor Gothic-esque 19th-century exterior belies the delights within. Rebuilt by Sir Frederick Peel, son of Sir Robert Peel, the manor house has a cool feel, with spacious rooms filled with laid-back Scandi-style furnishings and a smattering of floral prints. It is run with energy by the Hill family and their bright young team. Bedrooms (suites, really) have a huge bed and a separate sitting area with great garden views, plus freshly ground coffee, Bluetooth audio system, home-baked cookies and 100 Acres toiletries in the bathroom. In the Michelin-starred restaurant, innovative takes on British staples showcase local produce: smoked eel, kholrabi, samphire; turbot, asparagus, wild garlic. Breakfast has as-you-like-it full English.

MAP 3:C6
Shadowbrook Lane
Hampton-in-Arden B92 0DQ
T: 01675 446080
W: hamptonmanor.com

BEDROOMS: 15. 1 suitable for disabled, plus 4-bedroom cottage in Victorian walled garden.
OPEN: all year, except 24–26 Dec, restaurant closed Sun, Mon.
FACILITIES: bar, parlour, Peel's restaurant (wheelchair accessible), tasting room, breakfast room, free-Wi-Fi, in-room TV (Freeview), civil wedding licence, ramp, garden.
BACKGROUND MUSIC: in public spaces.
LOCATION: 4 miles from NEC Birmingham.
CHILDREN: not under 12.
DOGS: not allowed.
CREDIT CARDS: Amex, MC, Visa.
PRICES: per room B&B £190–£180. Dinner £75 (4 courses), £95 (7 courses).

HARROGATE Yorkshire
THE WEST PARK HOTEL

Across from The Stray's 200 acres of open parkland, this alluring town-centre hotel is in a seamlessly converted Victorian coach house. Nathan George manages for Provenance Inns & Hotels. Chef Pawel Cekala's seasonal menus of fresh fish and seafood, sharing platters and grills are served in the buzzy brasserie (zinc-topped bar, sea-green leather banquettes, designer lighting); in clement weather, the courtyard opens for alfresco dining. Well-appointed bedrooms (quieter ones at the back) have a large bed, a coffee machine and tasty nibbles; in the bathrooms, spoiling toiletries, under-floor heating and speakers. Two penthouse duplexes have room to stretch out, plus a lounge and dining area, and access to a roof terrace.

MAP 4:D4
19 West Park
Harrogate HG1 1BJ
T: 01423 524471
W: thewestparkhotel.com

BEDROOMS: 25. Some suitable for disabled.
OPEN: all year.
FACILITIES: bar, brasserie, meeting/private dining rooms, free Wi-Fi, in-room TV (Freeview), large walled terrace, adjacent NCP car park, pay and display street parking.
BACKGROUND MUSIC: in public areas.
LOCATION: town centre.
CHILDREN: all ages welcomed.
DOGS: well-behaved dogs allowed in some bedrooms, bar.
CREDIT CARDS: Amex, MC, Visa.
PRICES: per room B&B £225–£375, D,B&B £285–£435. Set lunch, Mon–Sat £12.95 (2 courses), £16.95 (3 courses), à la carte £30.

HEACHAM Norfolk
HEACHAM HOUSE

The wide sands and salt marshes of north Norfolk are within a flat, shortish walk of Rebecca and Robert Bradley's fine B&B. While the red brick Victorian house casts an eye over a duck-filled pond, twitchers may be more interested in the RSPB sites at nearby Snettisham and Titchwell. Tea and home-made cake are a tasty welcome to the lounge, warmed with a toasty fire in cooler months. Bedrooms are individually decorated; in common are fresh flowers, home-baked biscuits; bathrobes, fluffy towels, facecloths. A generous start to the day: home-baked bread, home-made preserves, award-winning sausages. Walking and cycling routes from the door. A drying room is much appreciated. Taxi and restaurant reservations can be arranged.

MAP 2:A4
18 Staithe Road
Heacham PE31 7ED
T: 01485 579529
W: heachamhouse.com

BEDROOMS: 3.
OPEN: all year, except Christmas, New Year.
FACILITIES: sitting room, breakfast room, free Wi-Fi, in-room TV (Freeview), garden, parking, bicycle storage.
BACKGROUND MUSIC: none.
LOCATION: centre of village overlooking large duck pond, 3 miles from Hunstanton.
CHILDREN: not under 14.
DOGS: not allowed.
CREDIT CARDS: none accepted.
PRICES: per room B&B single £70–£90, double £95–£105.

NEW

HELMSLEY Yorkshire

THE FEATHERS

Hunt the mice at this refurbished hotel, restaurant
and coffee shop, formed from two old buildings
on the bustling market square. The carved wood
trademark of Robert Thomas (The Mouseman
of Kilburn) runs on pillars, window sills, seating
and the counter of The Pickwick bar; low ceilings
and an open fire make it a cosy space for sampling
the wide selection of craft beers and ciders, many
from local breweries. Comfortable bedrooms
(some at the rear) are modern with plush fabrics.
Light meals, seasonal dishes and pub classics are
served in the Atrium restaurant, the Feversham
bar and Coffee Lounge; all desserts are home
made. The 'excellent, friendly service' continues
in the morning with a tasty breakfast. Part of the
Coaching House group.

MAP 4:C4
Market Place
Helmsley YO62 5BH
T: 01439 770275
W: feathershotelhelmsley.co.uk

BEDROOMS: 25.
OPEN: all year.
FACILITIES: 2 bars, restaurant, lounge,
room service, free Wi-Fi, in-room TV
(Freeview), courtyard.
BACKGROUND MUSIC: in public spaces.
LOCATION: on market square.
CHILDREN: all ages welcomed.
DOGS: not allowed.
CREDIT CARDS: Amex, MC, Visa.
PRICES: per room B&B single from £79,
double from £99.

HERTFORD Hertfordshire

NUMBER ONE PORT HILL

In a pleasant market town, Annie Rowley's artful
Georgian B&B is an Aladdin's cave of vintage
glassware, sculptures and 'an unbelievable
collection' of objects. The town house, featured
in Pevsner's guide to Hertfordshire, has
'immaculately kept' rooms; two are cosy, one
large, with French gilt bed, a bathroom with
a raised boat bath. Plentiful extras include
Belgian hot chocolate, sweet and savoury snacks,
bathrobes, 'eclectic' reading material. Traffic noise
is muted by 'very good' double glazing, though
some noise travels between rooms. A 'superb'
breakfast, with freshly ground coffee and home-
made preserves, is taken communally, or in the
shade of the walled garden's ancient wisteria.
A pop-up supper club is held most months.

MAP 2:C4
1 Port Hill
Hertford SG14 1PJ
T: 01992 587350
W: numberoneporthill.co.uk

BEDROOMS: 3.
OPEN: all year except Christmas.
FACILITIES: drawing room, free Wi-Fi,
in-room TV (Sky, Freeview), gardens,
limited street parking.
BACKGROUND MUSIC: none.
LOCATION: 5 mins' walk from town
centre.
CHILDREN: over-12s welcomed
('though exemptions may be made,
if discussed, for younger children').
DOGS: not allowed.
CREDIT CARDS: MC, Visa.
PRICES: per room B&B £130–£160.
Dinner £45 (dependent on number
of guests).

HEXHAM Northumberland
BATTLESTEADS

Formed from an 18th-century farmstead, Dee and Richard Slade's hybrid of pub and hotel in the empty reaches of Northumberland is liked for its unique blend of sustainable hospitality, 'beautiful grounds' and 'amazing dark sky observatory'. Both in the main building and in wood-built lodges at the back, the brightly decorated bedrooms are well equipped; some have a super-size spa bath. 'Our luxury lodge was superb, with every comfort.' 'Good wholesome food' on chef Edward Shilton's mainly British modern menus turns fine local produce, including bounty from the kitchen garden, into the likes of lamb shank, rich jus, mash and seasonal greens. 'After an excellent meal, a first-class bottle of organic wine, plus a visit to the moon, we slept like logs.'

MAP 4:B3
Wark-on-Tyne
Hexham NE48 3LS
T: 01434 230209
w: battlesteads.com

BEDROOMS: 22. 4 on ground floor, 5 in lodge, 2 suitable for disabled.
OPEN: all year except 25 Dec.
FACILITIES: bar, dining room, function facilities, drying room, free Wi-Fi, in-room TV (Freeview), civil wedding licence, 2-acre grounds (walled garden, kitchen garden, dark sky observatory).
BACKGROUND MUSIC: in bar, restaurant.
LOCATION: 12 miles N of Hexham.
CHILDREN: all ages welcomed.
DOGS: allowed in public rooms, some bedrooms (£10 per night), resident dog.
CREDIT CARDS: Amex, MC, Visa.
PRICES: per room B&B from £120. À la carte £33.

NEW

HEXHAM Northumberland
THE BEAUMONT

'Perfectly located' in the town centre, an independently run hotel in a Victorian building close to the sixth-century Abbey. Hadrian's Wall hikers beat a path to its door to join locals in the 'convivial' bar and dining space. The open kitchen serves 'excellent quality' food, perhaps stone bass, crab and coriander crust, cauliflower, Bombay spices, Puy lentils, lime and bay dressing. 'The choice was always interesting and varied.' Comfortable bedrooms may vary in size, but they are well appointed; a room at the top has its own roof terrace and separate seating area. 'Breakfast was splendid, too, using locally sourced produce.' 'All the staff were unfailingly welcoming, helpful and friendly.' Parking is limited.

MAP 4:B3
Beaumont Street
Hexham NE46 3LT
T: 01434 602331
w: thebeaumonthexham.co.uk

BEDROOMS: 33.
OPEN: all year.
FACILITIES: bar/lounge/restaurant, free Wi-Fi, in-room TV.
BACKGROUND MUSIC: in bar, restaurant.
LOCATION: in town centre.
CHILDREN: all ages welcomed.
DOGS: not allowed.
CREDIT CARDS: Amex, MC, Visa.
PRICES: per room B&B from £116. À la carte £35.

HITCHIN Hertfordshire

THE FARMHOUSE AT REDCOATS

With views across gently undulating countryside, this sprawling old building, with its outlying stables and barns, dates back to the 15th century. Extensively restored as a hotel and restaurant, it is part of the Nye family's Anglian Country Inns. They have retained many original features, with comfortable sitting areas and warming fires in myriad nooks and crannies. In the main house, bedrooms are classically furnished; simpler annexe rooms have stable partitions, original floors and tiling. Executive chef Sherwin Jacobs cooks farm-to-table produce (some from the kitchen garden), alongside seasonal game, served in the large conservatory restaurant. A six-course taster menu can be pre-arranged. Breakfast is hearty. A circular walk is nearby.

MAP 2:C4
Redcoats Green
Hitchin SG4 7JR
T: 01438 729500
W: farmhouseatredcoats.co.uk

BEDROOMS: 27. 23 in converted stables and barns, some on ground floor.
OPEN: all year.
FACILITIES: 2 bars, lounge, conservatory restaurant, 3 private dining rooms, free Wi-Fi, in-room TV (Freeview), civil wedding licence, 4-acre grounds, parking, unsuitable for disabled.
BACKGROUND MUSIC: 'subtle' in public areas.
LOCATION: 9 mins' drive from Stevenage.
CHILDREN: all ages welcomed.
DOGS: well-behaved dogs allowed in stable rooms (charge).
CREDIT CARDS: Amex, MC, Visa.
PRICES: per room B&B £120–£180, D,B&B £185–£225. À la carte £33.

HOLT Norfolk

BYFORDS

At the centre of a 'bustling' Georgian market town, a higgledy-piggledy old building with an all-day café, a store, 'very comfortable' accommodation and a lively holiday atmosphere. A winding staircase at the back of the deli leads up to bedrooms bursting with character, with stripped wood flooring and vintage furnishings. While each is different, all have home-made biscuits, a fridge containing fresh milk and water. The 'rustic' restaurant serves a seasonal menu. Breakfast sees hot dishes from the café menu. Picnic items, and more, are available in the deli. 'Staff were very friendly and helpful, making the stay very enjoyable.'

MAP 2:A5
1–3 Shirehall Plain
Holt NR25 6BG
T: 01263 711400
W: byfords.org.uk

BEDROOMS: 16. Plus self-catering apartment.
OPEN: all year.
FACILITIES: café, deli, free Wi-Fi, in-room TV (Sky), terrace, private secure parking.
BACKGROUND MUSIC: in café.
LOCATION: central.
CHILDREN: all ages welcomed.
DOGS: not allowed.
CREDIT CARDS: Amex, MC, Visa.
PRICES: per room B&B £165–£215, D,B&B £205–£255. À la carte £25.

HOOK Hampshire
TYLNEY HALL

'Peaceful' countryside views roll away from this 'very grand' Victorian mansion in 66 acres of 'spectacular' grounds. Designed by Gertrude Jekyll, they contain a formal Italian garden, water gardens and a lake. From the wood-panelled reception, a magnificent staircase sweeps up to country house bedrooms; others are in converted buildings dotted around the grounds. Young travellers are given a welcome pack; bowls, a bed and treats for Fido. 'Our second-floor room was spotlessly clean, well equipped (52 steps, no lift)'; ground-floor garden rooms have easy outside access. Golf carts whisk guests to and from the main house. Dine in style in the Oak Room restaurant. Menus in the lounge or on the garden-facing terrace are more informal. Popular for weddings.

MAP 2:D3
Ridge Lane
Hook RG27 9AZ
T: 01256 745532
W: tylneyhall.co.uk

BEDROOMS: 112. Some in cottages in the grounds, some on ground floor, 1 suitable for disabled.
OPEN: all year.
FACILITIES: bar, 2 lounges, restaurant, private dining rooms, free Wi-Fi, in-room TV (Freeview), civil wedding licence, conference/function facilities, health suite, indoor and outdoor pools, treatment rooms, 66-acre grounds, public rooms wheelchair accessible.
BACKGROUND MUSIC: occasionally piano in the restaurant or jazz in the Tylney Suite.
LOCATION: 7 miles E of Basingstoke.
CHILDREN: all ages welcomed.
DOGS: allowed in some rooms (£25 per night), not in lounges, restaurant.
CREDIT CARDS: Amex, MC, Visa.
PRICES: per room B&B from £163. À la carte £45.

HUDDERSFIELD Yorkshire
THE THREE ACRES INN & RESTAURANT

High on the hills', this 'friendly' roadside drovers' inn has 'detour-worthy food'; 'tremendous views to all sides' are nearly as impressive. The pub-with-rooms, which came on to the scene 40-odd years ago, is still owned by Neil Truelove, joined by his son, Tom. Bedrooms, spread across the main building and garden cottages, are 'comfortable, clean and functional, with an agreeable bed'; lighter sleepers might bring earplugs (some guests noticed noise from a neighbouring room). Locals join residents in the 'civilised' dining room for the 'high-quality' modern British menu: pomegranate molasses glazed rump of lamb or classic fish pie. The day starts well: home-made muesli, local bacon and sausage.

MAP 4:E3
Roydhouse
Huddersfield HD8 8LR
T: 01484 602606
W: 3acres.com

BEDROOMS: 17. 1 suitable for disabled, 8 in adjacent annexe.
OPEN: all year except evenings 25 and 26 Dec, midday 31 Dec, evening 1 Jan.
FACILITIES: bar, restaurant, free Wi-Fi, in-room TV (Freeview), civil wedding licence, small function/private dining facilities, terraced garden.
BACKGROUND MUSIC: in bar, restaurant.
LOCATION: 6 miles from Huddersfield town centre.
CHILDREN: well-behaved children welcomed.
DOGS: not allowed.
CREDIT CARDS: Amex, MC, Visa.
PRICES: per room B&B single £50–£100, double from £80. À la carte £50.

HURLEY Berkshire

HURLEY HOUSE

Rebuilt and reinvented by Bassam Shlewet, this award-winning boutique hotel brings 'great service', chic style and impressive cuisine to a picturesque stretch of the Thames Path. The smartly rustic bar has a cosy wood-burning stove, exposed brickwork, wooden beams. 'Excellent' British menus, 'promptly served by charming waiters', draw in diners to the sophisticated restaurant, where a huge window lets you observe the working kitchen. 'Lovely' bedrooms in creams and greys have urbane comforts (luxury bedlinen and towels, coffee machine, air conditioning, under-floor heating, a strong shower); calls to UK landlines are free. 'The ambience and superb staff are a feature.' Efficient insulation subdues noise from the adjacent busy road.

25% DISCOUNT VOUCHERS

MAP 2:D3
Henley Road
Hurley SL6 5LH
T: 01628 568500
W: hurleyhouse.co.uk

BEDROOMS: 10. Some suitable for disabled.
OPEN: all year.
FACILITIES: bar, snug, restaurant, private dining room, free Wi-Fi, in-room TV (Freeview), function facilities, civil wedding licence, spa treatments, terrace, lawn, barbecue pavilion, parking.
BACKGROUND MUSIC: in public areas until 11 pm.
LOCATION: 3 miles from Marlow, 5 miles from Henley-on-Thames, 5 miles from Maidenhead, 10 miles from Windsor.
CHILDREN: all ages welcomed.
DOGS: in bar area only.
CREDIT CARDS: Amex, MC, Visa.
PRICES: per room B&B £140–£315. À la carte £45.

IRONBRIDGE Shropshire

THE LIBRARY HOUSE

'Beautifully decorated' and properly bookish, this Grade II listed village library has been converted into a cheerful B&B near the River Severn. Run by Sarah and Tim Davis, the book-lined sitting room of the Georgian building retains the original library shelves; it's a cosy spot, especially in chilly weather when the log-burner blazes. Writers lend their names to the well-equipped bedrooms. Chaucer opens on to a private garden terrace; Eliot is all lofty ceiling and long views towards the river. In each: waffle dressing gowns, fresh milk, a hot-water bottle. Breakfast ranges from continental variations to a traditional English, freshly cooked. Convenient for visiting the UNESCO World Heritage site of Ironbridge Gorge and the open-air museum at Blists Hill.

MAP 3:C5
11 Severn Bank
Ironbridge TF8 7AN
T: 01952 432299
W: libraryhouse.com

BEDROOMS: 3.
OPEN: all year.
FACILITIES: sitting room, breakfast room, free Wi-Fi, in-room TV (Freeview), courtyard, mature garden, passes for local car parks.
BACKGROUND MUSIC: none.
LOCATION: town centre.
CHILDREN: not under 13.
DOGS: not allowed.
CREDIT CARDS: MC, Visa.
PRICES: per room B&B single £75–£95, double £100–£135.

KESWICK Cumbria

DALEGARTH HOUSE

A mile outside Keswick, Craig and Clare Dalton's welcoming, good-value Edwardian guest house is surrounded by splendid scenery. Visitors receive a warm greeting, starting outside with the riot of colourful potted plants leading up to the cherry red front door. After a day of outdoor activity, you can head for the bar with its grandfather clock, and the peaceful bedrooms. Each of the simply furnished rooms has a hospitality tray and flat-screen TV; most have memorable views of Derwent Water and the surrounding fells. In the morning, choose a daily-changing special, vegetarian or full English breakfast, all sourced from local ingredients, and served in the airy dining room – hearty fuel before another day out in the fresh air.

MAP 4: inset C2
Keswick CA12 5RQ
T: 017687 72817
W: dalegarth-house.co.uk

BEDROOMS: 10, 2 on ground floor in annexe.
OPEN: Mar–mid-Dec.
FACILITIES: lounge, bar, dining room, free Wi-Fi, in-room TV (Freeview), garden, parking, bicycle storage.
BACKGROUND MUSIC: occasional radio at breakfast.
LOCATION: 1½ miles W of Keswick.
CHILDREN: not under 11.
DOGS: not allowed.
CREDIT CARDS: MC, Visa.
PRICES: per person B&B £47–£59. 2-night min. stay preferred.

KESWICK Cumbria

LYZZICK HALL

'Glorious fell views', 'excellent food' and 'capable, obliging staff' are found at this family-friendly spot on the lower slopes of Skiddaw. The early Victorian hotel has been owned by the Fernandez family, now co-owners with the Lake family, for 25 years. The 'stunning scenery' can be enjoyed from most of the 'well-equipped' bedrooms; all overlook the lovely landscaped gardens, and have contemporary bathrooms with good toiletries. The lounge has a warming fire; the spa and indoor swimming pool is a blessing after a day's sightseeing or mountain hike. There are 'excellent' British dishes, 'divine desserts' and 'whatever the children fancy'. Breakfast has no buffet, but 'plenty of choice'. Many walks from the door.

MAP 4: inset C2
Underskiddaw
Keswick CA12 4PY
T: 017687 72277
W: lyzzickhall.co.uk

BEDROOMS: 30. 1 on ground floor.
OPEN: 8 Feb–4 Jan.
FACILITIES: bar, 2 lounges, orangery, restaurant, free Wi-Fi, in-room TV (Freeview), 10-metre heated indoor swimming pool, spa facilities, 4-acre grounds.
BACKGROUND MUSIC: 'discreet' in public areas.
LOCATION: 2 miles N of Keswick.
CHILDREN: all ages welcomed.
DOGS: allowed in 1 bedroom, if supervised at all times.
CREDIT CARDS: MC, Visa.
PRICES: per room B&B £172–£264, D,B&B £226–£318. À la carte £42.

KING'S LYNN Norfolk

CONGHAM HALL

Close to Sandringham, a Georgian country house
set amid lawns, orchards and woodland. The
herb garden contains 400 varieties of culinary and
medicinal plants that supply treatments for the
Secret Garden Spa, and flavourings and garnishes
for the kitchen. 'Beautifully decorated', the hotel
has 'attractive prints, good flower displays, plenty
of areas to sit'. Bedrooms, in the main property
and around the spa garden, blend classic and
contemporary styles. All have slippers, robes,
an espresso machine, a larder with home-made
biscuits, fresh milk. Dog-friendly garden rooms
('signs of usage') have a furnished terrace area.
In the light dining room, chef James O'Connor's
seasonal menus include pigeon breast, sea trout,
slow-cooked lamb – 'all delicious'.

25% DISCOUNT VOUCHERS

MAP 2:A4
Lynn Road
King's Lynn PE32 1AH
T: 01485 600250
W: conghamhallhotel.co.uk

BEDROOMS: 26. 6 garden rooms,
1 suitable for disabled.
OPEN: all year, packages at Christmas,
New Year.
FACILITIES: bar, sitting room, library,
restaurant, free Wi-Fi, in-room TV
(Freeview), civil wedding licence,
conference facilities, terrace, spa, 12-metre
pool, 30-acre grounds, public areas
wheelchair accessible, adapted toilet.
BACKGROUND MUSIC: in bar, restaurant.
LOCATION: 6 miles E of King's Lynn.
CHILDREN: all ages welcomed.
DOGS: allowed in some bedrooms,
public rooms.
CREDIT CARDS: MC, Visa.
PRICES: per room B&B £170–£350,
D,B&B £235–£450. À la carte £45.
1-night bookings sometimes refused
Sat.

KINGSBRIDGE Devon

THURLESTONE HOTEL

'Thoroughly dependable yet stylish in an old-
fashioned way', the Grose family have looked
after this 'family-friendly' hotel for more than 120
years. Approached by lanes 'resplendent with wild
flowers', it lies in 19 acres of sub-tropical gardens
on the South Devon National Trust coastline.
'Stunning' widescreen views are found in most of
the well-equipped bedrooms; family rooms have a
bunk bed, or extra space for a cot/additional bed.
Real ales and fresh seafood are found in the 16th-
century village inn or the terrace bistro, while in
the smart Trevilder restaurant the food was 'good
classic stuff'. Rock pools are five minutes away;
a plethora of on-site diversions includes croquet,
tennis, 9-hole golf course, a spa; a children's club
during the school holidays.

MAP 1:D4
Kingsbridge TQ7 3NN
T: 01548 560382
W: thurlestone.co.uk

BEDROOMS: 65. 2 suitable for disabled.
OPEN: all year.
FACILITIES: lift, lounges, bar,
restaurant, bistro, village pub, free
Wi-Fi, in-room TV (Sky), civil
wedding licence, function facilities,
terrace, spa, outdoor heated
swimming pool, tennis, 9-hole golf
course.
BACKGROUND MUSIC: none.
LOCATION: 4 miles SW of Kingsbridge.
CHILDREN: all ages welcomed.
DOGS: allowed in some bedrooms, not
in public rooms.
CREDIT CARDS: Amex, MC, Visa.
PRICES: per room B&B from £180.
À la carte £40. 2-night min. stay.

KINGSWEAR Devon

KAYWANA HALL

Across the estuary from Dartmouth, in its own hillside woodland, Tony Pithers and Gordon Craig's ultra-modern 1960s Butterfly house (one of four like it in Devon) has a curving staircase, angled zinc roof and glass walls. An adults-only B&B, it is intimate and discreet. Light-filled bedrooms each have their own entrance and private deck reached via steep steps. Abstract art dots the sleek, well-designed interiors; each room is well appointed, with plenty of extras (a mini-fridge, an iPod docking station, espresso machine, fudge, home-made biscuits). Breakfast, in an open-plan room overlooking the swimming pool, might start with freshly squeezed juices, locally baked bread, fruit compote; eggs Benedict, Florentine or other cooked dishes to follow.

MAP 1:D4
Higher Contour Road
Kingswear TQ6 0AY
T: 01803 752200
W: kaywanahall.co.uk

BEDROOMS: 4.
OPEN: Apr–end Oct.
FACILITIES: kitchen/breakfast room, free Wi-Fi in bedrooms, in-room TV (Freeview), 12-acre grounds, 9-metre outdoor swimming pool (heated in summer months), parking.
BACKGROUND MUSIC: none.
LOCATION: 5 mins from Dartmouth via ferry.
CHILDREN: not accepted.
DOGS: assistance dogs only.
CREDIT CARDS: MC, Visa.
PRICES: per room B&B £190–£240.

KNARESBOROUGH Yorkshire

NEWTON HOUSE

'Excellent accommodation and a breakfast that sets you up for the day.' Denise Carter extends a warm welcome at her 'good value' B&B in the centre of a 'lovely' market town. 'Spacious, well-appointed' bedrooms in the 'fascinating' 18th-century house are traditionally decorated; each has a comfortable bed, its own little library, a hospitality tray. Local beers, spirits and soft drinks are kept in the well-stocked honesty bar. In the evenings, light bites (soup, an omelette) might be 'rustled up'; the hostess can recommend nearby eateries for more substantial fare. Home-made sourdough bread, jams and compotes are a worthy start to 'organic "slow" breakfasts'. The small courtyard garden has a 'wildlife' area and 'Hibernation Hotel'. A bonus: on-site parking.

MAP 4:D4
York Place
Knaresborough HG5 0AD
T: 01423 863539
W: newtonhouseyorkshire.com

BEDROOMS: 12. 2 on ground floor suitable for disabled, 2 in converted stables.
OPEN: all year.
FACILITIES: sitting room, dining room, conservatory, free Wi-Fi, in-room TV (Freeview), courtyard garden, parking.
BACKGROUND MUSIC: Classic FM at breakfast.
LOCATION: town centre, 4 miles from Harrogate.
CHILDREN: all ages welcomed.
DOGS: allowed in 2 stable block rooms with outside access (home-made treats), not in public rooms.
CREDIT CARDS: Amex, MC, Visa.
PRICES: per room B&B single £70–£110, double £95–£145.

LANCASTER Lancashire

GREENBANK FARMHOUSE

A former cheese-making farm, where Sally and Simon Tait 'warmly welcome' visitors to their 'well-appointed', 'very affordable' B&B near the university. 'A good centre for exploring the area', it offers 'wonderful views of the moorlands'. Twitchers can take their field book into the conservatory, from where many bird species can be spotted flitting about in the gardens. The 'spacious' bedrooms have 'ample storage', 'adequate lighting'; 'even the loo' has sweeping views of the fells. Freshly cooked breakfasts, ordered the night before, are 'excellent': farm-fresh eggs, home-made bread, loose-leaf tea, local bacon and sausages. The hosts are a wealth of local information, including dining hot spots in neighbouring Dolphinholme

MAP 4:D2
Abbeystead Road
Lancaster LA2 9BA
T: 07512 520229
w: greenbankfarmhouse.co.uk

BEDROOMS: 4. 1 on ground floor.
OPEN: all year.
FACILITIES: conservatory breakfast room/sitting area, free Wi-Fi, in-room TV (Freeview), 6-acre grounds (some working farmland), parking.
BACKGROUND MUSIC: none.
LOCATION: 20 mins from centre of Lancaster (own transport essential).
CHILDREN: not under 12.
DOGS: not allowed.
CREDIT CARDS: Amex, MC, Visa.
PRICES: per person B&B single £60, double £70.

LANCHESTER Durham

BURNHOPESIDE HALL

Well placed for visits to Durham, Christine Hewitt's Grade II* listed home is surrounded by extensive gardens among acres of rolling farmland and forest. Engineer William Hedley, inventor of Puffing Billy, lived here. Inside, timeless elegance fuses with hospitable informality. Cosseting rooms include spacious, traditional bedrooms in the house or farmhouse, and cottage suites. Some have period windows, an open fireplace, a sleigh bed. Home-made, home-reared, home-grown fare features at breakfast; dinner may be requested in advance. A fantastic spot for cyclists, walkers and riders: trails lead to the river and the Lanchester Valley Railway Path. The house has cleaning facilities for muddy paws and boots; a drying room; stabling for guests' horses.

25% DISCOUNT VOUCHERS

MAP 4:B4
Durham Road
Lanchester DH7 0TL
T: 01207 520222
w: burnhopeside-hall.co.uk

BEDROOMS: 13. 5 in adjoining farmhouse, 3 in cottage in the grounds.
OPEN: all year, except when booked for exclusive use.
FACILITIES: sitting room, dining room, library, billiard room, free Wi-Fi, in-room TV (Freeview), 475-acre grounds, farmhouse rooms have a sitting room, dining room; cottages have a sitting room where breakfast can be served; all with log fires.
BACKGROUND MUSIC: none.
LOCATION: 5 miles NW of Durham.
CHILDREN: all ages welcomed.
DOGS: welcomed (resident dogs).
CREDIT CARDS: Amex, MC, Visa.
PRICES: per room B&B single £70–£85, double £100–£120. Dinner, by arrangement, £40.

LAVENHAM Suffolk
THE SWAN HOTEL & SPA

'So cosy and welcoming', this swish hotel is
formed from three timber-framed 15th-century
buildings in a medieval village. It is one of
The Hotel Folk group (see also The Crown,
Woodbridge, Shortlist). With a 'lovely' lobby and
interlinked areas separated by open wood-beamed
partitions, there is plenty of seating. Along twisty
corridors, the country house-style bedrooms each
have an oversized headboard, bathrobes, laptop,
safe, iron and board. Characterful suites have a
lounge, inglenook fireplace, mullioned windows.
Dining options abound: light bites in the Airmen's
bar; re-thought British favourites in the 'bright,
modern' brasserie overlooking the garden; refined
dishes in the Gallery restaurant. If you need to
revitalise, the Weavers' House Spa awaits.

MAP 2:C5
High Street
Lavenham CO10 9QA
T: 01787 247477
W: theswanatlavenham.co.uk

BEDROOMS: 45. 1 suitable for disabled.
OPEN: all year.
FACILITIES: lounges, bar, brasserie,
restaurant, free Wi-Fi, in-room TV
(Freeview), civil wedding licence,
private dining/function facilities, spa
(treatment rooms, sauna, steam room,
outdoor hydrotherapy pool), terrace,
garden, parking.
BACKGROUND MUSIC: occasional, in
public areas.
LOCATION: in village.
CHILDREN: all ages welcomed.
DOGS: in some rooms (£12 per dog
per night).
CREDIT CARDS: Amex, MC, Visa.
PRICES: per room B&B £105–£315.

LEATHERHEAD Surrey
BEAVERBROOK

Famous politicians and luminaries have pow-
wowed and partied in this country pile, once the
rural retreat of press baron Lord Beaverbrook.
A large white building on a Surrey hillside, it
has been transmuted into a lavish modern hotel.
Its illustrious past is celebrated with bedrooms
named after famous visitors. It has a well-stocked
library, glamorous Roaring Twenties-style bar and
Art Deco screening room. A grand staircase flows
up to floral-patterned bedrooms with an original
fireplace, a luxury bathroom; large windows or
a balcony look over the downs. Garden House
rooms are funkier, with woodland views. Dine
on beautifully presented Japanese cuisine,
seasonal Italian-inspired dishes or wholesome
food in the spa deli.

MAP 2:D4
Reigate Road
Leatherhead KT22 8QX
T: 01372 227670
W: beaverbrook.co.uk

BEDROOMS: 35. 18 in main house and
buildings in garden.
OPEN: all year.
FACILITIES: bar, lounge, 3 restaurants
(The Dining Room closed Sun night,
all day Mon), library, cinema, free
Wi-Fi, in-room TV (Sky), indoor
and outdoor pools, 400-acre grounds,
walled garden, woodlands, lake,
parking, cookery school, kids' club.
BACKGROUND MUSIC: in restaurant, bar.
LOCATION: on a 400-acre estate in the
Surrey hills.
CHILDREN: all ages welcomed.
DOGS: welcomed in some rooms,
public spaces.
CREDIT CARDS: Amex, MC, Visa.
PRICES: per room from £215. Breakfast:
continental £15, full £18, dinner set
menus £60, £90 (The Dining Room),
£54 (Garden House). 2-night bookings
only on Sat.

LECHLADE Gloucestershire

THE FIVE ALLS

Quirky and sophisticated, an 18th-century
Cotswold dining pub-with-rooms. Flagged
floors, stone walls and a huge fireplace are offset
by colourful textiles and playful wallpapers; a
pleasing concession to tradition is the leather
chesterfield sofas by the roaring log fire. The
popular bar and dining area are comfortably
informal and there's a wide choice of local ales,
the Five Alls house ale, craft beers and continental
lagers. On sunny days, European-influenced
dishes are served on the garden picnic tables.
Soft colours, neutral hues and cosy, locally made
woollen throws turn the upstairs bedrooms into a
calming retreat. Owned by the Barkby group. See
also The Plough, Kelmscott (main entry) and the
Bull Hotel, Fairford (Shortlist), nearby.

MAP 3:E6
Filkins
Lechlade GL7 3JQ
T: 01367 860875
W: thefiveallsfilkins.co.uk

BEDROOMS: 9. 5 in annexe.
OPEN: all year.
FACILITIES: snug, bar, restaurant
(closed Sun eve), free Wi-Fi, in-room
TV (Freeview), garden, parking.
BACKGROUND MUSIC: in public areas.
LOCATION: in scenic village of Filkins,
10 mins' drive from Lechlade.
CHILDREN: all ages welcomed.
DOGS: allowed in public rooms, not in
bedrooms.
CREDIT CARDS: Amex, MC, Visa.
PRICES: per room B&B £115–£180.
À la carte £38.

NEW

LECHLADE Gloucestershire

THYME AT SOUTHROP MANOR

'A village within a village.' An enclosed collection
of restored 17th-century farm buildings, houses
and cottages has been unified by founder Caryn
Hibbert over 15 years into a quintessentially
English country retreat. In the embrace of a
peaceful 150-acre estate, there is a pub, cookery
school, spa, shop and chic bedrooms (a roll-top
bath in some) decorated with lavish fabrics and
botanical prints. Join the flock for a cocktail in
the former lambing sheds; woolly sheep stools
add rural aptness to the smart green and gold
decor. Caryn's son, Charlie, uses produce from the
farm and kitchen garden for his seasonal dishes,
perhaps braised beef, pickled walnut, salsa verde
and mash, prepared in the open kitchen of the
lofty Ox Barn. Informal pub food in The Swan.

MAP 2:C2
Southrop Manor Estate
Lechlade GL7 3NX
T: 01367 850174
W: thyme.co.uk

BEDROOMS: 32. 8 in main building,
others in a lodge and cottages.
OPEN: all year.
FACILITIES: drawing room, cocktail bar,
restaurant, pub, free Wi-Fi, in-room
TV, event space, gardens, swimming
pool, spa.
BACKGROUND MUSIC: in public spaces.
LOCATION: on large Cotswold estate
N of Lechlade.
CHILDREN: not under 12, except for
1 cottage; younger children allowed in
the Ox Barn at lunchtime.
DOGS: in Old Walls cottage, pub.
CREDIT CARDS: Amex, MC, Visa.
PRICES: per room B&B £325–£1,250.
À la carte £45. 1-night bookings
refused bank holiday weekends.

LEDBURY Herefordshire

THE FEATHERS

Hosting travellers since 1564, this famous black-and-white-timbered building has many original features: a wonky staircase, leaded windows, a ghostly apparition. It is owned by the Coaching Inn group. 'Spacious' bedrooms, 'furnished in a somewhat quirky style', are well supplied (fruit, chocolates, robes). Coaching rooms have Tudor beams; high-ceilinged Dancing rooms are in the Victorian ballroom. In Quills restaurant, diners sit down to Suzie Isaacs's 'very good' modern British dishes, perhaps grilled monkfish tail, colcannon potato cake, broccoli, chorizo and clam butter, Serrano crumb. Fuggles brasserie is a laid-back alternative. Breakfast brings a 'good choice of cold and cooked options – the full English was particularly appreciated.

MAP 3:D5
High Street
Ledbury HR8 1DS
T: 01531 635266
W: feathersledbury.co.uk

BEDROOMS: 20. 1 suite in cottage, also self-catering apartments.
OPEN: all year.
FACILITIES: bar, lounge, brasserie, 2 restaurants, free Wi-Fi, in-room TV (Freeview), function facilities, spa, indoor swimming pool, gym, civil wedding licence, terraced garden, parking, restaurant suitable for disabled.
BACKGROUND MUSIC: none.
LOCATION: town centre.
CHILDREN: all ages welcomed.
DOGS: allowed in bedrooms, most public areas.
CREDIT CARDS: Amex, MC, Visa.
PRICES: per room B&B £70–£240, D,B&B £100–£320. À la carte £30.

LEVENS Cumbria

HARE AND HOUNDS

In the Lyth valley, Becky and Ash Dewar's 16th-century hostelry is a village pub 'with a modern twist'. Visitors mingle with regulars in the lively, slate-floored, beamed bar, where hand-drawn cask ales, craft beers and cocktails made with locally produced spirits are a big draw. Upstairs, distinctive bedrooms have duck-egg blue panelling, soft contemporary hues. Most offer a long view, all enjoy homely extras: home-made brownies, freshly ground coffee, fresh milk, a digital radio, Cumbrian-made toiletries. Home-made comfort food (seafood pot; 'unusual burgers') is served in the light-filled dining room. Breakfast starts with fruit, cereals and yogurt, and works up to a range of cooked fare. Muddy boots and dogs are welcomed.

MAP 4: inset C2
Levens
Kendal LA8 8PN
T: 015395 60004
W: hareandhoundslevens.co.uk

BEDROOMS: 5. 1 in barn annexe.
OPEN: all year, no accommodation 24/25 Dec.
FACILITIES: pub, lounge, restaurant, free Wi-Fi, in-room TV (Freeview), beer garden (½ acre), parking.
BACKGROUND MUSIC: in pub and restaurant.
LOCATION: in village.
CHILDREN: all ages welcomed (cots, Z-beds).
DOGS: allowed in pub and garden.
CREDIT CARDS: Amex, MC, Visa.
PRICES: per room B&B single £75–£135, double £85–£145. À la carte £50 for 2 people. 2-night min. stay for weekends booked 1 month in advance.

LEWANNICK Cornwall

COOMBESHEAD FARM

Attracting foodies from near and far, this hybrid of informal guest house and restaurant occupies a 16th-century farmhouse, among acres of meadows and woodland. Run by chef Tom Adams, it has 'delightful, enthusiastic young staff'. A convivial clientele ('it all felt very hipster') enjoys 'stupendous dishes', rustled up in an open kitchen in the 'feasting barn', using home-smoked, -cured and -pickled ingredients, Cornish organic produce and locally foraged food. Many of the wines come from Tom's brother's French vineyard. Handsomely rustic bedrooms have views stretching across to Dartmoor. Breakfast, naturally, is a feast: home-made yogurts, home-baked breads, freshly milled oats and grains. On-site sourdough bakery; monthly bread workshops.

MAP 1:D3
Lewannick PL15 7QQ
T: 01566 782009
W: coombesheadfarm.co.uk

BEDROOMS: 5. 1 with adjoining bunk-bedroom.
OPEN: all year except Jan, restaurant Thurs–Sun.
FACILITIES: living room, library, dining room, kitchen, bakery, free Wi-Fi, 66-acre grounds, parking.
BACKGROUND MUSIC: in evening in living room, dining room and kitchen.
LOCATION: in village, 3 miles from A30, 6 miles from Launceston.
CHILDREN: over-15s welcomed.
DOGS: not allowed in guest house, restaurant, but in grounds only, on a lead.
CREDIT CARDS: Amex, MC, Visa.
PRICES: per room B&B from £130. Set dinner menu £65.

LICHFIELD Staffordshire

SWINFEN HALL

Approached through 'well-maintained grounds', then entered through a magnificent hall (Grade II* listed) with a hand-carved ceiling and balustraded minstrels' gallery, the Wiser family's 'superb' Georgian manor is a 'very grand,' yet a 'relaxing experience' run by 'friendly' staff. Each spacious bedroom has an iPod dock, DVD-player views over formal gardens or parkland. Afternoon tea is served in the drawing room, overlooking the terrace. Cocktails are sipped in the 'lovely' Edwardian bar ('lots of wood panelling, stained glass'). À la carte and six-course tasting menus in the restaurant focus on produce from the kitchen garden, orchard and lamb and venison reared on the estate. The bar offers lighter bites, perhaps fish and chips or a superfood salad.

MAP 2:A2
Swinfen
Lichfield WS14 9RE
T: 01543 481494
W: swinfenhallhotel.co.uk

BEDROOMS: 17.
OPEN: all year except Christmas Day evening, Boxing Day, Four Sseasons restaurant closed Sun, Mon evenings.
FACILITIES: bar, lounge, cocktail lounge, restaurant, function/private dining rooms, free Wi-Fi, in-room TV (Sky), civil wedding licence, 100-acre grounds, courtyard garden, parking, restaurant wheelchair accessible.
BACKGROUND MUSIC: as appropriate' in cocktail lounge, bar, restaurant.
LOCATION: 2 miles S of Lichfield just off the A38.
CHILDREN: all ages welcomed.
DOGS: not allowed.
CREDIT CARDS: Amex, MC, Visa.
PRICES: per room B&B single £125–£330, double £155–£350. À la carte £52,

LINCOLN Lincolnshire
BRIDLEWAY BED & BREAKFAST

A smart trot up the bridleway reaches artist Jane Haigh's rural B&B. Always on hand, the hostess provides a welcoming tea (home-made scones, clotted cream); advice on local restaurants; even a lift into Lincoln, nearby. Country-cosy rooms in converted stables, all exposed brickwork, contemporary grey and pale hues, mellow wood, have their own entrance, bathrobes, under-floor heating; a coffee machine and baked treats. Breakfast, in the conservatory, brings fresh fruit salad, Aga-cooked porridge and pancakes, local honey, croissants, pains au chocolat, and a wide range of hot dishes, using eggs from Jane's hens; a continental option can be delivered to the room. Wellies and the family dogs can be borrowed for muddy walks. Stabling provided.

25% DISCOUNT VOUCHERS

MAP 4:E5
Riseholme Gorse
Lincoln LN2 2LY
T: 01522 545693
w: bridlewaybandb.co.uk

BEDROOMS: 4. All in converted outbuildings.
OPEN: 1 Jan–9 Dec.
FACILITIES: conservatory, free Wi-Fi, in-room TV (Freeview), ½-acre grounds leading to bridleway, 2 stables, manège, paddock for guests' horses.
BACKGROUND MUSIC: none, unless requested.
LOCATION: 3½ miles from Lincoln.
CHILDREN: not under 15.
DOGS: not allowed.
CREDIT CARDS: Amex, MC, Visa.
PRICES: per room B&B single £79–£110, double £93–£125.

LINCOLN Lincolnshire
THE CASTLE HOTEL

On the site of the Roman Forum, this sleek Bailgate area hotel is 'superbly' located between cathedral and castle. It is run by 'helpful, congenial, attentive staff, all positive promoters of the city'. 'Comfortable', compact bedrooms in the main building, modishly decorated in earthy hues, overlook the castle walls or have 'stunning views' of the medieval cathedral. Courtyard rooms ('signs of wear and tear') are in the peaceful 250-year-old coach house, all conveniently on the ground floor, with parking just outside. The hungry flock to consume Simon Hibberd's 'beautifully presented' modern European dishes in the Reform restaurant, perhaps braised blade of Lincolnshire beef. 'Our bar meal was excellent, quickly served and freshly cooked.'

MAP 4:E5
Westgate
Lincoln LN1 3AS
T: 01522 538801
w: castlehotel.net

BEDROOMS: 18. 1 suitable for disabled, plus 1 apartment, and 2-bed Castle Mews (available for self-catering).
OPEN: all year except 24–26 Dec.
FACILITIES: 2 small lounges, bar, restaurant, free Wi-Fi, in-room TV, wedding/function facilities, spa treatments, parking.
BACKGROUND MUSIC: in public areas.
LOCATION: 2-min. walk from cathedral.
CHILDREN: all ages welcomed.
DOGS: not allowed.
CREDIT CARDS: MC, Visa.
PRICES: per room B&B single £90–£140, double £90–£150, D,B&B £120–£220. Set menus £30–£35, à la carte £35.

LITTLE ECCLESTON Lancashire

THE CARTFORD INN

Just beyond the village, Julie and Patrick Beaumé's 17th-century coaching inn has winsome views over the River Wyre and is appealingly quirky inside. The eco-minded pair have used upcycled or locally crafted furnishings, and light fittings by a local glassblower. Chic bedrooms have snazzy wallpaper and a Juliet balcony overlooking the river. Lofty penthouse rooms display original beams, exposed brickwork; two treehouse-style 'pods' have a split-level bedroom, a spacious lounge. In the highly regarded kitchen, Lancastrian produce cooked by head chef Chris Bury has a Gallic tweak; in the convivial bar, regional cask ales and a house brew. Delicacies from the on-site deli, TOTI, can be picked up for the journey home.

MAP 4:D2
Cartford Lane
Little Eccleston PR3 0YP
T: 01995 670166
W: thecartfordinn.co.uk

BEDROOMS: 16. Some in riverside annexe, 1 suitable for disabled, 2 lodges in grounds.
OPEN: all year except 24–28 Dec, restaurant closed Mon lunch, except bank holidays.
FACILITIES: bar, restaurant, delicatessen, free Wi-Fi, in-room TV (Freeview), riverside terrace, garden, parking.
BACKGROUND MUSIC: in public areas.
LOCATION: near Blackpool, Cleveleys, Rossall and Garstang, easily reached from M6 and M55.
CHILDREN: all ages welcomed (some time restrictions in bar, restaurant).
DOGS: not allowed.
CREDIT CARDS: Amex, MC, Visa.
PRICES: per room B&B single £80–£150, double £130–£250. À la carte £33.

LIVERPOOL Merseyside

HOPE STREET HOTEL

In the buzzing heart of the city, opposite the Philharmonic Hall, a Venetian palazzo facade conceals this contemporary hotel, 'ideally placed' for discovering the city's wonderful history and architecture. The former carriage works' 'airy, modern' public spaces have a stripped-back style, all exposed brick walls, vintage metal supports and old beams. Varying in size, Scandi-minimalist bedrooms (white walls, birch floors, cherry wood furniture); some, at the top, have 'wonderful views' of the river or city landmarks. Further extension brings more rooms, together with a spa, pool and cinema. The restaurant is the place for 'delicious' modern British dishes using regional produce; in the bar, informal fare and made-to-order cocktails.

MAP 4:E2
40 Hope Street
Liverpool L19 DA
T: 0151 709 3000
W: hopestreethotel.co.uk

BEDROOMS: 89. Some interconnecting, 2 suitable for disabled.
OPEN: all year.
FACILITIES: lift, bar, lounge, restaurant, private dining rooms, free Wi-Fi, in-room TV (Sky, Freeview), civil wedding licence, functions, leisure facilities, limited parking nearby (£10 charge).
BACKGROUND MUSIC: in public spaces.
LOCATION: city centre, in Hope Street, the main artery through Liverpool's Georgian neighbourhood, bookended majestically by the city's two cathedrals.
CHILDREN: all ages welcomed.
DOGS: allowed in bedroom (£15 per night), public rooms except restaurant.
CREDIT CARDS: Amex, MC, Visa.
PRICES: per room B&B £102–£508, D,B&B £131–£537. À la carte £43.35.

LIVERPOOL Merseyside
THE NADLER LIVERPOOL

In an impressively restored former printworks near the Albert Dock, an 'efficient' hotel offering practical, 'affordably luxurious' accommodation. Well-designed, air-conditioned bedrooms to suit all needs range from a snug double to a two-level suite with a private courtyard. Triple-glazed windows and a compact kitchen (a microwave, a small sink, a fridge, crockery, cutlery) come as standard. Higher-floor rooms have views over the docks. In lieu of a restaurant or bar, guests are given exclusive discounts at selected eateries in the characterful surrounding Ropewalk area. A continental breakfast (ordered in advance) is taken in the lounge.

MAP 4:E2
29 Seel Street
Liverpool L14 AU
T: 0151 705 2626
W: nadlerhotels.com/the-nadler-liverpool

BEDROOMS: 106. Some suitable for disabled.
OPEN: all year.
FACILITIES: lift, lounge, meeting room, free Wi-Fi, in-room TV, 30 mins of free national landline calls per day, parking discounts.
BACKGROUND MUSIC: in public areas.
LOCATION: in Ropewalk area.
CHILDREN: all ages welcomed.
DOGS: assistance dogs allowed.
CREDIT CARDS: Amex, MC, Visa.
PRICES: per room £100–£174.

LOOE Cornwall
THE BEACH HOUSE

'A spoiling welcome' from hosts Rosie and David Reeve sets the tone at their 'ideally located' seafront B&B. Superb coastal views are shared across the comfortable garden room (where tea and home-made cake greet arriving visitors) and homely bedrooms. The latter are 'spotlessly clean' and stocked with teas, fresh coffee, a fridge with fresh milk, 'regularly replenished' bottles of Cornish water. Three rooms face the sea; two access the garden. In the morning, a help-yourself spread (fresh fruit, home-made muffins, yogurt) is followed by tasty cooked-to-order hot dishes. Steps away: coastal trails, rock pools and sandy beaches; fishing villages only a bit further on. The hosts have ready local knowledge.

MAP 1:D3
Marine Drive
Looe PL13 2DH
T: 01503 262598
W: thebeachhouselooe.co.uk

BEDROOMS: 5.
OPEN: all year except Christmas.
FACILITIES: garden room, breakfast room, free Wi-Fi, in-room TV (Freeview), terrace, ½-acre garden, beach opposite, spa treatments.
BACKGROUND MUSIC: classical music in breakfast room.
LOCATION: ½ mile from centre.
CHILDREN: not under 16.
DOGS: only assistance dogs.
CREDIT CARDS: MC, Visa.
PRICES: per room B&B £100–£130. 1-night bookings sometimes refused.

NEW

LUDLOW Shropshire

THE CHARLTON ARMS HOTEL

By Ludford Bridge, watching the River Teme
as it rushes past Cedric and Amy Bosi's popular
pub-with-rooms is an agreeable pastime. Built of
limestone, some of the building's stepped terraces
overhang the water, and afford panoramic views
to Ludlow. Further diversion is found in the
traditional bar, 'heaving' with locals and visitors,
and stocked with draft ales and well chosen
wines. At scrubbed wooden tables in the riverside
dining room, accomplished modern British dishes
and pub classics exhibit a French sway (Cedric
Bosi originates from Lyons). 'Excellent and very
prompt service.' Most of the simply furnished
bedrooms overlook the river; some have a balcony
and outdoor seating; one, a private terrace with
hot tub. Breakfast is a relaxing affair.

MAP 3:C4
Ludford Bridge
Ludlow SY8 1PJ
T: 01584 872813
w: thecharltonarms.co.uk

BEDROOMS: 9.
OPEN: all year.
FACILITIES: bar, restaurant, free Wi-Fi,
2 terraces.
BACKGROUND MUSIC: in bar, restaurant.
LOCATION: by Ludford Bridge, 11-min.
walk to town centre.
CHILDREN: all ages welcomed.
DOGS: well-behaved dogs welcomed.
CREDIT CARDS: MC, Visa.
PRICES: per room B&B from £110.

LUDLOW Shropshire

THE CLIVE ARMS

Just outside Ludlow, a red brick 18th-century inn
on the Earl of Plymouth's Oakly Park estate has
been recently remodelled to include an open-plan
'field-to-fork' restaurant, a cosy snug, spaces for
drinking and socialising. High-beamed rooms
are furnished by local designers; books, paintings,
botanical prints come from the Earl's collection.
Most of the contemporary bedrooms (some suitable
for a family) are in a converted building. At the
back, a new garden and courtyard area provides
all-year alfresco dining. Dana Tase is the new
general manager. Within walking distance, the
Ludlow Farm shop stocks meat and game from
the estate (much of it appears on the restaurant's
seasonal menus), along with artisanal products
from Shropshire and neighbouring regions.

25% DISCOUNT VOUCHERS

MAP 3:C4
Bromfield
Ludlow SY8 2JR
T: 01584 856565
w: theclive.co.uk

BEDROOMS: 17. Most in adjoining
annexes, some on ground floor,
1 suitable for disabled.
OPEN: all year except during the day
on 26 Dec.
FACILITIES: 2 bars, café, restaurant,
snug, private dining room, free Wi-Fi,
in-room TV (Freeview), conference
room, courtyard, beer garden.
BACKGROUND MUSIC: in public areas.
LOCATION: 4 miles NW of Ludlow.
CHILDREN: all ages welcomed.
DOGS: allowed in 1 bedroom, not in
restaurant.
CREDIT CARDS: Amex, MC, Visa.
PRICES: per room B&B £99–£250,
D,B&B £150–£350. À la carte £28–£40.

LUPTON Cumbria

THE PLOUGH

Ideally placed for exploring the Lake District and the Yorkshire Dales, Paul Spencer's laid-back inn sprawls comfortably on the road to Lupton. The 18th-century hostelry has a modern rustic look: wide wooden tables and mismatched chairs, a wood-burning stove, sheepskin-covered bar stools under oak beams. Diners come for well-considered British cooking, with good vegetarian options such as roasted squash, sage and goat's cheese pie. Andy Hoines has returned as acting head chef. Graceful country bedrooms (some snug) have pale furniture, perhaps a brass bed, squashy armchairs, a vast beamed bathroom with slipper bath. Many rooms have glorious views over Farleton Knott. Rooms away from the road are quietest.

25% DISCOUNT VOUCHERS

MAP 4: inset C2
Cow Brow
Lupton LA6 1PJ
T: 015395 67700
W: theploughatlupton.co.uk

BEDROOMS: 6.
OPEN: all year, no accommodation 24/25 Dec.
FACILITIES: lounge, bar, restaurant, free Wi-Fi (signal variable), in-room TV (Freeview), civil wedding licence, terrace, garden, restaurant suitable for wheelchairs, parking.
BACKGROUND MUSIC: in reception, bar and restaurant.
LOCATION: 1 mile off junction 36, M6, 4 miles from Kirkby Lonsdale.
CHILDREN: all ages welcomed.
DOGS: all but 1 bedroom, bar.
CREDIT CARDS: MC, Visa.
PRICES: per room B&B from £85, D,B&B from £115. À la carte £30.

LYME REGIS Dorset

ALEXANDRA HOTEL

With thrilling views over Lyme Bay, the Jurassic Coast and the Cobb, Kathryn Haskins's luxury hotel and restaurant is surrounded by lush clifftop gardens. Owned by her family for decades, the 'beautifully' renovated 18th-century house displays prints by the ornithologist John Gould, whose father was the head gardener. Traditionally styled bedrooms, furnished with plush fabrics and antiques, vary in size and shape; most have sea views; bathrooms are glossy. Two courtyard apartments are ideal for a family. Seasonal, locally sourced meals are served in the soothing restaurant in the orangery, overlooking the garden and sea. The terrace is a scenic spot for an alfresco meal. The hotel's aromatherapy treatments use hand-made Devonshire essential oils.

MAP 1:C6
Pound Street
Lyme Regis DT7 3HZ
T: 01297 442010
W: hotelalexandra.co.uk

BEDROOMS: 23. Plus 2 apartments in courtyard.
OPEN: all year, except 29 Dec–31 Jan.
FACILITIES: bar, sitting room, restaurant, orangery, free Wi-Fi, in-room TV (Freeview), treatment room, civil wedding licence, private functions, limited parking.
BACKGROUND MUSIC: in public areas at meal times.
LOCATION: close to the beach and harbour.
CHILDREN: all ages welcomed.
DOGS: allowed in bar, sitting room, garden.
CREDIT CARDS: MC, Visa.
PRICES: per room B&B single from £95, double £180–£370, D,B&B £256–£446. À la carte £38. 2-night min. stay weekends Apr–end Oct.

LYME REGIS Dorset
DORSET HOUSE

The eye-catching interior of Lyn and Jason Martin's Grade II listed Regency B&B is bested only by the coastal views from its lofty sash windows. Sympathetically furnished, the fire-warmed snug is tailor-made for absorbing a newspaper or book, or raising a toast with locally produced Castlewood bubbly from the honesty bar. Freshly styled bedrooms have clean lines, splashes of blue and mustard; many enjoy sea views. Each is provided with thoughtful extras: thick bathrobes, natural toiletries, artisan teas, home-made brownies. Breakfast treats, Aga-fresh and organic or local produce include apple and rhubarb juice, home-made granola, cake of the day, seasonal fruit, the full Dorset. Wellness and yoga breaks throughout the year.

MAP 1:C6
Pound Road
Lyme Regis DT7 3HX
T: 01297 442055
W: dorsethouselyme.com

BEDROOMS: 5.
OPEN: all year except Christmas.
FACILITIES: snug, breakfast room, reception, free Wi-Fi, in-room TV (Freeview), veranda, paid parking nearby.
BACKGROUND MUSIC: in breakfast room.
LOCATION: 300 yds from town centre.
CHILDREN: all ages welcomed.
DOGS: not allowed.
CREDIT CARDS: Amex, MC, Visa.
PRICES: per room B&B single £85–£165, double £95–£175. 2-night min. stay.

LYNDHURST Hampshire
THE BELL INN

Flanked by two golf courses, this 18th-century coaching inn, in a quiet New Forest hamlet, is 'a great option for a relaxed weekend away'. Updated in modern country style, the red brick building has been in the Eyre family since 1782. 'Simple, pleasant bedrooms', distinct in character, may have a lounge area, beams or a sloping ceiling. Dog-friendly rooms are on the ground floor and in spacious Manor Rooms, a few steps away; four-legged visitors receive a plethora of treats. The cosy bar serves hearty favourites (and a splendid range of gins), while 'more gourmet dishes' are found in the farmhouse-style dining room, perhaps pan-roasted estate partridge or a vegetarian option. A 'good choice' at breakfast includes eggs all ways, kippers.

MAP 2:E2
Lyndhurst SO43 7HE
T: 023 8081 2214
W: bellinn-newforest.co.uk

BEDROOMS: 28. Some interconnecting, 8 on ground floor.
OPEN: all year.
FACILITIES: bar, lounge, 3 dining areas, free Wi-Fi, in-room TV (Freeview), civil wedding licence, beer garden (games, boules pitch), patio, parking.
BACKGROUND MUSIC: in public spaces.
LOCATION: 1 mile from J1 of the M27, on the edge of the New Forest.
CHILDREN: all ages welcomed.
DOGS: allowed in some ground-floor bedrooms, bar, public rooms, not in dining room.
CREDIT CARDS: MC, Visa.
PRICES: per room B&B single from £84, double £109–£199, D,B&B double £159–£249. À la carte £30. 2-night min. stay Fri/Sat.

LYTHAM Lancashire

THE ROOMS

Renewed into a comfortably cool B&B, Andy Baker's Victorian house on the Fylde coast is a rejuvenating spot that takes good design seriously. Sleek and contemporary, the well-fitted bedrooms make a feature of a sloping ceiling, a skylight, a staircase leading to the bathroom; all have good technology (a flat-screen TV with built-in DVD, iPod docking station, DAB Radio), plus under-floor heating and a rain shower in the stylish bathroom. The morning meal (perhaps taken in the walled garden) highlights fresh local produce: a custom-blended smoothie, some locally baked bread, perhaps a Buck's Fizz; cooked dishes include smoked haddock, waffles and pancakes. The helpful host is a fount of knowledge; the best pizza-and-jazz hot spots, a speciality.

25% DISCOUNT VOUCHERS

MAP 4:D2
35 Church Road
Lytham FY8 5LL
T: 01253 736000
W: theroomslytham.co.uk

BEDROOMS: 5. ('Lots of stairs'), plus 2-bed serviced apartment.
OPEN: all year.
FACILITIES: breakfast room, free Wi-Fi, in-room TV (Freeview), meeting facilities, decked garden.
BACKGROUND MUSIC: in breakfast room.
LOCATION: ¼ mile W of town centre.
CHILDREN: all ages welcomed.
DOGS: assistance dogs allowed.
CREDIT CARDS: Amex, MC, Visa.
PRICES: per room B&B single from £110, double from £120.

MALVERN WELLS Worcestershire

THE COTTAGE IN THE WOOD

Everyone agrees about the 'stunning setting' of this 18th-century dower house high in the Malvern hills: 'One of the best views in the country.' A 'modern makeover' has added flamboyant touches. Some visitors found the reception and some public areas rather 'gloomy'; others wrote of a 'restful decor'. In three buildings, bedrooms (some snug, some recently refurbished) have comfortable beds, vintage pieces. The wood-floored bar and restaurant are uplifted by colourful seating; floor-to-ceiling windows give magnificent views across the Severn valley. 'We were pleased to detect real "cheffery" in the menu descriptions. We were satisfied with our starters and mains; vegetables were well executed.'

MAP 3:D5
Holywell Road
Malvern Wells WR14 4LG
T: 01684 588860
W: cottageinthewood.co.uk

BEDROOMS: 30, 4 in Beech Cottage, 19 in Coach House, 10 on ground floor, 1 suitable for disabled.
OPEN: all year.
FACILITIES: bar, restaurant, meeting room, free Wi-Fi, in-room TV (Freeview), 8-acre grounds, parking, public rooms wheelchair accessible, adapted toilet.
BACKGROUND MUSIC: 'quiet, relaxing music' in bar, restaurant.
LOCATION: 4 miles from Malvern Wells.
CHILDREN: all ages welcomed.
DOGS: allowed in some bedrooms (£10 per night), not in public rooms.
CREDIT CARDS: Amex, MC, V..
PRICES: per person B&B £44–£159, D,B&B £79–£149. À la carte £40.

MANCHESTER
THE COW HOLLOW HOTEL

In the hip northern quarter, Mujtaba and Amelia Rana have alchemised a Victorian textile warehouse into a glamorous hotel with a cool cocktail bar. The industrial design (brick walls, a metal stairway, beds made out of railway sleepers) comes with softer touches (a chandelier of laced tree branches), high technology and 'just-fussy-enough' staff. Tempting complimentary treats include bubbles and nibbles from the evening Prosecco cart; milk and cookies later. Come morning, a light breakfast-in-a-bag (granola, yogurt, toast, OJ, croissants, fruit) is brought up to chic, space-efficient bedrooms. Useful media include Netflix access, a Smart TV. The Aviary café offers guests free hot drinks day and night. No restaurant, but discounts at local eateries.

MAP 4:E3
57 Newton Street
Manchester M1 1ET
T: 0161 228 7277
w: cowhollow.co.uk

BEDROOMS: 16.
OPEN: all year except 25/26 Dec.
FACILITIES: cocktail bar, free Wi-Fi, in-room TV (Netflix).
BACKGROUND MUSIC: in cocktail bar.
LOCATION: in Manchester's Northern Quarter.
CHILDREN: all ages welcomed (sharing with one adult, max. room occupancy of 2).
DOGS: not allowed.
CREDIT CARDS: Amex, MC, Visa.
PRICES: per room B&B £89–£199.

MANCHESTER
DIDSBURY HOUSE

Between two parks in a leafy urban village, a sophisticated retreat in a refurbished Victorian villa within easy reach of the city. One of the Eclectic Hotels group (see Eleven Didsbury Park, next entry), the voguish B&B was designed with a boutique mindset: vintage prints and statement wallpaper, tempered by fresh flowers, books, open fires and sink-into sofas. At the top of a grand staircase, a beautiful stained-glass window. Tasteful bedrooms, some split-level, retain original features (high windows, delicate cornices). Inviting afternoon teas are followed by light bites and aperitifs in one of the relaxed lounges or on the walled terrace which has heating and a canopy. Leisurely weekends are de rigueur: breakfast is served until noon.

MAP 4:E3
Didsbury Park
Manchester M20 5LJ
T: 0161 448 2200
w: eclectichotels.co.uk/didsbury-house

BEDROOMS: 27. 1 suitable for disabled.
OPEN: all year.
FACILITIES: bar, 2 lounges, breakfast room, free Wi-Fi, in-room TV (Sky), civil wedding licence, meeting room, walled terrace.
BACKGROUND MUSIC: in public areas, volume adjusted to suit the time of day and atmosphere.
LOCATION: The city centre and airport are a quick train (or taxi) ride away.
CHILDREN: all ages welcomed.
DOGS: not allowed.
CREDIT CARDS: Amex, MC, Visa.
PRICES: per room £120–£300. Breakfast £16, à la carte £25.

MANCHESTER
ELEVEN DIDSBURY PARK

A peaceful haven, the spacious walled garden of this suburban Victorian town house is a tempting place to hang loose. Rattan chairs swing from beams, sun loungers, hammocks and a sofa in a shady gazebo await. Elsewhere, the relaxing vibe spreads to the sitting room's squashy sofas, cosy nooks and open fire, the high-ceilinged reception with its hand-crafted wood bar. Comfortable, snug bedrooms are spread over three floors; they have a private balcony, a roll-top bath. In all, spa-worthy toiletries, a minibar, a butler tray with fresh milk. Breakfast arrives in the bright conservatory. The city centre and airport are a short train-ride or drive away. (Eclectic Hotels group, see Didsbury House, previous entry).

MAP 4:E3
11 Didsbury Park
Manchester M20 5LH
T: 0161 448 7711
W: eclectichotels.co.uk/
    eleven-didsbury-park

BEDROOMS: 20. 1, on ground floor, suitable for disabled.
OPEN: all year.
FACILITIES: 2 lounge/bars, free Wi-Fi, in-room TV (Sky), veranda, walled garden, wedding/conference facilities, parking.
BACKGROUND MUSIC: all day in public areas.
LOCATION: Didsbury, Manchester.
CHILDREN: all ages welcomed.
DOGS: not allowed.
CREDIT CARDS: Amex, MC, Visa.
PRICES: per room from £150. Breakfast £16, à la carte £28.

MARAZION Cornwall
GODOLPHIN ARMS

Across the causeway from St Michael's Mount, which, 'caught in the evening sunset really is a magical prospect', James and Mary St Levan's 'fabulous (and fabulously dog-friendly)' inn wins praise for its 'excellent accommodation' and 'attentive, professional staff'. Uplifting coastal colours and local artwork brighten the bedrooms; many have superb views; village-view rooms, 'comfortable, smart, modern', have less character; in all are bathrobes, good toiletries. Some are accessed via 'steep stairs'. Caught-that-day seafood is a highlight of the 'fresh, tasty' menu in the light-filled restaurant with its breezy Scandi vibe (and spectacular terrace). 'The cod tasted as good as only fresh cod can.' Breakfast includes smoked salmon, buttermilk pancakes, the full Cornish.

MAP 1:E1
West End
Marazion TR17 0EN
T: 01736 888510
W: godolphinarms.co.uk

BEDROOMS: 10. Some suitable for disabled.
OPEN: all year.
FACILITIES: 2 bars, split-level dining area, free Wi-Fi, in-room TV (Freeview), wedding/function facilities, 2 terraces, parking, dining room wheelchair accessible.
BACKGROUND MUSIC: in public areas, occasional live acoustic music.
LOCATION: 4 miles E of Penzance.
CHILDREN: all ages welcomed.
DOGS: allowed in 2 bedrooms, designated dining area, on terrace.
CREDIT CARDS: MC, Visa.
PRICES: per room B&B £100–£295. À la carte £30.

MARCHAM Oxfordshire

B&B RAFTERS

Sigrid Grawert is the warm hostess of this inviting B&B on the edge of a pretty village, eight miles from Oxford. The stylish, modern bedrooms have delicate accents, leafy plants and upscale technology; some have a freestanding bath and a private balcony. The fluffy robes, welcoming drinks tray, power shower and clever bathroom storage are standard. Soft drinks and snacks can be sought from an honesty-box mini-fridge on the landing. The relaxing suntrap garden has an outdoor seating area. Award-winning breakfasts are communal gatherings over freshly squeezed orange juice, home-baked bread, home-made jams, a superb porridge menu. Vegetarian and special diets are catered for.

25% DISCOUNT VOUCHERS

MAP 2:C2
Abingdon Road
Marcham OX13 6NU
T: 01865 391298
W: bnb-rafters.co.uk

BEDROOMS: 4.
OPEN: all year except Christmas, New Year.
FACILITIES: lounge, breakfast room, free Wi-Fi, in-room TV (Freeview), garden, parking.
BACKGROUND MUSIC: none.
LOCATION: 3 miles W of Abingdon, 8 miles S of Oxford.
CHILDREN: over-11s welcomed.
DOGS: not allowed.
CREDIT CARDS: MC, Visa.
PRICES: per room B&B £67–£139. 2-night min. stay bank holiday weekends.

MARGATE Kent

THE READING ROOMS

On a Georgian square, Louise Oldfield and Liam Nabb have restored their townhouse B&B with a careful balance of a thoroughly 21st-century make-over with a 200-year-old history. In each airy bedroom, occupying an entire floor, technological flourishes (under-floor heating, flat-screen TV, etc) work with stripped wooden floors, enormous sash windows, original shutters and vintage plasterwork. Each design is different, but in common are the large Provençal-style bed, neutral hues, fresh flowers, vintage books; a 'cavernous' bathroom with a freestanding roll-top bath. Breakfast is a leisurely spread (freshly pressed juice, freshly baked sourdough bread, cooked options) at a bedroom table overlooking the square, 'beautifully served' at a time of your choosing.

MAP 2:D5
31 Hawley Square
Margate CT9 1PH
T: 01843 225166
W: thereadingroomsmargate.co.uk

BEDROOMS: 3.
OPEN: all year.
FACILITIES: free Wi-Fi, in-room TV (Freeview), parking vouchers available.
BACKGROUND MUSIC: none.
LOCATION: 4 mins' walk from the seafront and Old Town.
CHILDREN: not under 17.
DOGS: not allowed.
CREDIT CARDS: Amex, MC, Visa.
PRICES: per room B&B £95–£190. 2-night min. stay weekends and bank holidays.

MATLOCK BATH Derbyshire
HODGKINSON'S HOTEL

With 'superb views' of spectacular limestone cliffs, Chris and Zoe Hipwell's Georgian town house hotel near the River Derwent is 'a haven, in a quirky town'. Most of the restored features (tiled entrance hall, ornate glasswork, the wood-and-glass bar) originate from the ownership of Victorian wine merchant Job Hodgkinson, who also made use of the cave (dating back to Roman times) to store his wares. Some of the traditionally furnished bedrooms have river views; in one, a four-poster bed; another a roll-top bath; in each, a handsome bathroom or walk-in shower. Modern British menus are served in the restaurant; breakfast options include an omelette, kedgeree or a full vegetarian. 'Excellent walks, some challenging', straight from the door.

MAP 3:B6
150 South Parade
Matlock Bath DE4 3NR
T: 01629 582170
w: hodgkinsons-hotel.co.uk

BEDROOMS: 8.
OPEN: all year except Christmas week, restaurant closed Sun, Mon eve, except for guests who have pre-booked and bank holidays.
FACILITIES: sitting room, bar, restaurant, free Wi-Fi, in-room TV (Freeview), garden, limited parking (road parking nearby).
BACKGROUND MUSIC: radio (daytime), 'lounge, easy listening' (evening) in bar and restaurant.
LOCATION: centre of village, 1 mile from Matlock and Cromford.
CHILDREN: all ages welcomed.
DOGS: allowed in some bedrooms (£15 per night), not in lounge or restaurant.
CREDIT CARDS: MC, Visa.
PRICES: per room B&B single £77–£125, double £95–£165, D,B&B £149–£209. Set dinner £27–£30. 2-night min. stay on Sat.

NEW

MEVAGISSEY Cornwall
PEBBLE HOUSE

Blow all cares away with a welcoming glass of champagne on arrival at Andrea and Simon Copper's sleekly designed, child-free retreat. Perched high above a 14th-century fishing village, there are uninterrupted sea views stretching across the bay to historic Chapel Point and beyond. All but one of the modern bedrooms look towards the water; most have floor-to-ceiling windows, the better to marvel at the panorama over Mevagissey Bay. Breakfast, light lunches, Cornish cream teas are served in the breakfast room/lounge (comfy sofas, board games), or on the front terrace, in fine weather. Picnics can be ordered to take out on the South West Coast Path, steps away.

MAP 1:D2
Polkirt Hill
Mevagissey PL26 6UX
T: 01726 844466
w: pebblehousecornwall.co.uk

BEDROOMS: 3. 1 on ground floor with private terrace.
OPEN: Feb–Nov, self-catering only, Aug, Christmas.
FACILITIES: breakfast room/lounge, free Wi-Fi, in-room TV (Freeview), Sky in some rooms), terrace, small functions, parking.
BACKGROUND MUSIC: in breakfast room.
LOCATION: on South West Coastal Path, approx. 7 mins to Mevagissey, 25-min. drive from Truro.
CHILDREN: not under 17.
DOGS: not allowed.
CREDIT CARDS: Amex, MC, Visa.
PRICES: per room B&B £170–£215.

MIDHURST Sussex
THE CHURCH HOUSE

Visitors to Fina Jurado's genteel B&B, in a medieval market town, are in for a surprise: a string of four 13th-century cottages has been knocked through to create a 'wonderful' open space. Guests are welcomed with tea and home-baked cake in one of the elegant sitting rooms and eating areas, each with polished oak floors, oriental carpets, period features and vintage finds. Most bedrooms are up the curving staircase. Stylishly rustic, one has a dramatic, high-beamed ceiling, super king-size bed, stained-glass window and in-room roll-top bathtub; another has a velvet chaise longue, and makes full use of centuries-old timbers to create a mezzanine. Communal breakfasts bring organic yogurts, home-made preserves, locally sourced eggs and sausages.

MAP 2:E3
Church Hill
Midhurst GU29 9NX
T: 01730 812990
w: churchhousemidhurst.com

BEDROOMS: 5. 1, on ground floor, suitable for disabled.
OPEN: all year except Christmas.
FACILITIES: sitting room/dining room, conservatory, free Wi-Fi, in-room TV (Sky, Freeview), garden.
BACKGROUND MUSIC: none.
LOCATION: town centre.
CHILDREN: all ages welcomed.
DOGS: not allowed.
CREDIT CARDS: MC, Visa.
PRICES: per room B&B £140–£165.

MILLOM Cumbria
BROADGATE HOUSE

Visitors to Diana Lewthwaite's country house in Beatrix Potter country are guaranteed a colourful welcome – its grounds, designed into 'garden rooms', provide blooms across all seasons. With a dramatic backdrop of the Lakeland fells, the white-painted Georgian house has been home to the owner's family for almost 200 years. Flowery guest bedrooms have pretty country character and garden views. Bathrooms are shared (but only ever with members of the same party), and have a throne loo, freestanding bath. Handsome public spaces have antique furniture, ancestral portraits, plush fabrics, and an original fireplace or two. Keen birders should carry binoculars; snow buntings, flycatchers and other sorts have graced the gardens.

MAP 4: inset C2
Broadgate
Millom LA18 5JZ
T: 01229 716295
w: broadgate-house.co.uk

BEDROOMS: 5.
OPEN: all year except 1–23 Dec.
FACILITIES: sitting room, dining room, breakfast room, free Wi-Fi, 2-acre garden.
BACKGROUND MUSIC: none.
LOCATION: in Broadgate Estate, off A595.
CHILDREN: over-10s welcomed.
DOGS: not allowed in the house.
CREDIT CARDS: none accepted.
PRICES: per room B&B single £55, double £95. Dinner (by arrangement) £30.

MISTLEY Essex

THE MISTLEY THORN

Constable country reaches to the doorstep of this affable, historic restaurant-with-rooms in a village known for its swans. Transformed by chef Sherri Singleton and her husband, David McKay, the 18th-century coaching inn, on the site where Essex witches were tried, is a welcoming space. Menus specialise in well-prepared Mersea oysters and locally landed seafood, as well as interesting vegetarian options, all served by 'cheerful, willing, attentive' young staff in the lively beamed drinking and dining areas (smart tongue-and-groove panelling, a wood-burning stove). Accessed by steep stairs, bedrooms (quietest at the back) are soothingly decorated, with nice extras (dressing gowns, luxury toiletries, home-made biscuits); four have views down the Stour estuary.

MAP 2:C5
High Street
Mistley CO11 1HE
T: 01206 392821
W: mistleythorn.co.uk

BEDROOMS: 12. 3 with separate entrance, 1 suite in Little Thorn Cottage.
OPEN: all year except Christmas Day.
FACILITIES: bar, restaurant, free Wi-Fi, in-room TV (Freeview), outdoor seating, cookery workshops (special room rates for attendees).
BACKGROUND MUSIC: in restaurant during mealtimes.
LOCATION: village centre, 9 miles W of Harwich.
CHILDREN: all ages welcomed.
DOGS: small/medium dogs allowed in some rooms and in 'quiet part' of restaurant.
CREDIT CARDS: Amex, MC, Visa.
PRICES: per room B&B (Tues–Sat) £90–£170, D,B&B £120–£220.

MORECAMBE Lancashire

THE MIDLAND

In a 'superb position on the marine parade', this 'Art Deco wonder' was restored to its former glory by the small English Lakes group. The architecture, a backdrop for the Poirot series, 'adds a touch of historic enchantment'. 'The joy is the long dining room' in the 'lovely' Sun Terrace restaurant, where every table has a sea view through floor-to-ceiling windows, which follows the curve of the building. 'The food was excellent, the wine list extensive.' Reached up a 'charming' spiral staircase (or by a small lift), curved corridors, quirky bedrooms. 'Our spacious room had an excellent bed, a neat arrangement of cupboards; a fridge with milk.' Morning brings 'a good breakfast'. Ideal for the midday Isle of Man ferry.

MAP 4:D2
Marine Road West
Morecambe LA4 4BU
T: 01524 424000
W: englishlakes.co.uk

BEDROOMS: 44. 2 suitable for disabled.
OPEN: all year.
FACILITIES: lift, lounge, bar/café, restaurant, free Wi-Fi, in-room TV, function rooms, civil wedding licence, beauty treatments, parking.
BACKGROUND MUSIC: '1930s/1950s music' in bar, restaurant.
LOCATION: overlooking Morecambe Bay.
CHILDREN: all ages welcomed.
DOGS: welcomed (not in restaurant).
CREDIT CARDS: Amex, MC, Visa.
PRICES: per room B&B £148–£400, D,B&B £206–£456.

NEW

MAP 4:B4
St Mary's Lane
Morpeth NE61 6BL
T: 01670 293293
W: stmarysinn.co.uk

MORPETH Northumberland

ST MARY'S INN

There's a 'jovial, relaxed' feel at this modern pub-with-rooms. The 'cleverly' renovated former hospital building is in an unlikely setting, on the edge of a new housing estate. Bedrooms are styled with a mix of modern furnishings and antique pieces. 'Ours was uncluttered, clean and bright, with a well-lit bathroom and a generous supply of toiletries.' In the 'heaving' bar try a pint of the pub's own locally brewed St Mary's Ale. In the restaurant, classic pub grub or local specialities. Breakfast is served in a high-ceilinged room 'flooded with light': a buffet has 'excellent' juice, 'very good' croissants, pains au chocolat; pick from 'interesting' cooked. Jesmond Dene House, Newcastle upon Tyne (see main entry), is under the same ownership.

BEDROOMS: 11. 1 suitable for disabled.
OPEN: all year.
FACILITIES: lift, 4 bar areas, dining room, private dining rooms, free Wi-Fi, in-room TV (Freeview), grassed area at front.
BACKGROUND MUSIC: 'easy listening' in bar and dining areas.
LOCATION: 2½ miles W of Stannington.
CHILDREN: all ages welcomed.
DOGS: allowed in 1 bedroom, bar, not in restaurant.
CREDIT CARDS: Amex, MC, Visa.
PRICES: per room B&B £99–£119. D,B&B £129–£159. À la carte £27.

MAP 1:E2
Polurrian Road
Mullion TR12 7EN
T: 01326 240421
W: polurrianhotel.com

MULLION Cornwall

POLURRIAN ON THE LIZARD

Bird's-eye views of the Lizard peninsula, little luxuries and a relaxed air turn this cliff-top hotel into a stress-busting retreat. Its large gardens and 'wonderful position' above the beach provide activities to suit all ages, stretching from tennis or yoga sessions to sand-modelling, kayaking and surfing. Stunning coastal views extend into a range of bedrooms, many offering space for an extra cot; some interconnect to accommodate a larger family. In the restaurant, informal Mediterranean-inspired dishes made with Cornish ingredients include pizzas, cooked in a wood-fired oven. Perfect for panorama-watching, afternoon tea is taken in the Vista lounge or sun terrace on balmy days. Coastal paths lead from the doorstep; pampering treatments await in the spa.

BEDROOMS: 41. Some on ground floor, 1 suitable for disabled. Plus four 3-bedroom self-catering villas.
OPEN: all year.
FACILITIES: lift, lounge, snug, dining room, cinema, games room (table football, table tennis), spa, indoor pool, 9-metre outdoor pool (Apr–Sept), free Wi-Fi, in-room TV, civil wedding licence, function facilities, 12-acre grounds, terrace, tennis court, climbing frame.
BACKGROUND MUSIC: in public areas.
LOCATION: in Mullion village.
CHILDREN: all ages welcomed.
DOGS: allowed in some bedrooms, not in restaurant.
CREDIT CARDS: MC, Visa.
PRICES: per room B&B from £119, D,B&B from £159.

NETLEY MARSH Hampshire
SPOT IN THE WOODS

On the edge of the New Forest, this comfortable Victorian villa in large grounds is a reviving spot. Formerly TerraVina, it has metamorphosed into a large airy kitchen café offering a relaxed space for local get-togethers and respite for visitors after a long forest walk. An all-day menu, including breakfast and brunch, salads and afternoon tea is served until 4 pm by a 'happy team', overseen by Nina Basset. (Sadly, her husband, Gérard, died in January 2019.) Peaceful bedrooms have a little seating area, capsule coffee machine, good lighting. 'The sparkling clean bathroom had a claw-footed bath, organic toiletries, generous towels.' Three rooms have a patio garden, three a roof terrace. The terrace is 'a great place to sit in the summer'. Artisan products in the shop.

MAP 2:E2
174 Woodlands Road
Netley Marsh SO40 7GL
T: 02380 293784
W: spotinthewoods.co.uk

BEDROOMS: 11. 3 on ground floor, 1 suitable for disabled.
OPEN: all year.
FACILITIES: café, free Wi-Fi, in-room TV (Sky, Freeview), 1½-acre grounds, bicycle storage.
BACKGROUND MUSIC: none.
LOCATION: 8 miles W of Southampton, 4 miles N of Lyndhurst.
CHILDREN: all ages welcomed.
DOGS: allowed in some bedrooms, all public areas.
CREDIT CARDS: Amex, MC, Visa.
PRICES: per room B&B single £75–£145, double £85–£155. 2-night bookings preferred weekends.

NEWBY BRIDGE Cumbria
THE SWAN HOTEL & SPA

By an arched stone bridge, 'an imposing edifice' surrounded by gardens that sweep down to the River Leven, the Bardsley family's 'good-value', child-friendly former 17th-century coaching house is a welcoming spot. There's a playful vibe in the public areas (parrot-print wallpaper, modern florals, pompom-fringed lampshades); the spa is cool-contemporary. A spectrum of bedrooms: from top-floor adults-only suites, to interconnecting family rooms. 'Excellent' food in the restaurant and 'clearly popular' bar area, where low ceilings, good lighting, colourful furnishings create a 'pleasant brasserie atmosphere'. 'A 'truly outstanding' breakfast included home-made jams and hand-cut ham. Seating on a terrace is along the riverbank.

MAP 4: inset C2
The Colonnade
Newby Bridge LA12 8NB
T: 01539 531681
W: swanhotel.com

BEDROOMS: 54. Some suitable for disabled, plus 5 self-catering cottages.
OPEN: all year.
FACILITIES: sitting room, library, Swan Inn, restaurant, juice bar, free Wi-Fi, in-room TV (Sky), civil wedding licence, function facilities, spa (treatments), indoor pool, gym, terrace, 10-acre grounds, parking, mooring.
BACKGROUND MUSIC: in public areas.
LOCATION: 9 miles from Ulverston, Grange-over-Sands and Bowness-on-Windermere.
CHILDREN: all ages welcomed.
DOGS: allowed in pub only.
CREDIT CARDS: MC, Visa.
PRICES: per room B&B £110–£450. À la carte £30. 2-night min. stay bank holiday weekends.

NEWMARKET Suffolk

BEDFORD LODGE

Amid 'lovely' rose gardens and landscaped lawns, this family-run hotel combines old-fashioned comfort and modern flourishes with 'superb service'. The town's heritage races through the former Georgian hunting lodge; jockey silks and original artwork sit 'delightfully' against the regal palette and dark leather armchairs. In many of the 'well-maintained' bedrooms (some compact), guests awake to the sight of prize-winning steeds going through their paces on the training gallops next door; the best room has a pretty balcony. In the restaurant, the menu has plenty of healthy options as well as tempting indulgences (cakes, a champagne list). Breakfasts are 'excellent'. Outdoor dining on a 'delightful' terrace. Pampering treatments in the luxury spa.

MAP 2:B4
Bury Road
Newmarket CB8 7BX
T: 01638 663175
W: bedfordlodgehotel.co.uk

BEDROOMS: 77. Some suitable for disabled.
OPEN: all year.
FACILITIES: bar, sitting room, library, restaurant, private dining room, free Wi-Fi, in-room TV (Sky, Freeview), civil wedding licence, function facilities, 3-acre grounds, spa facilities, gym, indoor pool, parking.
BACKGROUND MUSIC: in public areas.
LOCATION: in heart of city, close to A14 and all motorways.
CHILDREN: all ages welcomed.
DOGS: allowed on the terrace only.
CREDIT CARDS: Amex, MC, Visa.
PRICES: per room B&B from £120.
2-night min. stay bank holiday weekends.

NEWQUAY Cornwall

THE HEADLAND HOTEL

Surf's up! Above Fistral Beach, the Armstrong family's child- and dog-friendly hotel overlooks one of Cornwall's surfing hotspots. Its Surf Sanctuary teaches kitesurfing, stand-up paddleboarding and coasteering. The impressive Victorian building (with self-catering cottages) offers plenty of less adventurous diversions. Buckets and spades for the beach; games, books and DVDs for rainy days. Pampering treatments in the luxury spa team with breathtaking seascapes. Most of the modern bedrooms (ask for one with a balcony) have coastal hues and views. Taken on the laid-back ocean-front terrace or in sophisticated restaurant Samphire, chef Christopher Archambault's menus highlight locally caught fish and Cornish produce.

MAP 1:D2
Headland Road
Newquay TR7 1EW
T: 01637 872211
W: headlandhotel.co.uk

BEDROOMS: 95. 1 suitable for disabled, plus 39 self-catering cottages in the grounds.
OPEN: all year.
FACILITIES: lounges, bar, 2 restaurants, free Wi-Fi, in-room TV, civil wedding licence, conference/event facilities, 10-acre grounds, indoor and outdoor heated swimming pools, spa, gym.
BACKGROUND MUSIC: in restaurant.
LOCATION: on a rugged headland overlooking Fistral Beach.
CHILDREN: all ages welcomed.
DOGS: allowed in bedrooms and public spaces (£24 per night).
CREDIT CARDS: Amex, MC, Visa.
PRICES: per room B&B single £70–£425, double £120–£475, D,B&B £180–£535.
À la carte £39.

NEWQUAY Cornwall
LEWINNICK LODGE

Wake to the sound of the sea and exhilarating
Atlantic views at Pete and Jacqui Fair's cliff-edge
hotel hovering on the edge of Pentire Headland.
Sleek and stylish inside, it has a laid-back vibe
and environment-friendly principles. Most of
the minimalist bedrooms watch over a vista that
stretches towards Towan Head and pristine
Fistral Beach; each has a large comfy bed, home-
made biscuits, binoculars, Bluetooth speakers and
DAB radios for music lovers; organic toiletries, a
slipper bath. Brasserie-style menus showcase the
freshest seafood, with monthly-changing specials.
Diners can sit by floor-to-ceiling windows in the
'busy, informal' restaurant and bar, or outside
on the spectacular decked terrace. Good walks
from the door.

MAP 1:D2
Pentire Headland
Newquay TR7 1QD
T: 01637 878117
W: lewinnicklodge.co.uk

BEDROOMS: 17. Some suitable for
disabled.
OPEN: all year.
FACILITIES: lift, bar, lounge, snug,
restaurant, free Wi-Fi, in-room
TV (Sky, Freeview), in-room spa
treatments, terrace, beer garden,
parking.
BACKGROUND MUSIC: in public spaces.
LOCATION: Pentire Headland,
Newquay.
CHILDREN: all ages welcomed.
DOGS: allowed in some bedrooms and
bar only.
CREDIT CARDS: MC, Visa.
PRICES: per room B&B £120–£300.
À la carte £29.50.

NORTHALLERTON Yorkshire
CLEVELAND TONTINE

Travellers between London and Sunderland
have long stopped at this Georgian hostelry
which skirts the North York moors. The
former coaching inn (Provenance Inns) is much
liked nowadays for its warm welcome, homely
atmosphere and 'delicious food'. The drama of the
'wonderful, light-filled' drawing room is as much
about its 'quirky' features (plasterwork starfish,
elephants, vines) as its bold styling. Equally
dramatic are the well-appointed, eclectically
designed bedrooms, some with a four-poster, a
stand-alone bath. Candlelit dinners are cooked
'with flair'; a generous breakfast is locally sourced.
Quintessentially English afternoon teas are served
in the garden or morning room. The Carpenters
Arms, Felixkirk (see main entry), is a sister hotel.

MAP 4:C4
Staddlebridge
Northallerton DL6 3JB
T: 01609 882671
W: theclevelandtontine.com

BEDROOMS: 7.
OPEN: all year.
FACILITIES: bar, lounge, morning
room, bistro, free Wi-Fi, in-room TV
(Freeview), room service, function
facilities, garden, parking.
BACKGROUND MUSIC: in public spaces.
LOCATION: 8 miles NE of
Northallerton.
CHILDREN: all ages welcomed.
DOGS: allowed in bar, lounge.
CREDIT CARDS: Amex, MC, Visa.
PRICES: per room B&B £130–£170,
D,B&B £200–£240. Set menu from
£22, à la carte £35.

NORWICH Norfolk
NORFOLK MEAD
By the River Bure, 'perfect peace and quiet' drifts across 'lush grounds' up to James Holliday and Anna Duttson's 'splendid', wisteria-hung Georgian house. The relaxed atmosphere is in part thanks to 'informal, attentive' staff; spa treatments and plenty of cosy nooks do the rest. 'Well-equipped, individually decorated bedrooms' have uplifting decor; some have a fireplace, a four-poster, an in-room egg bath. 'Our room was spacious, comfortable, light, with its own seating area.' The summer houses and cottages would suit groups. The dining room serves 'excellent, beautifully fresh and elegantly presented' dishes. 'Home-made marmalade and excellent black pudding, sausages and smoked bacon' for breakfast. The hotel's day boat can be hired.

MAP 2:B5
Church Loke, Coltishall
Norwich NR12 7DN
T: 01603 737531
w: norfolkmead.co.uk

BEDROOMS: 15. 2 in cottages, 3 in summer houses.
OPEN: all year.
FACILITIES: lounge, bar, snug, restaurant, private dining, 2 beauty treatment rooms, free Wi-Fi, in-room TV (Freeview), civil wedding licence, 8-acre grounds, walled garden, fishing lake.
BACKGROUND MUSIC: in public spaces.
LOCATION: approx. 20 mins' drive from Norwich.
CHILDREN: all ages welcomed.
DOGS: allowed in some rooms in grounds (£20 per night).
CREDIT CARDS: MC, Visa.
PRICES: per room B&B £135–£360, À la carte £38.50.

OUNDLE Northamptonshire
LOWER FARM
Adjoining their small arable farm, a series of outbuildings has been converted by the Marriott family into homely B&B rooms. Surrounded by fields and fresh air, it's a wholesome setting. Robert Marriott and his brother, John, run the farm; Caroline Marriott is the 'friendly, accommodating' hostess. Simple, attractive bedrooms, arranged around a central courtyard, occupy the former milking parlour and stables; several may be connected to suit a family. The hearty farmhouse breakfast might include porridge with fresh cream, a farmer's butty, steak and eggs (a speciality); ideal for tackling walking and cycling tracks from the door, including the Nene Way footpath which runs through the farm. The village pub is a short stroll away.

25% DISCOUNT VOUCHERS

MAP 2:B3
Main Street
Oundle PE8 5PU
T: 01832 273220
w: lower-farm.co.uk

BEDROOMS: 10. All on ground floor, 1 suitable for disabled.
OPEN: all year.
FACILITIES: breakfast room, free Wi-Fi, in-room TV (Freeview), courtyard garden, parking.
BACKGROUND MUSIC: radio 'if guests wish' in breakfast room.
LOCATION: 3 miles from Oundle.
CHILDREN: all ages welcomed.
DOGS: allowed in 2 bedrooms, not in public rooms.
CREDIT CARDS: Amex, MC, Visa.
PRICES: per person B&B £50–£90.

OXFORD Oxfordshire

THE BELL AT HAMPTON POYLE

Owner George Dailey revitalised this honey-stone roadside pub, north of Oxford, from a tired boozer into a popular village hub. Locals flock for pub classics, British dishes and pizzas, cooked in a huge wood-fired oven with a viewing window in the open kitchen. Served with butter sauces, fish and shellfish is simply grilled; meat comes from local producers. In the pub, flagstone floors and 18th-century beams have been preserved; deep leather chairs are set around a large log fire. Bedrooms, 'very comfortable and very clean', are well stocked with tea-/coffee-making facilities and posh toiletries; a bath or a monsoon shower. Blenheim Palace and Bicester Village are not far away.

MAP 2:C2
11 Oxford Road
Oxford OX5 2QD
T: 01865 376242
W: thebelloxford.co.uk

BEDROOMS: 9. 1 on ground floor.
OPEN: all year.
FACILITIES: bar, restaurant, free Wi-Fi, in-room TV (Freeview), function facilities, terrace, parking.
BACKGROUND MUSIC: in bar.
LOCATION: 10 miles from Oxford, Bicester Village and Woodstock.
CHILDREN: all ages welcomed (no extra beds or facilities).
DOGS: allowed in bar, not in bedrooms.
CREDIT CARDS: Amex, MC, Visa.
PRICES: per room B&B single £95–£130, double £120–£175. À la carte £30 (£12.50 2-course, £17.50 3-course set menus Mon–Thurs, 6 pm–7.30 pm).

PENZANCE Cornwall

ARTIST RESIDENCE CORNWALL

Tucked into a sloping street behind the harbour, this 'achingly cool' 17th-century house has 'lovely staff', 'well-appointed bedrooms' and 'tasty breakfasts'. Typical of Justin and Charlotte Salisbury's eclectic collection (see main entries for Artist Residence in London, Brighton and South Leigh, Oxfordshire), it brims with 'intriguing artwork' and vintage flourishes. Bedrooms, mildly eccentric, are all different: one is small; another has expansive views; a third, a hand-painted mural soaring up the walls and across the ceiling. Informal meals draw diners to the 'quirky' Cornish Barn restaurant, and fully stocked bar and smokehouse in the covered garden. 'Doorsteps of sourdough bread; first-rate' orange juice at breakfast.

MAP 1:E1
20 Chapel Street
Penzance TR18 4AW
T: 01736 365664
W: artistresidence.co.uk/our-hotels/cornwall

BEDROOMS: 23. 1 suite, plus a 3-bedroom cottage in grounds.
OPEN: all year.
FACILITIES: bar, restaurant, garden, free Wi-Fi, in-room TV (Freeview).
BACKGROUND MUSIC: in public areas.
LOCATION: town centre.
CHILDREN: all ages welcomed.
DOGS: allowed in some rooms, restaurant.
CREDIT CARDS: Amex, MC, Visa.
PRICES: per room £85–£440. À la carte £35. 1-night stay sometimes refused weekends.

PENZANCE Cornwall

VENTON VEAN

A frisbee fling from the waterfront, Philippa McKnight and David Hoyes's intimate B&B is a soothing place to be beside the seaside. Avid art collectors, the owners' use of striking colours, vintage furnishings and arty flourishes complement the house's Victorian stained-glass panels and fireplaces. There's a lush garden, full of unusual plants; an airy sitting room with plenty of books. Spacious bedrooms in contemporary hues, some with painted floorboards, have a king-size bed and thoughtful extras (refreshments, bathrobes, eco-friendly toiletries); one has an antique chandelier, hooks reclaimed from the Savoy's cloakroom in London. Breakfasts keep food -miles low, creativity high: perhaps Mexican tortillas with hot salsa and fried eggs.

MAP 1:E1
Trewithen Road
Penzance TR18 4LS
T: 01736 351294
W: ventonvean.co.uk

BEDROOMS: 5. 1 with adjoining single room, suitable for a family.
OPEN: all year except 25/26 Dec.
FACILITIES: sitting room, dining room, free Wi-Fi, in-room smart TV, garden.
BACKGROUND MUSIC: at breakfast in dining room.
LOCATION: 7 mins' walk from the centre of Penzance and Penzance seafront.
CHILDREN: over-4s welcomed.
DOGS: not allowed.
CREDIT CARDS: MC, Visa.
PRICES: per room B&B single £74–£93, double £84–£103. 2-night bookings preferred peak season (May–Sept).

PRESTON Lancashire

BARTON GRANGE HOTEL

In the former country pile of a cotton mill owner, the Topping family's large hotel is 'a quality product in all respects', and within easy access of the M6, makes 'an excellent stop-over spot'. Some of the well-appointed bedrooms are compact, but are 'well designed to maximise space'. Time spent enjoying the residents-only spa facilities, including a swimming pool and new treatment rooms, rejuvenates before dinner. Served in the Walled Garden restaurant, the locally sourced 'beautifully cooked' dishes include butter-poached Goosnargh chicken breast, mushroom risotto, sweetcorn purée, asparagus, and Dijon sauce. Unhurried mornings call for savouring the breakfast buffet, followed by a copious cooked; a 'grab-and-go' breakfast bag speeds things up.

MAP 4:D2
746–768 Garstang Road
Preston PR3 5AA
T: 01772 862551
W: bartongrangehotel.com

BEDROOMS: 51. 8 in Garden House in the grounds, 1 suitable for disabled.
OPEN: all year.
FACILITIES: lift, lounge, snug, bistro/wine bar, meeting/private dining room, free Wi-Fi, in-room TV (Sky), civil wedding licence, leisure centre (swimming pool, sauna, gym), parking.
BACKGROUND MUSIC: none.
LOCATION: 6 miles from Preston city centre.
CHILDREN: all ages welcomed.
DOGS: not allowed.
CREDIT CARDS: Amex, MC, Visa.
PRICES: per room B&B from £69. À la carte £25.

NEW

RAMSGATE Kent

ALBION HOUSE

Breathe the sea air at Ben and Emma Irvine's beautifully restored hotel atop Ramsgate's East Cliff. Enwrapped by a wrought iron balcony, the Regency building overlooks the beach and Royal Harbour. In the past, it has hosted politicians, actors, even Princess Victoria while recuperating from an illness. Inside, a sense of grandeur remains, with high ceilings, ornate cornices, carved fireplaces. Pale fabrics, pendant lighting, mirrors and plants contrast with deep heritage-coloured walls. Bedrooms, some high up in the eaves, one on the lower ground floor, are softly decorated and have modern bathrooms. (A busy road at the front may affect light sleepers.) Brunch, lunch and dinner are served in Townley's restaurant, where sea views are assured.

MAP 2:D6
Albion Place
Ramsgate CT11 8HQ
T: 01843 606630
W: albionhouseramsgate.co.uk

BEDROOMS: 14.
OPEN: all year.
FACILITIES: bar, restaurant, free Wi-Fi, in-room TV, private dining room.
BACKGROUND MUSIC: in public spaces.
LOCATION: above Ramsgate's Main Sands beach.
CHILDREN: all ages welcomed.
DOGS: allowed, by arrangement.
CREDIT CARDS: MC, Visa.
PRICES: per room B&B £105–£215.

RAMSGATE Kent

THE FALSTAFF

Two 'tastefully refurbished' Regency town houses near the harbour combine into this 'buzzy, friendly' pub-with-rooms. Guests can take a real ale by the wood-burning stove, or have coffee with 'a slice of obviously home-made cake'. Recent visitors enjoyed 'a nice lunch, personable service, good atmosphere'. Sometimes there's live piano music. 'It's all a bit pleasantly unpredictable.' Heritage shades, vintage furnishings, oriental rugs and fine prints characterise the well-liked bar and neatly done bedrooms. Each room is different, with 'a terrific bathroom'. 'Really pleasing breakfasts: good coffee and full English, not a cornflake packet in sight'; four nights a week, 'an interesting dinner menu'. The large garden has plenty of seating and hosts summer barbecues.

MAP 2:D6
16–18 Addington Street
Ramsgate CT11 9JJ
T: 01843 482600
W: thefalstafframsgate.com

BEDROOMS: 8. Plus 2 self-catering apartments.
OPEN: all year.
FACILITIES: bar, restaurant, deli, free Wi-Fi, in-room TV (Freeview), garden, parking, bicycle storage.
BACKGROUND MUSIC: in restaurant.
LOCATION: in town, a minute's walk to the seafront.
CHILDREN: all ages welcomed.
DOGS: allowed in 1 bedroom (garden access).
CREDIT CARDS: Amex, MC, Visa.
PRICES: per room B&B £89–£139.

REETH Yorkshire
CAMBRIDGE HOUSE

In Herriot country, Robert and Sheila Mitchell's 'relaxing, welcoming' B&B offers great walking and cycling routes, straight from the door – and 'splendid' facilities for wet or muddy kit. The 'genuinely caring' hosts provide packed lunches, a drying room, a boot-cleaning service and bicycle storage. Comfortable south-facing bedrooms with 'superb views' over Swaledale have fresh milk, biscuits, chocolates (all except the single have a bath and shower). Afternoons bring tea and home-made cake to the conservatory; the lounge has deep armchairs, a log fire in winter, wines and local beers from an honesty bar. The 'excellent' breakfast is a gastronomic adventure. Every taste is catered for, from fruit compote to smoked haddock, speciality crumpets or a full Yorkshire.

MAP 4:C3
Arkengarthdale Road
Reeth DL11 6QX
T: 01748 884633
W: cambridgehousereeth.co.uk

BEDROOMS: 5.
OPEN: all year, except 20 Dec–7 Feb.
FACILITIES: lounge, dining room, conservatory, free Wi-Fi, in-room TV (Freeview), small garden, terrace, parking.
BACKGROUND MUSIC: none.
LOCATION: 500 yds from centre of Reeth.
CHILDREN: not under 12.
DOGS: 1 well-behaved dog allowed, by arrangement, in bedroom, conservatory (not to be left unattended, £5 per night).
CREDIT CARDS: MC, Visa.
PRICES: per room B&B single £80–£100, double £95–£110.

RICHMOND Yorkshire
EASBY HALL

Overlooked by the ruins of Easby Abbey, Karen and John Clarke provide luxurious B&B accommodation in a rustic country house setting. Afternoon tea in the drawing room is a relaxed affair. Spacious suites, in a separate wing from the Georgian house, are sumptuous: a huge bed dressed with a velvet coverlet, throws and piles of cushions; a log-burner or open fire – a champagne fridge in each adds to the ambience. The dreamy gardens are fringed by woodland walks, an orchard, a paddock. Breakfast, at a time to suit the guest, has home-made preserves with fruit from the kitchen garden; poached pears from the orchard; local bacon; eggs from resident hens. Richmond and the gateway to the Dales is a short walk along the riverbank.

MAP 4:C3
Easby
Richmond DL10 7EU
T: 01748 826066
W: easbyhall.com

BEDROOMS: 3. 1 suitable for disabled, plus 2-bed self-catering cottage.
OPEN: all year.
FACILITIES: drawing room, dining room, free Wi-Fi, in-room TV (Freeview), 4-acre gardens, paddocks, loose boxes and stables for horses.
BACKGROUND MUSIC: none.
LOCATION: less than 2 miles E of Richmond.
CHILDREN: all ages welcomed.
DOGS: obedient, house-trained dogs allowed.
CREDIT CARDS: none accepted.
PRICES: per room B&B from £216.

RIPLEY Surrey

BROADWAY BARN

Just a few minutes' drive from RHS Wisley, Mindi McLean's refurbished B&B in a 200-year-old listed barn is filled with little luxuries. Creatively decorated bedrooms have fresh flowers, dressing gowns, slippers, chocolates, home-made shortbread. Bathrooms, with under-floor heating, are stocked with fine toiletries; one has a raised slipper bath set against illuminated brick walls. Taken in the conservatory, breakfast has plenty of choice. Tables, overlooking the walled garden, are laden with fresh fruit, home-baked bread, home-made granola and preserves, village honey; daily specials might include waffles with strawberries and maple syrup. In the evening, perhaps a foray to the Michelin-starred Clock House restaurant in the village High Street.

MAP 2:D3
High Street
Ripley GU23 6AQ
T: 01483 223200
W: broadwaybarn.com

BEDROOMS: 4. Plus self-catering flat and cottages.
OPEN: all year.
FACILITIES: conservatory sitting room/breakfast room, free Wi-Fi, in-room TV (Freeview), small garden.
BACKGROUND MUSIC: soft music during breakfast.
LOCATION: centre of small historic village.
CHILDREN: not under 12.
DOGS: not allowed.
CREDIT CARDS: Amex, MC, Visa.
PRICES: per room B&B £120.

NEW

RUDGEWAY Gloucestershire

OLD CHURCH FARM

On the edge of the village, Christopher Trim and Kathryn Warner's Grade II listed manor house is on a site dating back to the Domesday Book. It takes its name from the 12th-century church that lies in ruins in the grounds (a national monument). Inside, the spacious rooms have stone mullioned windows, impressive fireplaces; the wood-panelled snug has a Tudor plaster ceiling. Comfortable, country house bedrooms, each with refreshments and home-made biscuits, an alarm clock, CD-player, DAB radio, have a view of the rose garden, the surrounding countryside or serene churchyard. Breakfast makes full use of fruit, vegetables and herbs grown in the walled garden. 24 hours' notice is required for Kathryn's home-cooked dinners.

25% DISCOUNT VOUCHERS

MAP 3:E5
Church Road
Rudgeway BS35 3SQ
T: 01454 418212
W: old-church-farm.co.uk

BEDROOMS: 7.
OPEN: all year.
FACILITIES: snug, drawing room, breakfast room, dining room, free Wi-Fi, in room TV (Freeview), conference facilities, civil wedding licence, skittles alley, croquet, table tennis, terrace, 8-acre gardens.
BACKGROUND MUSIC: classical or guests' own choice, in drawing room, dining room.
LOCATION: on the edge of a South Gloucestershire village.
CHILDREN: not under 12.
DOGS: not allowed.
CREDIT CARDS: Amex, MC, Visa.
PRICES: per person B&B single £115–£175, double £130–£190, D,B&B £165–£262. À la carte £25.

RYE Sussex

THE HOPE ANCHOR

The shipbuilders, boozy sailors and notorious Tenterden smuggling gang that once formed the clientele of this 18th-century watering hole have been replaced by peace-seeking travellers bent on finding a decent meal. At the end of a cobbled street, high above the town, guests of the family-run hotel stay in cosy rooms that have old-fashioned tendencies but are 'warm and comfortable', and supplied with good essentials: a hospitality tray, a clock radio, slippers. Some rooms have a four-poster bed; many offer long views across the quayside, the Marshes and Camber Castle. Traditional English dishes dominate the menu; meat from Romney Marsh; daily fish specials showcase catch of the day, straight from Rye Bay.

MAP 2:E5
Watchbell Street
Rye TN31 7HA
T: 01797 222216
W: thehopeanchor.co.uk

BEDROOMS: 16. 3 in cottage and apartments, 10 yds away, 1 on ground floor with patio.
OPEN: all year.
FACILITIES: bar, lounge, restaurant, private dining room, free Wi-Fi, in-room TV (Freeview), wedding facilities, parking permits supplied.
BACKGROUND MUSIC: in public areas.
LOCATION: in the citadel of a medieval town.
CHILDREN: all ages welcomed.
DOGS: allowed in some bedrooms, not in restaurant.
CREDIT CARDS: Amex, MC, Visa.
PRICES: per room B&B £100–£140, D,B&B £160–£180.

ST ALBANS Hertfordshire

SOPWELL HOUSE HOTEL

This country retreat occupies an extended 300-year-old manor house, once the home of Lord Louis Mountbatten. The 'well-run' hotel has plush seating in the cosy cocktail lounge and an 'airy, pretty conservatory'. A choice for diners: the 'bustling brasserie' for classic bistro dishes, or the restaurant's sophisticated dining. 'Modern, clean lines' abound in the 'neat, if slightly characterless' bedrooms, which have 'an excellent shower'; in the stable block are stylish mews suites. A gallery of signed football shirts reflects the hotel's popularity with top teams (Barcelona stayed here). There is a popular spa; several walled gardens are within the extensive grounds. Breakfast was 'plentiful, nicely served with freshly squeezed orange juice'.

MAP 2:C3
Cottonmill Lane
St Albans AL1 2HQ
T: 01727 864477
W: sopwellhouse.co.uk

BEDROOMS: 128. 16 mews suites.
OPEN: all year.
FACILITIES: cocktail lounge, bar, 2 restaurants, meeting and conference facilities, free Wi-Fi, in-room TV (Sky, BT), civil wedding licence, spa, indoor pool, gym, 12-acre grounds.
BACKGROUND MUSIC: in cocktail lounge.
LOCATION: 1½ miles from the city centre and rail station.
CHILDREN: over-11s welcomed.
DOGS: not allowed.
CREDIT CARDS: Amex, MC, Visa.
PRICES: per room £154–£394, D,B&B £249–£499. 3-course set dinner menu £31.50 (brasserie), £39.50 (restaurant).

ST AUSTELL Cornwall

LOWER BARNS

A faintly bohemian B&B on the Roseland peninsula throws riotous colour and eye-catching features together in joyful combinations. Each well-equipped, spacious, sybaritic bedroom in Janie and Mike Cooksley's Cornish abode (and in several quirky buildings accessed through the garden) has its own style. One has a stone-built sauna; another a gypsy caravan parked outside its front door; some have a chandelier, perhaps a modern four-poster. Informal dinners, arranged in advance, are served in the 'party shed' in the wild flower garden. Guests in three garden suites have breakfast delivered to the room; the rest gather in the conservatory for fresh fruit compotes, home-baked muffins, locally smoked fish, farm sausages, eggs all ways.

MAP 1:D2
Bosue
St Austell PL26 6EU
T: 01726 844881
w: lowerbarnswedding.co.uk

BEDROOMS: 8. 4 in the grounds, 1 suitable for disabled.
OPEN: all year.
FACILITIES: conservatory breakfast room, dining room, free Wi-Fi, in-room TV (BT), civil wedding licence, small function facilities, garden, gym, spa treatments, outdoor hot tub, parking.
BACKGROUND MUSIC: equipment 'so guests can play their own music' in one dining room.
LOCATION: 7 miles SW of St Austell, 1 mile past Lost Gardens of Heligan.
CHILDREN: all ages welcomed.
DOGS: allowed in 2 suites, with own bedding.
CREDIT CARDS: MC, Visa.
PRICES: per room B&B £130–£175, D,B&B £230–£280. Set dinner £50 (BYOB). 2-night min. stay weekends.

ST IVES Cornwall

HEADLAND HOUSE

A tranquil retreat from the bustle of nearby St Ives, Mark and Fenella Thomas's chic Edwardian house stands above Carbis Bay. Characterful, well-equipped bedrooms share marine and pale hues, but are otherwise individual; a garden room has loungers on a private deck; in another, beach views are best admired from a broad window seat; some rooms have a stand-alone bath near exposed stone walls. Afternoons bring home-made cake to the room, while a garden hammock is a relaxed spot to tackle a book from the lounge's collection, or a complimentary evening drink. Cornish breakfasts, hearty and organic, kick-start the day with a view across the water.

MAP 1:D1
Headland Road
St Ives TR26 2NS
T: 01736 796647
w: headlandhousehotel.co.uk

BEDROOMS: 9. 3 off the courtyard garden.
OPEN: Apr–mid-Oct.
FACILITIES: snug lounge, conservatory breakfast room, free Wi-Fi, in-room TV (Freeview), large front garden, terrace, parking.
BACKGROUND MUSIC: none.
LOCATION: 1½ miles from St Ives centre, 5 mins from Carbis Bay beach.
CHILDREN: over-15s welcomed.
DOGS: allowed.
CREDIT CARDS: MC, Visa.
PRICES: per room B&B from £139. 2-night min. stay preferred.

ST IVES Cornwall

TREVOSE HARBOUR HOUSE

'A great deal of effort has been put in by the owners and it shows.' Angela and Olivier Noverraz's 'beautifully appointed' 1850s mid-terrace house has bags of style and an eco-conscious ethos. Unique pieces are upcycled from old furniture; sustainable products used throughout. Tip-top tech mingles with vintage finds, coastal hues wash over the design-conscious decor. The cosy lounge has deep-cushioned chairs to sink into, books to borrow and cocktails to mix in the honesty bar. Individually styled bedrooms each have a large bed and organic toiletries; most overlook the harbour and the bay. Breakfast (outside or in the bright breakfast room) has home-made preserves, 'smoothie shots', good veggie-friendly cooked choices.

MAP 1:D1
22 The Warren
St Ives TR26 2EA
T: 01736 793267
w: trevosehouse.co.uk

BEDROOMS: 6. 1 in rear annexe.
OPEN: 22 Mar–Dec.
FACILITIES: snug, breakfast room, free Wi-Fi, in-room TV (BT), in-room treatments, terrace, limited parking close by.
BACKGROUND MUSIC: in snug.
LOCATION: town centre.
CHILDREN: over-11s welcomed.
DOGS: not allowed.
CREDIT CARDS: Amex, MC, Visa.
PRICES: per room B&B £170–£295. 2-night min. stay.

NEW

ST LEONARDS-ON-SEA Sussex

THE CLOUDESLEY

A short walk from the seafront, photographer Shahriar Mazandi has created an artistic, eco-friendly B&B. This offbeat bolt-hole brims with books, African masks and original art in the two sitting rooms. Restful bedrooms, named after Persian poets, each have a large, comfy bed with organic bedlinen, eclectic decor featuring the host's own photography, a mosaic-tiled shower in the bathroom; no TV, but plenty to read. The semi-wild flower garden testifies to Shahriar's Chelsea Flower Show gold medal. Organic breakfasts, eaten in the room, in the bright dining room or out on the bamboo terrace, are sourced locally; choose from fresh kippers, a raw vegan breakfast salad, an Armagnac omelette. Fantastic fuel for exploring Derek Jarman's garden nearby.

MAP 2:E4
7 Cloudesley Road
St Leonards-on-Sea TN37 6JN
T: 07507 000148
w: thecloudesley.co.uk

BEDROOMS: 5.
OPEN: all year.
FACILITIES: dining room, 2 sitting rooms, honesty bar, no TV, garden, free Wi-Fi, patio, treatment rooms.
BACKGROUND MUSIC: none.
LOCATION: 10 mins from St Leonards-on-Sea town centre.
CHILDREN: not under 17.
DOGS: not allowed.
CREDIT CARDS: MC, Visa.
PRICES: per room B&B from £90. 1-night stays sometimes refused.

ST LEONARDS-ON-SEA Sussex

ZANZIBAR INTERNATIONAL HOTEL

Brimming with an 'interesting collection' of curios from far-flung lands, Max O'Rourke's seafront hotel is both 'splendidly quirky' and 'utterly relaxed'. While guests enjoy a welcome drink, 'efficient staff' take care of luggage. The distinctive bedrooms are set over several floors. Decorated to reflect different destinations, they have a 'huge variety': Antarctica is dazzlingly white, with a faux polar bear throw, floor-to-ceiling windows and 'wonderful sea views'; Manhattan is a loft with jukebox and aquarium coffee table. 'The busy road in front quietens at night.' A beachy bar offers cocktails and water views. Breakfast comes with the day's newspapers, plus suggestions for outings and eateries.

MAP 2:E4
9 Eversfield Place
St Leonards-on-Sea TN37 6BY
T: 01424 460109
W: zanzibarhotel.co.uk

BEDROOMS: 8. 1 on ground floor.
OPEN: all year.
FACILITIES: bar, breakfast room, free Wi-Fi, in-room TV (Freeview), garden.
BACKGROUND MUSIC: 'quiet' in bar.
LOCATION: seafront, 650 yds W of Hastings pier.
CHILDREN: not under 5.
DOGS: allowed in bedrooms, public areas (£30 per night).
CREDIT CARDS: Amex, MC, Visa.
PRICES: per room B&B from £115.

NEW

ST MARTIN'S Isles of Scilly

KARMA ST MARTIN'S

Facing powdery white sand on a stunning stretch of coastline, this low-built, stone-clad building (the only hotel on the island) has panoramic views across to Teàn Sound and Tresco. Tranquil bedrooms include bathrobes, a safe and seating. De-stress with a glass of chilled wine, dispensed from a card-operated machine in the book-lined bar. Seafood platters, lobster, crab and foraged plants are menu mainstays in Cloudesley Shovell restaurant, or eaten alfresco in the sub-tropical gardens. Staff are friendly, laid-back. Four-legged companions are welcomed with a bowl and blanket, and can relish a dish from Karma's Kanine Kitchen, and toast their good fortune with a 'Pawsecco' or 'Dog Beer'. Exotic spa treatments reflect the hotel group's Asian connection.

MAP 1: inset C1
Lower Town
St Martin's TR25 0QW
T: 01720 422368
W: karmastmartins.com

BEDROOMS: 30.
OPEN: (Easter) 10 Apr–end Oct.
FACILITIES: bar, restaurant, 2 lounges, free Wi-Fi, in-room TV (Freeview), civil wedding licence, treatment room, games room for children, 7-acre grounds.
BACKGROUND MUSIC: jazz in bar, restaurant, muted on request.
LOCATION: 2 mins' walk from Lower Town Quay.
CHILDREN: all ages welcomed.
DOGS: dogs allowed in lower dining room, some bedrooms.
CREDIT CARDS: Amex, MC, Visa.
PRICES: per room B&B £150–£600, DB&B £230–£680. À la carte £50.

ST MARY'S Isles of Scilly

ST MARY'S HALL HOTEL

Just beyond Hugh Town, this 'consistently good' hotel is minutes from two sandy beaches, and across from the Victorian church that shares its name. It is run by the 'knowledgeable, helpful' manager, Roger Page; it has 'unfailingly friendly, efficient' staff. A wide staircase leads to bright, comfortable bedrooms with a large bed, luxury toiletries, home-made biscuits on a well-stocked tray; fresh milk, delivered daily in an insulated flask. Most rooms overlook the sub-tropical garden; one has spectacular views over the harbour to neighbouring islands. Chef Ben Hingston's 'delicious' dishes exploit fresh local seafood, meat from the owners' rare breeds farm. Breakfast brings freshly squeezed juice, smoked Devon trout with scrambled eggs.

MAP 1: inset C1
Church Street
St Mary's TR21 0JR
T: 01720 422316
W: stmaryshallhotel.co.uk

BEDROOMS: 27.
OPEN: 16 Mar–16 Oct.
FACILITIES: bar, 2 lounges, restaurant, free Wi-Fi, in-room TV (Freeview).
BACKGROUND MUSIC: in public areas.
LOCATION: 5-min. walk to the town centre, 10-min. walk to quay.
CHILDREN: all ages welcomed.
DOGS: allowed in ground-floor suites, public rooms.
CREDIT CARDS: MC, Visa.
PRICES: per room single from £89, double from £173, D,B&B double from £217. À la carte £45.

ST MAWES Cornwall

THE ST MAWES HOTEL

With long views across to St Anthony's Head, David and Karen Richards's casual, quayside spot is liked for its seaside charm and 'very good situation'. No residents' lounge, rather 'a large, open-plan ground-floor area'; 'beautiful' interiors are all cheerily striped seating, local art, seafaring paraphernalia. Cocktails, nibbles and locals' salty tales are served in the lively bar; great plates, perhaps fish pie and seasonal vegetables or pizza in the Upper Deck restaurant, where 'provenance is important'. 'Very comfortable' bedrooms sport marine stripes; and under-floor heating in the bathroom. Some suit a family. Breakfast includes toasted brioche with seared banana, peanut butter, Cornish honey. Big-sister hotel The Idle Rocks is up the street (see main entry).

MAP 1:E2
Harbourside
St Mawes TR2 5DN
T: 01326 270270
W: stmaweshotel.com

BEDROOMS: 7. 4 in annexe around the corner.
OPEN: all year.
FACILITIES: bar, lounge, restaurant, function/private dining room, free Wi-Fi, in-room TV (Freeview).
BACKGROUND MUSIC: all day in public areas, occasional live music in bar.
LOCATION: village centre.
CHILDREN: all ages welcomed.
DOGS: allowed in bar, 2 bedrooms (bed, towel, bowl, treats, maps of local walks, £30 per stay).
CREDIT CARDS: Amex, MC, Visa.
PRICES: per room B&B from £195. 2-night min. stay weekends.

ST MELLION Cornwall
PENTILLIE CASTLE

Historic grounds tumble away from this
'magnificent, lovingly restored' castellated
mansion on the banks of the Tamar river. The
Coryton family home for nearly 300 years, the
grand country B&B has stately sitting rooms filled
with antiques, old mirrors and original artwork;
the open fires are ideal spots for afternoon tea or
pre-dinner libation. On sunny days, the terrace
takes over. Glorious views pour into the spacious
bedrooms, each named after a family character.
The morning meal hinges on estate-produced
jams, honey, apple juice and eggs. Come evening,
a three-course dinner every Thursday; on others,
a 'DIY' Aga-warmed supper – a selection includes
Looe Bay fish pie; slow-cooked beef shin lasagne
(order in advance).

MAP 1:D3
Paynters Cross
St Mellion PL12 6QD
T: 01579 350044
W: pentillie.co.uk

BEDROOMS: 9. 1, on ground floor,
suitable for disabled.
OPEN: all year, exclusive use Christmas
and New Year.
FACILITIES: morning room, drawing
room, dining room, guest kitchen, free
Wi-Fi, in-room TV (Freeview), civil
wedding licence, 55-acre grounds,
terrace, heated outdoor pool.
BACKGROUND MUSIC: during meals.
LOCATION: near St Mellion.
CHILDREN: all ages welcomed.
DOGS: assistance dogs allowed in
downstairs area, other dogs restricted
to heated boot room, on lead in garden.
CREDIT CARDS: Amex, MC, Visa.
PRICES: per room B&B single
£145–£225, double £160–£240. Set
menu £35.

SALCOMBE Devon
SALCOMBE HARBOUR HOTEL

'It was not only the view that made our stay, but
the whole ambience,' writes a Guide regular this
year, about this Victorian hotel and spa on the
Salcombe estuary. Most of the soothingly yachtie
bedrooms have a balcony, huge windows, and
binoculars to exploit the 'stupendous' panorama.
Inside, maritime stripes and shades of blue mix
with porthole mirrors and the occasional lifebelt.
Ice and lemon slices are delivered to the bedroom
each evening, to complement gin or sherry from
the decanters. Devon produce and the day's catch
are served in Jetty restaurant and on the sunny
terraces. While 'expensive', the final bill was 'a
pleasant surprise'. The Chichester Harbour Hotel
and Southampton Harbour Hotel (see Shortlist
entries) are sisters.

MAP 1:E4
Cliff Road
Salcombe TQ8 8JH
T: 01548 844444
W: harbourhotels.co.uk/hotels/salcombe

BEDROOMS: 50. Some suitable for
disabled.
OPEN: all year.
FACILITIES: bar/lounge, Jetty
restaurant, free Wi-Fi, in-room TV
(Freeview), civil wedding licence, spa,
private moorings.
BACKGROUND MUSIC: in public areas.
LOCATION: town centre.
CHILDREN: all ages welcomed.
DOGS: allowed in some bedrooms, not
in public rooms.
CREDIT CARDS: Amex, MC, Visa.
PRICES: per room B&B £185–£235,
D,B&B £225–£445. À la carte £50.
1-night bookings sometimes refused.

SALCOMBE Devon

SOUTH SANDS

This lively hotel, in a sheltered cove, is surrounded by a wide terrace which faces the beach. Coastal colours fill the 'informal' lounge and breezy bedrooms. Rooms, including suites large enough for a family, have seaside touches (seascape paintings; a seagull sculpture); those at the front have sea views. Preprandials out on the terrace might be followed by fresh-as-can-be seafood and other locally sourced fare, perhaps pan-fried monkfish, savoy cabbage, caramelised cabbage purée, pickled vegetables. Breakfast is extensive. Coastal paths start from the back door; a beautiful National Trust garden, Overbeck's, is up the hill. For pedestrians, the most fun way to reach the lively town centre is by taking the sea tractor, then the small ferryboat.

MAP 1:E4
Bolt Head
Salcombe TQ8 8LL
T: 01548 845900
W: southsands.com

BEDROOMS: 27. 1 room suitable for disabled.
OPEN: all year.
FACILITIES: bar, restaurant, free Wi-Fi, in-room TV (Freeview), civil wedding licence, terrace.
BACKGROUND MUSIC: in restaurant and bar area.
LOCATION: on South Sands Beach just outside Salcombe town centre (a little bit more than a mile).
CHILDREN: all ages welcomed.
DOGS: allowed in some bedrooms.
CREDIT CARDS: MC, Visa.
PRICES: per room B&B £225–£595. À la carte £45. 1-night bookings refused weekends in peak season.

SALISBURY Wiltshire

LEENA'S GUEST HOUSE

A 15-minute walk from the cathedral, the Street family's 'first-rate guest house' provides good-value B&B accommodation. Headed by Gary Heikki Street, the 'informative, very helpful', multilingual hosts enjoy practising their French, German and Suomi with guests. The Edwardian house is modest and traditionally styled, but 'well decorated, comfortably appointed'. 'Immaculate' bedrooms have 'a comfortable bed, a choice of pillows', modern bathrooms; the hospitality tray is supplied with chocolates and biscuits; some road noise might be expected. Served on pretty blue-and-white crockery, 'imaginative' breakfasts have 'good' granola, and delicious cooked dishes with healthy alternatives; in season, berries from the garden. A riverside footpath leads to the centre.

MAP 2:D2
50 Castle Road
Salisbury SP1 3RL
T: 07814 897907
W: www.leenasguesthouse.co.uk

BEDROOMS: 6. 1 on ground floor.
OPEN: May–Dec.
FACILITIES: lounge, breakfast room, free Wi-Fi, in-room TV (Freeview), garden, parking.
BACKGROUND MUSIC: ambient from kitchen during breakfast.
LOCATION: 12 mins' walk via pretty riverside footpaths to town centre and Salisbury cathedral.
CHILDREN: all ages welcomed.
DOGS: not allowed.
CREDIT CARDS: none accepted.
PRICES: per room B&B £90–£150.

SCARBOROUGH Yorkshire

PHOENIX COURT

MAP 4:C5
8–9 Rutland Terrace
Scarborough YO12 7JB
T: 01723 501150
w: phoenixcourt.co.uk

Overlooking the surf-licked sands of North Bay and within walking distance of the town, Donna and Mike Buttery's welcoming guest house is in two cream-painted Victorian town houses. The front leads directly on to the cliff-tops and paths down to the sea. Many of the spacious, no-nonsense bedrooms (two suitable for a family) have superb sea views through large bay windows; all have a hospitality tray, toiletries. In the dining room, in contemporary grey and pale hues, a 'great breakfast': a Yorkshire smoked kipper, Wensleydale cheese and fruit bread, a full English (Mike's big breakfast), and vegetarian and vegan versions. Walkers and cyclists welcomed; a packed lunch (£6) can be ordered in advance. The private car park is a bonus.

BEDROOMS: 12. 1 on ground floor.
OPEN: Mar–Nov.
FACILITIES: lounge (bar area), breakfast room, free Wi-Fi, in-room TV (Freeview), drying facilities, parking.
BACKGROUND MUSIC: local radio in breakfast room.
LOCATION: 10 mins' walk from the town centre and South Bay.
CHILDREN: all ages welcomed.
DOGS: not allowed.
CREDIT CARDS: MC, Visa.
PRICES: per room B&B £44–£95. 2-night min. stay weekends.

SEDBERGH Cumbria

THE MALABAR

MAP 4:C3
Garths
Sedbergh LA10 5ED
T: 01539 620200
w: themalabar.co.uk/rooms

At the foot of the Howgill fells in the far western Dales, the Lappins' B&B is surrounded by glorious scenery. Guests are welcomed with cakes and sandwiches on arrival; connoisseurs will appreciate the 12 different loose leaf teas. The restored 18th-century cattle barn now houses chic, spacious rooms with original stone walls and oak beams; warm colours and block-print fabrics reflect the owners' time spent in India and south-east Asia – as does the freshly made lassi at breakfast. Taken in the dining room or in the garden (at a time to suit), it also offers home-baked bread, seasonal juices, local specials, perhaps wild boar bacon, venison sausages. Weekday suppers, a monthly Indian supper club, Friday Feasts (Apr to Oct) may be pre-booked.

BEDROOMS: 6. 1 family suite with private entrance.
OPEN: all year except for arrivals on Sun, Mon, Tues, Wed in Jan, Feb.
FACILITIES: bar, sitting room, dining room, free Wi-Fi, in-room TV (Freeview), ⅓-acre garden, parking.
BACKGROUND MUSIC: in public areas during afternoon tea and in the evenings.
LOCATION: 2 miles W of Sedbergh.
CHILDREN: all ages welcomed.
DOGS: allowed in 1 suite.
CREDIT CARDS: MC, Visa.
PRICES: per room single £120–£190, double £140–£260. À la carte £30. 1-night bookings sometimes refused Easter, Christmas, New Year.

SEDGEFORD Norfolk

MAGAZINE WOOD

The wild Norfolk coast is minutes away from
the rustic luxury of Pip and Jonathan Barber's
chic B&B in the countryside. Each luxurious
suite has light, contemporary hues, harmonious
prints and artwork, its own entrance and terrace.
Boutique styling supplies each with a large bed,
mood lighting; in the bathroom, a deep bath
and separate shower. Thoughtful extras add to
the cocoon: books, DVDs, binoculars; a tablet
computer serves as online concierge, to summon
breakfast, download a newspaper, create a
bespoke itinerary. The day begins 'anytime': a
well-stocked cupboard contains muesli, cereals,
fruits and croissants; milk, organic yogurts are
in the fridge. Cooked breakfasts are ordered the
night before (charged extra).

MAP 2:A5
Peddars Way
Hunstanton PE36 5LW
T: 01485 750740
W: magazinewood.co.uk

BEDROOMS: 3. all on ground floor, 2 in
converted barn.
OPEN: all year except Christmas.
FACILITIES: free Wi-Fi, in-room
TV (on-demand movies), in-room
treatments, 3-acre grounds, parking.
BACKGROUND MUSIC: none.
LOCATION: 5 miles from Hunstanton.
CHILDREN: infants welcomed.
DOGS: allowed (not unattended) in
1 bedroom.
CREDIT CARDS: MC, Visa.
PRICES: per room B&B £105–£144.
Cooked breakfast £5–£7. 2-night min.
stay most weekends.

NEW

SHANKLIN Isle of Wight

HAVEN HALL

Above the glistening ocean, Arielle and David
Barratt's clifftop Arts and Crafts house lies in
gated seclusion at the end of a cul-de-sac; a
coastal path leads down to Sandown Bay and
the beach. For four years, the engaging owners,
who live in a separate wing, painstakingly
remodelled the interior, adding unusual furniture
and modern-day essentials to existing features.
Distinctive bedrooms are equipped with air-
conditioning; thick towels, LED mirrors and
old-style washstand basins in indulgent, modern
bathrooms. Most of the bedrooms, the restful
drawing room and a flowery terrace overlook
the award-winning gardens and out to sea. The
breakfast buffet, laid out in a bright, airy room,
makes a satisfying start to the day's activities.

25% DISCOUNT VOUCHERS

MAP 2:E2
5 Howard Road
Shanklin PO37 6HD
T: 07914 796494
W: havenhall.uk

BEDROOMS: 14. 7 available for self-
catering.
OPEN: Apr–Oct.
FACILITIES: bar, lounge restaurant,
free Wi-Fi, in-room TV (Freeview),
civil wedding licence, outdoor pool
(heated May–Sept), grass tennis court,
croquet, 2-acre grounds.
BACKGROUND MUSIC: none.
LOCATION: on E side of island,
overlooking the English Channel.
CHILDREN: not under 12.
DOGS: welcomed in 3 rooms.
CREDIT CARDS: Amex, MC, Visa.
PRICES: per room B&B £420–£875.

SHANKLIN Isle of Wight

RYLSTONE MANOR

Atop the cliffs of Sandown Bay, Mike and Carole Hailston's 'delightfully relaxing' island B&B enjoys a 'lovely' setting: it stands within the perimeter of public gardens with steps leading down to the sands. There is plenty of space inside the 19th-century gentleman's residence, where homely sitting rooms and bar sport rich hues, period furnishings and leaded windows. Some of the traditionally styled bedrooms offer tantalising glimpses of the sea through leafy trees. A secluded private garden surrounds the house. It's an easy walk to the shops and restaurants in Old Shanklin. The Hailstons are founts of Isle of Wight information.

MAP 2:E2
Rylstone Gardens
Shanklin PO37 6RG
T: 01983 862806
W: rylstone-manor.co.uk

BEDROOMS: 8.
OPEN: 8 Feb–2 Nov.
FACILITIES: drawing room, bar/lounge, dining room, free Wi-Fi, in-room TV (Freeview), terrace, ¼-acre garden in 4-acre public gardens.
BACKGROUND MUSIC: none.
LOCATION: Shanklin old village.
CHILDREN: over-16s welcomed.
DOGS: assistance dogs allowed.
CREDIT CARDS: MC, Visa.
PRICES: per room B&B single £110–£125, double £135–£165, D,B&B double £193–£223. 2-night min. stay peak season.

SHEFFORD WOODLANDS Berkshire

THE PHEASANT INN

Popular with the racing fraternity and couples in search of a weekend escape, this old sheep drover's inn is on the village outskirts, with wide views over the Berkshire Downs. Its modern rural revamp from owner Jack Greenall has given the cosy, traditional snug a rich colour scheme. The old settle and deep armchair by an open fire are ideal to sink into with a good book – and there are plenty to borrow. Fresh, comfortable bedrooms have well-chosen fabrics, wallpaper and artwork, along with a Roberts radio, Bramley toiletries, plush robes. Chef Andy Watts's elevated pub food (locally sourced where possible) is served in the large, light-filled restaurant. Breakfast is an occasion worth rising for.

MAP 3:E6
Ermin Street
Shefford Woodlands RG17 7AA
T: 01488 648284
W: thepheasant-inn.co.uk

BEDROOMS: 11.
OPEN: all year.
FACILITIES: bar, restaurant, private dining room, free Wi-Fi, in-room TV (Sky), courtyard, garden, parking.
BACKGROUND MUSIC: in public areas.
LOCATION: 15 mins from Newbury.
CHILDREN: all ages welcomed.
DOGS: allowed, by arrangement.
CREDIT CARDS: Amex, MC, Visa.
PRICES: per person B&B £115–£135. À la carte £28.

SHERBORNE Dorset

THE EASTBURY HOTEL

The 'lovely' walled garden surrounding this small hotel gives it a country house vibe in the middle of this historic market town. The 'pleasant retreat', taken over in 2018 by Peter and Lana de Savary, has been restored to its Edwardian splendour. Bedrooms are 'comfortable, well furnished', all different. Some have a private garden. The bar and lounge serve afternoon teas and light bites, also available on the terrace in good weather. Come evening, the restaurant offers 'tasty' seasonal menus with such dishes as venison loin, salt-baked swede, kale, toasted oats, crispy sage. Plans are afoot for a spa and new garden suites. Sherborne Abbey is close by.

MAP 2:E1
Long Street
Sherborne DT9 3BY
T: 01935 813131
W: theeastburyhotel.co.uk

BEDROOMS: 21. 4 with external access, 1 suitable for disabled.
OPEN: all year.
FACILITIES: drawing room, lounge, bar, library, conservatory restaurant, private dining room, free Wi-Fi, in-room TV (Freeview), wedding/function facilities, parking, terrace, 1-acre walled garden.
BACKGROUND MUSIC: in bar and restaurant.
LOCATION: town centre.
CHILDREN: all ages welcomed.
DOGS: allowed in some rooms (£20 per night), and some public rooms.
CREDIT CARDS: Amex, MC, Visa.
PRICES: per room B&B £135 single executive, £135 double/twin, £375 Superior Four Poster Garden Suite. Dinner B&B add £39. Tasting menu £45.

SHERBORNE Somerset

THE KINGS ARMS

Hands-on chef/patron Sarah Lethbridge and her husband, Anthony, run this restored stone-walled country pub in Charlton Horethorne, a pretty village four miles outside Sherborne. Some of the colourful, individually styled bedrooms overlook the terrace, croquet lawn and gardens; each has a marble wet room, with rainfall shower, towelling bathrobes. Though roadside, 'I wasn't aware of any noise.' The day's newspapers are stacked in the snug, which is warmed by a wood-burning stove. Public rooms have myriad artwork (all for sale). 'Very friendly' bar staff serve local ales and ciders in the modern country-style bar. Innovative takes on classic pub grub in the restaurant include Jospered free-range chicken breast, new potato, savoy cabbage, butternut squash, parsley broth.

MAP 2:E1
North Street
Sherborne DT9 4NL
T: 01963 220281
W: thekingsarms.co.uk

BEDROOMS: 10. 1 suitable for disabled.
OPEN: all year, limited service over Christmas, New Year.
FACILITIES: lift, snug, bar, restaurant, free Wi-Fi, in-room TV (Freeview), terrace, garden, free use of local sports centre, discounts at Sherborne Golf Club, parking.
BACKGROUND MUSIC: none.
LOCATION: in village 4 miles NE of Sherborne.
CHILDREN: all ages welcomed.
DOGS: allowed in bar.
CREDIT CARDS: MC, Visa.
PRICES: per room B&B from £145. À la carte £30–£35.

NEW

SHERBORNE Somerset

THE QUEENS ARMS

'Warm, welcoming and extraordinarily good value for money.' Guide inspectors in 2019 join the local admiration society in their praise of Jeanette and Gordon Reid's 18th-century inn on the Dorset/Somerset border. James Cole's 'standout' menu of modern British dishes are served in the rustic, dining room (comfortable seating, a huge fireplace). Enjoy 'beautifully presented, generously portioned' plates of beetroot-cured gravlax; honey-glazed duck; harissa cauliflower, Israeli basil couscous. 'An impressive wine menu.' Smart, colourful bedrooms overlook rolling countryside, and have a roll-top bath, 'a wonderfully large and comfy bed'. Breakfast, served communally, features eggs and bacon from the village.

MAP 2:E1
Corton Denham
Sherborne DT9 4LR
T: 01963 220317
W: thequeensarms.com

BEDROOMS: 8.
OPEN: all year.
FACILITIES: restaurant, bar, function room (meetings), terrace, free Wi-Fi, in-room TV (Freeview), garden.
BACKGROUND MUSIC: none.
LOCATION: 3 miles from Sherborne town centre, 4 miles from railway station.
CHILDREN: all ages welcomed.
DOGS: allowed (not in restaurant), £15 supplement.
CREDIT CARDS: MC, Visa.
PRICES: per room B&B from £95, D,B&B from £130. 3-night minimum at Christmas.

NEW

SHIPSTON-ON-STOUR Warwickshire

THE BOWER HOUSE

At the heart of the historic market town of Shipston-on-Stour, this well-restored Georgian house, built in 1731, is now home to a welcoming restaurant-with-rooms. Downstairs, the stylish restaurant hits all the right marks, with both a steak menu on Wednesdays and a separate vegan menu. Upstairs, bedrooms are filled with quirky appeal. A family suite combines two separate bedrooms, with bumblebee wallpaper and plenty of bedtime storybooks; on the floor above, Room 5 has Aztec colours, a wrought iron bed, a freestanding roll-top bath in the bathroom, and stunning views across the Warwickshire countryside. No need to rush in the mornings: breakfast is till 11 on Saturdays, while brunch lingers till a leisurely 2 pm.

MAP 3:D6
Market Place
Shipston-on -Stour CV36 4AG
T: 01608 663333
W: bower.house

BEDROOMS: 5.
OPEN: all year, except 25/26 Dec, restaurant closed Sun evening, Mon.
FACILITIES: restaurant, free Wi-Fi, in-room TV (Freeview), restaurant partially wheelchair accessible.
BACKGROUND MUSIC: 'iscreet' in restaurant.
LOCATION: in historic market town.
CHILDREN: all ages welcomed.
DOGS: allowed in bar area of the restaurant.
CREDIT CARDS: Amex, MC, Visa.
PRICES: per room B&B £130–£185. À la carte £32.

SHREWSBURY Shropshire
CHATFORD HOUSE

'All-round first-class hosts', Christine and Rupert Farmer offer guests a slice of the good life at their B&B on a small organic farm – and greet them with a piece of home-baked cake. Close to the Shropshire Way, the 18th-century farmhouse has cottage-style bedrooms full of spoiling touches: fresh flowers, magazines, and a regularly topped-up hospitality tray. In each, views of the pretty garden or towards the Wrekin. Come morning, Aga-cooked breakfasts use the owners' produce; home-made jams and local honey sweeten the feast. Great walks from the garden gate, beginning with the orchard and a visit to the farm animals. Not much further afield is Lyth Hill.

MAP 3:B4
Chatford
Shrewsbury SY3 0AY
T: 01743 718301
W: chatfordhouse.co.uk

BEDROOMS: 3.
OPEN: all year, limited service over Christmas, New Year.
FACILITIES: sitting room, breakfast room, free Wi-Fi, in-room TV, garden, orchard, parking.
BACKGROUND MUSIC: none.
LOCATION: 4 miles S of Shrewsbury.
CHILDREN: all ages welcomed.
DOGS: assistance dogs allowed, all others allowed by prior arrangement only.
CREDIT CARDS: none accepted.
PRICES: per room B&B single £60, double £75–£85.

SHREWSBURY Shropshire
LION AND PHEASANT

Original character and voguish style combine at this centrally located 16th-century coaching inn 'with easy access to all parts of the city'. Much liked are the 'friendly staff' and buzzy bar which has regional real ales, flagstone floors, exposed beams and open fireplaces. Upstairs, the bedrooms (quieter at the rear) display minimalist design; in some, river views; a contemporary four-poster; a magnificent array of exposed loft timber; in all, 'a comfortable bed; a good shower'. Innovative menus, in the split-level restaurant, might include duck breast, dauphinoise potato, roasted pear, confit duck and date rillette, port jus, prepared by chef Paul Downes and his brigade, using seasonal local ingredients. Breakfast is varied and plentiful.

MAP 3:B4
50 Wyle Cop
Shrewsbury SY1 1XJ
T: 01743 770345
W: lionandpheasant.co.uk

BEDROOMS: 22.
OPEN: all year except 25/26 Dec.
FACILITIES: 2 bars, restaurant, function room, free Wi-Fi, in-room TV (Freeview), garden terrace, parking (narrow entrance).
BACKGROUND MUSIC: in public areas, occasional live music in bar.
LOCATION: central, near English Bridge.
CHILDREN: all ages welcomed.
DOGS: allowed on garden terrace only.
CREDIT CARDS: MC, Visa.
PRICES: per room B&B single £120–£230, DB&B £165–£290. À la carte £38.

SISSINGHURST Kent

THE MILK HOUSE

Guests to Dane and Sarah Allchorne's 'enjoyable' pub-with-rooms may well feel like the cats that got the cream. The 16th-century hall house blends a buzzy, village-hub feel with a jocund dairy theme. Bedrooms with such names as Byre, Buttery, Churn, are unfussily voguish, decorated in a creamy palette, and with a 'very comfortable bed', and fresh flowers in milk pails. Rear rooms are quietest. Proper pub food, cask ales and local beers are served alongside wood-fired pizza under the bar's timber beams. The Tudor fireplace is lit on cold days. More creative, modern plates are served in the rustic dining room, perhaps chargrilled pork chop, champ mash, spring leeks, sage butter. Breakfast is a feast.

MAP 2:D5
The Street
Sissinghurst TN17 2JG
T: 01580 720200
w: themilkhouse.co.uk

BEDROOMS: 4.
OPEN: all year.
FACILITIES: bar, restaurant, private dining room, free Wi-Fi, in-room TV (Freeview), sun terrace, large garden, parking.
BACKGROUND MUSIC: in bar and restaurant.
LOCATION: in village.
CHILDREN: all ages welcomed.
DOGS: allowed in bar and garden only.
CREDIT CARDS: Amex, MC, Visa.
PRICES: per room B&B from £90. 2-night min. stay weekends.

SOMERTON Somerset

THE WHITE HART

A foodie destination skirting the Somerset Levels, this chic pub-with-rooms gathers praise for its 'superb meals' and quirky bedrooms. Its menu of British pub classics and more innovative fare is 'top-notch'. Hungry guests flock to the cosy bar with its wood-burning stove, and the conservatory dining room; on clement days, outdoor picnic benches are laden. Playful details (Moorish tiles, a listing Pink Panther clinging to a lampshade) bring a whimsical air to the well-equipped rooms; each has a large bed, fluffy towels, natural toiletries. Breakfast (served till 11 am) includes smashed avocado on malted toast, chilli sauce, slow-roasted tomatoes. Part of the small Stay Original Company; see also Timbrell's Yard, Bradford-on-Avon (Shortlist).

MAP 1:C6
Market Place
Somerton TA11 7LX
T: 01458 272273
w: whitehartsomerton.com

BEDROOMS: 8.
OPEN: all year.
FACILITIES: bar, restaurant, free Wi-Fi, in-room smart TV, large courtyard garden, bicycle storage.
BACKGROUND MUSIC: in bar.
LOCATION: in town centre.
CHILDREN: all ages welcomed.
DOGS: allowed in bedrooms (£10 per dog per stay).
CREDIT CARDS: MC, Visa.
PRICES: per room B&B from £85, D,B&B from £120. À la carte £27.

SOUTH ALKHAM Kent

ALKHAM COURT

'We were very well looked after,' report readers in 2019. From on high, 'warm, attentive' Wendy and Neil Burrows's farmhouse enjoys stunning sunsets over the Alkham valley. B&B guests are offered 'delicious' home-made cake on arrival; a picnic for walks on the Kent Downs; an evening bowl of soup; the spa barn with hot tub and sauna to unwind in. Discreet bedrooms each have a private entrance; within the country-style rooms: fresh flowers, robe and slippers, coffee machine, mini-fridge, biscuits and complimentary sherry; expansive rural views. Two restored vintage shepherd huts within the grounds have log-burners. An 'excellent' breakfast brings home-baked muffins, local pressed apple juice, farm-fresh eggs.

MAP 2:D5
Meggett Lane
South Alkham CT15 7DG
T: 01303 892056
w: alkhamcourt.co.uk

BEDROOMS: 4. Plus shepherd's hut, 1 suitable for disabled.
OPEN: all year except 24/25 Dec.
FACILITIES: sitting/breakfast room, free Wi-Fi, in-room TV (Freeview), spa barn, large garden, 60-acre farm.
BACKGROUND MUSIC: none.
LOCATION: in a rural location near Dover; 5 mins from M20, 10 mins from Eurotunnel.
CHILDREN: all ages welcomed.
DOGS: allowed in Garden Room, in Sun Room,; on lead at all times outside because of livestock (£10 per night).
CREDIT CARDS: MC, Visa.
PRICES: per room B&B single £85–£100, double £145–£175. 2-night min. stay on bank holiday weekends and in high season.

SOUTHAMPTON Hampshire

SOUTHAMPTON HARBOUR HOTEL

A taste of life at sea is creating waves at this large, contemporary hotel jutting out over Ocean Village Marina. It is managed by Lukasz Dwornik for Harbour Hotels. Ship-shape inside, it is bright, with colourful fabrics; porthole-shaped mirrors, vintage glass fish floats, a giant lobster, add nautical fun. A chunky white stairway leads up from the wood-floored lobby. Bedrooms have pale-toned walls, retro furnishing, a marble bathroom. A bathrobe, slippers, coffee machine and complimentary grog (decanters of gin and sherry) are supplied. For cocktails and light bites, the buzzing sixth-floor HarBar has wonderful (if also industrial) harbour views. Sea-sourced dishes features in the award-winning Jetty restaurant.

MAP 2:E2
Ocean Village
Southampton SO14 3QT
T: 02381 103456
w: harbourhotels.co.uk/southampton

BEDROOMS: 115. 8 suites, some suitable for disabled.
OPEN: all year.
FACILITIES: bar, restaurant, café, free Wi-Fi, in-room TV (Freeview), indoor swimming pools, gym, valet parking.
BACKGROUND MUSIC: in public areas.
LOCATION: on marina.
CHILDREN: all ages welcomed.
DOGS: assistance dogs only.
CREDIT CARDS: Amex, MC, Visa.
PRICES: per room B&B £206–£506, D,B&B £256–£556. Breakfast £17, set menu from £35, à la carte £25.95. 2-night min. stay during Southampton Boat Show and Cowes Week.

SOUTHAMPTON Hampshire
WOODLANDS LODGE HOTEL

Touring dogs and their discerning owners are warmly welcomed at Imogene and Robert Anglaret's 'perfect little dog-friendly hotel' which has walkies straight into the surrounding New Forest. Seven spacious bedrooms in the former hunting lodge (two with direct garden access) are set aside for man's best friend, who receives a treat, a blanket and a towel on arrival; the owner will perhaps be more pleased by the smart, modern, country design, and the wide garden and woodland views. Dogs may accompany owners eating in the bar and lounge; Hunters restaurant serves all-day light bites, while the Cattle Grid offers more substantial fare using locally sourced and grown ingredients.

MAP 2:E2
Bartley Road
Southampton SO40 7GN
T: 02380 292257
W: woodlands-lodge.co.uk

BEDROOMS: 17. 2 with garden access, 1 suitable for disabled.
OPEN: all year.
FACILITIES: lounge, bar, conservatory, restaurant, free Wi-Fi in public areas, in-room TV (Freeview), civil wedding licence, business facilities, 3-acre garden.
BACKGROUND MUSIC: radio or 'easy listening' in bar and restaurant.
LOCATION: 4 miles outside Lyndhurst, approx. 1 mile from Ashurst train station, 15 mins' drive from Southampton.
CHILDREN: all ages welcomed.
DOGS: allowed in some bedrooms, bar, lounge.
CREDIT CARDS: MC, Visa.
PRICES: per room B&B from £99, D,B&B from £129.

SOUTHWOLD Suffolk
SUTHERLAND HOUSE

In a handsome 15th-century building on the High Street, Andy and Kinga Rudd's restaurant-with-rooms casts modern fabrics, and contemporary and vintage furnishings against aged beams, elm floorboards and medieval windows. It is rich with history: the Duke of York (later James II) was a frequent visitor when commanding the English navy during the Anglo-Dutch war. Upstairs are characterful bedrooms, each different: one has a double-ended slipper bath on a platform before an original fireplace; in another, French doors open on to the walled garden; another has a sleigh bed under a sublime 17th-century pargeted ceiling (an architectural feature also found in the bar/dining area). The buzzy restaurant specialises in seasonal dishes, especially just-caught harbour-fresh fish.

MAP 2:B6
56 High Street
Southwold IP18 6DN
T: 01502 724544
W: sutherlandhouse.co.uk

BEDROOMS: 5. 1 suitable for disabled.
OPEN: all year, restaurant closed every Mon, 25 Dec.
FACILITIES: bar, restaurant, free Wi-Fi, in-room TV (Freeview), garden.
BACKGROUND MUSIC: in public areas.
LOCATION: town centre.
CHILDREN: not under 17.
DOGS: not allowed.
CREDIT CARDS: MC, Visa.
PRICES: per room from £139.50.
À la carte £28. 2-night min. stay Sat.

NEW

SOUTHWOLD Suffolk

THE SWAN

Brightening up the coastline, this well-refurbished Georgian hotel owned by the Adnams brewing group imports London cool to timeless Southwold. The drawing room gathers green velvet sofas around a log fire, 18th-century portraits, theatrical wallpaper; a buzzy setting for a refreshing G&T (using Adnam's own gin). Rooms spill between the main hotel and a garden annexe overlooking the lighthouse. In each a breezy seaside palette, crisp bedlinen on the bed, Bose speakers, coffee pod machine, complimentary gin. Rory Whelan's innovative British dishes are served in the Still restaurant: pan-fried sea bass, smoked almond; Tandoori-style roasted cauliflower. Breakfast is a winner, from fresh pastries to a full English with farm-fresh eggs.

MAP 2:B6
Market Place
Southwold IP18 6EG
T: 01502 722186
W: theswansouthwold.co.uk

BEDROOMS: 35. 12 in annexe.
OPEN: all year.
FACILITIES: 2 restaurants, lounge, free Wi-Fi, in-room TV, large garden, civil wedding licence, suitable for disabled.
BACKGROUND MUSIC: in the Still Room during operating hours.
LOCATION: on market square.
CHILDREN: all ages welcomed.
DOGS: allowed in selected garden rooms but not in the main hotel building.
CREDIT CARDS: MC, Visa.
PRICES: per room £200–£450, D,B&B £260–£480. À la carte £35.

STAMFORD Lincolnshire

THE BULL AND SWAN AT BURGHLEY

In the late 17th century, the Honourable Order of Little Bedlam (an aristocratic drinking club) rampaged through this stylish coaching inn – today an altogether more upstanding crowd crosses its mellow stone threshold. They come for the modern pub grub, cinema nights and the garden's 'pizza potting shed' (open on warm-weather weekends). Characterful bedrooms mix vintage furnishings and modern conveniences. Some have exposed stones or feature wallpaper, perhaps an original fireplace, mullioned window. Extras include fancy tea, 'proper coffee', biscuits, a mini-bottle of organic vodka. Burghley House is nearby. One of the small Hillbrooke Hotels group (see The Master Builder's, Beaulieu, main entry).

MAP 2:B3
St Martins
Stamford PE9 2LJ
T: 01780 766412
W: hillbrookehotels.co.uk/
    the-bull-and-swan

BEDROOMS: 9.
OPEN: all year.
FACILITIES: bar, private dining room, free Wi-Fi, in-room TV (Freeview), garden, terrace.
BACKGROUND MUSIC: in bar.
LOCATION: 5-min. walk into town centre.
CHILDREN: all ages welcomed.
DOGS: allowed (in 3 rooms; dog bed, bowls, special treats, room-service menu, £20).
CREDIT CARDS: Amex, MC, Visa.
PRICES: per room B&B £85–£180, D,B&B £135–£220. À la carte £30.

NEW

STOW-ON-THE-WOLD Gloucestershire

THE OLD STOCKS INN

Blending Scandi style and careful restoration, this 17th-century inn stands at the heart of a quaint Cotswolds town. Hosts Jim and Charlotte Tuck headed up the refurbishment; now ceilings restored with horsehair and lime, a brass-topped bar and wooden beams meet black-and-white tiles, mid-century modern furnishings and pastel hues. Upstairs, each room has a large bed, bold fabrics, woollen throws, a freestanding bathtub in the bathroom; a free minibar stocked with fresh milk, local snacks. Chef Ian Percival uses local produce in his 'great British grub', perhaps slow-cooked lamb, hay-baked celeriac. Breakfast, served in the restaurant, has granola, fresh pastries, cooked-to-order classics such as ham hock and poached eggs.

MAP 3:D6
The Square
Stow-on-the-Wold GL54 1AF
T: 01451 830666
w: oldstocksinn.com

BEDROOMS: 16.
OPEN: closed 24/25 Dec.
FACILITIES: restaurant, bar, library, coffee shop, private dining room, terrace, free Wi-Fi, in-room TV,
BACKGROUND MUSIC: in all public areas.
LOCATION: in town centre.
CHILDREN: all ages welcomed.
DOGS: allowed in 3 bedrooms, bar, library, coffee shop.
CREDIT CARDS: Amex, MC, Visa.
PRICES: per room B&B £129–£289, D,B&B £210–£350. Breakfast £15, à la carte £35. 1-night bookings sometimes refused Sat night.

NEW

STRATFORD-UPON-AVON Warwickshire

THE TOWNHOUSE

Characterful low ceilings and beams mix with extravagant modern touches at this style-savvy hotel and restaurant (Brakspear Pubs), in a 400-year-old Grade II listed building within minutes of the Royal Shakespeare Theatre. Contemporary bedrooms vary in size, but all have a large bed and a flair for the theatrical, with an elaborately framed mirror here, a suede chaise longue there, perhaps a claw-foot bathtub in the bathroom. Rub shoulders with locals, tourists and a thespian or two in the bustling all-day bistro and atmospheric bar: hung with heavy drapes, and decorated with interesting photographs and ornaments, it's a quirky, inviting spot for breakfast, lunch or dinner.

MAP 3:D6
16 Church Street
Stratford-upon-Avon CV37 6HB
T: 01789 262222
w: churchstreettownhouse.com

BEDROOMS: 12. 1 on ground floor suitable for disabled.
OPEN: all year.
FACILITIES: bar, library, dining room, free Wi-Fi.
BACKGROUND MUSIC: in public areas.
LOCATION: central.
CHILDREN: not under 16.
DOGS: not allowed.
CREDIT CARDS: MC, Visa.
PRICES: per person B&B £45–£80. À la carte £28. 1-night bookings generally refused weekends.

STRATFORD-UPON-AVON Warwickshire

WHITE SAILS

Close to the farmhouse where Anne Hathaway lived as a child, Tim and Denise Perkin's restful B&B is in a suburban house, a 20-minute stroll from the RSC theatres and town. Beyond distinctive blue entrance pillars, there is a home-from-home atmosphere. The lounge has help-yourself extras (sherry, espresso coffee, home-made treats). 'Clean and comfy' bedrooms in pretty colours, including one containing a four-poster, are well supplied with bathrobes, a digital radio/iPod docking station, home-baked cake; chilled water and fresh milk are left in a silent fridge. Breakfast is a feast of home-made granola, bread and cakes; cooked-to-order dishes include eggs Benedict or smoked haddock with poached eggs. Stratford racecourse is around the corner.

MAP 3:D6
85 Evesham Road
Stratford-upon-Avon CV37 9BE
T: 01789 550469
w: white-sails.co.uk

BEDROOMS: 4.
OPEN: all year except Christmas and New Year's Day.
FACILITIES: lounge, dining room, free Wi-Fi, in-room TV (Freeview), garden.
BACKGROUND MUSIC: yes.
LOCATION: 1 mile W of centre.
CHILDREN: not under 12.
DOGS: not allowed.
CREDIT CARDS: Amex, MC, Visa.
PRICES: per room B&B single £90–£115, double £105–£130. 2-night bookings required May–Sept.

NEW

SUMMERHOUSE Co. Durham

THE RABY HUNT
RESTAURANT AND ROOMS

Way above par, James Close, a former golf professional and self-taught chef, has scored two Michelin stars for his simple, visually stunning cooking. His tiny restaurant-with-rooms, in a creeper-covered 19th-century drover's inn (Grade II listed), is in a rural hamlet. An open-view kitchen in the modern restaurant allows diners to watch the drama as a busy team prepares 15 to 18 courses for the tasting menu. Up close, the Kitchen Table has front-row seats for six diners. A chocolate skull is a theatrical finale to plate after palate-thrilling plate – dishes such as razor clam, almond and celeriac, Wagyu sandu, mango with yuzu and coconut tart. Stay for breakfast: there are three contemporary, comfortable bedrooms.

MAP 4:C4
Summerhouse
Darlington DL2 3UD
T: 01325 374237
w: rabyhuntrestaurant.co.uk

BEDROOMS: 3.
OPEN: all year, except Christmas, New Year, restaurant closed Sun, Mon, Tues.
FACILITIES: free Wi-Fi, in-room TV, restaurant (wheelchair accessible).
BACKGROUND MUSIC: in restaurant.
LOCATION: 6 miles NW of Darlington.
CHILDREN: not under 12.
DOGS: not allowed.
CREDIT CARDS: Amex, MC, Visa.
PRICES: per room B&B from £195. Tasting menu (15–18 courses) £140 per person, Kitchen Table menu £170 per person.

TAUNTON Somerset

THE CASTLE AT TAUNTON

In the town centre, a 'beautifully furnished, traditional, very comfortable and cheerfully run' hotel stands inside a wisteria-festooned medieval castle. Extended and rebuilt over centuries, it has character and history to spare. The buzzy brasserie has 'delicious' food with inventive flavours and textures. The 'charming' Castle Bow restaurant has a more sedate ambience. for chef Liam Finnegan's à la carte and tasting menus featuring Brixham turbot, Exmoor venison or Lyme Bay cod. 'Individual and comfortable', 'airy' bedrooms have high-quality bedlinen; a turn-down service at night. But lighting may be 'rather dim'. 'Excellent' breakfasts include an extensive buffet with home-made bread and jams, muesli and 'piping hot' cooked dishes.

MAP 1:C5
Castle Green
Taunton TA1 1NF
T: 01823 272671
W: the-castle-hotel.com

BEDROOMS: 44. 2 suitable for disabled.
OPEN: all year, Castle Bow restaurant closed Sun–Tues for dinner, Jan.
FACILITIES: lounge/bar, snug, 2 restaurants, private dining/meeting rooms, free Wi-Fi, in-room TV (Freeview), lift, ramps, civil wedding licence, ¼-acre garden. public rooms wheelchair accessible, adapted toilet.
BACKGROUND MUSIC: 'easy listening' in bar, restaurant, brasserie.
LOCATION: town centre.
CHILDREN: all ages welcomed.
DOGS: allowed in bedrooms, bar.
CREDIT CARDS: Amex, MC, Visa.
PRICES: per room B&B £165–£255, D,B&B £209–£299. À la carte Castle Bow £60, BRAZZ bar £30.

TAVISTOCK Devon

TAVISTOCK HOUSE HOTEL

Pristine throughout, Brad and Gill Walker's small hotel is a harmonious mix of spruce amenities and well-maintained original features. The house, built by the Duke of Bedford in 1850, is five minutes' walk from the town square. Chic bedrooms (some snug), with grey and white hues and the odd splash of colour, are well appointed, with luxurious bedlinen, a capsule coffee machine, smart TV, a tablet computer to access free online newspapers; bath- and shower rooms have underfloor heating. Hearty breakfasts and all-day light bites are served in a serene room with marble fireplace, half-panelled walls and contemporary art, plus a well-stocked honesty bar. The large front garden has outdoor seating. The neighbourhood's eateries are nearby.

MAP 1:D4
50 Plymouth Road
Tavistock PL19 8BU
T: 01822 481627
W: www.tavistockhousehotel.co.uk

BEDROOMS: 6.
OPEN: all year except 25/26/31 Dec, 1 Jan.
FACILITIES: breakfast room/lounge with honesty bar, free Wi-Fi, in-room TV (Freeview, Netflix), front garden.
BACKGROUND MUSIC: in public areas.
LOCATION: in town centre.
CHILDREN: over-9s welcomed.
DOGS: not allowed.
CREDIT CARDS: MC, Visa.
PRICES: per room B&B £104–£144. Breakfast £14.

THORNHAM Norfolk

THE LIFEBOAT INN

With 'open views' across salt marsh and sea, this 16th-century inn has rescued travellers from storms and hunger for over 500 years. This year, its location also impressed Guide regulars. Its oak-beamed bar has warming fires, settles and stone walls hung with vintage agricultural equipment. Seasonal dishes, daily specials and a good selection of vegetarian/vegan options are served in the restaurant and under the conservatory's 200-year-old vine. Good weather draws diners on to the terrace. 'Our comfortable room had an ingenious hanging rail.' Most of the cosy bedrooms, each named after a crew member of a Hunstanton lifeboat, look out to the North Sea. At breakfast, even Fido gets a sausage. An Agellus Hotel (see also The Ship at Dunwich, Shortlist).

MAP 2:A5
Ship Lane
Thornham PE36 6LT
T: 01485 512236
W: lifeboatinnthornham.com

BEDROOMS: 13. 1 on ground floor, in cottage.
OPEN: all year.
FACILITIES: bar, 2 lounge areas, conservatory, restaurant, meeting room, private dining room, free Wi-Fi, in-room smart TV (Freeview), terrace, garden, parking.
BACKGROUND MUSIC: all day in public areas.
LOCATION: in a small coastal village 14 miles NE of Hunstanton.
CHILDREN: all ages welcomed.
DOGS: allowed in bedrooms, public rooms (£10 per stay).
CREDIT CARDS: MC, Visa.
PRICES: per room B&B £145–£225. À la carte £28. 2-night min. stay preferred.

THORNTON HOUGH Merseyside

MERE BROOK HOUSE

Within a dell of mature trees, this relaxed Edwardian country house B&B invites visitors to the Wirral peninsula. Lorna Tyson and her husband, Donald, a farmer, have a laid-back approach – 'no notices/rules anywhere!' Unfussy yet pretty bedrooms occupy the original building and a converted coach house; individually decorated, they overlook the garden or countryside. Both buildings have their own lounge and a residents' kitchen stocked with home-made cakes, snacks and hot drinks (home-made ready meals are available for re-heating). Come morning, the conservatory provides a breakfast of super-local ingredients including honey from the garden beehives; milk from the Tysons' dairy cows; apple juice from orchard fruit.

MAP 4:E2
Thornton Common Road
Thornton Hough CH63 0LU
T: 07713 189949
W: merebrookhouse.co.uk

BEDROOMS: 8. 4 in main house on first floor, 4 in coach house (3 on ground floor).
OPEN: all year, limited availability over Christmas, New Year.
FACILITIES: 3 lounges, conservatory, dining room, guest kitchens, free Wi-Fi, in-room TV (Freeview), wedding/function facilities, 1-acre garden in 4-acre grounds.
BACKGROUND MUSIC: none.
LOCATION: centre of Wirral peninsula, 20 mins' drive from Chester and Liverpool.
CHILDREN: all ages welcomed.
DOGS: assistance dogs only.
CREDIT CARDS: MC, Visa.
PRICES: per room B&B £75–£130.

THURNHAM Kent

THURNHAM KEEP

A long drive through landscaped gardens reveals this 'simply wonderful' B&B where visitors are rewarded by a sweet welcome from 'charming host' Amanda Lane: 'The best shortbread ever.' Built from the ruins of Thurnham Castle, the 'magnificent place', her childhood home, stands on the crest of the North Downs. Up an oak staircase, each traditionally furnished bedroom has its own personality; in two, a huge, original Edwardian bath in the bathroom; in all, soft pastels, splendid period furniture; in converted stables, a spacious suite. A 'lavish and tasty' breakfast, served communally, brings home-made jams, garden honey, fresh-from-the-coop eggs. Supper might be arranged in advance; plenty of nearby pubs, too. 'We'd love to return.'

MAP 2:D4
Castle Hill
Thurnham ME14 3LE
T: 01622 734149
w: thurnhamkeep.co.uk

BEDROOMS: 3. Plus self-contained suite in grounds.
OPEN: Mar–Oct.
FACILITIES: sitting room, dining room, conservatory, billiard room, free Wi-Fi, in-room TV (Freeview), 7-acre terraced garden, terrace, heated outdoor swimming pool (May–Sept), tennis, parking.
BACKGROUND MUSIC: none.
LOCATION: 3 miles from Maidstone.
CHILDREN: not under 10.
DOGS: not allowed.
CREDIT CARDS: Amex, MC, Visa.
PRICES: per room B&B £150–£165.

TILLINGTON Sussex

THE HORSE GUARDS INN

Walk across Petworth Park to this 350-year-old, quintessentially English village inn, once a regular stop-over for the Household Cavalry, who would rest their horses en route to Portsmouth. The rambling, updated interiors have stripped floorboards, scrubbed pine tables, eye-catching curiosities and log fires. Pretty florals add country charm to simply decorated bedrooms, some snug, some with low beams. A short daily-changing menu uses the inn's own vegetables, or locally foraged ingredients. A Guide regular this year enjoyed 'interesting starters', followed by a 'richly flavoured' duck leg goulash. Breakfast was 'tasty, well cooked'. Staff were 'invariably friendly and obliging'. The suntrap garden is strewn with hammocks, deckchairs and straw-bale seats.

MAP 2:E3
Upperton Road
Tillington GU28 9AF
T: 01798 342332
w: thehorseguardsinn.co.uk

BEDROOMS: 3. 1 in cottage.
OPEN: all year, limited availability over Christmas, New Year.
FACILITIES: bar, restaurant, free Wi-Fi, in-room TV (Freeview), garden, secure bicycle storage.
BACKGROUND MUSIC: none.
LOCATION: in village, close to Petworth House and Park.
CHILDREN: all ages welcomed.
DOGS: well-behaved dogs allowed.
CREDIT CARDS: MC, Visa.
PRICES: per room B&B from £110.

TISBURY Wiltshire
THE COMPASSES INN

A local hot spot 'in the middle of nowhere', this thatch-roofed 14th-century inn is worth the trip down a winding country lane. Inside are cosy nooks and crannies; owner Ben Maschler has retained the pub's flagstone floors and ancient beams, and the inglenook fireplace that keeps things warm. Paddy Davy's sophisticated pubby menu changes daily, using seasonal and local produce; cocktails, local ales and European wines make good accompaniment. Dinner was 'exquisitely cooked'. Airy and simply furnished bedrooms, above, have a cheerful cottagey feel, updated with Anglepoise lamps, a Roberts radio and a stack of Penguin Classics. Visitors recently had 'an excellent stay'. The footpaths and sheep trails of the Nadder valley start from the door.

MAP 2:D1
Lower Chicksgrove
Tisbury SP3 6NB
T: 01722 714318
W: thecompassesinn.com

BEDROOMS: 4. Plus 2-bed self-catering cottage.
OPEN: all year except 25 Dec.
FACILITIES: bar, restaurant, free Wi-Fi, in-room TV (Freeview), ¼-acre garden.
BACKGROUND MUSIC: none, occasional live music events.
LOCATION: 2 miles E of Tisbury.
CHILDREN: all ages welcomed.
DOGS: allowed in bedrooms, public areas.
CREDIT CARDS: MC, Visa.
PRICES: per room B&B single from £90, double from £110. À la carte £26. 2-night min. stay summer and bank holiday weekends.

TOPSHAM Devon
THE SALUTATION INN

A stone's throw from the River Exe, this characterful property with a rich history has welcomed the weary since the 1720s. Now sleekly updated with a nod to its maritime past, the inn is owned and run by the Williams-Hawkes family. It has hosted some dashing events in its time, from inaugural hot-air balloon trips, to a horse-leaping stunt over a dining room table. Today's excitement is more genteel and gastronomic: afternoon teas, lunches in the atrium café, and weekly-changing tasting menus, expertly executed by Tom Williams-Hawkes. Restrained, modern bedrooms share a galley kitchen for help-yourself hot drinks, toast, fruit and home-made biscuits. The RSPB Bowling Green Marsh nature reserve is nearby.

MAP 1:C5
68 Fore Street
Topsham EX3 0HL
T: 01392 873060
W: salutationtopsham.co.uk

BEDROOMS: 6. 2 suites.
OPEN: all year except 25 Dec evening, 26 Dec, 1 Jan.
FACILITIES: 2 lounges, restaurant, café, meeting/function room, free Wi-Fi, in-room TV (Freeview), walled seating area, parking, restaurant wheelchair accessible, adapted toilet.
BACKGROUND MUSIC: in public areas.
LOCATION: town centre.
CHILDREN: all ages welcomed.
DOGS: allowed.
CREDIT CARDS: MC, Visa.
PRICES: per room B&B £135–£225, D,B&B £200–£295. Set menu £43. 2-night min. stay weekends May–Oct.

TORQUAY Devon
MEADFOOT BAY

Close to the beach, Phil Hartnett and Vicki Osborne's recently refurbished B&B makes a tranquil 'home from home'. Run by manager Jody Miller and a friendly team, the Victorian villa has comfortable, light-filled sitting areas, painted in calming colours and with plush seating, mirrors, chandeliers. Individually designed bedrooms, each named after a South Devon cove, have clean lines, contemporary hues, a smart bathroom, along with fresh milk in the fridge, complimentary sherry, plenty of storage; three have a private terrace. Freshly cooked dishes accompany home-made muesli, granola, compotes and preserves at breakfast. Guests wishing to avoid the short trip into town can order sharing platters and light bites in the evening.

MAP 1:D5
Meadfoot Sea Road
Torquay TQ1 2LQ
T: 01803 294722
W: meadfoot.com

BEDROOMS: 15.
OPEN: all year, except Dec–Feb, restaurant closed Sun evenings, Mon, bar menu always available.
FACILITIES: lounge, bar, dining room, library, in-room free Wi-Fi, TV (Freeview), terrace, parking.
BACKGROUND MUSIC: in public areas.
LOCATION: 3 mins' walk behind Meadfoot beach, 15 mins' walk from Torquay harbour.
CHILDREN: over-13s welcomed.
DOGS: allowed in 1 room, not inside the hotel.
CREDIT CARDS: Amex, MC, Visa.
PRICES: per room B&B £70–£205, D,B&B £125–£260. 2-night min. stay in high season and on bank holidays.

TORQUAY Devon
ORESTONE MANOR

In sub-tropical gardens with views over Lyme Bay, the D'Allen family's hotel occupies a grand Georgian manor house, once home to John Callcott Horsley, designer of the first Christmas card. Its greetings now extend far beyond Yuletide. In the public rooms, comfortable leather settees join an 'eclectic assortment of artefacts', from colourful Persian-style carpets to Victorian artwork. Some ornate, some capacious, each bedroom has a 'state-of-the-art bathroom'. Most have sea views, some an outdoor hot tub. In the restaurant, Devonshire produce prevails: Exmoor lamb, Teign River mussels, Torbay scallops; fruit and vegetables from the kitchen gardens. Breakfast includes freshly squeezed juice, kippers, West Country ham with poached eggs.

MAP 1:D5
Rockhouse Lane
Torquay TQ1 4SX
T: 01803 897511
W: www.orestonemanor.com

BEDROOMS: 14. 3 in grounds.
OPEN: all year except Jan.
FACILITIES: bar, 2 lounges, 2 dining rooms, free Wi-Fi, in-room TV (Sky), patio, 2-acre grounds, parking.
BACKGROUND MUSIC: in public areas.
LOCATION: 4½ miles N of Torquay.
CHILDREN: all ages welcomed, over-9s only in main restaurant at dinner.
DOGS: not allowed in bedrooms.
CREDIT CARDS: Amex, MC, Visa.
PRICES: per room B&B single £95–£335, double £110–£350, D,B&B double £164–£404. Table d'hôte menus £27, à la carte £40.

TORQUAY Devon
THE 25 BOUTIQUE B&B

Gleeful design and a zesty touch fill 'charming, personable hosts' Andy and Julian Banner-Price's 'meticulously maintained', award-winning Edwardian B&B near Torre Abbey. The decor has a playful air (a zebra in sunglasses here, a psychedelic colour scheme there) – 'edgy but comfortably short of giddy'. A refreshing drink and slice of cake welcome arriving visitors. Bedrooms, each utterly different, have 'plenty of storage space and proper hangers', a hi-tech shower room with mood lighting; 'lavish amenities including fresh-baked treats'. Breakfast brings a fruit smoothie, followed by fruit salad, home-made yogurt and granola, and a choice of hot dishes. A short walk takes you to the seafront, and the harbour's shops, restaurants and bars.

25% DISCOUNT VOUCHERS

MAP 1:D5
25 Avenue Road
Torquay TQ2 5LB
T: 01803 297517
w: the25.uk

BEDROOMS: 6.
OPEN: Feb–Nov.
FACILITIES: drawing room, dining room, free Wi-Fi, in-room smart TV (movies on demand), patio, parking.
BACKGROUND MUSIC: at breakfast.
LOCATION: 5 mins' walk from the sea, 20 mins' walk from town.
CHILDREN: not under 17.
DOGS: not allowed.
CREDIT CARDS: Amex, MC, Visa.
PRICES: per room B&B single £99–£179, double £129–£199.

TRESCO Isles of Scilly
THE NEW INN

Just off the beach, the only pub on Robert Dorrien-Smith's private, car-free island is a 'relaxed' gathering place for locals and holidaymakers alike. It has 'lovely accommodation', and Michelin-rated menus showcasing bountiful Scillonian produce. Bryher lobster and chargrilled Tresco beef; pesto rösti is among the good veggie dishes, many sourced from Tresco Abbey Gardens. By the 'well-stocked bar', a wood-burning stove is a welcome haven on chilly days. In good weather, move into the 'very pretty' canopied garden. Many of the simple bedrooms are done in a beachy palette; many have views of the harbour. Welcoming treats include freshly ground coffee, home-made biscuits, high-end toiletries. Those in the modern annexe are more spacious.

MAP 1: inset C1
New Grimsby
Tresco TR24 0QQ
T: 01720 422849
w: tresco.co.uk/staying-on-tresco/
    the-new-inn

BEDROOMS: 16. Some on ground floor.
OPEN: all year (limited in winter months).
FACILITIES: bar, residents' lounge, restaurant, free Wi-Fi, in-room TV (Freeview), patio, garden, pavilion, heated outdoor swimming pool (seasonal), use of Tresco Island Spa facilities (extra fee).
BACKGROUND MUSIC: in pub and restaurant, occasional live music events.
LOCATION: near New Grimsby harbour.
CHILDREN: all ages welcomed.
DOGS: allowed in public bar, beer garden, assistance dogs allowed in bedrooms.
CREDIT CARDS: MC, Visa.
PRICES: per room B&B £120–£205.
À la carte £35.

TROUTBECK Cumbria
BROADOAKS

On a wonderfully scenic perch above Windermere, Tracey Robinson and Joanna Harbottle's 19th-century stone-and-slate country house is a 'very welcoming' retreat. Set in seven acres of landscaped grounds, it has 'helpful, charming staff'. 'Gorgeous bedrooms' have bold wallpaper, antique furnishings; perhaps a roll-top bath or a sunken spa bath in the bathroom. One suite lets a family spread out over two bedrooms and a lounge; another has a Victorian four-poster, its own log fire and views of the Langdale Pikes. The panelled sitting room serves pre-dinner canapés, before Sharon Elders's 'excellent' French-accented Cumbrian fare in the Oaks brasserie, including daily-changing vegan and vegetarian dishes. Plentiful choice at breakfast.

25% DISCOUNT VOUCHERS

MAP 4: inset C2
Bridge Lane
Troutbeck LA23 1LA
T: 01539 445566
w: broadoakscountryhouse.co.uk

BEDROOMS: 20. Some on ground floor, 5 in coach house, 3 detached garden suites.
OPEN: all year except Jan.
FACILITIES: sitting room, music room, bar, restaurant, orangery, free Wi-Fi, in-room TV (Freeview), civil wedding licence, 8-acre grounds, complimentary access to nearby spa.
BACKGROUND MUSIC: on low volume' in public areas.
LOCATION: 2 miles N of Bowness-on-Windermere.
CHILDREN: over-4s welcomed.
DOGS: allowed in some bedrooms, on lead in garden, bar and lounge.
CREDIT CARDS: MC, Visa.
PRICES: per room B&B £155–£335, D,B&B from £185. Set menu £47.50.

TRUSHAM Devon
THE CRIDFORD INN

Possibly the oldest inn in England, with a medieval wooden window pre-dating glass, this thatched village pub in the Teign valley is 'a gem'. A traditional Devon longhouse, it was a nunnery, property of Buckfast Abbey, when it was listed in the Domesday Book. Today, reached via a single-track road across a brook, the dog-friendly pub is owned by Paul and Ness Moir, and wins praise for the warm welcome and attentive staff. Among the four inn rooms, Teign has a pretty iron bedstead, a leaded glass casement window. The restaurant's 'delicious' locally sourced food includes Brixham fish pie, tenderstem broccoli; a Sunday roast (booking essential). A suntrap terrace has outside tables and seating for alfresco meals. All served with rural peace, just a short drive from Exeter.

25% DISCOUNT VOUCHERS

MAP 1:D4
Trusham TQ13 0NR
T: 01626 853694
w: thecridfordinn.co.uk

BEDROOMS: 4. Plus 2-bedroom cottage.
OPEN: all year.
FACILITIES: bar, restaurant, private dining room, free Wi-Fi, in-room TV (Freeview), terrace. Pub and restaurant wheelchair accessible.
BACKGROUND MUSIC: 'very light' in bar.
LOCATION: 12 miles SW of Exeter.
CHILDREN: all ages welcomed.
DOGS: allowed in 3 bedrooms, public rooms.
CREDIT CARDS: MC, Visa.
PRICES: per room B&B single £69–£109, double £89–£129, cottages per person £43, based on full occupancy, extra bed £25. À la carte £25. One-night bookings refused high-season weekends.

TUNBRIDGE WELLS Kent
THE MOUNT EDGCUMBE

With a leafy garden overlooking the common, Robert and Sally Hogben's nattily refurbished Georgian building is an appealing spot for an alfresco rendezvous. Families, dog-owners and real ale connoisseurs gather at picnic tables under parasols, while cooler months signal a retreat to the cosy bar's log fire and remarkable snug, with leather sofas in a 6th-century sandstone cave. On two floors, the informal restaurant offers a broad, seasonally changing menu of sharing platters, healthy options and classic pub dishes. At the top, six uniquely decorated bedrooms have harmonious hues, antiques, plantation shutters and colourful cushions patterned with wildlife. Various extras include an in-room roll-top bath, views of the common or Edgcumbe rocks.

MAP 2:D4
The Common
Tunbridge Wells TN4 8BX
T: 01892 618854
W: themountedgcumbe.com

BEDROOMS: 6.
OPEN: all year.
FACILITIES: bar, restaurant, free Wi-Fi, in-room TV (Freeview), garden.
BACKGROUND MUSIC: in bar, restaurant.
LOCATION: ½ mile from station.
CHILDREN: all ages welcomed (cot).
DOGS: in bar, restaurant, garden, not in rooms.
CREDIT CARDS: Amex, MC, Visa.
PRICES: per room B&B single from £95, double from £110. À la carte £30.

ULVERSTON Cumbria
THE BAY HORSE

By the water's edge, watching the tide race in at Robert Lyons and Lesley Wheeler's pub-with-rooms is a thrilling sight. The inn was once a stop-over for coaches and horses crossing the sands to Lancaster. These days, its 'amiable' comforts draw back birdwatchers, cyclists, walkers, dog owners and fishermen year after year. Afternoon tea in one of the cosy sitting areas is enjoyed. Freshly decorated bedrooms have a seasidey touch, each supplied with board games, books, magazines; six rooms have balconies that overlook the Levens estuary. Robert Lyons's candlelit dinners (between 7 pm and 8.15 pm) are popular with residents and locals; reservations may be needed. 'Everything was beautifully done; we especially enjoyed the excellent fish dishes.' Breakfasts are 'exceptional'.

MAP 4: inset C2
Canal Foot
Ulverston LA12 9EL
T: 01229 583972
W: thebayhorsehotel.co.uk

BEDROOMS: 9.
OPEN: all year, restaurant closed Mon lunchtime (light bites available).
FACILITIES: bar/lounge, restaurant, free Wi-Fi, in-room TV (Freeview), picnic area, parking, bar and restaurant wheelchair accessible.
BACKGROUND MUSIC: in bar and restaurant.
LOCATION: 1½ miles from town centre.
CHILDREN: not under 9.
DOGS: well-behaved dogs allowed in bedroom (2 dogs max.), not in restaurant.
CREDIT CARDS: Amex, MC, Visa.
PRICES: per room B&B £95–£115, D,B&B £165–£185. À la carte £40. 2-night min. stay preferred.

UPTON MAGNA Shropshire
THE HAUGHMOND

'It's a good place and clearly very popular.' Locals with their dogs, ramblers and cyclists unwind in the bustling bar at Mel and Martin Board's white-washed 17th-century village inn. 'Very good' country fare (whipped up by the host, a self-taught cook) is served in the bustling restaurant. 'First class trio of pork – shoulder, belly, faggot.' Above the bar, cottage-style bedrooms, all solid oak and crisp bedlinen, have a well-supplied refreshments tray, a smart TV with on-demand movies; one, in the eaves, has a Juliet balcony overlooking the fields; two are in a separate barn. A reader this year liked the personal service: 'I was greeted by name on several occasions.' The deli/farm shop has picnic hampers, takeaway lunches.

MAP 3:B5
Pelham Road
Upton Magna SY4 4TZ
T: 01743 709918
w: thehaughmond.co.uk

BEDROOMS: 7, 2 in annexe.
OPEN: all year except Christmas Day, New Year's Day.
FACILITIES: bar/brasserie, breakfast room, conservatory, free Wi-Fi, in-room smart TV, terrace, ½-acre garden, parking.
BACKGROUND MUSIC: 'on low volume' in public areas.
LOCATION: 4 miles from Shrewsbury.
CHILDREN: all ages welcomed.
DOGS: allowed (not unattended) in bedrooms, on lead in public areas (£10 per night, own bed required).
CREDIT CARDS: MC, Visa.
PRICES: per room B&B single £80–£110, double £90–£120. À la carte £30.

WADDESDON Buckinghamshire
THE FIVE ARROWS

At the gates of Waddesdon Manor, a half-timbered, ornately patterned Grade II listed house, originally built to accommodate the architects and craftsmen constructing the manor. Now a 'comfortable' hotel, it retains its wrought ironwork, medieval designs, gables and Elizabethan chimney stacks. Pleasing bedrooms, refurbished in contemporary style, have natural hues and soft fabrics. A 'busy' road may affect light sleepers. The restaurant produces 'carefully presented' seasonal menus, perhaps Five Arrows fish pie or wild mushroom ragout, alongside wines from the family's vineyard. Afternoon tea can be taken in the pretty garden. The hotel is run by the Rothschild family trust and National Trust; guests receive free entry to the manor house.

MAP 2:C3
High Street
Waddesdon HP18 0JE
T: 01296 651727
w: fivearrowshotel.co.uk

BEDROOMS: 16. 5 in Old Coach House, 3 on ground floor in courtyard.
OPEN: all year.
FACILITIES: bar, restaurant, free Wi-Fi, in-room smart TV (Freeview), civil wedding licence, 1-acre garden.
BACKGROUND MUSIC: in restaurant.
LOCATION: in Waddesdon village near the gates of Waddesdon Manor.
CHILDREN: all ages welcomed.
DOGS: allowed in some bedrooms, not in food service areas.
CREDIT CARDS: Amex, MC, Visa.
PRICES: per room B&B from £155, D,B&B single from £125, double from £215. À la carte £38.

WADEBRIDGE Cornwall
TREWORNAN MANOR

'A different but special experience.' Near the
mouth of the Camel estuary, Paul and Lesley
Stapleton have lovingly transformed their listed
early 13th-century manor house into a 'very
relaxing' B&B. Through the pillared gateway,
mature gardens provide an idyllic spot for a cream
tea. The log-warmed lounge has a well-stocked
bar. Spacious bedrooms have an emperor-size
bed, a tray with home-made treats, views of the
courtyard or gardens. Some bathrooms have a
freestanding bath and walk-in shower. Hospitable
owners, the Stapletons offer a small snack menu
to late-arriving guests. Hearty Cornish breakfasts,
which include blueberry pancakes with clotted
cream, can be walked off on the footpath to the
village. Mountain bikes can be borrowed.

MAP 1:D2
Trewornan Bridge
Wadebridge PL27 6EX
T: 01208 812359
W: trewornanmanor.co.uk

BEDROOMS: 7. 2 in courtyard annexe,
1 on ground floor.
OPEN: all year.
FACILITIES: lounge, snug, dining room,
free Wi-Fi, in-room TV (Freeview),
civil wedding licence, 8-acre gardens.
BACKGROUND MUSIC: in dining room,
lounge.
LOCATION: 1 mile N of Wadebridge.
CHILDREN: not under 14.
DOGS: not allowed.
CREDIT CARDS: MC, Visa.
PRICES: per room B&B single
£117–£198, double £130–£220.

NEW

WARMINSTER Wiltshire
BISHOPSTROW HOTEL & SPA

Deep in Wiltshire countryside, the River Wylie
runs past this Grade II listed Georgian country
mansion, now a welcoming hotel and spa. It
offers plenty to occupy the whole family from
swimming pools and tennis courts to exploration
of the Doric temple with rotunda and a Neolithic
long barrow in the extensive grounds. Wellies
and umbrellas are supplied for rainy days; for
indoor types, a board game in the lounge, or
perhaps a Rasul mud treatment in the spa. 'We
had a marvellous time.' Country-style bedrooms,
many with verdant views, range from cosy spaces
to duplex suites with a little patio; all have comfy
seating. British and international dishes are served
in the restaurant, or conservatory, with garden
views large windows display garden views.

MAP 2:D1
Boreham Road
Warminster BA12 9HH
T: 01985 212312
W: bishopstrow.co.uk

BEDROOMS: 32. Some in courtyard.
OPEN: all year.
FACILITIES: bar, lounge, library, dining
room, private dining rooms, free
Wi-Fi, in-room TV (Freeview), spa
(indoor and outdoor pools, thermal
suite, treatments, gym), indoor
and outdoor tennis courts, 27-acre
grounds.
BACKGROUND MUSIC: in public spaces.
LOCATION: 1½ miles from Warminster
railway station.
CHILDREN: all ages welcomed.
DOGS: welcomed (£20 per night).
CREDIT CARDS: Amex, MC, Visa.
PRICES: per room B&B from £120,
D,B&B from £193.

WARTLING Sussex

WARTLING PLACE

'Very convenient for Glyndebourne and the coast', 'every need is catered for' at Rowena and Barry Gittoes's Grade II listed former Georgian rectory. In three acres of 'beautiful' gardens it has rural views towards the South Downs. Tidy public spaces brim with interesting prints, and cosy nooks. 'Delightful' bedrooms have 'real coffee', Fairtrade teas; a DVD library; two have an antique four-poster. A 'wonderful' leisurely breakfast, taken in the bedroom or in the spacious dining room, has fresh fruit, cereals, honey from local bees; smoked salmon from Hastings, local meats, herbs from the garden. 'Delicious.' Picnic hampers can be arranged. An 'absolutely brilliant stay'.

MAP 2:E4
Wartling,
Hailsham BN27 1RY
T: 01323 832590
W: wartlingplace.co.uk

BEDROOMS: 4. Plus 2-bed self-catering cottage suitable for disabled.
OPEN: all year.
FACILITIES: drawing room, dining room, free Wi-Fi, in-room TV (Freeview), 3-acre garden, parking.
BACKGROUND MUSIC: none.
LOCATION: 5 miles E of Hailsham.
CHILDREN: all ages welcomed.
DOGS: not allowed.
CREDIT CARDS: Amex, MC, Visa.
PRICES: per room B&B single £100–£115, double £135–£160.

WARWICK Warwickshire

PARK COTTAGE

Hanging baskets of colourful blooms, along with wonderfully wonky timbers, front Janet and Stuart Baldry's 15th-century B&B next to the entrance to Warwick Castle. Warm and welcoming, the owners exhibit 'one of the great advantages of the British B&B – truly attentive care and concern for their guests'. Across sloping floors and up a steep staircase, the 'comfortable bedrooms' are all different – one has an antique four-poster bed, another a king-size spa bath; a third, access to the pretty patio garden, home to a 300-year-old listed tree. 'Splendid breakfasts, expertly cooked by Stuart Baldry', are served to tables set on the original sandstone floor of the former castle dairy.

25% DISCOUNT VOUCHERS

MAP 3:C6
113 West Street
Warwick CV34 6AH
T: 01926 410319
W: parkcottagewarwick.co.uk

BEDROOMS: 7. 2 on ground floor, plus 2 adjoining self-catering cottages.
OPEN: all year except Christmas, New Year.
FACILITIES: reception/sitting area, breakfast room, free Wi-Fi, in-room TV (Freeview), small garden, parking.
BACKGROUND MUSIC: none.
LOCATION: Warwick town centre.
CHILDREN: all ages welcomed.
DOGS: allowed by prior arrangement (not unattended) in bedrooms, on lead in public areas (£10 per night, own bed required).
CREDIT CARDS: Amex, MC, Visa.
PRICES: per room B&B single £82, double from £92. 1-night bookings sometimes refused.

WATCHET Somerset
SWAIN HOUSE

Watched over by a 150-year-old lighthouse, this coastal spot inspired Samuel Taylor Coleridge; his Ancient Mariner is commemorated with a statue on the harbour. Any entrapment in Jason Robinson's bijou B&B is of an altogether indulgent sort. The 18th-century house and shop in the town centre has a stylish verve, with an inviting mix of slate floors, soft velvet and warm wood. In each chic bedroom, a king-size bed stands under a mural of an Old Master painting; thoughtful extras abound: waffle bathrobes, fluffy towels, chic toiletries, an iron and ironing board, a safe; a roll-top slipper bath and separate walk-in shower in the bathroom. Breakfast has a range of home-cooked dishes, including a full veggie option. A light charcuterie supper can be arranged.

MAP 1:B5
48 Swain Street
Watchet TA23 0AG
T: 01984 631038
w: swain-house.com

BEDROOMS: 4.
OPEN: all year except Christmas, New Year.
FACILITIES: lounge, dining room, free Wi-Fi, in-room TV (Freeview).
BACKGROUND MUSIC: none.
LOCATION: 100 yds from harbour marina.
CHILDREN: not under 12.
DOGS: not allowed.
CREDIT CARDS: Amex, MC, Visa.
PRICES: per room B&B single from £115, double £135.

WATERGATE BAY Cornwall
WATERGATE BAY

'A very good environment.' Whether testing the surf for the first time, or paddleboarding like an old pro, there's a pursuit to suit at Will Ashworth's 'great' beachside hotel. The modern building stands on a stretch of sandy beach, where the on-site Extreme Academy hosts adrenalin-driven activities (kitesurfing, wave-skiing). Off the sands, the sleek Swim Club has every facility for deep relaxation; the Kids Zone gives children three areas to play. At mealtimes, choose between: 'excellent' American-style classics at Zacry's; seasonal grub in the Living Space; fresh seafood at the Beach Hut, Italian-inspired dishes at Jamie Oliver's Fifteen. Finally, a quiet night beckons from 'extremely comfortable' bedrooms, each with a coastal vibe (many with views to match).

MAP 1:D2
On the beach
Watergate Bay TR8 4AA
T: 01637 860543
w: watergatebay.co.uk

BEDROOMS: 71. 2 apartments, 2 suitable for disabled.
OPEN: all year.
FACILITIES: lounge/bar, 3 restaurants, free Wi-Fi, in-room TV (Freeview), civil wedding licence, terrace, sun deck, indoor/outdoor swimming pool, terrace, spa treatments.
BACKGROUND MUSIC: all day in public spaces.
LOCATION: 5 miles N of Newquay.
CHILDREN: all ages welcomed.
DOGS: allowed in some bedrooms, 2 restaurants (£15 per night, dog-friendly beach).
CREDIT CARDS: MC, Visa.
PRICES: per room B&B £185–£365, D,B&B £240–£420. À la carte (Zacry's restaurant) £40.

WEDMORE Somerset

THE SWAN

A 'good value, friendly' pub-with-rooms, with
a 'lovely, informal atmosphere', the pleasingly
updated 18th-century beer house has real ales,
comfy seating, stripped wooden floors. Come
summer, locals and residents decant on to the
cheery terrace. Upstairs, 'smart' modern bedrooms
(well stocked with ground coffee, old-fashioned
sweets, 'super toiletries') have much personality:
a pink-painted claw-footed bath; Beatles LP
covers on a wall. Chef Tom Blake's unpretentious
gastropub menu exploits local produce for such
dishes as Old Spot pork belly, fennel and sea salt
crackling. 'Breakfast is a real treat.' Part of the
Stay Original Company, like Timbrell's Yard,
Bradford-on-Avon (see Shortlist).

MAP 1:B6
Cheddar Road
Wedmore BS28 4EQ
T: 01934 710337
W: theswanwedmore.com

BEDROOMS: 7.
OPEN: all year.
FACILITIES: bar, restaurant, free
Wi-Fi, in-room TV, function facilities,
terrace, large garden, parking.
BACKGROUND MUSIC: in bar.
LOCATION: village centre.
CHILDREN: all ages welcomed.
DOGS: allowed (£10 per dog per stay).
CREDIT CARDS: MC, Visa.
PRICES: per room B&B £75–£135,
D,B&B from £100. À la carte £27.

WESTBROOK Herefordshire

WESTBROOK COURT B&B

Tucked behind a rambling 17th-century
farmhouse overlooking the Wye valley, an
architect-designed timber-clad building is
home to five voguish B&B suites. Kari and
Chris Morgan have transformed the space into
something sleek and unexpected. Bold colour and
quirky flourishes (a bird-cage lampshade; trompe
l'oeil book-lined wallpaper) are splashed about
the spacious, light-filled rooms. Each has its own
lounge area and a private suntrap deck; in four,
a mezzanine bedroom yields views of Merbach
hill. At weekends, the Morgans invite guests to
share a home-baked, garden-reared breakfast in
the farmhouse kitchen; weekdays, a hamper is
brought to the door first thing. 'Speedy suppers'
and beauty treatments available.

MAP 3:D4
Westbrook HR3 5SY
T: 01497 831752
W: westbrookcourtbandb.co.uk

BEDROOMS: 5. 1 suitable for disabled.
OPEN: all year.
FACILITIES: breakfast room/kitchen,
free Wi-Fi, in-room TV (Freeview),
5-acre grounds, terrace, cycle and
kayak storage.
BACKGROUND MUSIC: classical in
breakfast room.
LOCATION: 3 miles E of Hay-on-Wye,
2 mins' drive to Dorstone Village.
CHILDREN: all ages welcomed.
DOGS: allowed in bedrooms, not in
breakfast room (£5 per dog per night).
CREDIT CARDS: MC, Visa.
PRICES: per room B&B £90–£140.

WESTGATE Co. Durham

WESTGATE MANOR

'Absolutely fantastic', Kathryn and Stuart Dobson's large Victorian manor house in the heart of Weardale is decorated in fine style. Its red front door opens on to chandelier-lit rooms filled with antique furniture and displays of fresh flowers. In the sitting room, a log-burner; comfy sofas under huge windows gazing across sheep-speckled hillsides. 'Beautiful' traditional country-house bedrooms have exposed beams and views; a splendid bathroom with a walk-in shower, roll top bath, underfloor heating; some have a four-poster or half-tester bed. The orangery is an inviting dining spot any time; pre-booking may be necessary for 'superb' evening meals.

25% DISCOUNT VOUCHERS

MAP 4:B3
Westgate DL13 1JT
T: 01388 517371
W: westgatemanor.co.uk

BEDROOMS: 5, 1 suitable for a family.
OPEN: all year, except Christmas, New Year.
FACILITIES: lounge, dining room, orangery, garden room, in-room TV (Freeview), free Wi-Fi, patio, secure bike storage, parking.
BACKGROUND MUSIC: in reception, dining room.
LOCATION: 40 mins' drive from Durham.
CHILDREN: all ages welcomed.
DOGS: not allowed.
CREDIT CARDS: Amex, MC, Visa.
PRICES: per room B&B £129–£145. À la carte £30.

WESTLETON Suffolk

THE WESTLETON CROWN

A bird call from the RSPB nature reserve at Minsmere, birders convene with locals at this 12th-century coaching inn, much-liked for its friendly atmosphere. 'Hearty yet sophisticated dishes', perhaps herb-crusted hake fillet, roast artichoke, mash potato, tomato and tarragon coulis, are served before the fire in the cosy parlour, or in the airy Garden Room; on fine days, dining heads into the terraced garden. A separate menu and colouring book for children. Country-style bedrooms have magazines, ground coffee, home-made biscuits. Visiting dogs are welcomed with treats, a blanket and breakfast sausage. For their owners, perhaps eggs Benedict with Suffolk ham. A circular walk calls for a pitstop at sister inn, The Ship at Dunwich (see Shortlist).

25% DISCOUNT VOUCHERS

MAP 2:B6
The Street
Southwold IP17 3AD
T: 01728 648777
W: westletoncrown.co.uk

BEDROOMS: 34. Some in cottages and converted stables in grounds, 1 suitable for disabled.
OPEN: all year.
FACILITIES: bar, snug, lounge, conservatory, 2 dining areas, free Wi-Fi, in-room TV (Freeview), civil wedding licence, terraced garden.
BACKGROUND MUSIC: all day in dining areas.
LOCATION: in countryside, 3 miles from Dunwich beach.
CHILDREN: all ages welcomed.
DOGS: allowed in bedrooms and public rooms (£7.50 per night, outdoor dog wash).
CREDIT CARDS: Amex, MC, Visa.
PRICES: per room B&B £110–£215. À la carte £30.

WHEATHILL Shropshire

THE OLD RECTORY

Off the beaten track, a cheerful welcome awaits
horses, hikers and hounds at Izzy Barnard's wild
flower-filled Georgian house in prime Shropshire
hacking and walking country. A blazing fire in
the drawing room and piles of books help guests
wind down; the soothing sauna completes the job.
A candlelit four-course dinner may be served (by
arrangement); or perhaps simple home-made soup
and a sandwich. The country-style bedrooms have
home-away-from-home comforts, with a large
bed, antique furnishings and biscuits to nibble on
(horses and dogs have their own accommodation).
At breakfast, home-made bread and jams, home-
cured bacon; knitted cosies keep warm eggs
from the resident ducks. Guides and route cards
detailing nearby bridleways are available.

MAP 3:C5
Wheathill
Ludlow WV16 6QT
T: 01746 787209
W: theoldrectorywheathill.com

BEDROOMS: 3.
OPEN: all year except Christmas, Jan.
FACILITIES: drawing room, dining
room, sauna, free Wi-Fi, in-room TV
(Freeview), 7-acre gardens, boot room,
tack room, loose boxes for horses.
BACKGROUND MUSIC: none.
LOCATION: 7 miles from Ludlow.
CHILDREN: all ages welcomed, by
arrangement.
DOGS: allowed in boot room (£10 per
night).
CREDIT CARDS: MC, Visa.
PRICES: per room B&B single £80–£125,
double £95–£139. Set dinner £35,
supper tray £10. 2-night min. stay
preferred for Yellow Room.

WHITSTABLE Kent

THE CRESCENT TURNER HOTEL

Above the town, a newly built hotel with a
'distant view of sea' across fields and houses.
The decor is contemporary, bold, slightly brash.
A deluxe double ground-floor room was 'very
swish, spacious and shiny, with flowery wallpaper,
a posh shower room'. Behind net curtains there
were doors to the lawn and a small terrace. A
warning to those seeking a quiet stay: road noise
is audible from the A299; barking dogs are heard
from an animal sanctuary next door. 'I lunched in
the sunshine on a nice terrace, with flower boxes
and baskets.' In the restaurant, 'with big windows
looking towards the sea', mainly locally sourced
dishes ('not modern or fancy'). For breakfast, a
buffet and good cooked choices include the full
English, smoked haddock and eggs all ways.

MAP 2:D5
Wraik Hill
Whitstable CT5 3BY
T: 01227 263506
W: crescentturner.co.uk

BEDROOMS: 18. 5 on ground floor,
4 suitable for disabled.
OPEN: all year.
FACILITIES: bar/lounge, restaurant,
function room, free Wi-Fi, in-room
TV (Freeview), civil wedding licence,
terrace, 2¼-acre garden, public areas
wheelchair accessible, adapted toilet.
BACKGROUND MUSIC: in public areas.
LOCATION: 2 miles SW of town centre.
CHILDREN: all ages welcomed.
DOGS: not allowed.
CREDIT CARDS: MC, Visa.
PRICES: per room B&B single £75–£135,
double £110–£365. À la carte £40–£50.

WINCHESTER Hampshire

THE WYKEHAM ARMS

Bursting with character, a 'top-rate pub-with-rooms', in an 18th-century coaching inn (Fuller's Hotels and Inns) near the cathedral. Under a different name, the pub hosted Lord Nelson on his way to Portsmouth. Jon Howard manages the establishment with 'helpful, friendly staff'. The cosy bar has real ales (five usually on tap), a log fire, school-desk tables, walls crammed with pictures and breweriana. Chef Allen Sorrell's fresh pub classics are served in a panelled dining room. Some of the individually decorated bedrooms are up a narrow staircase; all are equipped with a coffee machine, free-of-charge minibar. Chatter heard from below ('perfectly bearable') stops around 11 pm. Breakfast is 'excellent'. A tea room has afternoon refreshments.

25% DISCOUNT VOUCHERS

MAP 2:D2
75 Kingsgate Street
Winchester SO23 9PE
T: 01962 853834
W: wykehamarmswinchester.co.uk

BEDROOMS: 14, 7 in adjacent building.
OPEN: all year.
FACILITIES: bar, 2 restaurants, 2 function rooms, free Wi-Fi, in-room TV (Freeview), tea room, small patio with outdoor seating, parking.
BACKGROUND MUSIC: none.
LOCATION: central.
CHILDREN: not under 14.
DOGS: allowed in 2 bedrooms and bar, not in restaurant (£15 per night).
CREDIT CARDS: Amex, MC, Visa.
PRICES: per room B&B single £100–£120, double £149–£189, D,B&B £189–£229. À la carte £32. 2-night min. stay on Sat.

WOLTERTON Norfolk

THE SARACEN'S HEAD

In 'a beautifully rural setting', the north Norfolk countryside stretches away on all sides from Tim and Janie Elwes's ivy-covered Georgian inn. The Elweses have recently refurbished the house (designed in 1806 to mimic a Tuscan farmhouse) from top to bottom. Bright public spaces, decorated in earthy tones, have a zingy feel; wood-burners keep the place as cosy as ever. The bedrooms are cheery, with splashes of colour amid simple, country furnishings. In the restaurant, Norfolk plates include local North Sea mussels, Brancaster smoked salmon, Cromer crab or beetroot and parsnip hash cakes with poached egg and watercress. The comfy first-floor sitting area has books and maps about the area, perfect for planning jaunts to the Broads or the coast.

MAP 2:A5
Wall Road
Wolterton NR11 7LZ
T: 01263 768909
W: saracenshead-norfolk.co.uk

BEDROOMS: 6.
OPEN: all year, except 5 days over Christmas.
FACILITIES: lounge, bar, restaurant, free Wi-Fi, in-room TV (Freeview), courtyard, 1-acre garden, restaurant and bar wheelchair accessible, no adapted toilet.
BACKGROUND MUSIC: in bar and dining rooms.
LOCATION: 5 miles N of Aylsham.
CHILDREN: all ages welcomed.
DOGS: allowed in bedrooms, back bar, not in restaurant.
CREDIT CARDS: MC, Visa.
PRICES: per room B&B single £75, double £110–£120, D,B&B £175. À la carte £36.

WOODBRIDGE Suffolk

THE CROWN

A 'comfortable, welcoming' spot in a small market town close to the Suffolk coast, this popular 16th-century coaching inn offers 'cool', modern interiors alongside traditional hospitality. The wooden sailing skiff suspended above the bar is a nod to the area's nautical heritage. The restaurant makes the most of Suffolk's seasonal larder with such dishes as grilled sea bream resting on a bed of green vegetables and crushed new potatoes. Diners spill out on to the large terrace in warmer weather. Upstairs, 'relaxing bedrooms' are swathed in soothing, natural tones; in each, goose-down pillows, under-floor heating, 'a well-stocked refreshment tray; traffic noise may be audible. Biscuits, books and local magazines are a nice touch.

MAP 2:C5
The Thoroughfare
Woodbridge IP12 1AD
T: 01394 384242
W: thecrownatwoodbridge.co.uk

BEDROOMS: 10.
OPEN: all year.
FACILITIES: restaurant, bar, private dining room, free Wi-Fi, in-room TV (Sky), terrace, parking, restaurant and bar wheelchair accessible.
BACKGROUND MUSIC: in public areas, plus regular live music.
LOCATION: town centre.
CHILDREN: all ages welcomed.
DOGS: allowed in bar.
CREDIT CARDS: Amex, MC, Visa.
PRICES: per room B&B £100–£210, D,B&B £150–£260. À la carte £34. 1-night bookings refused Sat.

NEW

WOODCHESTER Gloucestershire

WOODCHESTER VALLEY VINEYARD

Surrounded by fields corduroyed by vineyards, Fiona Shiner has turned a sympathetically restored barn into an artful B&B. Suites have their own cosy sitting area downstairs, with under-floor heating, a gas log-burner and epic views across the valley or vine-covered hills from floor-to-ceiling windows; a private terrace is the perfect spot to sip the vineyard's own Bacchus white. Afternoons can be spent touring the vineyard and winery, followed by sampling through the list at a taster evening. Breakfast (optional) is a locally sourced hamper of fresh bread, croissants, preserves, yoghurt, fresh fruit, orange juice. Stop by the Cellar Door shop to stock up on bottles from the vineyard before heading home.

25% DISCOUNT VOUCHERS

MAP 3:E5
Convent Lane
Woodchester GL5 5HR
T: 07808 650883
W: woodchestervalleyvineyard.co.uk

BEDROOMS: 3. 4 dog-friendly in farmhouse.
OPEN: all year.
FACILITIES: tasting room, free Wi-Fi, in-room TV (Sky), vineyard, winery, tours, suitable for disabled.
BACKGROUND MUSIC: none.
LOCATION: in south Cotswolds, 3 miles from Stroud.
CHILDREN: over-12s welcomed.
DOGS: in farmhouse.
CREDIT CARDS: MC, Visa.
PRICES: per room £130–£180. Breakfast £20. 1-night bookings sometimes refused.

WOODSTOCK Oxfordshire
THE FEATHERS

Near Blenheim Palace, old-world charm and
modern facilities unite at this child-friendly
hotel with bags of personality in a Cotswolds
market town. The cosy bar (popular with locals)
is 'just the place to unwind', perhaps with one of
its collection of more than 400 gins (a Guinness
world record). Up the winding staircases,
'spotless' bedrooms have a comfortable bed,
'playful decor', bright splashes of colour, quirky
touches (a jar of Jelly Babies, a sloping wooden
floor). In the busy restaurant, with its wood
panels and vibrant statement carpet, innovative
country-style dishes include slow-cooked beef and
ale pie, mashed potatoes and hispi cabbage. Sister
hotel Lords of the Manor is in Upper Slaughter
(see main entry).

MAP 2:C2
16–20 Market Street
Woodstock OX20 1SX
T: 01993 812291
w: feathers.co.uk

BEDROOMS: 21. 1 suitable for disabled,
5 in adjacent town house.
OPEN: all year.
FACILITIES: study, bar, restaurant,
free Wi-Fi, in-room TV (Freeview),
courtyard.
BACKGROUND MUSIC: none.
LOCATION: town centre.
CHILDREN: all ages welcomed.
DOGS: allowed in some bedrooms,
public rooms, not in restaurant.
CREDIT CARDS: Amex, MC, Visa.
PRICES: per room B&B from £99,
D,B&B from £219. À la carte £42.

WOOLACOMBE Devon
WATERSMEET

On the South West Coastal Path, this former
Edwardian gentleman's retreat has cliff-top views
of the three-mile-long beach. Owned by Amanda
James, and run with 'friendly, helpful staff', the
'comfortable, relaxed' hotel is decorated in coastal
hues and makes full use of its 'beautiful' location.
All but three of the bedrooms look out to Lundy
Island and Baggy Point. The lounges, terrace and
gardens have spectacular seascape panoramas
and glorious sunsets. In the informal bistro and
candlelit restaurant (every table with a lovely
view over the sea), chef John Prince features local
produce on his British menus. Breakfast is 'good
and plentiful'. Great walks through National
Trust land and a beach are on the doorstep.

MAP 1:B4
Mortehoe
Woolacombe EX34 7EB
T: 01271 870333
w: watersmeethotel.co.uk

BEDROOMS: 29. 3 on ground floor,
1 suitable for disabled.
OPEN: all year.
FACILITIES: lift, lounge, snug, bar,
restaurant, bistro, free Wi-Fi, in-room
TV (Freeview), terrace, civil wedding
licence, function facilities, ½-acre
garden, indoor and heated outdoor
swimming pool, treatment room,
restaurant wheelchair accessible.
BACKGROUND MUSIC: in public areas.
LOCATION: behind beach, slightly to
N of village centre.
CHILDREN: all ages welcomed
(children's tea).
DOGS: not allowed.
CREDIT CARDS: MC, Visa.
PRICES: per room B&B £120–£300,
D,B&B £210–£410. À la carte £50.

WORCESTER Worcestershire

THE MANOR COACH HOUSE

In a 'unique and peaceful' location, yet within easy reach of the town centre and Worcester cathedral, Chrissie Mitchell's 'spotless' and 'very reasonable' B&B is 'surrounded by delight'. The converted outbuildings are set around a courtyard; there are old cartwheels and farm paraphernalia in front, a lush garden behind. Arriving guests are offered tea, cake and helpful local information. 'Comfortable and immaculate' bedrooms (one a duplex family suite with a kitchenette; suitable for children over four because of the stairs) have 'excellent lighting', small fridge, bathrobes, fresh milk available on request. Local pubs are within walking distance.

MAP 3:C5
Hindlip Lane
Worcester WR3 8SJ
T: 01905 456457
w: manorcoachhouse.co.uk

BEDROOMS: 5. All double, in converted outbuildings, 3 on ground floor.
OPEN: all year except Christmas.
FACILITIES: breakfast room, free Wi-Fi, in-room TV (Freeview), 1-acre garden.
BACKGROUND MUSIC: none.
LOCATION: 2 miles from city centre.
CHILDREN: all ages welcomed.
DOGS: not allowed.
CREDIT CARDS: MC, Visa.
PRICES: per room B&B £74–£95, D,B&B from £89.

YELVERTON Devon

CIDER HOUSE

In the former brew house, Bertie and Bryony Hancock's sophisticated B&B is surrounded by the National Trust's Buckland Abbey estate. Impeccably designed in country house style, the elegant drawing room has an open fire, fresh flowers; maps and guidebooks. Mullioned windows in the airy, pretty first-floor bedrooms reveal glorious views; bathrooms are glamorous, with a roll-top bath. Breakfast includes eggs from the owners' rare breed chickens, meat from their saddleback pigs, and groat's pudding, a Devon speciality. Residents receive passes for the abbey, one-time home of Sir Francis Drake, and its gardens. For romantics, luxury shepherd's cabins have a glass ceiling above the bed; a wood-burner; DIY provisions in the galley kitchen.

MAP 1:D4
Buckland Abbey
Yelverton PL20 6EZ
T: 01822 259062
w: cider-house.co.uk/index.php

BEDROOMS: 4. Plus 2 adult-only self-catering shepherd's huts.
OPEN: Mar–Oct.
FACILITIES: drawing room, free Wi-Fi, in-room TV (Freeview), terrace, garden, 700-acre grounds, parking.
BACKGROUND MUSIC: none.
LOCATION: 1 mile from village, 4 miles N of Plymouth.
CHILDREN: not under 16.
DOGS: not allowed.
CREDIT CARDS: MC, Visa.
PRICES: per room single £125–£175, double B&B £140–£190. 2-night min. stay preferred weekends.

YORK Yorkshire

BAR CONVENT

Serenity is assured at this B&B in England's
oldest active convent, next to the city's medieval
walls. The Grade I listed building still houses a
community of sisters, who share their peaceful
garden, domed chapel and antique religious
texts with guests. Simple, immaculate bedrooms
(some designed by Olga Polizzi) have a
'wickedly comfortable' bed and a well-equipped
refreshment tray. Open during the day, the café,
in a Victorian atrium, serves an award-winning,
slap-up breakfast, beers and wine, meals, coffee
and cake. There's a communal kitchen for DIY
dinners; the pick of York's eateries are on the
doorstep. Guests enjoy a discounted entrance
to the exhibition in the on-site Living Heritage
Centre, and the convent, founded in 1686.

MAP 4:D4
17 Blossom Street
York YO24 1AQ
T: 01904 643238
w: bar-convent.org.uk

BEDROOMS: 20. 4 with shared
bathrooms.
OPEN: all year except some days over
Christmas.
FACILITIES: lift (to 1st and 2nd floors),
sitting room, kitchen, licensed café,
meeting rooms, free Wi-Fi, in-room
TV (Freeview), ¼-acre garden,
Victorian atrium, 18th-century chapel,
museum, shop.
BACKGROUND MUSIC: none.
LOCATION: 5 mins' walk from the
railway station.
CHILDREN: all ages welcomed (well-
equipped guest kitchen, with a
washing machine (small additional
charge)).
DOGS: assistance dogs only.
CREDIT CARDS: MC, Visa.
PRICES: per room B&B £40–£140.

NEW

YORK Yorkshire

THE BLOOMSBURY

A scenic riverside walk away from the city centre,
Steve and Tricia Townsley's three-storey Victorian
town house B&B offers an exceptional Yorkshire
welcome. The 'charming' hosts greet guests with a
hot drink and 'something sweet' on arrival. Most
of the traditionally furnished bedrooms are up the
original staircase. 'Extremely comfortable' and
well equipped, they are supplied with tea- and
coffee-making facilities, a safe, iron and alarm
clock. In the sedate dining room overlooking
a flowery courtyard garden, the 'very tasty'
breakfast offers locally sourced fare: sausages and
thick-cut bacon from the butcher 200 yards away;
roasted ground coffee from an independent coffee
merchant nearby; 'fabulous porridge with a tot of
whisky!' Off-street parking is a bonus.

25% DISCOUNT VOUCHERS

MAP 4:D4
127 Clifton
York YO30 6BL
T: 01904 634031
w: thebloomsburyguesthouse.com

BEDROOMS: 4. 1 on ground floor.
OPEN: all year except 23 Dec–end Jan..
FACILITIES: sitting/dining room, free
Wi-Fi, in-room TV (Freeview),
terrace, 'secret' courtyard garden,
parking.
BACKGROUND MUSIC: 'relaxing hits
from the 1950s to the present day' in
dining room at breakfast.
LOCATION: within a mile of the City
centre, 10–15-min. walk from York
Minster.
CHILDREN: not under 17.
DOGS: not allowed (resident dog).
CREDIT CARDS: MC, Visa.
PRICES: per person B&B single £60–£70,
double £40–£60. 2-night min. stay.

ABERDEEN Aberdeenshire
ATHOLL HOTEL

Soaring skywards, the spires of this granite Victorian Gothic Revival building make this traditional hotel within reach of the city centre an easy-to-spot beacon. Convenient for the airport, it's popular with business travellers. Fuss-free bedrooms have cheery tartan bedcovers and cushions; an array of necessary amenities includes a tea and coffee tray, hairdryer, iron and ironing board. Spacious suites suit a family. The restaurant, bar and lounge serve generously portioned, straightforward locally sourced dishes, such as baked salmon, samphire, spring onions, lemon and basil dressing. At breakfast, try tattie scones or smoked Finnan haddie. Golf courses are close to gloved hand.

MAP 5:C3
54 Kings Gate
Aberdeen AB15 4YN
T: 01224 323505
W: atholl-aberdeen.co.uk

BEDROOMS: 34. 2 suitable for disabled.
OPEN: Mar–Oct, shepherd's huts all year except Feb.
FACILITIES: lift (to 1st floor), lounge, bar, restaurant, patio, free Wi-Fi, in-room TV (Sky Sports), wedding facilities, functions, parking.
BACKGROUND MUSIC: in restaurant.
LOCATION: 1½ miles W of city centre.
CHILDREN: all ages welcomed (special menu, £10 per night).
DOGS: not allowed.
CREDIT CARDS: Amex, MC, Visa.
PRICES: per room B&B single £99, double £119. À la carte £32.

NEW

ABERFELDY Perth and Kinross
FORTINGALL HOTEL

At the entrance to Glen Lyon and close to Loch Tay, this small country hotel in an old coaching inn is at the centre of an Arts and Crafts conservation village. The Fortingall Yew, believed to be over 3,000 years old (Britain's most ancient tree), stands in the churchyard. Bedrooms are decorated in muted tones, with splashes of colour provided by the tartans and tweeds of local estates. 'Our room was fresh and bright with an enormous bathroom. A decanter of whisky, coffee, shortbread were supplied.' There's a choice of dining area for chef David Dunn's daily menus. 'The venison loin and sirloin steak were particularly fine.' A place to mingle, Ewe bar has live folk music on Friday nights. Walking, cycling, climbing, fishing and shooting on the doorstep.

MAP 5:D2
Old Street
Aberfeldy PH15 2NQ
T: 01887 830367
W: fortingall.com

BEDROOMS: 10. 2 in annexe.
OPEN: all year.
FACILITIES: bar, lounge, library, dining room, function room, wedding facilities, garden.
BACKGROUND MUSIC: in restaurant, live fiddle music in bar on Friday nights.
LOCATION: 7 miles W of town.
CHILDREN: all ages welcomed.
DOGS: allowed.
CREDIT CARDS: MC, Visa.
PRICES: per room B&B single £100, double £190–£230, D,B&B single £150, double £260–£300.

ALLANTON Scottish Borders
ALLANTON INN

'Helpful hosts' Katrina and William Reynolds offer a 'warm welcome' at their 'good-value' 18th-century restaurant-with-rooms in a Borders village. The former coaching house has 'a happy blend of modern furnishings, contemporary artwork, and the feel of a traditional country pub'; the bar has a 'spectacular' menu of over 30 gins. Borders-sourced produce is used for Craig Rushton's menus, who has returned as chef. Bedrooms have been refreshed. 'Very good breakfasts' start the day with 'a generous choice of fruit compotes; good-quality sausages, bacon, haggis'. The hosts provide bike storage, a drying room and a wealth of knowledge about the area. A large beer garden has wide-open country views. Day permits for trout and salmon fishing.

MAP 5:E3
Main Street
Allanton TD11 3JZ
T: 01890 818260
W: allantoninn.co.uk

BEDROOMS: 6.
OPEN: all year except 25/26 Dec.
FACILITIES: bar, 2 restaurant areas, free Wi-Fi, in-room TV (Freeview), large garden, parking.
BACKGROUND MUSIC: in bar and restaurant.
LOCATION: village centre.
CHILDREN: all ages welcomed.
DOGS: allowed in some areas, by prior arrangement.
CREDIT CARDS: Amex, MC, Visa.
PRICES: per room B&B £80–£105, D,B&B £120–£150.

APPLECROSS Highland
APPLECROSS INN

At the end of an 11-mile stretch of winding single-track road, visitors might breathe a sigh of relief on reaching Judith Fish's white-painted hostelry. The small dining room takes full advantage of its isolated setting on the Applecross peninsula, serving feasts of ocean-fresh seafood, perhaps dressed prawns or king scallops straight from the bay. The seashore beer terrace has outdoor tables and seating; in spring and summer, a retro food truck sells fish and chips, ice cream, cakes and coffees. In the buzzy bar, Scottish gins, single malts and local craft ales are served before the log fire. Superlative views across the Inner Sound of Raasay extend from the clean, comfortable bedrooms; there may be some pub noise. Cyclists, walkers, kayakers welcomed.

MAP 5:C1
Shore Street
Applecross IV54 8LR
T: 01520 744262
W: applecrossinn.co.uk

BEDROOMS: 7. 1 on ground floor.
OPEN: all year, no accommodation for 2 weeks over Christmas, New Year, restaurant closed 25 Dec, 1/2 Jan.
FACILITIES: bar, dining room, free Wi-Fi, beer garden, bicycle storage, bar, dining room wheelchair accessible, adapted toilet.
BACKGROUND MUSIC: in bar.
LOCATION: 85 miles W of Inverness, opposite the Isle of Skye, approx. 2 hours' drive.
CHILDREN: all ages welcomed, not in bar after 8.30 pm.
DOGS: allowed in 2 bedrooms, on lead in bar (£15 per stay).
CREDIT CARDS: MC, Visa.
PRICES: per person B&B single £95, double £150. À la carte £35.

ARINAGOUR Argyll and Bute

COLL HOTEL

The buzzy hub of this Inner Hebridean island, the hotel (run by the Oliphant family for three generations) offers sublime sea views from Coll's only village. Recently expanded, the spacious restaurant features just-landed lobsters, crabs, langoustines, and Coll-reared lamb on the daily specials board. Upgraded bedrooms have an understated style and plentiful homely extras (home-made biscuits, board games, Scottish-made toiletries); four look over to the Treshnish Isles. In the cosy bar, local photographs, nautical memorabilia and an open fire; spectacular seascapes from the large garden overlooking the bay. After sunset, the rooms' glow-in-the-dark sky scopes and star maps show a sky untainted by light pollution. Complimentary shuttle.

25% DISCOUNT VOUCHERS

MAP 5:C1
Arinagour
Isle of Coll PA78 6SZ
T: 01879 230334
w: collhotel.com

BEDROOMS: 6.
OPEN: all year, Christmas and New Year whole house parties only.
FACILITIES: lounge, 2 bars, restaurant, residents' lounge and dining room, free Wi-Fi, in-room TV (Freeview), garden, helipad, bicycles to borrow.
BACKGROUND MUSIC: none.
LOCATION: village centre.
CHILDREN: all ages welcomed.
DOGS: allowed in bar areas, not in bedrooms.
CREDIT CARDS: MC, Visa.
PRICES: per room B&B £80–£165. À la carte from £25.

BALLYGRANT Argyll and Bute

KILMENY COUNTRY HOUSE

At a handsomely furnished 19th-century house on the Isle of Islay, 'fabulous hosts' Margaret and Blair Rozga offer guests a sweet welcome with home-baked treats and tea. The 'superb' B&B is surrounded by Hebridean farmland. Country house decor and antiques style the traditional, individually designed bedrooms. A bonus in each: 'spectacular views' across hills, glen and countryside. Some rooms are pleasingly capacious (a generous suite with its own kitchen suits a family); others have access to a sheltered garden; all have tea, coffee, home-made biscuits, a fridge with fresh milk. A complimentary dram of whisky makes a thoughtful nightcap. Substantial farmhouse breakfasts with home-made bread, oatcakes and preserves are 'worth getting up for'.

MAP 5:D1
Ballygrant
Isle of Islay PA45 7QW
T: 01496 840668
w: kilmeny.co.uk

BEDROOMS: 5. 2 on ground floor.
OPEN: Mar–Oct.
FACILITIES: drawing room, dining room, sun lounge, free Wi-Fi, in-room TV (Freeview), ½-acre garden.
BACKGROUND MUSIC: none.
LOCATION: ½ mile S of Ballygrant, 10 mins' drive to Port Askaig.
CHILDREN: over-4s welcomed.
DOGS: allowed in some bedrooms.
CREDIT CARDS: none accepted.
PRICES: per room B&B £138–£172. 1-night bookings sometimes refused.

NEW

MAP 5:D2
Balquhidder
Lochearnhead FK19 8PQ
T: 01877 384622
W: monachylemhor.net

BALQUHIDDER Stirling
MONACHYLE MHOR

'An experience not to be missed.' A four-mile track skirting Loch Voil in the Trossachs national park leads to this pink-painted 18th-century stone farmstead, where Tom and Lisa May Lewis run their restaurant-with-rooms. Inside, 'a delightful warren of corridors and imaginatively used spaces' is creatively decorated in shades of grey. Handsome bedrooms are a quirky mix of rustic pieces and contemporary furnishings and artwork; Sprocket has a large bed on a raised platform giving views of the hills and lochs. Head chef Marysia Paszkowska's 'beautifully cooked' dishes use produce from the family farm, venison from the hills, Isle of Mull scallops. 'Never before have I admitted to enjoying a turnip!' Sandwiches and freshly baked scones are available all day.

BEDROOMS: 14. 3 on ground floor, 6 in courtyard, Ferry Cabin and a restored 1950s Pilot Panther showman's wagon.
OPEN: all year.
FACILITIES: sitting room, bar, conservatory restaurant, free Wi-Fi, in-room TV, wedding facilities, garden.
BACKGROUND MUSIC: in bar/restaurant.
LOCATION: 4 miles off the A84, down a single-track lane skirting Loch Voil.
CHILDREN: all ages welcomed.
DOGS: allowed in 3 bedrooms, bar and lounge.
CREDIT CARDS: Amex, MC, Visa.
PRICES: per room B&B £195–£360 per person. Set menu £65.

MAP 5:D1
Mill Farm
Barcaldine PA37 1SE
T: 01631 720125
W: ardtorna.co.uk

BARCALDINE Argyll and Bute
ARDTORNA

Light, bright and full of life, Sean and Karen O'Byrne's super-modern, eco-friendly house is all Scandi style and floor-to-ceiling windows offering memorable views of Loch Creran. Afternoon pastries are part of a generous greeting, while a help-yourself home-made whisky cream liqueur remains a temptation. Spruced-up bedrooms have bright splashes of colour, a king-size bed and under-floor heating, plus many extras: handmade chocolates, complimentary treats. Breakfast is served in the glass-fronted dining room: home-baked soda bread, griddled waffles, Scottish platter with Stornoway black pudding and tattie scones. The hosts can help plan day trips; a longbow lesson is an unexpected alternative – Sean is a former world champion.

BEDROOMS: 4.
OPEN: Apr–Nov.
FACILITIES: dining room, free Wi-Fi, in-room TV (Freeview), 1-acre farmland, parking.
BACKGROUND MUSIC: traditional in restaurant.
LOCATION: 12 miles N of Oban.
CHILDREN: not under 12.
DOGS: not allowed.
CREDIT CARDS: MC, Visa.
PRICES: per person B&B £75–£100.

BORVE Western Isles

PAIRC AN T-SRATH

On the west coast of Harris, Lena and Richard MacLennan's small, 'lovely, comfortable' guest house overlooks Borve's golden sand beach, and has 'superb views' over the sound of Taransay. It's all simply and unfussily done, without compromising comfort. Harris tweed blankets drape the bed in the neat, wood-floored bedrooms; fresh flowers and shelves of books bring lightness to a sitting room warmed by a peat fire. A surprising touch: a sauna in which to ease tired muscles after a day exploring the island. Breakfasts are a 'feast' (Uist scallops, Stornoway black pudding).

MAP 5:B1
Borve
Isle of Harris HS3 3HT
T: 01859 550386
w: paircant-srath.co.uk

BEDROOMS: 4.
OPEN: all year, except Christmas, New Year.
FACILITIES: sitting room, dining room, free Wi-Fi, sauna.
BACKGROUND MUSIC: none.
LOCATION: in village.
CHILDREN: all ages welcomed.
DOGS: allowed in 1 bedroom, by arrangement.
CREDIT CARDS: MC, Visa.
PRICES: per person B&B £54. Set 3-course dinner £38 (not available on Sat night May–Sept).

NEW

BRAEMAR Aberdeenshire

THE FIFE ARMS

At every turn, contemporary artwork, artefacts, taxidermy specimens and striking features catch the eye in this imposing 19th-century coaching inn. Now more country lodge than pub, it has been lavishly revitalised by gallery owners Iwan and Manuela Wirth. Paintings by many Scottish artists are among the 14,000 works on display. A Picasso hangs in the tartan-walled drawing room, below Chinese artist Zhang Enli's remarkable hand-painted ceiling; Louise Bourgeois's huge spider sculpture lurks in the courtyard. Richly furnished suites and bedrooms pay homage to a place, person or event with links to the area; Croft rooms are cosy and simple with box beds. Wood-fired cooking is showcased in the dining room; hearty dishes in the Flying Stag bar.

MAP 5:C2
Mar Road
Braemar AB35 5YN
T: 01339 720200
w: thefifearms.com

BEDROOMS: 46.
OPEN: all year, restaurant closed on Sun evenings.
FACILITIES: bar, drawing room, library, free Wi-Fi, in-room TV, pub, restaurant, 2 meeting rooms, 2-acre gardens.
BACKGROUND MUSIC: in public spaces.
LOCATION: in town centre.
CHILDREN: all ages welcomed.
DOGS: in some bedrooms, pub.
CREDIT CARDS: Amex, MC, Visa.
PRICES: per room B&B from £200. À la carte £46.

BROADFORD Highland
TIGH AN DOCHAIS

'Equal to any first class hotel', Neil Hope and
Lesley Unwin's 'beautiful' modern, architect-
designed B&B is across a galvanised footbridge.
Huge windows bring 'glorious views' of
Broadford Bay and the Cuillin mountains right
into the house. The book-lined, open-plan lounge/
dining area has a log-burning stove. Plump sofas
enable comfortable enjoyment of the panorama.
On the floor below, a sliding door leads from
each tartan-accented bedroom to larch decking.
Neil Hope cooks a 'delicious' locally sourced
breakfast, served communally: Skye sausages,
black pudding, home-made bread, muffins,
yogurt. 'Perfect' evening meals can be arranged;
restaurants are close by. The 'friendly hosts' offer
'helpful information' for planning excursions.

MAP 5:C1
13 Harrapool
Broadford
Isle of Skye IV49 9AQ
T: 01471 820022
W: skyebedbreakfast.co.uk

BEDROOMS: 3. All on ground floor.
OPEN: Mar–end Nov.
FACILITIES: lounge/dining area, free
Wi-Fi, in-room TV (Freesat).
BACKGROUND MUSIC: traditional,
occasionally, during breakfast.
LOCATION: 1 mile E of Broadford.
CHILDREN: all ages welcomed (must
take own room).
DOGS: not allowed.
CREDIT CARDS: MC, Visa.
PRICES: per room B&B single £90,
double £120, D,B&B £170. Set menu £25.

BRODICK Ayrshire
AUCHRANNIE HOUSE HOTEL

South of Goat Fell's pyramidal peak, this child-
friendly destination is a large resort on the Isle of
Arran. Employee-owned, the hotel in a 19th-
century country house is one of two established
by the Johnston family on the sprawling estate.
Rooms have earthy hues, hints of tweed. Some
of the large, contemporary rooms enjoy access
to an outdoor terrace and hot tub. All rooms
have fresh milk, tea-/coffee-making facilities.
There are plush lounges (some with an open
fire), a well-stocked library, swimming pools; a
play barn for children. Dining options include
grilled fare and West Coast seafood in informal
Brambles; Scottish-themed tapas in a conservatory
restaurant, eighteen69. Nearby, walks, bike and
horse rides await.

MAP 5:E1
Auchrannie Road
Brodick
Isle of Arran KA27 8BZ
T: 01770 302234
W: auchrannie.co.uk

BEDROOMS: 28. Some suitable for
disabled, plus Spa Resort rooms and
30 self-catering lodges.
OPEN: all year.
FACILITIES: bar, lounges, 3 restaurants,
spa, two 20-metre indoor pools, gym,
free Wi-Fi, in-room TV (Freeview),
wedding facilities, function facilities,
60-acre grounds, tennis, parking,
complimentary shuttle bus to/from the
ferry terminal.
BACKGROUND MUSIC: in public areas.
LOCATION: 1 mile from ferry terminal.
CHILDREN: all ages welcomed.
DOGS: allowed in some bedrooms,
some public rooms.
CREDIT CARDS: Amex, MC, Visa.
PRICES: per room B&B £79–£229,
D,B&B £109–£259. À la carte £35.
1-night booking sometimes refused on
Sat during peak periods.

BRUICHLADDICH Argyll and Bute

LOCH GORM HOUSE

'What more could one ask for?' On the northern shore of Islay, this 'charming, beautifully appointed' B&B is run by 'wonderfully welcoming' Fiona Doyle. The stone-built house is fronted by well-kept gardens, and has 'amazing views over the bay'. A florist, the hostess displays 'magnificent' flower arrangements in the large drawing room. 'Cosy, comfortable and bright', the prettily furnished bedrooms gaze seaward or inland across the fields and have superb bathrooms. 'Fiona made dinner reservations for us – a nice touch.' Breakfast ('such a feast') is a 'scrumptious' start to the day. Wellies, coats and beach towels are provided for coastal wanderings. Justly famous for its malt whiskies, the island currently has eight working distilleries.

25% DISCOUNT VOUCHERS

MAP 5:D1
Bruichladdich
Isle of Islay PA49 7UN
T: 01496 850139
w: lochgormhouse.com

BEDROOMS: 3.
OPEN: Mar–Dec.
FACILITIES: drawing room, dining room, free Wi-Fi, in-room TV (Freeview), 1-acre garden, drying facilities.
BACKGROUND MUSIC: none.
LOCATION: outside village on seafront.
CHILDREN: all ages welcomed.
DOGS: well-behaved dogs allowed in bedrooms, bar.
CREDIT CARDS: MC, Visa.
PRICES: per room B&B £135–£155.

DORNOCH Highland

2 QUAIL

'A good stay.' Close to the cathedral and the Royal Dornoch Golf Club, Kerensa and Michael Carr's 'pleasant' sandstone guest house provides homely, well-executed accommodation. A contented visitor praises the 'very friendly and thoughtful hosts, comfortable bed, warm room in winter'. The late Victorian town house has a wood-burning stove, tartan carpet and well-stocked library in the cosy lounge; many family antiques are displayed throughout the property. Traditionally decorated bedrooms have a hospitality tray, a 'good' power shower, 'fluffy towels' in the bathroom. A 'delicious breakfast' is served from 7 am ('for those with an early tee time'). The sands of Dornoch Firth are nearby.

MAP 5:B2
Castle Street
Dornoch IV25 3SN
T: 01862 811811
w: 2quail.com

BEDROOMS: 3.
OPEN: all year except Christmas.
FACILITIES: fully licensed lounge/library and dining room, free Wi-Fi throughout, in-room TV (Freeview), tea and coffee, hairdryer.
BACKGROUND MUSIC: none.
LOCATION: town centre.
CHILDREN: 'babes in arms', over-10s welcomed.
DOGS: only assistance dogs.
CREDIT CARDS: Amex, MC, Visa.
PRICES: per room B&B from £110.

DULNAIN BRIDGE Highland
MUCKRACH COUNTRY HOUSE HOTEL

Surrounded by the Cairngorms national park, the Cowap family's restored Victorian shooting lodge is zesty inside, with local artwork, modern furnishings and Scottish flourishes in the panelled public areas. Outside, the terrace overlooks pond and pastureland. Bright bedrooms have bathrobes, technology (smart TV, iPod dock, ceiling speakers). An all-day menu of cake, coffees and nibbles keeps you going, but dinner is a feast: 'home-style cooking with a twist', served in the candlelit conservatory restaurant, perhaps Highland venison, black pudding potato cake, red cabbage, redcurrant jus. The range of 70 whiskies merits a nightcap. An extensive breakfast might have Inverawe smoked kippers; croque madame.

MAP 5:C2
Dulnain Bridge
Grantown-on-Spey PH26 3LY
T: 01479 851227
w: muckrach.com

BEDROOMS: 16. Some in garden annexe, 2 interconnecting rooms suitable for a family, plus a 3-bedroom self-catering lodge with hot tub.
OPEN: all year.
FACILITIES: drawing room, library, bar, conservatory restaurant/coffee shop, private dining room, free Wi-Fi, in-room TV (Freeview), 1-acre grounds, terraced patio, wedding facilities, meetings, drying room.
BACKGROUND MUSIC: in public areas.
LOCATION: outskirts of Dulnain Bridge, 5 miles from Grantown-on-Spey.
CHILDREN: all ages welcomed.
DOGS: well-behaved dogs allowed in 5 bedrooms in adjacent building, on lead in library.
CREDIT CARDS: Amex, MC, Visa.
PRICES: per room B&B from £99, D,B&B from £159. À la carte £27.

NEW

DUNDEE
TAYPARK HOUSE

Stunning grounds and outstanding views of the River Tay and hills of Fife surround this baronial mansion. Sympathetically restored to its former glory, it is now a tidy hotel with romantic inclinations. Tucked amid award-winning gardens is an outdoor gin bar, popular with locals and residents for a quick snifter before shifting into the original library or drawing room for haddock ceviche and Ayrshire pork belly. When the sun shines, the wood-fired pizza oven burns in the garden for alfresco dining. Fresh, spacious rooms have a muted palette, poetry etched on the walls; Victorian fixtures and luxury toiletries in the bathroom. Start the day with French toast, fruit salad, gallons of coffee. Go on to explore Scotland's design heritage at V&A Dundee.

MAP 5:D3
484 Perth Road
Dundee DD2 1LR
T: 01382 643777
w: tayparkhouse.co.uk

BEDROOMS: 14. 1 suitable for disabled.
OPEN: all year.
FACILITIES: café, restaurant, free Wi-Fi, in-room TV, mature gardens, wedding facilities, functions.
BACKGROUND MUSIC: none.
LOCATION: in Tayside area of city, 1½ miles from Dundee University.
CHILDREN: all ages welcomed.
DOGS: assistance dogs allowed.
CREDIT CARDS: MC, Visa.
PRICES: per room B&B single from £60, double from £80. 1-night booking refused weekends.

EDINBURGH
THE BALMORAL

An Edinburgh icon for over a century, this
Victorian railway stop-over is today a thoroughly
21st-century hotel (Rocco Forte Hotels). Greeted
by a kilted doorman, visitors cross the threshold
into grand public spaces. Most of the elegant
bedrooms, designed by Olga Polizzi, look towards
the castle. Suites have Scottish flourishes, wide
views. Guests who look beyond the Michelin-
starred restaurant or award-winning spa might
spend an afternoon taking tea in the glass-domed
Palm Court, or sampling some of the bar's 400-
plus whiskies. Informal dining is in Brasserie
Prince. 'We had an excellent, if expensive, meal of
scallops, monkfish and steak.' A place where time
waits: the hotel clock has been set three minutes
fast since 1902, so no one misses their train.

MAP 5:D2
1 Princes Street
Edinburgh EH2 2EQ
T: 0131 556 2414
W: roccofortehotels.com/hotels-and-
    resorts/the-balmoral-hotel

BEDROOMS: 188. 3 suitable for disabled.
OPEN: all year.
FACILITIES: drawing room, 3 bars,
restaurant, brasserie, free Wi-Fi,
in-room TV, wedding facilities,
conferences, indoor swimming pool,
spa, gym, valet parking.
BACKGROUND MUSIC: in restaurant,
brasserie, bars and lobby.
LOCATION: city centre.
CHILDREN: all ages welcomed.
DOGS: allowed in some bedrooms.
CREDIT CARDS: Amex, MC, Visa.
PRICES: per room B&B from £270.
À la carte £80 (restaurant), £42.50
(brasserie).

EDINBURGH
BROOKS HOTEL EDINBURGH

Within easy reach of the city's sightseeing trail,
Andrew and Carla Brooks's spruced-up 1840s
West End hotel has a relaxed, clubby feel. The
modern lounge is given a vintage edge with
handpicked statement pieces including a black
chandelier, deep leather seating, animal horns;
periodicals, board games, an honesty bar and a
DVD library are on hand. Unfussy bedrooms
(some suitable for a family) have their own
temperature control and comfortable beds with a
choice of down or micro-fibre bedding. No need
to rush at weekends: breakfasts, served until 11
am, include a full Scottish embracing haggis and
a tattie scone. See also Brooks Guesthouse, Bristol
(main entry).

MAP 5:D2
70–72 Grove Street
Edinburgh EH3 8AP
T: 0131 228 2323
W: www.brooksedinburgh.com

BEDROOMS: 46. Some in annexe,
1 suitable for disabled.
OPEN: all year except 23–26 Dec.
FACILITIES: lounge, breakfast room,
dining room, free Wi-Fi, in-room
TV, courtyard garden, paid parking
nearby (£12 per day), public areas
wheelchair accessible, adapted toilet.
BACKGROUND MUSIC: in lounge,
breakfast room (jazz/contemporary).
LOCATION: 10 mins' walk to
Haymarket station.
CHILDREN: all ages welcomed.
DOGS: not allowed.
CREDIT CARDS: Amex, MC, Visa.
PRICES: per room B&B single £65–£135,
double £75–£150, 1-night bookings
rarely refused.

EDINBURGH
CITYROOMZ EDINBURGH

Ideal for city walkers on a budget, this affordable
hotel, with its bright, pared-down style, makes
a cheerful base for exploring the surrounding
landmarks. Rooms on the upper floors look out
at Old Town and New Town. Basic, and varying
in size, rooms can be boxy or capacious, but they
have all the essentials of a city stay: blackout
curtains or blinds, an iron and ironing board, a
laptop safe; a bedside nook for a cup of tea. BYO
takeaway meals may be eaten in the communal
dining area (crockery and cutlery provided).
Breakfast – a continental buffet or a grab-and-go
bag – is available at an extra charge.

MAP 5:D2
25–33 Shandwick Place
Edinburgh EH2 4RG
T: 0131 229 6871
W: cityroomz.com

BEDROOMS: 45. 9 family rooms with
bunk bed.
OPEN: all year.
FACILITIES: lift, dining room, free
Wi-Fi, in-room TV, discounts for
parking at Castle Terrace car park,
nearby.
BACKGROUND MUSIC: in public areas.
LOCATION: city centre.
CHILDREN: all ages welcomed.
DOGS: well-behaved dogs allowed in
some bedrooms, on lead in library.
CREDIT CARDS: MC, Visa.
PRICES: room only from £85.50.
Breakfast (continental) £6.95.

EDINBURGH
THE DUNSTANE HOUSES

Heathery tones and tweedy fabrics bring a breath
of fresh Orkney air to this family-owned hotel in
a peaceful area just beyond the city centre. It is
run in two Victorian villas, Dunstane House, and
Hampton House, opposite. Luxurious suites have
a high ceiling, a deep copper bath; all rooms have
heritage styling and a comfortable bed, pampering
Scottish products, home-made shortbread. In Ba'
bar, rich hues, leather bar stools, monochrome
photographs and a wide selection of craft spirits;
in the lounges, colourful velvet chairs and sofas. In
the dining lounge and bar (in Dunstane House),
modern Scottish dishes (crispy haggis bonbons,
hand-dived scallops) are available throughout the
day. Buses to the centre; those to the airport stop
right outside.

25% DISCOUNT VOUCHERS

MAP 5:D2
4 West Coates and 5 Hampton
Terrace
Edinburgh EH12 5JQ
T: 0131 337 6169
W: thedunstane.com

BEDROOMS: 35. In 2 buildings, 18 in
Hampton House.
OPEN: all year.
FACILITIES: bar, 2 lounges,
conservatory, free Wi-Fi, in-room TV
(Freeview), wedding facilities, garden,
parking.
BACKGROUND MUSIC: in bar and
lounges.
LOCATION: Murrayfield, West End of
Edinburgh.
CHILDREN: all ages welcomed.
DOGS: not allowed.
CREDIT CARDS: Amex, MC, Visa.
PRICES: per room B&B single from
£149, double £154–£525, D,B&B
double £204–£595. À la carte £30.
2-night min. stay preferred Sat night
in peak season.

NEW

EDINBURGH
FINGAL

All is shipshape on this plush former Northern Lighthouse supply ship, floating moments away from buzzy Leith. Once serving Scottish islands, today this now luxury liner serves up classic cocktails and fine dining before rocking visitors to sleep in decadent berths. The Art Deco interiors gleam glamour (curving wood, high-gloss brass, thick carpets, rich leather). Porthole-lined cabins have a huge bed draped in a custom-woven throw; rain shower, under-floor heating, good toiletries in the bathroom. First-class cabins open on to the deck; those on the starboard have the best views. Find modern Scottish fare in the dining room come evening. At breakfast, haggis and black pudding complete the full Scottish; waffles are tempting alternatives.

MAP 5:D2
Alexandra Dock
Edinburgh EH6 7DX
T: 0131 357 5000
W: fingal.co.uk

BEDROOMS: 23.
OPEN: all year except Christmas, New Year.
FACILITIES: bar, ballroom, dining room, deck, free Wi-Fi, in-room TV.
BACKGROUND MUSIC: none.
LOCATION: Port of Leith.
CHILDREN: all ages welcomed.
DOGS: not allowed.
CREDIT CARDS: Amex, MC, Visa.
PRICES: per room B&B from £300.

EDINBURGH
THE RAEBURN

In the 'very attractive' Stockbridge district, the Maclean family practise the art of hotel-keeping in their extended late Georgian mansion. Guests are 'warmly greeted' and shown to a chic bedroom, 'furnished to the highest standards', with a marble-finished rainforest shower – some also have a roll-top bath. 'Our room was large, well lit, free of noise from the popular bar below,' write readers in 2019. The restaurant, adjoining the bar, has a terrace where overhead heaters allow alfresco dining with a view on to the fields of Edinburgh Academical rugby club. Building work on a new stadium and shops is in progress. 'A few glitches' but 'the staff were kind and helpful; there were many good touches', like fresh milk in the minibar, a capsule coffee machine.

MAP 5:D2
112 Raeburn Place
Edinburgh EH4 1HG
T: 0131 332 7000
W: theraeburn.com

BEDROOMS: 10. 1 suitable for disabled.
OPEN: all year except 25 Dec.
FACILITIES: bar, garden and club room (dining), private dining area, library/function room, conference room, free Wi-Fi, in-room TV (Freeview), beer garden, dining terrace, limited parking, public areas wheelchair accessible, adapted toilet.
BACKGROUND MUSIC: in public areas.
LOCATION: ½ mile from city centre.
CHILDREN: all ages welcomed.
DOGS: allowed in bar, only guide dogs allowed in bedrooms.
CREDIT CARDS: Amex, MC, Visa.
PRICES: per room B&B from £150. À la carte £34.

EDINBURGH
TIGERLILY

Refreshingly spirited, this hotel in an elegant
Georgian house in the heart of New Town does
not go in for half measures. Every room has
swagger, with rakish prints, jewel tones, wildly
patterned wallpaper and shimmering mirror-ball
surfaces; a lush wall of greenery. Uncluttered
bedrooms rein it in, with soothing hues, stripped
wooden floor, a sleek bathroom, but can't resist
the odd splash of colour. All are packed with
amenities: plush bathrobes, slippers, a pre-loaded
iPod, an iPad concierge. The bars are popular
with locals on a night out; so are the brasserie-
style plates served in the buzzy restaurant.
Come morning, laid-back yet on the ball staff
dispense restorative detox juices, breakfast baps
and good coffee.

MAP 5:D2
125 George Street
Edinburgh EH2 4JN
T: 0131 225 5005
W: tigerlilyedinburgh.co.uk

BEDROOMS: 33. Some smoking.
OPEN: all year except 24/25 Dec.
FACILITIES: lift, 2 bars, restaurant, free
Wi-Fi, in-room TV (Freeview).
BACKGROUND MUSIC: in bar and
restaurant.
LOCATION: city centre.
CHILDREN: all ages welcomed.
DOGS: not allowed.
CREDIT CARDS: Amex, MC, Visa.
PRICES: per room B&B from £203.
À la carte £30.

EDINBURGH
21212

Take a Michelin-starred kitchen, throw in equally
impressive bedrooms and a soupçon of laid-back
glamour, and you have Paul Kitching and Katie
O'Brien's splendid restaurant-with-rooms. Airy
spaces within the Georgian town house, which
faces the Royal Terrace Gardens, have been given
a light, quirky touch: a vast copy of a painting
by Caravaggio; a sculpted Greek-style head; a
dazzling chandelier. An epicurean evening begins
in the handsome first-floor drawing room with an
aperitif, followed by an accomplished weekly-
changing menu in the elegant dining room with
clear sight into the kitchen. Top-notch dishes,
including 2- to 5-course lunches, have French
influences. In the crisply styled bedrooms, plush
seating, city or firth views.

MAP 5:D2
3 Royal Terrace
Edinburgh EH7 5AB
T: 0345 22 21212
W: 21212restaurant.co.uk

BEDROOMS: 4.
OPEN: all year, restaurant closed
Sun–Tues.
FACILITIES: drawing room, restaurant,
private dining rooms, free Wi-Fi,
in-room TV (Freeview).
BACKGROUND MUSIC: none.
LOCATION: 5 mins' walk from city
centre.
CHILDREN: not under 5.
DOGS: not allowed.
CREDIT CARDS: Amex, MC, Visa.
PRICES: per room B&B £95–£295.
À la carte £70. 2-night min. stay
preferred at weekends in Aug.

EDINBURGH
THE WITCHERY BY THE CASTLE

By the gates of Edinburgh Castle, James
Thomson's spellbinding restaurant-with-suites
is sited within 16th- and 17th-century buildings.
There are dramatic nooks and crannies, fine
carvings and rich tapestries. An indulgent Scottish
menu is served in candlelit dining rooms under
a painted ceiling, with such dishes as roast loin
of Cairngorm venison, creamed kale, pommes
dauphine, garden vegetables, bitter chocolate oil.
French windows open on to a secluded terrace.
No lounge, but each of the eclectic, Gothic-style
bedrooms has a bottle of champagne on arrival,
a bath made for sharing, a huge four-poster,
high-spec technology. Sybarites can have a
breakfast hamper delivered to the room. See also
Prestonfield, Edinburgh (main entry).

MAP 5:D2
Castlehill
Edinburgh EH1 2NF
T: 0131 225 5613
W: thewitchery.com

BEDROOMS: 9 suites.
OPEN: all year except 24/25 Dec.
FACILITIES: 2 dining rooms, free Wi-Fi,
terrace.
BACKGROUND MUSIC: in public areas.
LOCATION: by the castle, on the Royal
Mile.
CHILDREN: not under 16.
DOGS: not allowed.
CREDIT CARDS: Amex, MC, Visa.
PRICES: per room B&B from £345.
À la carte £50.

NEW

ELGOL Highland
CORUISK HOUSE

Two miles from the harbour of a tiny Skye
fishing village, a single-track road leads to Clare
Winskill's peaceful restaurant-with-rooms; guests
are offered a glass of Prosecco on arrival. Over 300
years old, quaint and quirky, Coruisk House has
low ceilings, a stone-walled snug, a conservatory
dining room with mountain and island views.
Simply furnished bedrooms are bright and neat.
In the house next door, two luxurious suites
share a sitting room; bathrooms have robes,
fluffy towels, luxury toiletries. Chef Iain Roden's
cooking features seafood and Highland game;
bread and ice cream is home-made. The remote
setting offers scenic walks, opportunities for wild
swimming. The hosts will book boat trips (Mar–
Oct) to islands Soay, Rum and Canna.

MAP 5:C1
Elgol
Isle of Skye IV49 9BL
T: 01471 866330
W: coruiskhouse.com

BEDROOMS: 4. 2 suites in The Steading
next door.
OPEN: Mar–end Oct.
FACILITIES: sitting room, dining room,
conservatory dining room, free Wi-Fi,
TV (in some rooms), ½-acre garden.
BACKGROUND MUSIC: none.
LOCATION: wild and remote part of
Skye, NE of Elgol. 17 miles from Kyle
of Lochalsh station.
CHILDREN: not under 14.
DOGS: dog-friendly suite (resident
dogs).
CREDIT CARDS: Amex, MC, Visa.
PRICES: per room B&B £155–£400,
D,B&B £255–£600.

FORT WILLIAM Highland
THE LIME TREE

Quintessential loch views are a match for 'innovative food' and 'true hospitality' at David Wilson's hotel, restaurant and modern art gallery in a beautifully converted former manse. Works by the host, a Highland artist, and others are displayed throughout the building. 'Comfortable, well-equipped bedrooms' have bright fabrics, solid furnishings and lots of natural light (loch-facing rooms book quickly). Spacious lounges have an open fire. The 'cosy' dining room's modern Scottish dishes are 'tasty, and served in generous portions'. Breakfast is a feast: 'a very good buffet, followed by perfectly cooked hot dishes'. Along with contemporary Scottish artists, previous exhibitions at the gallery have included works by Goya, Matisse and Hockney.

MAP 5:C1
Achintore Road
Fort William PH33 6RQ
T: 01397 701806
w: limetreefortwilliam.co.uk

BEDROOMS: 9. Some in modern extension.
OPEN: all year except Christmas.
FACILITIES: 3 lounges, restaurant, gallery, free Wi-Fi, in-room TV (Freeview), garden, drying room, bicycle storage, parking.
BACKGROUND MUSIC: none.
LOCATION: edge of town centre (5-min. walk).
CHILDREN: all ages welcomed.
DOGS: allowed, separate dining area.
CREDIT CARDS: Amex, MC, Visa.
PRICES: per room B&B £80–£150. À la carte £50.

GLASGOW
15GLASGOW

As a former home of Glasgow merchants, Lorraine Gibson's 'outstanding' listed B&B was built to provide rest and peace in a leafy neighbourhood – it still does today. The late Victorian town house is an elegant haven close to the city centre, minutes from galleries and museums. Sash windows, original fireplaces and intricate cornicing are complemented by a delicate Scottish design. Spacious, high-ceilinged bedrooms have a super-king-size bed, mood lighting; from two vast suites, huge windows overlook gardens front or rear. Ordered the night before, breakfast ('freshly squeezed orange juice, a fruit salad bursting with variety, a piping hot Scottish cooked, all first class') is eaten in the room, or communally in the lounge.

MAP 5:D2
15 Woodside Place
Glasgow G37 QL
T: 0141 332 1263
w: 15glasgow.com

BEDROOMS: 5.
OPEN: all year.
FACILITIES: lounge, free Wi-Fi, in-room TV (Sky, Freeview), small garden, parking.
BACKGROUND MUSIC: none.
LOCATION: between town centre and West End.
CHILDREN: not under 6.
DOGS: allowed in bedrooms, not in public spaces.
CREDIT CARDS: MC, Visa.
PRICES: per room B&B £110–£180.

GLENEGEDALE Argyll and Bute
GLENEGEDALE HOUSE

Amid large gardens, Graeme and Emma Clark's well-placed whitewashed house, midway between Bowmore and Port Ellen on Islay, gazes across the Mull of Oa to the Atlantic beyond. Consummate hosts, the Clarks dispense local knowledge, freshly baked cakes, a dram each night in front of the fire, to appreciative B&B guests. Smart bedrooms, decorated with antiques and judicious plaid, are supplied with spoiling extras: toiletries, Scottish-blended teas, chocolates from a Highland chocolatier. The award-winning breakfast spread includes poached and fresh fruit, porridge laced with whisky (from one of the eight working distilleries on the island). Golden beaches and archaeological sites are nearby. Close to the small island airfield; ferry terminals a short drive away.

MAP 5:D1
Glenegedale
Isle of Islay PA42 7AS
T: 01496 300400
W: glenegedalehouse.co.uk

BEDROOMS: 4. Plus 4-bed self-catering house.
OPEN: all year, except during Christmas and New Year.
FACILITIES: bar, morning room, drawing room, dining room, music room, free Wi-Fi, in-room TV (Freeview), wedding facilities, garden, parking, public rooms wheelchair accessible.
BACKGROUND MUSIC: none.
LOCATION: 4 miles from Port Ellen, 6 miles from Bowmore.
CHILDREN: not under 12.
DOGS: not allowed.
CREDIT CARDS: MC, Visa.
PRICES: per room B&B £115–£195.

NEW

GRANDTULLY Perth and Kinross
THE GRANDTULLY HOTEL

Resurrected with flair, Chris, Rachel and Andrew Rowley's Victorian hotel has become the sophisticated hub of a small Perthshire village. The contemporary bar and informal dining room draw a convivial gathering of locals and guests for inventive daily-changing menus. Sharing plates, large and small (perhaps venison haunch, horseradish crème fraîche, or monkfish fillet, fennel, rocket, salsa verde), use foraged, home-grown or local ingredients. Vibrantly coloured bedrooms have wide beds draped with locally woven tweeds; some overlook the River Tay; four have a bathroom with a cast iron bath. Breakfast is best walked off in the surrounding glens. The partnership also runs Ballintaggart Farm cookery school nearby.

MAP 5:D2
Grandtully PH9 0PL
T: 01887 447000
W: ballintaggart.com

BEDROOMS: 8. Some interconnecting, suitable for a family.
OPEN: all year.
FACILITIES: restaurant, private dining room, free Wi-Fi, terrace, shop.
BACKGROUND MUSIC: in public spaces.
LOCATION: in village.
CHILDREN: all ages welcomed.
DOGS: not allowed.
CREDIT CARDS: Amex, MC, Visa.
PRICES: per room B&B from £150, D,B&B from £200.

INNERLEITHEN Scottish Borders
CADDON VIEW

Praise pours in for Stephen and Lisa Davies's 'great-value', 'very welcoming' Victorian guest house in the Tweed valley – 'a little patch of undiscovered Scotland'. Outdoorsy adventures in the Borders, many from the door, are plentiful. Indoor pursuits, too, with books, board games, and a blazing fire in the high-ceilinged drawing room where the 'super hosts' offer tea and home-baked treats. Simply furnished bedrooms have tea-/coffee-making facilities, fresh milk, a radio/alarm clock, and 'spotless' modern bathrooms; secondary glazing reduces traffic noise. Five nights a week, Stephen Davies cooks 'excellent' seasonal Scottish food in the atmospheric dining room. Breakfast is served until 10 am; 'poached eggs done to perfection'. A coffee shop is planned.

MAP 5:E2
14 Pirn Road
Innerleithen EH44 6HH
T: 01896 830208
W: caddonview.co.uk

BEDROOMS: 8.
OPEN: all year except Christmas.
FACILITIES: snug bar, drawing room, dining room, coffee shop, free Wi-Fi, in-room TV (Freeview), ½-acre mature garden, storage for bicycles and fishing gear, parking.
BACKGROUND MUSIC: in dining room.
LOCATION: 400 yards from the centre of Innerleithen.
CHILDREN: well-behaved children of all ages welcomed.
DOGS: allowed in 1 bedroom, bar, drawing room 'if no other guests object' (£5 per night).
CREDIT CARDS: MC, Visa.
PRICES: per room B&B £55–£135. Set menus (except Mon eve) £22–£28.

NEW

INVERNESS Highland
BUNCHREW HOUSE

'A wonderful experience.' Back in the Guide after rave reviews, this handsome 17th-century mansion gazes across Beauly Firth. Guide readers in 2019 praise the 'friendly efficient staff, lovely restaurant and great location'. The intimate bar (impressive gin menu) overlooks sweeping grounds rolling into woodland laced with trails. Traditionally styled rooms have period details, garden or lake views; some have a high four-poster, conservatory or hot tub. Chef Jon-Paul Saint serves Scottish cuisine with a twist in the wood-panelled restaurant; perhaps caramelised Tatin, charred petals, Parmesan. At breakfast, fuel up on a Highland Scottish Grill, pancakes with maple-glazed bacon; great coffee. 'We will definitely return.'

MAP 5:C2
Inverness IV3 8TA
T: 01463 234917
W: bunchrewhousehotel.com

BEDROOMS: 16.
OPEN: all year, except Christmas, New Year.
FACILITIES: drawing room, cocktail lounge, terrace, free Wi-Fi, in-room TV, garden, woodlands.
BACKGROUND MUSIC: none.
LOCATION: on the A862 Beauly/Dingwall road, 3 miles from Inverness city centre.
CHILDREN: all ages welcomed.
DOGS: accepted (charge).
CREDIT CARDS: Amex, MC, Visa.
PRICES: per room B&B from £250, D,B&B from £360.

INVERNESS Highland

MOYNESS HOUSE

A few minutes' stroll from the city's bustling centre, John and Jane Martin's good value B&B, within its own grounds on a quiet residential street, remains a restful retreat. The modest Victorian villa, built in 1880, was once home to Highland literary giant Neil M Gunn. His books line the peaceful sitting room overlooking the garden. Upstairs, the individually styled bedrooms – named after Gunn's works – are supplied with bathrobes, toiletries, a hospitality tray. The garden hens provide eggs for the 'tasty breakfasts'. The Martins have plentiful tips about the city and surrounding area, and happily help arrange tours.

MAP 5:C2
6 Bruce Gardens
Inverness IV3 5EN
T: 01463 236624
w: moyness.co.uk

BEDROOMS: 7.
OPEN: Feb–Dec, except 25 Dec.
FACILITIES: sitting room, dining room, free Wi-Fi, in-room TV (Freeview), ¼-acre garden, parking.
BACKGROUND MUSIC: at breakfast.
LOCATION: 10 mins' walk from the town centre.
CHILDREN: all ages welcomed.
DOGS: not allowed.
CREDIT CARDS: MC, Visa.
PRICES: per room B&B single from £86, double from £98.

KELSO Scottish Borders

THE OLD PRIORY
BED AND BREAKFAST

The friendly Girdwood family provides a 'home from home' at their elegant late 18th-century house in a cobbled market town in the Scottish Borders. The B&B has traditionally furnished bedrooms with antiques, original shutters, silk-filled duvets; 'a tray with good tea bags, a teapot, fresh coffee and cafetière'. One ground-floor suite, with a separate twin-bedded room, is ideal for a family. Modern bathrooms have a plentiful supply of hot water. In the spacious, light-filled dining room, fresh flowers, views over the pretty enclosed garden and the old parish church. A 'very good breakfast buffet, and plenty of cooked choices, too, even a vegetarian haggis!' Kelso Abbey and many restaurants are a stroll away.

MAP 5:E3
33/35 Woodmarket
Kelso TD5 7AT
T: 01573 223030
w: theoldpriorykelso.com

BEDROOMS: 5. 2 on ground floor (suitable for disabled), 1 family suite.
OPEN: Feb–Dec, open at Christmas, New Year.
FACILITIES: dining room, conservatory/ sitting room, free Wi-Fi, in-room TV (Freeview), garden, parking.
BACKGROUND MUSIC: none.
LOCATION: in town centre.
CHILDREN: all ages welcomed.
DOGS: allowed in 1 room (resident dogs).
CREDIT CARDS: not accepted.
PRICES: per room B&B single £80–£110, double £90–£120.

KIPPEN Stirling

THE CROSS KEYS

A gateway to the north for 300 years, Debby
McGregor and Brian Horsburgh's unassuming
inn – one of the oldest in Scotland – stands in
a village on the edge of Loch Lomond and the
Trossachs national park. Today, its refined,
award-winning pub grub includes such dishes
as guineafowl, tarragon mousse, mushroom and
pea barley risotto, greens. In summer, locals,
walkers, families and their dogs head to the beer
garden for views of the Gargunnock and Fintry
hills. In winter, an open fire warms the rustic bar
with its exposed stone walls, antlers and decent
range of whiskies and real ales. Neat, good-value
bedrooms have oak furnishings, crisp linens, a
small DVD library; there is under-floor heating in
the bathroom.

MAP 5:D2
Main Street
Kippen FK8 3DN
T: 01786 870293
W: kippencrosskeys.com

BEDROOMS: 3.
OPEN: all year except Christmas Day,
New Year's Day.
FACILITIES: bar/dining areas, private
dining room, free Wi-Fi, in-room TV
(Freeview), wedding facilities, terrace,
beer garden.
BACKGROUND MUSIC: in bar.
LOCATION: 10 miles W of Stirling.
CHILDREN: all ages welcomed.
DOGS: allowed (£10 per night).
CREDIT CARDS: MC, Visa.
PRICES: per room B&B single £59,
double £79–£99. À la carte £26.

LOCHMADDY Western Isles

HAMERSAY HOUSE HOTEL

A paradise for wildlife and wilderness lovers,
Amanda and Niall Leveson Gower's laid-back
modern hotel sits in a small village within an
easy drive of dazzling white sand beaches. It is
run with the 'same high standards and very good
food' as sister hotel Langass Lodge, Locheport
(see main entry). A maritime air breezes through
the bright lounge and the modish brasserie, where
inventive menus use local game, just-landed
seafood, vegetables and herbs from the garden.
'Cosy bedrooms' sport tweedy touches; four rooms
open on to the garden. The landscaped grounds,
with a decked area for surveying the bay, pose a
striking contrast to the rugged surroundings.
Well placed for the ferries; a village shop and
pub are close by.

MAP 5: inset A1
Lochmaddy
Isle of North Uist HS6 5AE
T: 01876 500700
W: hamersayhouse.co.uk

BEDROOMS: 9.
OPEN: 28 Apr–Dec, closed Christmas,
New Year.
FACILITIES: bar, restaurant, free Wi-Fi,
in-room TV (Freeview), gym, garden,
parking.
BACKGROUND MUSIC: at low volume in
restaurant in evening.
LOCATION: on the edge of the village.
CHILDREN: all ages welcomed.
DOGS: not allowed.
CREDIT CARDS: MC, Visa.
PRICES: per room B&B £95–£145.
À la carte £30.

MELROSE Scottish Borders

BURT'S

After a day spent fishing on the River Tweed, golfing or walking, a warm welcome awaits at this 'excellent', well-established 18th-century hotel on the High Street of a pretty Borders town. It offers unobtrusive staff and individually styled bedrooms with earthy hues, and a bathroom with Scottish toiletries. In the restaurant, dark wood, light tartans, trophy fish, and modern Scottish dishes, including fillet of beef, dauphinoise potatoes, sautéed wild mushrooms, baby carrots, thyme jus. Lunch and supper menus and 'mash' single malts are served in the Bistro bar. A sustaining breakfast supports the next day's activities. The Henderson family, who have been at the helm for nearly 50 years, also own The Townhouse, across the street.

MAP 5:E3
Market Square
Melrose TD6 9PL
T: 01896 822285
w: burtshotel.co.uk

BEDROOMS: 20.
OPEN: all year, no accommodation 24–26 Dec.
FACILITIES: lobby lounge, residents' lounge, bistro bar, restaurant, private dining room, free Wi-Fi, in-room TV (Freeview), wedding facilities, function facilities, ½-acre garden, parking.
BACKGROUND MUSIC: in public areas.
LOCATION: town centre.
CHILDREN: all ages welcomed (restaurant over-8s only).
DOGS: allowed in some bedrooms, bar, bistro, not in restaurant.
CREDIT CARDS: Amex, MC, Visa.
PRICES: per person B&B £70–£90, per room D,B&B double £95–£115. À la carte £42.

MOFFAT Dumfries and Galloway

HARTFELL HOUSE & THE LIMETREE RESTAURANT

A short detour off the scenic Southern Upland Way reveals a 'pleasant town' where Robert and Mhairi Ash's 'lovely Victorian house' overlooks the surrounding hills. Returning visitors 'come for the exquisite views, fantastic cooking, and good-value accommodation'. Each of the 'comfortable bedrooms' is supplied with a memory foam mattress and pleasing extras: Scottish biscuits, fine toiletries. In Limetree restaurant, chef Matt Seddon's short, frequently changing, Michelin-approved modern Scottish menu (vegetarians are well catered for, with advance notice) includes such 'delicious' dishes as roast supreme of guineafowl with black pudding. Breakfast is equally excellent.' Easy access to the M74.

MAP 5:E2
Hartfell Crescent
Moffat DG10 9AL
T: 01683 220153
w: hartfellhouse.co.uk

BEDROOMS: 7. Plus self-catering cottage in the grounds.
OPEN: all year except Mon, Christmas, restaurant closed Sun, Mon.
FACILITIES: lounge, restaurant, free Wi-Fi, in-room TV (Freeview), garden, cooking classes, bicycle storage, parking.
BACKGROUND MUSIC: in restaurant.
LOCATION: 5 mins' walk from town centre.
CHILDREN: all ages welcomed.
DOGS: not allowed.
CREDIT CARDS: MC, Visa.
PRICES: per room B&B single £55–£75, double £80–£95, D,B&B double £142–£157. Set menu £25 (2 courses), £31 (3 courses).

NAIRN Highland
SUNNY BRAE

On one of the sunniest stretches of the Scottish coast, John Bochel and Rachel Philipsen ensure that their 'good-value' B&B lives up to its name and catches every ray. 'The panorama of the sea' is caught through the south-facing glass front; pretty suntrap gardens have plentiful seating. Coastal sands and marine blues cheerfully decorate bright bedrooms, each provided with bottled water and bathrobes; four have views over the Moray Firth. A cheese board or charcuterie platter can be arranged for an evening meal. The owners have more than 100 malt whiskies waiting to be sampled. Minutes from the beach, the day might start with sand between the toes before heading back for a generous breakfast – 'very good indeed', with a wide choice of cold and cooked options.

MAP 5:C2
Marine Road
Nairn IV12 4EA
T: 01667 452309
W: sunnybraenairn.co.uk

BEDROOMS: 8. 1 suitable for disabled.
OPEN: Mar–end Oct.
FACILITIES: lounge, dining room, free Wi-Fi, in-room TV (Freeview), terrace, front and rear gardens, parking.
BACKGROUND MUSIC: none.
LOCATION: 5 mins' walk from the town centre, 2 mins from beach.
CHILDREN: all ages welcomed.
DOGS: only guide dogs.
CREDIT CARDS: MC, Visa.
PRICES: per room B&B £85–£145. À la carte £35.

OBAN Argyll and Bute
GREYSTONES

A fresh, bijou air wafts through this hillside B&B in a baronial pile offering epic views of Oban Bay. Owned by John and Cathy Gavigan, the mansion's original stained-glass windows, moulded ceilings and fine staircase have been retained, accompanied by modish furnishings, contemporary art. Uncluttered bedrooms have every amenity: fluffy bathrobes and Scottish toiletries in a spacious bathroom, tea-making facilities, wine glasses, a corkscrew; in most, superb views. Unusual breakfasts, served in the turreted dining room, may include porridge with raspberry cranachan or a cheesy spinach frittata. The helpful hosts have ideas aplenty for trips around the Inner Hebrides. The town centre, harbour and seafood restaurants are within walking distance.

MAP 5:D1
1 Dalriach Road
Oban PA34 5EQ
T: 01631 358653
W: greystonesoban.co.uk

BEDROOMS: 5.
OPEN: Apr–Oct.
FACILITIES: sitting room, dining room, free Wi-Fi, in-room TV (Freeview), ½-acre garden, parking.
BACKGROUND MUSIC: none.
LOCATION: 5 mins' walk from town centre.
CHILDREN: not under 16.
DOGS: not allowed.
CREDIT CARDS: MC, Visa.
PRICES: per room B&B £100–£185. 2-night min. stay preferred.

PEEBLES Scottish Borders

CRINGLETIE HOUSE

A 'little jewel' in a secluded setting, this small baronial mansion is enveloped by sweeping manicured lawns within acres of woodland. Inside, 'friendly' staff, mainly local, impart a homely feel. Log fires, a wooden staircase, hand-painted ceiling and an old service bell in public rooms add to the grand ambience. Each of the pristine bedrooms is unique, all beautifully appointed, with a comfy bed and 'lovely toiletries'. Some are snug, some modern; each has garden and hillside views. The extensive grounds include sculptures, a walled kitchen garden. Seasonal Borders produce is used for unpretentious dishes and seven-course tasting menus, served under a frescoed ceiling in the restaurant, overlooking lawns and down the valley to Peebles.

MAP 5:E2
off Edinburgh Road
Peebles EH45 8PL
T: 01721 725750
W: cringletie.com

BEDROOMS: 13, 1 suitable for disabled, family cottage in grounds with hot tub.
OPEN: all year except 2–3 weeks Jan.
FACILITIES: bar, lounge, conservatory, garden room, restaurant, free Wi-Fi, in-room TV (Freeview), lift, wedding facilities, 28-acre fully accessible grounds, parking.
BACKGROUND MUSIC: in public areas.
LOCATION: 2 miles N of Peebles.
CHILDREN: all ages welcomed.
DOGS: allowed in bedrooms, garden room.
CREDIT CARDS: MC, Visa.
PRICES: per room B&B single £105–£205, double £145–£245, D,B&B £185–£325. À la carte £42.50.

PEEBLES Scottish Borders

THE TONTINE

A welcoming sanctuary, Kate and Gordon Innes's hotel was built in the early 19th century by French prisoners of war. It is now a popular spot for afternoon teas, cocktail evenings. At weekends, keen cyclists and golfers join locals and residents over real ales beside the lounge's open fire, or in the informal bistro. 'The atmosphere was very friendly; staff greeted us with ease and a smile.' In the high-ceilinged, chandelier-lit restaurant, Alejandro Wunderlin's seasonal cooking includes 'original, tasty' starters and Tastes of the Scottish Borders. In both the main building and an annexe (connected by a glass-sided corridor), neat bedrooms have tweedy accessories; some overlook the river to the hills beyond. Dogs are made welcome; maps point the way to country walks.

MAP 5:E2
High Street
Peebles EH45 8AJ
T: 01721 720892
W: tontinehotel.com

BEDROOMS: 36. 20 in annexe.
OPEN: all year.
FACILITIES: lift, bar, lounge, bistro, restaurant, private dining/meeting room, free Wi-Fi, in-room TV (Freeview), wedding facilities, 2 garden areas, drying room, secure bicycle storage, parking.
BACKGROUND MUSIC: in public rooms.
LOCATION: on the High Street in town centre.
CHILDREN: all ages welcomed.
DOGS: allowed in 10 annexe bedrooms, bar, bistro, garden (£10 per dog).
CREDIT CARDS: MC, Visa.
PRICES: per room B&B single £55–£95, double £70–£130, D,B&B £95–£180. À la carte from £25.

PERTH Perth and Kinross
SUNBANK HOUSE

A tranquil retreat within easy walking distance of
the bustling centre and all of Perth's attractions,
Finlay and Agnes Gillies's 'lovely, comfortable'
Victorian house is set amid mature gardens.
Traditional by design, unfussy bedrooms have
plenty of space to stretch out. Two rooms suit a
family; light sleepers might request a room at the
back. Guests mingle over preprandial drinks in
the fire-lit lounge, before sampling the dining
room's locally sourced take on classic dishes such
as pan-fried chicken breast rolled in Parma ham,
with white wine, lemon and sage sauce, fresh
vegetables, baby potatoes. There is a separate
vegetarian menu. 'Excellent' breakfasts cater for
everyone, and include a buffet, smoked salmon,
the full Scottish.

MAP 5:D2
50 Dundee Road
Perth PH2 7BA
T: 01738 479888
w: sunbankhouse.com

BEDROOMS: 10. Some on ground floor,
2 suitable for disabled.
OPEN: all year except Christmas.
FACILITIES: lounge/bar, restaurant,
free Wi-Fi, in-room TV (Freeview),
function facilities, terrace, ½-acre
garden, parking.
BACKGROUND MUSIC: in restaurant.
LOCATION: ½ mile from centre.
CHILDREN: all ages welcomed.
DOGS: allowed in allocated rooms only
(£15 charge).
CREDIT CARDS: Amex, MC, Visa.
PRICES: per room B&B £79–£125.
À la carte £30.

PITLOCHRY Perth and Kinross
CRAIGATIN HOUSE
AND COURTYARD

A lofty glass-fronted, cedar-beamed extension
creates a cathedral of light in this B&B in a former
surgeon's house set amid two acres of gardens
and woodland. 'Delightful, bright' bedrooms,
spread between the main house and converted
stables, mix mountain views with contemporary
flair. Some rooms are compact, some have original
Georgian wooden shutters, others a skylight; all
have splashes of colour and are supplied with
a hospitality tray, an umbrella and 'extremely
comfortable' chairs. The double-height extension
with wood-burning stove, overlooking the
gardens, is the site of a good breakfast, perhaps
porridge, with a choice of topping; a full Scottish,
local honey. New owners took over in June 2019.

25% DISCOUNT VOUCHERS

MAP 5:D2
165 Atholl Road
Pitlochry PH16 5QL
T: 01796 472478
w: craigatinhouse.co.uk

BEDROOMS: 14. 7 in courtyard, 2 on
ground floor, 1 suitable for disabled.
OPEN: Mar–Dec, closed Christmas.
FACILITIES: lounge, 2 breakfast rooms,
free Wi-Fi, in-room TV (Freeview),
2-acre garden, lounge/breakfast room
wheelchair accessible.
BACKGROUND MUSIC: none.
LOCATION: central.
CHILDREN: not under 14.
DOGS: not allowed.
CREDIT CARDS: MC, Visa.
PRICES: per room B&B single
£100–£128, double £110–£138. 1-night
bookings sometimes refused Sat.

PITLOCHRY Perth and Kinross
PINE TREES HOTEL

'Hill walking from the door, yet walkable into town', this secluded white-painted Victorian mansion is in a 'delightful setting' on the outskirts of Pitlochry. Recent refurbishment by new owners has brought verve to the hotel's stately public spaces; Ben Strutton is manager. An impressive wood-and-wrought iron staircase leads to comfortable, traditionally styled bedrooms with modern bathrooms; ground-floor rooms are in a converted coach house or annexe nearby, and have dedicated parking; all rooms are equipped with tea-/coffee-making facilities, iron and board, radio and alarm clock. In the restaurant, Scottish provender includes haggis tartlet or pigeon in sherry sauce, cheese from the Isle of Mull. In the extensive grounds, red squirrels and roe deer.

MAP 5:D2
Strathview Terrace
Pitlochry PH16 5QR
T: 01796 472121
w: pinetreeshotel.co.uk

BEDROOMS: 31. 3 in annexe, 6 in coach house, 7 on ground floor, plus 2-bedroom apartment.
OPEN: all year, special packages at Christmas, New Year.
FACILITIES: bar, 3 lounges, restaurant, free Wi-Fi (in lounge), in-room TV (Freeview), 7-acre grounds, parking.
BACKGROUND MUSIC: in bar and restaurant.
LOCATION: ¼ mile N of town centre.
CHILDREN: all ages welcomed.
DOGS: well-behaved dogs allowed (£10 per night), only guide dogs allowed in restaurant and bar lounge.
CREDIT CARDS: Amex, MC, Visa.
PRICES: per room B&B £85–£125, D,B&B from £95. À la carte £34.50.

PORTREE Highland
MARMALADE HOTEL

Overlooking the beautiful harbour town, an Edwardian country house in landscaped gardens with a sleekly modern interior. Skye-crafted natural fabrics, in soft greys and heathered mustards, feature alongside local materials and artwork. Bedrooms vary in size, but most look over the garden, the bay, the Cuillin hills beyond; extra touches: a sound system, capsule coffee machine, luxury toiletries. Large period windows in the coolly contemporary restaurant give far-reaching views. Local specialities include a traditional chargrill; fresh oysters delivered daily. The bar opens on to a patio overlooking the bay. Breakfast includes porridge with cream, brown sugar, perhaps whisky, followed by a full Scottish. Marmalade is part of the Perle Hotels group.

MAP 5:C1
Home Farm Road
Portree IV51 9LX
T: 01478 611711
w: marmaladehotel.co.uk

BEDROOMS: 11. 2 ground-floor rooms in annexe, 1 suitable for disabled (22 additional bedrooms in an extension are planned).
OPEN: all year, except 25/26 Dec.
FACILITIES: bar/restaurant, lounge, free Wi-Fi, in-room TV (Freeview), wedding facilities, 2-acre grounds.
BACKGROUND MUSIC: in bar, restaurant.
LOCATION: town centre.
CHILDREN: not under 12.
DOGS: not allowed.
CREDIT CARDS: Amex, MC, Visa.
PRICES: per room B&B £120–£299, D,B&B £190–£369. À la carte £35.

ST ANDREWS Fife
RUFFLETS

One of Scotland's first country house hotels, the turreted 1920s mansion in tranquil, 'elegant gardens' is owned by Mark and Christopher Forrester, grandsons of two of the original founders. Its traditional standards are upheld by long-serving manager, Stephen Owen, who runs it with 'extremely welcoming', 'helpful' staff. The 'superb' bedrooms are packed with thoughtful touches (home-made shortbread, a hot-water bottle for a chilly night, Rufus the teddy bear); some feature a four-poster bed or a private balcony. Chef David Kinnes serves a seasonal Scottish menu, incorporating produce from the kitchen garden and local suppliers. The ever-popular afternoon tea is taken on The Terrace on clement days.

MAP 5:D3
Strathkinness Low Road
St Andrews KY16 9TX
T: 01334 472594
W: rufflets.co.uk

BEDROOMS: 23. 4 on ground floor (2 in Gatehouse, 2 in Rufflets Lodge), 1 suitable for disabled, plus 3 self-catering cottages in gardens.
OPEN: all year.
FACILITIES: bar, drawing room, library, restaurant, free Wi-Fi, in-room TV (Freeview), wedding facilities, function facilities, 10-acre grounds (formal gardens, kitchen garden and woodland).
BACKGROUND MUSIC: in bar, restaurant.
LOCATION: 2 miles W of town.
CHILDREN: all ages welcomed.
DOGS: allowed in some bedrooms, by arrangement, bar.
CREDIT CARDS: Amex, MC, Visa.
PRICES: per room B&B £145–£315, D,B&B £180–£385. À la carte £45.

SOUTH GALSON Western Isles
GALSON FARM GUEST HOUSE

Part of a small crofting community on the dramatic north-west coast, Elaine Fothergill and Richard Inger's traditional Hebridean farmhouse displays rugged views across to the Butt of Lewis. Welcoming, and charmingly decorated, the guest house has comfortable, blue-toned bedrooms with locally crafted pottery, paintings, soft furnishings; a silent mini-fridge contains fresh milk and water. The quiet reading lounge overlooks the surging Atlantic; hot drinks are available all day. Served communally, a simple two-course, Aga-fresh supper (arranged in advance) showcases local produce, alongside an extensive selection of tipples. 'Excellent' breakfasts and packed lunches fuel a day's exploration of beaches, mountains and burns; vigour for observing the abundant wildlife.

MAP 5:B1
South Galson
Isle of Lewis HS2 0SH
T: 01851 850492
W: galsonfarm.co.uk

BEDROOMS: 4.
OPEN: all year, except Christmas, New Year.
FACILITIES: 2 lounges, dining room, free Wi-Fi, ¼-acre garden, drying facilities, parking, bicycle storage,
BACKGROUND MUSIC: in dining room, lounge.
LOCATION: around 8 miles S of Ness port, on NW coast, 20 miles from Stornoway.
CHILDREN: not under 16.
DOGS: assistance dogs allowed (animals on site).
CREDIT CARDS: Amex, MC, Visa.
PRICES: per room B&B single £70, double £95–£110. Dinner £22.

STIRLING
POWIS HOUSE

Buffered by trees and fields, Jane and Colin Kilgour's secluded Georgian mansion has the feel of a sedate world, yet is just ten minutes' drive from the city centre. The house has been carefully preserved (there are records of every resident since it was built in 1746). In the gardens, a listed sundial and well-kept lawns are protected from resident sheep by a ha-ha. Inside, sash windows, high ceilings and polished wooden floors set the tone. Board games and DVDs are available in the sitting room. Harris tweed curtains and throws complement the bedrooms' original features (in one a cast iron bath); broad views scan the horizon from each. Local ingredients and garden-fresh eggs for traditional breakfasts.

MAP 5:D2
Stirling FK9 5PS
T: 01786 460231
w: powishouse.co.uk

BEDROOMS: 3.
OPEN: Mid-Apr–end Oct.
FACILITIES: lounge, dining room, 9-acre garden, in-room TV (Freeview), free Wi-Fi.
BACKGROUND MUSIC: during breakfast.
LOCATION: 3 miles from town centre.
CHILDREN: all ages welcomed.
DOGS: not allowed.
CREDIT CARDS: MC, Visa.
PRICES: per room B&B single £75, double from £110.

STIRLING
VICTORIA SQUARE

Within strolling distance of the city centre, Kari and Phillip Couser's serene Victorian guest house overlooks the tree-lined square that shares its name. The elegant bedrooms, decorated in heritage hues, might have a king-size sleigh bed and views of Stirling Castle or a four-poster and a seating area in a bay window on the square. In The Orangery restaurant, afternoon tea is a sit-down indulgence, with delicate sandwiches and toasted Osborne pudding loaf (a favourite of Queen Victoria's). A table d'hôte and chef's taster menu is served in the evening, Wednesday to Sunday. Breakfast has a generous buffet, plus cooked dishes: VS Benedict – toasted muffin with haggis (or vegetarian haggis) and a poached egg topped with hollandaise sauce.

MAP 5:D2
12 Victoria Square
Stirling FK8 2QZ
T: 01786 473920
w: victoriasquare.scot

BEDROOMS: 10.
OPEN: all year except Christmas, restaurant closed Mon, Tues.
FACILITIES: lounge, breakfast room, orangery restaurant, free Wi-Fi, in-room TV (Freeview).
BACKGROUND MUSIC: quiet, in The Orangery.
LOCATION: town centre ½ mile.
CHILDREN: not under 12.
DOGS: not allowed.
CREDIT CARDS: MC, Visa.
PRICES: per room B&B £70–£175, D,B&B £95–£200. Table d'hôte £29.50 (2 courses), £37.50 (3 courses).

THORNHILL Dumfries and Galloway

TRIGONY HOUSE

In mature woodland and gardens, Jan and Adam Moore's relaxed and pet-friendly Scottish country house hotel is in an 18th-century former sporting lodge. Bedrooms range from 'small but fine' classics to the Garden Suite, with lobby area. All are supplied with home-made shortbread, fresh coffee, organic toiletries. Views are of hills, woodland or the garden, home to a Scandinavian sauna cabin and hot tub. You can eat in the bar (dogs allowed) or dining room. Evening menus feature Solway scallops, free-range, rare breed chicken, fruit, herbs and vegetables from the organic kitchen garden (vegetarians and vegans happily catered for). Home-made granola, Ayrshire-cured bacon, award-winning black puddings, local kippers in the morning.

25% DISCOUNT VOUCHERS

MAP 5:E2
Closeburn
Thornhill DG3 5EZ
T: 01848 331211
W: trigonyhotel.co.uk

BEDROOMS: 9. 1 on ground floor.
OPEN: all year except 25–27, 31 Dec.
FACILITIES: bar, lounge, dining room, free Wi-Fi, in-room TV (Freeview), spa treatment room in private garden (outdoor wood-fired hot tub, sauna cabin), wedding facilities, 4-acre grounds.
BACKGROUND MUSIC: in bar in evening.
LOCATION: 1 mile S of Thornhill.
CHILDREN: all ages welcomed.
DOGS: 'well-behaved' dogs 'not only allowed but welcomed' in bedrooms, bar, grounds; not in dining room (dog-sitting, beds, bowls, towels).
CREDIT CARDS: Amex, MC, Visa.
PRICES: per room B&B £125–£170, D,B&B £175–£240. À la carte £35. 1-night bookings sometimes refused Sat.

THURSO Highland

FORSS HOUSE

'Scottish country house living on a grand scale.' Near the mainland's northern tip, this Georgian mansion is surrounded by woodland and waterfall on the Forss river, a fishing hot spot. Guests also come for the shooting, deer stalking and single malts. Warm hospitality and angling anecdotes are provided by 'delightful' manager Anne Mackenzie. The main house's bedrooms have a high ceiling, comfortable seating, generous en suite bathroom, river views; patio doors in annexe rooms open on to woodland. Neighbouring estates and local waters supply the ingredients for head chef Andrew Smith's seasonal menus: Caithness lamb rump and slow-cooked leg with fondant potatoes, Madeira sauce; whole poached Scrabster lobster, golden potatoes, lobster jus.

25% DISCOUNT VOUCHERS

MAP 5:B2
Forss
Thurso KW14 7XY
T: 01847 861201
W: forsshousehotel.co.uk

BEDROOMS: 14. 3 in main house on ground floor, 6 in 2 neighbouring annexes, 1 suitable for disabled.
OPEN: all year except 23 Dec–4 Jan.
FACILITIES: bar, dining room, breakfast room, lounge, free Wi-Fi, in-room TV (Freeview), meeting room, wedding facilities, 19-acre grounds with river and waterfall.
BACKGROUND MUSIC: in public areas breakfast and evening.
LOCATION: 5 miles W of Thurso.
CHILDREN: all ages welcomed (under-5s free).
DOGS: allowed in Sportsmen's Lodges.
CREDIT CARDS: Amex, MC, Visa.
PRICES: per room B&B single £99–£135, double £135–£185, D,B&B single £137–£170, double £205–£260. À la carte £35.

ABERGAVENNY Monmouthshire

THE HARDWICK

In an 'attractive rural setting' outside the town, chef/patron Stephen Terry has transformed a former roadside pub into a destination restaurant-with-rooms. The bar and trio of dining areas have rafters, old beams, candles, mismatched tables and hanging copper pans. A wide-choice menu makes deciding difficult: 'Merthyr Pudding' – braised beef shin, oxtail and sourdough, baked with a little mustard, Cheddar cheese and beef stock; or duck hash, fried duck egg and caramelised orange dressing? 'Service can be a little slow at times.' Bedrooms occupy a timber-clad annexe around a courtyard. Most have countryside views, a bath with shower, some with walk-in shower. All have Welsh textiles, a Roberts radio. 'Ours was lovely, spotless, with a very comfortable bed and pillows.'

MAP 3:D4
Old Raglan Road
Abergavenny NP7 9AA
T: 01873 854220
w: thehardwick.co.uk

BEDROOMS: 8. 5 on ground floor, 1, with wet room, suitable for disabled.
OPEN: all year except 24–26 Dec.
FACILITIES: bar, restaurant, private dining facilities, free Wi-Fi, in-room TV (Freeview), courtyard (seating 40), small garden, public areas wheelchair accessible.
BACKGROUND MUSIC: 'unintrusive' in public areas.
LOCATION: 2¾ miles S of Abergavenny.
CHILDREN: all ages welcomed.
DOGS: only assistance dogs allowed.
CREDIT CARDS: MC, Visa.
PRICES: per room B&B single (Mon–Thurs) £115, double £120–£150, D,B&B £199. À la carte £46.50.

ABERGELE Conwy

THE KINMEL ARMS

In the verdant Elwy valley, this handsome sandstone inn is well placed for country and coastal walks. It is now part of the Tir Prince Leisure group. Heddwen Wheeler remains as general manager. In the popular bar, proper ales, local ciders; in the conservatory restaurant, chef Simon Roberts's seasonal brasserie-style meals are served throughout the day. Afternoons are for relaxing over home-baked cakes and loose-leaf tea, served in the tea room, a sweet alternative to walking, swimming and playing golf, all nearby. Landscape-inspired bedrooms (some parts in need of updating) have oak flooring, and perhaps a 'good walk-in shower', a vast slipper bath, a decked balcony. In the evening, a generous continental breakfast is placed in your fridge.

25% DISCOUNT VOUCHERS

MAP 3:A3
St George
Abergele LL22 9BP
T: 01745 832207
w: thekinmelarms.co.uk

BEDROOMS: 4. 2 on ground floor.
OPEN: all year.
FACILITIES: bar, restaurant, private dining room, deli/shop, tea rooms, free Wi-Fi, in-room TV (Freeview), small garden, parking.
BACKGROUND MUSIC: in public areas.
LOCATION: 15 mins' drive from Llandudno.
CHILDREN: not under 13.
DOGS: in public rooms, not in bedrooms.
CREDIT CARDS: MC, Visa.
PRICES: per room B&B £135–£175, D,B&B from £195. À la carte £32.

AMROTH Pembrokeshire

MELLIEHA GUEST HOUSE

With easy access to the Pembrokeshire Coastal
Path and the beach, Julia and Stuart Adams's
tranquil ranch-style B&B nestles in a forested
valley, on the edge of the National Trust's Colby
Woodland Garden. Tea and 'the lightest of scones'
or home-baked cake are part of the 'generous
welcome', served in the 'immaculate' garden or
conservatory – good spots for observing wildlife
from birds to badgers. A log-burning stove warms
the cosy lounge in cooler months. The pretty
bedrooms have thoughtful extras (bathrobes, a
torch for dark nights) and views across the garden
to the sea. Laver bread and cockles might form
part of the 'excellent, well-presented' breakfasts.
A delightful coastal walk leads to Saundersfoot;
restaurants and shops aren't far away.

25% DISCOUNT VOUCHERS

MAP 3:D2
Amroth SA67 8NA
T: 01834 811581
W: mellieha.co.uk

BEDROOMS: 5.
OPEN: all year, except 21 Dec–3 Jan.
FACILITIES: lounge, dining room, free
Wi-Fi, in-room TV, no mobile signal,
1-acre garden, parking.
BACKGROUND MUSIC: none.
LOCATION: 150 yds from Amroth sea
front, 2 miles E of Saundersfoot.
CHILDREN: not under 12.
DOGS: only assistance dogs.
CREDIT CARDS: MC, Visa.
PRICES: per room B&B £85–£108.
2-night min. stay weekends preferred
May–Sept.

BALA Gwynedd

PALE HALL

Rich in antiques, fine wood panelling and painted
ceilings, this sumptuous, well-refurbished country
house hotel, in an historic Victorian manor house,
lies on the edge of Snowdonia national park.
Sustainably run, the hotel is powered by one of
the country's oldest running hydro-electric plants;
it bottles its own spring water, and has the pick
of local suppliers for Gareth Stevenson's seasonal
fine-dining menus in the formal restaurant.
Spacious bedrooms have original features, with
added luxuries (a complimentary decanter of
sherry, a TV disguised as a gilt-framed mirror).
Two suites are in a turret; another room has
rich chinoiserie decor. Board games in the
library; lawn games, animals for petting outside.
Travelling dogs are properly pampered.

MAP 3:B3
Bala LL23 7PS
T: 01678 530285
W: palehall.co.uk

BEDROOMS: 18.
OPEN: all year.
FACILITIES: Grand Hall, 2 drawing
rooms, library, 3 private dining rooms,
free Wi-Fi, in-room TV (Freeview),
civil wedding licence, 50-acre grounds,
parking.
BACKGROUND MUSIC: in public areas.
LOCATION: 2 miles from Bala.
CHILDREN: all ages welcomed.
DOGS: allowed in 5 bedrooms, Grand
Hall, library (£25 per dog).
CREDIT CARDS: Amex, MC, Visa.
PRICES: per room B&B £275–£860,
D,B&B £385–£970. Taster menu
£70 (6 courses), £90 (10 courses),
à la carte £70.

CARDIFF
CATHEDRAL 73

Royal treatment awaits visitors to this stylishly refurbished Victorian town house hotel; a butler, personal chef and chauffeur-driven vintage Rolls-Royce are at the ready, if required. Sitting across the park and the River Taff from Cardiff Castle, it has soothing soft grey interiors with the occasional flare of colour. Smart, pale-hued bedrooms and chic apartments (with a kitchen) have top-shelf amenities: high-quality bedlinen, good toiletries, fresh milk. The tea room serves light lunches, afternoon tea with home-baked cakes; come evening (Thurs–Sat), it transforms into a cocktail and gin bar with Art Deco flourishes, tapas-style dishes, live piano music. Alongside trips to the station, theatre or opera, the bright yellow Rolls can be booked for a half-day tour.

MAP 3:E4
73 Cathedral Road
Cardiff CF11 9HE
T: 029 2023 5005
W: cathedral73.com

BEDROOMS: 9. 1, on ground floor, suitable for disabled, 2 apartment suites, 2-bed coach house.
OPEN: all year, except 25–26 Dec, 1 Jan (guests receive minimum housekeeping, towels only; no breakfast on these days).
FACILITIES: sitting room, bar/tea room, restaurant, free Wi-Fi, in-room TV (Freeview), civil wedding licence, terrace, limited parking, restaurant wheelchair accessible.
BACKGROUND MUSIC: in public spaces.
LOCATION: ½ mile from city centre.
CHILDREN: all ages welcomed.
DOGS: allowed in apartments, public rooms, not in restaurant.
CREDIT CARDS: MC, Visa.
PRICES: per room from £130, cooked breakfast around £10. À la carte £20. 1-night bookings sometimes refused on international rugby weekends.

CARDIFF
HOTEL INDIGO CARDIFF

Inconspicuous amid shops, bars and restaurants, this quirky hotel, alchemised out of an old office block, sits on a pedestrianised street, close to the station and castle. Inside, all things Welsh – heritage, industry and artistes – are celebrated with bright hand-woven textiles, slate signage, an upcycled miner's helmet light, and photographs of music icons (Shirley Bassey, Tom Jones, Stereophonics). Stylish bedrooms are similarly inspired (the Industry rooms have a coal-scuttle waste bin); there are dramatically tiled bathrooms, powerful showers. Many rooms have fabulous views. A lift ascends to the top-floor Marco Pierre White Steakhouse Bar & Grill; the rooftop terrace (well stocked with Welsh-made booze) overlooks the city skyline.

MAP 3:E4
Dominions Arcade
Cardiff CF10 2AR
T: 08719 429104
W: hotelindigo.com/hotels/gb/en/
    reservation

BEDROOMS: 122. 4 suitable for disabled.
OPEN: all year.
FACILITIES: lounge, restaurant, lift, free Wi-Fi, in-room TV, gym, discount at NCP car park nearby.
BACKGROUND MUSIC: in public areas.
LOCATION: city centre.
CHILDREN: all ages welcomed.
DOGS: not allowed.
CREDIT CARDS: Amex, MC, Visa.
PRICES: per room from £109. Breakfast from £15.95.

NEW

MAP 3:E4
Thornhill
Cardiff CF14 9UA
T: 02920 520280
W: townandcountrycollective.co.uk

CARDIFF

NEW HOUSE COUNTRY HOTEL

Nestling in the hills in Thornhill (a northern Cardiff suburb) is this welcoming, dog-friendly hotel in a Georgian manor house with sprawling views over the city and Severn estuary. At the front, a gravelled terrace with a three-tiered fountain adds country house appeal to the creeper-covered Grade II listed building; stone steps lead to elegant rooms where large windows with heavily draped curtains or wooden shutters look out on to lush greenery. Afternoon tea may be taken by the fire in a comfortable, blue-walled lounge. Spacious bedrooms are enlivened with feature wallpaper and bright cushions; three rooms have garden access. If the city's too far, Sequoias restaurant serves lunch, tea and dinner. Part of Town & Country Collective.

BEDROOMS: 37.
OPEN: all year.
FACILITIES: bar, lounge, seating area, restaurant, free Wi-Fi, in-room TV, ramp, 9-acre grounds, civil wedding licence, gym.
BACKGROUND MUSIC: quiet' in bar, lounge, restaurant,
LOCATION: in Thornhill, 7 miles from Cardiff city centre.
CHILDREN: all ages welcomed.
DOGS: allowed in 3 bedrooms.
CREDIT CARDS: Amex, MC, Visa.
PRICES: per room B&B from £113, DB&B from £183. À la carte £35.

25% DISCOUNT VOUCHERS

MAP 3:E3
63 High Street
Cowbridge CF71 7AF
T: 01446 774814
W: townandcountrycollective.co.uk

COWBRIDGE Vale of Glamorgan

THE BEAR

Long a popular stop-over, this well-located hotel has for centuries been the hub of a fashionable, cobbled market town surrounded by cow-flecked hillsides in the Vale of Glamorgan. Locals and tourists rub shoulders, attracted by its locally brewed drinks, modern pub dishes and rejuvenating bedrooms. Individually designed, some are compact, others sprawling. Local produce ('grown from Welsh soil and reared on Welsh grass') supplies the well-considered menus, served in the bar, lounge, courtyard or stylish Cellars dining room (vegetarians and vegans are well catered for with such dishes as Glamorgan leek, carrot and Cheddar hash, leek and Y-Fenni sauce). Mornings start with a buffet breakfast. A Town & Country Collective hotel.

BEDROOMS: 33. Some suitable for disabled, some in annexe, plus self-catering apartments.
OPEN: all year.
FACILITIES: lounge, restaurant, grill/bar, free Wi-Fi, in-room TV, civil wedding licence, conference facilities, courtyard, parking.
BACKGROUND MUSIC: in restaurant.
LOCATION: town centre.
CHILDREN: all ages welcomed.
DOGS: allowed in bedrooms, Grill bar.
CREDIT CARDS: MC, Visa.
PRICES: per room B&B from £99.
Locally sourced gastro-style menu £30.

CWMBACH Powys

THE DRAWING ROOM

Charmingly intimate, Melanie and Colin Dawson's 'wonderful little restaurant-with-rooms' is in a Georgian stone-built property near the scenic Elan valley. It has 'appealingly' decorated sitting rooms, and three bedrooms; bathrooms (one with a freestanding bath) have under-floor heating. In the open-plan kitchen, the 'helpful hosts' use garden-fresh fruit and vegetables, along with meats from local farms, to produce 'ambitious, complex and delicious' three-course set menus, for which guests must dine in: perhaps Welsh beef with shallot 'tarte Tatin', potato and roots, horseradish cream; mountain lamb, herb crust, ragout of vegetables, potato galette. At breakfast: fresh fruit, home-made muesli, wild mushrooms with pancetta and duck egg.

MAP 3:D4
Cwmbach
Builth Wells LD2 3RT
T: 01982 552493
w: the-drawing-room.co.uk

BEDROOMS: 3.
OPEN: all year.
FACILITIES: lounge, restaurant, private dining room, free Wi-Fi, in-room TV (Freeview), small garden.
BACKGROUND MUSIC: in restaurant.
LOCATION: 3 miles N of Builth Wells.
CHILDREN: not under 12.
DOGS: not allowed.
CREDIT CARDS: MC, Visa.
PRICES: per room D,B&B £225–£250. Set menu £40. Min. 2-night bookings bank holiday weekends.

DOLGELLAU Gwynedd

Y MEIRIONNYDD

On the Mawddach trail, Marc Russell and Nicholas Banda's stone-built restaurant-with-rooms stands at the southern gateway to Snowdonia national park. Days spent hiking and biking the mountain paths end in cosy, tweedy rooms, where wide beds have luxurious linen, Welsh blankets, robes and slippers; modern bathrooms have a walk-in shower or a bath, good toiletries, a slate floor. Guests and locals mingle in the friendly bar (perhaps over one of the vast selection of gins). Chef Robin Agnew creates comforting, seasonal plates in the smart cellar restaurant, set within the exposed stone walls of the former county jail. The next day's activities are sustained by a hearty breakfast and (pre-ordered) packed lunch.

25% DISCOUNT VOUCHERS

MAP 3:B3
Smithfield Square
Dolgellau LL40 1ES
T: 01341 422554
w: themeirionnydd.com

BEDROOMS: 5.
OPEN: all year except 12–27 Dec, restaurant closed Sun, Mon.
FACILITIES: bar, restaurant, free Wi-Fi, in-room TV, terrace.
BACKGROUND MUSIC: in bar, restaurant.
LOCATION: town centre, Snowdonia national park.
CHILDREN: not under 6.
DOGS: assistance dogs only.
CREDIT CARDS: Amex, MC, Visa.
PRICES: per room B&B £89–£135, D,B&B £141–£187. À la carte £29.50. 2-night min. stay weekends.

LLANARTHNE Carmarthenshire

LLWYN HELYG

With 'an unexpected wow factor', 'genuinely kind' Fiona and Caron Jones have given their modern house a 'glossy luxury' touch – all elegant granite, marble and honey-coloured wood. The acoustically designed, vaulted Listening Room is equipped with a state-of-the-art sound system. Guests are invited to bring their own music or choose from the hosts' large library. A welcoming tea on one of the squashy sofas is accompanied by the sounds of the great composers. The 'very comfortable' bedrooms have a 'top-quality' bed, a 'luxurious' bathroom. The sunny breakfast room overlooks a formal pond, with views of the tranquil Tywi valley. Dining recommendations are readily supplied. In 'magnificent countryside', the National Botanic Garden of Wales is nearby.

MAP 3:D2
Llanarthne SA32 8HJ
T: 01558 668778
W: llwynhelygcountryhouse.co.uk

BEDROOMS: 3.
OPEN: all year except 10 days over Christmas.
FACILITIES: 4 lounges, listening room, breakfast room, free Wi-Fi, in-room TV (Freeview), 3-acre garden.
BACKGROUND MUSIC: none.
LOCATION: 8 miles W of Llandeilo, 9 miles E of Carmarthen.
CHILDREN: not under 16.
DOGS: not allowed.
CREDIT CARDS: MC, Visa.
PRICES: per room B&B single £110, double £135–£155.

LLANDDEINIOLEN Gwynedd

TY'N RHOS

On a secluded farmstead, Hilary and Stephen Murphy and daughter Laura's hotel is 'in lovely countryside' overlooking the Isle of Anglesey. Sheep and cattle graze in fields beyond the gardens; binoculars are provided for watching the many varieties of birds. Each named after a wild flower, bedrooms are in the creeper-covered house or the courtyard; some have patio doors opening on to the lush garden. An aperitif can be enjoyed in the bar, lounge or conservatory, or on the patio in fine weather. 'Large portions of a good dinner' include pan-roasted silver hake, creamy mashed potatoes, clam chowder or cuts of Welsh Wagyu beef. In the morning, choose from the large breakfast buffet; cooked dishes include eggs Benedict and the full Welsh.

MAP 3:A3
Llanddeiniolen LL55 3AE
T: 01248 670489
W: tynrhos.co.uk

BEDROOMS: 19. 7 in converted outbuilding, 2 on ground floor, suitable for disabled.
OPEN: all year, except Christmas, New Year.
FACILITIES: lounge, bar, restaurant conservatory; free Wi-Fi, in-room TV, 1-acre garden, parking, some public areas wheelchair accessible, no adapted toilet.
BACKGROUND MUSIC: in public areas.
LOCATION: 12 mins from the Llanberis train, 4 miles from Bangor and Caernarfon.
CHILDREN: all ages welcomed.
DOGS: by arrangement, not in public areas.
CREDIT CARDS: MC, Visa.
PRICES: room B&B single £80–£94, double £90–£190, D,B&B single £115–£225, double £160–£255 (2-night min. stay). Set menu £36.50 (2 courses), £42.50 (3 courses).

LLANDUDNO Conwy
ESCAPE

Urbane cool design and personal touches fill
Sam Nayar and Gaenor Loftus's stylish B&B in a
white stucco Victorian villa just up the slopes of
the Great Orme. Period features (stained-glass
windows and oak-panelling) form a backdrop
to modern and vintage furnishings and fabrics.
Regularly updated bedrooms, each different,
might have a copper bath, a pair of velvet-covered
cocktail chairs, mood lighting in an overhead
canopy. The Boudoir has wallpaper encrusted
with crystals, an aubergine bed and black
chandelier. In every room, high-end toiletries and
high-spec technology. A DVD library and piles
of wool throws and crocheted granny-square
blankets invite a cosy evening in. Occasional pop-
up dining events. A short stroll from the beach.

MAP 3:A3
48 Church Walks
Llandudno LL30 2HL
T: 01492 877776
w: escapebandb.co.uk

BEDROOMS: 9.
OPEN: all year except 18–26 Dec.
FACILITIES: lounge, breakfast room,
free Wi-Fi, in-room TV (Freeview),
front garden, limited parking.
BACKGROUND MUSIC: at breakfast.
LOCATION: 1 mile from town and coast.
CHILDREN: not under 10.
DOGS: not allowed.
CREDIT CARDS: Amex, MC, Visa.
PRICES: per room B&B £99–£149.
Min. 2-night bookings weekends,
3 nights bank holidays.

LLANFERRES Denbighshire
THE DRUID INN

A lively gathering spot for locals, this 'lovely',
unpretentious pub close to Offa's Dyke Path
makes an ideal base for the area's many walks and
bike trails. Luggage transfers can be arranged.
Promising 'a real taste of Wales', the 'friendly
hosts' provide a welcoming atmosphere, and
good beer in the cosy bar (low, beamed ceilings,
roaring log fire), and tasty home-made fare in the
traditional dining room. Neat, modest bedrooms
are comfortable, with en suite shower rooms; a
separate guest bathroom has a tub for a relaxing
soak. When the sun shines, folk spill outside to
enjoy gorgeous views of the woods, fields and hills
of the Clwydian area. The Grade II listed church
of St Berris is next door.

MAP 3:A4
Ruthin Road
Llanferres CH7 5SN
T: 01352 810225
w: druid-inn.co.uk

BEDROOMS: 5.
OPEN: all year.
FACILITIES: bar, snug, restaurant,
pool room, free Wi-Fi, in-room TV
(Freeview), garden, parking.
BACKGROUND MUSIC: in public spaces.
LOCATION: edge of village, close to
Offa's Dyke Path.
CHILDREN: all ages welcomed (but no
family room).
DOGS: allowed in some bedrooms, bar,
pool room.
CREDIT CARDS: MC, Visa.
PRICES: per room B&B single £72,
double £85. À la carte £24.

LLANGAFFO Anglesey

THE OUTBUILDINGS

Glorious views to Snowdonia spill away from a quirky restaurant-with-rooms surrounded by sheep-spotted fields. Millie Mantle manages the 'much-enjoyed' place for Judith 'Bun' Matthews. Bright, modern and uncluttered, the well-appointed bedrooms in the converted stone-built barn and granary (one with a four-poster) are playfully named (Pink Spotty Jug, Button's Room); a pink-painted shepherd's hut in the grounds looks out to Snowdon. Plentiful extras include a hot drinks tray, home-baked treats, a quality music system. A communal breakfast initiates discussions of the evening's 'excellent' set menu, using local produce and foraged ingredients. Twenty-five minutes' drive to the Holyhead ferry terminal.

25% DISCOUNT VOUCHERS

MAP 3:A2
Bodowyr Farm
Llangaffo LL60 6NH
T: 01248 430132
W: theoutbuildings.co.uk

BEDROOMS: 5. 1 on ground floor, 1 in garden.
OPEN: all year.
FACILITIES: bar, sitting room, restaurant with sitting area, free Wi-Fi, in-room TV, civil wedding licence, private dining/function facilities, spa treatments, garden, tennis, parking.
BACKGROUND MUSIC: in sitting room, dining room (but 'happy to turn it off').
LOCATION: 10 mins from Menai Bridge and 10 mins from Llanddwyn beach.
CHILDREN: babes-in-arms and over-12s welcomed.
DOGS: small, well-behaved dogs in 1 bedroom, not in public areas.
CREDIT CARDS: MC, Visa.
PRICES: per room B&B single £65–£75, double £85–£100. Set dinner £35.

LLANSTEFFAN Carmarthenshire

MANSION HOUSE LLANSTEFFAN

'Overall, a very enjoyable stay.' With extensive views over the Tywi estuary, David and Wendy Beaney's restaurant-with-rooms brings 'stylish minimalism down to a fine art'. Tasteful refurbishment has kept original features: a marble-tiled entrance hall, grand staircase, stained glass, ornate plasterwork. 'Fabulous bedroom: airy, a huge comfortable bed; separate dressing area and a big bathroom with walk-in shower and stand-alone bath.' Eaves rooms lie up narrow stairs. All have countryside or estuary views, home-made treats, Welsh toiletries, bathrobes. 'Staff are brilliant, efficient and friendly.' Paul Owen's seasonal menus are served in the garden-facing restaurant. Breakfast brings 'decent' fruit, 'OK' home-made croissants, 'good' jams and marmalades.

MAP 3:D2
Pantyrathro
Llansteffan SA33 5AJ
T: 01267 241515
W: mansionhousellansteffan.co.uk

BEDROOMS: 8. 2 on ground floor are interconnecting, 1 suitable for disabled.
OPEN: all year.
FACILITIES: large open-plan bar/reception area, lounge, restaurant (closed Sun eve, Mon, Nov–Feb), free Wi-Fi, in-room TV (Freeview), civil wedding licence, conference facilities, 5-acre grounds, parking.
BACKGROUND MUSIC: in public spaces.
LOCATION: 2 miles to Llansteffan village, beach and castle.
CHILDREN: all ages welcomed (extra bed £25, children's menu).
DOGS: not allowed.
CREDIT CARDS: Amex, MC, Visa.
PRICES: per room B&B from £109, D,B&B from £142. À la carte £30.

LLANTWIT MAJOR Vale of Glamorgan
THE WEST HOUSE

Close to the centre of a historic village and the Glamorgan Heritage Coast, a small hotel in a lovingly restored 17th-century country house. It has a peaceful bar and lounge, enlivened with the occasional antique, vintage typewriter, old portrait – good for a leisurely afternoon tea. Pristine bedrooms, some compact, have a breezy palette; dog-friendly rooms are provided with a towel, dog bed, 'lovely doggie treats', and have hardwood flooring and easy access to the walled garden. All-day light bites and British classics (including vegan and vegetarian options, perhaps leek, carrot and Cheddar hash) are served in the atmospheric restaurant; on fine days, the courtyard beckons. A Town & Country Collective hotel (see also Shortlist for The Bear, Cowbridge).

MAP 3:E3
West Street
Llantwit Major CF61 1SP
T: 01446 792406
W: townandcountrycollective.co.uk

BEDROOMS: 22. 1 on ground floor.
OPEN: all year.
FACILITIES: bar, restaurant (closed Sun evenings), snug, free Wi-Fi, in-room TV, conservatory, terrace, garden, civil wedding licence, parking, public areas wheelchair accessible, no adapted toilet.
BACKGROUND MUSIC: in lounge, restaurant.
LOCATION: a 10-min. walk from Llantwit Major.
CHILDREN: all ages welcomed.
DOGS: allowed in some bedrooms, dining room.
CREDIT CARDS: MC, Visa.
PRICES: per room B&B £95–£130, D,B&B £120–£150. À la carte £20.

LLANWRTYD WELLS Powys
LASSWADE COUNTRY HOUSE

A gateway to the Cambrian mountains, this semi-rural Edwardian restaurant-with-rooms is a home from home with high green credentials. An electric vehicle charging point is available; incentives encourage visitors to arrive by public transport. Decoration may be dated ('boutique and high luxury we are not'), but the Stevenses are welcoming hosts and offer helpful information on the area. Pre-dinner drinks are served in the sitting room, which has squashy sofas, plenty of books and a log fire. Roger's 'ample' three-course menus are 'very good' ('he makes a mean zabaglione'); Emma's service 'exemplary'. The bedrooms have 'superb mountain views'. A small patio garden has a pond, and seating for admiring 'outstanding' countryside panoramas.

25% DISCOUNT VOUCHERS

MAP 3:D3
Station Road
Llanwrtyd Wells LD5 4RW
T: 01591 610515
W: lasswadehotel.co.uk

BEDROOMS: 8.
OPEN: 1 Mar–19 Dec, Sun, Mon.
FACILITIES: drawing room, restaurant, conservatory, free Wi-Fi, in-room TV (Freeview), function room, patio, small garden, parking.
BACKGROUND MUSIC: pianola in restaurant.
LOCATION: edge of town.
CHILDREN: all ages welcomed, over-8s allowed in restaurant.
DOGS: allowed by arrangement (not in bedrooms, restaurant).
CREDIT CARDS: MC, Visa.
PRICES: per room B&B single £70–£85, double £90–£125, D,B&B £160–£180, except during Royal Welsh Show week. Set menu £36.

MOYLEGROVE Pembrokeshire

THE OLD VICARAGE B&B

A woodland walk leads from the sea to this imposing Edwardian vicarage on a hill above the village. Owners Meg and Jaap van Soest have refurbished the light-filled house in pared-back style, with wooden flooring and modern furniture draped with Welsh blankets. The airy sitting room has a high ceiling, large windows and a horde of books; maps and guides for walkers and cyclists. Unfussy bedrooms have a large bed, crisp linen, fresh milk and coffee, a shower room with Welsh toiletries. Organic breakfasts are served in a twin-aspect room with views across the valley. They include apple and Pembrokeshire honey bircher muesli; a veggie full Welsh (grilled halloumi, home-grown spinach, tomatoes, free-range eggs, mushrooms). Dinner is available on request.

25% DISCOUNT VOUCHERS

MAP 3:D2
Moylegrove SA43 3BN
T: 01239 881711
W: oldvicaragemoylegrove.co.uk

BEDROOMS: 5.
OPEN: all year, evening meals provided by request.
FACILITIES: bar, sitting room, dining room, free Wi-Fi, in-room TV (Freeview), 1-acre garden.
BACKGROUND MUSIC: in dining room during the evening.
LOCATION: a few hundred yards outside village, 13 miles N of Fishguard.
CHILDREN: all ages welcomed.
DOGS: allowed, not in dining room.
CREDIT CARDS: Amex, MC, Visa.
PRICES: per room B&B £100–£110. Dinner £35.

MUMBLES Swansea

PATRICKS WITH ROOMS

Across from the seafront, this long-established, family-run restaurant-with-rooms is helmed by two husband-and-wife teams, Sally and Dean Fuller, Sally's sister, Catherine Walsh and her husband, Patrick. Relaxed and 'so friendly', the interior is lively in style. Colourful, individually decorated bedrooms (some interconnecting) sprawl across a converted pub and boathouse. Some have a balcony and views over the bay. 'Ours had a colossal shower and a big bath in the spacious bathroom.' The monthly-changing menu, using Welsh produce, might have beef fillet, grilled asparagus, rocket and horseradish slaw. Breakfast is perhaps smoked salmon, soft cream cheese frittata, or the choice of an English, or a Welsh breakfast with cockles and laver bread.

MAP 3:E3
638 Mumbles Road
Mumbles SA3 4EA
T: 01792 360199
W: patrickswithrooms.com

BEDROOMS: 16. 1 suitable for disabled, 6 in converted boathouse.
OPEN: all year except last 10 days in October, 25/26 Dec, 2 weeks in Jan.
FACILITIES: lift, lounge/bar, restaurant (closed Sun eve), free Wi-Fi, in-room TV (Freeview), civil wedding licence, meeting room, gym, on-street parking, public areas wheelchair accessible.
BACKGROUND MUSIC: in public areas.
LOCATION: close to seafront, 10 mins' drive from Swansea.
CHILDREN: all ages welcomed.
DOGS: not allowed.
CREDIT CARDS: Amex, MC, Visa.
PRICES: per room B&B single £100–£155, double £125–£185. À la carte £35.

NEW

NANT GWYNANT Gwynedd
PEN-Y-GWRYD HOTEL

At the foot of Snowdonia, the Pullees' 'eccentric' hotel is run by the same family who hosted Sir Edmund Hillary and Tenzing Norgay as they trained to climb Everest, and not a lot has changed since. Built in 1810, the farmhouse-turned-coaching inn retains the spirit of a mountaineers' hostel. Wi-Fi has found its way into the common areas, TV into some bedrooms, though not all have an en suite bathroom. The compensations are many, not least the beautiful surroundings and the hotel's own swimming lake, sauna and chapel. Lounge about in three snugs, with a reliquary of Everest memorabilia, a dartboard and table tennis. Breakfast is 'hearty'. In the evening, when the gong sounds, head to the dining room and a sustaining set dinner.

MAP 3:A3
Nant Gwynant LL55 4NT
T: 01286 870211
W: pyg.co.uk

BEDROOMS: 18. 1 on ground floor, 5 in annexe, 1 suitable for disabled (bathroom not adapted).
OPEN: Mar–mid-Nov, occasional weekends Dec, New Year.
FACILITIES: bar, games room, lounge, dining room, free Wi-Fi in some bedrooms, in-room TV (Freeview) in some rooms, chapel, 1-acre grounds (natural swimming lake, sauna), bar, dining room wheelchair accessible (no adapted toilet).
BACKGROUND MUSIC: none.
LOCATION: between Beddgelert and Capel Curig.
CHILDREN: all ages welcomed.
DOGS: allowed in some bedrooms, public rooms except dining room.
CREDIT CARDS: MC, Visa.
PRICES: per person B&B £47–£75, double £95–£150, D,B&B £76–£104. Set dinner £29. 1-night bookings often refused weekends.

NARBERTH Pembrokeshire
CANASTON OAKS

The friendly owners 'go the extra mile' at their well-restored Pembrokeshire longhouse, a short drive from a pleasant market town. Eleanor and David Lewis run the 'very good' B&B with their daughter, Emma Millership. Spotless bedrooms, in converted barns or a lake-view lodge, have thoughtful extras (dressing gowns, candles; 'the fresh milk in the room was a lovely touch'). A family might request a suite of interconnecting rooms with a countryside-facing terrace. In the morning, feast on thick and creamy Welsh yoghurt, heather honey, home-poached fruit, porridge with a dash of Penderyn whisky and smoked haddock fishcakes before an amble by the river. 'Five star at every level.'

25% DISCOUNT VOUCHERS

MAP 3:D2
Canaston Bridge
Narberth SA67 8DE
T: 01437 541254
W: canastonoaks.co.uk

BEDROOMS: 10, 7 around a courtyard, 2 suitable for disabled, plus 1-bed self-catering apartment.
OPEN: all year except Christmas.
FACILITIES: lounge, dining room, free Wi-Fi, in-room TV (Freeview), 1-acre grounds, parking.
BACKGROUND MUSIC: at breakfast in the dining room.
LOCATION: 2 miles W of Narberth.
CHILDREN: all ages welcomed.
DOGS: well-behaved dogs in 3 barn suites, not in dining area; must be kept on a lead.
CREDIT CARDS: MC, Visa.
PRICES: per room B&B £90–£175. 1-night bookings sometimes refused peak times.

NEWTOWN Powys
THE FOREST COUNTRY GUEST HOUSE

Home comforts and good value proliferate at Paul and Michelle Martin's family-friendly oasis in undulating mid-Wales countryside. The peaceful, muzak-free, Victorian country house B&B is ringed by large, flower-filled gardens. Inside: books, maps and games, plus an antique Bechstein grand piano to play, and a suit of armour with a sword that children are allowed to brandish. Up the 19th-century oak staircase, pleasantly old-fashioned, country-style bedrooms have period furniture, views of fields graced by a herd of rare breed sheep; one large room has a four-poster bed. DIY snacks and meals are easy in a kitchenette for guests' use. Eggs from the Martins' free-range hens supply the organic breakfasts.

MAP 3:C4
Gilfach Lane
Newtown SY16 4DW
T: 01686 621821
W: bedandbreakfastnewtown.co.uk

BEDROOMS: 5. Plus 4 self-catering cottages (1 room adapted for limited mobility is accessed by stairs).
OPEN: all year except Christmas, New Year, self-catering cottages open all year.
FACILITIES: sitting room, dining room, kitchenette, games room, free Wi-Fi, in-room TV (Freeview), 4-acre garden, tennis, parking, secure bicycle storage.
BACKGROUND MUSIC: none.
LOCATION: 1 mile from Kerry village, 3 miles from Newtown.
CHILDREN: all ages welcomed.
DOGS: allowed in cottages and in kennels in the grounds.
CREDIT CARDS: MC, Visa.
PRICES: per room B&B single £70–£85, double £80–£115. 1-night bookings sometimes refused bank holidays and busy weekends.

NEW

PENALLY Pembrokeshire
PENALLY ABBEY

'Worth the journey!' Overlooking the Pembrokeshire coast, the Boissevain family's 19th-century neo-Gothic house is 'an attractive building' in a 'beautiful' location. Architectural features include striking ogee-headed doors and windows, moulded plaster ceilings, an Adam-style fireplace. Public rooms are extensive and comfortable. Bright, chic bedrooms sport cool coastal shades. 'Housekeeping is 5 star.' A superior double has a four-poster, a sofa bed for an extra guest, views across to Caldey Island. Dog-friendly rooms in the coach house lead directly to the garden. In the new restaurant, Rhosyn, head chef Richard Browning's unpretentious menus focus on the area's produce. An atmospheric restored chapel is available for private hire.

MAP 3:E1
Penally
Tenby SA70 7PY
T: 01834 843033
W: penally-abbey.com

BEDROOMS: 11. 4 in coach house (40 yds from main house), 2 on ground floor.
OPEN: all year except first 2 weeks of Jan, restaurant closed to non-residents Sun, Mon.
FACILITIES: drawing room, snug bar, sunroom, restaurant, private function room, free Wi-Fi, in-room TV (Freeview), civil wedding licence, in-room massages and beauty treatments, terrace, 1-acre lawns.
BACKGROUND MUSIC: 'very gentle' in bar and restaurant.
LOCATION: 1½ miles SW of Tenby.
CHILDREN: all ages welcomed.
DOGS: allowed in coach house bedrooms (not unattended), bar, sunroom, not in restaurant.
CREDIT CARDS: MC, Visa.
PRICES: per room B&B £145–£265. À la carte fixed-price dinner £40, tasting menu £79.

PENARTH Vale of Glamorgan

HOLM HOUSE

High on a cliff-top, overlooking Penarth Pier and the Bristol Channel, a hotel and spa in a neatly designed garden with water channels, gravel and lawns; seating offers views over the sea. The house, built in 1926, is contemporary inside. Cocktails and mocktails are dispensed from a sleek, curved bar under a feature chandelier; the snug, a homely alternative, has a flickering open fire. In the coastal-hued dining room (candlelit at night), a steak menu and seasonal dishes, perhaps fillet of cod, fresh turmeric, clams, sweetcorn, samphire; fresh produce from the kitchen garden. Understated bedrooms have 'every luxury' (soft bathrobes, home-baked Welsh cakes, teas and cafetière coffee); many have a sea view. The spa is a soothing space.

MAP 3:E4
Marine Parade
Penarth CF64 3BG
T: 029 2070 6029
W: holmhousehotel.com

BEDROOMS: 13. 2 in annexe.
OPEN: all year.
FACILITIES: bar/lounge, snug, restaurant, free Wi-Fi, in-room TV (Sky), civil wedding licence, large garden, spa, gym.
BACKGROUND MUSIC: in public areas.
LOCATION: seafront location on the edge of town, 5 miles from Cardiff.
CHILDREN: all ages welcomed.
DOGS: allowed in annexe bedrooms, snug.
CREDIT CARDS: MC, Visa.
PRICES: per room B&B £130–£260. À la carte from £30.

PORTMEIRION Gwynedd

HOTEL PORTMEIRION

Clustered on the edge of a spectacular tidal estuary, this mansion house hotel – the focal point of Sir Bertram Clough Williams-Ellis's Italianate village – has welcomed guests including H G Wells, George Bernard Shaw and Bertrand Russell. 'A pleasant experience', it 'combines old-world touches with stylish modernity'. Its traditional bedrooms have estuary and mountain views; more contemporary rooms in Castell Deudraeth overlook the walled garden; the bedrooms in the colourful village cottages enjoy use of a fully equipped kitchen. Mealtime options include the informal brasserie or the Art Deco dining room; the cooking is thought 'somewhat outdated'. Places to explore include a shell grotto, a bell tower, a dog cemetery, a temple.

MAP 3:B3
Minffordd
Portmeirion LL48 6ER
T: 01766 770000
W: portmeirion.wales

BEDROOMS: 58. 14 in hotel, some on ground floor, 1 suitable for disabled, 11 in Castell Deudraeth, 33 in village.
OPEN: all year, Castell Deudraeth rooms closed 5–10 Jan.
FACILITIES: lift, 3 lounges, bar, restaurant, brasserie in Castell, free Wi-Fi, in-room TV, civil wedding licence, function facilities, 130-acre grounds, outdoor heated swimming pool (summer).
BACKGROUND MUSIC: in public areas.
LOCATION: 2 miles SE of Porthmadog.
CHILDREN: all ages welcomed.
DOGS: assistance dogs allowed.
CREDIT CARDS: Amex, MC, Visa.
PRICES: per room B&B £124–£344, D,B&B £184–£404. Set menu £47–£55, à la carte £55. 2-night min. stay preferred on Sat.

NEW

MAP 3:A2
High Street
Rhosneigr LL64 5UX
T: 01407 253102
W: sandymounthouse.co.uk

RHOSNEIGR Anglesey
SANDY MOUNT HOUSE

A rustic beach-house vibe breezes through this
restaurant-with-rooms in a small seaside village
in the south-west of Anglesey. Owners Louise
and Philip Goodwin, with designer Michelle
Derbyshire, have transformed the former public
house into a laid-back space: wicker chairs on
sand-bleached floors, weathered wooden tables,
thick rope features, pendant lighting. Still a
welcoming haven, locals are joined by kitesurfers,
dog-walkers and families off the beach, in the
lively bar and dining areas; outside, in summer
months. Chef Hefin Roberts's robust dishes
are cooked in an open kitchen; perhaps fillet of
Anglesey-reared beef. Modern, well-equipped
rooms have a bathroom with a rainfall shower.
Breakfast choices include a full Welsh.

BEDROOMS: 7.
OPEN: all year, limited hours over
Christmas period.
FACILITIES: bar, restaurant,
conservatory, private dining, garden,
free Wi-Fi, in-room TV, bar,
restaurant are wheelchair accessible.
BACKGROUND MUSIC: in bar, restaurant.
LOCATION: in village, close to beach.
CHILDREN: all ages welcomed.
DOGS: allowed in 2 bedrooms, bar,
front terrace, adapted toilet.
CREDIT CARDS: Amex, MC, Visa.
PRICES: per room B&B £140–£360.
À la carte £35.

NEW

25% DISCOUNT VOUCHERS

MAP 3:D1
Roch
Haverfordwest SA62 6AQ
T: 01437 725566
W: rochcastle.com

ROCH Pembrokeshire
ROCH CASTLE HOTEL

A 12th-century castle graced with 21st-century
design. In a dramatic setting on a rocky outcrop
high above the Pembrokeshire landscape, the
commanding property has panoramic views
over St Brides Bay and the Preseli hills. B&B
guests may hold court on dark suede seating in a
sleekly contemporary sitting room with arches,
stone alcoves, a blazing fire; a tapestry depicts the
castle's history. Up many steps, the Sun Room
merits the climb – floor-to-ceiling glass walls and
an alfresco viewing platform display magnificent
scenes below. Moody bedrooms have robes,
slippers, a fridge, iron, iPod dock, aromatherapy
toiletries. Freshly cooked breakfasts include
Welsh laver bread, local honey. Free transfers take
guests to a sister hotel for dinner.

BEDROOMS: 6.
OPEN: all year.
FACILITIES: lounge, study, dining room,
sunroom (honesty bar), free Wi-Fi,
in-room TV (Sky), civil wedding
licence, 19-acre grounds.
BACKGROUND MUSIC: lounges, dining
room.
LOCATION: 7 miles NW of
Haverfordwest.
CHILDREN: not under 12.
DOGS: not allowed.
CREDIT CARDS: Amex, MC, Visa.
PRICES: per room B&B £220–£260,
D,B&B £290–£340. 2- or 3-night min.
stay weekends and peak times, also
available for exclusive use.

ST DAVID'S Pembrokeshire
CRUG-GLAS

On their Pembrokeshire working farm, the Evans family 'warmly welcome' visitors to their laid-back, restaurant-with-rooms. The Georgian farmhouse, perhaps austere on the outside, is a family home, filled with photographs and inherited pieces – the handsome, generations-old dresser houses the honesty bar. Janet Evans serves 'excellent' dinners – 'good local produce, cleverly cooked'. 'The duck breast with plums in port and wine sauce was very enjoyable; a lovely "proper" apple crumble for dessert.' 'Idiosyncratic' cottage-style bedrooms (in the main building, a converted milk parlour and a coach house) might have a double-ended copper bath, a separate sitting room. An 'excellent breakfast' has 'superb choice'. St David's is three miles away; the coast is close.

MAP 3:D1
Abereiddy
St David's SA62 6XX
T: 01348 831302
w: crug-glas.co.uk

BEDROOMS: 7, 2 in outbuildings, 1 on ground floor.
OPEN: all year except 24–26 Dec.
FACILITIES: drawing room, dining room, free Wi-Fi, in-room TV (Freeview), civil wedding licence, function facilities in converted barn, 1-acre garden.
BACKGROUND MUSIC: classical.
LOCATION: 3½ miles NE of St David's.
CHILDREN: babes in arms and over-11s welcomed.
DOGS: allowed in cottage (£10 per night).
CREDIT CARDS: MC, Visa.
PRICES: per room B&B £150–£210. À la carte £35.

ST BRELADE Jersey

LA HAULE MANOR

A Provençal air whirls through this white-painted Georgian manor house overlooking St Aubin's Bay. Ola Przyjemska runs the show, supported by 'helpful and efficient' staff. Complimentary transfers are provided to and from the airport; a complimentary glass of bubbly on arrival sets a warm tone. The high-ceilinged sitting room has chandeliers and ornate furnishings. Many of the traditionally decorated bedrooms, each different, mix whites, creams and Louis XV-style pieces; some have broad sea views. Parasol-shaded loungers encircle the swimming pool. All-day light bites are served in the bar. For dinner, free transport takes guests to sister hotel La Place; other eateries are a short walk away. A bus for getting around the island stops right outside.

MAP 1: inset E6
La Neuve Route
St Brelade JE3 8BS
T: 01534 746013
W: lahaulemanor.com

BEDROOMS: 16. Some on ground floor, plus 2 self-catering apartments.
OPEN: all year.
FACILITIES: bar, sitting room, TV room, breakfast room, free Wi-Fi, in-room TV, terrace, garden, outdoor heated swimming pool, hot tub, parking.
BACKGROUND MUSIC: in bar, breakfast room.
LOCATION: close to St Aubin village.
CHILDREN: all ages welcomed.
DOGS: only assistance dogs allowed.
CREDIT CARDS: MC, Visa.
PRICES: per room B&B £107–£225.

ST MARTIN Guernsey

BELLA LUCE HOTEL

Renoir was once drawn to this spot, above Moulin Huet Bay, to capture the ever-changing scene in his Guernsey paintings. Today, it's the 'delightful staff', 'comfortable bedrooms' and 'outstanding food' that attract visitors to this luxurious small hotel. The Wheadon family has tastefully restored the handsome, extended Norman manor house, finishing the stylish bedrooms and suites with a superb bathroom, good technology; some have a four-poster bed, a separate lounge area. Diners tuck into modern European dishes by candlelight in the garden-facing restaurant. The courtyard's shady tulip tree is perfect for summer afternoons; the vaulted cellar lounge's leather sofas overlook the copper stills of the on-site gin distillery.

MAP 1: inset E5
La Fosse
St Martin GY4 6EB
T: 01481 238764
W: bellalucehotel.com

BEDROOMS: 23. 2 on ground floor.
OPEN: Apr–Oct.
FACILITIES: bar, snug, 2 restaurants, cellar lounge, free Wi-Fi, in-room TV (Freeview), ramps, civil wedding licence, private dining room, function facilities, 2-acre garden, courtyard, outdoor swimming pool, spa, parking.
BACKGROUND MUSIC: in public spaces.
LOCATION: 2 miles from the town centre and airport, above a valley, with a beach below.
CHILDREN: all ages welcomed.
DOGS: not allowed.
CREDIT CARDS: Amex, MC, Visa.
PRICES: per room B&B £120-£160, D,B&B £170–£250. À la carte £38.

ST PETER PORT Guernsey

LA COLLINETTE HOTEL

The Chambers clan encourages a family-friendly atmosphere at their white-painted Georgian hotel fronted with cheerful window boxes. The relaxed, unpretentious place near the waterfront is managed by the long-serving Cyril Fortier. Most of the bright bedrooms have splashes of ocean blue and glittering views of the sea; all have a choice of pillow, a thick mattress topper, and a hospitality tray with tea, coffee, biscuits. The informal restaurant serves uncomplicated dishes using much local produce. Breakfast brings a buffet; a Guernsey 'full house', a grilled kipper. A German Naval Underground Museum is sited under self-catering accommodation in the grounds. On the other side of Candie Gardens, shops, and island-hopping from the port.

25% DISCOUNT VOUCHERS

MAP 1: inset E5
St Jacques
St Peter Port GY1 1SN
T: 01481 710331
W: lacollinette.com

BEDROOMS: 23. 14 self-catering cottages and apartments.
OPEN: all year.
FACILITIES: lounge, bar, restaurant, free Wi-Fi, in-room TV (Sky, Freeview), 2-acre garden, outdoor heated swimming pool, children's pool, play area, gym, spa treatments, restaurant and bar wheelchair accessible.
BACKGROUND MUSIC: in bar and restaurant.
LOCATION: under a mile W of town centre.
CHILDREN: all ages welcomed.
DOGS: not allowed.
CREDIT CARDS: MC, Visa.
PRICES: per person B&B from £60.

ST PETER PORT Guernsey

THE DUKE OF RICHMOND

Above the town, this modern, family-friendly hotel (Red Carnation Hotel Collection) overlooks a park, and has views as far as Herm and Sark. A safari theme pervades the 19th-century building, and runs wild in the striking Leopard bar. Copies of Impressionist masterpieces hang throughout. Complimentary sweet snacks are replenished all day; a range of loose-leaf teas is served for afternoon tea, in the conservatory or on the terrace. Young travellers receive treats and a DVD-player for their entertainment; pets' needs are met by a 'preference form'. In the restaurant, the wholesome menu is supplemented with daily specials. Bedrooms might be modern or traditional, with sea view or balcony. At breakfast, eggs Benedict, Florentine, Royale; pancakes or waffles.

MAP 1: inset E5
Cambridge Park Road
St Peter Port GY1 1UY
T: 01481 726221
W: dukeofrichmond.com

BEDROOMS: 73. 14 self-catering cottages and apartments.
OPEN: all year.
FACILITIES: bar, lounge, restaurant, free Wi-Fi, in-room TV (Sky, Freeview), 2-acre garden, outdoor swimming pool, gym, spa treatments, restaurant and bar wheelchair accessible.
BACKGROUND MUSIC: in bar and restaurant.
LOCATION: under a mile W of town centre.
CHILDREN: all ages welcomed.
DOGS: allowed, not in restaurant.
CREDIT CARDS: MC, Visa.
PRICES: per room from £183.

BELFAST
THE OLD RECTORY

A good-value base for the university, Mary Callan's Victorian guest house is in a leafy suburb, a short bus ride from the centre. A visitor in 2019 was made 'very welcome'. 'I enjoyed my stay very much.' The well-maintained villa has books and board games in the 'nicely furnished' drawing room; hot whiskey for cool days. 'Comfortable' bedrooms are supplied with biscuits, reading material, tea-/coffee-making facilities; fresh milk in a mini-fridge on each landing. A 'splendid' breakfast (ordered the night before) has freshly squeezed orange juice, cereals, fruits and yogurt, home-baked Irish breads. 'I had a plate of delicious smoked salmon with scrambled eggs on my first morning; shredded duck on baked eggs with herbs, the next. Coffee was excellent.'

MAP 6:B6
148 Malone Road
Belfast BT9 5LH
T: 028 9066 7882
W: anoldrectory.co.uk

BEDROOMS: 6. 1, on ground floor, suitable for disabled.
OPEN: all year except Christmas, New Year, 2 weeks mid-July.
FACILITIES: drawing room, dining room, free Wi-Fi, in-room TV, garden, parking.
BACKGROUND MUSIC: 'quiet' at breakfast.
LOCATION: just under 2 miles from city centre.
CHILDREN: all ages welcomed.
DOGS: not allowed.
CREDIT CARDS: MC, Visa.
PRICES: per room B&B single from £55, double from £98. 2-night min. stay May–Sept.

BELFAST
RAVENHILL HOUSE

A short bus ride from the city centre, this handsomely restored red-brick B&B is also close to popular restaurants, shops and a leafy park. Hosts Olive and Roger Nicholson provide a warm welcome for arriving guests, with tea and oven-fresh treats. Cosy bedrooms in the Victorian house are decorated with floral prints; in each, good seating, pleasing extras: home-baked shortbread; a vintage Hacker radio. Weekends are leisurely, with a wide-ranging breakfast served till 10 am in a dining room with wood-burning stove and book-lined shelves; fuel for the day includes home-made marmalades and jellies, spiced fruit compote. The Nicholsons mill their own flour from organic Irish rye grain for the freshly baked sourdough bread; good vegetarian options.

MAP 6:B6
690 Ravenhill Road
Belfast BT6 0BZ
T: 028 9028 2590
W: ravenhillhouse.com

BEDROOMS: 4.
OPEN: Feb–15 Dec.
FACILITIES: sitting room, dining room, free Wi-Fi, in-room TV (Freeview), small garden, parking.
BACKGROUND MUSIC: Radio 3 at breakfast.
LOCATION: 2 miles S of city centre.
CHILDREN: not under 10.
DOGS: not allowed.
CREDIT CARDS: Amex, MC, Visa.
PRICES: per room B&B £85–£140. 2-night min. stay preferred busy weekends.

BUSHMILLS Co. Antrim

BUSHMILLS INN

A short stroll from the world's oldest distillery, this amiable 17th-century coaching inn on the Causeway Coastal Route is an eclectic jumble of ancient and modern. The public rooms have wooden booths, higgledy-piggledy snugs, inglenook turf fires, a 'secret' library. Many of the spacious bedrooms in the mill house, each with its own sitting area, overlook the River Bush. In the bar, still lit by Victorian gaslights, whiskey cocktails and Irish music; in the garden-facing restaurant, modern Irish plates, perhaps Dalriada Cullen skink (poached smoked haddock with hen's egg and sautéed potatoes). Well-considered top-ten lists suggest itineraries for days outdoors and indoors ('Ten things to do when it's raining', 'as a family', etc).

MAP 6:A6
9 Dunluce Road
Bushmills BT57 8QG
T: 028 2073 3000
W: bushmillsinn.com

BEDROOMS: 41. Some on ground floor, some suitable for disabled.
OPEN: all year, no accommodation 24/25 Dec.
FACILITIES: lift, bar, lounge, restaurant, gallery, loft, cinema, free Wi-Fi, in-room TV (Freeview), conference facilities, patio, 2-acre garden, parking.
BACKGROUND MUSIC: in public areas, live traditional Irish music sessions every Sat in bar.
LOCATION: village centre, on river, 2 miles from Giant's Causeway.
CHILDREN: all ages welcomed.
DOGS: only permitted on outside patio area.
CREDIT CARDS: Amex, MC, Visa.
PRICES: per room B&B £160–£460.
À la carte £60.

CAHERSIVEEN Co. Kerry

QUINLAN & COOKE BOUTIQUE TOWNHOUSE

In a town on the Ring of Kerry, Andrew and Kate Cooke's 'buzzing' destination restaurant and 'quirky, boutique-style' bedrooms provide 'a brilliant base for a boat trip to the Skellig Islands'. 'Kate is a charming owner/manager'; 'service is friendly and efficient'. In the intimate restaurant, a short menu based on wild local fish (supplied by the family business) is served 'in generous portions'. 'Spacious and comfortable' bedrooms have wooden floors, an iPod docking station, a safe, 'eclectic reading matter'; a Nespresso machine, a fridge full of treat-bearing Kilner jars (fresh fruit salad, fruit compote and yoghurt, granola, fresh milk). Come morning, croissants and muffins appear in a bag on your door handle.

MAP 6:D4
3 Main Street
Cahersiveen V23 WA46
T: 00 353 66 947 2244
W: qc.ie

BEDROOMS: 11.
OPEN: Apr–Oct, weekends only Nov–Mar, open Christmas/New Year.
FACILITIES: bar, lounge, free Wi-Fi, in-room TV (Sky), courtyard, gym, parking.
BACKGROUND MUSIC: in restaurant.
LOCATION: village centre.
CHILDREN: all ages welcomed.
DOGS: allowed.
CREDIT CARDS: Amex, MC, Visa.
PRICES: per room B&B from €135.
À la carte €40.

NEW

CARAGH LAKE Co. Kerry
ARD NA SIDHE
COUNTRY HOUSE HOTEL

In a magical place on the shores of Lake Caragh, a serene hotel in a Victorian-style manor. Its name translates as 'Hill of the Fairies', after a tree-covered knoll nearby. Each bedroom (in the main house or a building within a rustic courtyard) has fine linen, antique furniture, garden views; tranquillity is preserved by the absence of TV or radio. In the elegant restaurant, candlelit dinners include fish from the Atlantic or Kerry lamb. Afternoon tea is in a fire-warmed lounge, or on the terrace in fine weather. A picnic basket, maps, guides are supplied for days out: boating and fishing on the lake; discovering green glades in the extensive grounds. Complimentary leisure facilities at a sister hotel.

MAP 6:D4
Caragh Lake
Killorglin V93 HV57
T: 00 353 66 976 9105
w: ardnasidhe.com

BEDROOMS: 18. 8 in Garden House.
OPEN: 17 Apr–3 Oct.
FACILITIES: lounge, library, restaurant, free Wi-Fi, terrace, 32-acre grounds.
BACKGROUND MUSIC: in lounge, library.
LOCATION: on the shores of Caragh Lake.
CHILDREN: all ages welcomed.
DOGS: not allowed.
CREDIT CARDS: Amex, MC, Visa.
PRICES: per room B&B €230–€350, D,B&B €320–€440 (for two sharing).

CARLINGFORD Co. Louth
GHAN HOUSE

A tree's length from medieval Carlingford, this pretty Georgian house sits in mature walled gardens. It has been the Carroll family home for almost 30 years. Now Paul Carroll runs the hotel; his mother, Joyce, tends the garden and adorns the rooms with freshly cut flowers. The house is filled with family photographs and heirlooms, squashy sofas, antique French beds and claw-footed baths. Log-burners warm the drawing room and the 'elegant' dining room where menus based on abundant produce from lough and countryside include lapsang souchong smoked tea consommé, Lough Neagh eel, beetroot and turnip. Traditionally decorated bedrooms have an iPhone dock, biscuits, a modern bathroom and mountain views; most are in a garden annexe.

MAP 6:B6
Carlingford A91 DXY5
T: 00 353 42 937 3682
w: ghanhouse.com

BEDROOMS: 12. 8 in annexe, 1 on ground floor.
OPEN: all year except 24–26, 31 Dec, 1/2 Jan.
FACILITIES: bar, lounge, restaurant, 2 private dining rooms, free Wi-Fi, in-room TV (Freeview), wedding facilities, 3-acre garden, parking, charging point for electric cars.
BACKGROUND MUSIC: in bar, restaurant.
LOCATION: near Carlingford.
CHILDREN: all ages welcomed.
DOGS: allowed in kennels in converted stables.
CREDIT CARDS: Amex, MC, Visa.
PRICES: per person B&B €85–€125, D,B&B €125–€175. 6-course tasting menu and à la carte from €52.50.

CASTLETOWN BEREHAVEN Co. Cork
BEARA COAST HOTEL

'A real discovery.' In a 'first-rate setting' on the Beara peninsula, this good-value hotel on the water's edge, overlooks a harbour brimming with fishing boats and big ships. The contemporary interior was revamped by Mark Golden, who runs it with chef Mark Johnston. Their philosophy: source the best local produce, respect it, serve it in a relaxed setting. 'The staff are helpful and smiley.' Substantial, 'very good' food (scallops with orange and rocket; smoked salmon risotto, award-winning chowder) is served in the 'lively' Arches bar; an à la carte menu in the more formal plaid-seated dining room. 'Bright, comfortable bedrooms' have floral-patterned feature walls; many have a balcony with panoramic views of the harbour, the town, surrounding islands.

MAP 6:D4
Cametringane Point
Castletown Berehaven
T: 00 353 27 71446
w: bearacoast.com

BEDROOMS: 16. 1 suitable for disabled.
OPEN: all year, except 25/26, 31 Dec, after 4 pm.
FACILITIES: lift, bar, sunroom, library, restaurant, function facilities, free Wi-Fi, in-room TV, wedding facilities, terrace, public rooms wheelchair accessible, adapted toilet.
BACKGROUND MUSIC: in public areas.
LOCATION: on headland, overlooking harbour.
CHILDREN: all ages welcomed.
DOGS: allowed, by arrangement.
CREDIT CARDS: Amex, MC, Visa.
PRICES: per room B&B €120–€220, D,B&B €160–€260. Set menu dinner €27.50, à la carte €40.

CLIFDEN Co. Galway
BLUE QUAY ROOMS

Painted an unmissably bright blue, Paddy and Julia Foyle's good-value B&B in a 200-year-old building above the harbour is minutes from the town centre. It is sister to The Quay House on the waterfront (see main entry), and managed by son Toby and Pauline Petit. The interiors are playfully decorated: white-painted antlers hang opposite gilt-framed portraits, close to a ship's wheel; a zebra skin is stretched across a wall. In cosy sitting areas, bold black-and-white flooring lies beneath blue ceilings; a large metal lobster cooks atop the wood-burning stove. All but one of the pretty, modern bedrooms look across the harbour. Breakfasts are imaginative and plentiful. An ideal base for walkers and cyclists.

MAP 6:C4
Seaview
Clifden H71 WE02
T: 00 353 87 621 7616
w: bluequayrooms.com

BEDROOMS: 8. Plus 2-bed self-catering apartment.
OPEN: Apr–Oct.
FACILITIES: sitting area, breakfast room, free Wi-Fi, garden.
BACKGROUND MUSIC: none.
LOCATION: close to town centre.
CHILDREN: not under 10.
DOGS: not allowed.
CREDIT CARDS: none accepted.
PRICES: per room B&B single €65–€75, double €80–€90.

COBH Co. Cork

KNOCKEVEN HOUSE

High above Cork harbour, on the outskirts of this historic port town, the flower-laden garden of this grand Victorian house creates a cheering welcome. Pam Mulhaire is the friendly hostess. Arriving guests are treated to a hot drink and home-baked scones in the elegant drawing room, where a blaze crackles on cool days. B&B accommodation is found in spacious, high-ceilinged bedrooms filled with period pieces, flower arrangements; bathrooms have thick towels, terry cloth robes, high-end toiletries. Communal, organic breakfasts, served at a mahogany table in the light-washed dining room overlooking the garden, have seasonal fruits, preserves and home-baked brown bread. Pam has good advice on local attractions and restaurants.

MAP 6:D5
Rushbrooke
Cobh P24 E392
T: 00 353 21 481 1778
W: knockevenhouse.com

BEDROOMS: 5.
OPEN: 1 Jan–20 Dec.
FACILITIES: drawing room, dining room, free Wi-Fi, in-room TV, 2-acre grounds.
BACKGROUND MUSIC: at breakfast.
LOCATION: 1 mile W of centre.
CHILDREN: all ages welcomed.
DOGS: not allowed.
CREDIT CARDS: MC, Visa.
PRICES: per person B&B single from €30, double €60–€65.

COLLINSTOWN Co. Westmeath

LOUGH BAWN HOUSE

Off the beaten track, four generations of Verity Butterfield's family have lived in this 'impressive' Georgian house, with 'divine' views down rolling meadow to a spring-fed lough. The 'lovely hostess' welcomes guests with afternoon tea before an open fire in the homely drawing room packed with family heirlooms, books and an abundance of flowers. The 'lovely' home-cooked dinner, served (by pre-arrangement) in an elegant dining room, 'is a real treat'. Pretty, country house-style bedrooms overlook the garden or lake; two share a 'wonderful' bathroom (wooden floors, a shuttered window, vast bathtub, 'glorious walk-in shower'). At breakfast, soda bread, granola and preserves are all home-made; free-ranging chickens provide the eggs.

25% DISCOUNT VOUCHERS

MAP 6:C5
Lough Bane
Collinstown
T: 00 353 44 966 6186
W: loughbawnhouse.com

BEDROOMS: 4.
OPEN: all year except Dec.
FACILITIES: 2 sitting rooms, dining room, free Wi-Fi, 50 acres of parkland, wild swimming lake.
BACKGROUND MUSIC: none.
LOCATION: beside lake, near village.
CHILDREN: all ages welcomed.
DOGS: allowed in 2 bedrooms, public rooms (resident dogs).
CREDIT CARDS: MC, Visa.
PRICES: per room B&B from €80, D,B&B €120–€170. Dinner €45. 2-night min. booking weekends in May, June.

COLLON Co. Louth

COLLON HOUSE

'Meticulously' renovated and richly furnished, Michael McMahon and John Bentley-Dunn 's house in the Boyne valley 'exudes class, from bedroom to table'. Built in 1740, it was once the home of John Foster, last Speaker of the Irish House of Commons. Filled with antiques and paintings, the hosts add 'a big welcome, big winter fires and an unhurried flexibility'. The enclosed gardens, with an intricate sunken box parterre and Greek-style summer house, are surrounded by mature trees and a ten-foot-high hedge. Preprandials might be taken in the former ballroom; 'sumptuous' dinners (by arrangement for groups of six or more) are served in the panelled dining room. The well-equipped bedrooms have a subtly disguised bathroom.

MAP 6:C6
Ardee Street
Collon A92 YT29
T: 00 353 87 235 5645
W: collonhouse.com

BEDROOMS: 3. Plus 2-room suite in adjacent mews house.
OPEN: New Year, Feb–Dec, except Christmas.
FACILITIES: 2 reception rooms, sitting room, dining room, free Wi-Fi, TV in mews house, wedding facilities, ¾-acre garden, parking.
BACKGROUND MUSIC: none.
LOCATION: middle of Collon village, near to the Boyne valley.
CHILDREN: not under 13.
DOGS: not allowed.
CREDIT CARDS: none accepted.
PRICES: per room B&B €160–€180. Set dinner (4 courses) €60. 1-night bookings Sat sometimes refused.

DONEGAL TOWN Co. Donegal

ARD NA BREATHA

A ten-minute walk along a quiet path from Donegal, Theresa and Albert Morrow's modern rustic B&B within a working farm provides 'great value'. A covered walkway leads to 'simple, cosy' bedrooms in a purpose-built annexe; there are king-size beds, wool rugs, pine furniture. The Morrows start their day at dawn (rising to lamb sheep when needed) but encourage guests to take their French toast and scrambled eggs (served in the main house, to order) at a more civilised hour. Books, an honesty bar and a turf fire create a peaceful atmosphere in the residents' lounge. Dinner is available only for groups of ten or more (by arrangement), but the hosts are helpful with advice and booking for local eating options.

MAP 6:B5
Dumrooske Middle
Donegal Town
T: 00 353 74 972 2288
W: ardnabreatha.com

BEDROOMS: 6. All in converted barn.
OPEN: mid-Feb–end Oct.
FACILITIES: bar, lounge, restaurant, free Wi-Fi, in-room TV (Freeview), 1-acre grounds, unsuitable for disabled.
BACKGROUND MUSIC: in bar and restaurant at breakfast.
LOCATION: 1¼ miles NE of town centre.
CHILDREN: all ages welcomed.
DOGS: allowed in bedrooms (not unattended), sitting room, garden.
CREDIT CARDS: MC, Visa.
PRICES: per person B&B €35–€63. À la carte €39 (for groups of 10 or more).

DONEGAL TOWN Co. Donegal
HARVEY'S POINT

On the shores of Lough Eske, a traditional hotel run with old-fashioned care. Rare Irish whiskeys are ready for sipping by a peat fire; sustaining supplies in the spacious bedrooms (fresh milk, fruit, biscuits). Lakeshore suites have a private entrance and lough-facing terrace; compact cabin-style rooms are available in the Lodge. Modern Irish dishes are served in the restaurant overlooking the water, including pan-roasted turbot, baby leek, brown shrimp, leek, parsley gnocchi, verjus. The day starts with freshly squeezed juices, organic porridge, Donegal bacon or a fish special. Stabling and grazing is available for equine travellers. Outdoorsy pursuits range from the active (fishing, golf) to the passive (leisurely walks, loughside picnics).

MAP 6:B5
Lough Eske
Donegal Town
T: 00 353 74 972 2208
W: harveyspoint.com

BEDROOMS: 64. Some suitable for disabled, plus 13 in Lodge for group bookings.
OPEN: all year.
FACILITIES: lift, drawing room, bar, restaurant, ballroom, free Wi-Fi, in-room TV (Sky), wedding facilities, conference facilities, beauty treatments, 20-acre grounds.
BACKGROUND MUSIC: in public spaces.
LOCATION: 4 miles outside Donegal Town.
CHILDREN: all ages welcomed.
DOGS: allowed.
CREDIT CARDS: MC, Visa.
PRICES: per room B&B from €239. Set dinner (4 courses) €59, 7-course tasting menu €69. 2-night min. stay at weekends.

DUBLIN
ARIEL HOUSE

There's nothing ethereal about this 'warmly welcoming' guest house near Ballsbridge village; rather 'helpful staff' encourage guests to feel solidly at home, day and night. Stone steps lead to the three interconnected Victorian town houses, sympathetically restored to retain plenty of original features including Flemish brickwork, ornate stained glass, sash windows. Steep stairs lead to comfortable bedrooms; the best are handsomely styled with antiques, Victorian-inspired fabrics; suites have a four-poster bed and Waterford crystal chandeliers. Guests mingle over afternoon tea in the 'comfortably grand lounge'. An 'excellent' locally sourced breakfast (full Irish, eggs Benedict, pancakes, continental). is served in a bright, sunny room.

MAP 6:C6
50–54 Lansdowne Road
Dublin 4
T: 00 353 1 668 5512
W: ariel-house.net

BEDROOMS: 37. 8 in mews, attached to main house.
OPEN: all year except 23 Dec–4 Jan.
FACILITIES: drawing room, dining room, free Wi-Fi, in-room TV, garden.
BACKGROUND MUSIC: none.
LOCATION: about a mile from city centre.
CHILDREN: all ages welcomed.
DOGS: not allowed.
CREDIT CARDS: Amex, MC, Visa.
PRICES: per room B&B from €121.

DUBLIN

WATERLOO HOUSE

On a quiet tree-lined street within walking distance of St Stephen's Green and many other city landmarks, the twin red doors to this 'attractive pair of houses' signal your arrival at this Georgian guest house. Classically styled bedrooms, with warm earthy tones, and plenty of period-appropriate furnishings, can be snug, but they have 'everything one might require'. Light sleepers may wish to discuss room choice. The 'extensive breakfast', served in the dining room or the adjoining conservatory, is ideal fuel for steaming through the city: home-made muesli and soda bread, cold cuts, an omelette, a full Irish breakfast or 'catch of the day'. The helpful staff have recommendations aplenty within the vicinity and further afield.

MAP 6:C6
8–10 Waterloo Road
Dublin 4
T: 00 353 1 660 1888
W: waterloohouse.ie

BEDROOMS: 19. Some suitable for disabled.
OPEN: all year.
FACILITIES: lift, lounge, dining room, conservatory, free Wi-Fi, in-room TV, garden, parking, restaurant wheelchair accessible.
BACKGROUND MUSIC: all day in lounge, at breakfast in eating areas.
LOCATION: 1 mile to St Stephen's Green, Dublin city centre.
CHILDREN: all ages welcomed.
DOGS: not allowed.
CREDIT CARDS: MC, Visa,
PRICES: per room B&B from €220. 2 night min. stay preferred peak weekends.

INIS MEAIN Co. Galway

INIS MEAIN RESTAURANT AND SUITES

Blending into the landscape, Ruairí and Marie-Thérèse de Blacam's design-led restaurant-with-suites is on a remote Aran island, a stronghold of Gaelic culture. Sustainably run, local materials – wood, lime, stone and wool – form the linear architectural bedrooms; each has vast views from a private outdoor seating area. Succinct menus exploit prime island produce, the restaurant greenhouse, the surrounding waters, with such dishes as lobster with aïoli; beetroot carpaccio; lamb chop with salsa verde. Breakfast is delivered to the door. Guests receive an exploration kit with all the essentials: bicycles, fishing rod, swimming towels, binoculars, nature guides, maps, a hotpot lunch in a backpack.

MAP 6:C4
Inis Meáin
Aran Islands H91 NX86
T: 00 353 86 826 6026
W: inismeain.com

BEDROOMS: 5 suites.
OPEN: Apr–Sept.
FACILITIES: restaurant (closed Sun, Mon nights), dinner served to non-residents on Wed, Fri and Sat nights only, free Wi-Fi, 3-acre grounds.
BACKGROUND MUSIC: none.
LOCATION: centre of a small island, 15 miles off the Galway coast. 40-min. ferry from Ros a' Mhíl; a 7-min. flight from Connemara airport.
CHILDREN: not under 12.
DOGS: not allowed.
CREDIT CARDS: MC, Visa.
PRICES: per suite B&B €300–€650, includes daily hotpot lunch, bikes, fishing rod, binoculars, collections to and from the island. Set 4-course dinner €75. 2-night min. stay.

KANTURK Co. Cork

GLENLOHANE

In the Blackwater valley, visitors to this fine, ivy-clad Georgian country house are invited to stay 'as if with friends' by the welcoming Sharp Bolster family. Beyond the beautiful walled garden and terraced lawns lie acres of meadows and farmland. Inside brims with heirlooms and memorabilia collected by more than ten generations of the family. Days might be spent nestled in a fireside armchair in the book-lined study, and having tea in the airy drawing room. Spacious country-style bedrooms are pleasingly old-fashioned, with original fireplaces; one has a four-poster. The hosts offer tips for decent nearby eateries; guests might alternatively give a day's notice and dine in. Vintage motorcycle or classic car tours can be organised.

MAP 6:D5
Kanturk
T: 00 353 29 50014
W: glenlohane.ie

BEDROOMS: 3. Plus 3-bed self-catering cottage nearby, suitable for disabled.
OPEN: all year.
FACILITIES: drawing room, library, dining room, free Wi-Fi, 250-acre gardens and farmland.
BACKGROUND MUSIC: none.
LOCATION: 1½ miles E of town.
CHILDREN: over-12s 'will be considered'.
DOGS: not allowed.
CREDIT CARDS: Amex, MC, Visa.
PRICES: per room B&B single €135–€150, double €235–€250, D,B&B €285–€300.

KILKENNY Co. Kilkenny

ROSQUIL HOUSE

Phil and Rhoda Nolan's friendly B&B is well located for exploring the medieval town with its castle and cathedral, just across the River Nore. Simple bedrooms are well equipped with a flat-screen TV and a hot drinks tray; larger rooms may have a seating area; families have a choice of rooms, including a separate self-catering apartment with its own entrance. The extensive, wholesome breakfast, made with locally sourced produce, is a point of pride: fruit (fresh and poached), house special granola, home-baked bread, local cheeses; cooked-to-order dishes include a full Irish, omelettes. The Nolans have plentiful, on-point advice on local hot spots and trips further afield. Kilkenny Golf Club is within reach of a decent 7 iron.

MAP 6:D5
Castlecomer Road
Kilkenny R95 P962
T: 00 353 56 772 1419
W: rosquilhouse.com

BEDROOMS: 7. 1 suitable for disabled, plus a self-catering apartment.
OPEN: Feb (Thurs–Sun), Mar–21 Dec, 28 Dec–1 Jan.
FACILITIES: lounge, dining room, free Wi-Fi, in-room TV, smoking patio, ¼-acre garden.
BACKGROUND MUSIC: Irish or classical music in reception and dining room.
LOCATION: near town centre.
CHILDREN: all ages welcomed.
DOGS: allowed, by prior arrangement.
CREDIT CARDS: MC, Visa.
PRICES: per person B&B single €40–€60, double €80–€120.

KILLARNEY Co. Kilkenny
THE BREHON

Overlooking Killarney national park, peaceful repose greets travellers on the Wild Atlantic Way at the O'Donahue family's large spa hotel encircled by a spectacular mountainscape. Elegant public spaces have marble, dark wood and vast wall hangings. Understated bedrooms, some small, some staid, give views of the countryside or the purple-hued McGillycuddy Reeks mountains from a bay window or balcony; some interconnecting rooms suit a family. Danú restaurant serves chef Chad Byrne's award-winning Irish fare, perhaps slow-cooked pork steak, creamy savoy cabbage with chorizo, cumin and squash jam; lighter bites in the bar. Guests enjoy complimentary access to Angsana spa and the kids' club at sister Gleneagle Hotel, next door.

MAP 6:D4
Muckross Road
Killarney V93 RT22
T: 00 353 64 663 0700
w: thebrehon.com

BEDROOMS: 125. Some suitable for disabled.
OPEN: all year.
FACILITIES: lift, lounge, bar, restaurant, private dining room, free Wi-Fi, in-room TV, wedding facilities, function facilities, playroom, spa (12-metre indoor Vitality pool, steam room, herb sauna, spa bath, fitness centre, treatments), parking.
BACKGROUND MUSIC: in public areas.
LOCATION: ½ mile from town centre.
CHILDREN: all ages welcomed.
DOGS: allowed.
CREDIT CARDS: Amex, MC, Visa.
PRICES: per room B&B from €155, D,B&B from €239. À la carte €42.

MAGHERAFELT Co. Londonderry
LAUREL VILLA TOWNHOUSE

A literary haven for Seamus Heaney fans, behind the bright red door of Eugene and Gerardine Kielt's elegant villa, B&B guests will find an intriguing collection of his books and memorabilia. Eugene Kielt, a Blue Badge guide, gives award-winning tours of the area, and reveals the landscapes and community that inspired the late Nobel prize-winning poet and playwright. Bedrooms, each named after a great Ulster poet, including Longley and Kavanagh, display framed works and portraits of the writers. Gerardine's breakfasts (fresh fruit salad, a full Ulster, gourmet scones) are served in the wood-panelled dining room, beneath Heaney poems on scrolls. A large collection of genealogical and historic materials can help guests trace their Northern Irish roots.

MAP 6:B6
60 Church Street
Magherafelt BT45 6AW
T: 028 7930 1459
w: laurel-villa.com

BEDROOMS: 4.
OPEN: all year.
FACILITIES: 2 lounges, dining room, patio, free Wi-Fi, in-room TV, ¼-acre garden, parking.
BACKGROUND MUSIC: none.
LOCATION: town centre.
CHILDREN: all ages welcomed.
DOGS: not allowed.
CREDIT CARDS: MC, Visa.
PRICES: per person B&B single £75–£90, double £60–£90.

MOYARD Co. Galway

CROCNARAW COUNTRY HOUSE

Minutes from Connemara national park, Lucy Fretwell's 'fabulously located', creeper-clad Georgian guest house has mountain views, 'excellent food' and a homely, lived-in feel. The whitewashed house stands in mature grounds fringed by a rustic stone wall. Quirky ornaments and comfy seating fill the airy public rooms. Afternoon tea with Aga-baked treats is served fireside in the flower-filled drawing room. Upstairs, bright and uncluttered bedrooms have more fresh flowers, a gloriously rustic outlook over a kitchen garden, an orchard and a meadow of donkeys. A generous breakfast of home-made soda bread and home-grown produce is served on sunshine-yellow crockery in the dining room. Private dinners by arrangement.

MAP 6:C4
Moyard H91 EF82
T: 00 353 95 41068
W: crocnaraw.ie

BEDROOMS: 4.
OPEN: May–Oct, over Christmas and New Year by arrangement only.
FACILITIES: dining room, drawing room, snug, free Wi-Fi, 2-acre garden in 20-acre grounds.
BACKGROUND MUSIC: none.
LOCATION: by Ballinakill Bay, 5 miles N of Clifden on N59.
CHILDREN: all ages welcomed.
DOGS: allowed in some bedrooms.
CREDIT CARDS: MC, Visa.
PRICES: per person B&B from €45.

NEWPORT Co. Mayo

NEWPORT HOUSE

Small wonder visitors linger at this inviting, creeper-covered Georgian mansion on the Clew Bay shoreline. The building is steeped in cosy country house charm, thanks to Kieran Thompson, who has owned and meticulously maintained the property for over 30 years. Airy public rooms have gilt-framed artwork, antiques and trophy fish in glass cases; comfy fireside sofas, full bookshelves. Classically furnished bedrooms are in the main house and two courtyard buildings. In the elegant dining room, seafood from the bay, Irish beef and farmhouse cheeses. Anglers might cast their eye – and their line – at the extensive fishing rights; basket lunches, ghillies, and smoking/freezing facilities are available.

MAP 6:B4
Newport F28 F243
T: 00 353 98 41222
W: newporthouse.ie

BEDROOMS: 14. 4 in courtyard, 2 on ground floor.
OPEN: early Apr–early Oct.
FACILITIES: bar, drawing room, sitting room, dining room, free Wi-Fi in reception, some bedrooms, in-room TV, 15-acre grounds, walled garden, private fishery, bicycle hire.
BACKGROUND MUSIC: none.
LOCATION: in village, 7 miles N of Westport.
CHILDREN: all ages welcomed.
DOGS: allowed in courtyard bedrooms, public rooms.
CREDIT CARDS: Amex, MC, Visa.
PRICES: per person B&B €120–€135, D,B&B €185–€195. 5-course dinner €58.

NEW

PORTMAGEE Co. Kerry

THE MOORINGS

A favourite haunt of the Star Wars cast and crew
while filming on offshore Skellig, this family-run
guest house on the harbour front is a force to be
reckoned with. Luke Skywalker (Mark Hamill)
learned to pull the perfect pint in the brightly
painted Irish tavern, which is full of all the nooks,
crannies and maritime memorabilia you'd expect;
the sitting room became production headquarters.
The lively spot is well liked by locals too for its
straight-off-the-boat fish and buzzy bar. Upstairs,
restful rooms feature beds draped in crisp linen,
vivid reds; a marble bathroom; handy extras
(iron, ironing board, drinks tray, good toiletries).
From many, magnificent views over the harbour.
Home-made breads, a full Irish, bolster a day of
wildlife watching along the coast.

MAP 6:D4
Main Street
Portmagee V23 RX05
T: 00 353 66 947 7108
w: moorings.ie

BEDROOMS: 16. Some in annexe.
OPEN: closed Christmas and New Year,
restaurant closed Mon/Tues Mar–Oct.
FACILITIES: bar, restaurant, free Wi-Fi,
in-room TV.
BACKGROUND MUSIC: in bar.
LOCATION: 10 miles from the Ring of
Kerry (N70).
CHILDREN: all ages welcomed.
DOGS: not allowed.
CREDIT CARDS: Amex, MC, Visa.
PRICES: per person B&B €50.

RAMELTON Co. Donegal

FREWIN

Restored with flair, Regina Gibson and Thomas
Coyle's ivy-hung former rectory is a warm and
welcoming outpost just outside a town on the
Wild Atlantic Way. Set within mature wooded
grounds, the Victorian family home has been
returned to its former glory with stained-glass
windows, a candle-holding chandelier above the
dining room table, antiques and comfy sofas in
the sitting rooms, and an elegant staircase. The
spacious, country house bedrooms, each with a
compact bathroom, might have a sitting room,
a four-poster bed, a roll-top bath. Communal
breakfasts are praiseworthy. The congenial hosts
will help with dinner reservations and places to
visit. Golf, fishing, horse riding and guided hikes
in the Bluestack mountains can be arranged.

MAP 6:B5
Rectory Road
Ramelton
T: 00 353 74 915 1246
w: frewinhouse.com

BEDROOMS: 3. Plus cottage in the
grounds.
OPEN: Apr–Oct, by special
arrangement for small groups in Feb
and Nov.
FACILITIES: sitting room, library, dining
room, free Wi-Fi, 2-acre garden, golf.
BACKGROUND MUSIC: none.
LOCATION: outskirts of town.
CHILDREN: not under 12.
DOGS: not allowed.
CREDIT CARDS: MC, Visa.
PRICES: per person B&B single
€90–€125, double €85–€95.

RATHNEW Co. Wicklow

HUNTER'S HOTEL

Far from the hustle and bustle of everyday life, this rambling property next to the River Vartry claims to be Ireland's oldest coaching inn. It has been owned by the same family for almost 200 years, and the current stewards, the brothers Gelletlie, have maintained its grand olde-worlde charm, with antiques, open fires and floral fabrics. Run with 'acceptable eccentricity' ('if you wanted Wi-Fi you had to sit on the oak settle by the front door'), it is 'extremely comfortable and the food was good'. Most of the chintz-filled bedrooms overlook the 'lovely' grounds; in each, extra blankets for chilly nights. The dining room has crisp linen, classic cuisine. Breakfast is 'up to the mark'. 'Well worth a stop-over from the Rosslare ferry.' Mount Usher Gardens are 5 minutes away.

MAP 6:C6
Newrath Bridge
Rathnew A67 TN30
T: 00 353 404 40106
w: hunters.ie

BEDROOMS: 16. 1 on ground floor.
OPEN: all year except 24–26 Dec.
FACILITIES: drawing room, lounge, bar, dining room, private dining room, free Wi-Fi, in-room TV (Freeview), 5-acre grounds, golf, tennis, fishing nearby.
BACKGROUND MUSIC: none.
LOCATION: 1 mile SE of Ashford.
CHILDREN: all ages welcomed.
DOGS: allowed by arrangement.
CREDIT CARDS: Amex, MC, Visa.
PRICES: per person B&B from €65, D,B&B from €95. Lunch from €22.75, set dinner from €30.75, à la carte from €28.75.

RECESS Co. Galway

LOUGH INAGH LODGE

In 'a spectacular position', cradled by a mountain range, this Victorian fishing lodge is a remote and peaceful place. It has been owned by the O'Connor family for over 30 years. A peat-fuelled fire burns in the cosy library and the well-appointed sitting room; both have warm hues, wood floors with rugs, antique furnishings and artwork. Dinner – Irish food cooked with a French flair, underpinned by local seafood – is served on the dining room's white tablecloths; the panelled bar has simpler fare. Upstairs, the comfortable bedrooms (named after Irish writers) are traditionally furnished, some with a four-poster. Lough-view bedrooms 'are worth the extra'. Days out include walks by the lake or fishing on a boat on the river accompanied by a ghillie.

MAP 6:C4
Recess
T: 00 353 95 34706
w: loughinaghlodgehotel.ie/en

BEDROOMS: 13. 4 on ground floor, 1 suitable for disabled.
OPEN: Mar–Dec.
FACILITIES: sitting room, bar, library, dining room, free Wi-Fi, in-room TV (Freeview), 14-acre grounds, wedding facilities.
BACKGROUND MUSIC: none.
LOCATION: 3 miles N of Recess, on the lough's eastern shore.
CHILDREN: all ages welcomed.
DOGS: allowed in bedrooms, public rooms.
CREDIT CARDS: Amex, MC, Visa.
PRICES: per room B&B €155–€220, D,B&B €250–€320. À la carte €50.

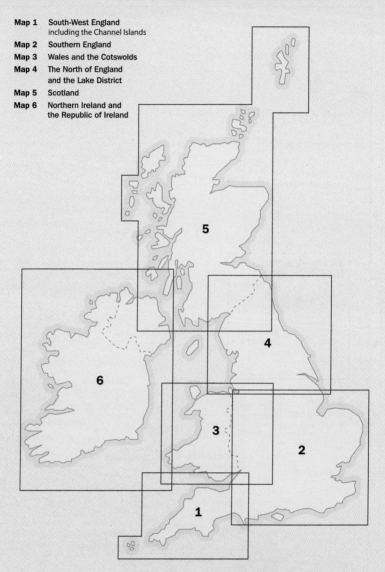

Map 1 South-West England
including the Channel Islands

Map 2 Southern England

Map 3 Wales and the Cotswolds

Map 4 The North of England
and the Lake District

Map 5 Scotland

Map 6 Northern Ireland and
the Republic of Ireland

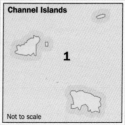

Channel Islands

1

Not to scale

MAP 1 • SOUTH-WEST ENGLAND

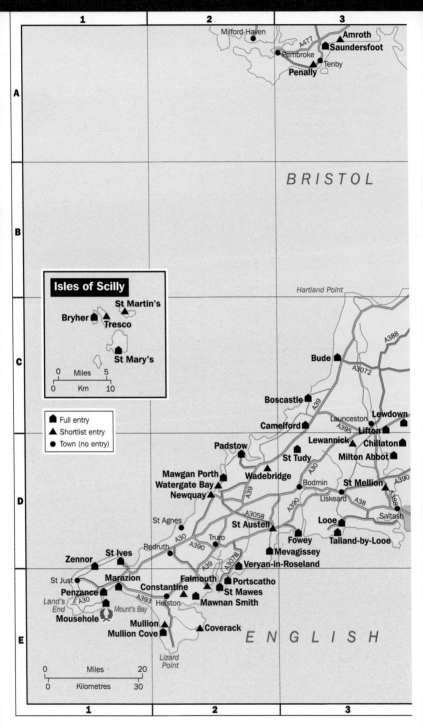

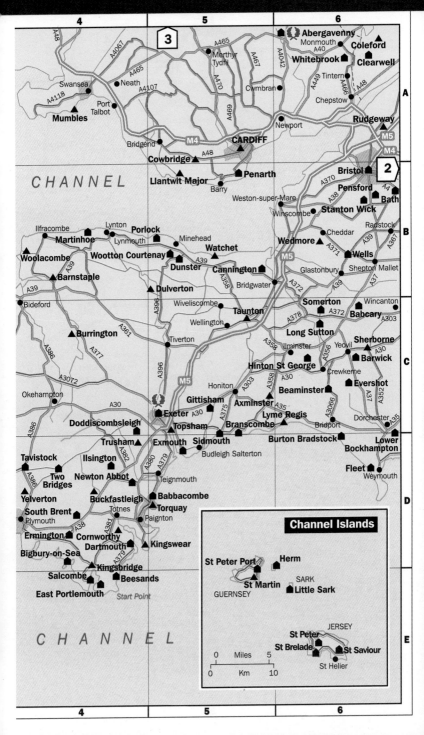

MAP 2 • SOUTHERN ENGLAND

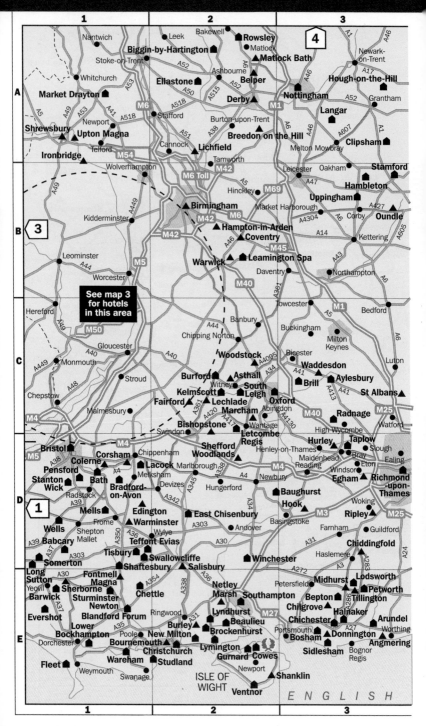

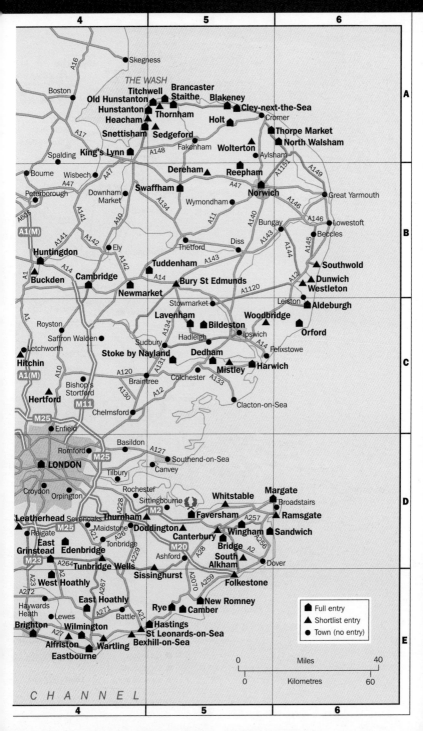

4 **5** **6**

Skegness

Boston

THE WASH

Titchwell Brancaster
Old Hunstanton Staithe Blakeney
Hunstanton Thornham Cley-next-the-Sea
Heacham Cromer
Snettisham Sedgeford Holt Thorpe Market
North Walsham
Spalding Fakenham Wolterton
King's Lynn Aylsham

Bourne Wisbech
Peterborough Downham Dereham Reepham
Market Swaffham Norwich Great Yarmouth
A1(M) Wymondham Lowestoft
Bungay Beccles
Huntingdon Ely Thetford Diss
Buckden Tuddenham Southwold
Cambridge Bury St Edmunds Dunwich
Newmarket Westleton
Stowmarket Leiston Aldeburgh
Royston Lavenham Woodbridge
Saffron Walden Bildeston Orford
Letchworth Sudbury Ipswich Felixstowe
Hitchin Stoke by Nayland Dedham Harwich
A1(M) Bishop's Mistley
Hertford Stortford Braintree Colchester
M11 Chelmsford Clacton-on-Sea
Enfield
Basildon
Romford Southend-on-Sea
M25 Canvey
LONDON Tilbury
Croydon Rochester
Orpington Sittingbourne Whitstable Margate
M2 Broadstairs
Leatherhead Sevenoaks Thurnham Faversham Ramsgate
Reigate Maidstone Doddington Wingham Sandwich
East Tonbridge M20 Canterbury
Grinstead Edenbridge Ashford Bridge
M23 Tunbridge Wells South Dover
West Hoathly Sissinghurst Alkham
Haywards East Hoathly Folkestone
Heath Lewes Battle Rye New Romney
Brighton Wilmington Camber
Alfriston Wartling Hastings
Eastbourne Bexhill-on-Sea St Leonards-on-Sea

■ Full entry
▲ Shortlist entry
● Town (no entry)

0 Miles 40
0 Kilometres 60

C H A N N E L

4 **5** **6**

MAP 3 · WALES AND THE COTSWOLDS

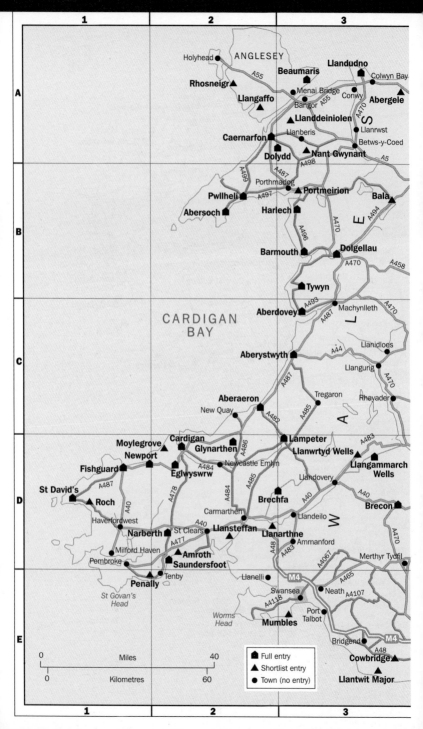

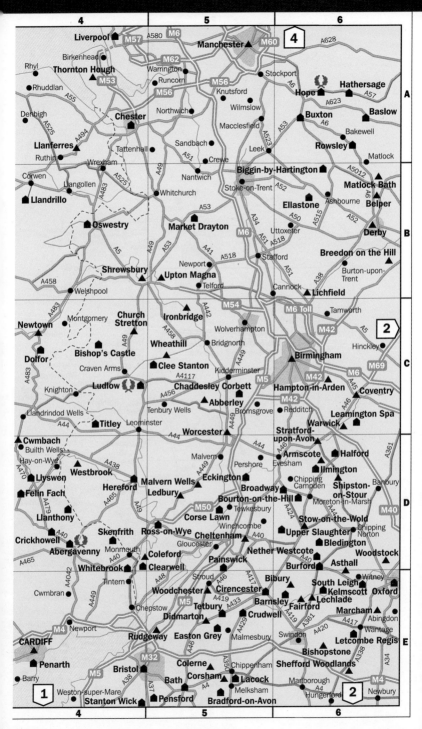

MAP 4 · THE NORTH OF ENGLAND AND THE LAKE DISTRICT

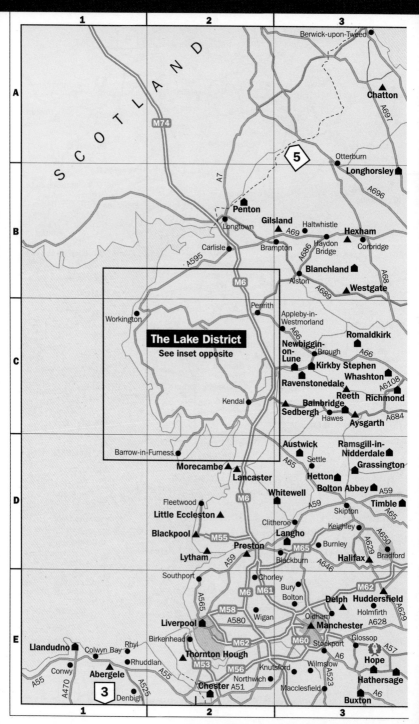

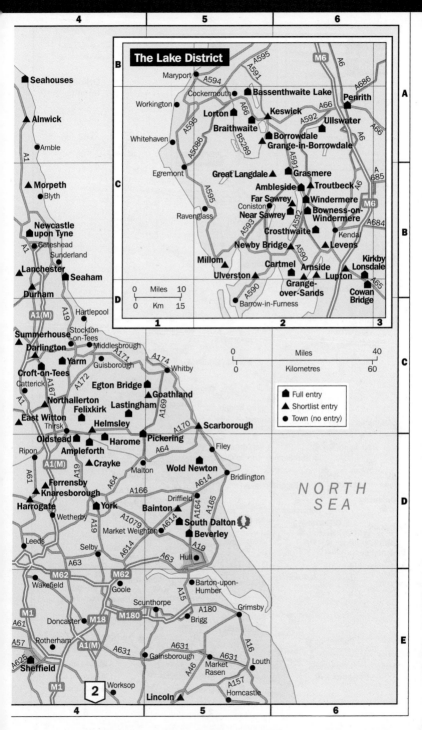

MAP 5 · SCOTLAND

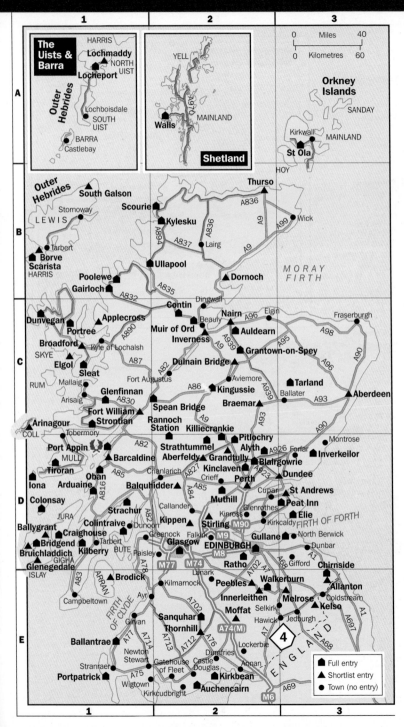

The Uists & Barra

HARRIS
Lochmaddy
NORTH UIST
Locheport
Outer Hebrides
Lochboisdale
SOUTH UIST
BARRA
Castlebay

YELL
Walls
MAINLAND
A970
Shetland

0 Miles 40
0 Kilometres 60

Orkney Islands
SANDAY
Kirkwall
MAINLAND
St Ola
HOY

A

B

Outer Hebrides
South Galson
Scourie
Stornoway
LEWIS
Kylesku
Tarbert
Borve
Scarista
HARRIS
Poolewe
Gairloch
Thurso
A836
A9
Wick
A99
A837
Lairg
A9
Ullapool
Dornoch
MORAY FIRTH
A835
A832

C

Dunvegan
Portree
Broadford
SKYE
Elgol
Sleat
RUM
Mallaig
Arisaig
Applecross
Kyle of Lochalsh
A890
A87
Contin
Dingwall
Beauly
Muir of Ord
Inverness
Nairn A96 Elgin
Auldearn
A939
A9
Fraserburgh
A98
Grantown-on-Spey
A95
Dulnain Bridge
A82
Fort Augustus
Aviemore
A86
Kingussie
A939
Tarland
Ballater
Aberdeen
A96
A90
A93
Glenfinnan
A830
Fort William
Strontian
Spean Bridge
Braemar
Rannoch Station
Killiecrankie
A9
A93

D

Arinagour
COLL
Tobermory
Port Appin
MULL
Tiroran
Iona
Oban
Arduaine
Colonsay
JURA
Ballygrant
Craighouse
Bridgend
Bruichladdich
GIGHA
Glenegedale
ISLAY
A82
Barcaldine
A85
Crianlarich
A816
Balquhidder
A85
Strachur
A82
Colintraive
Dunoon
A83
Aberfeldy
Strathtummel
Grandtully
Pitlochry
Alyth A926 Forfar
Blairgowrie
Kinclaven
A827
Crieff
Perth
A9
A93
Montrose
Inverkeilor
Dundee
A90
Cupar
St Andrews
Muthill
Callander
A84
Kippen
Kinross
Glenrothes
Peat Inn
Elie
Stirling
M90
Kirkcaldy
FIRTH OF FORTH
Balquhidder

E

Ballantrae
Portpatrick
Stranraer
A77
Newton Stewart
A75
Wigtown
Kirkcudbright
Campbeltown
FIRTH OF CLYDE
ARRAN
Brodick
A78
Ayr
Kilmarnock
A713
A714
Girvan
Sanquhar
Thornhill
A76
A712
Lockerbie
Dumfries
Annan
Gatehouse of Fleet
Castle Douglas
Kirkbean
Auchencairn
A75
A74(M)
M6
Greenock
Paisley
Glasgow
M77
EDINBURGH
M8
M9
M74
Ratho
Lanark
Peebles
Walkerburn
Innerleithen
Melrose
Moffat
Selkirk
Hawick
Jedburgh
A7
A68
North Berwick
Dunbar
Gifford
A1
Gullane
Chirnside
Allanton
Kelso
Coldstream
A697
A1
ENGLAND
A69
A68

4

Full entry
▲ **Shortlist entry**
● Town (no entry)

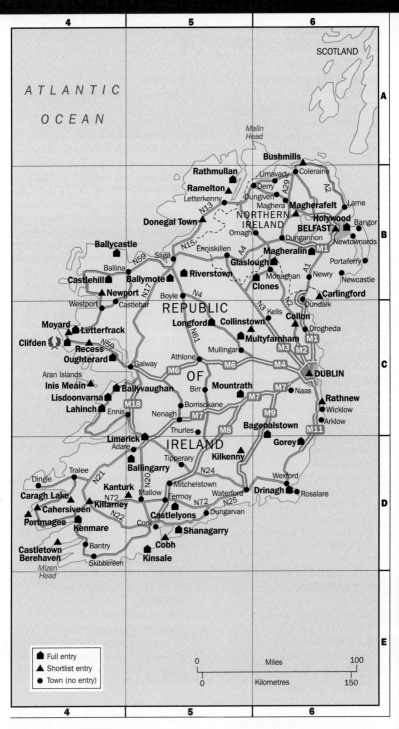

4 **5** **6**

SCOTLAND

A T L A N T I C

O C E A N

A

Malin
Head

Bushmills

Rathmullan
Limavady   Coleraine

Ramelton
Letterkenny   Derry
Dungiven

Maghera   **Magherafelt**   Larne

Donegal Town   N13
NORTHERN
IRELAND
Omagh   Dungannon   **Holywood**   Bangor
BELFAST

Ballycastle   N15
Enniskillen   **Magheralin**   Newtownards
B
N59   Sligo   A4   **Glasslough**   M1
Ballina   **Riverstown**   Portaferry
Castlehill   **Ballymote**   Monaghan   Newcastle
Newport   Boyle   N4   **Clones**   Newry
Westport   Castlebar   N3   **Carlingford**
N17   Kells   Dundalk

REPUBLIC   **Collon**
Moyard   **Longford**   **Collinstown**   Drogheda
Letterfrack   N61   **Multyfarnham**   M1
Clifden   **Recess**   N59   Mullingar   M3   M2
Oughterard   Athlone   M6   M4
Galway   M6   **DUBLIN**   C
Aran Islands   OF   Birr   **Mountrath**   Naas
Inis Meáin   **Ballyvaughan**   M7   **Rathnew**
Lisdoonvarna   M18   Borrisokane   M9   Wicklow
Lahinch   Ennis   Nenagh   M7   Arklow
Thurles   M8   **Bagenalstown**   M11
Limerick   IRELAND   **Gorey**
Adare   Tipperary   **Kilkenny**
Tralee   **Ballingarry**   N24   Wexford
Dingle   N21   Mitchelstown   **Drinagh**   Rosslare
Caragh Lake   **Kanturk**   N20   Mallow   Waterford
N72   Fermoy   N72   Dungarvan   D
Cahersiveen   **Killarney**   N25
Portmagee   N22   Cork   **Castlelyons**
Kenmare   **Shanagarry**
Castletown   Bantry   **Cobh**
Berehaven   Skibbereen   **Kinsale**
Mizen
Head

E

■ Full entry
▲ Shortlist entry
● Town (no entry)

0   Miles   100
0   Kilometres   150

4 **5** **6**

FREQUENTLY ASKED QUESTIONS

HOW DO YOU CHOOSE A GOOD HOTEL?

The hotels we like are relaxed, unstuffy and personally run. We do not have a specific template: our choices vary greatly in style and size. Most of the hotels in the Guide are family owned and family run. These are places where the needs and comfort of the guest are put ahead of the convenience of the management.

YOU ARE A HOTEL GUIDE – WHY DO YOU INCLUDE SO MANY PUBS AND B&BS?

Attitudes and expectations have changed considerably since the Guide was founded in the 1970s. Today's guests expect more informality, less deference. There has been a noticeable rise in the standards of food and accommodation in pubs and restaurants. This is demonstrated by the number of such places suggested to us by our readers. While pubs may have a more relaxed attitude than some traditional hotels, we ensure that only those that maintain high standards of service are included in our selections. The best B&Bs have always combined a high standard of accommodation with excellent value for money. Expect the bedrooms in a pub or B&B listed in the Guide to be well equipped, with thoughtful extras. B&B owners invariably know how to serve a good breakfast.

WHAT ARE YOUR LIKES AND DISLIKES?

We like
* Flexible times for meals.
* Two decent armchairs in the bedroom.
* Good bedside lighting.
* Proper hangers in the wardrobe.
* Fresh milk with the tea tray in the room.

We dislike
* Intrusive background music.
* Stuffy dress codes.
* Bossy notices and house rules.
* Hidden service charges.
* Packaged fruit juices at breakfast.

WHY DO YOU DROP HOTELS FROM ONE YEAR TO THE NEXT?

Readers are quick to tell us if they think standards have slipped at a hotel. If the evidence is overwhelming, we drop the hotel from the Guide or perhaps downgrade it to the Shortlist. Sometimes we send inspectors just to be sure. When a hotel is sold, we look for reports since the new owners took over, otherwise we inspect or omit it.

WHY DO YOU ASK FOR 'MORE REPORTS, PLEASE'?

When we have not heard about a hotel for several years, we ask readers for more reports. Sometimes readers returning to a favourite hotel may not send a fresh report. Readers often respond to our request.

WHAT SHOULD I TELL YOU IN A REPORT?

How you enjoyed your stay. We welcome reports of any length. We want to know what you think about the welcome, the service, the building and the facilities. Even a short report can tell us a great deal about the owners, the staff and the atmosphere.

HOW SHOULD I SEND YOU A REPORT?

You can email us at editor@goodhotelguide.com. Or you can write to us at the address given on the report form on pages 735–6, or send a report via the GHG's website: www.goodhotelguide.com.

ALPHABETICAL LIST OF HOTELS
(S) indicates a Shortlist entry

Cary Arms & Spa Babbacombe 77

Castle Bishop's Castle 100

Castle Lincoln (S) 577

Castle Cottage Harlech 438

Castle House Hereford 197

Castle Leslie Glaslough 477

Castle at Taunton Taunton (S) 619

Castleman Chettle 141

Cat Inn West Hoathly 339

Cathedral 73 Cardiff (S) 667

Cavendish Baslow 82

Cavens Kirkbean 385

Cedar Manor Windermere 344

Ceilidh Place Ullapool 414

Chapel House Penzance 269

Charlotte Street London (S) 497

Charlton Arms Ludlow (S) 580

Chatford House Shrewsbury (S) 612

Chatton Park House Chatton (S) 536

Chester Grosvenor Chester (S) 539

Chewton Glen New Milton 245

Chichester Harbour Chichester (S) 540

Chirnside Hall Chirnside 361

Church House Midhurst (S) 588

Cider House Yelverton (S) 637

CitizenM Bankside London (S) 497

CitizenM Tower of London London (S) 498

City Gate Exeter (S) 554

Cityroomz Edinburgh Edinburgh (S) 648

Clare House Grange-over-Sands (S) 561

Cleveland Tontine Northallerton (S) 593

Cley Windmill Cley-next-the-Sea 148

Clive Arms Ludlow (S) 580

Cliveden House Taplow 318

Cloudesley St Leonards-on-Sea (S) 602

Clow Beck House Croft-on-Tees 153

Cnapan Newport 447

Coach House Brecon 427

Coach House Derby (S) 548

Coach House at Middleton Lodge Richmond 279

Coast Bexhill-on-Sea (S) 522

Coes Faen Barmouth 423

Colintraive Colintraive 362

Coll Arinagour (S) 641

Collinette St Peter Port (S) 681

Collon House Collon (S) 687

Colonsay Colonsay 363

Compasses Inn Tisbury (S) 622

Congham Hall King's Lynn (S) 570

Cookie Jar Alnwick (S) 512

Coombe Abbey Coventry (S) 545

Coombeshead Farm Lewannick (S) 576

Coopershill Riverstown 492

Corse Lawn House Corse Lawn 150

Coruisk House Elgol (S) 651

Cottage in the Wood Braithwaite 114

Cottage in the Wood Malvern Wells (S) 583

Coul House Contin 364

Covent Garden London (S) 498

Cow Hollow Manchester (S) 584

Crab & Lobster Sidlesham 302

Craigatin House and Courtyard Pitlochry (S) 660

Creggans Inn Strachur 409

Crescent Turner Whitstable (S) 633

Cricket Inn Beesands 93

Cridford Inn Trusham (S) 625

Cringletie House Peebles (S) 659

Crocnaraw Country House Moyard (S) 692

Cross Keys Kippen (S) 656

Cross at Kingussie Kingussie 384

Crossways Wilmington 342

Fingal Edinburgh (S) 649

Fischer's at Baslow Hall Baslow 83

Five Alls Lechlade (S) 574

Five Arrows Waddesdon (S) 627

Fleur de Lys Shaftesbury 299

Fontmell Fontmell Magna (S) 558

Forest Country Guest House Newtown (S) 676

Forest House Coleford (S) 542

Forest Side Grasmere 183

Forss House Thurso (S) 664

Fortingall Aberfeldy (S) 639

Forty Winks Durham (S) 551

41 London (S) 502

Fowey Hall Fowey 181

Frégate St Peter Port 462

Frenchgate Richmond 280

Frewin Ramelton (S) 693

Fuzzy Duck Armscote (S) 514

G

Gallivant Camber 133

Galson Farm Guest House South Galson (S) 662

Gara Rock East Portlemouth 165

General Tarleton Ferrensby (S) 557

George Buckden (S) 531

George Hathersage 196

George in Rye Rye 286

George of Stamford Stamford 310

Ghan House Carlingford (S) 684

Gilpin Hotel and Lake House Windermere 345

Glazebrook House South Brent 306

Glenapp Castle Ballantrae 358

Glenegedale House Glenegedale (S) 653

Glenfinnan House Glenfinnan 373

Glenlohane Kanturk (S) 690

Gliffaes Crickhowell 430

Godolphin Arms Marazion (S) 585

Goldstone Hall Market Drayton 232

Gonville Cambridge (S) 534

Good London (S) 500

Gordon's Inverkeilor 379

Goring London 55

Grand Eastbourne 167

Grandtully Grandtully (S) 653

Grasmere Grasmere 184

Grasshoppers Glasgow 372

Grassington House Grassington 186

Gravetye Manor East Grinstead 163

Grays Bath (S) 519

Grazing Goat London 56

Great House Lavenham 215

Green House Bournemouth (S) 526

Green Park Pitlochry 393

Greenbank Falmouth (S) 555

Greenbank Farmhouse Lancaster (S) 572

Greenhills Country House St Peter 461

Gregans Castle Ballyvaughan 470

Greyhound Inn Letcombe Regis 217

Greystones Oban (S) 658

Greywalls Gullane 378

Grosvenor Arms Shaftesbury 300

Grove Narberth 446

Grove Lodge Bath (S) 519

Gunton Arms Thorpe Market 324

Gurnard's Head Zennor 351

Gwesty Cymru Aberystwyth 422

H

H10 London Waterloo London (S) 504

Hack & Spade Whashton 340

Halfway Bridge Lodsworth 221

Ham Yard London (S) 501

Hambleton Hall Hambleton 190

Hamersay House Lochmaddy (S) 656

INDEX OF HOTELS BY COUNTY
(S) indicates a Shortlist entry

Cumbria

Please send your reports to:
The Good Hotel Guide, 50 Addison Avenue, London W11 4QP, England.

Unless asked not to, we assume that we may publish your name. If you would like more report forms please tick ☐ Alternatively, you can either photostat this form or submit a review on our website: www.goodhotelguide.com

NAME OF HOTEL: _____

ADDRESS: _____

_____

Date of most recent visit: _____ Duration of stay: _____

☐ New recommendation   ☐ Comment on existing entry

Report:

Please continue overleaf

I am not connected directly or indirectly with the management or proprietors

Signed: _____

Name: (CAPITALS PLEASE) _____

Address: _____

             _____

Email address: _____